Phenomenology of Practice

Max van Manen offers an extensively updated edition of *Phenomenology of Practice: Meaning-Giving Methods in Phenomenological Research and Writing* to provide an eloquent, accessible, and detailed approach to practicing phenomenology.

Phenomenology of practice refers to the meaning of doing phenomenology on experiences that are of significance to those in professional practice such as psychology, health care, education, and in contexts of ordinary living. A special feature of this update is the role of examples, anecdotes, stories, and vignettes, and the singularity of fictionalized empirical fragments in making the unknowable knowable. Accordingly, the various chapters are enriched with many intelligible examples of phenomenological essays and excursions on ordinary and extraordinary topics. These examples show that a phenomenological method can be engaged to explore virtually any lived experience or event. Max van Manen provides penetrating portrayals of depthful insights by brilliant phenomenologists. He identifies and distinguishes a variety of phenomenological orientations that are alive and current today.

This book is relevant to scholars, students, and motivated readers interested in the originary meanings and methods of phenomenological human science enquiry. Max van Manen's comprehensive work is of significance to all concerned with the interrelation between being and acting, thoughtfulness and tact, in human sciences research and the phenomenology of everyday life.

Max van Manen is emeritus professor at the University of Alberta, Canada. He has presented at numerous universities in the areas of education, psychology, health science, pedagogy, and the arts. His publications on phenomenology, pedagogy, and human science have been translated into many languages.

Phenomenology of Practice

Series Editor: Max van Manen
University of Alberta

The series *Phenomenology of Practice* sponsors books that are steeped in phenomenological scholarship and relevant to professional practitioners in fields such as education, nursing, medicine, pedagogy, clinical and counseling psychology. Texts in this series distinguish themselves for offering inceptual and meaningful insights into lived experiences of professional practices, or into the quotidian concerns of everyday living. Texts may reflectively explicate and focus on aspects of method and dimensions of the philosophic and human science underpinnings of phenomenological research.

For further manuscript details available from the Series Editor: please contact Max van Manen at vanmanen@ualberta.ca / +250-294 4345

Other volumes in this series include:

Phenomenology of the Newborn
Life from Womb to World
Michael van Manen

Visual Phenomenology
Encountering the Sublime Through Images
Erika Goble

Pedagogical Tact
Knowing What to Do When You Don't Know What to Do
Max van Manen

Classic Writings for a Phenomenology of Practice
Michael van Manen and Max van Manen

The Birth of Ethics
Phenomenological Reflections on Life's Beginnings
Michael van Manen

The Pedagogy of Special Needs Education
Phenomenology of Sameness and Difference
Chizuko Fujita

The Phenomenology of Observation Drawing
Reflections on an Enduring Practice
Rose Montgomery-Whicher

For a full list of titles in this series, please visit **www.routledge.com**

Phenomenology of Practice

Meaning-Giving Methods `
in Phenomenological Research and Writing

Second edition

Max van Manen

Routledge
Taylor & Francis Group

NEW YORK AND LONDON

Designed cover image: Laura Sava
The cover displays a digital painting of Orpheus and Eurydice.

Second edition published 2023
by Routledge
605 Third Avenue, New York, NY 10158

and by Routledge
4 Park Square, Milton Park, Abingdon, Oxon, OX14 4RN

Routledge is an imprint of the Taylor & Francis Group, an informa business

First edition published by Left Coast Press, Inc. 2014

ISBN: 978-1-032-13189-4 (hbk)
ISBN: 978-1-032-13193-1 (pbk)
ISBN: 978-1-003-22807-3 (ebk)

DOI: 10.4324/9781003228073

Typeset in ArnoPro
by Apex CoVantage, LLC

*To Mark and Michael
for your exemplary dedication to all you do*

Contents

CONTENTS

Preface

Some words possess an enigmatic quality. Phenomenology is such a word. And yet, the root word "phenomenon" is very ordinary. But perhaps that is quite fitting for the study of phenomenology. It focuses on an ordinary phenomenon, but as it fixes its view, the phenomenon becomes rather extra-ordinary. I first came across the term "phenomenology" when I was still a young student in the Netherlands. But at the time, the word was written in the older spelling as "phaenomenologie" derived from and modeled on the German *Phänomenologie*. The Dutch book *Persoon en Wereld* (Person and World) published in 1953 and edited by the psychiatrist Jan Hendrik van den Berg and the psychologist Johannes Linschoten was the first that had the term phaenomenologie on its cover. It contained essays such as "The Secret Place in the Life of the Child" (Langeveld), "The Conversation" (van den Berg), "Driving a Car" (van Lennep), "The Hotel Room" (van Lennep), "Face and Character" (Kouwer), "Aspects of Sexual Incarnation" (Linschoten), "The Disgust of One's Own Nose" (Rümke), and "The Freedom of the Prisoner" (van Ratingen). These and many other studies truly fortified my fascination with the project of phenomenology and it began to expand my understanding of it.

On the inside pages and back cover of *Persoon en Wereld* van den Berg and Linschoten explain that this book was the first publication in the Netherlands that presented a collection of writings that exemplified the existence of a phenomenological tradition. This phenomenological movement had developed in the 1920s and became known in the 1950s as the Utrecht School of Phenomenology. It was unique in that many of its informal members were professionals in fields such as psychiatry, psychology, pedagogy, law, and health science fields. There are many names associated with phenomenology in the Netherlands, especially after World War II, but one of the first to apply phenomenological method in the Netherlands was the philosopher and linguist Hendrik Pos. He invited Edmund Husserl in 1928 to give the so-called *Amsterdamer Vorträge* (Amsterdam Lectures) on phenomenological psychology.

After moving to Canada in the late 1960s, I dedicated my interest and efforts to two projects: phenomenology and pedagogy. Neither of these academic enterprises was well known yet in professional fields in North America. In fact, a frequent question was: Phenomenology? What is that? What does it look like? So, I translated some better-known German and Dutch phenomenological studies for publication in English. In the seventies, it was not clear how to approach phenomenological texts formatively and how to assist researchers (in a field such as social science and curriculum studies) in the challenging work of phenomenological inquiry, investigations, and writing. As a professor, I opted to involve graduate students in the basics of phenomenological thinking directly on concrete and down-to-earth topics, rather than concentrate on traditional philosophical exegesis and abstract theorizing. It became clear to me that phenomenology could be approached and practiced as a transformative kind of liberated human science that abstains from unnecessary technical obsessions and theoretical shackles: a phenomenology of practice that is driven by a desire for a meaningful and originary understanding of human experience.

Phenomenology is not just the name of a philosophical perspective, it is also the source for questioning life meaning as we live it and the nature of responsibility for personal actions and decisions. What was true for me in those early days is still true today: nothing is more meaningful than the quest for meaning, the mystery of meaning, how meaning originates and occurs—as well as the meaning of our responsibility for others and for the organic, material, and technological world we inhabit. Phenomenology is about wonder, words, and world.

The reflective philosophical thoughtfulness of phenomenology respects the reality of our experience-as-lived, and the meaningfulness of our lives. Important readings by the Dutch phenomenologists became the phenomenological, philosophical, and existential writings of Maurice Merleau-Ponty, Jean-Paul Sartre, Martin Heidegger, Simone de Beauvoir, Albert Camus, Max Scheler, Eugène Minkowski, and these formed the backdrop of novels, plays, and poetry of authors such as André Gide, Hermann Hesse, Rainer Maria Rilke, Franz Kafka, Jean-Paul Sartre, Albert Camus, Anna Blaman, Samuel Beckett, and artists experimenting with Dadaism, Surrealism, Pop-art, Happenings, and other avant-garde development.

The ethical-philosophical attitude of phenomenology eminently seems to empower subjectivity to radicalize itself and to struggle to dislodge and confront the unexamined assumptions of our personal, cultural, political, and social beliefs, views, and theories. And, I strongly believe it still does. Phenomenology, in its multiple contemporary manifestations and historical orientations, continues to make us mindful to be critically and philosophically aware of how our lives (and our cognitive, emotional, embodied, and tacit understandings) are socially, culturally, politically, and existentially fashioned. But phenomenology also reminds us that these constructions themselves are always in danger of becoming imperatives, rationalities, epistemologies, and ontologies that need to be bracketed, deconstructed, and substituted with more reflective portrayals. In the contemporary scientized world, theoretical experience is always already part of the so-called natural attitude.

My personal library houses a true travelogue of theories that I have explored and theorists who I have "visited." And yet, in spite of these fascinations with theoretical experiences, I sometimes admit an ambivalent relation with "theory"—not any specific theory, but theory as such: theory as an intellectual achievement and property, theory as membership into the "circle of initiates." Theory can be a staple that feeds our intellectual and moral hunger, and it can be the addictive substance that induces a cognitive amnesia. Wakefulness requires that we constantly try to work in the tension between the theoretic and what lies outside of it.

In 1953 Merleau-Ponty published his *Phenomenology of Perception*. In the famous Preface he started with the question "What is phenomenology?" and he thought it was strange that half a century after Husserl, the brilliant founder of phenomenology, this question still had to be asked. Well, it is more than three-quarters of a century after Merleau-Ponty posed this question and it seems strange indeed that we still have to ask the question: What is phenomenology? Merleau-Ponty posited that "phenomenology is the study of essences" (2012, p. lxx), such as the essence of perception, and that it also means that we have to place these essences back into existence.

But now, we seem to have more variations of phenomenology than answers to the original question of what is phenomenology. Or perhaps the problem is that we have an abundance of phenomenological literature, and we see enormous stylistic variations but we do not seem to know how phenomenology is done, in its original down-to-earth manifestation. Compared to other disciplines, phenomenology might be considered an outlier.

An encyclopedia entry would undoubtedly link phenomenology to philosophy. And it is true that some treat phenomenology as if it consists primarily of philosophical exegesis, such as historical and comparative studies of technical and theoretical philosophical issues and disputes. But such approaches unwittingly may lead to reducing phenomenology to philosophy. The main source from which phenomenology draws its inspiration is phenomenological literature itself, as well as the various kinds of humanities, arts, ethics, and aesthetics that give phenomenology its rich and depthful foundational grounds and perspectives. Phenomenology is not just plain philosophy. Rather, phenomenology adopts ways of thinking and seeing and expressing that fall outside the paths and boundaries rationalized by the traditions and genres of orthodox philosophy. Phenomenology lies in part on the outside. And there are advantages of taking an outlier position. It allows for greater flexibility.

Some philosophers have remarked that there exists a peculiar inconsistency in the foundational writings of some of the most famous phenomenological thinkers, including Edmund Husserl himself, and their actual practice of doing phenomenology. In their foundational works they strongly assert that phenomenology always must start from experience, from the concrete things that matter in our world. And yet, many actually fail to follow their own guidelines and advice. This is odd because, from my perspective, "starting from experience" and "investigating the existential meaning structures and self-showing of concrete phenomena and events in consciousness" is the utmost unique and singularly identificatory feature of phenomenological thinking and acting.

When the first edition of this book was published in 2014, I was sometimes asked why I included certain phenomenologists but left out certain others. Of course, it was not my intent to claim that all the great authors and thinkers who practice phenomenological studies would need to be represented. I simply included the names and works of many phenomenologists whose works I greatly admire and whose reputations are beyond doubt. I chose phenomenologists whose texts may help to understand the research and approach of the broad domain and variations of phenomenology.

I do not believe that phenomenology should be regarded a unified field of study. But by following the course that phenomenology has taken through the works of many very talented thinkers and authors we may get an inkling how to understand its past and future along the path of a phenomenology of practice: not only asking what phenomenology *is* but also how it *is done*.

It is for this reason that I wrote this book. This is not an introduction to the philosophy of Husserl or Heidegger or Merleau-Ponty, though they feature importantly in the various sections of this text. Rather the aim of this book is to engage the reader directly in phenomenological reflecting, seeing, reading, and writing.

Phenomenological writing is the foundational practice for phenomenological research. But reading and writing is a tangled process. Writers are the first reader of their texts, but the texts were already read before writing. This is a strange linguistic entanglement. It is in the act of reading and writing that phenomenological insights emerge, and this means that reading is already a form of writing since they are phenomena entangled by the body (of) text of thinking, feeling, and acting. As author I have striven to make this a text that asks for active and engaged reading rather than mere passive reading. In other words, reading phenomenology can require doing phenomenology.

This book is divided into three sections. The first section gives the reader the opportunity to gain a feeling and understanding for what "doing phenomenology on the things" looks like. It includes seven short sample essays that start from experience (see Chapter 2). While the text of this book is philosophical it does not aspire to turn into a philosophical system. Therefore, no attempts are made to engage in technical philosophical exegesis regarding the numerous issues and contradictions that historically beset the field of academic philosophy.

The second section (Chapters 7–10) contains a selection of readings from the wide array of approaches by diverse phenomenological authors, which may serve to spark readers' interests in reading and exploring further topics and themes across the variety of phenomenologies in the literature. It is worth noting that these phenomenological thinkers and authors have been responsible for expanding the diversity of phenomenological approaches in the literature. Many of these great minds such as Jean-Paul Sartre, Maurice Merleau-Ponty, Simone de Beauvoir, Jacques Derrida, Hélène Cixous, Jan Hendrik van den Berg, Jean-Luc Nancy, Franz Fanon, Michel Serres, and Alphonso Lingis started influential phenomenological movements and approaches simply because their writings became infectious and influential.

The third section engages the reader in material that can serve the pursuit of self-guided concerns, topics, and activities. The focus here is especially on the understanding of phenomenology as essentially method oriented. The methodologies include not only open-minded interpretations of the famous epoché and the reduction, but also a deeply anchored idea of the phenomenological attitude as a way of seeing and thinking. And then there is the creative moment of being visited by the secret charm of serendipity in the struggle for in-seeing and insights.

Throughout, readers of this book are invited to interact with primary texts that clarify the assumptions and practices of "doing phenomenology on the phenomena" and that avoid the slippery slopes of excessive philosophical jargon. My earlier *Researching Lived Experience* (1990/1997) contains an outline of pointers, principles, and practices to conduct a phenomenological research project. I ask my readers to consider, though, that *Researching Lived Experience* was prepared in the 1970s when the term "phenomenology" was still virtually unknown in the English language professions and the human sciences and humanities fields. Phenomenology is sometimes referred to as human science. The term "human science" derives from the German word *Geisteswissenschaften*, translated as the study or science (*Wissenschaft*) of mind (*Geist*). I hope that the present text succeeds to show in some detail and by example how fascinating phenomenology as a human science can become in its determination to explore the existential and ethical meaningfulness of the phenomena and events of human life.

This book is a second edition and an extensive update of the 2014 edition. Since then my books have been moved between publishers, from Left Coast Press to Routledge. And Routledge now also publishes a book series, which I edit, called Phenomenology of Practice.

Acknowledgments

The study and struggle for the possibility of an experiential understanding of phenomenology and pedagogy has been a major part of my professional life. I appreciate the many colleagues and past students who have joined this trek with me: Bas Levering has been my Utrecht friend and colleague who has regularly kept me engaged with Dutch contestations; Catherine Adams attentively and sensitively co-wrote reflections about subtle phenomenological aspects of pedagogical technology and writing online; Vangie Bergum wrote the inceptual transformation of woman to mother, the meaning of birthing pain, and the feminine power of language; Tone Saevi showed her insightful skills of pedagogically watching children; Rod Evans attested that the phenomenology of ministrative service is pedagogically consequential to the lives of students; Chizuko Fujita showed how to understand the interior and tangled lives of special needs children who are different from others and yet the same; Rose Montgomery-Whicher presented how the draw of writing can be expressed in the art of drawing; Erika Goble explored how the artistic polarity of awe and beauty confronts us with the fatal finalities of the sublime; Shuying Li offered insights into the ancient scholarly source of Chinese pedagogy. I owe grateful thanks to them and to Carol Olsen, Hae-Ryung Yeu, Philo Hove, Andrew Foran, Keun Ho Lee, Patrick Howard, Brenda Cameron, Wendy Austin, and many other unnamed talented colleagues and brilliant friends who touched my soul.

Many of you have kept me motivated and in touch with your fascinating projects of phenomenology and pedagogy and furthered my understanding of the reach, possibilities, and challenges through some hundred fascinating doctoral research endeavors that I was honored to contribute to in some way. This book is dedicated to you.

I thank Mitch Allen for providing helpful advice in preparing this update as he was the first publisher of this book, and Hannah Shakespeare, chief editor of Routledge, for inviting me to prepare an update of the first edition. With a last name like hers, how could I decline? I thank Christopher Taylor, Lucy Kennedy and Matt Bickerton for their patience and expert follow-through in the production process. And I appreciate the smooth assistance from Neil Dowden, who, in his words "lightly copyedited" the hundreds of pages.

I thank Michael van Manen, for assisting with the update of this book. He should have co-written it. And, last but not least, I am grateful to Judith, for her enduring positive spirit and constant nudging me to keep reading and writing and listening, even when so much seems to go wrong with our world where so much is at stake.

About the Cover Image

Orpheus and Eurydice by Laura Sava

The book cover displays a creative image of *Orpheus and Eurydice* by the Romanian artist Laura Sava. The mythical allegory of Orpheus and Eurydice is a well-known tragedy, but it is about the mistake of a glance of the eye that has become famous in the literature of myths. And, surprisingly perhaps, this glance converts the classic romantic tragedy into a poetic story of human obsession.

It happened that shortly after their marriage Eurydice sadly dies from the poison of a snakebite. Her lover, the grieving poet and singer Orpheus, descends into the dark caverns of the underworld to implore the gods with his plaintive songs to reunite him with Eurydice and allow them to return to the daylight world of the living. He enchants the ferryman Charon, the hellish three-headed dog Cerberes, and the monstrous vengeful Erinyes. Orpheus' poetic power and songs are so moving that finally Hades and Persephone take pity on him and grant his wish to take Eurydice with him from the realm of the dead, but on one condition: that he will not turn around to look at her till they should have reached the upper air of daylight.

As the story goes, Orpheus and Eurydice proceed in total silence: "They took the upward path, through the still silence, steep and dark, shadowy with dense fog, drawing near to the threshold of the upper world. Afraid she was no longer there, and eager to see her, the lover turned his eyes" (Ovid, 2000, p. 486). It is said, that in a moment of unguarded forgetfulness, as if to assure himself that she was still following him, Orpheus casts a quick glance behind. At that very instant she is borne away. Eurydice is snatched from him so fast that their stretched-out hands, attempting a desperate last embrace, fail to reach each other. Orpheus grasps only the air, and her last words of farewell recede with such speed that they barely reach his ears.

> In an instant she dropped back, and he, unhappy man, stretching out his arms to hold her and be held, clutched at nothing but the receding air. Dying a second time, now, there was no complaint to her husband (what, then, could she complain of, except that she had been loved?). She spoke a last 'farewell' that, now, scarcely reached his ears, and turned again towards that same place. (Ovid, 2000, p. 486)

Now they had lost each other for a second time and forever. All that Orpheus is left with is the image of that fleeting glance that he saw of his love Eurydice. This is the way the story is usually told. But the phenomenologist Maurice Blanchot describes Orpheus as not forgetful at all.

According to Blanchot the glance of Orpheus was no accident. The glance was motivated by human desire. What Orpheus really wanted was to see Eurydice in her death, in her true immortal being, stripped of the accoutrements that belong to the imperfect world of everyday living, of mortality. He wanted to see her immortal soul and risked losing her because of his selfish artistic desire. But such a glance is not permitted to mortals. What lies on the other side of death is darkness and not to be known or seen by humans. And so the glance that Orpheus cast behind him expresses a desire that can never be completely fulfilled: to grasp the phenomenology of death, beyond mortality. Yet, it is this veil of mystery that every artist, every thinker, may hope to lift. And so, when Orpheus descends toward Eurydice, art is the power by which night opens, says Blanchot. And what happens is this: Orpheus tries to use song, lyrics, and words to "see" and reclaim love from death and death from love.

At first it seems that his words bring his lifeless love into presence, from the dark of death to the light of day. But no one can see what is beyond death unpunished. The price to pay is one's own death. Death is something that belongs to each of us mortals so essentially that it cannot be apprehended except in the realization of our own dying. It is said that Orpheus should have been courageous and willing to die and so unite with Eurydice. But he wanted to perceive Eurydice in her infinite otherness. Orpheus would need to die to reach the other side of death itself. But he wanted to see while entering the twilight of dying alive. Thus, in a momentary glance Orpheus sees and does not see, touches and does not touch, hears and does not hear his beloved while she still belongs to the night darkness of death, to the realm of wild being beyond mortality.

Orpheus is the writer and Eurydice's death is the existential secret that the writer's work seeks or desires to uncover and reveal. Thus, the glance of Orpheus and the fleeting image he sees of Eurydice belong to the essential act of writing. Orpheus is a poet, a writer, who desires to capture true meaning in words, to capture what truth Eurydice brings in her being: the essence of love and death. Capturing meaning in writing is a desirous act. To write one must come to terms with the limits of meaning that lies at the edge of existence where things simply *are*, but no longer perceivable as objects, artifices of the human cogito. Only when truly engaging in writing may the writer experience the privilege of the gaze of Orpheus: the gaze that has penetrated the dark and momentarily has glanced inside. But at what cost?!

At the level of raw existence there is only the darkness of the night from which all human insight and meaning arises and vanishes. And yet, our desire directs our gaze to the mystery of meaningfulness, and thus impels us to write. Immediately after he returned, Orpheus tried again to go back and find Eurydice in the underworld. But he was no longer allowed entry. So, Orpheus became obsessed with the desire to actually die and be with Eurydice. A version of the myth tells that Orpheus was assaulted by the vindictive Maenads, female followers of Dionysus, who vengefully tore his body to pieces in an ecstatic frenzy. They threw his remains in the fast-flowing River Hebrus. But his head remained fully intact, glancing and singing his love for Eurydice while floating down to the sea.

While the myth is ancient and complex, it is recounted with different twists by the phenomenological philosophers Maurice Blanchot, Michel Serres, and Jean-Luc Marion (see Section Two). With these phenomenologists the epic poetic tale by Ovid receives repeated and surprising translations or poetic interpretations that are phenomenologically compelling and revealing. They seem to give us insights into the meaning of the glance of Orpheus in Blanchot's obsessive desire to write, in Serres' linguistic evocation to read, and in Marion's wonder how we see a painting in the paint.

Meanwhile, when returning to Ovid we read that Orpheus has died:

> The ghost of Orpheus sank under the earth, and recognised all those places it had seen before; and, searching the fields of the Blessed, he found his wife again and held her eagerly in his arms. There they walk together side by side; now she goes in front, and he follows her; now he leads, and looks back as he can do, in safety now, at his love Eurydice. (Ovid, 2000, p. 532)

So, we learn that only in death can we glance back and ahead, and "see." But what do we see? Death? Our beloved? The union of love itself? We wonder: is the significance of the quotidian theme of glancing back a literal looking back into the past? Or is it a temporal looking for what is there in the presence? Because then the glance is always already too late. Or is glancing back an existential reminiscing on the search for essence and originary meaning? That might be the prerogative of phenomenological thinking, seeing, reading, and writing.

Ways of Understanding Phenomenology

CHAPTER ONE

Doing Phenomenology

Phenomenology is the study of the meaning of lived-through experiences—phenomena, as they appear, reveal, and show themselves, and as they give themselves in our consciousness, before they have even been named, conceptualized, abstracted, and/or theorized. "Doing phenomenology" involves a certain way of seeing and thinking—it is not a doctrine but rather a philosophic way (*methodos*) to meaning, not a body of knowledge but rather an attitude or disposition. If it were a doctrine then phenomenology would include a study of the canons, creeds, and courses of the particular traditions that are historically associated with the various philosophical perspectives. But since phenomenology is primarily a philosophic method, attitude, and way of thinking and seeing, the (writing) practice of phenomenology is actually flexible and can be quite creative. It primarily requires an insightful and a sensitive orientation to the meaningfulness of the things and events that matter and that we encounter and experience in everyday life.

Interest in phenomenology has awakened in a very different settings—the domain of public policy and professional practice. These domains are characterized by priorities that arise from everyday practical concerns and experiences, not necessarily from abstract scholarly questions that are inherent in the traditions of (phenomenological) philosophy. In the professional fields, context sensitive research seems to have become especially relevant in recent years. It requires approaches and methodologies that are adaptive of changing social contexts and human predicaments. And that is perhaps how we may explain emerging non-philosophical trends in phenomenological developments.

Over the years, philosophers have occasionally urged that philosophy should find a way of making phenomenology more accessible to professional practitioners and researchers who would be interested in phenomenology but who do not possess a strong, deep, and systematic philosophical background. Some of the various philosophical "introduction to phenomenology" texts that are available in the literature are helpful for developing preliminary understandings. To "introduce" means to bring into a circle of knowledge. But introductions are often regarded as simplifications or popularizations of the ideas of great thinkers. When introductions are simply palatable versions of the real thing, then they may slide into seductions. Seducing, *sēdūcĕre*, is to lead away: to tempt, entice, and also to beguile to do something wrong or unintended. So, sometimes introductions may not be adequate for the tasks of entering a phenomenology of practice.

Thus, a new direction needs to be taken with this book: an agogical approach to phenomenology. The term "*agogic*" derives from Greek, ἀγωγός, which means

DOI: 10.4324/9781003228073-2

orienting, showing, accompanying, or guiding. Agogy is the root word of andragogy (adult focused), pedagogy (child and youth focused), gerontagogy (old-age focused)—agogy means pointing out directions, providing support. Agogical phenomenology aims to show access to phenomenological thinking and research in a manner that makes manifest, in a reflexive mode, what the phenomenological attitude consists of. The *Oxford English Dictionary* shows a relation between *agogics* and *paradigm*: to show through example is to be *paradigmatic*. An agogical approach tries to be an example of what it is showing—a writing practice for those who are interested in doing phenomenological research and writing. An agogical approach to phenomenology aims to orient the person to the project of phenomenological inquiry and to help stimulate personal insights and sensitivities for a phenomenology of practice.

Phenomenology of Practice

The phrase *phenomenology of practice* is meant to articulate the resolve of doing phenomenology directly on the things—especially the quotidian and ordinary aspects of professional practices. The word "practice" is used in the manner that professionals in medicine, law, and other occupations regard practice the core of their calling. The term "practice" is neither used to refer to exercise or training, nor is it used as "applied," in relation to theory, or as a form of critical praxis. Phenomenology of practice wants to be sensitive to the concerns of practices in professional fields, and also to the personal acting and social practices of everyday living. In this way, "phenomenology of practice" distinguishes itself from the more punctilious philosophical phenomenologies that deal with more abstract theoretical and technical philosophical issues.

As well, phenomenology of practice is sensitive to the realization that life as we live and experience it is not only rational and logical, and thus transparent to systematic reflection—it is also subtle, enigmatic, contradictory, ambiguous, sometimes mysterious, and saturated with existential and transcendent meaning that can only be accessed through poetic, aesthetic, and ethical languages. Phenomenology is a perpetual practice, an eternal practicing to get, explore, and disclose meaning in all its complexity.

So, the practice of "doing phenomenology" is thinking and seeing our world phenomenologically. And to think phenomenologically is to be swept up in a spell of wonder about the originary meaningfulness of this or that phenomenon or event as they appear, show, present, or give themselves to us in experience or consciousness. In the experiential encounter with things and events of the world, phenomenology assists us by directing our gaze toward the regions where understandings, emotions, meanings and feelings originate, well up, and percolate through the porous membranes of past existential sedimentations—then infuse, permeate, infect, touch, stir us, and exercise a formative and affective effect on our being and becoming. In this sense phenomenology tells us who we are.

Doing phenomenological research is making intelligible the originary meaningfulness of experiential phenomena and events that we explore in a methodical phenomenological manner through written texts. This need for intelligibility is a characteristic of phenomenology as a mode of inquiry and as an intellectual discipline. Phenomenology starts with experience. But some current phenomenological discourses are so rooted in academese and technical philosophical vocabulary and argument that they are virtually unintelligible jargon, even to well-educated readers. This has led some philosophers to urge their philosopher colleagues to practice phenomenology in a manner that is understandable to non-philosophers. But ironically even some of these philosophers, wittingly or unwittingly, do not seem to know how to follow their own advice and not raise the unnecessary threshold of comprehensibility by remaining as much as possible jargon-free for genuinely interested readers.

Of course, every professional and academic language has its characteristic idiom and etymology of its special technical terminology. That is unavoidable and such nomenclature needs to be clarified and carefully scrutinized if it is meant for its readers. This book too may have some texts that are less clear to those who lack the vocabulary. But we can endeavor and insist that the content and form of phenomenologies of practice strive to remain intelligible while also attempting to appeal, allure, fascinate, and captivate. That is only possible if it avoids getting entangled in unnecessary jargon. Phenomenologies of practice may find its inspiration in a great variety of professional fields and thus the idioms of those fields.

Now, methodologically speaking, phenomenological texts are in some sense always descriptive and interpretive, linguistic and hermeneutic. But it is true that Edmund Husserl (main initiator of phenomenology) emphasized description rather than interpretation, for the simple reason that an accurate description of the essence of a phenomenon should not need to be interpreted. If I can provide a perfect and clear description of a phenomenon then I would not need to interpret it. From a Husserlian perspective, a description is either true and accurate or it is not. But in this book, I assume that language always is inherently and inevitably ambiguous and therefore the meanings of words contain interpretive challenges.

In this book, the term "phenomenology" usually is taken to mean "descriptive-interpretive phenomenology." But while all phenomenology is in some sense interpretive or hermeneutical not all hermeneutics is phenomenological. Indeed, it would appear that some forms of hermeneutics are so wildly interpretive that they have lost all phenomenological (descriptive, concrete, evidential) bearings in lived experience or the lifeworld.

Perhaps phenomenology is better understood as a form of heuristic questioning and wondering than as a kind of determinate answering. Deeper insights tend to come to us in modes of musing, reflective contemplation, or being entangled in primal sources of meaning. This wondering obsession with the meaning of pre-reflective experience and focusing on the singularity of a phenomenon is a main feature that characterizes the various phenomenologies discussed in this book. Ultimately, phenomenology is less a determinate code of inquiry than an inceptual search for originary meanings of prereflective experiences. It will be shown in these chapters that there are many phenomenologies, but that does not mean that the name phenomenology may be used arbitrarily or indiscriminately.

The Phenomenality of a Phenomenon

Etymologically, the term "phenomenon" means "that which appears" and *logos* means "word or study." On first sight, then, the term "phenomenology" seems to be formed like "psycho-logy," "socio-logy," "bio-logy," and so on. The first part of the word refers to the subject or domain of study: psyche (spirit, soul), socio (society, community), bio (life), and so on. The second part, "logos," designates the science or inquiry into the domains of the subjects of the psyche, social, or bios. However, phenomenology does not have a subject matter or subject domain in the same sense as psychology, biology, or sociology—a phenomenon is not a subject in a disciplinary sense.

In the methodological Introduction to *Being and Time*, Heidegger carefully unpacks his provisional ontological formulation of the etymological meaning of the Greek word *phenomenology*. He points out that *logos* means "to let something be seen" and *phenomenon* means "that which shows itself from itself."

> Hence phenomenology means: to let what shows itself be seen from itself, just as it shows itself from itself. That is the formal meaning of the type of research that calls itself "phenomenology." But this expresses nothing other than the maxim formulated above: "To the things themselves!" (Heidegger, 2010, p. 32)

In other words, phenomenology is done on the things themselves by turning to the things that matter themselves. This famous explication by Heidegger has been cited in numerous texts, even though it may have been interpreted differently and the various interpretations may not be very clear methodologically. But perhaps it is important to see that Heidegger wanted to bring forward the notion that what phenomenology aims to "let show itself" is something that is *concealed* or hidden, something that lies *hidden* but that "belongs to what shows itself so essentially as to constitute its meaning and ground" (2010, p. 33). Conceivably, the universal theme of the various traditions of phenomenology is indeed that phenomenology is an inquiry that involves a dynamic play of showing and hiding. It should also be noted that the showing and hiding dimensions of meaning are understood in different modalities. Heidegger clarifies the methodological expression "descriptive phenomenology" as follows:

> Here description does not mean a procedure like that of, say, botanical morphology. The term rather has a sense of a prohibition, insisting that we avoid all nondemonstrative determinations. The character of description itself . . . can be established only from the "content" ["*Sachheit*"] of what is "described" . . . in the way phenomena are encountered. (2010, p. 32)

Phenomenology is the way of access to the world as we experience it prereflectively. Prereflective experience is the ordinary experience that we live in and that we live through for most, if not all, of our day-to-day existence. Whether we are eating a meal, going for a walk, driving a car, gardening, daydreaming, texting a message, hugging a loved one, presenting a lecture, having a conversation, remembering an incident, reading a novel or reflecting on the novel—these are all prereflective experiences when regarded from a phenomenological point of view. Indeed, even the experience of phenomenological reflection can be treated as prereflective and become the focus of reflection. In fact, much of this book is trying to do just that: reflecting on the results of phenomenological reflection and analysis. However, not just any kind of reflection is phenomenological. That is why we must understand the notion of phenomenology as method that involves the somewhat enigmatic coupling of the epoché and the reduction.

From a philosophical point of view, phenomenology is a meaning-giving and meaning-clarifying method of inquiry. But it is not a method in the usual more technical sense of the term. Quantitative and qualitative scientific method often refers to the commonly employed set (or sets) of tools, rules, experiments, trials, treatments, and procedures for conducting investigations, research, and inquiries that are particular to a specific intellectual discipline or scientific practice. Scientific method generally assumes a mode and code of conduct that is impartial, impersonal, and free from the idiosyncrasies or personal styles of the persons who employ such scientific method—although practicing scientists would no doubt say that doing science is often messy, hit-and-miss, going on hunches, and so on.

As we regard the history of phenomenology—from the early Edmund Husserl through Martin Heidegger, Edith Stein, Maurice Merleau-Ponty, Emmanuel Levinas, to Maurice Blanchot, Jacques Derrida, Michel Henry, and Jean-Luc Nancy, and now to contemporaries such as Alphonso Lingis, Giorgio Agamben, Jean-Luc Marion, Günter Figal, Michel Serres, and Jean-Louis Chrétien—we notice an increasing awareness that the phenomenality of human experience cannot be adequately captured with the clarity of analytic concepts, objectifying themes, the purity of philosophical prose, the laws of logic, the abstractions of theory, the codifications of scientific method, and the traditional rationalities of philosophical systems. Instead, there is an acknowledgment that inquiries into the phenomenality (originary or inceptual meaning) of human experiences and truths require the full measure and complexity of the language of prose, the poetic, the cognitive, and the pathic.

Especially in the works of contemporary phenomenologists, reflexive reflections on the eidetic, inceptual, and enigmatic nuances of our experiences go far beyond the pure prose of traditional argumentative and concept-driven qualitative discourses. Some of these meaning-giving methodical features of phenomenological method are described in this book by means of the notions of the vocative, the pathic, the image, the anecdote, the vignette, the model, and the example. When we examine exemplary phenomenological texts, we do indeed find methodical features that are rarely discussed or described in the more orthodox phenomenological philosophical literature. So, we need to explore the relation between meaning and method—where method does not merely mean procedural, technical, repeatable features of inquiry. Phenomenological method is always a matter of attempts, bids, and hopeful risks. Within a phenomenological context, method is never just a smooth or sputtering engine that will unerringly produce insightful outcomes.

Phenomenology is primarily a philosophic *method for questioning*, not just a method for answering or discovering or drawing determinate conclusions. But in this questioning there exist the possibilities and potentialities for experiencing openings, understandings, insights—producing cognitive and noncognitive or pathic perceptions of existentialities, giving us glances of the meaning of phenomena and events in their singularity. Phenomenology contrasts with other qualitative methods and approaches that require repetition and may involve calculation, technicization, and comparison of outcomes, trends, and the indexing of data. But, the further we delve into the phenomenological literature, the clearer it should become that phenomenological method cannot be fitted to a rule book, an interpretive schema, a set of steps, or a systematic set of procedures.

Phenomenology is sometimes referred to as human science. The term "human science" derives from the German word *Geisteswissenschaften*, translated as the study or science (*Wissenschaft*) of mind (*Geist*) (see "Human Sciences and Phenomenology" in Merleau-Ponty, 2010a, pp. 316–372). In North America, human science may refer to a variety of qualitative disciplines such as ethnography, ethnomethodology, narrative inquiry, and so on. It is also regularly equated with the humanities, which would include the arts, literature, philosophy, classics, divinity, ethics, and the social science humanities. But, phenomenological human science differs from the stricter phenomenological philosophy in that some of the human sciences embraces, in addition to the philosophical phenomenological methods, certain empirical and analytical methods that find their roots in the behavioral social sciences. However, by importing methodical activities such as interviewing, observation, participation, and the like into the phenomenological process of inquiry, these methods need to acquire the same underlying methodological signification as the basic project of phenomenology. For example, the phenomenological interview differs markedly in approach and intent from the psychological or the ethnographic interview, as will be shown in a later chapter.

This text aims to touch on a full range of methodological practices that may be engaged in conducting phenomenological human science research. Some phenomenological projects would emphasize or engage some methods over others. The problem is, however, that none of these methodical dimensions of phenomenological inquiry can be reduced to instrumentally procedural schemes or series of steps that would lead to insightful phenomenological studies. Some of such schemes are periodically proposed in the qualitative research literature, but they fail for the simple reason that, as Gadamer points out, there is no method to human truths. Any method, in a procedural sense, inevitably technologizes and objectifies what it studies and thus fails to grasp what is singular, subtle, or what can only be grasped with inventive and vocative means of reflective writing.

Thus, the serious researcher is confronted by the challenge to focus on those parts of the phenomenological literature that would be of relevance to their research interest. The present book attempts to be an agogy in this process and point the reader to original sources. It is more helpful to gain an authentic understanding of primary phenomenological notions and methods than to rely mostly on some simplified scheme that is several "steps" removed from the inspiring works of original and leading phenomenological authors.

In this text I try to be sensitive to the different ways that phenomenology has been understood in the philosophical tradition of phenomenological scholarship. However, I also introduce some terminology that may not be as commonplace in the philosophical literature: notions such as the vocative and the pathic, the anecdote and the example, and the notion of serendipitous insights. These ideas may contribute to the pedagogical project of making phenomenology as a reflective writing practice understandable and doable. The meanings of the vocative and the pathic for phenomenological writing are inherent in the literature, but perhaps they do not often surface explicitly since writing (composing practical phenomenological studies) is so taken for granted in philosophy that it is rarely reflected upon in a practical manner. Even in the professional phenomenological literature, little attention is paid to the fact that, in the end, the reflective process of phenomenological inquiry largely happens in the practice of writing. Notions such as lived experience descriptions (LEDs), the anecdote, the phenomenological example, incept, punctum, descant, serendipity, tact, and so on, may help with the know-how of practicing phenomenology. Some of these notions I have borrowed, interpreted, and extended from the works of authors such as Sartre, Merleau-Ponty, Blanchot, Barthes, Derrida, and Agamben—though these terms may carry even richer meanings in their original texts. For example, Michel de Montaigne frequently used anecdotes in his essays as tools for his meditative reflections about the meanings of his topical interests such as notions of happiness, experience, friendship, names, virtue, and so forth. And he was famous for his skeptical saying "What do I know?" (*Que sais-je?*) which expresses the sense of doubt that inheres in the concept of *essay* as a literary contrivance. The figure of *anecdote* and the expression of *phenomenological essay* for the research texts of phenomenological enquiries are used in this book as methodological models for the genre of phenomenological writing, even though they have been ripening for 500 years in the works of Montagne.

Finally, and importantly, phenomenology does not necessarily have to follow the standard social science practice of empirical data-gathering through interview, observation, written solicitations, or the narrowly conceived procedural practices of thematic analysis and the like. Phenomenology can be practiced in a reflective manner on topics that may require a fundamental knowledge of cinematography, photography, experiences gained through travel, the study of the novel or stories, the phenomenological study of visual and graphic arts, new creative art forms and expressions, and topics that may arise in the development and encounters with new media, technologies, Internet-related phenomena and events, and topics that present themselves in the reflective actions of professional practices. I hope to demonstrate that the various appearances of phenomenology show that there are many methodical possibilities in engaging in a phenomenology of practice: phenomenologies that may enrich and guide our professional and every day actions and experiences. The ultimate aim of a phenomenology of practice is modest: to nurture a measure of insightful thoughtfulness and discretionary tact in the practice and understanding of our professions and in everyday life.

Bringing the Reader to Wonder

By the time students who were enrolled in my doctoral phenomenology seminar selected a topic for their course paper, my first writing assignment was: make the reader wonder about the meaning of your phenomenological topic (phenomenon).

Only one page should be an adequate beginning. Let others read your first one-page draft and test to see if their response is genuine wonder: "Yes, what is that phenomenon, that thing, that event, or that object?" I knew that simply selecting a topic for a paper was not enough. The students had to come to the point of fundamentally starting to wonder with respect to the meaning of the human experience that they themselves had chosen to study.

Of course, we examined some interesting examples. For instance, the Dutch phenomenologist David van Lennep was spending a few days with his partner sightseeing in Paris. But sightseeing is tiring and after some hours walking through a museum, he suggested they "Go home for a few hours and read a bit." The partner laughed and said, "You mean go back to the hotel room?" They both laughed. Yes, the hotel room had become their temporary home. And yet it does not look in the least like their real home. So, van Lennep remarked:

> Someone once said: a room is like a sacred garment. This expression points to the fact that we dwell in a room not because it is our room, but because it becomes our room when we live in it. What is this mysterious inhabiting through which a room becomes ours? For the most part we believe that it is very important for the inhabiting whether or not, for example, we have placed furniture of our choice in it and that through this choice a room becomes a personal expression of ourself. However, the room as an expression of our personality is to a great extent an unfulfillable dream: there are too many factors which do not depend upon our free choice. (van Lennep, 1987a, p. 209)

Next, van Lennep wonders how it is that an impersonal hotel room seems to turn into "our home" after a few days or even after a few hours living in it. Appropriately van Lennep alludes to the way that a piece of clothing such as a coat or some other garment becomes our own. "The Hotel Room" is a wonderful example of how a text can make us wonder. Van Lennep makes us question all kinds of stereotypical prejudgments that we have about the way that a space becomes our own and it is a great example of how to conduct a phenomenological inquiry about a seemingly ordinary phenomenon.

Van Lennep shows how a phenomenological study of a phenomenon or event is a search for its inceptual meanings and originary significance. But indirectly he helps the reader to understand Heidegger's notion of inceptuality. The idea of phenomenology is that it is the original science of life, says Heidegger. Original refers to the primal beginnings of meaning of life phenomena. Originary means primary in the sense of underived inceptuality.

Therefore, Heidegger says, "all questioning related to phenomenology should itself be phenomenological and should be settled phenomenologically" (2013a, p. 4). The phrase phenomenology as an original science should not be confused with qualitative empirical inquiries that are based on the factualities of life. And we must not reduce a phenomenon or event to an objectifying concept, theory, causal, or scientific explanation.

So where to begin? If phenomenology is the study of phenomena then what is a "phenomenon"? Any object and event can be considered a phenomenon, but phenomenologists have a special meaning in mind. To see something phenomenologically, one needs to assume a special attitude so that the taken-for-granted meaning of a phenomenon turns phenomenal, which means that the obvious becomes questionable and enigmatic. That special attitude that one needs to assume or adopt is described by Merleau-Ponty as the heuristic of wonder (Merleau-Ponty, 1962, p. xiii). But how can wonder be a method?

As readers we know how the spark of wonder can alight: when a text infects us with a sudden realization of the unsuspected enigmatic nature of ordinary reality. Wonder is this infectious evocation when one is overcome by awe or perplexity—such as when something familiar has turned profoundly unfamiliar, when our gaze has been drawn by the gaze of something that stares back at us.

From a philosophical perspective it is not at all surprising that wonder is the central methodological feature of phenomenological inquiry. Phenomenology is a philosophical project and ancient philosophy posed that all philosophical thought begins in wonder, but we may also turn it around and say that philosophical reflection is the product of wonder. In other words, wonder is both the condition and the primary principle of phenomenological method (Verhoeven, 1967, pp. 30–50). Phenomenological writing not only finds its starting point in wonder, it must also induce wonder. For a phenomenological text to "lead" the way to human understanding, it must lead the reader to wonder. Our text must induce a questioning wonder. But what is wonder? Can we make someone wonder?

Let me give another simple example. But this is an example of a child's experience of wonder. Unfortunately, philosophers rarely if ever discuss children's experiences as worthy of including in their reflections. I just want to ask what it is like to wonder about seeing something in a manner that is perhaps childlike. This was an occasion when my children were still quite young. As a parent I recall one late night, many years ago, that my family and I were returning home, the long seven-hour journey from my wife's hometown to our home in the big city. This drive takes us through some of the most desolate landscapes of the Canadian prairies. For hours the traveler may not see any sign of human settlement. Here is mostly dry bare country. No trees, no bushes, nothing. The only thing to watch out for is the rare bundle of tumbleweed that, driven by a fickle wind, may suddenly bounce across the highway. But that night the desolation hardly mattered since we were traveling in the dark. No moon in the sky to light the landscape. Except for the beam of light of the headlights, the car was spinning its way through a time cocoon. No markers outside the dark windows tell where one is, how far one has come, and how far one still has to go. My eyes were fixed on the strip of road ahead, and I began to notice a strange event.

It was as if the dark was being lifted from the landscape. Some invisible hand drew curtains of sheer crisscross against the sky. It was the theater of the Northern Lights. I stopped the car, and my wife, our two children, and I got out. There we were! Out there in that open country. Darkness all around and the immense expanse of stars above. The sheets of aurora borealis were offering a truly incredible spectacle all across the deeply black sky right above us. It is at moments like this, when one is all surrounded by the stupendous starry sky and its immensely wondrous phenomenon of the aurora, that I teeter at the edge of my agnosticism. Truly there must be something deeply meaningful in the universe around us. Gazing into the sky, one may experience a strange sensation of being gazed at in return by something beyond oneself. It is as if one gazes into a cosmic mirror, and in a moment of extreme reflexivity one experiences the reflection of one's own gaze as uncannily strange: Who am I? What is my place in all this? Why are we here? But these are questions without answers. They call for a turning away of the eyes.

To my satisfaction the children, too, were unbelievably quiet—unbelievably, since they had had some conflict in the backseat of the car just prior to our stopping. I was happy because I thought that for them, too, this must be an experience of true wonder. This is an experience that one cannot plan for. As we stepped back into the car and resumed our journey, I asked them for their impression. Oh, sure, they thought it was quite "cool," but I was surprised that they were much more interested in talking about other things. Things such as: Was I afraid to be in the dark all by myself? Would there be wolves around where we stopped? Had I heard the rustling in the grass on the side of the road? What could it have been? What if something would have jumped on us? What would we have done? What if we would have to remain in that dark all night? Yes, we had lots of good talks, and it helped us pass the time, another hour of dreary driving. I realized that I had not succeeded in helping my children to experience a moment of true wonder about the aurora. And yet, the children had been stirred by their own sense of wonder about things that had eluded me completely. I had directed my gaze upwards to the aurora. But my children had gazed directly into the night. And the night had gazed back at them, and they seemed to have sensed its terrifying mystery.

As we drove on I had to think of Heidegger's reflections on the nature of wonder. He made a special effort to explain that wonder should not be confused with admiration, puzzlement, curiosity, or amazement. Of course, we may inquire into the physics of the aurora and thus give an interesting scientific explanation of its appearance. Natural science approaches the aurora with a sense of curiosity. Science wants to understand the physical processes that cause the aurora. The point is that wonder affects us more profoundly than curiosity. The experience of wonder is the depthful state of a special dispositioning. It displaces our sense of being. And it may pose questions that only lead to the realization of more questions.

Merleau-Ponty cites Eugen Fink when he described the import of meaningfulness of the phenomenological reduction as the sense of "wonder in the face of the world" (Merleau-Ponty, 1962, p. xiii). Such experience of wonder evokes an attitude of fundamental questioning of the meaning of things that matter: the phenomenal meanings of life as we experience them. What gives the appearance of the aurora such spellbound draw? This is indeed a phenomenological questioning. And phenomenological questions should not be confused with explanatory, informational, conceptual, or cause-and-effect type questions that may lead to an attitude of curiosity, amazement, or admiration. The last types of questions are resolved once we hear the proper answers to the question. For example, the curiosity about the aurora borealis may be stilled by an atmospheric explanation: auroras are caused by the emissions of photons in the earth's upper atmosphere that are excited to emit light by the collision of particles. While the scientific explanation may be complex and intellectually challenging, in principle the question of the aurora borealis can be answered and then the curiosity has been killed, so to speak. But the attitude of wonder of the experience of the aurora borealis, also called polar lights or aurora polaris, might not be stilled with a scientific explanation. The mere fact *that* this phenomenon exists is already wondrous. The "what" question of a phenomenon is rooted in a "that" that searches for the existential transcendental meaning of "what" something is in its phenomenality, and the realization "that" it exists and that it shows itself.

To reiterate, wonder should not be confused with terms such as amazement, admiration, or curiosity. Amazement is an inability to explain a certain phenomenon or event, but once we do explain it, the wonder is gone. Similarly, the admiration we may feel for an action or a person that we admire or with whom we are greatly impressed is not really wonder, because once the admiration is gone, so is the wonder. Wonder is different also from astonishment. But what nevertheless may unify these (false or superficial) conceptions of wonder is that they presuppose that the wondrous is something "extraordinary." False conceptions of wonder are therefore nothing more than different forms of curiosity or amazement. But curiosity or amazement is superficial. It has no interest in wondering. So, what then is wonder?

Heidegger points out that the experience of wonder is dispositional: wonder dispositions us. It puts us in a special mood by displacing us and dispositioning our relation with the things of the world. Wonder brings us to awaken a sense of aporia: questioning perplexity. But real questioning does not lead to positivistic answers. Wonder is the experience of a question for which there is not really a ready answer, says Wittgenstein. For a thoughtful inquiry wonder needs to linger. If wonder is converted too quickly into the action of posing and solving problems then it may already have lost its heuristic power and potential.

We may be caught in a moment of wonder before we have even started to think. Phenomenology aims to radicalize this experience of wonder. And vice versa, the radical sense of wonder is the method of phenomenology. Of course, it may be difficult to make someone wonder about a phenomenon or the meaning of an experience and yet that is precisely what needs to be accomplished in adopting an attitude of radical openness. This openness is called the phenomenological epoché. When a phenomenon or event passes the gaze of wonder it can potentially become a *phenomenon* or *event* in the full sense of the word.

The Intimate Pleasure of the Secret Soul

The main challenge of phenomenological inquiry (researching, writing) is to gain insights into a phenomenon that presents itself and that is being investigated. But as Wassily Kandinsky says: no matter how common or trivial the object of a phenomenon, everything has a secret soul:

> Everything that is dead quivers. Not only the things of poetry, stars, moon, wood, flowers, but even a white trouser button glittering out of a puddle in the street . . . Everything has a secret soul, which is silent more often than it speaks. (2009, p. 75)

When Kandinsky says that everything has a secret soul, then he is speaking not only of things but also of his inner self as artist. There is a nostalgia in Kandinsky's pronouncement. Only the one who can hear or see the silent soul in a thing as trite as a button in a gutter, only that person is in touch with the true essence of that thing. That person experiences life meaning. When the inner essence of the artist entangles the outer essence of a thing then this contact is experienced as meaningful. One gains insight into the essence of something. And those who have experienced such moments know that experiencing or having an insight is highly pleasurable or fulfilling. There is almost something cosmic in this realization of a moment of entanglement that asks for an insight.

What entanglement? When two particles, such as a pair of photons or electrons, become entangled, they remain connected even when separated by vast distances. So, particles can appear independent—yet are entangled and mysteriously connected, so that when the one particle quivers the other quivers. We sense the mystery. Even if the mystery would get solved by an explanation—it will likely remain mysterious. Apparently Einstein mockingly called the idea of this apparent mysterious entanglement "spooky action at a distance." But for Einstein the mystery was unacceptable because it was just an idea and unrealistic. Now we know that particle entanglement is a physical phenomenon that can be measured, demonstrated, and explained. But the explanation still remains a mystery. And yet, we may feel great pleasure experiencing an insightful moment.

What makes phenomenology so rewarding is that it is pleasurable to read about existential insights: to passively and actively read and write insightful moments. In his book *The Pleasure of the Text*, Roland Barthes (1975) reminds us that the act of reading and writing itself can be highly pleasurable. He calls it *jouissance*, carnate pleasure. He poses the question of what we do when we enjoy a text. But we should remind ourselves that reading and writing a phenomenological essay is pleasurable in a different sense than reading a novel or writing a novel. The practice of doing phenomenology may not even be regarded as pleasurable though it can be experienced as highly gratifying. Pleasure is an ambiguous word that can evoke very different experiential emotions and feeling.

Barthes' book *The Pleasure of the Text* contains a series of fragments about reading and writing; in the table of contents the fragments are indicated with one-word titles with page numbers. The book is actually a highly original series of reflections on linguistic issues and topics such as "Right, Exchange, Hearing, Emotion, Boredom." But each fragment is joyful to read as it offers meaningful insights into the question what makes textual reading and writing joyful. The question is how such ideas and insights come to us. Roland Barthes gives this response:

> To be with the one I love and to think of something else: this is how I have my best ideas, how I best invent what is necessary to my work. Likewise for the text: it produces, in me, the best pleasure if it manages to make itself heard indirectly: if, reading it, I am led to look up often, to listen to something else. I am not necessarily *captivated* by the text of pleasure; it can be an act that is slight, complex, tenuous, almost scatterbrained: a sudden movement of the head like a bird who understands nothing of what we hear, who hears what we do not understand. (Barthes, 1975, pp. 24, 25)

Insights are at the core of all science but there are at least two kinds of insights, cause-and-effect insights and meaning insights, that deserve attention.

Cause-and-Effect Insight

A famous example of cause-and-effect insights was given by the neuroscientist Otto Loewi. But he is especially known for the way that the insight came to him. On Easter Saturday 1921, he dreamed of an experiment that would prove once and for all that transmission of nerve impulses was chemical, not electrical. He tells how this insight occurred to him as a dream when he wondered how to determine whether the causal nexus for the transmission of nerve impulses is chemical or electrical. He woke up, scribbled the experiment onto a scrap of paper on his night-stand, and went back to sleep. But the next morning, he found, to his horror, that he couldn't read his midnight scribbles. That day, he said, was the longest day of his life, as he tried to remember his dream, in vain. The next night, however, he had the same dream. This time, he woke up and immediately went to his lab to perform the experiment. Thirteen years later, Loewi shared in the Nobel Prize in Physiology or Medicine.

Often scientific "insights" are associated with research and technologies in the physical and medical sciences, nanotechnologies, and so forth. In Canada, there is a national radio program, Quirks and Quarks, that once a week features the latest scientific insights and discoveries. But these are predominantly problem–solution insights. Meaning insights are rarely addressed in this otherwise fascinating program about the progress of human insights into natural, physical, and cosmic phenomena.

Meaning insights are different from problem–solution and cause–effect insights. Problem–solutions and cause–effect insights may occur in a single instant, as when Archimedes reportedly jumped out of his bathtub and ran into the street yelling, "Eureka, I found it!" This is the eureka moment that occurred to Archimedes when he suddenly realized, while taking a bath, how to measure the volume of an irregular object or body. A cause-and-effect insight also is characterized by a sudden insight after a period of incubation. The cause-and-effect insight describes the moment of suddenly seeing the causal nexus of a physical, psychological, or epidemiological situation. Pure jouissance! But meaning insights too are pleasurable.

Meaning Insights

Meaning insights generally do not offer themselves in a single coup. Once revealed in an insightful moment, they have to be wrestled with to gain depth and clarity, and their complexity often requires further insights, as in Heidegger's increasingly depthful insights into the phenomenon of boredom in *The Fundamental Concept of Metaphysics*. Similarly, meaning insights do not so much require a period of incubation, as in the chicken which must be physically ready to lay the egg.

Rather, meaning insights depend on a "latency" that eventuates an experience of clarity. This clarity of a sudden meaningfulness may also be sudden but is more associated with a sense of opening oneself and a constant searching for understanding the meaning of something. Indeed, this opening and searching may be associated with the phenomenological epoché (opening up) and the reduction (focusing on something). A meaning insight may come to us as when suddenly remembering the name of someone or something. Other meanings are less like names but more like memories that present themselves like an eidetic anamnesis, reminiscences of essences of our fundamental humanness. These may come to us when most unexpected, and yet they require a charged preoccupation, being haunted by the need to understand or "see" something for what it is or for how it gives itself. Meaning insights must be written or they escape like Kairos moments (Marramao, 2007; Sipiora and Baumlin, 2012; Hermsen, 2014). The sudden ingrasping of an inceptual insight is the writerly experience of the gaze of Orpheus who was haunted by the desire to see Eurydice in her essence: her perfect incarnation of the immortality of love itself.

The term "insight" literally means in-seeing. The *Oxford English Dictionary* provides a definition of "insight" that hints at the very phenomenology of its meaning: "The fact of penetrating with the eyes of the understanding into the inner character or hidden nature of things; a glimpse or view beneath the surface; the faculty or power of thus seeing." Insight is related to inseeing, ingrasping, and inception. The poet Rainer Maria Rilke confesses that the greatest feeling that has moved him is always a certain kind of inseeing: moments of seeing into the heart of things (Rilke, 1987, p. 77). His description of inseeing as that fleeting swift moment of seeing into the heart of things is a Kairos moment. Inseeing can be regarded a vocative poetic description of the phenomenological method of the epoché-reduction: glancing the essence of something (a phenomenon or event). We might paraphrase another artist, Wassily Kandinsky, that everything has a secret essence, which is silent more often than it speaks.

The insight of phenomenological inseeing is grasping the primal structure of meaning of something. But the insight of phenomenological inseeing must be distinguished and not be confused with the more common definitions of insight as suddenly seeing the solution to a problem.

There exists quite an extensive literature on the philosophy and psychology of insight (for example, Sternberg and Davidson, 1994; Kounios and Beeman, 2015), yet almost all this literature is concerned with problem–solutions and cause-and-effect insights. Problem–solution insights tend to occur when experiencing an impasse in solving a previously puzzling or incomprehensible problem. Sometimes, a solution will suddenly occur as an "eureka" moment or an "aha" epiphany when an issue or problem has been simmering below the surface, on the back-burner of the always active brain, for some time.

Inceptuality or Ingrasping

Meaning insights tend to occur when we wonder about the sense or the significance of the originary meaning of an experiential phenomenon. Originary does not mean new or original. Originary means inceptual: originary insights reveal the primal meaning and significance of a phenomenon (lived experience). For Heidegger the notion of inceptuality assumes critical significance in his later work. The originary meaning of a phenomenon or event lies in its inceptuality, its primal meaning, which must be sought in the epoché (openness) of the beginning of its meaningful beginning. An incept is a grasping of the epitome, quintessence, or what is essential in the sense of the original-unique (Heidegger, 2012b, p. 52). According to Heidegger, "in-grasping [inceptuality] is a knowing awareness that comes out of in-abiding which is not a propositional knowing" (1999, p. 45). Inception connotes origination, birth, dawn, genesis, beginning, and opening. When Heidegger describes an inceptual insight, it tends to occur as a "flash of beying" (Heidegger, 2012a, pp. 70, 71), meaning a flash of inceptual meaning.

Insightfulness should not be confused with creativity. From a phenomenological perspective, the occurrence of a "flash of insight" is more intriguing than understanding it as a creative act. In a creative act the subject is the creator, the agent of the creation, the creative production. But inceptual insights do not necessarily depend on my creative agency, rather an inceptual thought may happen to me as a gift, a grace—an event that I could neither plan nor foresee. That is why Heidegger describes the inceptual experience in terms of an appropriative event or happening. In a manner, the inception may be regarded as the birth of meaning. The problem for phenomenological researchers is that a meaningful insight often cannot be secured by a planned systematic method. There are no technicalities, procedures, schemes, packages, or programs that will somehow produce or capture an insightful thought or creative insight.

The Active Passivity of Patience

Illogically perhaps, human phenomena tend to be both active and passive. From the simplest phenomenon (like falling asleep) to the more complex phenomenon (like gaining an insight), activity and passivity are inextricably entwined. This also means that "producing" insights in doing phenomenological analysis is not just a function of active mental processes. Inceptive insights, just as poetic words, cannot always be forced into fixed concepts. Any attempts at treating inceptual moments as conceptual "data" with pure data-processing procedures are profoundly misdirected. Instead, an active passive attitude and patience may be required for an inceptual happening to happen. Rilke speaks of the extreme patience as well as the slow preparedness that are conditional for a creative moment to occur. He describes evocatively the many living experiences and the passive receptivity that is required for a vocative gift of a poetic word or phenomenological insight to present itself in the creative tumult of a rare or unexpected fleeting movement of time. For Rilke, the gift is the first word that passes as fast as a fleeting feeling, but the true gift is not the feeling itself, but it is the secret experience that the pathic word or the verse is able to evoke.

verses are not, as people imagine, simply feelings (those one has early enough)— they are experiences. For the sake of a single verse, you must see many cities, people and things, one must know the animals, one must feel how the birds fly and know the gesture with which the little flowers open in the morning. One must be able to think back to roads in unknown regions, to unexpected meetings and to partings one had long seen coming; to days of childhood that are still unexplained, to parents whom one had to hurt when they brought one some joy and one did not grasp it (it was a joy for someone else); to childhood illnesses that so strangely begin with such a number of profound and grave transformations, to days in rooms withdrawn and quiet and to mornings by the sea, to the sea itself, to seas, to nights of travel that rushed along on high and flew with all the stars,—and it is not yet enough if one may think of all this. One must have memories of many nights of love, none of which was like the others, of the screams of women in labour, and of light, white, sleeping women in childbed, closing again. But one must also have been beside the dying, must have sat beside the dead in the room with the open window and the fitful noises. And still it is not yet enough to have memories. One must be able to forget them when they are many, and one must have the great patience to wait until they come again. For it is not yet the memories themselves. Not till they have turned to blood within us, to glance and gesture, nameless and no longer to be distinguished from ourselves—not till then can it happen that in a most rare hour the first word of a verse arises in their midst and goes forth from them. (Rilke, 1964, pp. 26, 27)

Indeed, we need to be tolerant of a certain level of genuine frustration and real struggle while actively trying to gain phenomenological insights. Or better, we need to expect becoming frustrated—in the hope that insights may come when least expected, though unfortunately this hope may, of course, prove to be idle. It should be clear as well that the phenomenology of research-writing shows that writing does not just happen when sitting behind the keyboard or leaning against a tree with pen and paper. We are still writing when going for a walk and we are suddenly "overcome," as it were, by some new thought. Yes, we may even be "writing" still when falling asleep. Phenomenology tries to understand consciousness, meaning(fulness), and our sense of self and otherness, and the way that these phenomena manifest themselves.

The Brain: Consciousness, Experience, Self

While neuroscience cannot tell from brain monitoring what the phenomenology of our experiences consists of, scientists have been able to show how demonstrable brain activity is associated with thinking. Neuroscience shows that the brain is always more active than we can possibly be conscious of in our daily lives. Amazingly, the brain is said by science to consists of 86 billion neurons all of which are constantly active and tied into trillions of intricate connections with other neurons and neuron receptors. And yet, strangely, we do not know and notice these brain activities (for accessible background readings see: Wolf, 2007; Damasio, 2010; Eagleman, 2011). Should we therefore say that these activities of the brain are unconscious, nonconscious, subconscious, or preconscious? Or are the words conscious and consciousness inappropriate in describing the operations or processes of the brain that can be observed at the chemical-electronic cellular level and with functional brain imaging machines?

No wonder that some neuroscientists have declared the brain to be the most complex and miraculous structure in the universe. What happens when we stir from deep sleep when there is no human awareness of any cognitive or affective kind, and we wake up? This simple moment of waking up is utterly mysterious. And neuroscience still does not know how to convincingly explain human consciousness, meaningfulness, the nature of experience, and related core phenomena of human existence. After all, it is precisely this awareness, consciousness, meaningfulness, awakening of the unconscious and profoundly miraculous mind that is the stuff of phenomenology. Meaning is the word that lies at the core of phenomenological interests. Meaning and meaningfulness point at phenomenal experiences that matter to us and that we care about in our everyday lives. The neuroscientist can observe and study the clever behaviors of brain cells but they cannot describe the contents of the meaningful life of the continuous interactions of the synaptic junctions, connections, fusions, and diffusions of the neurotransmitting chemical-electric brain-cell structures, programs, and centers.

The brain is constantly interacting with the world outside of our skull, although in some sense the world is already inside our brain and the brain is inside or part of the world. When we wonder about questions such as "Who am I?" then the answer lies somehow in the trillions of complex interactive relations or spheres that the brain actively maintains with the world around us. But it is a mystery why and how at certain moments the question "Who am I?" presents itself. The vast majority of brain activity is concerned with our daily physical and mental states, conditions, and behaviors that are unconscious, automatic, and somehow constantly being "controlled" or programmed in the neural network connections of the brain. Only a tiny fraction of the electro-chemical activities of the brain is associated with consciousness and/or self-consciousness. And yet that is precisely where our sense of "I" and "being me" emerges in the awareness and self-awareness of our lived experiences.

Scientific monitoring of the activities of the brain suggests that past experiences continually seem to be being "processed," especially in periods or moments of active passivity, even just before falling asleep when the brain seems even more active than when fully awake. This phenomenon can be observed in situations when we forget a name and no matter how hard we try, the name cannot be recalled. Then, to our surprise, some time later, when the whole name thing has been forgotten, the name unexpectedly occurs. The name jumps to mind. We may suddenly call out the name. "Yes, that is what I was trying to remember!"

So, strangely, it is in passive moments of seeming inactivity that the brain is especially active. It is in such moments of active passivity that sudden insights may come to us. From a neuroscience perspective, these brain activities likely lead to new changes in the unique mental organization and "the internal or mental model" of the world in the mind of each person. In everyday life situations, we may be talking with someone who asks us about something that we do not know how to respond to immediately. In such situations what happens is that we tend to pause while looking up and away from our interlocutor. In a sense, the brain does the same kind of thing: it momentarily passes into a state of active passivity.

Measuring brain activity while stimulating sudden insights in a person shows that new and sudden insights tend to occur when the person momentarily looks away or closes the eyes. Just so, when we are engaged in conversation and we are searching for a word or an idea, the brain seems to momentarily pause, look away, or close its eyes, so to speak, in order to create an instant when looking for an insight or when an insight may occur. Sudden insights (such as in the sense of inceptive thoughts) often tend to occur when we are not doing anything particular. Or insights may happen in moments of active passivity, such as when we go for a lone walk, when doing a routine task, when pedaling on an exercise bike, or when absent-mindedly staring into the distance.

For the purpose of phenomenological insight, we must realize, however, that, when we are not struggling and not preoccupied with a question, or when we are not really actively and painstakingly wondering about the meaning of something, then there is no emergent emergency of stored up experiences or thought that may unexpectedly lead to insights for our writing. There is truth in the cliché: no pain no gain. If nothing is cooking or simmering on a back burner, no meal will be ready. We may experience moments that we suddenly awaken during the night with the realization that an important idea has struck us. Better write it down because it may be forgotten again in the morning.

If we place them in sharp contrast then phenomenology tries to *describe* and *understand* the meaningful experiences of consciousness. Neuro-science tries to *explain* and *predict* the existence and causalities of meaningful experiences of consciousness. Neither can quite do the other's task, or so it seems.

Streams of Phenomenology

When discussing the subject matter of phenomenology, awkward questions may arise. What kind of phenomenology is most relevant for researchers in fields such as psychology, pedagogy, nursing, and medicine? Are some phenomenological studies more helpful than others for understanding professional practices? What do such studies look like? Which phenomenological texts are appropriately accessible for reading? One obvious suggestion would be to peruse journals and books that publish phenomenological papers and in which reputable phenomenologists publish. If published texts are structured for reading, what types of structures of texts and publications do we find with the term "phenomenology" in the title or with the obvious intent to be considered works of phenomenology? To gain a sense of the variety of phenomenology publications one would have to cast the net quite wide, and one would soon discover that some books, journals, magazines, and other media contain texts that are highly specialized and technical while others are quite accessible to human science researchers and scholars, and also possibly appeal to the spheres of interest of the educated reader. But in perusing the literature, one will discover that the range of phenomenological publications is quite large and that they consist of different streams.

With the intent to provide some order in the plethora of published phenomenological studies, the philosopher Joseph Kockelmans distinguished three kinds of phenomenological publications (for a contextual discussion, see also van Manen and van Manen, 2021). These distinctions can be helpful to the reader. Kockelmans says the following:

> Over the past decades many books and essays have been written on phenomenology. Some of these publications are historical in character and were designed

to give the reader an idea of the origin, meaning, and function of phenomenology and its most important trends. Others are theoretical in nature and were written to give the reader an insight into the ways in which various authors conceive of phenomenology and how they attempt to justify their views in light of the philosophical assumptions underlying their conceptions. Finally, there are a great number of publications in which the authors do not talk about phenomenology, but rather try *to do* what was described as possible and necessary in the first two kinds of publications. Some attempts to do the latter have been quite successful; in other cases the results have been disappointing. (1987, p. vii)

On the basis of Kockelmans' suggestion, the kinds of publications that appear in the broad literature under the name "phenomenology" may be grouped into three streams or currents: foundational, exegetical, and phenomenal. The foundational kinds of writings and publications establish the nature, conditions, and assumptions of phenomenology. The exegetical kinds of phenomenological writings and publications explore the ways that phenomenological perspectives, principles, and starting points may speak to the varieties of phenomenological concepts, themes, topics, theories, and interests that are addressed in the literature. And the phenomenal kinds of writings and publications distinguish themselves by actually doing or practicing the method of phenomenology on concrete phenomena and everyday events. In Kockelmans' view, and he cites Spiegelberg (1975), it is doing phenomenology, rather than mostly theorizing about it, that is needed. Here follows an interpretive clarification of Kockelmans' distinction of three kinds of phenomenological works.

The Foundational Stream

The first stream of publications that Kockelmans mentions include the most original works that are of historical relevance, and generally foundational to the field of phenomenology. These are the writings by leading philosophy authors and human science and humanities scholars. Edmund Husserl, Martin Heidegger, Edith Stein, Jean-Paul Sartre, and Maurice Merleau-Ponty are probably among the best-known originators, though their work is not always easy to read and comprehend. Still, the foundational structures of these writings offer fundamental insights that are inexhaustible in their philosophical significance for those seriously interested in understanding phenomenology.

Husserl and Heidegger are the highly gifted thinkers who took their leads from the works by Aristotle, Nietzsche, Brentano, Hegel, and others. Husserl's works (1970, 1983) gave us the method of the reduction that must establish the phenomenological attitude; the mode of *intentionality* of consciousness that allows the things of the world to give themselves as phenomena; the epoché that involves the suspension of the *natural attitude* in favor of the *transcendental reduction*, the *lifeworld* as the source of our *lived experiences*, and the means of *bracketing* to assist in identifying eidetic aspects of phenomena. Heidegger's works (1962, 1977, 1982, 2001) gave us the focus on the *Being of being*; human ontology as *Dasein*; the characterization of the phenomenological method as to let that which shows itself be seen from itself in the very way in which it shows

itself from itself; his notions of *zuhanden* and *vorhanden*; and his writings on *technology* whereby technology is not to be understood instrumentally but as the explication of the general comportment by which technology may shape our existential ways of being.

Following them there are other early and subsequent phenomenological publications that offer founding phenomenological ideas, such as in the writings of Wilhelm Dilthey (1985, 1987), Jean-Paul Sartre (1956, 1991), Simone de Beauvoir (1967, 2011), Maurice Merleau-Ponty (1962, 1968), Max Scheler (1970), Emmanuel Levinas (1979, 1981), and more contemporary originary works of thinkers such as Jean-Luc Nancy (1997b, 2007b), Jacques Derrida (1995a, 1995b), Michel Henry (2008, 2009) and Jean-Luc Marion (2002a, 2007) (see Chapters 7–9). These works are indeed recognized as brilliant, original, and pathbreaking texts offering convergent and divergent paths of thought. The significance of these publications is that they are foundational to the development and understanding of the philosophical project of phenomenology itself. For example, the philosophical phenomenologist Dermot Moran has done more than most in dedicating himself to making the founding works of Husserl and Heidegger as well as the foundational texts of a dozen of the most central phenomenological thinkers from Franz von Brentano to Paul Ricoeur accessible to readers. Moran's *Introduction to Phenomenology* (2000) and Moran's and Mooney's *The Phenomenology Reader* (2002) focus on exemplary and founding dimensions of the works of some of the most talented phenomenological authors to date.

The Exegetical Stream

As for the second stream that Kockelmans distinguishes, this is the dominant literature that in the past and present continues to address and explore exegetical, technical, historical, and theoretical issues of phenomenology. Exegetics is the critical discourse or philosophical commentary, explanation, or argumentative interpretation of a text. Exegetical publications tend to take up in a critical, and philosophical manner the arguments and positions of the founding authors mentioned above as well as address theoretical issues of more exegetical philosophers and scholars of phenomenology. This literature is enormously variegated and extensive, sometimes offering interesting comparative studies and probing thought-provoking topics, other times texts that are steeped in "language" and only of interest and readable by specialized philosophers, and there are publications that are engaged in energetic hair-splitting, cleverly raising fault-finding objections, and serving academic exegetical arguments. The exegetical structures of these enormously diverse and numerous texts unfortunately may be seen to include an almost interminable array of historical, theoretical, and liberal topics that are sometimes tedious, pretentious, intellectualist, and captious.

The etymology of the term "exegesis" and "exegetics" borrows from Latin and Greek, meaning exposition, narrative, and explanation, also numerical exegesis of mathematical solutions. Exegetical phenomenology tends to be meta-phenomenology and meta-meta-phenomenology. How to recognize this form of phenomenological publications? The general style of these publications is that they offer explanations *of*, theories *about*, comments *on*, and introductions *to* other published (meta-)phenomenological works, topics, and concerns that tend to be technical and/or historical in a philosophical or specialized disciplinary phenomenological sense.

Some of these philosopher scholars may spend much of their entire life's efforts on studying some aspects of the works of certain selective foundational phenomenologists or defending their grasp of the technical intricacies of a certain phenomenological ideas or concepts—such as the meaning and upshot of the phenomenology of empathy, the transcendent meaning of consciousness in the reflexivity of the self, the significance of poetry in the work of Heidegger, and so forth. Thus, a majority of phenomenological texts may actually be more identifiable as belonging to the genre of traditional philosophy rather than with the more lifeworld oriented part of the exegetical stream of phenomenology. Perhaps there is virtually no clear indexical approach to describe the breadth, uniqueness, variety, quality, and levels of (ir)relevance of these phenomenological texts.

So, for many interested in reading the truly brilliant varieties of exegetical phenomenology I would recommend you read Chapter 9, discussing the variety of phenomenological orientations and the protagonists of these orientations. In highlighting aspects of the works of these leading phenomenologists I aim to offer justifications for scrutinizing any of their works. These writings are often exceptionally gifted and also deeply luminous, moving and worthy of contemplative reading.

The Phenomenal Stream

Kockelmans' third stream of phenomenological publications features studies that return to and start out from experience. This stream neither establishes phenomenological foundations, nor addresses theoretical topics, arguments, and contestations. Instead, the third stream of publications is composed of phenomenological texts that aim to "practise" or "do" phenomenology on concrete experiential topics of the lifeworld. Authors of the third stream try to do, as Kockelmans says, what was described as possible and necessary in the foundational, theoretical, and exegetical writings of phenomenologists. They "do" what the works of the two streams of founding originators and brilliant exegetical scholars and academic commentators suggest or imply are the possible, original, and necessary task of phenomenology: to explicate the phenomenality of phenomena as they give themselves *in* and *as* human consciousness and experience. So, this phenomenal stream includes phenomenological works that address topics that are primarily concrete and relevant to the experiential lives of clinical professional practitioners as well as the experiential concerns of everyday lives. It will be shown in this book that it is inherent in the original conception and practice of phenomenology that it minimizes or even avoids the role of theory and abstraction in the practice of phenomenological description and research.

The perceived relevance of the various titles and themes of the third stream of phenomenological publications is dependent on one's personal and professional interests, clinical practice, or research project. But, in principle, the stream of phenomenal publications may include most any kind of experience that is part of human existence. In fact, in the various chapters of this book all kinds of phenomena and events are mentioned that could be explored through phenomenological study and exploration. Think of the experience of being stroked by the hand of the mother or father, or a lover as the basic experience of the sensuality of our body. Van den Berg describes how the body of a healthy person as a faithful ally:

> At one time a mother's hand bathed it—and through her gestures he learned to dwell in it. A loving hand caressed it, and the affectionate touch gave the person the wonderful knowledge that his or her body is good, as good as it was desired by the other person. The healthy person is allowed to *be* his or her body and makes use of this right eagerly: he *is* his body, she *is* her body. (van den Berg, 1966, p. 66)

But then van den Berg shows how illness disturbs this assimilated experience. Our body becomes foreign to us. And we may begin to imagine what is wrong on the inside of our body and our skin.

> An intruder makes it his headquarters and it becomes uninhabitable to the sick person. An ailment governs it, and makes it a proliferating tissue, excreting organs, a troublesome sore or a disturbing tumor. The body has become unfaithful. The trusted ally has become an antagonist, a fierce enemy. The sick person has to revolt against it. The caressing hand which made it his body and which perhaps still desperately tries to overcome its faithlessness, has become powerless. (van den Berg, 1966, pp. 67, 68)

Alphonso Lingis also describes the act of stroking someone or being confirmed by a person we love. And he describes the ambiguous experiential realization of the fact that the skin we stroke is on the outside of our bodies, but many of us also have experienced the uncanny realization that stroking a human body is stroking a body that has also an inside of our skin. How do we sensually perceive the inside of our skin while stroking or being stroked?

> Contained and also protected by our skin, the inner contents of our bodies are concealed from others and also from us. They keep what they are doing secret. We do feel, vaguely, something of what is going on in there, in a mix of attachment and aversion. We are attached to the beating of our heart and to the crisp air swelling our lungs. We feel distaste in a brief thought of our kidneys, our liver, our pancreas, the slabs of yellow fat, the grisly kinks of our intestines that are pushing along chunks of mush turning brown with dead bacteria. We feel repugnance over substances expelled from our bodies—gases, excrement, vomit, mucus, pus. What we call filth, what provokes disgust outside are things we come upon that resemble what comes out of our bodies or what is inside them. (Lingis, 2018, p. 3)

In the same short essay entitled "Outside" Lingis reflects on the irrevocable limit of the human skin in communicative body experience. We may, in a friendly manner, have conversations with someone and realize that we are involved in emotional interactions that can be read from their and our faces. But what makes the face so expressible and readable? Or how does the physiognomy of the face show itself? What is hidden and revealed in this self-showing of the face?

> We know that we are frowning, expressing skepticism, looking surprised or sarcastic. We know that our expression looks quizzical, shocked, or ironic. But we have no view or feeling of the muscle contractions and dilations, nervous circuitry, and pulses of blood behind our skin that engineer those surface expressions. Our expressiveness, our convictions, attitudes, character, our personality are on our skins. Remove the skin and you remove the expression, the attitude, the personality. At the "Body Worlds" exhibition by Gunther von Hagens cadavers are on display that were preserved not by replacing the blood with formaldehyde but by replacing the blood, body fluids, water, and fat with liquid plastic. There we see that those whose faces are skinned are now anonymous. We cannot imagine what these individuals were like. (Lingis, 2018, p. 4)

But most of us rarely or never think about the body mass, fluids, and skeleton structures behind and below the skin.

> We move, we act by not seeing how we move. We dance when we stop watching where we are putting the right foot, then the left foot; we type not looking at where we are pressing our fingers. When we move we look outside. We scan the environment for open spaces and for pathways toward objectives in the distance, catching sight of moving obstacles. We can see the environment about us because we do not see anything behind our skin. (Lingis, 2018, pp. 4, 5)

These excerpts from van den Berg and Lingis are examples of doing phenomenology directly on the things or events of our world. They are examples of "doing phenomenology" in a manner that should not be confused with theoretical philosophizing about technical topics or engaging in philosophical exegesis, or deliberating argumentatively about philosophical entanglements of concepts and contradictions of the so-called phenomenological literature, however interesting that may be in its own right. The point is that these types of publications by van den Berg and Lingis are examples of the third stream of literature, they begin with the experience of the body and orient to the originary aspects of the experience of the body in its various modalities.

To do phenomenology *on* the things, we must turn *to* the things that matter and attend to our experience of them. Maurice Merleau-Ponty says that this means that we must begin by reawakening the basic experience of the world and by practicing a "direct description" of this world in which we live and that lives in us:

> the efforts [of phenomenology] are concentrated upon re-achieving a direct and primitive contact with the world … it also offers an account of space, time and the world as we "live" them. It tries to give a direct description of our experience as it is, without taking into account of its psychological origin and the

causal explanations which the scientist, the historian or the sociologist may be able to provide. (1962, p. vii)

Giving a "direct description" of experience is not a narratively reporting, copying, or providing information about something. Rather to describe, to compose a description, is to *write* (unravel or uncover) what remained hidden or concealed. Doing phenomenology on the phenomena means taking up the attitude of immediate and direct seeing and practicing an attentive awareness to the things of the world as we live them rather than as we conceptualize, categorize, or theorize them. Direct description is making existential sense of the originary meanings of lived or inceptual experience (the primal phenomena and events as given in or as consciousness).

Lived Experience as Starting Point

The modified and updated version of the standard *Oxford English Dictionary* (June 2022) does not (yet) recognize the term "lived experience." The search function of the online *OED* states, "No dictionary entries found for 'lived experience'." Several other dictionaries do contain the term "lived experience" but they define it as "what you see, hear, feel" or as "personal experience." This new quotidian meaning is partly a shift away from the original phenomenological usage of the term lived experience.

As I am writing this, I am half-listening to a radio talk show about health care. The topic is excessive wait times in the Canadian health-care system. The moderator is asking listeners to phone in with their experiences of having to wait for a diagnosis, especially serious diagnoses that deal with potentially life-threatening illnesses such as cancer. The host peaks my interest when she uses the word "lived experience." She says that she wants "to hear people's lived experiences of waiting times for a medical diagnosis." Many people phone in and share how traumatic the waiting for a diagnosis has been, especially when the wait was many weeks or even several months long. People's stories are filled with emotive adjectives describing the waiting experience as filled with anxiety, pain, and worry.

It occurs to me that the radio host's pronounced interest to hear people's "lived experiences" might make it an appropriate topic for phenomenological research. However, the responses she receives from her listeners are largely limited to personal and emotional reactions. Most of the testimonials contain strong opinions, critiques, and include adjectives such as unbearable, nerve-wrecking, frightening—but they are not truly descriptions of lived experiences in the sense of narrative accounts—they lack experiential concreteness, vividness, and descriptive detail. As a listener, I am not presented with the opportunity to reflect on the experience itself of waiting for a diagnosis. Still, I appreciate the program, recognizing that it is important that the concerns of the public and patients should be voiced to health practitioners, policy makers, and the community at large.

Lived Experience Is Meaningful, yet Not Necessarily Profound

The term "lived experience" (*Erlebnis*) probably has its origin in German and/or philosophical and phenomenological sources. But it is gradually being more widely adopted in the English language, even though these usages may have little to do with phenomenology. The term lived experience is often used to refer to personal experience and to the authority that those who have had certain experiences speak about them. It is not unusual nowadays to hear the phrase "lived experience" in television shows, podcasts, or radio shows like the one I have been listening to.

People seem to feel that the term "lived experience" is loaded with special profundity—it seems to hint at certain deeper meanings. But ironically, the phenomenological term "lived experience" simply means lived-through experience. Historically it does not refer to any kind of deep experience, fundamental event, or hidden source of meaning—on the contrary, lived experience (as translated from the German term *Erlebnis* or the Dutch term *belevenis*) is just the name for ordinary life experience as it carries us on in its lived everyday stream. That is why Heidegger can suggest that everyday lived experience is meaningful, yet superficial. There is nothing unusually "rich," "deep," "hidden," or "mysterious" about our everyday living of experience—until we take up a phenomenological questioning—until we ask: "What is the meaning and significance of the phenomenon expressed in this or that *lived experience*?" Then we are challenged by the phenomenality of the phenomenon. "What is the phenomenal meaning of this lived experience?" "How does the phenomenal meaning of this lived experience give itself to our consciousness, our awareness?"

The Natural Attitude

A phenomenology of practice may deal with experiences that are common or less common. For example, the experience of driving a car or riding a bike is common for many people, while the experience of moving about in a wheelchair is common only for some. Everyday experiences that are common tend to be experienced in a taken-for-granted manner. But what is the everydayness of daily life? When we speak of matters of everyday life, we tend to think that such matters are simple and less worthy of our academic attention. We are more interested in things that are exotic and less common. And yet, phenomenology shows that the quotidian everydayness of daily life experiences are much less simple than we tend to think.

In everyday life we are able to engage in our daily practices because they are to a certain degree habituated, repeatable, common, reproducible. That is why we speak of common or everyday language. Ordinary language consists of words that allow us to communicate common meanings and develop interpersonal understanding. The language of everyday life is reproducible even though the common words may be used to describe uncommon and novel situations. So, the reproducibility of language allows us to go about our daily business. However, at the origin of the reproducibility of everyday thought and language are hidden the originating thoughts and poetic images that make the reproducibility of life possible. Phenomenology aims to grasp and express these originating meanings; as well, it aims to open itself to new originating beginnings that form the inceptualities of phenomenological inquiry.

Husserl reserved the notion of "natural attitude" not just to point at the taken-for-grantedness of everyday thinking and acting. For him, the natural attitude is manifested in our natural inclination to believe that the world exists out there, independent of our personal human existence. The challenge for phenomenology is not to deny the external existence of the world, but to substitute the phenomenological attitude for the natural attitude in order to be able to return to the beginnings, to the things themselves as they give themselves in lived-through experience—not as externally real or eternally existent, but as an openness that invites us to see them as if for the first time.

Heidegger warns us against a reliance on method, yet he and others describe phenomenology in terms of method: "Phenomenology is only accessible through a phenomenological method," says Merleau-Ponty (2012, p. xxi). How do we reconcile these claims? It appears that these scholars are warning against reducing phenomenology to a set of standard strategies and techniques. Merleau-Ponty refers to method as something like a way of thinking and feelingly understanding: "phenomenology allows itself to be practiced and recognized as a manner or as a style" (2012, p. xxi). So, it may be best to think of the basic method of phenomenology as the taking up of a certain attitude and practicing a certain attentive awareness to the things of the world as we live them rather than as we conceptualize or theorize them, and as we take them for granted. "Doing phenomenology," as a reflective method is the practice of the bracketing, brushing away, or reducing what prevents us from making primitive or originary contact with the primal concreteness of lived reality.

The predicament of the search for method in phenomenological inquiry is somewhat akin to what happens in Kobo Abé's novel *The Woman in the Dunes*. The protagonist, an entomologist, gets lost while taking a long walk along the beach and through a landscape of dunes. He happens upon a strange village with homes at the bottom of deep sand pits. It is late, and he needs a place to stay. Somehow he gets trapped in one of these houses inhabited by a woman. From then on, every night he must work alongside her, shoveling and lifting away buckets of sand and soil that inevitably and ceaselessly keep flowing from the edges into the living space of the pit. He soon discovers that "you'll never finish, no matter how long you work at it." But that is the nature of life—a metaphor for the ceaseless task of brushing and excavating the matter that keeps drizzling and dispersing across the raw reality of our world. There is something authentic about the human task of attempting to uncover, literally by digging up and exposing the ground of our living existence—and thus to safeguard our being.

This picture of phenomenology, as continuously brushing away in order to reach a primitive contact with the world-as-experienced, is complicated by the realization that the "matter" that constantly keeps covering the ground of our being is also the ground itself. As we lift to remove this matter, it already has taken certain shape or meaning. Lived experience is the name for that which presents itself directly—unmediated by thought or language. Yet in a fundamental sense, lived experience is already mediated by thought and language in a broad sense, and accessed only through thought and language. Just so, the phenomenological reduction consists of the attempt not only to clear away (bracket), but simultaneously to confront the traditions, assumptions, languages, evocations, and cognitions in order to understand the existential "facticities" of everyday lived experience.

28

To reiterate, lived experience is experience that we live through before we take a reflective view of it. For the researcher it is important to realize that experience, as we live it from moment to moment, is always more complex, more nuanced, more richly layered than we can fathom, and meanings emerging from reflecting on lived experience are always ambiguous, enigmatic, and ultimately unfathomable. The problem is that as we focus on an experience or on a certain aspect of experiential meaning, this focus fixes experience into an object for study. This objectification inevitably strips the living meanings of lived experience of depth and subtleties. Philosophers like Gadamer have pointed out that once we make an experience into an object (as happens when employing a method), then the truth of the lived meaning of the experience will remain beyond reach. Issues like this will be discussed in subsequent chapters of this book.

Back to the Thing Itself—What Is the Concrete?

For phenomenological research, it is especially imperative to understand what the concrete can mean and signify. What is the concrete? Some equate the concrete with the empirical and the factual. The concrete is the thing-in-itself. It can also be understood as the essence or originary ground of a thing. Or the concrete may be referred to as the particular. But in *The Phenomenology of Mind* (1977), Hegel argues that what is referred to as the particular and the concrete is actually the most abstract and the most general and therefore poor in its specificity. What we consider as the concrete is linguistically determined with language and may give the illusion of concrete reality but that is actually ultimately fictional. Perhaps the concrete is phenomenologically best understood as the phenomenality of the experiential meaning of a phenomenon. In this way we can keep apart the idea of the thing-in-itself that is the starting point for phenomenological inquiry and ideas generated through abstract theorizing but that have no meaningful anchor in experiential existence.

Wilhelm Dilthey (1987) had already explicated how lived experience (*Erlebnis*) is a nexus of lived relations to the world. He suggested that in its most basic form lived experience involves our immediate, prereflective consciousness of life: a reflexive or self-given awareness which is, as awareness, unaware of itself:

> A lived experience does not confront me as something perceived or represented; it is not given to me, but the reality of lived experience is there-for-me because I have a reflexive awareness of it, because I possess it immediately as belonging to me in some sense. Only in thought does it become objective. (1985, p. 223)

An analysis of the structural nexus involves an exploration of the relation between experiences, the ways the experience is expressed (in language, art, architecture, etc.), and the understandings these expressions make possible. However, Dilthey's explication of lived experience still lacks the primal sense of a Husserlian phenomenality of intentional consciousness. More simply put, phenomenological research and inquiry is commonly described as turning back *zu den Sachen*, to "what matters in lived or primal experience." What appears in consciousness is the phenomenon or event that gives itself in lived experience. And the significance of the idea of "lived experience" is that we can ask the basic and seemingly overly simple phenomenological question: "What is the Lived Meaning of this (originary) Experience?" Or: "What is this Phenomenon or Event Like and How Does it Show Itself in or as Experience?"

Of course, from a general qualitative research point of view there would be many valid ways of exploring topics such as the experience of having a conversation, the experience of meeting someone, or the experience of waiting for someone. Different qualitative methodologies might explore a variety of issues, empirical questions, policy practices, perception and opinion surveys related to gender, social group, sex, education, etc. But phenomenology focuses on the eidetic and originary meanings of a phenomenon. The famous dictum *zu den Sachen* means "to the things" in the sense of turning to experience that matters. And the methodological meaning and significance of the concept of lived-through experience is that we can ask the basic phenomenological question: "How is this experience given in consciousness?"

The point is that we usually do not think about, or phenomenologically reflect on our experiences while we actively live through them. And yet, as Heidegger says, even though we are not explicitly conscious of our prereflective, a-theoretic everyday experiences, they carry the meaningfulness-character of the concrete context of life. In his 1919/20 Freiburg Lectures Heidegger provides some telling portrayals of the ordinary and taken-for-granted meaningfulness of the lived experience of lived experiences:

> Even if it is not explicitly conscious, I live in a context of anticipation. Unbroken, without having to surmount barriers, I slide from one encounter into another, and one sinks into the other, and indeed in such a way that I do not bother about it. I do not at all conceive of the idea that there is anything to notice [*beachten*] anyway. I swim along with the stream and let the water and the waves crash behind me. I do not look back, and living into the next one, I do not live in the encounter that has just been lived or know about it as having just been lived. I am engrossed in the temporally particular situation and in the unbroken succession of situations and to be sure in that which encounters me in the situations. I am engrossed in it, i.e. I do not view myself or bring myself to consciousness: now this comes along, now that. But in that which comes, I am captured and arrested, fully and actively living it. I live the context of meaningfulness, which is produced as such in and through my experiencing, insofar as I am just swimming here and there in this direction of expectation. (Heidegger, 2013a, p. 92)

Of course, some of our experiences such as waiting for a medical diagnosis may be weighty, shocking, unbearable, dramatic, or tragic. Lived experiences may lead or involve us in difficult or serious reflections. Still, from a phenomenological perspective these lived experiences, as we live through them, are usually raw: prereflective, non-reflective, pre-predicative, or a-theoretic as Heidegger suggests.

From the perspective of Heidegger's hermeneutic-phenomenology, it does not help to speak gravely and emphatically of our "lived experiences" as if they are pregnant with meanings that will "emerge" or "spill out" as soon as we press the magic methodological phenomenological analytical button. And yet, it is true that the term "lived experience" (or "phenomenon") points to a central methodological feature of phenomenology: it announces the interest of phenomenology to turn to the epoché and the reduction to investigate the primal, eidetic, or inceptual meanings that are passed over in everyday life. The phenomenological gesture is to lift up and bring into focus with language any such raw moment of lived experience and orient to the living meanings that arise in the experience. Any and every possible human experience (event, happening, incident, occurrence, object, relation, situation, thought, feeling, and so on) may become a topic for phenomenological inquiry. Indeed, what makes phenomenology so fascinating is that any ordinary lived-through experience tends to become quite extraordinary when we lift it up from our daily existence and hold it with our phenomenological gaze. Wondering about the meaning of a certain moment of our lived life may turn into the basic phenomenological question: "what is this experience?" How does the experience present itself?

Heidegger gives a special twist to the primordiality of lived meaning with the notion of "fading":

the fading of meaningfulness. It is not a disappearing but a fading, i.e., a transition into the stage and into the mode of non-primordiality where the genuineness of the enactment and beforehand the renewal of the enactment are lacking, where even the relations wear themselves out and where merely the content that itself is no longer primordially had 'is of interest'. Fading has nothing to do with 'losing something from memory', 'forgetting' or with 'no longer finding any interest in'. The content of factical life experience falls away from the existence relation towards other contents: that which falls away remains available; the available itself can, however, for its part fade as sense character of the relation and pass into that of mere usability . . . i.e. they have fallen away from the primordial existence relation. (Heidegger, 2013a, pp. 26, 27)

If there is no concealing, hiding, or fading of meaningfulness, then we would not need phenomenology because we would sense with perfect clarity the lived meanings of our everyday existence. So, this quote taken from the lecture of 1920 may give us a hint of how Heidegger thought about the concealment and unconcealment of the meaning of lived experience. He uses the notion of fading of meaningfulness to describe the passing of experience into taken-for-grantedness. Heidegger seems to suggest that when studying a certain phenomenon or event (lived experience) we have to try to question what has faded and how phenomena give themselves. Ultimately this questioning is a matter of the reduction and the primordial source of meaningfulness. Our challenge is to see how any phenomenological description should become a "learning how to see" and "seeing into or through" the faded meaningfulness to the inceptuality (beginning) of the deeper or primal meaning of human existence and lived experience.

Experience Is Always Self-Experience

Wilhelm Dilthey said, "the reality of lived experience is there for me because I have a reflexive awareness of it, because I possess it immediately as belonging to me in some sense" (1985, p. 223). In other words, experience is always self-experience. For Dilthey, consciousness is equivalent to lived experience. "There-fore, lived experience is not merely something present, but already contains past and future within its consciousness of the present" (p. 225). These words were written around the same time that Husserl wrote on his internal time consciousness, and they seem to echo each other. It is the idea of primal consciousness that may refer to some kind of pre-consciousness of lived experience that is yet fundamentally pre-reflective, pre-theoretic, pre-predicative. Husserl uses the term "experience" as a comprehensive concept for all acts of consciousness. We have and undergo experiences.

Human experience is the main epistemological basis for qualitative research. But the phrase "lived experience," as suggested above, possesses special methodological significance. The notion of "lived experience," as used in the works of Dilthey, Husserl, Merleau-Ponty, and their contemporary proponents, announces the intent to explore *directly* the prepredicative or prereflective dimensions of human existence: life as we live through it. The etymology of the English term "experience" does not contain the sensibility of "lived"—it derives from the Latin *experientia*, meaning "trial, proof, experiment, experience." But in the German language the word for experience, *Erlebnis*, already contains the word *Leben*, "life" or "to live." The same is true for Dutch language. The German term *erleben* translates into the English compound term *lived experience*; and in French the equivalent is *expérience vécue*.

The German verb *erleben* literally means "living through something," so the English compound translation "lived experience" is this active and passive living through experience. The Dutch term *beleven* also already contains the word *leven*, meaning to live. But the English word "lived experience" should not be translated back into the German, Dutch, or Scandinavian as if it now must mean experience in a profound, fundamental, deep, or weighty sense. That is not the case. "Lived experience" should simply mean "experience" in the lived sense of *erleben* or *beleven*. In other words, Dutch and German *erleben* or *beleven* usually simply means experiencing. But the word "experience" may refer to ordinary as well as extraordinary, quotidian as well as exotic, routine and surprising, dull and ecstatic moments and aspects of experiences as we live through them in our human existence.

Wilhelm Dilthey (1976, 1985, 1987) offers the first systematic explication of *Erlebnis* (lived experience) and its relevance for the human sciences and the humanities, in the late nineteenth century. He describes "lived experience" in 1907 as a reflexive or self-given awareness that inheres in the temporality of consciousness of life as we live it. "Only in thought does it become objective," says Dilthey (1985, p. 223). He suggests that our language can be seen as an immense linguistic map that names the possibilities of human lived experience. There is an obvious distinction between "having experiences" and "undergoing experiences." Experiences that we *have* might be accumulative, while experiences that we *undergo* tend to be transformative in their impact on our sense of who we are. To have undergone many experiences may imply that we have learned about life.

Edmund Husserl uses the concept *Erlebnis* alongside *Erfahrung*, which expresses the full-fledged acts of consciousness in which meaning is given in intentional experiences. "All knowledge 'begins with experience' but it does not therefore 'arise' from experience," says Husserl (1970, p. 109). *Erfahrungen* (as meaningful lived experiences) also can be seen to have a transformative effect on our being. Generally, experience can be seen in a passive modality as something that befalls us, overwhelms us, or strikes us, and experience can be understood more actively as an act of consciousness in appropriating the meaning of some aspect of the world. And we can speak of an "experienced" person when referring to his or her mature wisdom, as a result of life's accumulated meaningful and reflective experiences.

In *Truth and Method*, Hans-Georg Gadamer suggests that there are two dimensions of meaning to lived experience (*Erlebnis*): the immediacy of experience and the content of what is experienced. Both meanings have methodological significance for human science. They refer to "the immediacy with which something is grasped and which precedes all interpretation, reworking, and communication" (1975, p. 61). Thus, lived experience forms the starting point for inquiry, reflection, and interpretation. This thought is also expressed in the well-known line from Merleau-Ponty, "The world is not what I think, but what I live through" (1962, pp. xvi–xvii). If one wants to study the world as lived through, one has to start with a "direct description of our experience as it is" (p. vii). Both Gadamer and Merleau-Ponty put in their own words the meaning of the prereflectivity of prereflective experience.

In contemporary humanities and human sciences, "lived experience" remains a central methodological notion (see van Manen, 1990, 1997) that aims to provide concrete insights into the qualitative meanings of phenomena in people's lives. For example, phenomenological human science investigates lived experience to explore concrete dimensions of meaning of an illness such as multiple sclerosis (Toombs, 2001) or pain in the context of clinical practice (Madjar, 1998). This contrasts with the epistemology of medical science that provides for strategies of intervention and action based on diagnostic and prognostic research models. The point is that predictions about the clinical path of an illness do not tell us how (different) people actually experience their illness.

Even in the deconstruction and postmodern work of the more language-oriented scholars such as Jacques Derrida, the idea of lived experience reverberates in phrases such as the "singularity of experience" or "absolute existence." Derrida speaks of this originary experience as "the resistance of existence to the concept or system," and says, "this is something I am always ready to stand up for" (Derrida and Ferraris, 2001, p. 40). In the human sciences, the focus on experience remains so prominent because of its power to crack the constraints of conceptualizations, codifications, and categorical calculations. And the critical questioning of the meaning and pursuit of the originary or inceptual source of lived experience assures an openness that is a condition for discovering what can be thought and found to lie beyond it.

Qualitative methodology is often difficult since it requires sensitive interpretive skills and creative talents from the researcher. Phenomenological methodology, in particular, is challenging since it can be argued that its method of inquiry constantly has to be invented anew and cannot be reduced to a general set of strategies or research techniques. Methodologically speaking, every notion has to be examined in terms of its own assumptions, even the idea of method itself is reinvented. Heidegger stated: "When a method is genuine and provides access to the objects, it is precisely then that the progress made by following it . . . will cause the very method that was used to become necessarily obsolete" (1982, p. 328). Moreover, it is difficult to describe phenomenological research methods since even within the tradition of philosophy itself "there is no such thing as one phenomenology, and if there could be such a thing it would never become anything like a philosophical technique" (Heidegger, 1982, p. 328).

The project of phenomenology includes becoming familiar with some of the great philosophical phenomenological texts. It is here that we may become infected by the attitude that drives phenomenological thought and that makes "thinking" such a compelling engagement into the exploration of lived meaning of human life and existence. Günter Figal makes the strong claim that every true philosophy is originary: "A philosophical discussion that is not originary is not a philosophy, but, rather, only makes a contribution to a philosophy" (2010, p. 30). This is especially true for phenomenology that, as a philosophical approach, aims to be constantly renewing. Originary means that there is something about a certain phenomenological text that is not derived from a prior phenomenology.

When it comes to the great "minds" in the tradition of phenomenology, what sets them apart from many other philosophers is that they write in an originary manner of phenomenology while actually "doing" it. A classic example is the "Preface" by Merleau-Ponty from his *Phenomenology of Perception*. In this Preface he asks "What is phenomenology?" and then sets out to provide an insightful portrayal written in a powerful phenomenological pathic prose that is still originary in its inception and compelling in its style. Indeed, the scholarly writings of thinkers such as Heidegger, Bergson, Binswanger, Stein, Reinach, Merleau-Ponty, Sartre, de Beauvoir, Levinas, Derrida, Lingis, Marion, Nancy, Chrétien, Serres, and Agamben are so compelling in that they practice phenomenology with phenomenological sensitivity, logical consistency, poetic precision, and passionate pathos, and they do so from an originary position.

The Instant of the Now Is Always Late—Too Late

We do not normally reflect on or name the everyday lived experiences we go through. But the irony is that as soon as we do name and reflect on certain experiential aspects of living we may already have lost touch with the living sensibility of these lived moments. Somehow the problem lies in the momentary temporality of the moment itself.

While we are alive, we always and inevitably live in the moment, in the instant of the "now." How can we not? Even when remembering or anticipating an event, we always do so in this moment, the "now" (this second, minute, hour, day, year). But, as soon as we try to (re)capture this "now," it is already gone, absent. Neuroscience can tell us quite exactly how long it takes for the brain to process the information that our neurons are constantly receiving, detecting, altering, constructing, composing, re-composing, re-working, every second of the day of what the neuroscientist calls the reality that the sensory organs and equipment of our body and brain give us.

How far in the past do we live? And how does it matter? The challenge for phenomenology is that it is precisely the experience as we live through it, this living moment that we must recover and investigate for its phenomenal meanings. But not only does it take time for our sensory organs to perceive the things of our world, we must become aware of the things that we normally live unthinkingly, automatically, unconsciously, in a taken-for-granted manner and all the other modes of existence that we live through from moment to moment in the instant of the now. Putting it more methodologically: what gives itself has to be determined through the method of the phenomenological epoché and reduction. These are the originary insights that are the basic purpose of phenomenological research and inquiry. But the originary or inceptual existence and meanings of experiential insights are elusive. Not only is our sensory uptake slow and always lies in the past, so to speak, but our reflectivity is elusive too and depends upon our attentiveness, interest, alertness, awakeness, and so forth. It takes a moment to shift from the prereflective attitude into the reflective attitude in our daily existence.

Someone who practices meditation in order to live more consciously in the present moment, is constantly aware how the present seems to slip away into distractions: thoughts, reminiscences, anticipations. Even for the meditator it is hard to stay in the "now of the present" because the person who meditates tries to focus *on* the lived now while living *in* the now and that focal awareness is constantly slipping away into an absent minded (non-reflective) absence of the presence. Meditating is a constant erasing of the distractions that keep pressing themselves into the taken-for-granted consciousness of everyday lived experience.

Phenomenology orients to the prereflective life of human existence. Prereflective experience is composed of the experiences that we go through from moment to moment and from day to day. But what is the relation between prereflective experience and experiences that are gathered and accessed through reflection? Indeed, phenomenological method consists of phenomenological reflection on the prereflective life of our daily existence. But the point here is that we need to realize that we are always too late in recovering our perceptions that we experience in the instant of the now. Our brain is always about half a second late (or a fraction of a second late) in registering and processing our sensory stimuli. And second, our phenomenological reflections (our inner reflective sensations) that make up our reflective experiences and attitude through which we aim to capture the meanings of our prereflective experiences also are too late when we try to make sense of our experiences.

Phenomenologists are highly aware of this dual elusiveness of the living meaning of lived experience. Indeed, those who claim to conduct phenomenological analysis through the use of methods or techniques of categorizing, abstracting, dissecting, counting, etc., tend to misunderstand the basic idea of phenomenology. Phenomenological analysis does not involve coding, sorting, calculating, or searching for patterns, synchronicities, frequencies, resemblances, and/or repetitions in data. However, fascinating such research may be in its own right, it cannot achieve what a phenomenological study aims to achieve: to let a phenomenon (lived experience) show itself in the way that it gives itself while living through it. Phenomenology in its original sense aims at retrospectively bringing to our awareness some experience we lived through in order to be able to reflect phenomenologically on the living meaning of this lived experience.

35

When the later Heidegger becomes critical of the concept of lived experience, he is critical not of the inceptual presumptions of lived meaning, but of the shallowness and meaninglessness of contemporary life. Likely, his words can be read also pejoratively as an uncanny early critique of empirical-analytical qualitative inquiry that has become obsessed with the academese of (lived) experience, while, according to Heidegger, in these superficial contexts, the terms "lived" and "experience" have become popular and yet have lost all their phenomenological meaning and significance. Somewhat mockingly, Heidegger says:

> Now for the first time everything is a matter of "lived experience," and all undertakings and affairs drip with "lived experiences." And this concern with "lived experience" proves that now even humans themselves, as beings, have incurred the loss of their beying and have fallen prey to their hunt for lived experiences. (2012b, p. 98)

Modern existence has become a life of calculation and machination. With the term "machination" Heidegger means that our lives and concerns now stand increasingly under the sign of producing, constructing, making, and what is makeable and consumable. This has special significance for the contemporary conceptualizations of qualitative methods that are ever more governed by systems and programs of "machination."

To Do Phenomenology on the Things that Matter

Among a divergent range of philosophers there has been an effort to search for a phenomenological approach that is explicitly oriented to the idea of doing phenomenology directly on the things, on the phenomena themselves. In other words, it is justified to regard the approach of a *phenomenology done directly on the things* as a qualitative genre of a phenomenological style. This phenomenological style is also implicitly evident in the diverse themes addressed by authors such as Henri Bergson (*Le Rire*), Eugène Minkowski (Death), Martin Heidegger (Boredom), Jean-Paul Sartre (*Nausea*), Maurice Blanchot (Writing, *The Gaze of Orpheus*), Jean-Luc Nancy (*L'Intrus*; *The Fall of Sleep*), and Alphonso Lingis (*Abuses*). In some parts of their diverse works, these phenomenologists all engage in the genre that is characterized by the peculiar style of classic and contemporary phenomenological writing, as it subscribes to the concrete dictum of *back to the things*.

Heidegger warns that we should not misunderstand phenomenology as if it were a kind of body of knowledge we amass. To grasp the meaning of phenomenology a certain attitude of attentiveness is required. Of course, to read and conduct phenomenological inquiry does not mean that one must take an oath to Husserlian principles or become partisan to a Heideggerian following. Therefore, we should not confuse the essence of the project of phenomenology with the usual philosophical activity of arguing and contesting abstract issues and technicalities. Phenomenology is a preoccupation with the meaningfulness of human lives. What do we do with our life? Are we prepared to truly care for existential being? Authenticity is not just the quality of knowledge that we realize that we are all mortal: born to live and die. More urgently we must understand that we also live in the face of the fact that we may be destroying the very world that is the source of human life. In these times, caring for planet earth, it is not good enough to be a pessimist or an optimist, one must aim to be and act as a realist.

Epistemology and Ontology of Practice

The *Oxford English Dictionary* defines a "practitioner" as a person engaged in practicing a particular practice requiring particular skills, arts, and discipline. Latin, French, and British sources go back to the fourteenth century in phrases such as the practice of medicine (*practizare in medicina*), and putting something in practice (French *pratiquer*), to act and to work. More recently, the term "practice" has become associated with exercise, and also with frequent repetition, drill, memorizing, and learning of a skill. Practice can make relentless demand on faultless training and performance, as reflected in proverbs such as "practice makes perfect." But the phrase "phenomenology of practice" aims to restore the meaning and significance of the notion of practice to its ethos of care as in the calling of the practice of the professional medical practitioner or the attention paid to the values of the meaningfulness of life, and the ethos of the practice of searching for the originary meaning of the relations and things of our world.

The idea of "phenomenology of practice" is operative with respect to the everyday practice of living. In other words, phenomenology of practice is *for* practice and *of* practice. Adolf Reinach, a promising and early student of Edmund Husserl and Martin Heidegger, turned to phenomenology to investigate the performative function and meanings of the legal practice of jurisprudential phenomena such as "the promise" in law. Edith Stein, another brilliant and early student of Edmund Husserl and Martin Heidegger, dedicated herself to pursue the phenomenology of the empathic understanding of the inner and spiritual lives of others. Hannah Arendt studied with Heidegger, on the concept of love and contributed in her work to a politics of practice. Jan Patočka, who was also an early student of Edmund Husserl and Martin Heidegger, already spoke of the essential primacy of practice that lies at the proto-foundation of thought, of consciousness, of the being of human being. When we understand something, we understand practically. For Patočka this means that phenomenology needs to "bring out the originary personal experience. The experience of the way we live situationally, the way we are personal beings in space" (Patočka, 1998, p. 97).

The coinage of the term "phenomenology of practice" pertains also to the pathbreaking work of practitioners such as Martinus Langeveld, Jan Hendrik van den Berg, Frederik Buytendijk, Henricus Rümke, David van Lennep, Nicolaas Beets, and Jan Linchoten who were academics as well as clinicians as professional practitioners in their fields of pedagogy, psychology, psychiatry, education, law, medicine, and health science. At the time, they may not have used the phrase "phenomenology of practice" in describing their research and publications, but in hindsight the term perfectly fits their phenomenological attitude and work.

The idea of phenomenology of practice is meant to refer to the practitioner of phenomenological research and writing that reflects *on* and *in* practice, and prepares *for* practice. A phenomenology of practice does not necessarily aim at addressing philosophical technicalities—rather, it serves to foster and strengthen thoughtful and tactful action. Phenomenology is usually described as a method. This text aims to present a variety of phenomenological possibilities that may be regarded, in a broad philosophical sense, as meaning-giving methods for doing inquiry. These phenomenologies are associated with the works and texts of leading phenomenological thinkers and authors.

Being a Phenomenologist

What does it take to practice a thoughtful thinking and insightful in-seeing into the meaningful primordialities of human existence? A few years ago, Cornelis Verhoeven (1972) made a troubling observation. He suggested that traditional philosophical knowledge of phenomenology does not make a person a phenomenologist any more than scholarly knowledge of poetry makes a person a poet. Verhoeven made a distinction between those who study, analyze, and criticize poetry and those who actually *do* poetry: there are those who are connoisseurs or critics and "write *about* poetry," and then there are those who "write poetry."

Of course, some critics may also be poets, but the poems of critics may lack motivation, depth, and inspiration. Verhoeven's warning gives pause to reflection. He even went a step further and suggested that some philosophers who only talk about philosophy are nothing but a nuisance. The entitled philosopher just talks about philosophy but fails to "do" it. Verhoeven originally made these comments in his phenomenological study *The Philosophy of Wonder*. But we might still insist that his assertions are relevant today for the literature of phenomenology.

If Verhoeven is right, then we have to admit that someone may be a famous philosopher, a learned scholar who writes about phenomenology, but perhaps who is unwilling or unable to actually write phenomenologies. "They who have no talent for life do philosophy," says Michel Serres (2008, p. 133). To paraphrase Jean-Luc Nancy, "there are many examples of talented philosopher technicians whose philosophical faculty doesn't get beyond tepid academic compositions" (2007c, p. 64).

The fact that we can say, "doing phenomenology" implies that it is a special activity—it says what we do (phenomenology) and how we do it (phenomenologically). For example, it is the special act of explicating originary meanings of a phenomenon or event such as making eye contact, caring for one's sick child, dealing with feeling verklempt, listening to music, the act of writing, feeling obsessively compelled about something, experiencing a sudden meaningful insight, looking what time it is, etc. To do phenomenology is to engage in the descriptive-interpretive process of determining the essential meaning of a human phenomenon or event.

Don Ihde asserts that he would make the strong claim that "without doing phenomenology, it may be practically impossible to understand phenomenology." True, much traditional philosophy is traditionally learned by studying its history, traditions, and its structures of inquiry, but phenomenology makes additional demands: "without entering into the doing the basic thrust and import of phenomenology is likely to be misunderstood" or missed at all (1986, p. 14). Merleau-Ponty also suggests in the Preface to *The Phenomenology of Perception* that to understand phenomenology one must do it oneself. One must be able to internalize and express the attitude and style of phenomenological thinking. It is not enough to be a learned exegetical philosophical scholar. To be a scholar of phenomenology one must be able to *do* phenomenology.

There are many talented technicians, but they may do philosophical exegesis and argue about philosophical technicalities rather than bringing things to life. At best, they are really doing meta-phenomenology or meta-meta-phenomenology that is some steps removed from the actual practice of doing phenomenology directly on experiential phenomena. Some of the most productive scholars, in terms of sheer quantity of so-called phenomenological publications, have ironically actually little association with phenomenology as performed on the concrete things and events of the experiential lifeworld as seen in Kockelmans' third stream of phenomenological publications and as described by the work of the protagonists included in the next section.

Since the defining feature of phenomenology is its method, then the question should be: method in what sense? The answer to this question would have to point to the core notions of phenomenological method: the epoché and the reduction, as well as the related methodological elements such as intentionality. It makes no sense, however, to speak of "applied phenomenology" and suggest that applied phenomenology can do without the epoché or the reduction. If the term "application" means "the action of bringing something to bear upon another" then all phenomenology is applied or none of it is. The online *Oxford English Dictionary* defines application as: "The action of putting something to a use or purpose." But Heidegger already pointed out that it is not helpful to ask what the usefulness is of phenomenology. The question is not so much what can we do with phenomenology (as if it were an applicative tool) but what can phenomenology do with us. Throughout this book I suggest that phenomenology is inherently valued for its thoughtfulness and the pleasure that meditative thinking brings to life.

Now, we might ask whether Roland Barthes' sense of the "pleasure of the text" (1975) and the ability to read phenomenological studies is something that can be expected of all readers or whether some people (even some philosophers) simply are not inclined or interested to read reflective meditative phenomenological material—just as not every person who has learned to read prose is inclined or prepared to read poetry. It is also true that one does not have to be a scholar of poetry to be able to understand poetry. Just so with phenomenology. One may not be a professional philosopher and yet understand and enjoy the meaningful experience of reading and writing insightful phenomenological studies.

These reflections about being a phenomenologist and doing phenomenology rather than theorizing and talking about phenomenology are somewhat sobering and should instill a sense of modesty and caution in our confidence of writing insightful lifeworld studies. But they also grant hope and optimism: one may not be a professional philosopher and yet have studied phenomenological philosophy sufficiently to possess the talented and tactful ability of pursuing fascinating projects and writing insightful texts.

Re-interpretive Meaningfulness

The Danish philosopher Herman Tønnessen told a challenging tale entitled "Happiness is for the Pigs."

> Our predicament is that of a sleepwalker. Imagine, we live in an apartment near the top of a skyscraper as tall as the Empire State Building. We have gotten out of bed and walk onto the veranda. But still asleep we do not realize that we just fell over the railing of the balcony. Next, the fall wakes us up. We open our eyes and looking down in horror at our situation. What do we do? Some people wake up and realize that their death is near and inevitable. They try to go back to sleep as quickly as they can. Others realize their predicament and declare: "this free-falling experience is actually quite comfortable; as long as it lasts, let us make the best of it." Still others exclaim, "let us at least do something useful while we can." As they fall they start counting the windows of the building on the way down. And, then there are people who cry, "don't worry, this is not really happening. It must be an illusion." Or they declare, "surely we will be saved. Right now, they must be busily engineering a scientific way to catch us before we hit and splash to death on the concrete ground below." (Adapted from Tønnessen, 1966/67, pp. 188, 189)

Only the apathetic ignorant people will confuse authenticity with blissful happiness. Herman Tønnessen compared the person who seeks out a life of "permanent sedation" with "the happy-go-lucky pigs, grunting with whole-hearted contentment and a complete peace of mind, with no demands beyond the garbage, a 'vital' and 'useful' life in unawareness of their existence and destiny" (p. 199).

Happiness is for the pigs, said Tønnessen. But that is an insult to pigs. Realists know that simple optimism (just like simple pessimism) is superficial. The attitude we choose to adopt reveals our tendency to suification—to try to occupy our lives with hebetants such as drugs, alcohol, self-deceptive, and superficial activities to give us a false sense of existential security. And to divert ourselves from recognizing our desperate "situation," and to abstract, as it were, every single moment of the "fall" out of its irreparable totality, to deny our reality, to think that everything will end well, or to cut our lives up into small portions with petty, short time-span goals. Tønnessen's point was that our existential situation is indeed such that we are sleep-walkers. And, considering the state of our planet, the destructive lives we lead, and our failure or apparent unwillingness to save ourselves and our children, we should face the possibility that the end may actually be quite near and in plain sight. To live authentically in our world would mean to live insightfully and to act ethically upon our insights.

Heidegger's investigation into authenticity and anxiety reflects indeed an existential predicament and the realization that care for the self and others in a fundamental sense would wake us up from sleepwalking our way through life. The realization is not just that I am falling from this tall building but that the children who I have helped into this world, and for whom I must care, also may come to experience this anxiety. It is perhaps significant that Heidegger did not reflect on the terrifying responsibility that each of us must experience authentically in caring for our children. Not only am I responsible for my child's birth and life, I am also responsible for my child's mortality. How can I forgive myself for "giving" my children not only life but also the inevitable prospect of death? The command of authenticity requires that we must give the fact of mortality back to our children— as if they ever asked us for it. Even profound philosophers like Husserl and Heidegger rarely seem to think about the pedagogical care we owe the children and our companions for whom we are responsible. These reflections too belong to the task of a phenomenology of practice, though we need to understand that phenomenology requires a constant creative attentiveness to possibilities and responsibilities of re-interpretive meaningfulness.

CHAPTER TWO

Samples of Phenomenological Texts

One of the brilliant students of Husserl had been Adolf Reinach who was a university-educated lawyer. Reinach started his public talks about phenomenology from the perspective of law with these words: "I have not set myself the task of telling you what Phenomenology is. Rather, I would like to try to think with you in the phenomenological manner" (Reinach, 1968, p. 234). This pedagogical invitation by Adolf Reinach at Marburg in 1914 to come to an understanding of phenomenology by thinking phenomenologically is felicitous and convincing. Reinach resolves to think phenomenologically, which is meant to be done directly on the phenomena themselves. His public lecture with the title "What Is Phenomenology?" was a study performed on the experience of jurisprudential practice. When exploring the significance of legalistic terms such as "claim, obligation, and promise," Reinach started his talk in 1914 like this:

> One person makes a promise to another. A curious effect proceeds from this event, an effect quite different from the effect of one person informing another of something, or making a request. The promising produces a unique bond between the two persons in virtue of which the one person—to express it for the time being very roughly can claim something and the other is obliged to perform it or to grant it. (Reinach, 1983, p. 8)

By reflecting on the experience of uttering a promise and by comparing it to other utterances, Reinach shows that this promise statement is not only descriptive or informative, the statement is also a performative act in that something is being granted in making a promise. Reinach's phenomenology of the speech act antedates the famous linguistic phenomenology of John Austin's performative speech act as well as John Searle's indirect speech acts of doing by talking. Reinach addressed methodological concerns such as the "a priori" which makes possible the formulation of the essence of a phenomenon like the promise.

An early development of doing phenomenology "on the things" came to be known as "the Utrecht University" or "the Dutch School" of phenomenology even though some of the authors were German or French or wrote in some other languages. The Utrecht studies were probably among the first to explicitly claim to do phenomenology on ordinary and concrete phenomena.

Some of the well-known topics and subjects that were explored in books and manuscripts by the proponents of the so-called Utrecht Circle or Utrecht Movement of phenomenology were "The Hotel Room" (David van Lennep, 1953a), "Aspects of Sexual Incarnation" (Johannes Linschoten, 1953a), "The Psychology

DOI: 10.4324/9781003228073-3

of Driving a Car" (David van Lennep, 1953b), "The Sickbed" (Jan Hendrik van den Berg, 1966), "Falling Asleep" (Johannes Linschoten, 1987), "Some Aspects of Touch" (Frederik Buytendijk, 1970b), "Paediatric Diagnosis" (Nicolaas Beets, 1952), and so forth. It is not difficult to discern the difference between the more theoretical exegetical publications and these examples that may be called "phenomenologies of practice," in the sense of professional practices and the practice of everyday life phenomena and events.

The work of the authors of these phenomenological writings is unique in that it speaks to the practice of doing phenomenological research to better understand aspects of professional life. The first mention of the Utrecht movement of phenomenology is probably on the back cover of *Persoon en Wereld* (*Person and World*) (1953), edited by van den Berg and Linschoten. They stated, "one could say that in the fifties at Utrecht University, a phenomenological movement had emerged under the leadership of F.J.J. Buytendijk." Van den Berg and Linschoten (1953) further declared programmatically that the phenomenologist resolves to stay as close as possible to the everyday life's ordinary events. Indeed, these phenomenologists were driven by a quotidian interest in ordinary life phenomena, even as these topics often were born in the contexts of professional practices. These writings are challenging and demanding, not only because of their scholarly resourcefulness, but also because of the required talents for perceptive phenomenological insights of these early leading proponents (see van Manen and van Manen, 2021).

Subsequent phenomenologists have produced similar fascinating works (writings) that exemplify doing phenomenology on the phenomena: *The Glance* by Edward Casey (2007), *Abuses* by Alphonso Lingis (2001), *The Thinking Hand* by Juhani Pallasmaa (2009), *The Fall of Sleep* by Jean-Luc Nancy (2007b), *The Five Senses of Veils, Boxes, Tables, Visit, Joy* by Michel Serres (2008), and similar studies that offer surprising and compelling phenomenological insights into the meaningfulness of concrete everyday human experiences and lifeworld events. In addition, there are fascinating works that comprise foundational and exegetical works.

Yet, these phenomenological reflections "done directly on the things" are surprisingly less common than the numerous exegetical texts that deal with phenomenology at levels more removed from the concrete reality of human experience.

This chapter offers seven reflective texts or essays in order to show what phenomenological texts may look like. When I started to offer phenomenology seminars and workshops as an approach to research in psychology, pedagogy, education, and health science, the term "phenomenology" still had little currency in the US, Canada, and the UK. In the seventies, philosophy was still dominated by concept analysis and language analysis. So, as mentioned in the Preface, a frequent question was: what does a phenomenological text look like? It appeared necessary to translate some texts from Dutch and German into English so these could be studied for their inherent phenomenological methodology.

The following essays and studies aim to show how an everyday phenomenon, experience, or event may be approached and interpretively described: topics such as eye contact, touching and being touched, looking at the time, experiencing boredom, the experience of worry in caring, writing about writing, and the experience of forgetting someone's name. These are just a handful of brief phenomenological studies (by Max van Manen) in order to give the reader a feel for what phenomenological texts may look like. They are sample studies in the sense of essays, trials, attempts, or approximations (Montaigne). The intent of each phenomenological text is to invite the reader to think phenomenologically along with the text and observe how it researches reflectively the prereflective meaningfulness of a certain experiential phenomenon or event of everyday life. It is assumed that each text may be extended, deepened, improved, and probed further by the reader.

Each text is titled with a basic phenomenological question: What is this experience like? And the intent of the opening paragraphs is to bring the reader to wonder about the meaning of this experience (phenomenon or event). In other words, each reflective essay probes the question of phenomenological meaning and the coming into being of this meaning. The last paragraph of each text usually attempts to provide a summative eidetic statement that focuses on the unique or exemplary essential meaning of the phenomenon. Of course, the topic of each essay could be further explored since no phenomenological text is final.

The Play of the Eyes: What Is It Like to Make Eye Contact?

I have settled in the window seat and the plane has just taken off. I am not looking forward to an eight-hour flight and have opened a book that I will probably finish by the time the plane arrives at my destination. As I am sliding back in my seat, in an effort to find some comfort for my body, I read by holding the book at eye level. Then it happens: a small head of hair with dark eyes suddenly bobs up from the seat in front of me. But before I can have a good look, it has disappeared already. I hear a small giggle. I continue reading, but slide the book sideways when again the head of hair has appeared, this time in the space beside the seat and the window: and then I see two eyes look at me—and dash away again the next moment. I realize that I know what this is: a child has engaged me in the play of the eyes: peekaboo. As soon as I make eye contact, the eyes quickly disappear behind the back of the airplane seat. There is even more giggling. I raise the book and make myself invisible to the playful eyes. Then I slowly lower it and as I peer cautiously over the edge of the book, I am caught by the child's eyes again. The eyes say, "I see you!" We both smile. The child's head quickly ducks away again. This playful hiding and mutual seeking is a seeing-and-knowing-that-you-are-being-seen. After a few seconds of hiding, the child's head appears again—but now with the eyes wide open and accompanied by full boisterous laughter. We both laugh cheerfully, and after a few more of these "peekaboos," I hear the mother admonish the child to sit still and not bother the other passengers. The game lapses.

I wonder, what really was happening just now? What is it about the play of the eyes that makes it so universally attractive? What is it about eye contact that is such compelling experience? There are many ways to be in touch with others, but eye contact is certainly most enigmatic. Our eyes cross and we look each other in the eyes, and yet the contact is usually brief, even if it is not peekaboo. Soon we look away again. But when we have a conversation or we need to catch the attention of the other person then our eyes will meet again and again. So what touch is the touch (tact) of eye contact? How and where do we look the other in the eyes?

Peekaboo is an infant variation on the game "hide 'n' seek" that is played universally by children, though with cultural variations. The *Oxford English Dictionary* defines it as "a game played with a young child which involves hiding and suddenly reappearing, saying 'peekaboo'" or "boo" (Stevenson and Waite, 2017, p. 1056). This showing and hiding of the eyes is generally accompanied by smiling, pulling a face, or grimacing in surprise as if one did not expect the reappearance of the face. Indeed, some developmental psychologists have explained that peekaboo proves that the young child is not yet capable of understanding the perception of object-permanency, as originally argued by cognitive psychologists.

At any rate, the essential significance of these games is a dialogue of eye contact: being seen by the eyes is "being caught by the eyes." To know you are caught is to see yourself being seen. This constant back-and-forth of appearing and disappearing, this seeing and hiding movement of peekaboo, is the essence of the meaning of play. In some fashion, play is always the movement of to-and-fro, says Gadamer (1975). Peekaboo shares this play movement of to-and-fro with hide 'n' seek.

During my own childhood in a Dutch town, older children in the neighborhood spontaneously used to gather in the early evening to play hide 'n' seek. The seeker had to count aloud to ten and then shout, "Ready or not, here I come!" or "Who has not hidden, will be seen!" Meanwhile, the children scattered and quickly sought hiding places where they would not be seen. The thrill, of course, was that the seeker wanted to catch you, in other words "see you," and loudly call your name to prove that you had been found. The other players might risk running and rush to safety, the home-base. The entire game relies on the ambivalent experience of (not) wanting to be caught by the one who is "it" (the child who plays the seeker is "it"). Everyone had to be found, and the last successful hider had won that particular turn of the game. It would be terrible for a child to be still hiding while all the other children have left. It would mean that you are not worthy to be sought and caught.

But normally, the rules of the game are clear: If the seeker sees you, he or she calls you by your name: "I see you, Jan!" Jan might sometimes wonder if he or she was really seen. But when, while peeking at the seeker, there is the clear moment of eye contact then it means that Jan is found. When the pupils of the eyes momentarily "lock" or make "contact," then there is no denying that one is seen. The moment you are found and "look" the other in the eyes, you recognize in the experience of the mutual "touch" of the eyes that the seeker has found you or made eye contact. The term "contact" derives from *contingere*, which means to touch closely, connectedness. Eye contact of peekaboo is not just the indifferent glance or look as may happen when we pass someone in the street, rather the "look" of peekaboo is a to-and-fro playful but real touching and seeing the other in the pupil of the eye. The notion of the significance of the pupils of the eyes between the adult and the infant, as the eyes "touch" each other in a to-and-fro movement of showing and hiding, is a phenomenological aspect of the peekaboo game.

Seeing Where Nothing Can Be Seen

But, we might ask, more specifically, what is the phenomenology of this "touch" or "contact" of the pupils of the eyes? The philosopher-phenomenologist Jean-Luc

Marion is interested in how we experience the look, as when we make eye contact with another person. He asks, "what gives itself in the look of the other?" He notes that, obviously, we cannot look at the "look." The look is what passes between the two people who experience the crisscrossing of the eyes—but the look itself is invisible to the looking eye. Therefore, Marion says that we must look where the look gives itself, in the face of the other. But here, too, there is an ambiguous invisibility. Marion asks,

> what do we look at in the face of the other person? Not his or her mouth, nevertheless more expressive of the intentions than other parts of the body, but the eyes—or more exactly the empty pupils of the person's eyes, their black holes . . . in the face we fix on the sole place where precisely nothing can be seen. Thus, in the face of the other person we see precisely the point at which all visible spectacle happens to be impossible, where there is nothing to see. (2002b, p. 115)

What a wonderful realization: Unlike the surrounding iris, the pupil of the eye is hollow and therefore black. And yet, if we check our experience, we would probably admit that when we make eye contact, we do so with the pupil of the eye. It is in the pupil of the eye of the other person where we meet when our eyes touch. Now, there are two aspects to this observation by Marion: first, there is the insight Marion is offering about the curious phenomenon of the pupil, and second, there is the sudden serendipitous occurrence of the insight itself.

As I am interested in understanding how qualitative (phenomenological) insights are arrived at in the inquiry process, I want to ask, where or how did Marion procure this delightful insight? What kind of analysis did he perform to discover that, when we look someone in the eye, we tend to focus on the "ocular hollow" of the pupil? Obviously, this insight did not involve coding, counting, calculating, or conceptualizing. True, some might say that this is such simple insight that it seems hardly worthy of our attention. Yet, no one else has expressed this insight that may lead us to wonder about the significance of the invisibility of the very thing that we look at in eye contact.

So, I am curious: Did Marion have supper with his family and suddenly realize, while talking with his spouse and children and exchanging glances, that we see each other by looking in the pupils of the eyes where there is nothing to be seen? A serendipitous moment? Did Marion then rush to write down this seemingly trivial and yet striking insight? Indeed, ordinarily in a face-to-face relation, we do not just see the face, the eyelids, or the colored iris of the eyes, we make contact by looking at the pupils. Yet, as Marion observes, the pupil is black, it actually is a hollow, and there is nothing to be seen in the pupil itself. Or is there?

What is the phenomenology of the dark or invisibility of the pupil? Proverbially, the eyes are the windows to the soul. And the soul is regarded as the mysterious essence of the other person. Therefore, it is no wonder perhaps that the ultimate mystery of the other person as "other" can only be "seen" in the invisibility of the black depth of the hollow space of the pupil of the eye. It is a non-seeing seeing through the eye contact made possible by the meeting of the "nothingness" of the dark pupils. When we look someone in the eyes, we see that ultimately the other, who we may know so well, is a mystery to us. That is what the infinite darkness of the window of the pupil reveals: a strange invisibility, the familiar other as mystery. Indeed, sometimes we may experience even the person who is closest to us as stranger. Years ago, when looking at my young child asleep, or who was just about to go to sleep but needed one more hug—it happened that I was struck by this thought: here is this person who I know so well and yet who is an utter mystery to me.

Is it not fascinating that we make eye contact with others by looking at that part of their eyes where there is only invisibility? To be sure, when we talk with someone and when we make eye contact, then we also see the face and we may be aware of the visual surroundings and other visible things going on around us. But the point is that we make contact with the pupil. Without the pupil, eye contact would be creepy or even impossible. If we were to look someone in the eyes and there are no pupils, but just white eyeballs or only a colored iris, as in some zombie movies, then the face-to-face contact would be highly unsettling. Similarly, we may be disturbed when a photograph shows the red-eye pupil effect, when the flash or light of the camera bounces back against the retina behind the pupil, inside the eye. Therefore, there are programs available to correct this red-eye in digital portrait images or digital photos of people's faces.

One might counter that, physiologically, the pupil is not really empty as it is covered by the lens that projects images through the pupil's transparent chamber to the retina behind it. However, we do not normally see the retina, situated deeply behind the pupil, when we make eye contact. True, we may be struck by the aesthetic beauty of the iris. Different people have differently colored irises, but the ocular pupil at the center of the iris is always black, a black or dark hollow. In this all people are alike. Visually, we orient to the pupil when we look someone in the eye. But the pupil is a dark entity: the ocular pupil is where the invisible parts of the eyes cross and make contact.

When looking the other in the eyes then this is experienced as highly personal and sensitive to a person's core being. We soon look away, as looking the other in the actual pupil of the eye for more than a brief moment is like encountering and entering his or her very intimate essence—it might be felt as an intrusion, as if we enter the other's inner soul. Indeed, when a person is dead, we close the eyelids, to give dignity, respect, and peace to the face and to show that no contact is possible any longer, as no light will enter or leave the pupils after passing. I invite you, the reader, to be attentive to the presence of the pupils when having face-to-face encounters with others in our everyday lives. Even when the pupils are hardly visible, they are experientially still "seen" and fill the important function of making eye contact possible. It is a liminality of seeing and invisibility. Without the pupils, eye contact would not be possible.

Eye contact is not necessarily the same as face-to-face contact. When we recognize a person from a crowd at the airport, it is the body schema, idiosyncratic movements, personal gestures, and the unique physicality and physiognomy of the face that make it possible to distinguish and recognize one person from thousands of others. Of course, this unique physiognomy is true, and it is quite remarkable that we can pick out the singular identity of a person's face from a million others.

Facial recognition is presumed to involve face-to-face contact. Yet, facial recognition is a superficial meeting of the other. Emmanuel Levinas (1985) pointed out that it is not the physicality of the facial features but the "naked face" that is the primal quality of the physiognomic face and that is the place where we might truly see the otherness of the other. The otherness (ethical alterity) of the other is (in)visible to the seeing eye, as the naked face cannot be reduced to a set of facial recognition data points.

Looking Is Taking Possession of the World

Normally, all seeing is essentially appropriation, says Levinas (1995). And in describing the things and people of my world, I reduce them to my own perceptions and conceptions. But the naked face of the other cannot be reduced to the self—it is invisible to the seeing eyes of the person who has appropriated the image of the other as his or her personal possession. Levinas points out that when we focus on the external features of the face of the other then we do not really "see" the otherness of the other. Therefore, when we are struck by the beautiful shape of the eye of the other person, or when we cannot help but notice the striking color or presence of the iris of the eyes, then we are still centered in our own self. But when we suddenly see the "naked" face of the other—such as when we experience the vulnerability of the other person who makes an ethical demand or appeal on us—then we no longer notice the outer physiognomy of the other's face. Thus, in this sense, the invisibility of the look in the pupil is related to the invisibility of the phenomenon of the naked face, when we truly make "contact" with the alterity of the other.

In our technological screen-dominated world, true eye contact should not be taken for granted. Skype, FaceTime, and similar face-to-face social networking programs do not really allow us to look each other in the eye in the sense of real eye contact. Such programs allow us to see each other's faces but this is not real pupil-to-pupil eye contact—it is facial recognition but not soul recognition. Of course, facial recognition is now used as a key to unlock the software of a computer screen. You can look directly at the camera of your computer or your smart phone so that the other sees you looking directly at them (or so it seems)—but there (in the camera lens-eye) you will not meet the pupil of the other. With a smaller screen where the camera is located closer to the center of the screen, there may be the impression that you are looking directly in the other person's pupils. But, short of new technologies that might actually provide the experience of a genuine "locking of the pupils," it would appear that real eye contact is at best always technologically simulated.

Now, with this insight, the game of peekaboo also acquires new phenomenological significance. Indeed, peekaboo is a game of the pupils of the eyes: to see each other directly, in the invisible hollow of the pupil. It is the contact that the eyes of the child make with the eyes of the adult. Peekaboo is often played by young children from the safety of the mother's or father's presence with a stranger, as happened to me in the airplane. And yet, in the to-and-fro, back-and-forth playful meeting of the facial glances, there occurs a contact that is given meaning by the innocent play character of the game. Eye contact occurs when the pupils of the eyes touch each other. Peekaboo can only work when the pupils of the eyes make contact.

When talking conversationally together, the moment of eye contact may occur in various guises. Often, people are engaged in conversation and yet hardly look each other in the eye. They may sort of quickly or fleetingly look at each other while talking but not in a direct and candid manner. Some people are even in the habit of closing their eyes for moments while relating a memory or telling a story. Other people may converse while looking up and away from their interlocutor. Some people actually may be doing something else while talking, such as checking their mobile, making a sandwich, or looking at something or someone else. But then there is the person, who, while talking with you, looks you straight in the eyes. This is real eye-to-eye contact, really looking the other in the eyes. Anyone who has paid attention to these different conversational modalities may have been struck by the compelling, gripping, and candid directness of the affect and quality of the straight and unguarded look of the open eye-to-eye contact of such moment. When really looking someone in the eyes, the open and straight look gives an uncanny authenticity and power to the play of pupil-to-pupil contact of the eyes.

The term "play" and "playful" is used in many broad contexts to refer to actions, movements, and operations; to certain free or unimpeded motions and conditions; and to moments of joy, spontaneous diversion, and related dimensions. Here I use the term "play" broadly and narrowly to refer to the experiential sense of human actions and activities that carry the inner phenomenal purpose of play and playful existence. The behaviors of young children often give the appearance of play. And yet, we have no difficulty distinguishing moments of real play from other activities. For example, a child may be playing car-racing with a self-made car from a kitchen utensil, but when a "wheel" gets sticky or falls off then the relation to the car changes from play-thing to a thing that needs fixing. The play object is a utensil again. Now the child stops playing and looks at the utensil with investigative eyes: what is the problem? When a child examines a thing to see how it works or what is wrong with it, then the child is not playing, but is back in the real world. In fact, after half an hour of trying in vain to fix the problem, the child may protest to the interfering parent, "I have not played yet."

In her early studies of children playing, the phenomenological psychologist Vermeer warned already that too often play is used by adults for children to learn something. The toys become instruments that are meant for the child to practice certain skills and acquire certain knowledge. Thus, play becomes confused with other kinds of activities and experiences. Eugen Finke already had made this warning in 1960 in his famous German text *Play as Symbol of the World*. Many modern educators flounder, says Fink (2016), because they are not able to distinguish the meaning and pedagogical significance of "play" from "the playful" (p. 269). Playfulness may merely mean to be fond of amusement, light-heartedness, but it may not mean the playfulness of true play. For example, when a child is teasingly trying to make another child cry but is claiming to be "just playing" then this is not play in the phenomenal sense of play as described in this text.

In the true play-world, objects are not what they are in the "real" world. In the real world, a thing is only what it is intended or meant to be: a chair is a chair for sitting, a bowl is a vessel for storing, a fork is a utensil for picking food, and so on. But in the play-world, these things can turn into imaginary things that have no determinate or intended meanings: a chair can be turned over and become a castle, a bowl becomes a flying saucer, and a fork turns into an animal. For the child, the magical power of play is still unexhausted (Fink, 2016). Yet, the play-world needs the real world for its backdrop and design. The world of play is always projected onto the everyday familiarities of the real world and thus play is charac-terized by double meanings, ambiguities: a table can be a table, but because it is a table, it can also be a dwelling to hide under, or a ship on a journey to magical lands. Play challenges us to dwell on the meaning of things and events. Indeed, the central method of the phenomenological epoché and the reduction consists in the insightful search for meaning through the practice of variation in imagination. But play does not have to be light-hearted, amusing, and easy.

Play is a luring of some other or some-thing into a sphere of openness: to be surprised, touched, moved, and engaged. In everyday life, objects have relatively fixed meanings, while in the play-world, they have "possible" meanings. A table is a table, a chair is a chair—objects with certain characteristics. But, when the chair or table becomes objects of play, they change into undetermined, changeable things. Things become images that tempt, entice, and lure the players into intimations of variations of meaningful imaginations and insight.

A friend said to me, "You know something special happened this morning in the coffee shop: as I ordered my coffee the woman beside me gave me a real 'look.'" I said, you mean she was flirting? But my friend said, "No, I just felt that the meeting of her look was a very pleasurable moment. People don't do that very often. When someone gives you a real look, it sort of confirms that you are being seen, that you exist." But he hastened to add, "this eye contact only took a second." What is this special "look" like when our eyes cross and catch the eyes of another? What hap-pens in this moment of real eye contact? To be sure eyes often meet in common and contingent circumstances (see Casey, 2007). We glance at the eye of the driver of the other car to check his or her traffic intention. We catch the eye of the sales person at the store, who greets us. We catch the eye of a person who walks by us. But those are fortuitous "looks," incidental and accidental kinds of eye contact. Phenomenologically, it may not really be appropriate to speak of real "eye contact" in this common type of glancing of the eyes. No real encounter, meeting, or con-tact has been made in this contingent touching of the eyes. Or to say it differently, this was not a meaningful contact, not a meaningful touch.

Soon after birth, newborn babies begin to show preference looking at the face of the mother or father, the one who holds and feeds them. This look is still more like a gaze that may wander from one object to another, fixing on this then on that visual thing. The baby looks and stares at the face (see Michael van Manen, 2019). But many parents have noticed that between around six and eight weeks a new-born baby will "make" eye contact. This is a thrilling sensation of really meeting each other's eye. It is the magic moment when the innerness of the infant seems to announce and reveal itself in the pupil of the eye. The pupils of the eyes "touch," make contact. But at the same time the pupil creates a distance between the self and the (m)other as the child may be regarded as (an-)other looking at the mother.

Furthermore, Buytendijk describes how in this moment the smile may occur in the facial encounter between mother and the young child—a first recognition or awareness of the innerness of the other. The smile is not just an expression, says Buytendijk, it is also a response to the person "toward whom our heart has affectionately opened" (Buytendijk, 1988, p. 4). Undoubtedly, the look where the pupils really "meet" is different from the look that merely sees the external face. A different kind of consciousness or awareness is at stake—but this awareness or sense of experienced subjectivity is difficult to gauge.

Of course, when we talk with someone and when we make normal eye contact then we also see the general face in that field of vision and we may be aware of the visual surroundings and other visible things going on around us. Indeed, we may be struck by the beautiful blue, brown, or dark iris of the eyes of the person with whom we make eye contact. But the true tact (touch) of eye contact consists in this: the pupil of the eye (touching) making contact with the pupil of the eye of the other. Without the pupil, the look of eye contact would be strange or even impossible. If we were to look someone in the eyes and there are no pupils, but just white eyeballs or only a colored iris, then there is no meeting of the look. In fact, the meeting of eyes that do not have pupils may be an unsettling experience, as if we are looking at the faces of zombies or the walking dead.

But what is the phenomenology of eye contact, in the encounter with the face of the other person we meet? Do we "look" the person in the face? Although he does not mention the pupils of the eyes, Emmanuel Levinas suggests that we experience the face of the other more immediately:

I wonder if one can speak of a look turned toward the face, for the look is knowledge, perception. I think rather that access to the face is straightaway ethical. You turn yourself toward the Other as toward an object when you see a nose, eyes, a forehead, a chin, and you can describe them. The best way of encountering the Other is not even to notice the colour of the eyes! When one observes the colour of the eyes one is not in social relationship with the Other. The relation with the face can surely be dominated by perception, but what is specifically the face is what cannot be reduced to that. (Levinas, 1985, pp. 85, 86)

In a television commercial we see a woman, from the agency soliciting our support in financial donation, holding up a child of poverty in a caring embrace, and then she says to us, the television viewers, "Look into these eyes and do what you would do if you were face-to-face." At the very moment that she utters these words, the child turns and stares directly into the camera. Now, no matter what we think of these kinds of commercials, if we really are captured by this child's eyes and if we did not just look and click to another television channel, then we may have experienced an uncanny sensation. The pupils of the child's eyes hold us virtually and yet so compellingly that, before we know what has happened, they burn us, as it were. In the pupils we experience the demand of the child's look. In real eye contact we look the other in the empty black space of the pupil where nothing can be seen. What marvelous insight! Reading phenomenological texts often gives me great pleasure. I love the "meaningful insights" that phenomenological studies may offer.

51

The Eidos of Eye Contact

The phenomenology of looking someone in the eyes, eye contact, is not to see but to touch and meet. Literally it is the touch of in-touchness, contact. Looking the other in the dark center, the pupils of the eyes is looking for the unseeing look of true eye contact. There is nothing to be seen or possessed in the pupils of the eyes. In this mutual touching of the eyes, this ephemeral moment when the pupils catch and momentarily lock each other in the look, we encounter the other's infinite otherness or secret. Only when the eyelid blinks may we suddenly be self-conscious of the pupil of the look in the intimacy of eye contact.

Indeed, ordinarily in a face-to-face relation we make contact by looking at the eye, and yet, as Marion observes, the pupil is black, it actually is a hollow, so, unlike the surrounding iris of the eye which may be colored and drawn, there is nothing to be seen in its center: the pupil. Isn't it fascinating that we make eye contact with others by looking at that part of their eyes where there is only invisibility? Marion might have noted as well a further insight, that in eye contact we experience the eidetic difference between a certain kind of looking and seeing. Normally when we look we see something. And in seeing we appropriate the world. The look claims what it sees. It possesses. But the look of eye contact has a unique essence. It does not claim. It does not see but touch—it touches the essence of the other. The phenomenology of eye contact is pure touch. That is why we feel as it were the eyes "catch" each other in the look.

What Is It Like to Forget Someone's Name?

"Well, hi . . . How are you?" I say, trying not to betray my lapse of memory. I have seen his face before, this I am sure of. But what is his name? I smile, overly cordial, as if to cover up my feeble-mindedness. On the outside I show a friendly demeanor but, on the inside, I feel uneasy and awkward.

As we continue talking, I purposefully adopt an intimate tone of familiarity. I nod agreeably to his comments. Yet I do not know clearly who this person is. Without a name an integral part of this person's identity seems missing. It is as if I have misplaced the key that will unlock the screen door that stands between me and my recognition. My non-remembering is like a state of deafness. As he continues talking to me, I do not really hear the meaning of what he says because I am too busily engaged in chasing a clue: a circumstance, a shared happening, a common acquaintance. While trying out several names (Bill, Mike, John, Jim, Robert) I answer in monosyllabic words. "Yes . . . yes . . . oh yes . . ." I say, responding only enough to maintain the conversation. I try several strategies that will hopefully help bring back to awareness the misplaced name so that I can step out of this awkward and embarrassing situation.

. . . Tony! Suddenly the name has cropped up. From where I do not know— Tony, that's it. What a joyous occasion. What relief! I feel a genuine smile of satisfaction spread across my face. In a casual tone, acting like I knew the name all along, I say, "Yes, Tony," as I re-enter the conversation, but now as a fully engaged participant, ready and willing to discuss all of the other memories that follow in the wake of remembering Tony's name.

Forgetting someone's name seems a common occurrence. You run into someone you know or should know and you just cannot remember the person's name. You are about to introduce guests to each other and, to your horror, the guest's name just won't come. Or it may happen that someone greets you by your name but you just cannot do likewise. There are two obvious aspects to this experience: the issue of forgetting and the fact that it is someone's name that is being forgotten. But why is the situation of name-forgetting so charged with affect? What is so meaningful about the occurrence of forgetting a person's name? I don't feel the same having forgotten a person's phone number. So why is the name so important?

The written accounts that people have provided of this experience seem highly recognizable:

> Recently, a woman came up to me and greeted me by my name. I looked at her with an awkward smile, trying to hide the panic in my eyes. "Oh, helloooo . . .! I'm fine. How are you doing?" I replied, hoping that she wouldn't notice that I didn't use her name. Outwardly, our conversation continued. Inwardly, I began having a conversation with myself—an attempt to recall this woman's name, the context in which we must have met, anything that would end this feeling of awkwardness.
>
> She inquired, "Do you see much of her, your sister?"
>
> "Um, every few months or so." I tried to answer in as calm a manner as possible, overcompensating with a tone of attentiveness so as not to give away my secret. I began to carefully study her face for distinguishing clues, the sound of her voice, her words. She doesn't look familiar. I don't remember telling anyone a story about my sister. Have I heard this voice before?
>
> "I don't see much of my sister either but I guess, given our situation, that's probably all for the best . . . ."
>
> "Um, yeah. You're probably right."
>
> At this point, she looked at me quizzically, "You do remember me, don't you?"
>
> I felt my cheeks flush, thinking we've had this intimate conversation and I can't even remember this person's name. At this point, how can I tell her that I don't know who she is without insulting her. I feel so insensitive. "Oh, sure. I remember us talking about our sisters." The words just seemed to fall out of my mouth. I had given myself no choice but to carry on with this masquerade.
>
> Our conversation turned to matters of children, schedules—the life of a mother. On the outside, I tried to maintain a normal flow of conversation, smiling and nodding when I thought that it was appropriate. On the inside, my mind was racing: Where was I when I met this woman? Why was I talking about my sister? Do I know her sister? Is that where we met? Nothing. I still couldn't seem to remember her, her name, or her face . . .
>
> I experienced a strong feeling of disconnectedness, of not being able to grasp on to anything—orally or visually. I could hear the woman's voice but I wasn't making real sense of what she was saying. I knew that she was there in front of me but I could not even recall her face. Putting her into any sort of context was

impossible. There was no reference point, no clue that would allow me to attach myself to her. When our conversation finally ended, I stood for several minutes in the same spot hoping that her absence would suddenly trigger my memory. It didn't.

Weeks later, when I met this woman on the street, I felt the same sense of disorientation and confusion in her presence. It wasn't until she retold my story about my sister pinning me under a rocking chair that I remembered. Upon hearing the words "rocking chair" I suddenly knew her name and where I had met her. We continued to talk and reminisce—this time together—about our childhood memories of our sisters.

The concern with memory, in connection with proper names and face naming, has a long theoretical history in the psychological literature. But this research is largely experimental, developmental, neuropsychological, computational and oriented to developing cognitive maps and models. It is clear that many people at times experience forgetting names. The concern with proper names has been discussed primarily by language philosophers. But few philosophical references are made to the issue of remembering or forgetting proper names. Admittedly the theme of forgetfulness and good memory in everyday situations could be seen as a more appropriate problem for the popular self-improvement press—simply not serious enough for philosophers to bother with.

But, in contexts of pedagogy, teaching, and other professional practices the problem of forgetting people's names has obvious practical relevance. And I am not just referring to the Dale Carnegie types of concerns for learning how to use people's names in workshops that teach how to win friends and influence people. When we are in situations where we meet and greet people the experience of saying someone's name, forgetting someone's name, misnaming, or hearing one's name seems to have phenomenological significance. In particular, it may have consequences for one's sense of self and self-identity, the recognition of others, the sense of feeling recognized or acknowledged, one's ability to be in relation, and so forth.

Proper Names

The proper name differs in certain respect from the common name since a proper name belongs to a unique individual or entity rather than to a group or type. The basic distinction is simple. In an early text about proper names, Mill (1843) argued: "Proper names are not connotative: they denote individuals who are called by them: but they do not indicate or imply any attributes as belonging to these individuals." In other words, a proper name is a word that has no meaning as such. Similar notions are associated with the work of Frege (1892), Wittgenstein (1922), and Kripke (1980) who distinguish between two aspects of meaning: sense and reference. Proper names only are used for reference in that they denote individuals (or entities) that are called by these proper names, but unlike common nouns they do not connote sense or meaning, they do not describe a quality, attribute or property.

It has been long known that proper names are more easily forgotten than other words (Cohen and Burke, 1993). Many empirical studies have been done on the problem of face naming and on the question of the forgettability of proper names. An interesting example is the Baker–baker paradox, an often-cited experiment by McWeeny, Young, Hay, and Ellis (1987). In the experiment people were shown a face where sometimes the name Baker was given as the proper name and other times the word baker was used to indicate that this face belonged to someone whose occupation was a baker. The occupation baker was more easily recalled upon seeing the face than the name Baker. So, it appears, that remembering that someone's name is Mr. Baker is more difficult than remembering that someone is a baker. The reason may have something to do with the fact that proper names tend to be experienced as more arbitrary and meaningless; as well, proper names are virtually detached from other semantic networks. People usually have only one name (first and surname) and so we cannot substitute other names for them. In contrast when we know that someone is a baker we may surmise several proper-ties: that the person probably makes bread, gets up early in the morning, works with dough and ovens, etc. But the name Baker gives none of these clues, except that it is from Anglo-Saxon origin and perhaps some other trivial information or associations.

Name Calling

When we get to know someone or something really well we sometimes use a spe-cial name, a nickname. A nickname is really a name over and above the name that something or someone already carries. The original meaning of sur-name (French *surnom*) is that it is a re-naming, the placement of a second name above or on top (sur) the first name. With the nickname we indicate our special relation to some-thing or someone. We make our world knowable by giving names, assigning labels to them. But nicknames and proper names serve a special function. They (re)name the often more subjectively felt meanings of our relations with others.

Giving names is a most peculiar act. What occurs when one gives a name? asks Derrida (1995b). What does one give? One does not offer a thing. One delivers nothing. And yet something comes to be. What is this something? We may look for a clue in the act of renaming. We seem to rename when the usual name is found to be lacking of something. Sometimes, ordinary words have become too ordinary; we feel the need to get at what is unique, personal, singular. It appears that there is something untranslatable about that what the proper name names.

On first glance we call people by their name because we recognize them. "Naming is recognition," says Merleau-Ponty. But of course, he meant this in a general sense. We are able to recognize aspects of our world by naming them. And just as we call things into being by naming them so we ourselves need to be named to exist for others and for ourselves. "To name is to call into existence," said Gusdorf (1965, p. 38). Things that fall outside of our linguistic reach may stay more indeterminate. And this is also true for proper names of people. The strange thing is that even people who we think we know do to some extent remain indeterminate until we remember their names. Somehow, by being able to call them by their name we seem to be able to reach them, and stand in meaningful relation to them. But if their name escapes us then the relation seems to remain frustrated, unfulfilled.

We have arrived at my wife's staff party. I knew beforehand that I hardly know anyone there. The hostess takes us into the living room where some dozen people are sitting around on sofas and chairs. The room quiets as Anne announces us with some kind words. Then she proceeds to introduce each person by name. People smile and nod in acknowledgement. Halfway through the circle Anne adopts a bit of an exasperated tone as she continues to introduce people by name. And that is Ron and his better half Teresa over there . . . And . . . next to Ron is Tom who belongs to Pamela, well you know Pamela. We wink and smile as she gets full circle to the last person: "And the handsome one over there is Peter and his lovely wife Jane. Just married. You can still see the glow." "Well, how did I do? she finally asks, as if to congratulate herself that she was able to produce all the names from memory. We praise her and then accompany her to the kitchen where some more people are milling around the drinks and the snacks. Obviously, Anne does not relish the prospect of going through all the names here. Besides, people are talking in small groups. My wife has already joined in some discussion, so Anne takes me to a distinguished-looking gentleman and introduces me personally. "I like you to meet Dr. Hans Mollenhauer, he is head of the renal unit at the General Hospital . . ." The gentleman looks up and extends his hand while his eyes hold me for a moment. Anne adds a few more particulars about each of us and then slips away while I shake hands with Doctor what's his name. Almost as soon as I heard his name I had forgotten it. But then we enter an amiable discussion while he inquires whether I would prefer red or white wine as he hands me a glass.

In situations where we meet many new people it is very unlikely for most of us to remember everyone's name. Even when introduced to a single person we may immediately forget this name, unless we make special efforts (such as by asking the person how the name is spelled, by silently repeating the name, by trying to associate the name with a peculiar likeness, or some other mnemonic device). But with people whom we have not met before the fact that we do not know their name is not so critical. In being introduced to someone there is something about the immediate presence of the person that makes the name almost irrelevant. Thus, many of us will even have forgotten the name of the person to whom we were introduced only seconds after we were told. The name simply does not really matter, yet. But once we develop a history with this person, and upon renewed contact, then the name does become important. The problem is that if we have forgotten someone's name then the history may be vague or forgotten as well. The name tends to bring back the history.

The Spoken Name as Gesture

Often, we are not even aware that we successfully "remember" people's names. When my friend walks by and I say, "Hello, David," then the name is like a gesture of recognition. Sometimes I may just wave my hand or nod, sometimes I say, "Hi, David." The friendly smile that may accompany the verbal greeting is as much a gesture as the utterance—both may evoke between us a space of mutual recognition that is colored by our past encounters. Afterwards I may not always be sure whether my brief greeting was a body gesture or a verbal gesture. In this sense the utterance of the proper name is a merely gesturing act. Of course, Merleau-Ponty has tried to show that all language is gestural—corporeal acting: "The spoken word is a gesture and its meaning, a world" (1962, p. 184). Speech is a way of living our corporeality in the world in the same sense as our bodily movements are inherently expressive of our way of experiencing the world.

However, in addition to using the name as a verbal gesture in greeting, there is something more enigmatic to the experience of the name. A gesture (such as a wave of the hand, a smile, a nod, a wink) may constitute a greeting but they are in some sense universal codes. I may greet one acquaintance in the same body gesture as I may greet another acquaintance. In contrast, the verbal gesture of the proper name is unique to each of these encounters. If I forget Caroline's name or if I mistakenly call her Christine, then the moment of recognition and relational contact falters. In a peculiar sense my world grinds to a halt. And rather than having a relaxed chat with Caroline I am thrown into a turmoil. I cannot remember this woman's name. Yet her face may (or may not) look quite familiar.

For the person with a failing memory, when it comes to meeting or greeting someone whose name has been forgotten, the experience can be highly embarrassing or troubling. Lacking the memory for people's names often is maliciously interpreted as lacking a real interest in people. Perhaps that is why we sometimes hear a person say: "I really have a good memory for faces." Or: "I'll never forget a face, but I have a hard time with names." In other words, "I really am a people person and I like people very much but the name just happens to escape me right now." The point in all this is that it is difficult to prove whether such statements are true. Visual memory is quite different in that we may recognize not only the uniqueness of a particular person's face, we also tend to recognize the type of person. Indeed, everyone has some features in common with others who fall within the same type.

Especially as people grow older they may discover, to their dismay, that their memory for names seems to deteriorate. And yet, a failing memory (as long as it isn't a sign of some debilitating disease) does not need to threaten fundamentally one's sense of who we are: our identity or self-worth. There is something arbitrary about people's names: a name can be as easily forgotten sometimes as a phone number. We do not mind admitting to forgetfulness since we despair the irrationality of memory. There is little reason to be proud of the arbitrariness with which we remember some things and forget others. Why do we recall some seemingly trivial events from childhood and not others? Why do we remember one person's name but not another's? And so, as far as mental faculties are concerned, one is much more inclined to admit to a poor memory than to a poor intellect. If we thought that our capacity for being thoughtful and our facility for judicious judgment were deteriorating then we might be more alarmed. Our ability to think and feel seems to be more closely intertwined with our sense of identity and personal dignity than our ability to recall. Indeed, forgetting people's names may even be seen as an excusable problem for someone who is very busy or who has achieved status or leadership in life. One simply cannot be expected to know everyone.

The Pain of Forgetting

We should not trivialize that in everyday life the experience of forgetting some-one's name easily remains a source of embarrassment, hurt, and pain. While the embarrassment itself may not be so important it does alert us to the question of what is at stake in the encounter when someone's name is forgotten.

While mingling with newly graduated students and their parents following the graduation ceremony, I heard a voice from behind calling my name. I turned around to encounter a former student, whose name I had forgotten. How could this happen when only two years ago I had this student in my class for six hours a week working with her on a one-to-one basis in a clinical practice setting? Just looking at her face I could recall aspects of her personality and performance as a student, but not her name. Right away I smiled in pleasant recognition, said "Hi!" very emphatically, touched her upper arm and told her what a pleasant surprise it was to see her. I then immediately proceeded to ask her questions regarding her life and well-being: "How are you doing? What are you doing? Do you like your job? Have you heard from or seen any of your classmates? How are they doing?" etc.

I thought that surely within the time frame of this conversation her name would come back to me and I would have a chance to use it before we concluded our encounter. Unfortunately, this did not happen, and for several hours after-wards I was preoccupied with trying to remember who she had been.

It so happened that much later that day her name came back to me, "out of the blue," so to speak. A lot of good it did me then! Why couldn't I have remem-bered it when it really mattered?

So, what is at stake in forgetting or remembering names? And what is the signif-icance of names and naming for our sense of self and social relations? The term memory comes from the Latin *memoria*, meaning mindful and also "to care for, to be anxious about, think, consider, remember" (Klein, 1979, p. 456). And to remember is etymologically associated with "to call to mind again, remember again, be mindful" (Klein, 1979, p. 628). Forgetting someone's name seems to show that we are uncaring, inattentive, inconsiderate.

The first few times that I meet my classes I remind myself to look over the class list to make sure I know all the names of the students. As I quickly rehearse the names I try to connect these names with the persons to whom these names belong. Soon some of these students I will know so well that I no longer have to remember them. I will simply know them. Other students I will have trouble remembering their names for quite some time.

For example, in my grade nine class I have a boy who looks very much like his older brother who was in my class last year. During the first few weeks of school I kept confusing and calling Tim by his brother's name Don. One day, when this happened again I could see that Tim was clearly annoyed even though he did not say anything. So spontaneously I made a public apology to him. Of course, I felt embarrassed having to do this and my confession was somewhat like self-punishment. But I knew it important to let Tim know that he mattered to me. I told him how sorry I was that I kept confusing his brother's name and how I appreciated him for who he was.

To be recognized literally means to be known, to mean something, to be memorable. I am known and therefore I exist. There is something very pleasant about hearing your name spoken out loud by another person. It is a kind of recognition of your presence, an acknowledgment of your being. Even should your name be spoken in anger it is still a recognition that you have significance, that you matter in some way or another to the person who is speaking your name. To hear your name spoken is a validation of your existence. It tells of your history and places you in time and space. Hearing your name spoken gives you a moment of pride, a second of spotlight. Conversely, if someone greets you by the wrong name, you may feel hurt or offended. Sometimes it is the other way around. You may remember the other person's name but it is clear that your name is forgotten.

I knew this person by name to whom I was slightly acquainted for almost 25 years. It wasn't until recently that he finally could recall and correctly use my name, in spite of several re-introductions. Over time it became laughable to me. Not only did he not know my name, he was calling me various incorrect names. To confound the matter, I used to respond to those names. It must have confused him all the more when others named me correctly. It would have been easy for me to pointedly reintroduce myself, but I was having too much fun. I distinctly recall the day when he actually correctly identified me. I felt a mild sense of victory: at last, I was someone in his mind.

Spheres of Recognition

Experientially the act of remembering often seems to come into focus precisely when it challenges or fails us. When we are asked for someone's phone number or how a word is spelled in a foreign language then we may have to make an effort. We can indeed have the sensation of recalling from somewhere these items of information. But there are many instances where our memory seems to be integrated with our living sensibilities in such a way that there is not really a question of using our memory at all. When my son comes downstairs in the morning, I may say: "Hi, Mark, how do you feel?" I did not, however, have to remember his name. I simply say: "Hi, Mark." And this is often how it goes when we greet people who belong to our personal sphere of intimacy.

It seems that there are different modalities in terms of which we experience the people we meet in our social life. On the one hand, we experience people on the inside sphere of our awareness, such that we tend to experience them as part of the prereflective sphere of our lifeworld. And on the other hand, we may experience people on the outside of this inner sphere. When I ask my wife "Is Michael home yet?" then I elicit an inside subjectivity that she also feels. But when I ask a distant neighbor whether he has seen my younger son then I have objectified to some extent my relation with my son. This neighbor may not know my son's name so I may have to describe him as "the kid in the blue coat." If I were to ask my wife

"Is my younger son home yet?" she would probably feel that I am playing with the inside–outside dimensions of our relation to our children. Now, it is probably the case that we may experience, at different times, some people on the inside as well as on the outside of the inner personal sphere. But there are people whom we only experience on the outside of this sphere. The latter we only know superficially and we easily forget their names while the people who do inhabit the inside sphere we feel we know in a manner that is more personal since we share a life with them. They belong to our sense of self and personal identity.

In fact, some things belong so closely to our personal sphere that it would be strange to say, "I remembered my wife's name" or "I remember my birthday." Also, it would be strange for me to say that I was just about to take a bite from a steak and suddenly remembered that I am a vegetarian. Many dimensions of the knowledge we "possess" are so much part of our personal being that they have little to do with the more arbitrary sphere of memory. And this is especially true for those aspects of personal being that belong to our moral inclinations, habituated skills, interpersonal sensitivities, innermost secrets, and so forth.

However, with some aspects of our personal world things may get more ambiguous. If I am asked the birthday dates of my children I may, indeed, feel that it is a character blemish if I have to think about it or if I confuse their birthdays. Why is this? Perhaps we assume that the births of one's children and their subsequent birthday festivities should have made such a significant impression that it is more than embarrassing if we cannot recall the dates of such events. These dimensions of personal knowing are usually so tied up in personal being that they should not need to rely on the faculty of memory. We do not have to remember the names of our loved ones or close friends since these names are part of the ongoing awareness and constitution of meaning that characterizes our primary reality. We are always in the process of temporal integration: appropriating the past and the future into the present.

Trying to Remember

I feel that someone is staring at me and I become self-aware or restless. Why is this person looking at me like this? This is not an uncommon experience. In our western culture one should not stare at others, unless this other is a loved one, our child, or such person to whom we stand in a close relation. But with strangers or with others who share our public space this is different. The look tends to objectify and depersonalize the relational space. If someone looks at us for too long then we tend to grow increasingly uncomfortable; indeed, we feel "looked at." That is why we teach young children not to stare at people. It is interesting, however, that the voice can repair such incidents. In contrast to the eyes, the voice personalizes. When someone speaks to me then the discomfort of the depersonalized space is more easily repaired. And if the person greets me in a friendly manner by calling me by my name then this further enhances the chance of experiencing a more personalized relational space. In some sense the word *is* the relation; however fleetingly or sustained the encounter may be, the names uttered in the greeting shows the audible existence of the relation, its vocative being.

As I was shopping one day, I heard someone call out "teacher, teacher." I turned around and looked but did not recognize anyone. However, I saw a young man rushing up. He said hello to me and told me how happy he was to see me. While he was greeting me by my name I found myself searching through my mind, through all the "files" marked school for a name to put to the face in front of me. But I couldn't find one. Nevertheless, I responded to his greetings and started to ask questions hoping the answers would give me a clue as to who he was. More than a few minutes went by (which seemed like hours). Feeling increasingly embarrassed, I told him that he must have grown and changed since I last saw him.

I saw the enthusiasm and excitement fade for a second as he reminded me of his name, Stephan Miller. As soon as he told me his name, I connected with him. The picture of him that I held in my memory, the class that Stephan had been in, and the history we had shared came flashing back.

Now I felt comfortable, at ease, and connected. As we talked about him, his classmates, and school, it all seemed like yesterday—the time between this meeting and the last one vanished—the conversation seemed to proceed from where we had last left it. I asked him what had become of his plans to become a veterinarian. He expressed disbelief at my remembering his dream; a disbelief I would have shared. But on hearing his name, my mind seemed to pick out from all my memories the events in which Stephan was a part and made me relive them.

But reflection of personal histories may not produce the forgotten name. Trying to bring back the name by recalling the possible experiences that we may have with a student often will not work well because we already have too much of the same history—for example, too many students who were also in the same class. In the prereflective experience things break down when we constantly try to reflect on the experience itself. And in the encounter with a person we meet and whose name we seem to have forgotten, memory actually becomes a destructive act that we perform when we try to recall the name. The more aware we are of the fact that we cannot remember this name, the more we try to recall the less able we seem to engage in an ordinary conversation.

As he maneuvers through the crowd, I glance at his face and our eyes meet. Is he familiar? I have given a casual smile and quickly look away. But he moves in: "High, Carol. How are things?"

"Fine. How are you?" I say to him. But those words convey a familiarity I do not feel. My mind is reeling now, as I am searching for some recall . . . Have I talked with this man? If so, when? Where? Was it important? Should I remember? Nothing comes. Amazing. All the possibilities and associations that I seem to be able to make in this very instant . . . Recollections of numerous moments. But it can't be done this time . . . My face betrays me; I can't even fake it . . . ! I really don't have the faintest idea who he is . . . Okay, I give up . . . I have to get out of here.

What we ordinarily recognize in meeting and greeting a person seems to be something unique that is made up of the various idiosyncrasies and contingencies that belong to each person's presence and physical appearance. We are able to recognize a person because he or she is and looks different from other people we know.

> When I am about to meet someone whose name I have forgotten I quickly go through the whole alphabet. I try every letter until the name occurs to me. This method works well for me, although occasionally I do get it wrong. Last term I had a graduate student in my seminar who often had brilliant ideas. I had lost the class list so I retrieved her name by going through the alphabet. For many weeks I called her Frieda. I addressed her as Frieda and kept referring to her as "Frieda really makes an excellent point . . ." and so forth. At the end of the term she came up to me and said: "I much appreciate how you acknowledged me in class but I want you to know that I am not Frieda. My name is Jane Friedman." I had confused the first name with something of the last.

Sometimes it can also be the case that we recognize something that is so unique that we realize that it lies beyond the trusted and ordered world of our normal existence. We recognize something that is other to us and that remains beyond our reach precisely because it exceeds us. In other words, what we recognize goes beyond the superficialities of mere difference. We sense that we are confronted by something that remains ungraspable and yet deeply seems to matter to us. So, the frightfulness of being in a situation where we have forgotten someone's name is not just the prospect of social embarrassment. The experience may have existential overtones: it offers the prospect of experiencing a relational situation of unrelation. The face confronts me with the mystery of the other person who is both recognizable and unrecognizable, familiar and alien.

> Recently I woke up in the middle of the night and could not get back to sleep. There was nothing in particular that seemed to have disturbed my sleep so I remained in a state of relaxed wakefulness, staring into the darkness around me. It was then that I glanced at my husband who was deeply asleep. And a strange thought arose. I looked at the contours of his face and a peculiar sensation came over me. What I saw was not my husband's familiar face but the mask of a stranger, a stranger who looked like my husband. I realized that, oddly, I did not know this person and yet I recognized in this face more clearly than ever something unique.
>
> I lifted myself on my elbows and looked at him squarely. It was as if his relaxed features showed me something that deeply belonged to him and that I knew and recognized even though I had never quite seen him like this. I began to wonder: who is this man with whom I have shared so many years of my life? But then it so happened that he suddenly must have woken up, because he opened his eyes for a moment, looked at me, and said "Hi, darling. Are you okay?" At that very moment the strange feeling had left me.

In the moment of recognizing someone we may experience a distance which becomes unbridgeable. This can happen even in our relation with someone who we know so well that ordinarily we would not speak of "recognizing" that person. Waking up in the morning and saying good morning to one's spouse is often so routine that there is no sense of recognition in this greeting. But it may happen that recognition breaks open this taken-for-grantedness in a manner that can be quite profound.

Unnaming—Trying to Forget

To name is to call into existence. But what is it to unname? The science-fiction author Ursula Le Guin experiments with epistemology. She fictionalizes a world without names. Or rather, she lets woman perform a radical act of unnaming her world, a kind of purposeful forgetting. Why? Because she wants to overcome the separation that language effects in our relation to the world. In the short story "She Unnames Them" Le Guin (1987) imagines what happens in unnaming. How would we experience others once we had unnamed them?

So, Le Guin tells the tale of woman who asks Adam to take back the name he had given her just as he had given names to all the animals that the Creator had brought before him. She had already persuaded the animals and the birds and the insects and the fishes to accept namelessness. They had agreed and decided to give back their names. For most of them the act of unnaming had been very easy since the names given to them had left them utterly indifferent. But Adam's woman must have suspected that for humans, for her, the effect of unnaming might be quite dramatic. The effect she had been after, of becoming more attached to the world, was even more powerful than she had anticipated. After the unnaming she had discovered with surprise how close she felt to the creatures around her.

> They seemed far closer than when their names had stood between myself and them like a clear barrier: so close that my fear of them and their fear of me became one and the same fear. (p. 195)

In a strange way, after the unnaming, things became indistinguishable from one another. The desire to smell one another's smells, to feel or rub of one another's scales, fur, feather, or skin now was so immediate and created such sense of presence that she decided that she could make no exception and she too needed to give back the name that had been given to her. So, she went up to him and said:

> "You and your father lent me this—gave it to me, actually. It's been really useful, but it does not exactly seem to fit very well lately. But thanks very much! It's really been very useful." (p. 196)

She found that it was not that easy to return a gift without creating the impression of being ungrateful. But Adam seemed preoccupied.

> He was not paying much attention, as it happened, and said only, "Put it down over there, OK?" and went on with what he was doing.
> [After some hesitation she said at last to him,] "Well, goodbye, dear. I hope the garden key turns up." (p. 196)

With this simple dialogue Le Guin produces a scene that is no less startling than the philosophical reflections of Derrida on the meaning of name. When things get unnamed we can no longer ignore the hidden contours of the phenomena that words tend to hide like blankets of snow. For Adam language was only a tool to gain dominion over the earth and its inhabitants.

> He was fitting parts together, and said without looking around, "OK, fine dear. When's dinner?"
>
> "I'm not sure," I said. "I'm going now. With the —" I hesitated, and finally said, "With them, you know," and went on. In fact, I had only just then realized how hard it would have been to explain myself. I could not chatter away as I used to do, taking it all for granted. My words now must be as slow, as new, as single, as tentative as the steps I took going down the path away from the house, between the dark-branched, tall dancers motionless against the winter shining. (p. 196)

What occurs when we unname is a question that is rarely asked. Can we truly erase or forget the words we give to those who are important to us? We do not live in that science-fiction world of Le Guin. We cannot unname everything, perhaps not even one thing. But unnaming does not have to mean that we completely discard the words. By putting them aside or by making them transparent we can orient to our world as if we were removing "a clear barrier" that stands between us and others. Certainly, we would not be able to take others around us for granted as we usually do. We would have to orient to them as other than being, as otherness, as a Thou, in the sense of Buber and Levinas. Levinas shows that, when we speak of human beings in the third person (he, she, they), we tend to experience them as belonging to the realm of the "It." In contrast, the I–Thou relation differs from the I–It to the extent that it designates a relation that is not an intentionality, says Levinas (1996b, p. 20). In other words, it is not a relation that issues from the self to the world.

Calling the other person by his or her name means that we allow ourselves to be addressed by the uniqueness of this person. Indeed, the name that has been given to the other to "bear" through life also gives expression to a fundamental vulnerability.

> Where is the other more naked than in his name—a name that he does not possess, but has received; a name that he does not coincide with, but which can neither leave him indifferent; a name that summons him to life, but that also will survive him? (Visker, 1998, p. 203)

The Eidos of Name-forgetting

On the one hand, it is important to be able to remember a person's name since that is how we recognize each other and stand in reciprocal relation to each other. The uniqueness of proper names reflects the uniqueness of each relation and unsubstitutability of each person in this relation. The Hegelian idea of recognition is that it requires its reasons. Recognition that is worth something has its reasons. Forgetting people's names seems to say that there is no reason for the other person to be worth remembering. Even the social practice of snubbing is in some sense an acknowledgment of the Hegelian notion of recognition—the person who snubs the other says: "I see you but I have no reason to acknowledge you. You are not worth recognizing." And, indeed, sometimes it may appear as if forgetting someone's name lies unfortunately close to a snub.

On the other hand, it is important to be able to "forget" a person's name since that is how we can truly orient to the other person as "other" without reducing the other to our own priorities (the self), or to an "it" in the sense of Levinas (1996b). A name is something to which the other can never be reduced, and yet without the name there would be no particular other. It is a paradox that precisely when we do not have to remember the other person's name, because the person belongs to the inner sphere of our being, that we may be able to experience both the greatest distance and the greatest closeness. In a strange sense we need to remember and forget the name of the other in order to understand him or her as other. To understand we would need to get really close to the other so that his or her hopes become our hopes, his or her pain becomes our pain—we would need to listen and speak in a manner that is attentive to his or her true otherness that is ultimately unnameable. Our words would now have to be "as slow, as new, as single, and as tentative" as if we were going down a path away from the familiar toward a world we had never navigated before.

Gnostic and Pathic Touch: What Is It Like to Touch or Be Touched?

During a graduate seminar, a nursing professor mentions several incidents that occurred during her teaching of student nurses. These were minor incidents that might have been quickly forgotten if they had not happened that same morning. Jean had introduced her students to palpation, a technique of physical examination. Student nurses must learn to rely on their sense of sight, touch, hearing, and smell to detect abnormalities in the physical condition of patients. These techniques include inspection, palpation, percussion, and auscultation. Quite literally, the nurse scrutinizes very closely and minutely the skin and body of the patient by utilizing all sensory organs: watching, feeling, sensing, touching, pressing, stroking, vibrating, tapping, blowing, striking, smelling, and listening. As we listened to Jean's explanations, the other graduate students in our seminar could not help but wonder how students experience touching or being touched when practicing palpation. Touch is perhaps the most intimate contact that one person can have with another person. So, what kind of touch is palpation? Is it different from other kinds of touch?

Most medical texts define palpation as "the act of feeling by the sense of touch" but this definition is too limited for the complex meanings that a practiced hand can extract (DeGowin and DeGowin, 1976, p. 35). The human hand is marvelously equipped to be receptive to different types of sensations. Physician and nursing handbooks provide a great deal of detail about the practice of palpation and the sensory discriminations detected through the use of the hand. Because of its anatomical structure, the hand possesses regional sensitivities and degrees of receptivity to different types of sensations. The finger pads are most sensitive to tactile discriminations for detecting moisture, contour, consistency, and mobility. Fingertips are especially suited to explore tiny skin lesions. And the dorsal surface and the ulnar edge of the hand and fingers are most sensitive to variations of temperature. Vibratory impulses are best detected with the palmar surface, or ball, of the hand.

Light palpation is used for detecting skin surface characteristics and structures located immediately below the skin. Deep palpation refers to the application of firmer pressure to examine the condition of deeper organs and structures. Light palpation with the various parts of the hands and fingers is the most common method for examining the patient's face, neck, axilla, chest, breast, abdomen, and extremities. Students must learn to let their fingers glide, roll, and gently push across the skin of the patient. The course guide describes in a matter-of-fact tone how the hand turns into a data-collecting instrument that is manipulated in a diagnostic manner:

> Manoeuvring the position of the palpating hand and varying the type of motion will affect the type of data collected. Gliding the finger pads over the skin surface in a horizontal and vertical plane will yield data on texture and surface contour. Information about the position and consistency of a structure can be obtained by using the grasping fingers. (Kot, n.d., p. 13)

Anyone who, as a patient, has been submitted to a palpation examination of a cystic breast or of an abdominal complaint may recall that this was hardly a pleasant experience. But student nurses who must practice palpation on each other find this experience unpleasant for more ambiguous reasons. Jean described the incident as follows:

> In a three-hour morning lab exercise I taught the students palpation and I noticed that they seemed to be uncomfortable. First, some students confided in me during the break that they were quite reluctant to have Ken, the only male student nurse in the class, participate in the peer practice. During peer practice, one student must put on the patient gown, and the other the nursing uniform. Even though Ken has many years of ambulance experience and though he is a very pleasant person, the female students felt uneasy having to pair up with Ken and practice palpation. We solved the problem by having Ken practice on a dummy. Some female students even felt uncomfortable doing the palpation on each other, and some asked if they could keep on their underwear under the gown. (JC)

Jean explained that, though being undressed in the company of one's peers may be experienced as embarrassing, nurses must learn to do palpation. Keeping on underwear is not allowed since it inhibits the process of sensitive discriminations of skin on skin, especially if the underwear is long or elastic.

The second incident happened when the students had to move out of the lab onto the ward where they had to apply their palpating techniques to elderly patients. The students kept postponing, lingering, and stalling. In Jean's words, they seemed willing to do anything to avoid doing palpations. When Jean finally confronted them, the student nurses admitted that they were quite hesitant. What if these patients did not want to be bothered? What if they were reading or taking a nap? What if they had different things on their minds? It is clear that potentially at least, palpation is highly charged with the intimacy of human touch.

Indeed, when Jane in her next class asked students to reflect on the nature of their reluctance to practice palpation, on each other and on patients, they were happy to talk about it. They admitted that their difficulties had to do with ambiguity. They felt acutely aware that there are different ways of touching and that some forms of touching are not fitting for palpation. When asked about these differences, students made a spontaneous distinction between what they called professional touching and nonprofessional touching.

What then is professional touching? Jean asked. Students responded by saying that "the professional touch is firm not light, confident and directed with purpose, goal, and intent." One student said: "When I was practicing palpation on my sister at home, I was too gentle. She told me not to touch in this way. She said it was too light and might be misinterpreted by the patient." When Jean asked the students to describe nonprofessional touching, they said, "It is hard to describe, but it is easy to know when it is not right."

One of the students had a bad experience. The patient, an elderly lady, was uncooperative and shirked away with a startle when the nurse tried to do her palpation examination. The woman seemed so upset that another nurse, who was present, put her hand on the woman's arm in a gesture of support. The patient surrendered to the nurse's hands and started sobbing. "Isn't it strange," remarked the nurse later, "that the patient rejected the hands of one nurse but reached out to the hands of another!" And, of course, it is somewhat ironic that while the young nurse had tried so earnestly to apply the correct touch, this was not received well by the patient. The irony is that it was not an issue of the professional touch versus a nonprofessional touch; rather, the patient actually needed not the gnostic touch of palpation but she needed the pathic touch of support.

So, it seems that there are at least two kinds of touch that we might distinguish in reflecting on the situation of the nursing students: the gnostic and the pathic touch.

The (Dia)Gnostic Touch

First there is the gnostic touch of palpation as described in medical texts. The objective of palpation is diagnostic. Literally *dia-gnostic* means "to know thoroughly" in the sense of seeing through the body. The palpating hand can bring about this diagnostic view. The medical text states: "The assessment of underlying anatomical structures is facilitated if the examiner makes a habit of mentally visualizing anatomical features while conducting the examination" (Kot, n.d., p. 9). Thus, we may say that palpation belongs primarily to the gnostic or medical side of health care. Both doctor and nurse apply the procedure with diagnostic intent. This is how a physician describes the uncannily effective (dia)gnostic expertise of palpation:

It was my clinical on ICU. The unit was to receive an admission from the ward momentarily. The previous evening the patient had undergone emergency surgery for a ruptured appendix and was now doing poorly. She presented with fever, tachycardia, and tachypnoea; she was definitely septic. I initially focused my exam on the patient's abdomen, as this was the site of the surgical incision.

Carefully, I removed the dressings and provided reassurance to the patient. I expected this exam to be difficult. On inspection, there was clear fluid oozing out of the incision. It was swollen, red, and looked angry. I began my exam with light palpation in the opposite corner and worked my way across the abdomen. I could feel the tenseness in the abdominal muscles, especially the rectus abdominis. Gently, I asked the patient to bring her knees up. I wanted to examine the abdomen with the muscles relaxed. My plan was to examine the surgical incision last, because I knew this would cause her the most pain. Following a normal light palpation, I performed a deeper palpation of the abdomen, attempting to feel for masses. As long as I avoided the surgical sight, she tolerated the procedure well.

It was time to move to the hot area. As I rolled my fingers lightly over the surgical incision, I had a passing feeling of bubbles, crepitations, in the abdominal wall. I knew this was not benign air in the muscles. Until proven otherwise, I had to treat the case as gas gangrene. I immediately called for a swab and requested a stat gram stain to confirm my clinical suspicion. I then continued with the rest of the abdominal exam. Upon deep palpation and rapid removal of the hands, there was marked rebound tenderness signifying inflammation around the surgical site. I had my answer.

Shortly after, the lab confirmed my diagnosis. Now I faced the real problem. I immediately marked the skin to demonstrate the extent of the crepitations and booked the patient for emergency surgery. In the following twenty-four hours, she had three debridement surgeries and thankfully survived. (TD)

In this example of the life-saving power of the gnostic touch, we sense the close relation between the expert gnostic eye, the gnostic mind, and the gnostic touch. While the physician remains aware of the vulnerability of the patient as a person, his care for her predicament is expressed in a gnostic approach to her suffering.

The term gnostic derives from the ancient Greek *gnostikos*, meaning "one who knows"; the notion is related to "mind, judgment; rationality, maxim and opinion." In our age, at the practical level, the gnostic attitude in medicine and the health sciences also proceeds on the principle that the process of healing is approached and defined in terms of rationalistic factors. It is not surprising, therefore, that we find the term "gnostic" in the most commonly used medical terminology of "diagnostic" and "prognostic." Indeed, to the layperson, gnostic knowledge may still command an element of awe and blind faith.

The Probing Gnostic Touch

The diagnostic touch can be seen as a specialization of the more general cognitive and probing aspects of touch. Touch is perhaps the most fundamental feature of human experience that lets us explore, discover, and know the world and ourselves in a perceptually unique manner. Touching is finding something tactile. And the hand is uniquely suited to its probing task. The touch of our hand lets us explore the materiality of the world around us. That is why we say that we learn to "handle" and "manipulate things." The phenomenology of touch is quite subtle and complex.

We all know from experience that to touch something and to be touched by something are two very different experiences—even though in both cases the objective pressure on the skin may be exactly the same. When something unexpectedly touches us, then we may shrink back at first.

Moreover, when something or someone touches us, then we do not only feel the other, we also feel our selves. When I suddenly experience the touch of the other person, I do not only feel the skin of the other's hand, I also feel myself, through my own skin. This is even true when, for example, the right hand touches the left hand. Merleau-Ponty called this phenomenon a kind of physical reflection (1964b, p. 166). When the right hand touches the left hand, then the left hand feels not only the right hand in a reciprocal mode, but the left hand also feels itself. Merleau-Ponty shows how in the handshake I feel the other's hand as if it were my own other. So, there is a dual aspect to the touch of things: through touch we get to know what is outside of us and through touch we become aware of ourselves together with that which is being touched (1962, pp. 90–97).

What does this mean for palpation? The patient who is being palpated is in the position of feeling the palpating hand of nurse or physician and at the same time feeling his or her own body. The probing hand turns anatomical, and it is quite possible that the patient begins to participate in the probing attitude. At least that is how one person describes the experience:

As I was lying prone on the hard, narrow examination table, the physician was probing my abdomen. Slightly embarrassed by this procedure, my eye caught the anatomical charts on the wall where an opened up torso exposed its various organs and muscle groups. While turning my face away from the doctor, I fleetingly focused on the intestines in the picture. I was imaging what the hand on my abdomen might be feeling and I was hoping that there would not be any evidence of some villainous lump or malignant growth. I tried not to be tense, but then the sudden push-pull movement of the physician's hands caused excruciating pain.

After I had rearranged my clothes the doctor explained that I probably suffered from diverticulitis, an infectious condition of the colon; not uncommon for someone my age. He drew me a picture of diverticular pockets on the colon wall. An X-ray would have to confirm the diagnosis.

As I left the doctor's office and walked onto the busy street, I felt a bit unsettled—as if my abdomen had been left exposed somehow. The doctor's hands had given me X-ray eyes. In the street, instead of people, I saw fleshy torsos marching by. Torsos filled with blood, organs, and intestines. How would I ever be able to just see people rather than stuffed torsos wrapped in skin and clothes? I had walked into the doctor's office with the simple complaint of a sore abdomen but now my diseased colon was in conspiracy with the unappetizing anatomies of the people passing me by in the street. (MV)

How many people, as patients, undergo this strange sensation of X-ray eyes? The phenomenologist van den Berg describes a similar experience as a young medical student in the 1930s in an anatomy lab in the Netherlands. He recalls a moment when he and a female medical student had to practice their anatomical skills on a corpse.

> I dissected at that moment the musculature of the shoulder and upper arm, my practicum companion dissected the lower arm and hand.—When I looked up at what she was doing I perceived two hands: the hand belonging to the corpse and the hand of my fellow student.
>
> The live hand was nicely tanned and slightly manicured. Slightly, because female medical students are not terribly preoccupied with manicure. One only needs to imagine a hand adorned with rings and heavily lacquered with nail polish holding the knife and scalpel. The difference between the two hands would have been spoiled. But now this strange difference presented itself. Two hands. Under the moving, easily manipulating hand of the living lay the hand of the dead. A parched, white, withered, dried-up hand. A dead hand. A pathetic hand. A split open, busted, jammed open, gaping hand. A terrible hand. A hand with muscles, tendons, veins, nerves, membranes, bands and bones. A full, stuffed filled hand. A belaboured hand. A fussed over hand.
>
> And above it, active, mobile, moving, a simple hand, a closed hand of the young woman. Only a slight sign, some blue veins on its back. (1961, p. 220)

Van den Berg argues that it was a significant event in human history, around the year 1300, when the ordinary closed body was first cut open and by Mundinus and soon by others. From this historical moment onward, it is possible to see the hand with two kinds of vision: with the gnostic eye and with the pathic eye. We can even see this gnostic eye portrayed in the painting of the anatomy lesson by Rembrandt.

But, of course, like the analytical eye, the hand itself has become gnostic as well. The two hands that van den Berg saw—one alive and dissecting, the other dead and anatomized—both belong to the gnostic domain. And yet, he could not help but see a different hand as well. And this difference lies in the distinction between the gnostic and the pathic. He also saw the closed and natural-looking hand of his fellow student—this is the pathic hand, the pathic body, that remains resistant to the X-ray eyes. The term pathetic is also related to pathic. Pathetic originally meant capable of feeling, emotion, and suffering. We can say, therefore, that van den Berg saw the two hands with an ambiguous attitude: the gnostic and the pathic. Van den Berg saw a nicely tanned and slightly manicured hand touching an anatomized hand that was being dissected in a gnostic manner. This pathic hand belonged to the female fellow student beside him. But, at the same time, her hand was performing a gnostic task. Thus, van den Berg saw the hands even more ambiguously than he himself described.

The Private Pathic Touch

The pathic touch is no less complex than the gnostic touch. The pathic touch may be experienced in a variety of modalities. Within the context of the discussion on palpation, I would distinguish between a private and a personal touch; though these too have several experiential dimensions. Thus, the private touch may be loving, friendly, erotic, or intimate; the personal touch may be experienced as supportive, caring, comforting, healing, therapeutic, and so forth. We all have experienced a hand that caresses us. And in this experience we know how the caress brings about a change in the hand. A caress transforms the body, even if the physiologist is unable to report on this transformation, suggests Buytendijk (1970b). Sometimes we all may feel our body as more or less foreign to us. Why do I have this particular body? These eyes? This nose? These hands? But then, when another person touches us—in friendship, care, or in love—then the contingencies of our own body are eliminated. A justification of the body takes place. The touch removes the distance between two bodies, and one is invited to be one with one's own body, to inhabit one's own body.

Precisely because the touch can accomplish so much, one can sense also the uncomfortable ambiguity of this private, sometimes intimate touch. The intimate touch is what the student nurses referred to as unprofessional; it was the touch they feared since it might be misinterpreted by the patient. Practicing palpation on each other leaves open all kinds of possibilities for ambiguity. As student nurse, how can I submit my self-conscious body to the scrutinizing palpation of my classmate without feeling touched in an intimate manner? Similarly, in palpating the body of my fellow student, how can I pretend that this is just a body, a body without a person who feels somewhat embarrassed and exposed beneath that hospital gown?

The same is true in real medical situations, a light palpation of the skin might be experienced by the patient as caressing, as too intimate. So, it would appear that it is the private touch that may render the nurse–patient relation ambiguous in a potentially confusing manner. The private touch might mean that the hand that touches has a special interest in the other. Again, this may manifest itself in significations of embarrassment.

The Personal Pathic Touch

Next there is the personal pathic touch, which the texts on palpation did not mention but which was evident in the patient's positive response to the comforting hand. Of course, the private touch is also pathic, but here the special quality of the hand does not touch with private but with professional intent. The pathic hand and the pathic knowledge that supports it can be seen to lie at the heart of nursing practice since its effect is that it reunites or reintegrates the patient with his or her body again. Thus, the gnostic aspect of health science works in the opposite direction as the pathic aspect. The gnostically healing attitude analyzes, anatomizes, dissects, and makes diagnoses and prognoses that tend to separate us from our body, so to speak. The pathically healing attitude of the act of healing aims to console and comfort, to wake in times of suffering, to be there in moments of need, to support in the process of convalescence, and so to assist the recovering patient in feeling whole and making life livable again—even if sometimes under constraints of chronic difficulties.

Strangely perhaps, the very notion of touch presupposes our lived distance from things and others. Without touch it would not be possible to go away, to let go, or to lose contact, and to get in touch again. "There is proximity, but only to the extent that extreme closeness emphasizes the distancing it opens up," says Nancy (2000, p. 5). This means that touch is the primordial medium to overcome separation and relational distance, and yet it opens up separation and distance. Still, touch is primal contact. Neither the ear nor the eye can give us an experience of human contact in the same pathically direct manner as the touch. Indeed, we may be deeply moved by a human voice or a meaningful glance, but the touch stirs us in a particularly intimate manner. It may even happen at times that we are touched to tears—as in the case of the elderly patient and nurse above.

So wherein lie some of the differences between gnostic and pathic thought and practice? When we compare the more gnostic medical relation to the more pathic medical relation, then we note that medical diagnostic practice first of all searches for symptomatic clues and determining factors in the patient's history. For example, the medical specialist may look for causal, symptomatic, or developmental patterns, for difficulties surrounding the birth, for psychological, physical, and genetic abnormalities in parents, grandparents, and other close family members. Psychiatric clinical thought operates in a similar manner: one does psychological analyses, administers diagnostic instruments, and applies intelligence tests, personality inventories, and other measuring devices. One searches for disease patterns *by looking back* into personal and family histories.

Thus, the gnostic mode of thinking and practicing leads to a certain idea of the meaning of healing: the gnostic approach is to locate the pathology and then to "cut out" the intrusion that has been festering there for days, weeks, or even years. Just as one frees someone from his or her appendix in the surgical room, so one searches for and removes the "psychological problem" by "cutting it out" of people's lives in the therapeutic room. How is this experienced by the patient? Sometimes it may seem that the physician, the psychologist, the psychiatrist "gives" the patient a tumor, a neurosis, a paranoia. And, of course, once the patient has been given (diagnosed with) the illness, now the medical treatment consists of cutting and taking it out again.

Of course, it would be wrong to suggest that the gnostic approach of the medical doctor would preclude a meaningful caring relation. "The 'gnostic' contact should not be interpreted as a cold, calculating, dry and therefore heartless association with the patient," says van den Berg (1972, p. 131). But it may be true, as van den Berg proposes, that the sense of caring and trust is different for the medical specialist who sees the patient only briefly and the family physician, hospitalist, or nurse who, hopefully, is to be present or available throughout a period of time. The patient tends to experience the specialist physician (such as a surgeon) with a different "nearness" that is not due to pathic qualities but to the knowing relationship of the doctor and his or her patient. "The medical contact combines a maximum of trust with a minimum of familiarity," says van den Berg (1972, p. 131). So, would van den Berg suggest that the gnostic contact may nevertheless be experienced pathically? And how would the pathic quality of this knowing relation be experienced differently from the caring attentiveness of the nurse or physician? Van den Berg does not speak about these concerns but, no doubt, we should see the gnostic as well as the pathic realized in the actions, knowledge, and attitudes of the physician as a tactful and knowledgeable practitioner.

If I have confidence in the physician, then I experience the palpating medical hand as an instrument of competence in whose knowledge and skills I have the trust of confidence. Bollnow (1988) has clarified the phenomenological difference between *confidence* and pure *trust*. Confidence lacks relationality and the intrinsic moral character of trust, says Bollnow. Confidence is basically concerned with performance, specific competencies, and proven expertise. For example, from the patient's point of view, it is reassuring to have confidence in one's surgeon, but the surgeon's expertise is not really dependent upon the patient's confidence.

In contrast with the knowing or gnostic hand of palpation, the nursing and medical hand is pathic when it applies the dressing, straightens the bedding, starts an intravenous, administers the medication, gestures supportively, cleans the skin, provides relief of pain, supports the aching body in its time of healing, or even when the nurse or physician is simply present. True, the medical hand is knowledgeable of medical science. But—outside of the highly technologized intensive care, emergency, or technical tasks—the patient still expects the healing hand to be a caring hand that touches not only the physical body, but also the self, the whole embodied person. This pathic quality may well constitute the core meaning of the healing act of medical care. If, as a patient, I trust this hand then it has the power to reunite me pathically with my body. It reminds me that I am one with my body and thus makes it possible for me to heal, to strengthen, to become whole.

Of course, a gnostic–pathic ambiguity can arise in many professional and social situations. For example, the physiotherapist may manipulate or massage the patient's body with gnostic intent while the patient would say that the treatment has the quality of a pathic experience. Many medical procedures that are primarily technical may give the patient a pathic trust in the physician, especially if the quality of the relation between patient and doctor is personal. What then makes pathic practice distinct? The difference is this: pathic thought turns itself immediately and directly to the person himself or herself. A pathic relation is always specific and unique. Even a relatively brief encounter between a patient and a health-care provider can have this personal quality. A personal relation is something you can have only with a specific other. The pathic orientation meets this concrete person in the heart of his or her existence, without trying to reduce the patient to a diagnostic picture, a certain kind of case, a preconceived category of patient, a psychological type, a set of factors on a scale, or a theoretical classification. In other words, there is something deeply personal or intersubjective to the pathic relation. That is also the reason that the pathic personal relation is easily confused with the private one.

What is quite compelling in medical practice is the way in which any particular person fails to match preconceived gnostic distinctions, how a particular patient consistently refuses to fit diagnostic judgment and prognostic projections. How with any particular patient the clinical path of an illness is always different from medical assessment. How the profile of a disease is never experienced in exactly the same manner by different persons. How patients often continue to live when they were expected to die, or die when they were supposed to recover. This constant "defying difference" between diagnosis or prognosis on the one hand and contingency and concreteness on the other is what makes each person, each patient, uniquely who he or she is—which is never the same as the diagnostic portrait that the expert constructs. The individual human being always falls to a certain extent "outside" of the dossier, the diagnosis, the description, the prognosis (see Beets, 1952/1975).

If we want to be sensitive to the pathic nature of professional practice, then we need to pursue forms of research that use pathic language. Pathic questions cannot be answered by texts that primarily communicate cognitive, intellectual, theoretical, or technical meaning. And gnostic insights cannot produce pathic experience. To construct texts that can address and reflect on the experience of illness, we need to get beyond the objectifying effects of naming the things of our world with labels that distance us from them. We need to write (and read) for tone and pathic understanding.

The Eidos of Touch

The eidos of the touch seems to lie in the gesture whereby the touch unites and reunites, integrates and reintegrates two bodies. A feature of the medicalization of increasing aspects of life and body functions is that the gnostic act tends to fragment. When a disease has been properly treated, when a surgical operation has been successfully completed, this does not necessarily mean that the patient has been re-integrated with his or her body or with his or her world. This needful moment of healing is exactly where the pathic practice enters. It may be appropriate to say that the pathic medical act complements the gnostic medical act, in the sense that *the pathic meaning of medical practice consists of reuniting the patient with his or her body, and thus make life livable again in whatever way this has to be learned by the patient.* For example, in the everydayness of nursing practice, there is the pathic process of taking the patient to the bathroom, prompting him or her to get out of bed, encouraging personal hygiene in the awareness that this has to do with relationships and with re-establishing relationships. One nurse said: When I see the patient look in the mirror, then I know that the healing is in progress, that the patient is getting "better."

Looking at the Clock: What Time Is It?

I glance at the clock: it is not supper time yet. So, I open the book again that I am reading. But then my son walks in the room. "What time is it," he asks. I look at the clock again and answer, "It is five o'clock." "Thanks." My son disappears again and I look at the clock again and wonder: why did I have to look at the clock again to tell my son what time it is? I just had looked at it less than a minute earlier. Am I getting forgetful? Or did I not really look at the clock when I looked at the time? What did I see when I looked at the time? Is looking *at* the time the same as looking *for* the time?

Looking at the time is probably one of the most common habits of our modern existence. We tell the time from the face of the ordinary clock, watch, or digital timepieces or screens. A common definition of a clock or timepiece might be that it is the device used to measure, verify, keep, and indicate time. So, how would we describe the experience of a clock phenomenologically as it presents itself and as we encounter it in our everyday life? A Husserlian phenomenologist may begin by asking how does the material clock appear? As we approach and examine the clock on the mantelpiece or on the wall in our room, how does the clock-thing show or give itself in our experience or consciousness?

We immediately seem to run into an issue. A Husserlian philosopher who observes a clock will note that no matter how we look at the clock, we always see it only from one of many possible points of view and shifting spatial and temporal vantage points. Fancy clocks may have an interesting look. But it is not really possible to see the whole clock in one conscious grasp. In other words, our knowledge of the clock in front of us is always partial. As we examine it from every side and from all kinds of angles, and as we examine it in the morning light and the evening shade, how can we really give a final description of its appearance? Our consciousness of the clock and the clock face is such that the clock always seems to give itself in profiles or adumbrations, suggests Husserl. This may seem somewhat trivial and yet it is a telling point that while we would think that we can easily know what a clock is just by looking at it, strictly speaking this assumption is problematic.

A Trompe l'oeil

What do we really see when we walk down the street and see a clock mounted on a shop window? As we notice a clock in a shop window, we may be surprised and confused because as we walk closer it seems to be only an image of a clock. It just looks like a clock, but it is a *trompe l'oeil* (optical illusion). But it is also possible that next, as we look closer we confirm that yes, it really appears to be a clock. A Husserlian philosopher may ask, but how do we know that the object or thing we see is a real clock? Is a painting of a clock still a clock? Well, not really, indeed the painter René Magritte asked exactly that: He painted a pipe and entitled the painting "This Is Not a Pipe." Even a material-looking pipe or clock may not be what it seems. Therefore, Husserl might ask, "How can we imaginatively vary aspects of the clock in our consciousness in order to determine its true nature?" Would this clock, this physical object still be a clock if we paint it a different color? Yes, it would still be a clock, so color is not an essential aspect of a clock. Would it still be a clock if it was made of wood or plastic? Yes, so wood or plastic are not essential aspects of a clock either. Would it still be a clock if we remove the hands of the clock? Well, no! A clock needs hands (whether analog or digital) to show us the time. Therefore, the hands (or analog time indicators or monitors) would seem essential to a clock. Even real or virtual "hands" or luminous numbers are time indicators and would be a necessary element of a real clock. Is it still a clock even if it does not seem to correspond with the time at that moment? One has to be able to read or perceive the time on a clock. The aim of the Husserlian philosopher is to establish epistemologically our knowledge of the essence of the clock. Indeed, an epistemological phenomenology orients to our possible knowledge of the clock.

When the Husserlian philosopher looks at the clock and describes how this particular clock appears, he or she may be inclined to use terms such as dial—pendulum—oscillator—gears—hands—hours—minutes—mechanism—glass—wood—plastic—brass—keys—spring—battery—metal works inside. But again, one can never perceive (describe and know) a material object such as a clock in its material or perceptual totality. Therefore, Husserl would point out that it belongs to the essence of the clock, as an empirical object or thing, that it only shows itself in profiles or adumbrations. Adumbrations are the sides, faces, segments, edges, areas, through which the thing presents or gives itself. Every material object such as a clock, a chair, a tree or a house always shows or reveals itself in adumbrations.

Therefore, the Husserlian phenomenologist says, that while we cannot have "perfect knowledge" of the clock empirically in its total perspectival presence, we can, however, know the clock in its phenomenal essence. This is a critical phenomenological insight into the essence of the material object: any object like a clock reveals itself in a constant showing and hiding of an endless series of adumbrational profiles. So, the phenomenological insight of the nature of the clock is that we can never have perfect empirical knowledge of the clock by looking at it or listening to its sounds. No matter how many times and in what manner we turn the clock around and look at it from different angles we still only see profiles of the clock. However silly it may sound, we can never see the clock from every possible vantage point at once.

Thus, the Husserlian philosopher discloses the clock by pointing at its profiles— the fact that perception of the object is always perspectival. However, and this is the surprising insight from Husserl's epistemology, we can know the essence of a clock by looking at it as a phenomenon. When we apply the phenomenological epoché then we suspend our belief in the empirical reality of this or that particular clock and yet we keep looking at it as a concrete example of a clock. And the phenomenological reduction reconstitutes the essence of the clock by bracketing all inessential aspects and features of the clock in front of us and yet regard the essential structure of our intentional experience of the clock. So, ironically, we cannot indubitably "know" a "thing" like this clock, or this house, or this car, or this book in a non-perspectival manner, but we can know its essence experientially with certainty, richness, and existential phenomenal precision. Ironically, the Husserlian philosopher "shows" how the clock "appears" by adopting a transcendent inceptual perspective. This is an important point.

The Phenomenal Clock

Now, how would a Heideggerian philosopher explicate the phenomenon of a clock? This philosopher would use an existential approach to describe the ontology (being) of a clock. From an existential and ontological Heideggerian perspective, one would ask again, "Is this really how we get to know the clock better?" How does a clock appear or give itself phenomenologically in its total phenomenality? How does the clock appear in our everyday experience?

Actually, the Heideggerian philosopher may suggest that the Husserlian descriptive concepts increasingly thematize and objectify the clock and thereby impoverish the concrete experiential character and experiential meaningfulness of the timepiece in front of us, or as it hangs on our wall. The problem is that the objectifying act of describing the clock is actually a de-living experience: only leaving a residue of the originally immediate, subtle, complex, and rich primordial experience of temporality and materiality. Instead, we should aim to describe the meaning of the clock in its phenomenal being, as it gives itself to us in experience, unmediated by conceptual or perceptual objectifications and abstractions.

As I am writing this sentence, I glance at the clock in my home office. This glance is a protentional gesture: I expect to see the time. But this expectation is more than simply seeing the clockface with its hands. I kind of expect to see where I am at in my activity of writing. And I see that it is almost bed time. But as I reflect on my momentary look at the face of the clock in my room, I should take note that I actually didn't really "observe" the face, dial, and hands of the clock. Rather by looking at the clock, I "saw" that the positional space of the hour and minute hands of the clock told me where I am with my writing in the context of the evening. If someone were to ask me at the next instant what time it is as I directed my eyes back to my work, I would probably have to glance at the clock again. I would say, "it is a quarter to twelve." As I glanced at the clock a moment earlier, it did not really register that it was fifteen minutes before twelve; instead, I saw that there was a spatial configuration that told me that there was little space left until midnight—when the hands gather at the top of the dial. And yet, I did not really study the dial and hands; I just "saw" that it was about bedtime. At the same glance, the clock lets me know how (dis)satisfied it feels with regards to my writing accomplishment. It also makes me conscious that it is too late now to still make that planned phone call to my colleague who lives in a city of a different time zone. I should really stop working but could try to finish writing this paragraph, about glancing at the clock, I am working on. But instead I realize that I am trying to describe the experience of this clock.

My clock is an antique wall clock that used to belong to my grandparents. Sometimes I look at this antique clock and am reminded of the bedroom under the eaves at my grandparents' Dutch farm. Being aware of the clock is a subjective and an objective experience. It shapes the way I experience time and how it regulates and dictates my daily activities. The clock makes me aware of, tells me, how I am spending my day, and it reproaches me for not being more productive. I reflect on how Heidegger asks if it is possible to thematize lived experience without falling into the trap of objectification as it occurs in positivistic forms of inquiry. Heidegger answers in the positive. But the phenomenological task of doing justice to the way we experience the things of our world remains a constant challenge and concern.

The acts of phenomenological description and thematization inevitably do violence to the meaningfulness of experience by unwittingly bringing experience to a halt. We cannot really capture experience in its unfolding in time. But Heidegger believes that it is possible for language to move beyond the traditional function of thematization, reification, representation, and objectification. For this purpose, Heidegger makes a distinction between traditional (epistemological) objectification as it occurs in social science, and between formal (ontological) objectification as practiced in phenomenological inquiry (1982, p. 281). Formal or ontological objectification safeguards the Being of beings as it lets ontological objectification be guided or informed by the preontological understanding of being as it is lived in a "subjective way."

Objective Clock Time

Objective clock time is contrasted with subjective time. Chronos, the personification of objective time, is often depicted as an aged Greek god showing an hour glass by which he holds time. He stares at the timepiece as if he is penetrating its temporal secrets. Chronos time is measurable, reproducible, plannable, and pre-dictable. "Time is what is counted," says Heidegger. The clock time is always the time of the "now."

> What is counted are the nows. And they show themselves "in every now" as "right-away-no-longer-now" and "just-now-not-yet." The world time "caught sight of" in this way in the use of the clock we shall call *now-time*. (Heidegger, 2010, p. 401)

Heidegger could have called it Chronos time. Chronos, the Greek god of time, is portrayed as an all-devouring force.

In contrast, Kairos is the Greek god of subjective qualitative time. Kairos always shows himself in the fleeting instant of a moment. He is the youngest and most rebellious son of Zeus, and grandson of Chronos. Kairos time may be considered the moment of the experiential now. This moment can be life-altering for the person who understands the importance of just this moment (Hermsen, 2014; van Manen, 2015, pp. 51–53).

And yet, as we measure time, we realize that time is not a substance. Time is not something that we can put or pour into a cup. The physicist who captures the movement of time with an atomic clock knows that from a cosmological point of view time is merely a label or name to describe a position in space. When looking at the clock, we do not see a material thing, but rather we immediately "see" time.

As we look at the clock, we are being looked at in return. But, this is a particular manifestation of Kairos time, an enigmatic realization of the nature of time. While working at my desk, I may not have been aware at all of the time. But as I glanced at the clock, I immediately experienced my temporal predicament. Instead of reg-istering the exact Chronos time, I saw how little time I had left to complete my work. The spatial configuration of the hands on the face of the clock immediately converted objective spatial distance into temporal subjective distance. Indeed, it shows how space and time are phenomenologically intertwined.

Clocks that are designed with digital faces may give us a different immediate sense of time. A digital clock that shows changing numbers rather than moving hands on a dial may not give us immediately the subjective sense of time. When I look at the digital clock on my smart phone and I see the number 11:45 then I translate the numbers into "a quarter to midnight" in order to determine the sub-jective clock time, which gives me a sense of how I am doing in what I am doing (writing this text).

The Kairos Moment

A phenomenological insight may be said to occur in a Kairos moment. We say "Kairos moment" because Kairos always shows himself in the fleeting instant of a moment (see Hermsen, 2014). But this instant can be life-altering for the person who encounters Kairos and understands the importance of just this momentary instant (Marramao, 2007).

From Greek mythology, we all know Chronos, the father of Zeus, but the strange thing is that Kairos (the rebellious grandson of Chronos) is little known.

Both Chronos and Kairos are gods of time and both are portrayed with wings. Chronos is the god of quantitative or cosmic time of the clock. Kairos is the god of qualitative time—but not just any kind of qualitative time: Kairos is pregnant time, the time of possibility. Chronos is often depicted as an aged bearded man with lots of hair, holding an hour glass by which he measures and keeps time. Even though he is an old man, Chronos is a bit of a bully, dominating and authoritarian. Chronos time is plannable, measurable, reproducible, and predictable. Underlying the distinction between Chronos time and Kairos time slumbers a significant philosophical controversy: the question whether we experience time as a continuous flow of duration or as discontinuous ruptured moments and instants.

In *Intuition of the Instant* (2013), Gaston Bachelard carefully examined in 1932 the generally accepted position of Henri Bergson (explicated in 1910) that we experience time as duration. He contrasts Bergson's (2001) sense of temporality as "the consciousness of pure duration" with his sense of streaming time as "multiplying conscious instants" (Bachelard, 2013, p. 50). Husserl also describes the streaming of time as a continual renewal of the "now" moment that constantly changes into the "just now." We have to pay attention to how the now gives itself, says Edmund Husserl,

> to the fact that a new now attaches itself to this now, and that a new and constantly new now attaches intrinsically to every now in a necessary continuity, and that, in unity with this, every current now changes into a "just now," while the "just now" changes in turn and continually into ever new instances of "just now" of the previous "just now" and so forth. The same holds for every now that has attached a new to a previous now. (Husserl, 2014, p. 157)

Husserl's phrase for describing the lived presence of the "now" that lies at the basis of our everyday existence is "primal impressional consciousness." In his *Phenomenology of Internal Time Consciousness* (1964b), Husserl famously uses the example of musical sound to show how the tones of a piece of music present themselves in the instant of the now, and how the successive retention (just now) and anticipated protention (next now) gives us the experience of melody: of time past, present, and future. In Husserl's epistemological language, it is the primal impressional consciousness and its retentional and protentional aspects that make our lived experiences potentially available for our reflection.

The curious fact of life is that we always seem to be in the "now," in the instance of the moment or the moment that spreads out over time. How could we not be? As I am writing these words, I am in the now of this moment of writing (I have been doing so for a couple of hours). Even when we dwell in memories, daydreams, or in anticipations, we do so in the experiential "now." And yet, when we try to capture the "now" of our experience, we always seem to be too late.

This is where the figure of Kairos becomes important for our understanding of the instant of the now as the source for phenomenological insights. Kairos offers us an understanding of time as the discontinuous instant of the now, the fleeting instant of the moment, or the experiential structure of time as momentary temporality. Kairos is indeed a very strange and complex figure of temporality. Since ancient biblical times a Kairos moment has been described as *carpe diem*, a transformative moment of chance and change, depending on our ability and willingness to recognize this moment and to seize the opportunity that is offered in it (Sipiora and Baumlin, 2012). Kairos is the god of the ephemeral moment. He is whimsical, rebellious, and creative. In old paintings and sculptures, he holds a razor, or else scales balanced on the sharp edge of a knife—illustrating the evanescent instant of a moment when Kairos may appear and disappear.

You also can see that he is double-winged, indicating that a Kairos moment is fleeting, propitious, instantaneous, and serendipitous. Kairos time is the presence of the now. The instant of the now. In such Kairos moment, time seems to stand still. We are in timeless time.

Yet, if Kairos comes your direction, he'll race by on his wild wings. At that "eye-wink" instant you have the chance to grab him by the hair as he flies by, but the moment he has passed you, you are too late. You may reach out for his hair but your hands will slip off the back of his bald skull. This is a provocative image, but one that is striking and clarifying of the human predicament when something hangs in the balance: of needing to deal with a crisis that confronts us in the now, but that will be too late to face when the now has passed. Then all there is left is regret that Kairos leaves in his trail. The figure of Metanoia often appears as a veiled and sorrowful woman companion of Kairos. Metanoia is there to perhaps console or blame us when we fail in Kairos moments of opportunity (Myers, 2011).

Like so many mythological tales and legends, the figure of Kairos speaks to the enigma of our humanness. Heidegger has pointed out that in our age we are all under the spell of Chronos: continuity, order, and machination. While living in a time dominated by technology and production, there are aspects to our humanity that are hard to grasp, such as human innerness, the imaginal, and the inceptual. And yet, however beyond comprehension this play of Kairos may sound, this is the sort of thing that seems to have happened to many of us. I trust it has happened to you the reader: I am trying to write some ideas, reflecting on the meaning of a certain question or phenomenon that interests me, but the insight won't come. Finally, when I seem to be hopelessly stuck with my writing I give up. To do what? Well, nothing: I do nothing—which means I may go for a walk, a bike-ride through the countryside, or spend half an hour mindlessly peddling on my exercise bike with music turned up really loud.

Now, it is in mindless moments like this (doing essentially nothing) that our most striking insights may happen. Afterwards we say, "it occurred to me"; "it crossed my mind"; "it came to me"; "I stumbled upon"; "I suddenly had this idea"; "it hit me"; "I had a dream"; "I suddenly thought"; "I suddenly felt I was onto something"; "as if from a hazy distance"; "the words just came to mind."

Subjective Clock Time

From the example of the clock we may have noticed that Husserl tends to approach the phenomenon of the clock epistemologically as a time-measuring object. It is 11:45 a.m. Heidegger focuses on the clock ontologically while thinking it is almost bedtime.

Both a Husserlian and a Heideggerian phenomenology explore how the clock appears, shows, or gives itself. Husserl uses epistemology to ask what kind of knowledge it is that we may gain from a phenomenological "seeing" while Heidegger explores the seeing of the appearance (self-showing) of the clock ontologically. The clock in this example is a thing or a phenomenon. But a thing or phenomenon may also be less material and thing-like. For example, how might we see the phenomenology of a mood like boredom?

I look again at the clock. What time is it? That is the question. Hélène Cixous probes the existential consequence of the question when it occurs:

In the wee hours, when I'm no longer sleeping but still dreaming and I'm in the midst of waking, it comes, the question, to spur me on, and in the same way in the middle of the day, it comes to rouse me. What time is it, do you know what time it is? As soon as I wonder what time it is, I'm lost.

What time is it, I mean to say where am I, I mean to say where have I gone— I don't know anymore, in this instant when I call out to myself, where I'm passing or where I'm going.

When do we wonder this? So often. We grope our way along in time, worried, distracted. And blindly we forefeel. (Cixous, 1998, p. 75)

Eidos of Looking for the Time

As I gaze again at my antique clock I become aware of its aging appearance. It was already more than a hundred years old when I inherited this clock some 50 years ago. So, it also tells the time of where I am in my life, my life-time. And, of course, it lets me know the time of this day, and what I accomplished today. I feel like the elderly White Rabbit of Lewis Carroll who keeps racing against the hands of the clock, exclaiming, "Oh dear! Oh dear! I shall be late!" But late for what? After Alice fell in the White Rabbit hole she is constantly in search of the White Rabbit, in her quest of grasping the meanings of the strange wonders she encounters. More symbolically Alice is ongoingly confronted by her sense of adolescent self-identity as she tries to deal with her world and of the all-encompassing significance of time in her growing up. We experience the pressing of the circadian rhythms in the changing of the seasons and the operation of our body clock and the psycho-biological clock that steers our sense of the space and time. Phenomenologically time is the profoundly enigmatic phenomenon of the personal life of each of us and the cosmic life of us all: time seems to create and be created by the impulse of the cellular clock of all life and the draw of the cosmic clock of the universe.

The Experience of Care-as-Worry: What Is the Language of Care?

It is a nice summer evening and we were all sitting around and talking about what it means to have children. I express the belief that both my sons have made a wonderful life for themselves and for their spouses and their own children. And I remark how happy I am that my grown-up children are doing so well and that I do not have to worry about them any longer. Then my son speaks up and says: "Papa I want you to keep worrying about me." I am somewhat taken aback because, though the comment may have seemed a bit flippant, he is utterly serious. Here is my son who holds advanced university degrees and a professional position, and he knows what I meant with my sense of not having to worry, because he has two young children himself. But, of course, I completely understood why he said what he said. And, of course, he knows that my continued concern and attention for him will always be there—like most every other parent, I will always care and worry about my children—no matter how mature and independent they have become. And yet, I wonder how can the experience of caring be at the same time the experience of worrying?

In Dutch, Belgian, and Scandinavian dictionaries, the English term "care" translates into the word "*zorg*" or "*Sorge*" but with the added meaning of worry. Generally, the word "*zorgen*" always possesses an element of what we may call in English happy-care as well as a good-natured worry or a low-grade sense of concern. Does that mean that the lived experience of *caring* in English is different from the lived experience of *zorgen* (which means care)?

People who are reasonably fluent in two or more languages know how some words and phrases in one language do not translate easily into another language, because they may have a different sentiment or *Stimmung* (mood, sphere). This difference in sensed meaning poses an interesting challenge for qualitative inquiry since this usually implies that the phenomenal meaning of a certain experience (phenomenon) does not easily lead to a linguistic rendition that corresponds to the immanent phenomenality of a similar experience in another language. Some of these translation issues are well known. For example, the word *gemütlich* in German or the word *hyggelig* in Danish or the word *gezellig* in Dutch share fairly common experiential qualities, but it proves difficult to find an English word or phrase that communicates quite the same meaning. These terms express a quality of intimate sociality that seems typically recognizable in Dutch, German, or Danish. But this felt meaning seems untranslatable into North American English language.

More philosophically, certain words that are everyday and quotidian in one language culture may be awkward in the currency of other language cultures of such experiential meanings. For example, the terms *Erlebnis* or *belevenis* are immediately felt to be understood by common German- or Dutch-language speakers, while the English translation "lived experience" became common place in human science and phenomenological texts, though it remained somewhat artificial. It is noteworthy, however, that recently the translation "lived experience" seems to have slipped into ordinary language. But now the term seems to carry the specific sense of emphatically meaningful experiences and personal experiences.

The English term "care" or caring pose especially interesting translation issues. In North American English the term "care" or caring appears to have changed its meaning. This is especially clear when care or caring is compared with the supposed equivalent Dutch, German, or Scandinavian terms *zorg*, *Sorge*, or *umsorge*.

For a person whose first language is Dutch, there occurs a strangely shifting emphasis of meaning in using the Dutch word "*zorgen*" as compared with the English word "caring." The word "care" or "caring" has generally very positive denotations and connotations in the English language. The meaning of the term "caring" includes *Oxford Dictionary* equivalents such as kind-hearted, warm-hearted, affectionate, loving, considerate, tender, thoughtful, cherishing, to be devoted, fond of, to love.

Most speakers of the English language would probably agree that the word "caring" carries generally a positive affectivity. Care seems primarily (but not exclusively) to be a nice and pleasant qualitative word and indeed many like to claim to be in the caring business, especially those who *are* in business: we can see advertisements for car care, lawn care, skin care, carpet care, and many other profitable caring enterprises. So how does that compare with the German *Sorge*, the Danish *omsorg*, and the Dutch *zorg*? Do they also feature as happy words in the Dutch, German and Scandinavian advertising industry?

Strictly speaking it seems that the North American term "care" or "caring" is untranslatable into Dutch, German, or Scandinavian, while the terms *zorg, Sorge*, and *umsorg* are untranslatable into North American English. These terms are not quite equivalent. It gets even more complicated when in the European languages the American term *care* or *caring* gets imported into the professional literature of health care and child care.

The Dutch terms *zorg* and *zorgen* translate into English language as *care* and *caring* but they also translate as *worry* and *worrying*. In the Dutch word "*zorg*" the two main meanings *care* and *worry* are totally intertwined. The statement "*ik zorg voor m'n kinderen*" translates as "I care for my children," and yet the connotation of worry adds an important different emphasis to these common phrases. The experiential shifts in meaning are worthy of phenomenological attention. It should make one wonder about the significance of the differing experiential correspondences of these terms: caring means *zorgen*, care means *zorg* in the relations between adults and children.

When consulting the English–Dutch dictionary for the equivalent of the English term "care" then one finds the Dutch term "*zorg*" and when one looks for the equivalent of the English term "worry" one also and again finds the Dutch term "*zorg*." Thus, while in English these two terms "care" and "worry" are kept separate, in Dutch, German, and Scandinavian languages these meanings are inextricably wound up or entangled in a singular mode of meaning. Even terms such as *verpleegzorg* or *kinderzorg*, meaning nursing care or child care, contain meaning associations that express this ambiguous sense of loving-care-as-worry, except that the element of worry or concern is semiotically embedded. In other words, *zorgen* for someone means to care for someone in a certain worrying kind of manner. Interestingly, even in the Google Translate program, the main equivalents for *zorgen* are care and worry. The same is the case for dictionary meanings of *Sorge* (German), *omsorg* (Danish, Norwegian and Swedish), and *huoli* (Finnish). Echoes of the meanings of "care, concerns, and worries" are also evident in words like *bekommer* (Dutch), *bekymring* (Danish, Norwegian), *Besorgnis* (German), *bekymmer* (Swedish), and *soargen* (Frisian).

Very likely, the "worry" aspect of meaning of the term "*zorgen*" would make it unattractive for the sales and service business in Dutch, German, and Scandinavian languages—after all, who wants a recommendation for a company that will care for your car while worrying about it or while getting itself and you worried! And yet, the worrying aspect in this compound meaning of "*zorg*" is experienced as an ethical sensibility rather than in the negative sense of an anxiety disorder that psychologists would like to help you get rid of. In other words, "caring for a child" in the affective sense, as in the pedagogical relation of mothering or fathering, is translated as *"zorgen voor een kind"* and this implies the normal affective significance of care as well as the sense of concern or worry that is always part of the affective relation. That is why many parents will say that once you have a child, life will never be the same again—not just in the sense of everyday happy responsibilities but especially in that you will discover that you now experience a sense of caring that is simultaneously a chronic parental concern or worry that will never quite leave you again. This is from here on the pedagogical aspect of the "being" of being a parent for the rest of your life—pedagogy means actively distinguishing good from bad ways of acting and dealing with children or young people and this is done with a sense of concern or worry.

To reiterate, it would appear that semiotically the Dutch words *zorg* and *zorgen* refer to the English terms "care" and "caring." But in the English word caring the sense of worry has been largely excised from the word caring while the Dutch, German, and Scandinavian words *zorg*, *Sorge*, and *omsorg* have retained the expressiveness of concern or worry in an emphatic sense. Does that mean that the lived experience of caring has lost much of the sense of concern and worry—as expressed in the popular song "Don't Worry Be Happy"?

Caring for the Faces of Those Who Are Faceless

I suggested that the worry of care as *zorgen* should not be confused with pathological fear and phobia, or with dominant anxiety disorder which involves excessive and uncontrollable worry as well as chronic somatic anxiety symptoms. And yet, in spite of this clarification, I like to suggest, somewhat tongue-in-cheek, that care-as-worry can be likened to a metaphor for illness—a chronic condition of concern and worrying for this other person who is dear to me, whom I love, or for whom I care and happen to feel responsible. And indeed, this condition of care-as-worry is truly somewhat like an affliction. Existentially the vulnerability of the other may be experienced as ethical pain—a pain that is symptomatic of the worrying condition engendered in the encounter with this other person who has made a claim on me. Many parents, many teachers, many nurses, many physicians, and many other helping professionals would readily agree that this worrying can be painful and troubling. But it is a form of worry that is also necessary. Why? Because worrying keeps me in touch with the presence of this other. Or, as Levinas says, "The presence of the other touches me" (in Rötzer, 1995, p. 62). And now that the ethical has entered my life, I feel I should *do* something, something is demanded of me, and this in-touchness is phenomenologically the ethical significance of care-as-worry.

As a father or mother, you may recognize this care-as-worry from personal experience: from those numerous moments when you suffered almost more from the stomach ache, the illness, the fear, or the anxiety experienced by your child than the child did him or herself. A teacher may feel a special responsibility for this or that student. And this care-as-worry is often expressed as, "I have to let her know that she is doing okay," or "I need to keep a special eye on him." But, of course, caring in a deeper sense can only happen where contexts, structures, teacher–student or patient–staff ratios, and schedules provide opportunities for the occurrence of genuine caring relations, even though we know that these relations cannot necessarily be planned or predicted.

Importantly, caring in this deeper sense remains the source for understanding every other kind of caring. It is intuitively obvious that care-as-worry cannot be legislated or prescribed through protocols, and it is impossible to care deeply for every person (child, student, patient) for whom we are responsible as professionals. But the sporadic and spontaneous occurrence of this originary kind of care in singular instances provides the basis for understanding the more practical pedagogical responsibilities that we do expect from professional educators and others on an everyday and routine basis in their care for a multitude of children, patients, or others for whom we carry responsibility.

The pedagogy of caring tends to happens in dyadic relations: between this adult and this child, or between this nurse and this patient. But it is because a teacher feels addressed by the "faces" of particular students, about whom he or she worries, that the teacher can remain sensitive to the sometimes "faceless" multitude of all the other students for whom the teacher is responsible. The point is that this deeper sense of care-as-worry is the source for understanding and nurturing the more derivative varieties of care for the faces of the faceless that are theorized and called for in our research literature and professional practices. This is as true for the teaching profession as it is for the nursing, counseling, medical, social work, and other health science and care staff.

The dyadic relation remains the source for understanding the pedagogy of care because of the reality of singularity. Ultimately each child is unique and every parent knows that in every family each child calls for certain kinds of caring concerns from the parent. This is true also for a ward of patients. Every patient experiences the unique path of their illness, even if the illness is caught by many.

There is also the terrifying reality of the thousands of young children who have lost their parents and for whom no one cares. We feel moved by the knowledge that right now, at this very moment, many young children are crying for their parents, they may have lost their parents in natural disasters or in circumstances of war or criminality. So, feeling the suffering care for this multitude of children may spur us into social action. And yet, when we meet the face of this or that singular child do we experience concretely the pure ethical care-as-worry. This dyadic relational pure care must inform the multivalent care relations.

Only by remaining attuned to our sense of unique responsibility can we insert into our professional ethical practices the general responsibility of caring in all its various modalities that our vocations require. This is true for many professional practitioners. True, for the cynics and the pragmatically minded, care-as-worry may still be an unrealistic or a "heavy" idea. A cynic might say that care-as-worry seems a burdening responsibility. But, so it is a burden. It may not always be pleasant or delightful, but, as Levinas says, it is good: "It's the experience of the good, the meaning of the good, of goodness. Only goodness is good" (in Rötzer, 1995, p. 61).

Care as Primordial Ethic

Famously, Martin Heidegger describes *Sorge* (care) as the basic mode and mood of being in the world of *Dasein* (the Being of human being). And this mode and mood is essentially that of concern (1962, p. 84). Related German terms and their translations are *besorgen* meaning to take care, to deliver, to attend to, to look after, and to get worried about; *fürsorge* meaning to care for, to nurse, to look after, to worry about. *Sorgen machen* is to get worried. *Sich sorgen um* is to worry, to be worried about. *Sorgenfrei* means free of worries. Heidegger does not focus on the special pedagogical sense of *sorge* and *fürsorge* in the adult–child relation. And yet, he stresses and elaborates on the mood of anxiety in his investigation of care (*Sorge*) as being-in-the-world. Care is the basic way of being-in-the-world: "Being-in-the-world itself is that in the face of which anxiety is anxious" (Heidegger, 1962, p. 232). The point to emphasize is that in the German language care (*Sorge*) is ontically understood as "worry" and "troubles." Concern and worry are very much retained in the self-interpretation of *Dasein* as "care" or *sorge*. Heidegger retells "an ancient fable" that shows that *Sorge* (care) belongs to the primordial being of human beings:

> Once when "Care" was crossing a river, she saw some clay; she thoughtfully took up a piece and began to shape it. While she was thinking about what she had made, Jupiter came by. "Care" asked him to give it spirit, and this he gladly granted. But when she wanted her name to be bestowed upon it, he forebade this, and demanded that it be given his name instead. While "Care" and Jupiter were arguing, Earth (Tellos) arose, and desired that her own name be conferred upon the creature, since she had furnished it part of her body. They asked Saturn to be the judge. And Saturn gave them the following decision, which seemed to be just: "Since you, Jupiter, have given its spirit, you should receive that spirit at death; and since you, Earth, have given its body, you shall receive its body. But since "Care" first shaped this creature, she shall possess it as long as it lives. And because there is a dispute among you as to its name, let it be called "homo," for it is made out of humus (earth). (Heidegger, 2010, p. 191)

Heidegger places extraordinary significance on the primordiality of the story about "care" as the source of the being and the characterization of the essence of humanness. Accordingly, "care" is here seen as that to which human *Dasein* belongs "for its lifetime." This being has the "origin" of its being in care. Care is the primordial way of being-in-the-world for the human being as *Dasein*.

> "Being-in-the-world" has the stamp of "care", which accords with its Being . . . . Thus, the pre-ontological characterization of man's essence expressed in this fable, has brought to view in advance the kind of being which dominates his *temporal sojourn in the world*, and does so through and through. (Heidegger, 1962, p. 243)

Heidegger continues:

> Burdach calls attention to the double meaning of "*cura*" [care] according to which it signifies not only "anxious exertion" but also "carefulness" and "devotedness" . . . In the "double meaning" of "care", what we have in view is a *single* basic state in its essentially twofold structure of thrown projection. (1962, p. 243)

Now, Heidegger was probably not aware that in the English language the term "care" no longer seems to express this double meaning. In expressions such as "car care," "skin care," and "lawn care" the connotations of anxiety and worry are largely worn away. Neither is Heidegger's mood of anxiety evident in the connotations of care in the professional education and health science literature. In *The Challenge to Care in Schools*, Nel Noddings features chapters on caring for self, caring for strangers, caring for animals, caring for plants, caring for ideas, and caring for the world. Her conversational narratives are eloquently spiced with recommendations, warnings, and discussions of a wide range of topics, and they are attentive to relational qualities and practical actions. Noddings' philosophical enumeration proves that the meanings of devotedness, dangers, and compassions associated with the term "care" and "caring" are very broad. But it also unwittingly shows how the concept of "care" in the English usage may have taken in too much and too little.

And yet, the notion of worry occasionally lingers in some English language expressions of care. We feel that young children should be carefree, free of worries. So why has the meaning of care-as-worry survived in some expressions but has been seemingly lost in most other usages? In the English-speaking cultures of North America and the UK we are encouraged to care for and about almost everything and anything, yet the subtler and ethically significant pedagogical aspect of care for children seems to have been suppressed from the positive felt-sense of the word "care" in the everyday language.

The *Klein Etymological Dictionary* associates the earliest meaning of care with providing protective attention. The etymology of the term "sorrow" derives from the Danish, Swedish, Dutch, and German equivalents of *Sorge, zorg* which carried the meaning of anxiety, sadness, and worry. The expression "sorry," meaning "it causes me pain and regret," also finds its origin in this etymology from *Sorge* and sorrow. When we say "I'm sorry" then we actually say, "I care." But when we say "I don't care" then we may be playing on the ambiguous sense of care-as-worry.

Modern dictionaries too retain the reference to protection and guardianship. So, when we consult the *Concise Oxford English Dictionary* an equivalent to the noun "care" is listed as worry and concern; and the *Oxford English Dictionary* lists the terms "mental suffering, sorrow, grief, trouble" and secondly "burdened state of mind arising from fear, doubt, or concern about anything." The term "careworn" means tiredness because of "prolonged worry." The noun "worry" has the etymological meaning of choking and "a troubled state of mind arising from the frets and cares of life; harassing anxiety or solicitude." And, worry lines or wrinkles on the forehead are formed by a "habitual expression of worry." *Webster's Dictionary*, too, lists the synonyms "care, concern, solicitude, anxiety, and worry."

Perhaps no wonder that some critics argue that the concept of care is too vague and that it may even be morally indifferent or insignificant. So, Peter Allmark asks rhetorically, "can there be an ethics of care?" (1995, p. 19). It seems that the concept of care has been watered down to the simple sense of "providing attention" and even with words like "child care" or "health care" we do not really expect that the meaning of "care" goes much beyond institutional practices. But perhaps the problem lies in the fact that the experiential-language meaning of the English notion of care has been depersonalized by the focus on the multitude at the expense of the dyadic meaningfulness of care-as-worry.

In her book, *Caring: Gender-Sensitive Ethics*, Peta Bowden comments on the works by Nel Noddings, Carol Gilligan, and others. She writes that she is less interested in theoretical explications of caring than in analyzing how agogical caring actually occurs in the practices of everyday life—in mothering, friendship, nursing, and citizenship. Indeed, the caring literature seems to need more phenomenological attention to how caring is actually experienced rather than as it is conceptualized, theorized, and criticized. And yet, in Bowden's text, too, there seems to be no mention (as far as I could tell) of the pervasive sense of worry and concern that is phenomenologically associated with the act of caring. Mostly Bowden engages in argument with the earlier professional and feminist texts and pays less attention to empirical accounts or literary sources that may reveal how caring is actually experienced in everyday life. I keep using the term "worry" because worry is the common translation "care" and "caring" for the Dutch, German, and Scandinavian terms *zorg, Sorge, umsorg*, etc.

Tronto (2005) makes distinctions of phases of care: caring about, caring for, caregiving, and care receiving. And she distinguished various questions that may guide caring judgments. But these distinctions do not speak to the subtle connotational meanings of care-as-worry (*Sorge*) and they do not address other possible meanings that care may carry in different languages and cultures.

In the early nineties Janice Morse and colleagues published two studies presenting a "Comparative Analysis of Conceptualizations and Theories of Caring" (1991), using the categories: human trait, moral imperative, affect, interpersonal interaction, and therapeutic intervention. They also included 23 definitions culled from the studies they examined. Even in these early studies, the term "worry" does not occur in the definitions although some definitions contain related notions such as solicitude, vulnerability, and concern.

But, why this absence of the term "worry" in the caring literature? Does the sense of care-as-worry not fit well into frames of professionalized ethical relations? Is worry too problematic or psychologically negative concept for care theorists in the health sciences and education?

There is one health science context where the notion of care-as-worry is broadly discussed in both a practical and a theoretical way. I am referring, of course, to baby-care literature. It is interesting that in the weeks following the death of Dr. Benjamin Spock early in 1998, all across North America debates raged on radio and television about the legacy of Spock's advice to young parents. Was his influence positive or negative? Apparently, his book *Baby and Child Care* helped millions of parents with their inevitable anxieties and worries associated with early childhood and caring for young children.

Ironically, Spock's main message has always been for parents to trust their own feelings and inclinations; and that there is no way to be a perfect mother or a perfect father. The first two sections of the opening chapter are entitled: "Trust Yourself" and "Parental Doubts Are Normal" (Spock and Rothenberg, 1992). However, critics have argued that, instead of alleviating worries, Spock actually instilled worries and anxieties—especially in mothers— since his books implicitly suggest that some ways of dealing with children are more appropriate than others ways. Thus, feminist critics argue that young mothers were made to worry that they could not live up to the idealized versions of the perfect mother that, because of Spock's book, they may have constructed for themselves or that society may have constructed for them. However, it is important to note here that for these critics of Spock, the issue of worrying has shifted from care for one's child to care for one's self.

Self-Care

Of course, the point is not that self-care is unimportant. There are literally thousands of books published with child care or nursing care or self-care in the title. Caring for others is difficult if not impossible if in an obvious as well as a deeper sense one's own house is not in order, so to speak. And yet I would like to place some question marks over the assumption that self-care must therefore have priority over care for others. Michel Foucault was concerned with the priority of caring for one's self (Foucault, 1988).

In his *Technologies of the Self*, Foucault establishes ancient relations between caring and self-knowledge (Foucault, 1988). He argues that the concern for "taking care of oneself" was one of the principles of practice in early Greek society. Even the oracular "know thyself" implied the requirement of knowing how to ask the right questions for the practice of self-scrutiny: the *techné* or practical wisdom regarding how to take care of one's body and soul. These technologies that Foucault has inventoried include self-disclosure, letter-writing, confession, self-training, the examination of self and conscience, and so forth.

Foucault finds a foothold for prioritizing the question of self-care in Plato's *Alcibiades*. In this dialogue Socrates becomes the spiritual teacher of Alcibiades in the latter's quest for self-knowledge. And Foucault asks: "In that relationship, why should Alcibiades be concerned with himself, and why is Socrates concerned with that concern of Alcibiades?" (1988, p. 24). In Plato's text we learn that Alcibiades wants to gain personal and political power over others but that Socrates is able to show him that power over others resides actually in power over self, which requires self-care for its edification. But what Foucault does not consider is that Plato's Alcibiades can also be interpreted as a narrative wherein the meaning of care consists in a pedagogical concern for the other's care as self-care.

In Plato's *Alcibiades* the figure of Socrates is involved in care, namely care for his pupil. This is the story: Socrates is worried about Alcibiades since the latter does not know how to take care of his self or soul. Thus, Plato shows, in the example of Socrates, that care as cultivation of self finds its roots in care as concern for others. We can easily translate this idea in everyday pedagogical terms—as parent I care for my child's care as self-care. My pedagogical concern is with the child's taking proper care of his or her body and soul. If I do this not just out of mere parental duty but from a genuine sense of care-as-worrying, then I cannot help but be preoccupied with this other person's welfare.

In this childhood experience of having your parents worry for you and worry about you, the child (as future parent) in turn is encouraged to recognize that the source of understanding this self-care lies in the care for other. Thus, teaching self-care also teaches care for the other. It is pedagogically desirable that the child not only demonstrates self-care but also, gradually, begins to demonstrate care-as-worrying for others. Ironically perhaps, while Foucault advocated an archaeology of knowledge, it appears that he was not interested in digging for any originary roots of self-care in the pedagogical example of Socrates' caring for others. For this kind of search, we need to consult another French thinker, Emmanuel Levinas (2003). Levinas has insistently proposed that caring responsibility can only be understood in its most basic modality if we can somehow transcend the self-centered intentional relation toward the world that accompanies all modes of being and thinking.

One may argue that it makes little sense to try to determine if there is any core or shared meaning to the idea of caring since the term obviously means different things in different contexts. One might wonder: perhaps the language-analytical literature of caring is so confused that it is better to simply impose a certain definition or behavioral equivalents on the concept of care? But there are dangers in either relativizing the meaning of care to shifting language games, or in stipulating functional definitions of care and taking it to mean whatever one wants it to mean. Either way, one stands in danger of forgetting the deeper human meaning of care as the ethical demand, as the Danish philosopher Løgstrup (1997) called it, and how the caring encounter may help us understand in a richer way the nature of our profession as a vocation and as a domain of ethical responsibility.

Levinas has insistently proposed that caring responsibility can only be understood in its most basic modality if we can somehow transcend the intentional relation toward the world that accompanies all modes of being and thinking. Levinas has aimed to show that it is only in the direct and unmediated relation to the other that we can gain a glimpse of the primordial meaning of the caring encounter that he discusses as the human responsiveness to the appeal of the other who needs my care. Usually we think of other people as selves who are in the world just as we are in the world as selves. And so, we are cohabitants, fellow human beings who live in reciprocal relationships. In these relations each of us cannot help but see others as objects of our personal perception and thinking. But this is not the only possibility. It also may happen that the other person bursts upon my world and makes a claim on me outside of my own intentional cognitive orientation. In other words, it is also possible to experience the other in the vocative: as an appeal that the other makes on me. This is especially true of situations where we meet the other in his or her vulnerability, as when we happen to be handed a hurt and helpless child, or when we suddenly see a person fall in front of us. What happens then is this: I have felt a response that was direct and unmediated by my intentions or thinking.

This is the originary caring encounter. And in this situation, says Levinas, thought comes too late. What happens is that this person in pain, this child in need has made an appeal on me already. I cannot help but feel responsible even before I may want to feel responsible. For Levinas, to meet the other, to see this person's face, is to hear a voice summoning me. This is the call of the other. A demand has been made on me and I know myself as a person responsible for this unique other. Levinas states this predicament even more provocatively. He says, the other is not only someone I happen to meet but this person calls me to responsibility, stronger yet, this person accuses me and takes me hostage. In this gesture I have experienced also my own uniqueness because this voice did not just call, it called me, and thus took me hostage.

Hostage? Is this not just metaphorical philosophical speech? Not if we recognize this experience in our own life: Is this not precisely what happens to us when we are claimed by our sick child as in the stories we just read? Here is this vulnerable child who exercises power over me. And I, the big and strong adult, is being held hostage by this small and weak person who relies on me. If, as a parent, I am careless (meaning: if I do not worry about my child) then I may inadvertently expose him or her unduly to risk and dangers. For example, I fail to keep my eye on my child when he or she wanders astray. Thus, a careless parent is not necessarily uncaring but unworrying. In George Eliot's *Silas Marner* there is the moment that the child, Eppie, has managed to slip from under his watchful gaze. And now Silas is suddenly overcome by a strange sensation: he experiences the worried searching of a parent whose child has strayed: "poor Silas, after peering all-round the hedgerows, traversed the grass, beginning with perturbed vision to see Eppie behind every group of red sorrel, and to see her moving always farther off as he approached" (Eliot, 1861, p. 180). When he finally finds her and knows that custom has it that one should punish a child who has willfully disobeyed by straying off when explicitly told not to, he cannot help but demonstrate that he has been afflicted by this chronic illness of caring-worrying. "Here was clearly a case of aberration in a christened child which demanded severe treatment; but Silas, overcome with convulsive joy at finding his treasure again, could do nothing but snatch her up, and cover her with half-sobbing kisses" (Eliot, 1861, p. 180).

Of course, in a real sense every human being is vulnerable; every human being is mortal and subject to fears and dangers. And so, every human being is my Other. Every other is actually or potentially weak and vulnerable—just as I know myself to be actually or potentially weak and vulnerable. However, the existence of Other does not merely manifest itself as my feelings of pity or compassion for the hurt or suffering of this other person. More importantly I experience the other as a voice, as an address, as an appeal to me. And this is what we mean when we speak of our living with children or caring for the sick as a vocation, as a calling.

For Heidegger, care is the Being of human being even if this means to recognize the profound predicament of the realization what life and the inevitability of death mean to us. What do we do with our life and the anxiety that an authentic answering of the question of care might bring? Are we prepared to truly care for the Being of being in an existential sense?

Caring for One and Caring for the Many

We need to be sensitive to the ethics of the singularity of the other. And the singularity of each person comes into sharp relief against the fact of his or her individual mortality. Ironically, we are given this mortality right at birth. Therefore, Derrida (1995a) calls this "the gift of death," as it is our own mortality that belongs to each of us more uniquely than anything else imaginable. No matter whatever else can be taken away from us, there is one thing that belongs to us so essentially that nobody can take it away—our own death. I may give my death in sacrifice to my child, and yet even that supreme gift cannot be substituted for their own death. Thus, it is the non-substitutional uniqueness of the other that

I must preserve and not "kill" by betraying it to the general. And yet, Derrida claims, this is precisely what we do every day:

> By preferring my work, simply by giving it my time and attention, by preferring my activity as a citizen or as a professorial and professional philosopher, writing and speaking here in a public language . . . I am perhaps fulfilling my duty. But I am sacrificing and betraying at every moment all my other obligations: my obligations to the other others whom I know or don't know . . . also those I love in private, my own, my family, my son, each of whom is the only son I sacrifice to the other, every one being sacrificed to every one else in this land of Moriah that is our habitat every second of every day. (Derrida, 1995b, p. 69)

It seems that we constantly betray the call of caring responsibility in our efforts to be caring in the general sense of duty, as in our professional practice of teaching, psychology, social work, nursing, or medical care. Derrida articulates the dilemma in such a way that his confession of failing to be responsive to the call of his own son becomes an unsolvable predicament:

> What can be said about Abraham's relation to God can be said about my relation without relation to *every other (one) as every (bit) other [tout autre comme tout autre]*, in particular my relation to my neighbor or my loved ones who are inaccessible to me, as secret and transcendent as Yahweh . . . Translated into this extraordinary story, the truth is shown to possess the very structure of what occurs every day. Through its paradox it speaks of the responsibility required at every moment for every man and woman. (Derrida, 1995b, p. 78)

In a way Derrida seems to let himself—and us—off the hook in our unique responsibility to care for the other as other. On the one hand, he suggests that we need to heed this call, and yet, on the other hand, his questioning strategy aims to show that we must constantly fail, as we cannot possibly be responsive to every other who is out there and who also makes an appeal to our caring responsibility. Because we can only worry about one thing at a time, we cannot worry about everyone and everything. So why worry? Why care in this deepened sense? Indeed, even as an educator or as childcare professional, one would have to agree with Derrida— we cannot really see how we could worry for each child in our charge.

Does that mean we must flee into the ethical domain of a professional responsibility that says that we must subsume our caring behaviors under some general obligatory moral code? The problem with Derrida's approach is that he has already fled into language when he deconstructs the prereflective occurrence of the caring encounter. In everyday life the experience of the call of the other, of care-as-worry, is always contingent and particular. It can happen to any one of us anywhere, anytime. Every situation like that is always contingent. I can only be here and now, in this home, in this classroom, in this street. Thus, it is the singularity of this child, or the multivalence of these children who address me in my singularity and particularity. We may experience this in a situation of being addressed or surrounded by the one or the many in the home, street, school, or community. Yet, the care for the faces of the multitude seems rooted in the care for the vulnerable singular face. As an attentive parent one would be aware how unique each of our children are and how different each one is from the other. It is this uniqueness that is the source for understanding the care and responsibility we may feel for others that needs to be guarded and that may not be overlooked for fear of becoming insensitive to the difference in the sameness of the many in our care, when we sing "Don't Worry Be Happy!"

The pediatrician Henryk Goldszmit who wrote under the pseudonym of Janusz Korczak founded a school and orphanage, taught and took care of many orphaned children. He heroically tried to save hundreds of Jewish children of the Warsaw orphanage from the gas chambers of the Nazi concentration death camp in Poland. Korczak refused many offers to be smuggled out of the Ghetto. He joined nearly 200 children and orphanage staff members who were rounded up for deportation to Treblinka, on August 5, 1942. There they were all put to death.

One of Korczak's popular and pedagogically inspiring books is entitled *Loving Every Child: Wisdom for Parents* (2007). Perhaps he could have entitled the book *Loving all Children*, but "loving all" may sound too generalized for an inceptual understanding of the pedagogy of love. Another popular book is called *How to Love a Child* (2018), but it is not called *How to Love Children*. Again, the title "How to Love Children" would sound more depersonalized by stressing plurality rather than singularity. Many of the stories in Korczak's writings are about this or that particular child. To understand the worry about this child is to understand the possible worry about any of the other children under one's care. We cannot separate the dyadic from the multivalent structures and qualities of the primordiality of care and *Sorge*. The motivation and understanding of loving care for the many finds its pedagogical root and primal significance in the dyadic-multivalence of care-as-worry for each and every one child.

A much discussed question is whether specific emotions are innately affected and formed, or whether emotions are culturally determined. This is not really a phenomenological question since phenomenology is not very well equipped to arbitrate causally determined phenomena. (Is caring not a more primal phenomenon?)

Nevertheless, Batja Mesquita's (2022) empirical research seems to show that understanding people's emotional lives and behaviors requires immersing yourself in their realities across culturally, racially, and geographically divided worlds. But if the emotional experience of caring for others is largely culturally determined and socially influenced then it is quite possible that in many societies caring becomes an emotion that is eroding.

Phenomenologically it may be possible to investigate whether the distancing of human relations, due to the decline and transformation of physical intimacy into virtual or digital intimacy, makes caring and worrying about and for others less intense or less likely. Especially the small-time care-as-worry that is expressed in, for example, the Dutch and German language of *zorgen* and *sorgen* and that consists of simple acts of kindness, sharing, sacrifice, and looking out for each other, that may be less expressed in the English term "care" but that is an aspect of culturally created emotions, and/or primal emotions that are sparked by socio-biologically aroused sensitive interactive conditions.

Eidos of Care as Leaping In and Leaping Ahead

The ethic of taking care for the other (*Fürsorge*) is described by Heidegger as *Dasein*'s state of Being as Being-with. It is the state of attentive care and protectiveness for others who matter to us. Heidegger sees two possibilities: We can *leap in* for the other or we can *leap ahead* of the other (1962, p. 158). In the moment of *leaping in* for the other we take away the care (worry) for the other. In the moment of *leaping ahead* we give it back. The latter looks more like an (ped)agogical action which Heidegger describes as "authentic care" since it has the intent to give the care back authentically to the other. To give back to the other is to assist the person to gain autonomy rather than dependency. "[To give] to the existence of the Other, not to a '*what*' with which the other is concerned; it helps the Other to become transparent to the self *in* its care and to become free for it" (1962, p. 159). Heidegger warns that his use of the terms care and solicitude does not necessarily cohere with the everyday usage in ordinary life. And Wittgenstein (1968, p. 77) has shown that the meaning of any term is always conditioned by the usage of that term within the social practices of the language games in which we are involved. Therefore, we should not confuse the meanings associated with parental caring with the way caring may be a term used in the discourses of, for example, nursing, medicine, professional childcare, advertising, business enterprises, or even philosophy.

Writing to *See*: Why Write?

It is evening and darkness is setting in. We are strolling through the narrow streets of the small medieval town of Freiburg in Germany. Passing by the house of the late professor Edmund Husserl, we peer unobtrusively through the partially drawn curtains. We imagine the great thinker at work, writing at his desk right in front of his window. There he sits concentrating on his subject! The white sheet of writing paper in front of him. The next moment he puts his pen to paper and continues to write—every now and then we see him look up and then stare pensively at the sheet of paper. If we move closer to the window we may gain a view of his text. It appears that he is writing about writing:

> Let us begin with examples. Lying in front of me in the semi-darkness is this sheet of paper. I am seeing it, touching it. This perceptual seeing and touching of the sheet of paper, as the full concrete mental awareness of the sheet of paper lying here and given precisely with respect to these qualities, appearing to me precisely with this relative obscurity, with this imperfect determinateness in this orientation, is a cogitatio, a mental process of consciousness. (Husserl, 1983, p. 69)

Husserl seems to suggest that for the writer the focus of awareness is not the process of writing but the sheet of paper; today it may be the computer screen. And yet, what is this physical aspect of writing? How do we experience the space afforded by this empty sheet? How do those letters, those words seem to inhabit a textual space? What is the textual space? Is it just a metaphor for the sheet of paper? What really is the meaning of this space to write? Husserl continues to write:

> The sheet of paper itself, with its Objective determinations, its extension, its Objective position relative to the spatial thing called my organism, is not a cogitatio but a cogitatum; is not a mental process of perception but something

94

perceived. Now something perceived can very well be itself a mental process of consciousness; but it is evident that such an affair as a material physical thing, for example, this sheet of paper given in the mental process of perception, is by essential necessity not a mental process but a being of a wholly different mode of being. (Husserl, 1983, pp. 69, 70)

What kind of "thing" is a text? And what mode of being belongs to the space of the text? Where are we when we are engrossed in the act of writing? What kind of consciousness is writing-consciousness? Husserl goes part way in answering these queries:

Around the sheet of paper lie books, pencils, an inkstand, etc., also "perceived" in a certain manner, perceptually there, in the "field of intuition." . . . Every perception of a physical thing has a halo of background-intuitions . . . and that is also a "mental process of consciousness" or, more briefly, "consciousness," and, more particularly, "of" all that which in fact lies in the objective "background" seen along with it. (Husserl, 1983, p. 70)

In spite of his dense prose, and the fragmentary nature of these selected paragraphs, it does not escape us that there is an experiential quality about Husserl's description. He ostensibly appeals to our sense of perception. He draws our attention to the way we would attentively "see" a sheet of paper in front of us on our desk. And he describes the way in which this sheet of paper is given to us in its "objective determinations." He then shows how the act of perceiving is an act of consciousness, while all the things that lie in the background belong to the periphery, the "halo of consciousness" (Husserl, 1983, p. 70).

Of course, Husserl's primary aim was to show how objects are given in the act of cognition, and how the cogito is given to us in the act of perceiving an object such as the sheet of paper on which we write. His project was not really to write about writing itself. In fact, nowhere in the *Ideas* do we gain a hint from Husserl that the "practice of phenomenological seeing" is precisely this reflective writing with language, this evocation of experienced meaning through words. His phenomenological reflection takes place in this writing, in the text, and in the space of the text. So, it is ironic that the act of cognition was executed in and through language, and yet language remains at the margin, while the "sheet of paper" itself, the *cogitatum*, was there as a reminder of the centrality of language.

Only in a rare case does Husserl comment on the significance of the written word. In an appendix to his posthumously published *The Crisis* (1970) we learn something of Husserl's late and changing view of the role of language and meaning in written text.

The important function of written, documenting linguistic expression is that it makes communications possible without immediate or mediate personal address; it is, so to speak, communication become virtual. Through this, the communalization of man is lifted to a new level. Written signs are, when considered from a purely corporeal point of view, straightforwardly, sensibly experienceable; and it is always possible that they be intersubjectively experienceable

95

in common. But as linguistic signs they awaken, as do linguistic sounds, their familiar significations. (Husserl, 1970, p. 360)

Here Husserl seems to subscribe to the commonly accepted idea of writing as expression. But he makes some additional observations that are suggestive of richer phenomenological explication. He suggests that writing puts out of play personal address. And he hints at the mode of passivity that accompanies writing and reading:

The awakening is something passive; the awakened signification is thus given passively, similarly to the way in which any other activity which has sunk into obscurity, once associatively awakened, emerges at first passively as a more or less clear memory. In the passivity in question here, as in the case of memory, what is passively awakened can be transformed back, so to speak, into the correspond-ing activity: this is the capacity for reactivation that belongs originally to every human being as a speaking being. Accordingly, then, the writing-down effects a transformation of the original mode of being of the meaning-structure . . . It becomes sedimented, so to speak. But the reader can make it self-evident again, can reactivate the self-evidence. (Husserl, 1970, p. 361)

From our present perspective, Husserl's view of the relation between phenom-enological meaning and text may seem somewhat unremarkable. He says that written words are signs that awaken idealities of meaning and that make human communication possible. Reading is first of all a passive affair, but the reader can use the sedimented meaning structures embedded in the text as a tool to reactivate the special process of intuitive understanding and reflection that leads to phenom-enological understanding.

The notion of reading as a passive awakening of meaning will not sit well with present-day constructivists and reading theorists who stress the importance of reading as active meaning-making. And yet, this passivity is a compelling feature of the experience of the text and of reading and writing. A sensitive phenomenol-ogy of reading and writing would show that words are immediately experienceable in a corporeal sense. This immediate corporeal dimension of reading opens the possibility of the text to passively awaken meaning in the reader; and it places a "responsibility" on the text to be active: the text must speak.

To write is to measure our thoughtfulness. Writing separates us from what we know and yet it unites us more closely with what we know. Writing teaches us what we know, and in what way we know what we know. As we commit ourselves to paper we see ourselves mirrored in this text. Now the text confronts us. We try to read it as someone else might, but that is actually quite impossible, since we cannot help but load the words with the intentions of our project. Yet, the text says less than we want, it does not seem to say what we want: we sigh: "Can't we do any better than this?" "This is no good!" "We are not coming to terms with it." "Why do we keep going when we are not getting anywhere?" "We need to scrap this." "Let's try it again that way." Writing gives appearance and body to thought. And as it does, we disembody what in another sense we already embody.

However, not until we had written this down did we quite know what we knew. Writing separates the knower from the known (see Ong, 1967, 1971, 1977, and 2013, for some distinctions in this section), but it also allows us to reclaim this knowledge and make it our own in a new and more intimate manner. Writing constantly seeks to make external what somehow is internal. We come to know what we know in this dialectic process of constructing a text (a body of knowledge) and thus learning what we are capable of saying. It is the dialectic of inside and outside, of embodiment and disembodiment, of separation and reconciliation.

Writing distances us from the lifeworld, yet it also draws us more closely to the lifeworld. Writing distances us from lived experience but by doing so it allows us to discover the existential structures of experience. Writing creates a distance between ourselves and the world whereby the subjectivities of daily experience become the object of our reflective awareness. The writer's immediate domain is paper, pen, or keyboard on the one hand and language or words on the other hand. Both preoccupations have an alienating effect. The author who writes about the experience of parenting must, temporarily at least, "slacken the threads" between himself or herself and the world. Every parent/author knows the tensions between the demands made by the two roles even if the object of interest in both cases is the child. Whereas on the one hand writing gets me away from immediate involvement with my child, on the other hand it allows me to create a space for pedagogic reflecting on my parenting relation with this child so that I may return to this child with a deepened understanding of the significance of certain realities of the lifeworld.

Writing decontextualizes thought from practice and yet it returns thought to praxis. Writing tends to orient us away from contextual particulars toward a more universal sphere. As we try to capture the meaning of some lived experience in written text, the text in turn assumes a life of its own. Thus, writing places us at a distance from the practical immediacy of lived life by being forgetful of its context. Or rather, writing focuses our reflective awareness by disregarding the incidentals and contingencies that constitute the social, physical, and biographic context of a particular situation. But as we are able to gain a deeper sense of the meanings embedded in some isolated aspect of practice, we are also being prepared to become more discerning of the meaning of new life experiences. And thus, reflectively writing about the practice of living makes it possible for the person to be engaged in a more reflective praxis. By praxis we mean thoughtful action: action full of thought and thought full of action.

Writing abstracts our experience of the world, yet it also concretizes our understanding of the world. Because language is itself abstractive, writing tends to abstract from the experience we may be trying to describe. This abstractive tendency is a problem for phenomenological human science research since its aim is precisely to return "to the things themselves," which means to return to the world as lived: "that world which precedes knowledge, of which knowledge always speaks, and in relation to which every scientific schematization is an abstract and derivative sign-language" (Merleau-Ponty, 1962, p. ix). What is the great paradox of language? That it always abstracts from the concreteness of the world which it was responsible for creating in the first place. Writing intellectualizes.

We recognize this intellectualizing in the image of Kien, Canetti's bookish person, who appears thoroughly alienated from real existence (Canetti, 1979). And yet, writing, true writing can concretize the experience of the world more pithily it seems, more to the shaking core (however strange it may seem) than the world as experienced. The narrative power of story is that sometimes it can be more compelling, more physically and emotionally stirring than lived life itself. Textual emotion, textual understanding can bring an otherwise sober-minded person (the reader but also the author) to tears or to exhilaration and to a more deeply understood worldly engagement.

Writing objectifies thought into print and yet it subjectifies our understanding of something that truly engages us. On the one hand, the inscribing, the writing of the text is the research. One writes to make conversationally available the author's idea, a notion being questioned. On the other hand, the text once completed and in print circulation is now a testimonial, a relic of embodied reflections. More so than long-hand writing, printed text is an object. We sense this in the greater ease with which we can take distance from our text once it has been converted into type-faced print. So, there is a subjectifying and an objectifying moment in writing and in the way that the word allows us to understand the world. Research is writing in that it places consciousness in the position of confronting itself, in a self-reflective relation. To write is to exercise self-consciousness. Writing plays the inner against the outer, the subjective self against the objective self, the ideal against the real.

Writing exercises the ability to see. Writing involves a textual reflection in the sense of separating and confronting ourselves with what we know, distancing ourselves from the lifeworld, decontextualizing our thoughtful preoccupations from immediate action, abstracting and objectifying our lived understandings from our concrete involvements (see Ong, 1967, and all this for the sake of now reuniting us with what we know, drawing us more closely to living relations and situations of the lifeworld, turning thought to a more tactful praxis, and concretizing and subjectifying our deepened understanding in practical action. Writing has been called a form of practical action. Writing is action in the sense of a corporeal practice. The writer practices his or her body in order to make, to "author" something. In one sense, the text is the product of the writer's practical action. But writing exercises more than our mere redactive skills.

Writing exercises and makes empirically demonstrable our ability to "see." Writing shows that we can now see something and at the same time it shows the limits or boundaries of our sightedness. In writing the author puts in symbolic form what he or she is capable of seeing. And so, practice, in the lifeworld with children, can never be the same again. My writing as a practice prepared me for an insightful praxis in the lifeworld. (I can now see things I could not see before.) Although I may try to close my eyes, to ignore what I have seen, in some way my existence is now mediated by my knowledge. And because we are what we can "see" (know, feel, understand), seeing is already a form of praxis—seeing the significance in a situation places us in the event, makes us part of the event. Writing, true writing, is authoring, the exercise of authority: the power that authors and gives shape to our personal being. Writing exercises us in the sense that it empowers us with embodied knowledge which now can be brought to play or realized into action in the performance of the drama of everyday life.

The methodology of hermeneutic phenomenology is more a carefully cultivated thoughtfulness than a technique. Phenomenology might be called a method
without techniques. The "procedures" of this methodology have been recognized
as a project of various kinds of questioning, oriented to allow an interrogation of
the phenomenon as identified at first and then cast in the reformulation of a question. The methodology of phenomenology requires a dialectical going back and
forth among these various levels of questioning. To be able to do justice to the
fullness and ambiguity of the experience of the lifeworld, writing may turn into a
complex process of rewriting (re-thinking, re-flecting, re-cognizing).

Sartre describes how writing and rewriting aim at creating depth: constructing successive or multiple layers of meaning, thus laying bare certain truths while
retaining an essential sense of ambiguity. This kind of writing cannot be accomplished in one straightforward session. Rather, the process of writing and rewriting
(including revising or editing) is more reminiscent of the artistic activity of creating an art object that has to be approached again and again, now here and then
there, going back and forth between the parts and the whole in order to arrive at a
finely crafted piece that often reflects the personal "signature" of the author. Sartre
calls this crafted aspect of a text "style" (1977, pp. 5–9). Naturally, he alludes to
something more complex than mere artistic idiosyncrasy or stylistic convention.

Schleiermacher's use of the notion of "style" refers both to the essential genius
of a text and to the thoughtfulness of the author as the producer of the text (1977,
pp. 166–173). To write, to work at style, is to exercise an interpretive tact, which in
the sense of style produces the thinking/writing body of text. For Schleiermacher
"style" was an expression of *Geist* (mind, culture, spirit), a *geistig* phenomenon.
More modern phenomenological formulations see style as the outward appearance of the embodied being of the person. In writing, the author stylizes in textual form the truth that is given signification in his or her contact with the world
(Merleau-Ponty, 1973, p. 59). "Style is what makes all signification possible," says
Merleau-Ponty (p. 58). But we should not confuse style with mere technique or
method, rather style shows and reflects what the author is capable of seeing and
showing in the way that he or she is oriented to the world and to language. It is this
blessed moment where style gathers language to "suddenly swell with a meaning
which overflows into the other person when the act of speaking [or writing] binds
them up into a single whole" (Merleau-Ponty, 1964b, p. 235).

What role does anecdote play in these semiotic considerations? The anecdote,
vignette, and story have become quite common methodological devices in human
science research in general. Anecdotes, in the sense that they occur in the phenomenological writings of, for example, Sartre, Marcel, and Merleau-Ponty, are not to
be understood as mere illustrations to "beautify" or "make more easily digestible"
a difficult or boring text. Anecdote can be understood as a methodological device
in the humanities and human sciences to make comprehensible some notion that
easily eludes us. The use of anecdote in human science discourse is analogous
to the use of metaphor. We use metaphor to explain or provide insight into the
nature of one phenomenon at the hand of another phenomenon. Anecdote too
is used as a methodological device to describe something indirectly when this
phenomenon resists direct description. However, anecdote has a stronger phenomenological quality than metaphor. While metaphor may tend to dwell at the

level of abstraction, anecdote turns the attention more naturally to the level of the concrete.

Only a text that knows how to "speak" can thus activate the reader to reflect on the meaning of experienced life and succeed in "reawakening the basic experience of the world" (Merleau-Ponty, 1962, p. viii). And perhaps we should question the assumption of activism that pervades so much of our thinking about thinking. Perhaps at its origin, in moments of wonder, there needs to be preserved the value of passivity that allows us to be open to the meaning of the things around us. Husserl seems to open a door to a phenomenology of writing and of the meaning of meaning, but it is a door that he himself did not enter.

Of course, we also know that Husserl was by training a mathematician, and that it should not be too surprising that he considered language primarily as a representational system of symbols and signs, serving the purpose of elucidating and communicating cognitive meaning. As mathematician Husserl did not have a concern for the fact that every living language is always particular, and that words have existential and linguistic contexts to which an author has to be sensitive. Sentences and phrases reflect not only individual uniqueness and personal style of the author, but also possess richness and a certain ambiguity, inviting readers to make interpretive sense.

For Husserl language is mainly there as an imperfect instrument of communication. Only towards the end of his career Husserl may have become more interested in the realization that the language of speaking and writing is intricately tied into the achievement of understanding. Merleau-Ponty (1964a, p. 82) puts words in Husserl's mouth when he lets him say that "to speak is not at all to translate a thought into words. It is rather to see a certain object by the word." Literally, language illumes the world and thereby makes the world available, accessible to consciousness. But Husserl did not draw the conclusion of this conviction for his own reflective writing practice. No wonder that translator David Carr (1969, p. xxii) says that Husserl's writing lacks the quality of attentiveness to language as compared, for example, to Heidegger's work.

Phenomenological description is for Husserl fundamentally a cognitive act, and in this act language remains muted, in the background, in the dark. This is not to say, of course, that even as prolific an author as Husserl may not have sighed at the dinner table that the writing had been difficult that day, that he did not get as much accomplished as he had hoped. In this sense Husserl may not have differed from contemporary authors. Today, many philosophers and human science researchers will complain how difficult the writing has been. And, like Husserl, they may fail to relate the challenge of writing to the challenge of research and reflection; they too may tend to overlook that the process of research and reflection is a writerly and readerly practice.

Descending into Darkness

"I'm dying to write again," a colleague says to me, "I have been so busy lately with other things, but I can't wait to get back to it!" Indeed, writing can be a highly enjoyable activity. And one may crave to get back to writing as one may desire to read a good book. But where exactly do we go when we write or read? Where do we go back to? And what is this strange desire for words? For sure, not all authors speak of their writing experience with unreserved enthusiasm. The successful fiction writer Mordecai Richler once mentioned that he was relieved when a book was finally finished since writing literally would make him quite ill. The philosopher Sartre could write only when he was under a heavy use of anti-depressive drugs. The poet Rainer Maria Rilke sought inspiration in solitude and existential loneliness. It appears that writing is often not without pain or difficulty.

There is a certain irony in the utterance "dying to write" since this phrase may express unwittingly a significance that is quite profound. To write, truly write, one must die. Of course, we all must die. Quite literally, from the moment we are born, we are on the way to our death. But we rarely reflect on this existential fact of life. Only individuals who are living in full face of the limit of meaning of their lives may be truly experiencing the presence of darkness that lies at the other side of the light of day.

On first glance "dying to write and writing to die" sounds rather excessive, another metaphor of the hermeneutics of exaggeration. But Maurice Blanchot (1981), who has reflected perhaps more patiently and more deeply than any other philosopher on the nature of writing, insistently returns to this theme: writing is the experience of dying, of gaining a glance of the limits of personal existence. Like Orpheus, the writer must enter the dark, the space of the text, in the hope of seeing what cannot really be seen, hearing what cannot really be heard, touching what cannot really be touched.

Blanchot refers to serious writing, the kind of writing—whether poetic, literary, or reflective—that is oriented toward themes of meaning of human life. In other words, he concerns himself with the kind of writing that is not afraid to come face to face with the proverbial darkness out of which human insight and understanding is wrestled. Blanchot agrees with Heidegger about the elusive nature of human truth. And so, truly reflective writing is oriented to capture in language what can ultimately not be apprehended. Blanchot uses the allegory of Orpheus to allude to what happens in the act of writing (1981 pp. 171–176; see the story about the cover at the beginning of this book).

Darkness Before the Dawn of (In)sight

There exists an obvious difference between oral and written discourse. In spoken conversational situations one cannot erase what one has said. One cannot restart a conversation in the way that one can restart a text. One cannot edit out a phrase and replace it with a more appropriate one. One cannot step back reflectively from one's spoken word to monitor and adjust the effects that selected words and phrases seem to exercise on other words we utter. But this difference is also what makes writing difficult.

We tend to think that written discourse is irrevocable. And, of course, this is true once text has been put into print. Written texts can be subject to forms of scrutiny, to destructive, constructive, and deconstructive critique that goes far beyond spoken discourse. Once we have put our word in print we have lost control over its fate. This condition is known as the autonomy of the text and an entire hermeneutic of reading and critical semiotics has been built on the notion of textual autonomy and authority. And yet, from an originating point of view, the spoken word is irrevocable in a manner that is rarely true of the written word.

In a normal conversation or discussion, what has been said and heard cannot be taken back. Of course, we can apologize for some things that may be a slip of the tongue. We may try to deny that we said what has been heard. We may correct ourselves, and say what it is that we "really meant to say." We may add meaning through a certain tone of voice or physiognomic expression. We may repeat or paraphrase our earlier points when we feel that we are being misunderstood or when we feel that our words do not seem to have their intended or hoped-for effect. And yet, what has been heard has been heard; therefore, what we say can never be completely revoked. Indeed, our spoken words someday may be brought back to us, to remind us of things we may wish forgotten. Of course, all of this is even truer when our words have been electronically recorded.

In comparison with writing, speaking is more improvisational and, in Gadamer's words, "speculative" in that our words and gestures thrive on a certain poetic and semantic ambiguity that allows us to constantly play with our intentions while sensing the content and tone of our conversational relations with others. Moreover, in the act of speaking we not only express our thoughts, we also find out what we are thinking and while thinking we find out what we can say, and what lets itself appear in words. So, in this sense oral discourse is more dynamic and more tolerant and even reliant on the rich ambiguities of the context and the content of our speaking. But because of the immediacy of the spoken word, and because of the irrevocability of the live utterance, we have less reflective control over what is heard in what we say.

As authors, we may feel sometimes that our written text is misinterpreted or over-interpreted. We may regret a thoughtless phrase. We may wish that we had not sent a letter, that we had not published a premature manuscript. Once a text is public, it is beyond our control. There exist obvious political and personal implications in this autonomous life of the text that we create. Furthermore, a written text can make a plea for its own immortality—in spite of its author's intentions. For example, we know that Max Brod, the executer of Franz Kafka's will, was requested by Kafka to destroy all of his unpublished manuscripts. But, in a manner of speaking, the will of Kafka's words was stronger than the words of Kafka's will. Luckily for us, Brod decided to publish Kafka's works anyway.

The upshot of all this for interpretive phenomenological inquiry is that the moment of writing is extremely consequential and differs from the moment of speaking in that we can weigh our words: we can check their semantic values, we can clarify their meanings, we can taste their tonalities, we can measure their effects on certain readers, we can explicate and then try to bracket our assumptions, and we can compose and recompose our language and come back to the text again and again to get it hopefully "just right" before we commit it to permanent record.

In the paper and ink days, the editing evidence of our writing was right there in the waste paper basket filled to the brim with crumbled up paper. In the present period of word processing the evidence of the messiness of our writing is temporarily saved in an embedded series of undo-redo moves on the computer keyboard, stored on back-up disks, or simply removed with a stroke of the delete button. But finally, the text is done and we have to let go of it. From now on it will lead a life of its own. It will constitute a textorium, a space for others to enter—to read and rewrite.

Darkness as Method

We intuitively know that wonder is not a cognitive state that can be simply produced or manipulated in others. One cannot even "will" oneself to wonder. Rather wonder is something that can at best only be evoked. And since wonder is at the heart of the phenomenological attitude this elusiveness of wonder raises epistemological and ontological issues. Not only do we try to lead the reader to a sense of wonder about this or that phenomenon, we also need to induce a wondering about wonder.

If we understand phenomenological method not as a controlled set of procedures but more modestly as a "way toward understanding" then it may be possible that someone can lead us a way to it, or into it. And even if we are open to it then wonder is still more a state of being than an intellectual activity. To be able to wonder about something one needs to be able to adopt a state of receptive passivity.

Receptive passivity seems to be both the condition for and the state of mind of the experience of wonder (Verhoeven, 1972). What does receptive passivity mean? And what does it signify? The term "passive" derives from *passivus* which means "capable of suffering" and the word "suffer" is formed from *sub* and *ferre* to bear, to carry. The term "passion" too is associated with the meanings of affection and suffering. Passivism (as opposed to the willful agency of activism) is the ability of being sensitive to the power of pathos—the capability of suffering a strong affect or feeling.

Now, passivity and receptivity are not highly valued epistemological categories. We are living in an aggressive era of hustling restlessness and bustling commotion. To activate is to put things in motion. It appears that activism is given to outward action that values speediness, quickness, energy, entrepreneurship, industriousness. The term activism is associated with performance, productivity, profitability, fecundity, and aggressive assertiveness. In results-based, productivity-oriented research we have become suspicious of categories that are associated with a philosophy of receptivity and passivity or with an approach to life that fails to take charge, get on with it, act on things.

One might have presumed that reflection implies a refraining from taking immediate action. But reflection is now commonly linked up with action—as in reflective action, or reflection in action—no longer do we sense that there is virtue in stepping back, holding off, simply looking and reflecting on what one sees. Even in the academic realm of the social and human sciences passivity and receptivity are no longer valued. The spirit of activism has overtaken the spirit of patient thinking, quiet wondering.

Anyone who has experienced wonder knows that wondering is initially not at all oriented to activity. On the contrary, wonder implies non-activity. The person who is struck with wonder is overcome, as it were, overwhelmed with something that defies a quick resolution, strategic action. For the person caught up in wonder, what seemed ordinary and commonplace has now become extraordinary.

Wittgenstein said that wondering is a form of questioning for which there is no answer—questions such as: Why is there something and not nothing? Why are things the way they are and not otherwise? Wonder shakes us into opening our eyes, and now we stare at the object of our wonder, almost mute, speechless, unable to act. Verhoeven (1967) points out that wonder should not be confused with questioning. This was Aristotle's inclination to see wonder primarily as the emergence of a question. And once the question has been answered the wonder stops. That is why he thought of all knowledge growth as the product of wonder and the questions that flow from it.

But perhaps true wonder does not ask questions, not yet, not immediately. True wonder only looks on, takes in, remains open to the things (Verhoeven, 1992). True wonder sweeps us up in a state of passivity, or perhaps it is passivity that makes it possible to be swept up in wonder. That is why Plato spoke of wonder as pathos, as something that literally overcomes us, comes over us. And so, a text that induces wonder is a pathic text.

The opposite of wonder is matter-of-factness. Indeed, the greatest hindrance to gaining access to the phenomenology of wonder and the wonder of phenomenological method is perhaps our cultural inclination to devalue passivity in favor of a pervasive activism and a valuing of information in all realms of inquiry. We are so inclined to convert research into action and usable "results" that this activism can limit our possibility for understanding—understanding that involves the experience of meaningfulness. We may say, therefore, that for writing as well as for reading what is required is a heightened sense of the pathic: an aggressive passivity and aggravated receptivity.

And yet, passivity is something prior to activity (Wall, 1999). Before passivity can be contrasted with activity it lies already outside of itself. Activity presupposes an agent, a self. But passivity is purely passionate, it suffers it-self before it has become a subject, a self. Passivity is both subject and non-subject. This is the case, for example, in the experience of reading, when passivity feels it-self as other: in reading a novel or a poem I forget who I am. The same is true for the experience of writing. To be a writer one must enter the space of the text where one is no longer oneself, no longer active in the ordinary reality of the light of day.

To be a writer. But what does that mean? What does phenomenology that requires writing ask of the person who wants to practice it? The act of writing is difficult and fraught with frustrations. Writing may give one the experience of being in the dark in a variety of ways. But reflecting on the phenomenology of trying to write may let one know "when" one is there, "where" one is when one is there, and where "there" is.

What happens when writing begins? One peculiar feature of writing is that, just as in reading, the words draw us in. And as words draw us, they open up a space. But this is not just an inner space, a space inside us (as is often supposed) but more accurately a space in language, a textorium—a literary or textual space. Writing is similar to reading in that we take leave of the ordinary world that we share with others. We step out of one world, the ordinary auditorium of daylight, and enter another, the textorium, the world of the text. In this world of shadows and darkness one is a writer: writing in the dark.

This is a world that possesses its own reality, even if this reality is referenced to the world outside of the text. Writing is not a productive activity in the sense that it changes the ordinary world (see Nordholt, 1997). However, in transporting writer/reader to the world of the text, scripture asks us to be receptive of experiences that we could not otherwise have. In the world of this text we are no longer the same. Writing puts out of play and negates everyday reality. Instead, there is the reality of the outside; this reality is present without being given. In writing one develops a special relation to language which disturbs its taken-for-grantedness. Thus, it may happen that in the attempt to write one loses one's very sense of language: one finds it impossible to write.

Writing Is Like Falling Forward into the Dark

Writing is first of all a solitary activity. While it is commonly assumed that writing is usually performed as a communicative act and therefore social in its intent, the experiential fact is that at the moment of writing I am here by myself at this writing desk or in this writing space. Many authors have commented on this intensely solitary, even lonely dimension of writing. Next, a peculiar change takes place in the person who starts to write: the self retreats or steps back without completely stepping out of his or her social, historical, biographic being. Just as the reader is no longer his or her own self when the reader loses himself or herself in a story, so the writer who writes is no longer this or that personal self. The writer becomes an "it," a neutral self.

The language of writing is scripture rather than the spoken language of oral discourse. That is why Blanchot says that the writer belongs to a language no one speaks. While engaged in the activity of writing, the words I write are not addressing in the conventional sense of the term. Even if the writer has some reader(s) in mind, these readers are not there as interlocutors. Furthermore, written words differ from ordinary discursive words in that these words lose their transparency and their ordinary currency. In the textorium, the world of script, words no longer mean what they mean in ordinary discourse; they tend to become denser and more ambiguous. They acquire a quality of transparency in a different sense.

More so than in the speaking, expressing, and communicating in ordinary language, the language of scripture foregrounds the resistance of language. The experience of resistance and difficulty of language are not accidental features of writing but they belong to written language itself that continually puts to question the nature and possibilities of words. In writing one develops a special relation to language which disturbs its taken-for-grantedness. Thus, it may happen that in the attempt to write one loses one's very sense of language: one finds it impossible to write. At the best of times, writing always falls short of its ambition to capture meaning. Levinas and Blanchot have argued that writing (and especially philosophical writing) cannot help but destroy what it tries to understand, it reduces the experiential to the conceptual, otherness to sameness. Words become the replacements for the things they name. Of course, words are not things. But it is in the nature of writing that it lets nothing (experience and meaning are no-"things") appear as something. Thereby, even words become things. More precisely, the word makes present the absence that it names, and thus it denies the enigmatic concreteness and strange singularity of existence. At the same time the word restores this absence through the constitution of meaning. Thus, the immediacy of lived experience is first lost but then fleetingly restored by the indirectness of meaning that is made possible by language. The experience of writing shows us reflexively that the immediacy of the lived world can never be recaptured in its original form.

The phenomenologist is constantly oriented to lived meaning. And the phenomenological text has the effect that it can make us aware of the meaningfulness of something in a manner that enriches our understanding of human experience. This grasping of meaningfulness is not merely a cognitive affair. The production of insight must proceed through the creation of a research text that speaks to our cognitive and noncognitive sensibilities (although it may be better not to make this distinction in the first place). Phenomenological understanding is existential, emotive, enactive, embodied, situational, and nontheoretic—a powerful phenomenological text thrives on a certain irrevocable tension between what is unique and what is shared, between particular and transcendent meaning, and between the reflective and the prereflective spheres of the lifeworld (van Manen, 1990). Without this tension, the phenomenological text tends to turn flat, shallow, boring, because it loses the power to break through the taken-for-granted dimensions of everyday life.

Commonly, texts that deal with phenomenological methodology focus on the substantive, conceptual, analytic, or thematic understandings that the text may offer the reader. This focus on the thematic aspect of the text is primarily concerned with what a phenomenological text says, its substantive, conceptual, semantic meaning, and significance. In contrast, when we focus on the mantic aspect of a text we try to capture the poetic, expressive, vocative or how the text speaks—how the text divines and inspirits our understanding. Both forms of meaning are methodologically of importance to hermeneutic phenomenological inquiry.

Don Ihde (1983) too has pointed out that while "phenomenology, particularly in its Husserlian form, may be seen to reciprocate with the analytic philosophies of language with respect to reference, its deeper concern lies with the other tendency [of] expression" (1983, p. 167). The difference between the designative, referential, semantic functions of language and the expressive, transcendent, poetic functions of a text is not simply an issue of interpretability. Both designative and expressive meaning involve interpretation, though in a different manner and to a different degree.

Of course, the language of semantic and mantic, designative and expressive meaning does not entail an either/or distinction. Phenomenological discourse depends on cognitive meaning: argument, logic, conceptual, intellectual, and moral intelligibility. But this is not enough. Phenomenological text must also appeal to our noncognitive mode of knowing—without expressive or transcendent meaning a phenomenological text is like a poem without poetic sensibility. In these vocative distinctions lie the challenge of phenomenological inquiry and writing. When analyzing classical phenomenological studies (by authors such as Linschoten, van den Berg, and Langeveld) for their inherent methodological features, certain scriptural qualities come into view, such as lived-throughness, evocation of meaning, intensification of language, textual tone, and transformative epiphany. They belong to the domain of textorium in which the writer dwells.

Therefore, Linschoten suggests that phenomenological meaning is not contained primarily in the terms of his analysis of a phenomenon; rather, phenomenological writing reaches its goal only if the reader is "continuously confronted with the phenomenon" (1987, p. 115). What Linschoten means is that the phenomenologist does not present the reader with a conclusive argument or with a determinate set of ideas or insights. Instead, the writer aims to be allusive by orienting the reader reflectively and unreflectively to that region of lived experience where the phenomenon dwells in recognizable form. More strongly put, the reader must become possessed by the allusive power of text—taken, touched, or overcome by the phenomenological effect of its engagement with lived experience. (Texts that are too self-absorbing or that are merely argumentative or derivative fail to open up such evocative space.)

And phenomenologists must become readers of their own texts too. As writers, we know that we have achieved something when we have managed to stir our own selves. Of course, there is always the danger that we are merely enchanted by the superficial haunt of shallow sentimentality or catchy formulations. But George Steiner expresses it well when he says that "the genuine writer is a self-reader" (1989, p. 126). To write is to stir the self as reader. This is not just a question of "feeling" or "emotion." It is simplistic to conceive of the stirring of self as the emotive or feeling dimension of language. Phenomenologically, feeling and knowing, ideas and emotions strongly implicate each other: understandings are what ideas feel like.

Eidos of Writing and Reading as Dwelling in Unreality

In writing and especially in fictionalizing a sensitive account it may happen that the space opened by the text becomes charged with a signification that is, in effect, more real than real. As readers, many of us know this phenomenon. Many readers have at one time or another been profoundly moved in the realization of being touched by a human insight. And this insight might not have affected us this deeply if we had undergone the experience in the sober light of day, rather than in the dark realm of the novel, story, or poem. There is something paradoxical about the unreality of a powerful text: it can be experienced by the writer or reader as real, as unreally real. This super-reality turns the insights we gain in the space of the text essentially virtual, unencumbered by the presence of all the other memories, impressions, and factualities that permeate the affairs of our everyday life. The phenomenologist as writer is an author who starts from the midst of life, but then is transported to that space where, as Robert Frost says, writing is "like falling forward into the dark," where meanings resonate and reverberate with reflective being.

Philosophizing Homesickness: How to Awaken from Boredom?

Heidegger refers to his early studies with Husserl as exercises in "phenomenological seeing." But Heidegger later redefined "phenomenological seeing." He turned his attention away from the cogito, toward elucidating the meaning of things as we live them in everyday life. Husserl was preoccupied with the issue of apodictic or indubitable knowledge and with the condition and possibility of phenomenological understanding. But Heidegger and like-minded existential phenomenologists turned toward a phenomenological examination of "ordinary" life experiences. In his book *The Fundamental Concepts of Metaphysics: World, Finitude, Solitude* (1995), Heidegger poses the question that is perhaps most central to his work: the very meaning of philosophy (metaphysics) itself. The opening chapters of this text are compelling. Why compelling? Because, when read patiently and carefully, one gets infected and affected by the sense of wonder that Heidegger evokes in his phenomenological reflections. In this text, Heidegger resolves to pursue the question of the meaning or essence of philosophy and philosophizing. His opening chapters are investigative of a certain attunement concerning the question of the meaning of world as our homesickness, finitude as our fundamental way of being, and individuation as a solitariness in our lived relation and nearness to the things of the world. Even though.

Phenomenology Awakens

It is likely justified to read the word "phenomenology" when Heidegger says that philosophy has "the task of awakening a fundamental attunement" that involves a radicalization of our understanding of finitude (our human way of being), individuation (the solitary), and world (home). Heidegger shows that the question of the meaning of philosophy can neither be answered by comparing it with art or religion, nor by comparing it with science or looking for historical antecedents. But we should keep in mind that Heidegger speaks of the task of awakening. Indeed, much of Heidegger's work is dedicated to awakening the originary or inceptual understanding of a certain existential phenomenon or event.

So, what is philosophy or phenomenology? After making several instructive "detours," Heidegger (1995) concludes that true philosophy must be sought in philosophy itself; it "*can be determined only from out of itself and as itself—comparable with nothing else* in terms of which it could be positively determined" (p. 2). He says, "no other choice remains than to ready ourselves and to *look metaphysics in the face*, so as not to lose sight of it again" (p. 4). Heidegger warns that we should not misunderstand philosophy (phenomenology) as if it were a kind of "knowledge we amass," which leads to "an inner loss" and, eventually, "to a smug contentment." To discover the meaning of phenomenology, "a different kind of attentiveness is demanded" (p. 10)—an attentiveness that does not argue or dispute but, "awakens." Heidegger (1995) refers to Plato:

> Plato says in one of his major dialogues that the difference between the philosophizing human being and the one who is not philosophizing is the difference between being awake and sleeping. (p. 23)

We are to awaken to this or that fundamental attunement. (p. 59)

When Heidegger asks "what is philosophy?" he spends more than 100 pages on concrete explications of the lived experience of boredom (Heidegger, 1995, pp. 74–185). But the explications of boredom are not just a means to an end but rather to show what it means to awaken our attunement to the project of phenomenology. Heidegger says in his early chapters of *The Fundamental Concepts of Metaphysics: World, Finitude, Solitude* that we need to "do" phenomenology rather than talk or read about it. It is a powerful explication of showing that philosophical phenomenology turns us to existential phenomena and events. For Heidegger, only *doing* phenomenology is wakeful. The reader will gain a sense of the inspired and poetic sensibility that empowers Heidegger's writings. And second, Heidegger's extensive lived experience excursions into the phenomenology of boredom are meant to provide us access to and awaken in us the fundamental attunement to the meaningfulness and the understanding of our own finiteness, our personal existence, and the existential world we inhabit and construct.

From a phenomenological point of view, Heidegger asks what it is to do philosophy, and he elicits experiential descriptions of levels of boredom. For Heidegger, the experience of profound boredom ultimately should lead to an awakening of an attunement to the meaning and meaningfulness of our existence. Phenomenology is the path to such awakening. It is too simplistic to comprehend the extensive excursion into the phenomenology of levels of boredom as mere "means." Rather, Heidegger brilliantly weaves the foundational question of the meaning of philosophy into the existential question of the meaning of boredom and awakening.

Heidegger also consults the poet Novalis in his quest for the meaning of philosophy (phenomenology) to show what an existential homesickness, as the fundamental attunement of philosophizing, is like: "philosophy is really homesickness, an urge to be at home everywhere," says Heidegger (1995, p. 5). His fascinating explication of boredom is not just a means to an end—rather our moving from becoming bored *by* something, through being bored *with* something, to *profound* boredom should arouse or awaken us to our existential predicament and thus attune us to the danger of meaninglessness and the positive possibility of meaningfulness of our worldy existence. Here I mostly mean to show that Heidegger's writing at times contains powerful evocative experiential descriptions.

There is another benefit to start a phenomenological investigation with an attentiveness to the concreteness of lived experience. It is the benefit that one may actually stand closer to the phenomenon (phenomenal life) that one is aiming to investigate. If we take Heidegger's writing on boredom as an example, then we may discern both the conceptual-argumentative and the showing-seeing dimension of phenomenological method. When Heidegger (1983) thematizes the lived experience of boredom, he "argues" that we can distinguish three kinds of boredom: becoming bored by, being bored with, and profound boredom. But when he engages in phenomenological explication or analysis, he "shows" or lets us see *how* these various kinds of boredom appear or show themselves in our lived experience.

Becoming Bored By, Being Bored With, and Profound Boredom

First, we may become bored by a person giving a lecture, by a guide on a tour, by a movie, or by waiting for an airplane connection. When we experience this kind of boredom, then we are really conscious of time passing by slowly. For many of us, Heidegger's description will resonate with our own personal experience of this kind of boredom.

Second, we may be bored with a visit, an event, or a social situation. For example, we come home from a party that seemed okay at the time. But when someone asks, "How was the party?" we answer, "It was rather boring." Because now, in hindsight, we realize that it actually was mostly empty chatter. During the party, we may not have been very conscious of time passing, but now we realize that the party was really wasted time.

The third kind of boredom is more difficult to describe. It may involve the experience of coming to a new and existential realization, such as in the recognition of what Heidegger calls profound boredom. For example, having spent time on a lonely hike, or encountering people who are very different from us, or facing unexpected life difficulties may awaken our sense of the value of life and the little things. We realize that these new and unexpected life experiences are not just the richest times of our life, but that they give us a deeper understanding of life meaning: time is life, time is who we are.

In presenting the different modalities of boredom, Heidegger uses examples that we can readily grasp, and we can think of similar examples ourselves. The experience of boredom is "shown" through examples and experiential description that we may have experienced. It is also possible that we may never have experienced the third kind of boredom. Or perhaps, we happen to be living a very meaningful life already. Or we won't come to the realization of how profoundly meaningless and boring our life has been until we reach an age where we can no longer change ourselves, such as the title character in Leo Tolstoy's novel *The Death of Ivan Ilyich*. On his deathbed Ivan Ilyich finally comes to the realization of how meaningless and wasted his life has been. Out of anguish, he begins three days of incessant screaming. Screaming "Oh! No!" and "went on uttering screams with that 'O' sound," writes Tolstoy (1981, p. 111), as if to remind us of the famous existential Edvard Munch painting "The Scream" of 1893. Just before his death, in a moment of clarity, Ilyich sees that he has not, after all, lived well—a powerful literary image exemplifying Heidegger's phenomenological description of profound boredom.

The point is that phenomenological explication and writing cannot be limited to the argumentative or propositional style that is commonly used in the natural and social sciences. Some philosophers tend to favor "argument" over "showing" the phenomenology of meaning—and so a philosopher may want to say, for example, that "Sartre claims that the body is primarily present to us in the *for-others* (*pour-autrui*) way," while Sartre is not just arguing but actually showing that this is how we experience the body. By using narrative examples from everyday life or literature, phenomenological inquiry interweaves the conceptual with the nonconceptual (or better, the inceptual), the argumentative with the evocative or more poetic form.

Eidos of Boredom

A phenomenology of boredom can show times of existential despair, but also moments for awakening to the meaningful dimensions of life. Children sometimes complain about feeling bored, but pedagogically sensitive parents know that moments of boredom can offer opportunities for creativity. So, it is unwise not to let children deal with being bored at times. And adults too can benefit from having to face boredom in their lives, and not always to seek empty distraction, for example, in superficial screen activity. The experience of profound boredom may bring us to the point where we contemplate the meaningfulness of an extraordinary insight in our existence: to live meaningfully is to philosophize, to do phenomenology.

Things and No-Things

The sample writings of the texts above are meant to show what working drafts of phenomenological texts may look like. They are meant to show the practice of doing phenomenology on the things. The so-called "things" can be phenomena or events of all kinds. In this sense the phenomena of "touch, name-forgetting, boredom, the clock, caring and worrying" are all "things" (or "no-things" but still things). They are meaningful phenomena and events, or relevant affairs that matter. They may be ordinary and extra-ordinary lived experiences. A phenomenology of practice can be performed on just about any lived experience. Inceptual phenomenological research is essentially composed of phenomenological writing on originary meaning. There are many exemplary instances of showing aspects of phenomenological writing throughout the book. For example, the section discussing the "inversion of meaning" is based on an analysis of Linschoten's phenomenological study of "falling asleep." It carefully traces how Linschoten's language makes extensive use of vocative devices in his implicit engagement of phenomenological method. Indeed, the research is the writing. And phenomenology is the name of the reflective and expressive method of this writing.

Chapter Three

On the Meaning of Meaning

Phenomenological Meaning

What is it about phenomenological meaning that distinguishes it from other forms of meaning in social inquiry? First, phenomenological meaning needs to be distinguished from psychological, sociological, ethnographic, biographic, and social science or human science disciplines. Generally, the social sciences such as sociology, psychology, and ethnography aim at explanation, while phenomenology aims at description and interpretation. But this is not always the case.

For example, ethnography has the task of describing a particular culture or subculture. Ethnography (*ethnos* means people; *graphy* means description) is interested in cultural meanings. Ethnographers generally use a participant-observation approach to study cultural scenes, scenic settings. The key to the process usually is an eloquent "informant." The ethnographer wants to understand what one has to know, acceptably as a member of a particular group or culture, to behave acceptably as a member of that group. Similarly, ethnomethodology applies cultural ethnography to social situations and studies social meanings in this context of "rule-use," "social accomplishments," and "taken-for-granted" or "seen-but-unnoticed" features of social practices, based in part on the social phenomenology of Alfred Schutz. Ethnomethodology argues that people themselves produce the facticity of their social world (the common-sense reality) and then experience it as independent of their production. So, ethnomethodology seeks to "uncover" the practices whereby the factual character of the social world is produced. Both ethnography and ethnomethodology aim to break through the taken-for-grantedness of social and cultural meanings. So, ethnography and ethnomethodology share some features with phenomenology. Still, the purpose and interest of these disciplines are quite different.

The distinction between psychological and phenomenological meaning is trickier. Psychology has a historical relation to phenomenology, in the sense that psychology originally grew from the disciplines of philosophy and medicine. Traditionally, philosophers had a special interest in the mind, consciousness, the self, and other concerns that fall also squarely within the purview of psychology. And many (continental) philosophers were also scholars of psychology. In North America, William James was a philosopher-psychologist who has been regarded as a phenomenologist; see, for example, the study of the works of James by Johannes Linschoten: *On the Way toward a Phenomenological Psychology: The Psychology of William James* (1954). Indeed, Husserl at times refers to phenomenology as

DOI: 10.4324/9781003228073-4

phenomenological psychology. But gradually he started to push off the evolving kinds of psychology that were shaped in the image of the natural sciences.

Phenomenological meaning differs from psychological meaning in that psychology wants to develop theories and conceptual systems that explain human behavior and psychological processes. Phenomenology may provide meaning structures that help to understand the significance of human phenomena such as fear, anxiety, and grief. However, phenomenology does not provide diagnostic or prognostic tools: it does not give us access to what the problems, state of mind, or mental conditions are of a particular individual. So, phenomenology cannot tell whether a particular person suffers from a certain kind of anxiety. As well, phenomenology is not well suited to investigate the meaning structures of abstract, theoretical, or technical psychological concepts. Terms such as "anxiety," "denial," or "transference" may carry special technical psychological meaning as well as ordinary life-world meaning. Phenomenology is best suited to investigate the meaning aspects of terms that clearly correlate with concrete lived experience.

The term *phenomenology* has been used (inappropriately) to describe narrative inquiries and qualitative methodologies that have little or nothing to do with phenomenology as discussed in this text and as represented by the phenomenologists discussed here. For example, among psychologists there is a lively interest in how individuals make sense of their own experiences. Interpretive sense-making of one's own life and personal experiences may indeed be helpful for therapeutic practices that aim to assist people to come to certain self-understandings. But interpretive sense-making of personal experiences falls within the domain of psychology and psychiatry, not pure phenomenology.

Further, it may be helpful to compare the distinction between phenomenological meaning and ordinary social science meaning by comparing the contrast with the meaning that inheres in the language of poetic literary texts and the meaning that inheres in the language of ordinary prose. The aim of this contrast is illustrative since poetry differs from prose in a similar manner that phenomenological text may differ from other social science discourses. This is not to say that writing poetry or novels should be confused with writing phenomenological texts. So, the aim of this comparison is methodological, since we may see that poetic thought plays a crucial role in generating phenomenological meaning, especially for scholars such as Heidegger, Sartre, Merleau-Ponty, Bachelard, Nancy, Serres, Lingis, and Chrétien. In other words, to the extent that phenomenological discourse makes use of poetic and literary language, it can benefit from an examination of how poetic and literary discourses are structured differently from ordinary propositional prose and scientific discourses that strictly adhere to logical forms of inductive or deductive reasoning, theoretical inference, empirical generalizations, and statistical proof.

The writings of phenomenologists such as Heidegger, Sartre, Merleau-Ponty, Bachelard, Blanchot, Serres, Chrétien, Marion, and Gosetti-Ferencei display "styles" that seem very personal and at the same time universal: their texts are able to communicate existential meanings that normally fall out of the range of traditional philosophy or ordinary social science. In Sartre's writings, this intellectual–experiential tension is most peculiarly demonstrated. We may see the strange split in his publications: his sometimes difficult philosophical texts on the one hand, and very readable novels and plays on the other. It appears that Sartre usually worked in the two methodological genres—the cognitive and the noncognitive dimensions of phenomenological understanding—more or less side by side, as if he felt that the relation between text and understanding required special mediation.

For example, in *Being and Nothingness* Sartre discusses at a cognitive or intellectual level the notion of bad faith: a person commits bad faith when denying his or her freedom to act and take responsibility for (in)actions. Some of his plays and novels, such as *Nausea* and *The Respectable Prostitute*, evoke an experiential understanding of bad faith at a noncognitive level of lived meaning. But it is also true that at times, in his philosophical treatise, the cognitive and the noncognitive are closely interwoven; this happens, for example, in the famous sections on "the body as seen by the other" in *Being and Nothingness*. Sartre shows how we may experience our body under the objectifying look of an observer, and he also shows the many subtle and contradictory elements involved in love and erotic desire (Sartre, 1956, pp. 252–302).

So, in the works of these phenomenologists, we see that phenomenological meaning is closely tied into the structure of the text. For example, it was said of Heidegger that he was sensitive to the effect of his lectures on his audiences. He prepared carefully for his talks by marking, with different colors, selected words, phrases, and sentences that needed a special tone, pause, emphasis, or repetition. His lectures were described as extraordinarily spellbinding, evocative, and stirring performances. More recent phenomenologists such as Hélène Cixous, Michel Serres, Jean-Louis Chrétien, Alphonso Lingis, and Jennifer Gosetti-Ferencei also write texts that at times are highly poetic and evocative.

Perception through sight, hearing, and touch is first of all primal. Similarly, there is the body knowledge that guides us through what we do. And we do not always "know" what we know when we do what we do. It is the unknowing consciousness, a noncognitive knowing, that guides much of our daily doing and acting. Our body knows how to pick up a coffee mug from the table with just the right grasp and lift. We almost blindly reach for the towel after the shower. When we arrive home after our daily commute, we may virtually have no memory of how many times we had to stop and wait for traffic lights. Our body has guided us safely through busy traffic. Some of this noncognitive knowing we may have gained in the way of habits. But it is more than habit that makes us ride our bike confidently through traffic.

Many things we do, we seem to do in a mode of unknowing knowing. And the opposite is true as well; sometimes the body itself seems forgetful in a corporeal and kinesthetic sense. We get up from our chair to do something but we have already forgotten for what purpose. Something may take us to walk into the kitchen, and when we get there we seem to have forgotten what brought us there. Did I just feel hungry? Or did I need to get something? And so, I trace my way back to the living room where I see the bottle of wine standing beside my chair. Oh, yes, I needed to get the corkscrew. Much of our day-to-day existence is probably guided by body memory and body knowledge, a noncognitive knowing controlled by the constant acting and checking of the neural network connections of the brain.

This noncognitive knowing is like a nonconscious consciousness that seems to reside and operate directly in and through our corporeal being: a body memory. Do we share this nonconscious consciousness, this body memory with animals? Or does human consciousness and self-consciousness separate us from other creatures? We need to be careful not to deny animals their own forms of consciousness, perhaps a proto-consciousness.

Strongly and Weakly Incarnated Meaning in Texts

Not only do words and texts have semantic and logical meaning, they also have stylistic or affective meaning, depending on how they are composed. Arnold Burms and Herman De Dijn (1990) suggest that meaning may be differently embedded or incarnated in texts and thus produce different types of texts. In poetic texts, meaning tends to be strongly embedded, while in informational texts meaning tends to be weakly embedded. To say that meaning is strongly embedded means that the relational tension between words and passages is tightly woven and that the meaning of the text would be disturbed if the words were interfered with. Surprisingly perhaps, strongly embedded meaning in texts tends to be fragile: when we alter or change the words or structure of the sentences, we immediately disturb the meaning of the text.

In contrast, weakly embedded texts tend to be robust: we can change the language of the text without basically altering its informational content. For example, news stories may be told by different sources in a different manner and yet produce basically the same news event and information. This distinction has important consequences for the reading and writing of phenomenological texts. A phenomenological text does not primarily communicate information, more importantly it also aims to address or evoke forms of meaning that are more expressive, elusive, or ambiguous, but that cannot be easily told in propositional discourse.

The best way to make an immediate distinction between strongly embedded and weakly embedded narrative is to observe how both a story and a poem might be paraphrased, restated, or retold. We can easily recount a newspaper article, tell what a journalistic story is about, retell a travel account, summarize a scientific report, or reiterate an argument. But it is not so easy to tell the meaning of a poem. It is true that the prosaic meaning of a poem can also be paraphrased. Just as with a report, we can tell what a certain poem is about. In both cases we end up with a recapitulated narrative about a certain topic. In fact, the topics of a poem and a travel report may be the same. For example, both the paraphrased report and the paraphrased poem may deal with travel in a foreign land. While a paraphrased report may leave out certain detail, it need not do injustice to the original version.

However, the same is not true for the paraphrased poem or poetic text. When a poem is paraphrased or retold, then something is bound to have happened in the rephrasing of the poem or poetic text: something essential has disappeared. The special meaning that renders the poem its felt meaning has nearly or completely vanished in the narrative restatement or paraphrasing. Few readers of poetry will contest this claim: the "precious idea" or "special meaning" contained in a poem cannot really be paraphrased or summarized. Indeed, even translating poetic texts from one language into another is a hazardous exercise; many readers will observe that the original meaning can never be quite captured—the best any translator can hope for is to come up with another poem or poetic expression that, as closely as possible, evokes the meanings of the first one.

Now, many scientific reports in the natural sciences, if they are unambiguously formulated, can be translated, summarized, or paraphrased. But qualitative scientific studies in the human sciences might not be easily translated or summarized when their qualitative dimension aims to express strongly embedded meaning. Phenomenological studies are often written in a manner that is heedful of strongly embedded meaning, and this poses special challenges for the vocative aspects of phenomenological writing.

Directness and Indirectness of Expressivity of Meaning

It would be wrong to suppose that strongly embedded, vocative, poetic dimensions of meaning are only the sentimental effect or emotional content of language. To understand what is evoked by a poem, a piece of music, an image, or a gesture is in essence no different from understanding words and sentences. Similarly, it is wrong to suppose that the meaning of a poem or vocative text is too complex, too rich, or too deep to be grasped by means of language. It is not that language falls short of reaching directly the iconic meaning of poetic texts, but rather that the indirectness belongs to the structure of poetic meaning. The fact that we cannot unambiguously summarize evoked meaning is both a function of the nature of meaning that is being expressed in phenomenological research as well as a function of the way in which meaning is embodied and embedded in the text.

The epistemological significance of this poetic language is that the structure of phenomenological texts helps to communicate forms of meaning that are unique to phenomenological understanding and that are impossible to mobilize in texts in any other way. Some (but not all) philosophers would suggest that poetic or expressive language is a necessary dimension of phenomenological inquiry; it contributes to the evocation of a special evidential quality of cognitive and noncognitive, intellectual and experiential meaning in phenomenological texts.

Thus, direct description of the phenomenality of human experience sometimes requires a certain indirectness. The subtler meanings of certain experiences cannot always be clearly named or described directly. When words of conceptual language seem to fall short of the felt meaning, then this meaning may need to be addressed indirectly by means of, for example, anecdote, example, or story. Or perhaps the phenomenologist may actually need to use the indirectness of some artistic material such as a novel, film, painting, or musical piece to point at the lived meaning that is being referenced, discussed, and evoked (see, for example, van den Berg in van Manen and van Manen, 2021).

On the Meaning of "Thing" and the Call "To the Things Themselves"

The famous dictum "to the things themselves" (*zu den Sachen*) is a widely quoted phrase from the texts by Husserl. Generally, it is understood as an urge to reawaken

116

us to the experience of the phenomena of our world, and (re)learning to reflect on our awareness of experience. In the *Logical Investigations* Husserl says, "we can absolutely not rest content with 'mere words.' . . . Meanings inspired only by remote, inauthentic intuitions—if by any intuitions at all—are not enough: we must go back to the 'things themselves'" (1982, p. 252). What are these "things" that we turn or return to? What do we really refer to when we study some thing, object, event, or phenomenon? Simply put, the thing or phenomenon for the researcher is a certain experience, a sensibility. Yet, ironically, the meaning or experiential nature of the thing as thing or the phenomenon as phenomenon tends to remain unaddressed and unquestioned in the qualitative literature. That is why we can argue about the (somewhat silly) question, whether we should use descriptive or interpretive methods. The point is that the various scholarly perspectives or traditions of phenomenological inquiry give us different understandings of what it is that we study when we study some "thing." The online *Oxford English Dictionary* defines "thing" as "something not specified by name" but it is specifically in the unnamedness where the enigma, strangeness, and otherness of the thingness of the thing resides.

The phenomenological reduction operates in the allusive tension of the space between the thing as object and the thingness of the thing: in naming the phenomenon, as it appears to us in consciousness or as an experiential event, the thing is, paradoxically, both annihilated and called into being precisely as it gives itself.

We need to be reminded as well that the idea of the thing-in-itself may refer to the Kantian distinction between phenomenon and noumenon. Kant argued that the human mind is only able to grasp the things of the world in a cognitive manner and through categories shaped by the structure of the human brain and human consciousness. Humans can only know things (the phenomena) as they appear in consciousness. But, according to Kant, the "real" reality of the thing-in-itself (the noumenon) is inaccessible to us because of the limiting structure or the limitations of the human mind. Object-oriented philosophers and speculative realists or speculative materialist proponents, like Graham Harmann (2011) and Quentin Meillassoux (2009), attempt to radically loosen the subject and consciousness from things and thus give things an independent self by perceiving them as "objects" or "individual entities of various different scales," which form "the ultimate stuff of the cosmos" (Harmann, 2013, p. 7). Even though this philosophic reflecting on the nature of reality, things, and objects is fascinating, up to now it seems removed from the more concrete and inceptual interests in the experiential meanings of phenomena.

It should be obvious that it would be wrong to limit and confuse a "return to the things themselves" with empirically given things. Rather, *zu den Sachen*, to the things, means a return to what matters. The question of the things themselves should orient to the question of what the things themselves are in an originary phenomenological sense. Phenomenology wants to respect the thing in its whatness, its genesis, and in its otherness. So, it is not just a matter of determining the identity of a thing or entity by describing its essence. Rather, it means that phenomenology must stand in awe at the wonder of the thingness of the thing as it acquires its meaning in relation to the other things that surround each other in the world. Not unlike the Levinassian awe of being addressed by the alterity of the

117

other, the face of the "thing" or of any "object" demands the same kind of respect (wonder) as the face of the person who is encountered in his or her otherness.

Body-I and Reflective-I

Another way to further pursue this distinction between prereflective life and the world is to follow the thoughts of phenomenological philosophers such as Husserl, Levinas, and Derrida, who have set out to describe the nature of lived experience and the ego or self in terms of internal time consciousness, presence and absence as pure subjectivity, the prereflective immediacy of the practice of living, or the moment of the "now" that precedes all reflection. It is not so strange to interpret the nature of experience by means of the "I" or the "self" because ultimately "experience" and "self" seem to coincide.

Emmanuel Levinas makes the distinction between a bodily self and a reflective self that is conscious of its body. This body-I and the reflective-I do not coincide. The first is always more actual or present-as-now than the second. In fact, it seems that the first "I" can never be directly grasped by the reflecting "I." For example, there is always an interval between *being* touched and *feeling* touched by something or someone. In the instant impression of feeling touched, we may look up to identify the nature of this physical intrusion, as portrayed in the above anecdote of meeting with a friend in a coffee shop. And in that glance of looking up, we reflectively appropriate the physical sensation of having been touched. If the touch is caused by a person who brushed up against us while passing, we may feel irritated. If it is a person who we recognize as a friend or a lover, the touch immediately receives a different significance. We may actually feel pleasure being touched this way.

But it is also possible that we had a prior disagreement or conflict with this friend and now, as we look up to see who or what touched us, we may feel ambivalent in the recognition of the friend. The point is that in this lived moment the instant perceptual impression of seeing the friend is also a moment that is unreflective (in a phenomenological sense) and, in the next instant, as we become conscious of the fact that it is this friend with whom we had a conflict, we may now become conscious of our changed mood.

As suggested above, the now of our lived experience is always constituted of what Husserl called "primal impressions" that flood our awareness before we are reflectively conscious of them. It is not strange that our entire existence is lived in the now, but that this now is always in the first instant unreflective. Even highly reflective experiences are in this sense unreflective or unthinking. Indeed, when I say, "I was thinking about something" then the "I" who says, "I was thinking" thought that he or she was thinking. The point is that, even when we are deeply and consciously reflecting on something, then we cannot simultaneously consciously reflect on this reflecting. The reflective-I always comes too late to grasp the body-I in the moment of its existence.

When I say, "I suddenly felt something touch me" or "I suddenly saw my friend" or "I thought it would be nice to have my friend join me for coffee," then who is the "I" who recounts those experiences? Is the "I" who says, "I felt something" the same as the "I" who actually felt it? Obviously, the two do not coincide. There is a difference between the preconscious "I" and the "I" that consciously reflects on the body. The first "I" is the lived body or center of the now—the living present that is somehow the primordial reality or raw existence that we live from moment to moment. For Husserl, every lived experience is always in the "now." The now is the moment of existence that we experience at present. Phenomenology asks, "What is the nature of the now, as we live it?"

How or when does an experience become a phenomenon? Husserl points out that we must distinguish the reflected aspect (which is temporal) from the prereflective now (which is not in time):

> We must therefore distinguish: the prephenomenal being of experiences, their being before we have turned toward them in reflection, and their being as phenomena. When we turn toward the experience attentively and grasp it, it takes on a new mode of being: it becomes "differentiated," "singled out." And this differentiating is precisely nothing other than the grasping [of the experience]; and the differentiatedness is nothing other than being-grasped, being the object of our turning-towards. (Husserl, 1991, p. 132)

But if reflection singles out and differentiates in a particular way, the givenness of our prereflective experiences, how then are we to understand their prereflective nature? Is there a kind of attentiveness that offers an awareness of prereflective experience without imposing cognitive screens or structures? When reflection sets in, then it initially seems to grasp something that has just elapsed. The reason that we can still grasp it is that the primal impression remains connected through retention to the living present—not as memory but as trace of the constantly renewal of the timeless instants or moments of the now. Phenomenology is preoccupied with the singularity of momentary human existence, with the identity of this difference and the difference of this identity.

The question is: how does the retention hold on to the primal impression? The answer that Husserl gave is that the retention (and the protention) are not separate events but part of the primal impression. "The now changes continually from retention to retention," every retention taking in the traces of the prior retentions that have been modified by their prior retentions (Husserl, 1964a, p. 50). Thus, the impressional consciousness passes over into an ever-fresh retentional consciousness. Because of what is held in retention (such as tones of sound), we are able to hear the melody of sound, through the sequence of retentions of tones. And protention anticipates the melodic tones that are about to come next. Husserl calls this constantly flowing continuum of retentions "primary remembrance." But since primary remembrance consists of retentions, it is not yet memory—rather, it is the passive self-constituting, self-temporalizing, and self-unifying of the living stream of the present that manifests itself as lived experience. In the *Phenomenology of Perception*, Merleau-Ponty provides a sensitive corrective to Husserl's notion of temporality. He shows how the flow of time is intertwined with our embodied world.

> Time, in the primordial experience of it that we have, is not for us a system of objective positions through which we pass, but rather a moving milieu that recedes from us, like the landscape from the window of a train. Yet we do not

really believe that the landscape moves; the attendant at the railway crossing whizzing by, but the hill in the distance hardly moves, and, in the same way, even if the start of my journey has already moved off, the start of my week remains a fixed point; an objective time is sketched out upon the horizon and must therefore be taking shape in my immediate past. (Merleau-Ponty, 2012, p. 443)

It is obvious that the notion of lived experience is much more enigmatic than we might have supposed.

The Living Moment of the "Now"—Presence and Absence

Lived experience may be considered the main theme and concern of doing phenomenological research on the phenomena. Now, it may be argued that many other qualitative research approaches also take human experience as the main epistemological and ontological source. This is true. But for phenomenology the concept of "lived experience" (*Erlebnis*) possesses special philosophical and methodological significance. The notion of "lived experience" announces the intent to explore *directly* the originary or prereflective dimensions of human existence. Husserl used the term *prepredicative experience* to refer to experience before it has been named and thematized. It is important to dwell on the question of the meaning of lived experience since an understanding of the enigmatic nature of the notion of lived experience allows us to adopt a proper phenomenological perspectival attitude necessary for doing phenomenological inquiry.

The focus on "lived experience" means that phenomenology is interested in recovering somehow the living moment of the "now" or existence—even before we put language to it or describe it in words. But, Heidegger asks, what is this "now"?

When we ask the simple questions: "what now is?" [*Was ist jetzt?*] . . . the question is already ambiguous despite its simplicity . . . As long as we do not thoughtlessly recite the question, the preliminary question already becomes necessary: "What does 'now' mean here?" Do we mean this "moment," this hour, this day, today? How far does today reach? By today, do we mean the "present time" [*Jetzt-Zeit*]? How far does this extend? Do we mean the twentieth century? What would this mean without the nineteenth century? Doe the "present-time" mean the entire modern era [*Neuzeit*]? Does the question, "what now is?" ask about what "is" in *this* time, the modern era? (Heidegger, 2011, p. 4)

We may wonder what happens in the fleeting moment of casting a glance at someone or how we experience being seen by someone. Or we may wonder how human beings experience technology now, as compared to the way humans experienced technology in the industrial age or in ancient times. And what "is" it when we study the experience of the glance or the experience of technology?

What do we mean by "is"? Is it and does it count as the beings that can appear before us as tangibly available? Or, do these beings ever remain only a fleeting appearance of what "really" "is" in the background and has being? What does one generally mean today, in the current time, and in the modern era, by "being"? (Heidegger, 2011, p. 4)

Phenomenology tries to show how our words, concepts, and theories inevitably shape and give structure to our experiences as we live them. For example, it is one thing to get lost in a novel, but it is another to retrospectively capture what happened to us, just now, as we slipped into this textual space and began to dwell in the story. Similarly, health science professionals identify, categorize, and rate with empirical descriptors the nature and intensity of various forms of pain. But the actual moment of suddenly being struck by pain or the condition of suffering a chronic pain somehow seems to be beyond words. Medical science is able to draw a diagnostic profile of clinical conditions such as obsessive compulsive disorder (OCD). But medical science has difficulty capturing in language what an actual moment of obsessive compulsive thought or behavior consists of: this strange moment of compulsively and simultaneously wanting-and-not-wanting to think or do something. Similarly, as teachers and parents, we talk about our children learning, and yet do we really know what happens experientially in that living moment of learning something?

The value of phenomenology is that it prioritizes how the human being *experiences* the world—for example, how the patient experiences illness, how the teacher experiences a pedagogical encounter with a child, how the student experiences a moment of success or failure, how a lover experiences the touch of a caress, how friends experience having a good talk, how a child experiences the admiring glance of a parent, how we experience being in touch with someone online, and so forth. Virtually any and every moment or event of our lives can be approached as a lived experience (a phenomenon or phenomenal event) and thus can become a topic for phenomenological inquiry. The phenomenological attitude keeps us reflectively attentive to the ways human beings experience and are conscious of the world before reflecting on it and thematizing it. From a methodological perspective, any (non)conscious experience can always be seen as a moment of prereflectivity: the experiential nonthematic pregivenness of the things of our world.

So, the curious fact of life is that we always seem to be in the "now," in the instance of the moment or the moment that spreads out over time. How could we not be in the now? As I am writing these words, I am in the now of this moment of writing (I have been doing so for a couple of hours). Even when we dwell in memories or in anticipations, we do so in the experiential "now." And yet, when we try to capture the "now" of our experience, we always seem to be too late. For example, when I say: "I write these words" or "I feel this pain," then I am already objectifying the moment and the subject "I" who writes these words or feels this pain. But before we reflect on experience, the I and the now are not separated. The "I" and the "now" seem to be the same, or coincide. I am the now when I am in the now. And yet, the present moment of the now is always already absent when we try to capture or reflect on it. So, the important realization is that while phenomenology always somehow is preoccupied with the instant of the now (however broadly this is conceived), the now is always absent. In a paradoxical sense we may even wonder if there ever was this "now" that we are trying to capture. And that is why the idea of "presence" in phenomenology is so problematic and wrought with issues.

Indeed, these simplified comments hide a host of philosophical issues and problems, but it is important to glimpse the basic idea of phenomenology. Phenomenology constantly questions the assumptions and presuppositions that prevent us from adequately understanding and expressing in words the living moments of immediate experience—no matter how analytically insightful, descriptively rich, or poetically evocative our words may be. The problem is that the living moment of immediate experience is by no means easily accessible or even conceivable. It must always be retrospectively retrieved as past or just past (that perhaps never "was" in the way that we think it).

So, as soon as we nod to the inevitable predicament that we can never grasp the present as present, we may also become aware that the matter is even more complex: the moment from the prereflective to the moment of the reflective exposes a gap. The past is always too late to capture the present as present. Therefore, some phenomenologists say that the past has never been present. The past is always already there. The living moment of the instant is prereflective in the sense that the living and the lived dimensions of "lived experience" are the same, and yet, paradoxically, they do not coincide. As Levinas enigmatically puts it, "a past more ancient than every representable origin" (Levinas, 1996a, p. 116). The present is already the past. But the past is a present that never was. Never quite like this.

In the later writings of Heidegger the "now" is the mere point of contact between the past and the future. In a sense we are constantly already living the future that rushes toward us. The present of the now is neither an eddy in a river flow of time nor a series of points on a temporal line that moves from past to future; rather, it is a constant absence, a continual losing of the future to the past—in the flash of the moment of the now. No matter how the moment of the now is conceptualized, the point is that we are always too late to capture it, and therefore we will never know its full meaning and significance. Indeed, its significance not only lies always already in the past, it also lies in the latency of its future. Our experiences may sometimes carry significance that we may only experience later, sometimes much later when certain events haunt us or return to us in memories that seem to come not from the past but from the future—the future latency of past events.

Lived time and the living moment of the now are indeed enigmas. But rather than shrug our shoulders and say that phenomenology is simply "impossible," we should actually acknowledge and embrace this "impossibility" as the condition for all true inquiry in the human sciences. This "impossibility" makes phenomenology so compellingly fascinating and ultimately necessary. Without the realization that human experience is related to an absent present that can only be accessed through an unrecoverable past, phenomenology would not be what it is: the most radically reflective and most demanding approach to the study of life as we experience it.

Originally, "phenomenology" was the name for the main philosophical orientation in continental Europe in the twentieth and twenty-first centuries. In the beginning of the twentieth century, philosophers such as Adolf Reinach and Alexander Pfänder were inspired by Husserl's early publications and became known as the Munich School. Since then many societies, organizations, circles, and schools of phenomenology have sprung up. Sometimes phenomenology is referred to as a movement, such as in Spiegelberg's (1982) encyclopedic two-volume compendium of internationally known phenomenologists. *The Phenomenological*

Movement offers a detailed study of national and geographical "phases" of historical phenomenological developments. But generally, to speak of phenomenological philosophy as a movement or a school may suggest more programmatic coherence than can actually be demonstrated.

After the pathbreaking work of Husserl and his immediate followers, phenomenology grew into a living body of practices that soon sprouted into a variety of distinguishable traditions and orientations. A living body of practices is a tradition that constantly reinvents itself. So, perhaps it is appropriate to regard phenomenology as a tradition of traditions.

Intentional, Retentional, Protentional Consciousness

To reiterate the question: how is it that we perceive the event of listening to or participating in a piece of music as an experiential phenomenon? From moment to moment we can attend to rhythm, melody, instants of silence and all the aesthetic phenomenal events that fuse into our sense of a song, a concerto, a chorus, and so on. If it is a new song that we are listening to then we may be surprised by the musical elements, if it is a song we have heard before we may anticipate the melodic elements that we recognize and that we may accompany by singing along. So how is time structurally linked to our experience of music? In his *Phenomenology of Internal Time Consciousness* (1964a) Edmund Husserl famously uses the example of musical sound to illustrate how the tones of a piece of music present themselves in the instant of the now, and how the successive retention and anticipated protention of melody gives us the experience of time past, present, and future.

In Husserl's epistemological language, it is the *primal impressional consciousness* and its *retentional* and *protentional* aspects that make our lived experiences potentially available in the form of *intentional* objects for our reflection. On the one hand, primal impressional consciousness is prereflective, and thus it manifests itself as an inexhaustible deposit of primordialities that constitute our experiential existence. On the other hand, the experiences that we live through present themselves to us as accessible to reflection and language. Husserl says:

> We must distinguish: the pre-phenomenal being of experiences, their being before we have turned toward them in reflection, and their being as phenomena. When we turn toward the experience attentively and grasp it, it takes on a new mode of being: it becomes "differentiated," "singled out." And this differentiating is precisely nothing other than the grasping; and the differentiatedness is nothing other than being-grasped, being the object of our turning-towards. (Husserl, 1991, p. 132)

So, when reflection lifts up and out from the prereflective stream of consciousness the lived experiences that give shape and content to our awareness, reflection interprets what in a prereflective sense already presents itself as a primal awareness. Obviously, there are many philosophical issues associated with these distinctions. For example, is the prereflective stream of consciousness already an explicitly conscious experiential awareness? And what is the relation between the passive reflection by which consciousness becomes aware of itself as world and the more active reflection of thinking? Is prereflective experience already experience of meaning, lived meaning? Or does meaning and intelligibility only emerge at a linguistic or more reflective level of the practice of living?

For Husserl the ultimate source of intelligibility seems to be the primal impressional stream of preconscious life that becomes interpretatively available to our understanding as lived experience. In Husserl's words, "the term lived experience signifies givenness of internal consciousness, inward perceivedness" (Husserl, 1964a, p. 177). However, to say that primal impressional intention–retention–protention is preconscious does not mean that it precedes consciousness, but rather that it is conscious in a primal prereflective sense. It points to the realm that for Husserl is the source and the condition for intelligibility of the experience or practice of living.

Primal Impressional Consciousness

Husserl's notion of primal impressions should not really be seen (as is sometimes done) as some kind of elemental building blocks or the contents of our perceptions or cognitions. Rather, one should think of the primal impressional intention–retention–protention as that form of consciousness that presents itself as time—time as we live through it—as the living present before it has been appropriated by reflection. Primal impressional consciousness points to the corporeal and temporal nature of existence. At the level of primal consciousness, there is not yet objectification of self and world. Lived experience is simply experience-as-we-live-through-it in our actions, relations, and situations. Of course, our lived experiences can be highly reflective (such as in making decisions or theorizing) but from a Husserlian phenomenological point of view this reflective experience is still prereflective since we can retroactively (afterwards) subject it to phenomenological reflection. Only through reflection can we appropriate aspects of lived experience, but the interpretability of primal impressional life is already in some sense given by its own givenness.

Husserl's introduction of primal impressional consciousness is attractive in that it provides a context for conceptualizing the notion of the phenomenological reduction and how phenomenological reflection is possible in relation to the everyday practices of the lifeworld. But not all phenomenologists subscribe to the distinction of primal impressional consciousness. From the perspective of Heidegger's ontology, Husserl's primal impressional consciousness is already an abstraction of how we find ourselves in the world. Heidegger says that we are always already practically engaged in the context of life. For Heidegger the origin of meaning is not found in some primal realm but right here in our actions and in the tactile things of the world that we inhabit.

For example, in contrast with Husserl's explication of the temporality of tone and music, Heidegger emphasizes the *meaning* of the sound we hear:

> We never really first perceive a throng of sensations, e.g., tones and noises, in the appearance of things . . . rather we hear the storm whistling in the chimney, we

hear the three-motored plane, we hear the Mercedes in immediate distinction from the Volkswagen . . . . We hear the door shut in the house and never hear acoustical sensations or even mere sounds. (2001a, p. 25)

When we hear the sound of a car, we hear it in the way in which it breaks in onto our world. To hear "bare" or pure sounds we would have to listen "away from things"—in other words, "listen abstractly" (2001a, p. 26).

Maurice Merleau-Ponty makes a similar point in the *Phenomenology of Perception*. Pure impressions are not only imperceptible but undiscoverable (1962, p. 4). We don't hear a pure sound sensation or "sense impression" rather we hear the barking of the dog or the ringing of the phone.

Time consciousness was Husserl's singular full-fledged description of a phenomenon. Through his theory of perception, Husserl was able to show that the universal features of objects, and general relations among objects, are not a product of our minds or of abstracting from particulars, but are intuited in perception itself.

The Existent

Only by exploring the epistemological and ethical consequences of our perceptions, sentiments, moral imperatives, and conceptions can we strive to "free" ourselves from their perspectival effects—and yet we cannot escape them. From a Husserlian view, the phenomenological reduction aims to grasp the intelligibility that lets the world "be" or come meaningfully into existence in experiential modalities. The methodical idea of the phenomenological epoché and reduction is less a technique than a "style" of thinking and orienting, an attitude of reflective attentiveness to the primordialities of human existence, to what it is that makes life intelligible and meaningful to us. Furthermore, language is decidedly implicit in the constitution and experience of meaning. And that is why phenomenological inquiry needs to start down to earth, by speaking and by letting speak the things of our everyday world, just as we experience and encounter them: see, feel, hear, touch, and sense them.

A fundamental issue of phenomenological method is that even in simply naming an experience we have already lifted it up, so to speak, from the seeming raw reality of human existence. That is why we have to constantly remind ourselves that we are trying to understand not the named concept, but the *existent*—that raw moment or aspect of existence that we "lift up," as it were, and bring into focus with language (verbal or otherwise). As we saw, Husserl termed the raw dimension of prereflective experience "primal impressional consciousness." In *The Phenomenology of Internal Time Consciousness*, he describes how these primal impressions are constituted in increasingly complex temporal layers of retentional and protentional structures of prereflective consciousness. To do phenomenology is to orient to these primal or inceptual beginnings:

But it is not through philosophies that we become philosophers . . . The impulse to research must proceed not from philosophies but from things and from the problems connected with them. Philosophy, however, is essentially a science of true beginnings, or origins, of *rizomata panton* [the roots of everything]. (Husserl, 1981, p. 196)

What Husserl is talking about is not just things at hand but the "matter at issue," which as the above quote makes clear, are the origins or *rizomata panton*, "the roots of everything" in the transcendental structures of consciousness. What do we name when we speak of "experience"? From a philosophical perspective, this is not a simple question. It may be helpful to regard experiences as the living of life. To experience something is "to live through something." But saying this may make us realize the enigmatic nature of meaning of the very notion of experience. How and what really is this temporal moment of living through something? The point is that experience refers to the livedness of this moment. Interestingly the German term *Erlebnis* and the Dutch term *belevenis* literally means the primality of living through: living or lived experience.

The issue is even more complicated when we try to sort how, for example, the moment of being touched is registered, received, or perceived by our "body" in relation to the functioning of primal impressions that are or become our lived experiences. In what sense are we aware (conscious) of the existence of primal impressions? Is primal impressional consciousness a pre-consciousness? In what sense is it primal? Does our "body" already give shape and meaning to these primal impressions before we have become aware of them? And is this prereflective moment already part of our lived experience? If so, how?

Husserl raised these questions in his famous text that has been called Husserl's most exemplary and prolonged phenomenological description: *The Phenomenology of Internal Time Consciousness*. Michel Henry hails it as an "extraordinary text, which is certainly the most beautiful of twentieth century philosophy" (2008, p. 21). And yet Henry himself, as well as other interpreters such as Emmanuel Levinas, Jacques Derrida, and Jean-Luc Marion, have argued that Husserl did not go far enough in pushing back to the originary beginning of phenomenology and that the question of the primordiality of consciousness and lived experience is ultimately the most fundamental issue that determines what phenomenology is and how it should be understood and practiced.

The issue of the precise nature of lived experience easily leads to confusion and ultimately remains a philosophical conundrum beset with assumptions. How do we focus on experience as we live through it? Can we recover moments of lived experience through reflective grasping or remembering? When we describe a particular event in experiential terms, are we really getting hold of the experience as we lived through it? Researchers who are trying to collect from individuals their experiential accounts of specific situations or events face the practical problem that many people find it much easier to tell *about* such events rather than "simply" tell them as they experienced them. Generally, people tend to have much less difficulty sharing their opinions, views, and perceptions than sharing sensitive experiential accounts. But, of course, direct experiential descriptions are not always easy to distinguish from descriptions that include perceptions, opinions, views, and interpretations. We should realize as well that even the most evocative experiential description will fail to capture the fullness and subtlety of our experience as we live it.

Should we, therefore, be less concerned about the existential validity (concreteness) of experiential descriptions? I think not. What distinguishes phenomenology from other kinds of inquiry is precisely that phenomenology wants to investigate the originary emergences of human experience and meaning. Many other interesting and worthwhile forms of qualitative inquiry focus on experiences described through perceptions (psychological perception studies), opinions (survey studies), cultural meanings (ethnographic inquiry), conceptual understandings (conceptual and language analysis), autobiographic or life meanings (narrative inquiry), psycho-analytic meanings (Lacanian inquiry), theorizing meanings (grounded theory), and so forth. But phenomenology takes a different angle on experience. Its method aims at uncovering and seeing through the presumptions and suppositions that shape our understanding of the world and understanding of life.

CHAPTER FOUR

Phenomenology Is the
Name of a Method

It may be somewhat confusing to see Husserl frequently point out that phenomenology must always start from concrete human experience (1981, p. 196, 1982, p. 252, 1991, p. 132), and yet Husserl's own texts are more often preoccupied with rather abstract and philosophically technical matters. Although Husserl's project was ostensibly "descriptive phenomenology," ironically, Husserl's writings are often abstract, focusing on technicalities, and notoriously "lacking in concrete examples," said Dermot Moran (2000, p. 63). And van den Berg remarked that Husserl remained too tied to his desk and hardly moved outside the philosophical world (Kruger, 1985). Even Husserl's home was an extension of his university office when he invited students for philosophy seminars. Indeed, it might be interesting to speculate how Husserl's followers might have been inspired and how the development of phenomenology might have unfolded in a richer fashion if Husserl himself had indulged some of the time to focus on concrete and down-to-earth lifeworld phenomena in his pursuit of a pure phenomenology. (His study of internal time consciousness might be regarded an exception since it is a study of musical time.)

This is true also for many philosophical phenomenological works by Husserl's followers and the writings of phenomenologically oriented philosophers who feel driven to try to solve historical issues or deal with challenging contradictory philosophical arguments. So, it is somewhat bemusing that, in the context of this apparent confusion, Heidegger warns against deformations of the idea of phenomenology in the literature: "Why, then, all these contrived detours, reminiscent of the notorious practices of the so-called epistemology, which constantly sharpen the knife without ever cutting anything?" (2013a, p. 4). Heidegger seems to suggest that many phenomenologists act like knife sharpeners who keep preparing their methodological tools to do phenomenology without actually doing what they are supposed to do: being attentive to what appears and how it appears in our living and lived meaningful experiences. It looks as if knife sharpeners are primarily busy with philosophical theorizing, metatheorizing, and exegetical projects. Indeed, they may be well-published phenomenological philosophers who have never really had an original insight into the meaning of a concrete phenomenon. These philosophers are busy commenting on and about phenomenology but that kind of exegesis is not necessarily as original as doing phenomenology in the basic sense of the term as explicated, somewhat ironically perhaps, by Husserl and Heidegger themselves.

DOI: 10.4324/9781003228073-5

Knife Sharpening

The phenomenological method is supposed to investigate a phenomenon in terms of the how and what of its appearance or how the phenomenon gives itself. But, when we read Heidegger's cutting remark, it is not clear if he was mockingly referring to an amusing story about Edmund Husserl whose brilliant and voluminous writings on phenomenology contain numerous painstaking refutations and elaborations of every conceivable objection to his philosophical writings. An amusing story had grown around Husserl whose voluminous writings on phenomenology contain painstaking refutations and elaborations of every conceivable objection to his philosophical system. The story is that as a boy Edmund wanted to sharpen his pocket knife. And he persisted in making the knife sharper and sharper until finally he had nothing left (de Boer, 1980, p. 10). The anecdote aptly illustrates the perfectionist qualities in Husserl's character.

Of course, it is important to recognize, that it is not wise to try do phenomenology without having a proper understanding of its approach and method. It is inevitable that a phenomenological researcher needs to sharpen their tools before aiming to shape something into a meaningful phenomenological project. But, it is fitting to read into this warning by Heidegger about phenomenologists who are so busy with philosophical theorizing, argumentation, and exegesis that they seem to forget what it means to actually do phenomenology: investigating phenomena and lifeworld topics with respect to the *how* and *what* of their givenness. In this sense, phenomenology is the primal study of the roots and meaning of phenomena, the true beginnings of their appearance and givenness. But, it is justified to ask, how should one engage in the phenomenological search for beginnings when one keeps beating about the bush in contrived detours, or when one still has not even begun?

Both, Husserl and Heidegger have pointed out that phenomenology is the name of a method. In his Göttingen lecture of 1907, on *The Idea of Phenomenology*, Husserl states: "Phenomenology . . . above all denotes a method and an attitude of mind" (1964a, pp. 18, 19). And exactly 20 years later, in his Marburg lecture on *The Basic Problems of Phenomenology*, Heidegger made a concurrent statement:

> Phenomenology is the name for the method of ontology, that is of scientific philosophy. Rightly conceived, phenomenology is the concept of a method . . .
>
> Like every other scientific method, phenomenological method grows and changes due to the progress made precisely with its help into the subjects under investigation. (Heidegger, 1982, p. 20)

Phenomenology is not a method in a technical instrumental sense—it is a method as "an attitude of mind" and a way of seeing. At a general methodical level phenomenology is often regarded as a philosophical tradition or as a human science or humanities movement. "Scientific method is never a technique. As soon as it becomes one it has fallen away from its own proper nature" (Heidegger, 1982, p. 21).

The Method of Abstemious Reflection

To reiterate, "hermeneutic phenomenology" is the name of *a method of abstemious reflection on the basic structures of the lived experience of human existence*. The term *method* refers to the way or attitude of approaching a phenomenon. *Abstemious* means that reflecting on experience aims to abstain from theoretical, polemical, suppositional, and emotional intoxications. *Hermeneutic* means that reflecting on experience must aim for discursive language and sensitive interpretive devices that make phenomenological analysis, explication, and description possible and intelligible. *Lived experience* means that phenomenology reflects on the prereflective or prepredicative life of human existence as living through it.

When the phenomenological historian Herbert Spiegelberg sets out "to give a minimum operational grasp of what it means *to do* phenomenology" (p. 14), he starts from the commonly accepted Husserlian phrase "To the Things" (*Zu den Sachen*) which indicates that doing phenomenology is doing a direct investigation into the phenomena or the things that can be described in terms of everyday, common, and uncommon experiences. Phenomenology wants to see the things in a new way, namely as phenomena, as they appear to us in all their richness and meaningful phenomenality (p. 15). This starting point implies "turning away from preoccupation with concepts, symbols, theories, and hypotheses" in favor of "a turn toward their concrete referents in experience, i.e., to the uncensored phenomena" (p. 58).

Spiegelberg points out that the philosophical development of phenomenology is really a reaction against the traditional preoccupation with philosophical texts and theories. But he argues that "no one, not even Hegel or Husserl, has proprietary rights to a term like "phenomenology." It is older than both, and it is in this sense anyone's for the taking—and defining.

Spiegelberg adds, "I do not want to restrict phenomenology to Husserl's increasingly radical—and esoteric—form of it. I intend to interpret the definiendum of a possible final definition in a broader sense" (1975, p. 14). However, Spiegelberg makes clear that he does not quite intend to take a casual position on the meaning of phenomenology. He defines phenomenology as a movement whose primary objective is the direct investigation and description of phenomena. He points out that phenomenology wants to see its data of experience "in a new way, namely as phenomena" (1975, p. 15), as they are given to us in their whatness and in their appearance—in all their richness, but also in their inevitable incompleteness, ambiguous covered-upness, and enigmatic hiddenness.

Doing phenomenology on the concrete phenomena and events of human existence is an acceptable description of phenomenology. And yet, when we examine the broad range of phenomenological literature within the domain of philosophy, we see that many phenomenological philosophers are actually doing something else. They theorize *about* phenomenological concepts, they argue and write *about* technical issues, they debate and contest important historical literature, and they engage in various kinds of philosophical exegesis. In other words, some of these scholarly activities are concerned with phenomenology at a meta-level. Or perhaps it is better to say that such scholars philosophize about phenomenology rather than do phenomenology.

From Doing Meta-Meta-Phenomenology to Actual Phenomenologizing

Someone can be occupied with writing scholarly articles and books about phenomenology at a meta-level or, as Spiegelberg wrote, at a meta-meta-level twice removed from the effort of actually doing phenomenology on the things as intended by Husserl and in his famous dictum "back to the things themselves" (*zu den Sachen selbst*). But writing *about* phenomenology is not the same as doing phenomenology directly on phenomena themselves. The difference is that one can "argue" philosophically about exegetical phenomenological issues and aim to develop philosophical systems while being purblind to phenomenological "seeing" and failing to demonstrate a genuine phenomenological attitude, able to explicate sensitively and insightfully originary meanings of selected life-world phenomena. Significantly, in the opening pages to his *Phenomenology as a Rigorous Science*, Husserl (1980, 1981) makes clear that he is not interested in building some "system" for which we yearn, which is supposed to gleam as an ideal before us in the lowlands where we are doing our investigative work. It is unfortunate that not more contemporary philosophers seek to pursue their phenomenological interests in the lower (concrete) regions of investigative work that should make our lives more thoughtfully livable (see van Manen and van Manen, 2021, p. 1073).

So, Spiegelberg suggests that it is helpful to distinguish between doing phenomenology and doing meta-phenomenology which is one or more steps removed from the actual practice of doing phenomenology directly on the things. The resolve of doing phenomenology directly on the phenomena by "going back to the things that matter" is consistent with the basic or original project of phenomenology starting from concrete phenomena. The ultimate source for all phenomenological research is the "things themselves" or the originary phenomenality of the phenomena. Therefore, Spiegelberg says (perhaps somewhat mockingly) in his discussion about doing phenomenology, "I wanted to lead from meta-meta-phenomenology via meta-phenomenology to actual phenomenologizing" (1975, p. 23). In his book *Doing Phenomenology* he gives examples of phenomenologizing on down-to-earth topics, such as his study of the phenomenon of "approval" (pp. 190–214).

Some philosophers propose that phenomenology can only be understood when returning to Husserl, the founder of phenomenology. According to them, all subsequent developments of phenomenology either help clarify or misconstrue the original Husserlian program. Of course, a basic understanding of phenomenology is constructive in that it commands us to keep returning to the original works of the great minds and learn from them. Yet, it does not mean that one should be imprisoned by the Husserlian perspective since it is tapped in a presumptive pathos that can be regarded to be no longer the original purpose of phenomenology. In other words, it is not helpful to insist that the term "phenomenology" should singularly refer to the writings of Edmund Husserl. The term "phenomenology" has come to represent a variety of new foundational starting points that have evolved into a phenomenological tradition of different movements, schools, streams, and indeed traditions.

Aspects of Phenomenological Analysis

Some researchers who engage in qualitative studies tend to think of "analysis" as the magic bullet for gaining positive results in their research activities. Doing analysis means using methods or techniques such as dissection, segmentation, separation, or taking apart the structural aspects of the object or subject being analyzed. For example, when Heidegger explicates the meaning of phenomenology he focuses on the two parts *phanestai* and *logos* to provide an understanding of the term. He does the same with the term *Dasein* and other terms and phenomena that he investigates. This is logical analysis by taking apart and examining the parts for further distinguishing elements. However, usually Heidegger engages in phenomenological analysis that does not take apart and separate but that orients to the whole integral structure of essential meaning of a phenomenon. This is characteristic of the notion of analysis in the practice of phenomenology. In discussing the idea of *phenomenological analysis* Spiegelberg takes his clues from this broad literature. He identifies the following four aspects that not only describe phenomenological analysis they simultaneously clarify the main idea of phenomenology:

1. Phenomenological analysis focuses primarily on the phenomena as they give or show themselves in lived experience or in consciousness, rather than on their conceptual linguistic expressions.
2. Phenomenological analysis aims primarily at a reflective study, as faithful as possible, of the phenomena in their directly presented articulation.
3. Phenomenological analysis pays special attention to the way in which these phenomena present themselves in consciousness.
4. The analysis contains at least two aspects for explicating the meaning of a phenomenon:
    a. One begins from a concrete example that aims to insightfully grasp the essential structure of meaning belonging to the phenomenon.
    b. The other begins with determining the generic distinctiveness and the possible modifications of the phenomenon.

(Spiegelberg, 1975, pp. 193–195)

Spiegelberg's first aspect of the analysis is the *focusing on a phenomenon as it gives or shows itself in lived experience or consciousness* (p. 193). Indeed, it is shown above that the term phenomenology means the study of what shows itself and how something shows itself in consciousness or lived experience.

An Example: The Experience of Getting Verklempt

In order to use a simple example, I will focus on the experience (phenomenon) of *becoming or being verklempt*. The term "verklempt" may not be immediately clear to everyone since it is less often used. If we were to focus on verklempt as a concept, then we would try to determine how the meaning of the concept is being used. A conceptual focus might involve language analysis and concept clarification. But as Spiegelberg first points out, phenomenology is not interested in a phenomenon as a concept but as the meaning of human experience.

First: *Phenomenological analysis focuses primarily on the phenomenon as it shows itself in lived experience or in consciousness.* So, if I am interested in the phenomenal meaning of verklempt, then I need to focus on the appearance of this phenomenon. How does the phenomenon of verklempt show itself in our experience or in consciousness? Well, something like this might happen: we are having a conversation in which we are describing or explaining to another person or group of persons some thoughts or feelings that are especially meaningful to us. But as we reminisce and talk we suddenly feel emotionally overcome and choked up. We stop talking for a moment. This experience is sometimes described as "becoming or being verklempt."

The *Oxford English Dictionary* says that verklempt means the experience of being overwhelmed by emotion. Anyone who has experienced an instance of being verklempt knows that what happens is that we cannot speak for a moment. We feel gripped by something as if we have to loosen something that obstructs us or we feel that we have to swallow away something. The word "verklempt" is borrowed from the Yiddish *farklempt*, and the German root is *klemmen* and *verklemmen*. The preposition *ver* intensifies the sense of pressure or the quality of squeeze of the verklempt facial physiognomy. A verklempt face shows the gripping, pressuring quality of the emotion as the lips may be pressured in a squeeze.

Second: Spiegelberg's next aspect of phenomenological analysis, *being faithful to the phenomenon* (1975, p. 193), means that we want to understand "what" a certain phenomenon is in its unique being or essence. So, we focus on the what-ness of the experience of verklempt and compare this phenomenon with other phenomena, but we do so with the intent on seeing what is singularly unique about the phenomenon of becoming or being verklempt. We want to understand it in the way that it shows itself in a directly presented manner. For example, we note that feeling verklempt strikes us when a certain memory, event, or occurrence emotionally overwhelms us, so that suddenly we have difficulty speaking. Our voice becomes emotionally affected. We may need a moment to come to ourselves as it were. Verklempt happens when we feel so choked up and overwhelmed with emotion that we cannot continue to speak normally. Most likely this overcomes us when in the presence of friends or people to whom we have opened ourselves with matters that matter and are meaningful to us. We have trouble talking about this, perhaps "simple" but meaningful or intimate matter, such as explaining why a piece of music or a song is so compelling to us or what a certain novel or poem means to us. Or why a certain memory is so meaningful to us. We get totally emotionally "caught" and entangled in such moments—making it hard to express ourselves.

Third: *Paying attention to the way things show themselves* (Spiegelberg, 1975, p. 194) means focusing on "how" a phenomenon shows itself or presents itself in consciousness. Being verklempt is a phenomenon of feeling emotionally blocked to talk but that experience differs from other kinds of experiential moments of being unable to speak. Becoming verklempt shows itself especially when we enter a moment in life of increased sensitivity or sentimentality, but saying this does not really help with understanding the experience of verklempt. Feeling verklempt may be experienced as annoying and embarrassing. We may feel weak or vulnerable. Yet, we cannot help getting stuck in such moment of being too verklempt to explain or talk about something that is obviously rather meaningful.

Still, becoming verklempt is not the same as being brought to laughter. In laughter we also may be unable to talk in a normal tone or manner. Of course, there are all kinds of situations that call for laughter: the laughter of a joke, the laughter of embarrassment, the giggle of the teenager, the laughter of a happy surprise, canned laughter, the laughter while hugging a friend. And there are types of laughter that correspond to various affective of emotional moods, such as belly laughter, nervous laughter, contagious laughter, polite laughter, embarrassed laughter. Yet, we sense that the meaning of these varieties of laughter are unlike being verklempt. While laughter is also an elusive phenomenon in its own right, it differs from the smile or chuckle of feeling verklempt. Often, we seem to start laughing in situations when we do not know what to say or do, it is an unanswerable situation, then the body simply surrenders and shakes with laughter, says Plessner (1970, pp. 111–115). We laugh when we expect something meaningful, but meet nothing, or when we encounter something that seems not worthy seriously considering. Then we feel at wits' end and simply laugh. Indeed, there is much to laughter that we simply do not realize unless we engage in phenomenological reflection. These are just some opening reflections. But they may help to distinguish verklempt from related phenomena with which we might otherwise confuse the meaningful aspects of the experience of being or becoming verklempt.

Fourth: Phenomenological analysis means *explicating the structure of meaning of a phenomenon* (Spiegelberg, 1975, p. 194). In other words, we need to determine the meaning of becoming verklempt so that this phenomenon becomes understandable in its structural and singular essence or meaning. The aim of phenomenology is to explicate the structure of meaning of a concrete lived experience so that it becomes understandable in its essence or basic sensibility. Spiegelberg distinguishes a dual aspect of the explication of meaning of a phenomenon:

(a) On the one hand, the analysis of the structure of meaning of a phenomenon *starts from a concrete example* (1975, p. 194). And this is a critical aspect of phenomenological analysis that many phenomenological philosophers seem to forget or consider unimportant.

By way of a concrete example I have chosen in this chapter to use the phenomenon of becoming and being verklempt. I now offer a concrete narrative example that may *evoke* the understanding of feeling verklempt. A good colleague and friend, a retired professor, reminisced about the decision, when he was still a young university student, of becoming a mountain botanist in Japan. I had asked him what made him become a botanist. But in his quiet Japanese manner Dr. Shuji Yukawa smiled as he quietly explained that he did not really decide himself to become a mountain botanist but that perhaps a little flower had decided for him:

> When I was still a student, I often explored the higher elevations of the mountains of Hokkaido, where certain flowers are rare but exquisite, if you find them. One day I had been hiking up the mountains for hours and realized that I might not be able to get back home before it would be pitch dark. How stupid of me.

To make matters worse a lightning storm had just started, and I became really worried that I was not very safe on these bare rock cliffs high up the mountain. I also realized that there must be a cabin nearby, especially for hikers and rock climbers, to take shelter. As I clambered up some steep rocky slopes it started to rain, and the rocks became slippery. I realized that if I could make it to the high ridge above me, I might be able to have a view of the area where there should be a cabin. With great difficulty I hoisted myself up the cliff with my hands grasping the edge. As I pulled myself up, I could just see something delicate waving in the wind, as if beckoning me. Should I go on or should I turn back? My eyes were peering over the naked rocky edge. And then it happened. I saw something beautiful: it was the loveliest lone little flower greeting me. I could not tell its name, but it looked like it might be related to the Edelweiss, a magical flower known for its mysterious medical powers. As I looked at it, it looked at me. The encounter made me feel elated and encouraged that I was not alone. In this moment I was a budding botanist. This little flower was surviving and so should I. Near the flower was the cabin where I spent the lone night, but not completely alone.

A week later I had to meet with my senior professor in Tokyo. As I sat in his office, I asked him what I should study for my doctoral research. He said: "I have something special for you in mind." He opened an old alpine book and put his finger on a picture of a beautiful white flower. "This one," he said, "the leontopodium discolor." Feeling emotional, I stared stunned at the tiny exquisite flower that had greeted me high up on the mountain rock. The professor looked at me expectantly. But I felt overwhelmed—I swallowed and nodded silently.

At this moment, my colleague, who had been recounting this memory with a smile, momentarily stopped talking. But as I looked at him I knew why: the reason is that he had become verklempt. Or rather, he had become verklempt again! As he had been slowly choosing his words, while recounting the reminiscence—he experienced the same thing that had overcome him as a young student in his professor's office, a lifetime ago. He was telling me a meaningful memory that was decisive for the career of his life, and he became overwhelmed, verklempt.

I tell this story as an "example" of how an exemplary narrative may constitute a phenomenological explication or "analysis" through intuitive grasping (*anschauen*). This may sound a bit strange as we tend to equate analysis with abstract dissecting of the thing or process that we aim to explain or understand. But a phenomenological example is an analytic tool that does not dissect but composes by keeping the analysis whole and distinctive.

(b) On the other hand, Spiegelberg suggests that the analytic explication of the structure of meaning of a phenomenon proceeds by *focusing on the generic distinctiveness of a phenomenon* (1975, p. 194). Applying this methical insight to the phenomenon of feeling verklempt should show the meaningful structure of the experience that is generic of the emotionality of experiencing the depth of something. While being verklempt is an experience of an emotionality that makes us lose control of the normal command of our speaking composure and of our physiognomic demeanor, we try to regain control by perhaps trying to not show that we feel verklempt. We try to resist the resistance of being verklempt, and ironically, we do it by resisting this resistance. And it shows in our facial, physiognomic and perhaps physical composure.

The moment of being verklempt may only last briefly. Therefore, if I feel verklempt I wait a moment, to pull myself together and then continue my interaction as if nothing happened. And yet I realize that my companion may have noticed what happened to me. And I appreciate when the moment passes discreetly.

The question is ultimately not what explains this concept of verklempt, though psychoanalysis may add something here. But rather, we ask what is distinctive about this experiential phenomenon? And how can we describe it meaningfully by showing how it speaks to our humanness? Indeed, we cannot help but show in our verklempt behavior that we are deeply touched by something that is of value to us.

To reiterate, phenomenology is not primarily interested in "units of meanings," "concepts," or "words"—rather it is interested in "the thing itself" the *concrete experience* that (in my example) we are provisionally pointing to with the word "verklempt" or with the utterance, or behavioral gesture about the sensation of feeling choked up and unable to speak. It should be noted as well that the stated topic of my colleague's reminiscence was how, when he was young, he had decided to become a botanist. But then the experiential moment that lies at the core of this topic turns interestingly to the question of the nature of a moment when we feel verklempt or in whatever terms we might provisionally orient to the phenomenality of this decisive moment. However, verklempt can also be seen as indeed just a word, a concept. It names the meaning of an experience but as a concept it does not really describe the primal meaning or, better, it does not describe the actual phenomenon until we approach it in the attitude of phenomenological analysis. There are moments when we feel so emotionally moved that we cannot talk. It is not that we do not know what to say, but rather that we are so choked up that we cannot bring ourselves to utter the words.

Intentional Analysis and Intuition

In the moment when we feel "emotionally" overwhelmed we are not over-whelmed by emotion (emotion is not an object) but by a third presence: the self-conscious self is suddenly so self-aware that it blocks the conversation. This happens when the self touches itself—as when we are writing and sometimes become so touched by our own words that they have become present as if uttered by a stranger. The presence of the third is experienced as a sudden depth and this moves us physically and spiritually which is the literal meaning of e-motion: to be moved out of. The motion is the rush we sense as being brushed by the intimacy of the reflective self that breaks the normal unreflective moment of the conversa-tional talk. So here we see that phenomenological analysis reveals what we may have become, emotionally and morally. The phenomenon of verklempt permits us an experiential glance at our own spiritual depth. This is part of the insightful gift that the existential structure gives us, that the phenomenological analysis of being verklempt reveals.

136

Phenomenological analysis is usually more complicated than some technical philosophical procedures. Phenomenological analysis is intentional analysis and should do the opposite to taking apart: the intentional analysis is descriptive and focuses on the whole rather than on the parts. Intentional analysis lies close to Henri Bergson's notion of intuition. He contrasts intuition with ordinary logical analysis:

By intuition is meant the kind of intellectual sympathy by which one places oneself within an object in order to coincide with what is unique . . . Analysis, on the contrary, is the operation which reduces the object to elements already known, that is, to elements common both to it and other objects.

To analyze, therefore, is to express a thing as a function of something other than itself. All analysis is thus translation . . . we note as many resemblances as possible between the new object we are studying and others which we believe we know already . . . analysis multiplies without end the number of its points of view . . . It goes on, therefore, to infinity. But intuition, if intuition is possible, is a simple act. (Bergson, 1955, pp. 23, 24)

Phenomenological analysis consists of investigating in an originary sense the primal or core meanings of a phenomenon or event. It serves to determine the phenomenality or essential meaning structures of a phenomenon. And the term "phenomenon" points at what and how something shows itself in consciousness or prereflective experience.

But if analysis implies a constant further separating, distinguishing of the analytical parts and elements of something then it is clear that the essential meaning of the phenomenon to be analyzed will always remain out of reach. In other words, analysis destroys what it tries to understand since it will never reach a final moment where the full and whole meaning and significance of the phenomenon or event will be perceived or grasped. In contrast, the phenomenological holistic analytic approach of intuitive grasping is the grasping of originary meaning or the essence of something.

Phenomenology as Method of Inquiry

In spite of the fact that we can now recognize many brilliant human scientists and philosophers who have played critical and foundational roles in developing phenomenology, two names remain most famous and influential: Edmund Husserl and his student, Martin Heidegger. These two thinkers are often referenced, but one must be careful not to adopt partisan philosophical positions regarding the works of either Husserl or Heidegger. It would be unfortunate if qualitative researchers believe that they must choose between the phenomenological canon of the works of Husserl or the canonical works of Heidegger for the tenets of their methodological inquiry. However, having offered this warning, it may nevertheless be helpful to look at some of the core distinctions between the epistemological foundation of Husserl's thinking and the ontological foundation of Heidegger's thought.

Husserl's original aim in the founding of a phenomenological science was to find a way, via the radical doubt of Descartes, to establish an epistemological philosophy that would be founded on the principle of absolute (doubtless) certainty. He sought this beginning in Descartes' famous *Discourse on the Method* in 1637, with the phrase "cogito, ergo sum" ("I think, therefore I am"). Not unlike the famous ambition of Descartes, Husserl set out to find a true beginning for all thinking by radically doubting the validity of all knowledge. This phenomenological science could then serve as foundation for the many empirical sciences such as psychology, anthropology, and other human and social science disciplines. So, the founding ambition for the construction of a phenomenological methodology for Husserl was to establish a certain foundation for scientific knowledge. A Husserlian philosopher who sets out to demonstrate how we should develop our knowledge of the things of our world would first of all point out that knowledge comes in the form of our experiential cognitions or consciousness. To study what something is we need to attend to what and how it appears or presents itself to us in consciousness. But in the works of Heidegger the ambition was for a way of doing philosophy that would be able to address the Being of human existence, the meaning of the Being of beings.

Understanding the concept of analysis is a common concern in phenomenological inquiry. Husserl is known for his phenomenological analysis of time in his study of primal impressional consciousness. Heidegger is known for his phenomenological analysis of technology in his explication of the polar attitudes of present-at-hand and ready-to-hand. But interestingly neither Husserl nor Heidegger regularly employ the term "analysis" as a methodological concept, and it is not listed in the indexes of works by either Husserl or Heidegger.

Husserl strove to build his phenomenology on an epistemological foundation of knowledge. He implied that he aimed to make the phenomenality (lived meaning) of a phenomenon transparent to our understanding. With Heidegger the question of the meaning of a phenomenon or event is sought at an ontological level. Heidegger notes that the phenomenological meaning of something that appears (gives or shows itself) is also something that simultaneously hides itself. This dynamic of showing and hiding is what phenomenology wants to probe in investigating the Being of the phenomenon (being) in which we are interested. According to Heidegger a phenomenon is

> that which proximally and for the most part does *not* show itself at all: it is something that lies *hidden*, in contrast to that which proximally and for the most part does show itself; but at the same time, it is something that belongs to what thus shows itself, and it belongs to it so essentially as to constitute its meaning and its ground. (Heidegger, 1962, p. 59)

Now, we may be happy to go through life without ever wondering what really is the deeper meaning of a phenomenon. But we can also become intrigued by such questions. Ontologically we would be investigating the meaningfulness of things, the phenomenality of a *phenomenon* or *event*. One might say that in such moment we are gripped by phenomenological wonder and by a desire for meaning and understanding.

Phenomenology and Psychology

For Husserl the first methodological question to be addressed and engaged is the essence and originary source of primal cognition in the constitution of a phenomenon or event. Heidegger likewise regarded phenomenology the basic method of a priori cognition: knowing or consciousness in its inceptuality. To understand the what and how of the appearance of a phenomenon one needs to trace it to its originary beginning. This quest for meaning or meaningful understanding is, in part, the appeal and the draw of phenomenology for Husserl, Heidegger, and many subsequent proponents of phenomenology: to investigate and witness the appearing and appearance of the phenomenal meaning of phenomena, as evidence and expressions of the meaningfulness of human existence.

In his early writings Husserl's main occupation was to be precise about phenomenological method and clearly distinguish between phenomenology and psychology, since phenomenology had from the beginning been confused with psychology. Psychology deals with empirical mental facticities but phenomenology deals with pure meanings. Once he had posited that the epoché and the reduction are needed to establish the primal phenomenological attitude and to engage the reduction in describing its phenomenal meaning, Husserl became clearer about a warning: "One must guard oneself from the fundamental confusion between the pure phenomenon, in the sense of phenomenology, and the psychological phenomenon, the object of empirical psychology" (Husserl, 1964a, p. 33).

One of the most fundamental assumptions about the project of phenomenology as a method is that it is driven by the couplet of the *epoché* and the *reduction;* however, this critical method may be conceived in various ways. Indeed, Husserl himself kept reconceiving, rewriting, editing, and revising the method and significance of the reduction into a variety of ways. And yet, the method of the epoché and the reduction remained at the core of phenomenological research.

Meanwhile, there are numerous essays and books dedicated to phenomenology that do not concern themselves much or at all with the method of the epoché and the reduction, or any other aspect or engagement of phenomenological method. One can do phenomenology on the phenomena, so to speak, without explicitly discussing methodological issues; and yet implicitly using the phenomenological methods of the epoché and the reduction. In contrast, one can obviously write *about* phenomenology without actually *doing* phenomenology in the originary sense. One does not need to be concerned with the epoché and the reduction when the discourse consists largely of philosophical, historical, theoretical, or critical exegesis of phenomenological themes, topics, issues, or applications.

Disclosing the Phenomenalities of Human Life

The more human science becomes qualitative and expressive, the more it needs to ask: what is required of writing and of language? What are the possibilities of writing and what are its limits? Qualitative writing that addresses itself to the phenomenality of phenomena of everyday life is surprisingly difficult. The more reflective the process becomes, the more it seems to falter and fail. Sometimes the difficulty of writing tends to be explained psychologically as a lack of creative thought, low motivation, poor insight, or insufficient language ability. Solutions to the difficulty of writing have been explicated pragmatically in terms of linguistic rules, inquiry procedures, reflective methods, scholarly preparation, and so on. But perhaps it is neither primarily the psychology nor the technology of writing that lies at the root of the challenge.

The difficulty of writing has specially to do with two things: First, writing itself is a reflective component of phenomenological method. Phenomenological writing is not just a process of writing up or writing down the results of a research project. Rather, from a phenomenological perspective, to write is to reflect; to write is to research. And in writing we may deepen and change ourselves in ways we cannot predict. Michel Foucault expressed this well:

> I don't feel that it is necessary to know exactly what I am. The main interest in life and work is to become someone else that you were not in the beginning. If you knew when you began a book what you would say at the end, do you think that you would have the courage to write it? What is true for writing and for love relationship is true also for life. The game is worthwhile insofar as we don't know what will be the end. (1988, p. 9)

Second, the pathic phenomenality of phenomena and the vocative expressivity of writing involve not only our head and hand, but our whole sensual and sentient embodied being. So, writing a phenomenological text is a reflective process of attempting to recover and express the ways we experience our life as we live it— and ultimately to be able to act practically in our lives with greater thoughtfulness and tact.

Meanwhile, writing as a cultural practice seems to be increasingly displaced by other forms of media. Are new technologies and media altering the nature of writing or displacing the process of writing altogether? These are questions that are pursued in the works of media scholars such as Vilém Flusser (2011a, 2011b) and Michael Heim (1987). They may have import for phenomenology as a writing practice and as the composing of phenomenological meaning through devices and gestures that extend the reach of traditional philosophical or rational discourse. Even though the medium of writing seems to be increasingly displaced by popular media of visual images, blogs, podcasts, and self-made movies (such as on YouTube), Flusser argues that the gesture of writing possesses culturally habituated and historically embodied structures that are so unique that they cannot really be substituted without a certain loss of reflectivity, expressibility, and the meaning associated with literacy (Flusser, 2012).

Just as we take for granted the material reality of the things of our physical world, so we take for granted the reality of the "things" of our mundane, symbolic, and spiritual world. It would be correct and yet silly to say that this table or this plate from which I eat my food is, at the subatomic level, largely composed of empty space and particles, and thus does not really exist in the way I know it in my daily life. Just as it would be silly to say that the look, the touch, the love, or the responsibility that I experience in my relation with others does not really exist. They are just the elusive and illusory constructions of an ineffable mind. And yet, the various qualitative inquiry models largely take the reality, the existence, and the meaning of these phenomena for granted—it is precisely the sensibility or meaning of this experiential reality that is at stake in phenomenological inquiry. In daily life, when I speak or write the names of my children, my spouse, or friends, I call their presence into being as it were. And this is true also of language in general. When I call someone a "friend" or "loved one," then I call into being a certain relational quality of friendship or love that pertains between this person and me. However, when I reflectively write this word "friend" or this word "lover," then a strange thing happens. The word now gazes back at me, reminding me that it is only a word. As soon as I wrote or pronounced this word, the meaning that I aimed to bring into presence has already fallen away, absented itself.

Naming Kills What It Calls into Being

Hegel (1979) wrote that the biblical Adam, in naming the things and creatures of his world, actually annihilated them. In the act of naming and gaining knowledge, we cannot help but rob the things that we name of their existential richness. And so, while trying to become sensitive to the subtleties, nuances, and complexities of our lived life, writers of human science texts may turn themselves unwittingly into annihilators—killers of life: a sobering realization and an unusual way perhaps for thinking about phenomenology, reflection, research, and writing.

A *phenomenology of practice* aims to be consistent with its various philosophical and human science antecedents: a practice of doing phenomenology and a phenomenology of the practice of living. As Jan Patočka pointed out, it is within the practical horizons of our personal everyday lives that phenomenological meaning is most clearly needed and seen. Contemporary phenomenology is based on many intellectual strands and traditions that are developed in response to current and earlier thoughts.

What is fascinating about phenomenology is that the influential thinkers who have presented diverse versions of phenomenological inquiry do not just offer variations in philosophies or method. They inevitably also offer alternative and radical ways of understanding how and where meaning originates and occurs in the first place. And yet, it is the search for the source and mystery of meaning that we live in everyday life that lies at the basis of these various inceptual phenomenological philosophies. In looking back at the landscape of phenomenological thought, we discern a series of mountains and mountain ranges from which certain views are afforded to those who are willing to make the effort scaling the sometimes challenging and treacherous ascents and descents. Phenomenology does not let itself be seductively reduced to a fixed methodical schema or an interpretive set of procedures. Indeed, relying on procedural schemas, simplified inquiry models, or a series of descriptive-interpretive steps will unwittingly undermine the inclination for the practitioner of phenomenology to deepen himself or herself in the relevant literature that true research scholarship requires, and thus acquire a more authentic grasp of the project of phenomenological thinking and inquiry.

The I, the Me and the Self

Another way in which we can make the distinction between the "now" of lived experience and the "now" of reflective experience is by paying attention to what happens to the sense of self when we are engaged in something versus when we reflect on this engagement. Generally, we do not explicitly experience the self as "I" when we are involved in something. Sartre famously suggested that there is no "I" when I am running to catch the bus. But the "I" suddenly appears when I tell someone that "I was running to catch the bus." In other words, only when I recall and reflect on a moment of lived experience do I actually say "I."

This is not to say that I would wonder whether it was I (and not someone else) who was trying to catch the bus while running after it. "I" am the "now" of my individual and social existence—I am the ongoing flux of my lived through life. For example, I am having a stirring experience while reading a novel. And after I put the book down, I may reflect on (my experience of) reading certain passages. However, the "I" who is now reflecting is not the same "I" as the one who was just now doing the reading. The reflecting "I" is making the "I" of reading into an object, but in objectifying the living I, we are already changing this I. So, in this sense, the "I" is not an entity or object that becomes recognizable until we reflect on it, but even in reflection it cannot be captured as it was lived (and not really there). The situation is that the pure "I" of the "present now" reflects on the "I" of the "just now"—which was absent and is now present as absence. So, it is important to realize as well that at this moment of reflecting on the "I," the "I" of the now is again not present as an entity or object of our awareness in the manner that the "I" of reflection has become an object. These kinds of distinctions between the prereflective sense of self in a lived moment and the "I" who reflects on the objectified "I" of this moment are concerns of rather technical discussions between philosophical perspectives grounded in Husserl and others.

Phenomenology Is Not the Psychology of Someone's Inner Life

It is sometimes thought that phenomenology is the study of the subjective experience of this or that person or group of persons. But, phenomenology should not be confused with psychology or with trying to understand what goes on in the inner life or the consciousness of a particular subject or a specific group of people. The point is that much qualitative inquiry naively assumes that we can just ask people what it is that they experience in certain moments. It assumes that people have straightforward or introspective access to their experience as they experience it, and it assumes that people can fully grasp and report what the meanings and meaning structures embedded in their experiences consist of. In contrast, phenomenology proposes that some kind of special reflective method or attitude is required that aims to establish access to the primordialities of life as it is lived and experienced from moment to moment. This special reflective method or attitude is known as the reduction (the confluence of the epoché and the reduction-proper)—as understood and, yes, also contested, within and from the various historical phenomenological perspectives.

In other words, if a person (adult, child, or old person) has apparent psychological or emotional problems then phenomenology is not the right tool to analyze and prescribe diagnostic profiles and solutions for the therapeutic problem. What phenomenology can do is analyze and give meaningful insights into the phenomenon (such as grief, anxiety, obsessive disorder, loss, loneliness) but psychology has to give insights into the therapeutic need of this particular person and whether the patient suffers from grief, anxiety, obsessions, loss, or loneliness. Psychology studies the patient, phenomenology studies the phenomenon. Phenomenology may give insight into the existential structure of a phenomenon, but psychology has to determine if the diagnosis is correct in this particular situation and what help should be provided to this particular person or patient who suffers from grief, anxiety, obsessions, loss, or loneliness.

Phenomenology aims to describe, in rigorous and rich language, the meaning of a phenomena or events as they give themselves, and it aims to investigate the conditions and origins of the self-givenness of these phenomena and events. To this end, phenomenology has developed certain reductive methods that aims to guard against the effects and assumptions induced by therapeutic theory, science, concepts, values, polemical discourses, and the taken-for-granted prejudices of common sense in everyday life.

Phenomenology Avoids Abstraction and Codification

Phenomenology differs from almost every other social and human science in that it attempts to gain insightful descriptions of the way we experience the world pre-reflectively and pre-predicately, largely without taxonomizing, classifying, codifying, or abstracting it. So, phenomenology does not offer us the possibility of effective theory with which we can now explain and/or control the world; rather, it offers us the possibility of plausible insights that bring us in more direct contact with the world. It is the experience that is the ultimate bearer of meaning, not some theory, linguistic formulation, or abstractive construction. Therefore, van den Berg can say, "the phenomenologist is obsessed by the concrete [and] distrusts theoretical and objective observations" (1972, p. 76). This is not to say that theorizing cannot be a fascinating and even an obsessively compelling activity. But, the difference is that a theorist observes and interprets the world through the optics and the vitreous vocabularies of the theoretical frame by means of which he or she thinks and within which he or she has been "captured," so to speak.

This project is both new and old. It is new in the sense that modern thinking and scholarship are so caught up in theoretical and abstract thought that the program of a phenomenological human science may strike us as a breakthrough and a liberation. It is old in the sense that, over the ages, human beings have invented artistic, philosophic, communal, mimetic, and poetic languages that have sought to (re)unite them with the meaningful layers of their lived experience.

It is true, some phenomenologists speak of phenomenological "explanations" (Lingis, 1986b, p. 19) or phenomenological theorizing. But here the terms *explanation* and *theorizing* do not refer to the question of "why" and the "causes" of phenomena, but rather how certain phenomena appear in consciousness. For example, Husserl made certain distinctions between description and explanation associated with static phenomenology and genetic phenomenology. Static phenomenology describes what things mean, and genetic phenomenology explains how meaning comes about. In other words, static phenomenology describes the "what" of phenomena, and genetic phenomenology describes the "how" of phenomena.

While generally phenomenology tries to push off theory in the sense of abstractive science, phenomenology may also bring in theory when exploring a human phenomenon or event.

First, phenomenology may bring in theory to show where the promise of theory fails to remain fulfilled. Especially in the field of psychology there are an abundance of fascinating and influential theories that should have contributed to human understanding—and yet, these theories may leave their central concepts impoverished of experiential and phenomenological meaning. Some theories that explain human problems and processes through psychological theories may be enriched by having these psychological concepts translated back into experiential realities.

Second, phenomenology may bring in theory where theory and phenomenology intersect in the understanding of human phenomena. For example, Maurice Merleau-Ponty (1962, 2012) criticizes Freudian theory for its reliance upon causal explanations between sexuality and human experience, but he agrees that Freud's thinking opens up phenomenological approaches to sexuality. And Bernard Stiegler (1998) extensively relates to archaeological, anthropological, neurophysiological, economic, and social theory in his exploration of technics as a conditioning force and as a force that is being conditioned by human beings.

Third, it should be mentioned that in the human science literature, phenomenological reflecting and analyzing is sometimes referred to as theorizing and theory. This is especially the case where the terms *theorizing* and *theory* are used in a very broad or philosophical manner.

The Primacy of Practice

The reason that professional practitioners in the health sciences, pedagogical disciplines, education, psychology, counseling, and so on are intrigued with phenomenological human science inquiry is indeed that it may offer plausible insight, and these insights speak not only to our intellectual competence but also to our practical capabilities. These practical abilities are not technical kinds of skills. Rather, phenomenology tends to foster ethical sensitivities, interpretive talents, and thoughtfulness and tact in professional activities, relations, and situations (for example, see van Manen, 1991).

Phenomenology does not assume that our experiential reality is necessarily rational, logical, noncontradictory, or even describable in propositional or scientific language. Rather, it tries to be sensitive to moments of thoughtfulness as well as moments of taken-for-grantedness, moments of insight, and even moments that we may experience our world in terms of mystery, confusion, disorientation, strangeness, or incongruity. After all, this is how life presents itself to us. At times, our sense of reality may be experienced as uncertain, excessive, hazy,

144

mad, bewildering, perplexing, or unintelligible. The mood of the morning may differ subtly from the mood of the evening. A lover's kiss may literally brighten our day and lighten the appearance of the things around us. A disturbing email may cloud our perception, a hostile comment from a colleague may clog our mind, an encouraging look may help us feel confident and resolute. These are the objective features of the subjectivities of our existence and events. Phenomenology aims to bring these experiential realities to language. But this expressiveness cannot be limited to the argumentative and propositional discourse of traditional philosophy and social science. To be sensitive to the rich realities of human existence, phenomenology must resort to descriptive and interpretive, cognitive and evocative, propositional and poetic, analytical and synthesizing textual means.

A good phenomenological text has the effect that it can make us "see" or "grasp" something in a manner that enriches our understanding of everyday life experience. This seeing of meaning is not merely a cognitive affair. The production of insight must proceed through the creation of a research "text" that speaks to our cognitive as well as noncognitive sensibilities. Phenomenological understanding is distinctly existential, emotive, active, relational, embodied, situational, temporal, technical, theoretic, and nontheoretic. A powerful phenomenological text thrives on a certain irrevocable tension between what is unique and what is shared, between immanent and transcendent meaning, and between the reflective and the prereflective spheres of the lifeworld. Without this tension, the research text tends to turn flat, shallow, boring—because it loses the power to break through the taken-for-granted dimensions of everyday life.

In-Seeing Versus Utility

But the practical value of phenomenology also should be found in the sheer pleasure of insight and feeling touched by things that reach the depth of our existence and confirm our humanness. The rewards phenomenology offers are the moments of "seeing meaning" or "in-seeing" into "the heart of things" as Rilke so felicitously put it:

> If I were to tell you *where* my greatest feeling, my universal feeling, the bliss of my earthly existence has been, I would have to confess: It has always, here and there, been in this kind of in-seeing, in the indescribably swift, deep, timeless moments of this divine seeing into the heart of things. (Rilke, 1987, p. 77)

Some of Rilke's poetry is called "seeing poems" (such as the famous poem "The Panther"). They are powerful examples of his in-seeing. And not unlike the poet and the artist, the phenomenologist directs their gaze not inwardly but outwardly onto the world. In-seeing takes place in a thoughtful relation to what Martin Heidegger (1985, p. 266) calls "in-being" or our everyday being involved with the things of our world. In-being is the constitution of the sense of being, in which every particular mode of being finds its source and ground. So, when Heidegger says, "Knowing is a mode of being of in-being," then this means that every moment of practical acting and knowing always already takes place in a mode of in-being (1985, p. 161). A phenomenology that is sensitive to the lifeworld explores how our everyday involvements with our world are enriched by knowing as in-being.

It is true, members of professional disciplines are interested in the promise that phenomenology can make to practice. But Heidegger warns that phenomenology "never makes things easier, but only more difficult" (Heidegger, 2000, p. 12). He agrees with those who feel that phenomenology lacks effectiveness or utility if one hopes to do something practically or technically useful with it:

> "Nothing comes" of philosophy; "you can't do anything with it." These two turns of phrase, which are especially current among teachers and researchers in the sciences, express observations that have their indisputable correctness . . . [It] consists in the prejudice that one can evaluate philosophy according to every-day standards that one would otherwise employ to judge the utility of bicycles or the effectiveness of mineral baths. (Heidegger, 2000, p. 13)

According to Heidegger, the practicality of a phenomenology of practice should not be sought in instrumental action, efficiency, or technical efficacy. And yet this does not mean that phenomenology cannot have practical value.

> It is entirely correct and completely in order to say, "You can't do anything with philosophy." The only mistake is to believe that with this, the judgment concerning philosophy is at an end. For a little epilogue arises in the form of a counter-question: even if *we* can't do anything with it, may not philosophy in the end do something *with us*, provided that we engage ourselves with it? (Heidegger, 2000, p. 13)

In some sense all phenomenology is oriented to practice—the practice of living. But from the perspective of pragmatic and ethical concerns, we may have a special interest in phenomenology. We have questions of how to act in certain situations and relations. This pragmatic-ethical concern I call the "phenomenology of practice." Thus, we explore how a phenomenology of practice may speak to our personal and professional lives.

By asking whether phenomenology may do something *with us*, Heidegger hints at the formative value of phenomenology. In practicing phenomenological inquiry, through the reflective methods of thoughtfulness and writing, the aim is not to create technical intellectual tools or prescriptive models for telling us what to do or how to do something effectively. Rather, a phenomenology of practice aims to open up possibilities for creating formative relations between being and acting, between who we are and how we act, between thoughtfulness and tact.

It may be helpful to remind ourselves that the word *practice* has long been used in contrast with the term *theory*. Valuing the theoretical life over the life of practice hints at high commitment to truth and contemplating the good life. Thus, theory can mean a rebuttal of practice, but it can also be seen in the service of practice, following practice, or as the essence of practice itself. In his *Praise of Theory* Hans-Georg Gadamer (1998) notes that *theoria* in its original Greek sense of *contemplatio* was conducted in a broader context of life and thus was also a way of comporting oneself. He says, it is a "'being present' in the lovely double sense that means that the person is not only present but completely present" (1998, p. 31). Gadamer questions the justification of the oppositional contrast between theory and practice. He asks whether it is perhaps not so much theory but practice itself that points to the sources of meaning of our lives:

> But what has happened to our praise of theory, then? Has it become a praise of practice? Just as the individual who needs relevant knowledge must constantly reintegrate theoretical knowledge into the practical knowledge of his everyday life, so also a culture based on science cannot survive unless rationalizing the apparatus of civilization is not an end in itself, but makes possible a life to which one can say "yes." In the end all practice suggests what points beyond it. (Gadamer, 1998, pp. 35, 36)

If we accept Gadamer's suggestion of praise of theory as praise of practice, then some provocative questions present themselves. What then remains of theory in an age where only few are still willing to sing its praises?

An example of a provocative questioning of the significance of theory is the book *life.after.theory*, which contains a series of interviews with prominent scholars such as Jacques Derrida, Frank Kermode, Christopher Norris, and Toril Moi (Payne and Schad, 2003). The title of the book was chosen first of all to indicate that the period of high theory appears to have passed and now it may be time to ask again about the relation of theory to life. The conjunction "after" in "life after theory" may be understood in different ways. "After" may simply mean the chronology of life following theory, referring to new forms of thought or practice now that theory has vanished, or "after" may suggest that theory has conditioned life, or, vice versa, that life is now after theory in an entirely different sense of that term.

In the opening dialogue of *life.after.theory*, Derrida offers a surprising portrayal of how he sees practice of his own life in relation to his writing. He says,

> I confess that everything I oppose, so to speak, in my texts, everything that I deconstruct—presence, voice, living, voice and so on—is exactly what I am after in life. I love the voice, I love presence, I love . . .; there is no love, no desire without it. So, I'm constantly denying, so to speak, in my life what I'm saying in my books or my teaching . . . [In my writing, there is] a Necessity which compels me to say that there is no immediate presence, compels me to deconstruct . . . Nevertheless, in my life, I do the opposite. I live as if, as if it were possible . . . somehow to be present with voice, or vocal presence. I want to be close to my friends and to meet them and, if I don't, I use the phone. That's life, consistent with and inconsistent with, following without following . . . it's because there is no pure presence that I desire it. There would be no desire without it. (Derrida in Payne and Schad, 2003, pp. 8, 9)

How should we interpret Derrida's provocative thesis? He seems to be saying that the pathos of his philosophical theorizing (phenomenological writing) is contradicted by the desires of his everyday life practice. He deconstructs the possibility of presence and yet desires real presence in his personal life.

147

Whereas for Gadamer, *theoria* refers to an exemplary manner of comporting oneself in such a way that one is "completely present," Derrida (in the footsteps of Heidegger) has deconstructed the possibility of being "completely present." But what is methodologically even more striking, perhaps, about Derrida's personal reflection is that he is living his personal life in a relation of distinct tension and discontinuity with his life as scholar. His confession is especially revealing to the extent that he goes to great pains to show that he strives for consistency in his scholarly (theoretical) work:

> Now, in my own case—I mean, theoretically—I have tried, the best I could, to avoid being inconsistent; I try to write and to say and to teach in a certain way which prevents me, as much as possible, from, let's say, contradicting myself or changing. I try. Even if I think, "Well, there are contradictions or aporias in my own texts", it is because I'm saying things which are self-contradicting or aporetic; so, I point to them and I try to formalize the aporia or the self-contradiction in order not to be inconsistent, not to say, "Well, that is what I wrote when I was 25." I try not to. (Derrida in Payne and Schad, 2003, p. 26)

Derrida could argue that there is still consistency in the sense that theorizing is also a form of life—in other words, a practice. Indeed, there are good reasons for shifting the focus from the tenuous issue of "life after theory" to the more contemporary concern of "life after practice"—the practice or practices that make up theory, that precede theory, or that make theory possible in the first place.

If we take the view that a primal notion of practice refers to our ongoing and immediate involvement in our everyday worldly concerns, then the mutual relations between practice and thought appear extremely complex and subtle. Numerous phenomenologists have aimed to find vantage points from which we may grasp the ways that reveal how our sensibilities and experiences of the world are formed or conditioned by the primordialities of our existence. Perhaps we need to understand the impossibility of perfect presence so we may long for perfect presence in life as we live it. In essence this predicament underlies all true art and all genuine inquiry. We need to be prepared to deconstruct phenomena such as true love, genuine friendship, and gift giving, so that we may thoughtfully and tactfully aim for the perfection of love, friendship, and gift giving in our actual personal lives. The experience of a practice that transforms a person in his or her inner depths can only be achieved through a phenomenological in-seeing into the essence of things. Such Orpheus gaze can be experienced as an inner upward rush or upwelling, enabled by a phenomenology of practice in its final textual performance.

CHAPTER FIVE

The Role of Stories, Anecdotes, and Vignettes

The person who begins a hermeneutic phenomenological study soon discovers that this form of inquiry is not a closed system. There are many paradoxes that mark the routes of a human science journey. As one develops a focus on the phenomena of lived experience, it soon appears that these phenomena are highly elusive and problematic. If I focus on an experience that strikes me as particularly interesting but that is not easily captured in language, then I may wonder: what word(s) do I use to describe this experience? Sometimes a story may help: "Has something like this . . . ever happened to you?" Sometimes a scene from a movie or a few lines from a poem may help to communicate the topic of our inquiry. And yet, experience is always more immediate, more enigmatic, more complex, more nuanced, and more ambiguous than any description can do justice to. The human science and humanities researcher is a scholar-author who must be able to maintain an almost unreasonable faith in the power of language to make intelligible and understandable what always seems to lie beyond language.

I am moved by an evocative musical passage. I feel strengthened by an encouraging hand on my shoulder. I recall a frightful childhood experience. I am struck by the loveliness of someone I meet. I wistfully reminisce on a holiday adventure. I exchange a meaningful glance with someone. How do we capture and interpret the possible meanings of such experiences? The things we are trying to describe or interpret are not really things at all—our actual experiences are literally no-things, nothings. And yet, we seem to create some-thing when we use language in phenomenological inquiry to create a narrative or an anecdote. Anecdotes are a common figure in everyday telling of events or happenings.

The term "anecdote" is perhaps too plain, too everyday, too vernacular, too low-bred, too mundane. An anecdote is not a commonly accepted form of literary expression. Among authors the notion of anecdote generally receives low status. And in the behavioral social sciences too the employment of anecdote is avoided or frowned upon. For behavioral scientists the presence of anecdotes in research reports may indicate possible flaws in the evidential basis of scientific reasoning (see Strasser, 1974, p. 298).

But this poor status of anecdote may be quite undeserving. It is worth noting that in everyday life the anecdote is probably the most common device by which people talk about their experiences. I am tempted to suggest that anecdote is the natural way by which particular concerns of everyday living are brought to awareness. My interest in anecdote resides especially in its power to enhance the phenomenological and hermeneutic quality of human science text. At the basis

DOI: 10.4324/9781003228073-6

of this interest in anecdotes, vignettes, fragments, stories, lies the methodological notion of seeing the process of human science research to be intrinsically a textual or writing activity (van Manen, 1989a). When we speak of our daily practices then we tend to do so at the hand of anecdotes. Barthes has argued provocatively that writing and textuality are at the heart of the method of human science inquiry.

> Some people speak of method greedily, demandingly; what they want in work is method; to them it never seems rigorous enough, formal enough. Method becomes a Law . . . the invariable fact is that a work which constantly proclaims its will-to-method is ultimately sterile: everything has been put into the method, nothing remains for the writing; the researcher insists that his text will be methodological, but this text never comes: no surer way to kill a piece of research and send it to join the great scrap heap of abandoned projects than Method. (Barthes, 1986, p. 318)

Writing fixes thought on paper. It externalizes what in some sense is internal (or intersubjective); it distances us from our immediate lived involvements with the things of our world. As we stare at the paper, and stare at what we have written, our objectified thinking now stares back at us. Thus, writing creates the reflective cognitive stance that generally characterizes the theoretic attitude in the social sciences. The object of humanities or human science research is essentially a linguistic project: to make some aspect of our lived world, of our lived experience, reflectively understandable and intelligible. Researchers recognize this linguistic nature of research in the imperative reminder: "Write!" Human science research requires a commitment to write. But writing for a human science researcher is not just a supplementary activity. The imperative "Write," as Barthes put it, "is intended to recall 'research' to its epistemological condition: whatever it seeks, it must not forget its nature as language—and it is this which ultimately makes an encounter with writing inevitable" (Barthes, 1986, p. 316). For Barthes, research does not merely involve writing: research is the work of writing—writing is its very essence (1986, p. 316).

The Significance of Anecdotes in Human Science Inquiry

An interesting case of the significance of anecdotes in human science thinking concerns the doctrine or philosophy of Diogenes Laertius, also called the cynic or dogman, or "a Socrates gone mad" (Herakleitos and Diogenes, 1979, p. 35). There are no authentic texts left from this thinker, who at any rate, considered living more important than writing. What is available are just anecdotes. Legend has it that the youthful Alexander the Great one day went to visit the philosopher Diogenes about whom he had heard such strange stories. He came upon the philosopher while the latter was relaxing in the beautiful sunshine.

ALEXANDER: I am Alexander the Great.
DIOGENES: I am Diogenes, the dog.

150

ALEXANDER: The dog?
DIOGENES: I nuzzle the kind, bark at the greedy, and bite louts.
ALEXANDER: What can I do for you?
DIOGENES: Stand out of my light. (p. 30)

While Alexander wanted to show his benevolence and generosity to the thinker, the latter showed that he knew only too well the nature of worldly temptations. But rather than to theorize and to get entrapped into the addictive sphere of theoretical knowledge, Diogenes "showed" his argument in verbal gesture: "get out of my sun." By means of this pantomimic demonstration Diogenes shows more effectively than theoretical discourse might do how the philosopher frees himself from the politician. He was the first person who was free enough to be able to put the mighty Alexander in his place. Diogenes' answer not only ignored the desire of power but also the overwhelming power of desire (Sloterdijk, 1983, p. 265). And so, this humble and wretched philosopher showed himself more powerful and autonomous than the feared ruler Alexander who went all the way to the borders of India to satisfy his need for power. Did Alexander recognize the sense of superiority of the moral life of the cynic? History has it that Alexander once said: "if I were not Alexander, I would be Diogenes" (Herakleitos and Diogenes, 1979, p. 36). Diogenes and Alexander the Great died on the same day, a fact to which people have attached superstitious significance.

So, Diogenes set out to teach his fellow citizens not by giving speeches or by writing books but by means of pantomimic exercise and by living example. A kind of street theater, one might say. Sloterdijk (1983) has argued that the aureole of anecdotes that surrounds the figure of Diogenes are more clarifying of his teachings than any writings could have been. And yet the reason that Diogenes' philosophy has not been more influential may also find its cause in the fact that it is only anecdotes that have been preserved.

Anecdotes have enjoyed low status in scholarly writings, since, in contrast to historical accounts or reports, they rest on dubious factual evidence. The shady reputation of anecdote may derive from the sixth-century Byzantine historian Procopius who called his posthumously published scandalous account of the Emperor Justinian *Anecdota* or *Historia Arcana* (Anecdotal or Secret History).

In everyday life, too, anecdotes may get negative reactions. For example, we may hear someone say that a certain account should be distrusted since "it rests merely on anecdotal evidence." Evidence that is "only anecdotal" is not permitted to furnish a proper argument. Of course, it is entirely fallacious to generalize from a case on the basis of mere anecdotal evidence. But empirical generalization is not the aim of phenomenological research. The point that the critics of anecdotes miss is that the anecdote is to be valued for other than factual-empirical or factual-historical reasons.

An historical account describes a thing that has happened in the past, but an anecdote is rather like a poetic narrative which describes a universal truth. Verhoeven (1987) argued that what Aristotle says about the poetic epic of his time applies to the anecdotal narrative of our time:

the poet's function is to describe, not the thing that has happened, but a kind of thing that might happen, i.e., what is possible as being probable or necessary . . .

poetry is something more philosophic and of graver import than history, since its statements are of the nature rather of universals, whereas those of history are singulars. (Poetics, 1451)

Anecdotes may have a variety of functions (see Verhoeven, 1987 for distinctions made here; and Fadiman, 1985). The ones that are of significance to human science discourse may include the following characteristics:

(1) Anecdotes form a concrete counterweight to abstract theoretical thought. The object of phenomenological description is not to develop theoretical abstractions that remain severed from the concrete reality of lived experience. Rather, phenomenology tries to penetrate the layers of meaning of the concrete by tilling and turning the soil of daily existence. Anecdote is one of the implements for laying bare the covered-over meanings.

(2) Anecdotes express a certain disdain for the alienated and alienating discourse of scholars who have difficulty showing how life and theoretical propositions are connected. Thus, anecdotes possess a certain pragmatic thrust. They force us to search out the relation between living and thinking, between situation and reflection. In this connection Fadiman (1985, p. xxi) too notes how anecdote has acted as a leveling device, how it humanizes, democratizes, and acts as a counterweight to encomium.

(3) Anecdotes may provide an account of certain teachings or doctrines which were never written down. Socrates and Diogenes are examples of great thinkers about whom anecdotal life stories form both their biographies as well as the essence of their teachings. This historical phenomenon also shows the great potential and generally unacknowledged power of the figure of "anecdote" in human science discourse. Plato's Dialogues are an anthology of anecdotes about Socrates, the philosopher. It differs markedly from the large body of philosophical writings that have followed it down the ages. At the methodological level Plato's writings are round-about or indirect reflections about fundamental human experiences such as friendship (Lysis), love (Phaedrus, Symposium), teaching virtue (Meno), and so forth.

(4) Anecdotes may be encountered as concrete demonstrations of wisdom, sensitive insights, and proverbial truths. Classical figures considered their anecdotes as narrative condensations of generally acknowledged truths (Fadiman, 1985, p. xxi). For example, the anecdote of the cave in Plato's *Republic* is offered by Plato as allegory or possible story. Plato's accounts are offered not as factual truths in the empirical or historical sense but, in Plato's words, as "likely stories." By their anecdotal quality we come to see what is possible and what is not possible in the world in which we live (Cairns, 1971, p. xv).

(5) Anecdotes may acquire the significance of exemplary character: they make the singular visible and graspable. This is an extraordinary feat because, by definition, something that is singular cannot be captured by concepts. Concepts are constructed through generalization from particulars. Even ordinary nouns are already too blunt to express the singular. And yet, an anecdote that is carefully honed can evoke a strong sense of singularity and concreteness.

Because anecdote is concrete and taken from life (in a fictional or real sense) it may be offered as an example or as a recommendation for acting or seeing things in a certain way. In everyday life an anecdote may be told as a tactful response (a "message") to let the recipient of the anecdote sense or perceive a certain truth that is otherwise difficult to put into clear language.

Anecdotal narrative as story form is an effective way of dealing with certain kinds of knowledge. "Narrative, to narrate," derives from the Latin *gnoscere, noscere* "to know." To narrate is to tell something in narrative or story form. The paradoxical thing about anecdotal narrative is that it tells something particular while really addressing the general or the universal. And vice versa, at the hand of anecdote fundamental insights or truths are tested for their value in the contingent world of everyday experience. And so, one may say that the anecdote shares a fundamental epistemological or methodological feature with phenomenological human science which also operates in the tension between sin particularity and universality.

D'Israeli termed anecdotes "minute notices of human nature and of human learning" (in Fadiman, 1985). Anecdotes can teach us. The use of story or of anecdotal material in phenomenological writing is not merely a literary embellishment. The stories themselves are examples or topics of practical theorizing. Methodologically speaking, story is important because it allows the human science text to acquire a narrative quality that is ordinarily characteristic of story. A hybrid textual form is created, combining the power of philosophic or systematic discourse with the power of literary or poetic language. Anecdote particularizes the abstracting tendency of theoretical discourse: it makes it possible to involve us prereflectively in the lived quality of concrete experience while paradoxically inviting us into a reflective stance vis-à-vis the meanings embedded in the experience. The important feature of anecdotal as well as phenomenological discourse is that it simultaneously pulls us in but then prompts us to reflect.

The significance of anecdotal narrative in phenomenological research and writing is situated in its power (see Rosen, 1986): (1) to compel: a story recruits our willing attention; (2) to lead us to reflect: a story tends to invite us to a reflective search for significance; (3) to involve us personally: one tends to search actively for the story teller's meaning via one's own; (4) to transform: we may be touched, shaken, moved by story; it teaches us; (5) to measure one's interpretive sense: one's response to a story is a measure of one's deepened ability to make interpretive sense. In short, the lacing of anecdotal narrative into more formal textual discourse, if done well, will create a tension between the prereflective and reflective pulls of language. Compare, for example, the phenomenological essay of Chapter 2, "I Never Forget What's-His-Name."

Language and Experience: The Look

What then is the relation between language and experience? It seems that words forever will fall short of our aims. Perhaps this is because language tends to intellectualize our awareness—language is a cognitive apparatus. And yet, language is also an expressive medium. What we try to do in phenomenological inquiry is to evoke understandings through pathic mediations of language such as fictivity, example, anecdote, and poetic image. Contemporary phenomenologies are able to bring about pathic forms of knowledge and understandings that transcend the common cognitive function of language. This matter is important because many professions (such as the practice of nursing, healing, counseling, educating) seem to require not only gnostic and diagnostic skills and specialized bodies of knowledge, but also sensibilities and sensitivities that have to do with discretionary, intuitive, pathic, and tactful capacities (van Manen, 1991). It seems that in these directions lie the relevant and continuing contributions of hermeneutic phenomenology for the complex and subtle ontological and ethical epistemologies of professional practice.

When phenomenologists use experiential narrative to explore the phenomenological meaning aspects of a certain phenomenon, they are likely to take as their material some factual, imagined, or fictional story. For example, in his famous reflections on the "Look," Sartre uses an imagined instant of spying on a couple in another room by listening at the door and looking through a keyhole:

> Let us imagine that moved by jealousy, curiosity, or vice I have just glued my ear to the door and looked through a keyhole. I am alone and on the level of a non-thetic self-consciousness. This means first of all that there is no self to inhabit my consciousness, nothing therefore to which I can refer my acts in order to qualify them. They are in no way *known*; I *am my acts* and hence they carry in themselves their whole justification. I am a pure consciousness *of* things, and things, caught up in the circuit of my selfness . . . This means that behind that door, a spectacle is presented as "to be seen," a conversation as "to be heard." The door, the keyhole are at once both instruments and obstacles . . . (Sartre, 1956, p. 259)

While looking through the spyhole in the door, I am totally engaged in what is going on at the other side of the door. I am not reflecting on my actions; rather, I am jealously immersed in this world of spying on the couple at the other side of the door. Even the jealousy is simply and unreflectively part of the experience.

> (there is a spectacle to be seen behind the door only because I am jealous, but my jealousy is nothing except the simple fact that there is a sight to be seen behind the door)—this we shall call *situation* . . . and since I am what I am not and since I am not what I am—I cannot even define myself as truly being in the process of listening at doors. (Sartre, 1956, pp. 259, 260)

Sartre stresses that while in the act of looking through the keyhole, I am so self-forgetful that I am unaware of myself—I escape myself. But, then, suddenly, I realize that I am not alone. Someone else has arrived on the scene and sees me spying at the door. And now something happens: I am no longer lost in the moment of doing what I am doing. I feel the eyes of the other and I feel myself objectified by the judging look of this third person.

> But all of a sudden I hear footsteps in the hall. Someone is looking at me! What does this mean? It means that I am suddenly affected in my being and that essential modifications appear in my structure—modifications which I can apprehend and fix conceptually by means of the reflective cogito. (Sartre, 1956, p. 260)

Sartre provides a detailed phenomenological analysis to show what happens to the self when the look of the other objectifies me and strips me of my subjectivity. The look of the other makes me into an object. This is a look that shames me and makes me self-conscious.

> First of all, I now exist as *myself* for my unreflective consciousness. It is this irruption of the self which has been most often described: I see *myself* because *somebody* sees me—as it is usually expressed. This way of putting it is not wholly exact.... The unreflective consciousness does not apprehend the person directly or as its object; the person is presented to consciousness *in so far as the person is an object for the Other*. This means that all of a sudden I am conscious of myself as escaping myself.... Now, shame ... is shame of *self*; it is the *recognition* of the fact that I am indeed that object which the Other is looking at and judging. I can be ashamed only as my freedom escapes me in order to become a given object. (Sartre, 1956, p. 260)

The example of the look allows Sartre to draw many fine distinctions in the pre-reflective experience of the self and other as they are engaged and subjected to the look. Sartre starts the anecdote with "Let us imagine that . . ." but we do not know whether Sartre's anecdotal account of the spying look is based on a factual incident or whether it is purely imagined. The important point for phenomenological inquiry is that it does not matter whether the story is factual or fictional. Any factual-empirical account of an experience immediately transfigures into the status of a fictional account when it is examined by phenomenological reflection of the reduction. Or, better, it does not help to distinguish between factual-empirical accounts and imagined empirical accounts. The only requirement is that the experiential account is *plausible* in its truth-value.

Edward Casey (1981) underscores the importance of the fictional nature of experiential accounts for phenomenological explication. He gives the example of Merleau-Ponty's discussion of the shared experience of the look while gazing at a landscape. What is the empathic sensibility and the meaning of shared world of such a moment? How do we partake in each other's gestures?

> Suppose that my friend Paul and I are looking at a landscape. What precisely happens? Must it be said that we have both private sensations, that we know things but cannot communicate them to each other—that, as far as pure, lived-through experience goes, we are each incarcerated in our separate perspectives—that the landscape is not numerically the same for both of us and that it is a question only of a specific identity? When I consider my perception itself, before any objectifying reflection, at no moment am I aware of being shut up within my own sensations. My friend Paul and I point out to each other certain details of the landscape; and Paul's finger, which is pointing out the church tower, is not a finger-for-me that I *think of* as oriented towards a church-tower-for-me, it is Paul's finger which itself shows me the tower that Paul sees, just as, conversely, when I make a movement towards some point in the landscape that I can see, I do not imagine that I am producing in Paul, in virtue of some pre-established harmony, inner visions merely analogous to mine: I believe, on the contrary, that

my gestures invade Paul's world and guide his gaze. When I think of Paul, I do not think of a flow of private sensations indirectly related to mine through the medium of interposed signs, but of someone who has a living experience of the same world as mine, as well as the same history, and with whom I am in communication through that world and that history. (Merleau-Ponty, 1962, p. 405)

Merleau-Ponty points out that we shall not understand this shared experience if we think of the world as an object or as something universal. But we will understand it immediately if the world is "the *field* of our experience and if we are nothing but a view of the world" (1962, p. 406).

Are we to say, then, that ... my world is the same as Paul's, just as the quadratic equation spoken of in Tokyo is the same as the one spoken of in Paris, and that in short the ideal nature of the world guarantees its intersubjective value? ... Paul and I "together" see this landscape, we are jointly present in it, it is the same for both of us, not only as an intelligible significance, but as a certain accent of the world's style, down to its very thisness ... It is precisely because the landscape makes its impact upon me and produces feelings in me, because it reaches me in my uniquely individual being, because it is my own view of the landscape, that I enjoy possession of the landscape itself, and the landscape for Paul as well as for me. (Merleau-Ponty, 1962, pp. 405, 406)

We can ask again, what sort of description is this account that Merleau-Ponty provides? Is it a description of a past and remembered experience? Or is it a purely imagined and fictional experiential description? And the point is, again, that for phenomenological inquiry it does not really matter whether the experience actually happened or whether it is fictional. If it is a plausible experiential account, then that means that the events may have happened more or less like this; yet, it may be imagined and purely fictional. Or, indeed, the account may have been borrowed from fictional literature or novels.

Using Merleau-Ponty's words, Casey notes that Merleau-Ponty's description is "suppositional in status; it is a possible description which is at once plausible and presumed" (1981, pp. 176–201). But it should be seen as well that the use of examples in phenomenological reflection is not peculiar only to Sartre and Merleau-Ponty. Virtually every phenomenologist, who does phenomenology on the things, makes use of experiential examples of this sort.

Retelling Myths for Understanding Life

Phenomenologists have used experiential material that is *factional* and *fictional*. As well, phenomenologists have borrowed literary fiction or fictional narratives from literary novels, short stories, poetry, diaries, and biographic texts—especially from existential kinds of authors such as Fyodor Dostoevsky, Marcel Proust, Friedrich Hölderlin, Rainer Maria Rilke, and Franz Kafka. Some of the most fascinating phenomenological thinkers have used biblical stories and the literature of mythology. For example, Søren Kierkegaard (1983) and Jacques Derrida (1995a) have produced profound phenomenological reflections on ethics by

156

means of the story of Abraham and Isaac. Maurice Blanchot, Michel Serres, and Jean-Luc Marion have used the myth of Orpheus and Eurydice in their reflections on the phenomenology of artistic expression. And Bernard Stiegler has used the myth of Prometheus and Epimetheus to explain the originary significance of technics in the evolution of human becoming. Similarly, Michel Serres uses various fables to explore how human relations are similar to those of parasites in the host body and pests (Serres, 2007). By retelling myths, new ways of interpreting and understanding life and human experiences are made intelligible.

For example, the myth of Eros and Psyche may help us gain an understanding of what it means "to fall" for someone. We "fall" for a new friend, for a love we encounter, or for a person we admire. We may meet someone whose mind fascinates us and we cannot help but feel inspired in the company of this person. We fall for something in this other person that is uniquely singular and that asks for our devotion.

Eros and the Fall for Love

The myth of "the fall for love" describes how Eros, armed with his arrow, happens to come upon the sleeping Psyche. As he bends over to gaze at her, he accidentally pricks himself with his own arrow and promptly falls for her. He falls for the beautiful Psyche who finds herself woken from sleep by the loving gaze of Eros. From then on, in the darkness of the night, Eros visits the beautiful Psyche. His touch is so sensual, his love so perfect that she surrenders to her secret lover, night after night. But gradually, as her mysterious lover leaves in the morning, Psyche starts to feel ambivalent. However wonderful and intimate she feels with her lover, she has never really seen Eros. So, one night, in spite of having been warned by Eros that she cannot look at him, she lights an oil lamp to "see" the identity of who she has fallen for. However, in the very moment of catching a glance at the source of her fall, some hot oil accidentally drips on Eros' body. He wakes, wounded, and startled—the next moment he has disappeared forever to the heavenly realm of the immortals.

But now, Psyche's desire for Eros cannot be stilled. Catching a glimpse has awakened in her a desperate desire. She has truly fallen. She has "seen" Love. In another famous legend, Tristan and Isolde fall in love by drinking a fateful potion, the potion of Love. It is not that they were already in love with each other, rather they unlock love in each other: they have fallen in love with Love. Similarly, Psyche has been struck with love by Love. And like every true lover, Psyche can only think of this Love. She is obsessed with Eros and her desire propels her onward in her journey to find him.

But what is frightening about Love is that ultimately it can never be attained. The separation of Psyche and Eros is symbolic of the separation that we all may have experienced in falling for someone, no matter how near our love is in space or time. However sweet our kisses, however sensual our embraces, it seems that this embodied being we so ardently want to touch and passionately engulf with our own aroused body always escapes our grasp. Even in the moment when we are most intimate, even in the instant of ecstatic pleasure, we also find that we are still separate. In the very gesture of stroking the lovely face of our beloved, this

157

face overwhelms us, becomes mystery, untouchable, infinitely deep. In this face we recognize the unrecognizable, the riddle of Eros whom we so desire. Love is the enigma of the otherness of the other. Or to speak in the language of the philosopher Levinas, the face of the other is ultimately invisible. Love presents a face that goes beyond the face, says Levinas. The face of the Other is not the face we see on the surface of the skin, the color of the eyes, the shape of the nose. The true face is the naked face that lies behind the surface features.

One version of the myth says that Psyche searched for Eros, but never found him and that Aphrodite turned her into an owl, forever haunting the forest. The other version is more commonly told: Psyche has to overcome near impossible tasks set by Aphrodite, who is jealous of Psyche's beauty. But we are told that love succeeds in the end—Psyche is made immortal and thus united with Eros through the divine intervention of Zeus. And from this perfect union of lovers was born the daughter named Pleasure. But, of course, this ending is indeed mythical. In the world of ordinary human beings there exists no perfect union. Eros, the embodiment of love, is divine, immortal, elusive, and essentially invisible to ordinary mortals. Love gives pleasure, but desires more: oneness.

Love and the Riddle of the Other

Hegel thought of love, i.e., falling for something in someone, as a special kind of recognition. Falling in love is not only a desiring and knowing of the other, it is also a strange and contradictory kind of self-knowing: as a knowing of myself in a unity with the other and the other in unity with me. Love is the most tremendous contradiction, according to Hegel. Why? Because in this unity the separation and difference remain. Levinas also talked of love as a relation between oneness and separateness, except that the desire for oneness is simultaneously achieved and not achieved: "Reference of love 'given' to love 'received', love of love, voluptuousity is . . . like a spontaneous consciousness . . . . In voluptuousity the other is me and separated from me" (1979, p. 265). According to Levinas, love is ultimately oriented neither to the person nor to the unique qualities of the loved one. Rather, falling for the other is oriented to the riddle of the Other, with that what always eludes us, remains ungraspable, making us one and yet separate in even the most intimate moment. Love is the recognition of what is simultaneously recognizable and unrecognizable in the other: his or her incognito.

The tale of Psyche's perfect union with Eros embodies the impossible desire of all those who have fallen for another. The desire to become one and melt in blissful union with one's love. The passionate desire of every lover is to want to touch, see, and hold his or her love—but ultimately, the lover wants to touch what is untouchable, see what is invisible, hold and embrace what is ungraspable. This most intimate love of my life lets me experience simultaneously the most incredible closeness and the most unbridgeable and immeasurable distance. The one who is closest to us in love is also the farthest. Isn't it strange that the person most difficult to describe is, ironically, the person for whom we have fallen deeply and know the best? And yet, herein lies also a recognition: that this one and only human being, this one (my own child, my close friend, my true love) whom I have sought to know more perfectly than any other person in my life, cannot be reduced to the qualities or particulars I know or attribute to this person. Myths and legends like Psyche and Eros may give us a phenomenological glimpse into the enigmatic experience of "falling for" someone, of unlocking a secret in each other—of the meaning of a possible human experience.

Empirical Descriptions Possess Fictional Status

Ricoeur suggests that myths are not just nostalgia for some forgotten worlds: they "constitute disclosures of unprecedented worlds, an opening on to other *possible* worlds which transcend the established limits of our *actual* world" (in Kearney, 2004, p. 124). Even more so, the hermeneutic reinterpretations of myths can make phenomenologically accessible the meanings of human realities that otherwise are hard to bring to our experiential understanding.

So, the important methodological point to make is that empirical phenomenological narrative descriptions possess a "fictional" methodological status. Whether the lived experience descriptions are derived from factually or historically observed events, whether they are recorded accounts from reliable witnesses, or whether these are personal experiences—no matter: once the accounts are engaged and mediated in phenomenological reflection, they are transfigured and reduced or, perhaps we should say, "elevated" to the status of "fiction" in the sense that they could have been imagined examples. Husserl already asserted the methodological importance of fiction for phenomenological inquiry:

> Extraordinary profit can be drawn from the offerings of history, in an even more abundant measure from those of art, and especially from poetry which are, to be sure, imaginary but which, in the originality of their invention of forms [*Neugestaltungen*], the abundance of their single features and the unbrokenness of their motivation, tower high above the products of our phantasy and, in addition, when they are apprehended understandingly, become converted into perfectedly clear phantasies with particular ease owing to the suggestive power exerted by artistic means of presentation.
>
> Thus, if one is fond of paradoxical phrases, one can actually say, and if one means the ambiguous phrase in the right sense, one can say in strict truth, that "feigning" [Fiktion] makes up the vital element of phenomenology as of every other eidetic science, that feigning is the source from which the cognition of "eternal truths" is fed. (Husserl, 1983, p. 160)

The important insight that Husserl confirms here is that essentially the data for phenomenological reflection are fictionalized or fictitious. Even so-called empirical data are treated as fiction since they are not used for empirical generalization or for making factual claims about certain phenomena or events. Of course, Husserl does not say that literary texts and novels are in themselves phenomenological descriptions. But they are resources for the process of phenomenological analysis. "Fictional" examples may be *drawn* from literature and the arts, from life, and from the imagination. Literature offers expressive sources such as mythology, poetry, biography, and, yes, paintings, cinematography, and other arts. Phenomenological investigations and analyses are mediated by empirical material drawn from life, such as anecdotes, stories, fragments, aphorisms, metaphors, memories, riddles, and sayings. And, the imagination may offer suppositional material that neither art nor life might present.

Empirical Data Are Stripped of Their Factuality

The implication for phenomenological research is that the researcher realizes that experiential material gained through interview, observation, written accounts, and other social science methods are essential data for phenomenological reflection. But the empirical data are stripped of their factuality once they become objects for phenomenological reflection and analysis. This does not mean that factual-empirical accounts are unimportant for phenomenological research. On the contrary: it means that the insights to be released from the experiential accounts may be increasingly depthful of lived meaning and resonant of human truths. It also does not mean that fictional accounts or poetry texts in themselves are already a form of phenomenology. But it can mean that, "human science starts there where poetry has reached its end point," as Linschoten (1953b, postscript) so felicitously put it.

To reiterate, it does not really matter whether a certain experience really happened or is only imagined to have happened. This realization may strike some qualitative researchers as problematic. But the important reminder is that, even though phenomenology employs empirical material, it does not make empirical claims. Phenomenology does not generalize from an empirical sample to a certain population, nor draw factual conclusions about certain states of affairs, happenings, or factual events. What then is the philosophical or methodological status of anecdotes, vignettes, stories, and other vocative texts (fictional or real) in phenomenological inquiry? In the following paragraphs I will show how certain kinds of examples (anecdotes, stories, fragments, and so on) function as "phenomenological examples" or "exemplary paradigms." However, it is important to remind oneself that these vignettes, anecdotes, stories, or accounts remain an aspect of phenomenological explications and reflections. Claiming to do vignette research or anecdote research without a phenomenological scaffold reduces such accounts to mere narratives, even if eloquently written in some biographic sense. The point is that such vignette or anecdote does not evoke a phenomenologically exemplary understanding as that was not their intentionality.

Writing Lived Experience Descriptions (LEDs)

When we tell about our daily experiences, then we tend to do so at the hand of anecdotes, vignettes, tales, sketches, accounts, or stories. Any of these narrative descriptors would be appropriate to reflect on the meaning of a phenomenological topic or event. But I will use the term anecdote for this discussion because ironically anecdotes are lowly rated for their evidential validity. Anecdotes are just stories but not necessarily factually true. Therefore, we say "that is just an anecdote" in order to stress that the account is not proven to be correct or true. And that is also the case for narratives such as vignettes, tales, sketches, or stories. Yet, the anecdote is the everyday manner by which particular concerns of living are brought to awareness. Better yet, anecdotal narrative allows the person to reflect in a concrete way on experience and thus appropriate that experience. "To anecdote" is to reflect, to think. Anecdotes form part of the grammar of everyday storying. Anecdotes recreate experiences, but now already in a transcended (focused, condensed, intensified, oriented, and narrative) form. And thus, the act of "anecdoting" as concrete reflecting prepares the space for phenomenological reflection. What makes anecdotes so effective is that they seem to tell something noteworthy or important about life, about the promises and practices, frustrations and failures, events and accidents, disappointments and successes of our everyday living.

So, the anecdote is a narrative device that is concrete and taken from life (in a fictional or real empirical sense) and that may be offered as an "example" in a phenomenological sense (see also van Manen, 1989a). The example (anecdote) can be seen as methodologically related but seen from a different vocative or writing perspective. Phenomenological reflection involves a stepping back from immediate experience by reflecting on it. Derrida has pointed out that this withdrawing from the world in the moment of reflection, in order to somehow recapture it, is actually already writing—we should say here: phenomenological writing.

Anecdotes, in the sense that they occur in the phenomenological writings of, for example, Sartre, Marcel, Merleau-Ponty are not to be understood as mere illustrations to "butter up" or "make more easily digestible" a difficult or boring text. Anecdote can be understood as a methodological device in human science to make comprehensible some notion that easily eludes us (see van Manen, 1990, pp. 116, 117).

Thus, ironically, the phenomenological use of anecdote should not be confused with untrustworthy empirical accounts. For example, we may hear someone say that a certain account should be distrusted since "it rests merely on anecdotal evidence." Evidence that is "only anecdotal" is not permitted to furnish a proper proof or argument. And, of course, it is entirely fallacious to generalize from a case on the basis of mere anecdotal evidence. But empirical generalization is typically not the aim of phenomenological research. The point that the critics of anecdotes, stories, or vignettes in qualitative research miss is that this genre is to be valued for other than factual-empirical or factual-historical reasons. Stories, vignettes, or anecdotes are so powerful, so effective, and so consequential in that they can indirectly evoke the meaning of things that resist straightforward explanation or conceptualization. Anecdotes bring things into nearness by contributing to the vividness and presence of the essence of an experience.

Webster's definition of anecdote is "a usually short narrative of an interesting, amusing, or biographical incident." And the online *Oxford English Dictionary* defines anecdote as "A short account of an amusing, interesting, or telling incident or experience; sometimes with implications of superficiality or unreliability"; also, as a secret, private, or hitherto unpublished narratives or details of history. It speaks of the narrative of an incident or event as "being in itself interesting or striking." Anecdotal accounts are regarded as a genre. Some people are considered skilled raconteurs of anecdotal accounts, and an anecdote-monger is a person who engages in the telling or retelling of anecdotes. Paintings and other visual images can also be expressed in anecdotal style.

The term "anecdote" derives from the Greek, meaning "things unpublished," "something not given out." And indeed, Cicero (and later Renaissance scholars as well) used to describe some of their unpublished manuscripts as anecdotes, "things not given out." Anecdotes are social products. In everyday life the anecdote usually begins its course as part of an oral tradition. Often, it is originally a fragment of the biography of some famous or well-known person. Thus, Samuel Johnson described anecdote as "a biographical incident; a minute passage of private life." Biographers and historians value anecdotes for their power to reveal the true character of persons or of times which are hard to capture in any other manner (Fadiman, 1985, p. xxi).

But often anecdote was information meant for insiders, stuff that for discretionary reasons did not make the written record. Sometimes the anecdote was used to characterize a way of thinking or a style or figure which was really too difficult to approach in a more direct manner. This is one epistemologically interesting feature of anecdote, that if we cannot quite grasp the point or essence of a subject and we keep looking at it from the outside, as it were, then we may be satisfied with an anecdotal story or fragment (Verhoeven, 1987). This is also the ironic intent of the reflective use of anecdote in phenomenological texts in this book and in my previous publications on the genre of anecdotes, stories, vignettes, etc. (see, for example, van Manen 1990, pp. 116, 117).

The Example Makes the Unknowable Knowable

For researchers, the methodological power of the "anecdote" or "narrative vignette, story, fragment, sketch, tale, account" serves the phenomenological status of the "example." The "anecdotal example" does not express what one knows through argument or conceptual explication, but, in an evocative manner, an "anecdotal example" lets one *experience* what one cannot define or describe in a conclusive manner (in an intellectual or cognitive sense). Yet, both the anecdote and the example (which may be the same textual unit) can make the singular knowable in a qualitative sense. They can do this because the exemplary anecdote, like literary fiction, always orients to the singular which becomes the source for understanding the rich possible contents of the experience. Indeed, any literary story or novel is always some unique story that brings out the particular or singularity of a certain phenomenon or event.

Suppose that someone came up with a definitive and final formulation of what it is like to fall in love. It would mean that we no longer have to approach love as an enigmatic phenomenon. Yet, we already know that this will never be possible. At best we can give examples of the experience of falling in love. If it were possible to say directly and satisfactorily what this [something] is, it would not be necessary to present it by means of examples, says Günter Figal (1998, p. vii). But that is precisely what phenomenology must do.

For instance, the Chekhov story "The Lady with the Dog" is a typical literary fiction in the sense that it describes an event that has never quite happened exactly like this. In this fictional story, Chekhov lets us experience what it is like to fall in love in a way that is out of the control of the protagonists in the story. He shows in this unique story not the conceptual meaning but the singularity of falling in love. Furthermore, the example as anecdote makes what is unexplainable knowable in a phenomenological sense. So, in a phenomenological text on falling in love, the use of an exemplary anecdote may make knowable and understandable the singularity of the experience. Methodologically speaking, using the paradigmatic form of example in writing a phenomenological research text is making the meaning of a phenomenon or event knowable in a way that the conceptual and argumentative dimensions of the text cannot achieve.

Another way of clarifying the phenomenology of singularity is with the notion of the moment. The phenomenological attitude comprises a fascination with the moment: the uniqueness or singularity of an experience or event. This moment is different and unique like every moment is always different and unique. For example, when I fall for someone and I think about the meaning and singularity of this event (falling in love), then I am compelled not by concepts or abstractions but by the concreteness and singularity of my experiences: the sweet taste of that last kiss, the tenderness I felt when I looked in my love's face, the longing I experienced when reading the love note, the pleasure of hearing her voice, the desire I feel in this moment of being the object of my lover's desire. A phenomenology of falling for someone is not primarily pursued through a theoretical discourse or a conceptual analysis of the notion of love; it is pursued through a language of the unique, the singular—the singular is like this: this example.

Examples in Phenomenological Texts

In the traditional and qualitative social sciences, examples are usually employed as concrete or illustrative "cases-in-point" to clarify an abstract idea or theory. This commonly used form of example-as-case-in-point is meant to make theoretical knowledge more accessible, concrete, or intelligible, although the example itself may not contribute to the knowledge. Indeed, examples are often used as informative illustrations. But, an example-as-illustration can be left out of the text without compromising the text. So, it is essential to realize that "phenomenological examples" differ radically from such explanatory, clarifying, or illustrative uses of examples. The phenomenological notion of "example" is methodologically a unique semiotic figure for phenomenological inquiry.

Examples in phenomenological texts have evidential significance because the example is the example of something experientially knowable or understandable that is not directly expressible—it is a universal singularity. If a singularity were to be expressed in ordinary prose, it would immediately vanish. Why? Because language cannot really express a singularity by naming or describing it. A singularity cannot be grasped directly through words because words are already generalized bits of language. Language universalizes. However, and this is paradoxical, the "phenomenological example" as a story can provide access to the phenomenon in its universal singularity. It makes the "singular" knowable and understandable. Every fictional story or novel has at its core a singularity: a unique theme or signification.

A Model Is a Definite Example

The etymology of the Greek word for model is to "show something in something and thus make it present" in an interpretive methodical sense. Günter Figal makes special use of the term "model" as an equivalent term for "example." He says, "a model is a definitive example" (Figal, 2010, p. 29). To reflect in a hermeneutic phenomenological manner on the meaning of something is to examine it as an originary model. The model is like an incept (as opposed to a concept). It points toward the originary meaning of something. Some models are more appropriate or better suited to get at the originary meaning of something. And so, models (as examples) must be well chosen because the essence of the matter has to be expressed in the model. In the words of Figal (2010), "models are supposed to be distinguished by their pregnancy; they must prove themselves as such by really letting something be shown in them" (p. 30).

Similarly, Giorgio Agamben (2002) uses the term "example" interchangeably with paradigm: "example" means *para-deigma*. According to Agamben "paradigm means simply 'example' . . . a single phenomenon, a singularity." A singularity is, by definition, single and unique—it does not share properties in common with anything else. In other words, a singularity has no specifiable identity (idem); it has no recognizable sameness except that it is self-same. A singularity is only identical to itself (ipseity). Interestingly, Agamben (1995) points out that a true example is neither particular nor universal.

To reiterate, it would be wrong to assume that the "example" in phenomenological inquiry is used as an illustration in an argument, or as a particular instance of a general idea, or as an empirical datum from which to develop a conceptual or theoretical understanding. Instead, the phenomenological example is a philological device that holds in a certain tension the intelligibility of the singular. How can the example do this? It can do this because the example mediates our intuitive (self-evidential) grasp of a singularity, which is precisely the project of phenomenology. Again, we need to sense the paradoxicality of this explication of a critical methodological aspect of phenomenological inquiry, thinking, and writing.

The singularity of the singular may show itself by way of the example. "The example lets the singular be seen," says Agamben (1995, p. 10). But one could perhaps equally say that the phenomenological example reconciles the incommensurable couplet of the particular and the universal. In other words, singularity emerges in the deconstructive fusion of the particular with the universal. In this sense, the phenomenological example expresses the singular as universal. So, the example is somewhat of an enigma and contradiction. This idea may be seen as a phenomenological variation on Georg Wilhelm Friedrich Hegel's notion that a lived experience originates as particularity but becomes recognizable as universal.

Phenomenology Is a "Science of Examples"

Phenomenology is a "science of examples," said Buytendijk. Phenomenological reflection and analysis proceed by way of example. But what does this mean? It means that the so-called data (stories) of phenomenological analysis may have the status of examples. As shown above, phenomenologists often speak of and reach for an "example" when examining an experiential phenomenon or event for its phenomenological features. When Gabriel Marcel (1978) discusses the phenomenology of hope, he gives the example of a mother who keeps a place at the dining table for her son who, she knows, died many years ago. Yet, says Marcel, the mother lives with hope. When Levinas describes the experience of the uncanny rumbling of the *il-y-a* (the there-is), he refers, by way of example, to a childhood experience of hearing the rumble of the there-is (the *il-y-a*) behind the wallpaper of his bedroom.

When Heidegger reflects on the meaning of the "thing," he uses the example of a jug. When Henry presents the idea of immanence and the "auto-affection of life," he uses the painting of Kandinsky as an example. When Sartre discusses the experience of negation and nothingness, he says that he needs an example, and he describes having an appointment with Pierre in the café where they are supposed to meet at 4 o'clock. But as he arrives at the café and looks around, Sartre finds, "He is not here." Next, Sartre explores how it is that we "see" this absence that is a nothing (not being there) and yet not a nothing (the absence of not being there). Interestingly, all these examples have acquired iconic fame in the philosophical phenomenological literature. They have become classic or well-known phenomenological anecdotes, fragments, vignettes, stories, and it matters not whether they are fictional, imagined, or real in an empirical or biographic sense.

In contrast, in the natural and social sciences, an example is commonly used as a concrete or illustrative "case in point" to further clarify an abstract idea or theory. Kant declares in the first draft of his *Critique of Pure Reason*, that

> examples and illustrations always appeared necessary to me, and hence actually appeared in their proper place in my first draft. But then ... I found it inadvisable to swell it further with examples and illustrations, which are necessary only for a popular aim. (1999, pp. 103, 104)

Indeed, examples are often used as informative illustrations. But, an example-as-illustration does not add new knowledge and such example-as-illustration could be left out of the text without damaging the text. So, it is important to realize that "phenomenological examples" differ radically from the explanatory, clarifying, or illustrative use of illustrative examples in texts.

Whether taking the form of vignettes, anecdotes, or narratives, "examples" may be understood as rhetorical and aesthetic devices for evoking phenomenological understandings or phenomenological knowledge that cannot necessarily be expressed, explained, or explicated in a straightforward propositional or prosaic manner. The use of "phenomenological examples" is a clear feature of phenomenological texts that focus on the phenomena themselves. Examples in this methodical sense are also found in the wider phenomenological philosophical literature: the example of "boredom" while waiting for the train in the study of metaphysics in Martin Heidegger (1995, p. 93), the example of the myth of "the Gaze of Orpheus" in the study of writing in Maurice Blanchot (1981, pp. 99–104), the example of the voyeur looking through the keyhole of the door in "the look" in

Jean-Paul Sartre (1956, pp, 259, 260), "Homer's Odysseus" as an example of The Homecomer in Alfred Schutz (1971, pp. 106–119), the example of "Morpheus" in *The Fall of Sleep* in Jean-Luc Nancy (2007b, pp. 8, 9), and so on.

Husserl rarely used detailed reflections of concrete examples to analyze and explicate the meaning of a concrete phenomenon or event, so I am using another translation of this well-known instance of "example" when he describes the cogito as an act. He says:

> Let us start with an example. In front of me, in the dim light, lies this white paper. I see it, touch it. This perceptual seeing and touching of the paper as the full concrete experience of the paper that lies here as given in truth precisely with these qualities, precisely with this relative lack of clearness, with this imperfect definition, appearing to me from this particular angle—is a cogitatio, a conscious experience. (Husserl, 2012, p. 65)

Husserl sets himself the task of describing the phenomenon of conscious experience (*Erlebnis*), meaning "lived experience." According to Husserl, the cogitatio, the stream-of-consciousness lived experience, in the fullness of its unity, can be seen to give access to the essence of every lived experience.

> The Eidos, the pure essence, can be exemplified intuitively in the data of experience, data of perception, memory, and so forth, but just as readily also in the mere data of fancy (Phantasie). Hence with the aim of grasping an essence itself in its primordial form, we can set out from corresponding empirical intuitions, but we can also set out just as well from non-empirical intuitions, intuitions that do not apprehend sensory existence, intuitions rather of a merely imaginative order. (Husserl, 2012, p. 14)

In his study *Imagining,* Casey (2000) takes his own experiences as a source for constructing narrative examples to investigate the meaning of the phenomenon "imagining." Furthermore, he affirms that it is not only fictional texts that can function as examples but also observed and fictive objects, events, and actions.

> Phenomenological method takes objects, events, or acts—whether real or imagined—as exemplifying an essence or essential structure. In this way their basic constitution is made perspicuous, and examples become the specific vehicles or privileged media of eidetic insights. (Casey, 2000, p. 24)

Casey wants to make the strong case that examples that exhibit an essence or essential structure with a maximum of evidential lucidity can achieve eidetic insights. Even carefully selected factual or empirical material may serve as phenomenological examples, but only after they have been fictionalized through the application or performance of the reduction.

It is important to keep in mind that phenomenology does not deal with facts. Accordingly, we may need to allow that some examples only partially serve the purpose of the phenomenological reduction; while they present evidentially perspicacious examples, they may remain linguistically ambiguous or enigmatic.

For the Utrecht phenomenologists, the methodological power of the "example" also serves an analytic purpose. The "example" does not express what one knows through argument or conceptual explication, but, in a vocative manner, an "example" lets one experience what one does not know. There is an indirectness in the turn to the narrative meaningfulness of phenomenological examples.

The example can make the singular experienceable and thus knowable as an indite method of phenomenological writing (see van Manen and van Manen, 2021). While the methods of the epoché and the reduction are engaged in an attempt to gain insights into the originary meaning of a phenomenon, it is the indite methods, the vocative aspects of writing, that assist in bringing phenomenological insights to textual understanding. The online *Oxford English Dictionary* defines the term "indite" in this way: "to put into words, compose (a poem, tale, speech, etc.); to give a literary or rhetorical form to (words, an address); to express or describe in a literary composition." The term indite is used here to focus on the semiotic or writing practices that present the linguistic, methodological dimension to phenomenological thinking, inquiring, and writing. An "example" often takes shape as a story (as in existential literary fiction) and thus orients to the singular. Indeed, any literary story or novel is always some unique narrative that brings out the particularity or singularity of a certain phenomenon, event, or life.

In the exegetical phenomenological literature, little attention appears to be paid to the methodological significance of the "example" in phenomenological writing. But some of the leading phenomenologists commonly speak of and reach for an "example" when examining a phenomenon or event for its phenomenal features. Unfortunately, many of Husserl's "examples" are seemingly overly simple, such as a reference to seeing a tree, in his explication of the noema and intentionality. But Husserl's (1964b) most famous and extended "example" is probably contained in his study of time consciousness. In his description of our inner consciousness of time, Husserl uses the example of hearing a familiar melody. In hearing a well-known musical melody, the present notes of the melody and the notes just past are retained in retention while the notes about to be heard are already anticipated as protention. Thus, Husserl explicates and shows the streaming structure of ongoing retentions and protentions as primal impressional consciousness in the exemplary experience of hearing a familiar melody (see primordialities in Chapter 3).

The phenomenological notion of "example" is methodologically a unique figure for phenomenological inquiry. Strictly speaking, phenomenology does not reflect on the factualities of examples—facts or actualities. Phenomenology reflects on examples in order to discover what is exemplary and singular about a phenomenon or event. Examples in phenomenological inquiry serve to examine and express the aspects of meaning of a phenomenon; examples in phenomenology have evidential significance: the example is the example of something experientially knowable or understandable that is not directly sayable—a singularity. If a singularity were to be expressed in ordinary prose, it would immediately vanish. Why? Because language cannot really express a singularity by naming or describing it. A singularity cannot be grasped through concepts because concepts are already generalized bits of language. Language universalizes. But, and this is quite enigmatic, the "phenomenological example" as story provides access to the phenomenon in its singularity. It makes the "singular" knowable and understandable; it lets the inexpressible essence be seen.

Lived Meaning

An eloquent revealing anecdote (story, vignette, tale, sketch) can be constructed from "lived experience descriptions" gathered through interview, observation, personal experience, related literature, written accounts, or from imagined accounts. Sometimes experiential descriptions are so well narrated that they already have the narrative shape of an anecdote.

By way of example, I present here two anecdotes from Diana McGowin's book on her experience with forgetfulness (compare also the text on name forgetfulness in Chapter 2). She describes autobiographically how her forgetfulness of other people starts to interfere with her office work, though she had not been diagnosed with any illness:

> As I sat down behind my polished, glass covered desk, a brightly dressed woman approached.
> "Yes?" I greeted her. "How may I help you?"
> "Diane!" The woman paused in obvious surprise.
> "Whatever do you mean?"
> I felt a throbbing in my chest as I realized the woman thought we knew each other, and on first-name basis.
> But who was she?
> Staring at me intently, the woman placed a sealed payroll envelope in front of me.
> "Payroll came while you were delivering the brief transcript," the woman said slowly. "I took your paycheck for you." (McGowin, 1993, p. 18)

When the forgetfulness becomes chronic and disruptive of daily functioning, then the memory failure takes on a more ominous appearance. Diane still had not fully realized that her forgetfulness was not just an ordinary kind of occurrence. But already she was trying to cope with unexpected situations:

> "Hey, Diane! Good to see you! How have you been?" He greeted me with a smile.
> Oh, God, not another one! I felt I was on a trip to never-never-land. This time, I attempted to bluff my way through small talk with the young stranger. As we walked along together, he asked me how long I had worked for this firm. I hesitated, then replied I had been with them for about three years. The lad nodded approvingly and said he was there to interview for a job as messenger or courier. Could I help him?
> I threw in the towel, and smiled resignedly at him.
> "Please forgive me. I know that I know you, but it is just one of those days! I simply can't bring your name to mind. I will be happy to put in a word for you, if you could write down your name and other relevant details."
> "I don't get it," he muttered.
> "Your name?" I did not waver.
> "Diane, I'm your cousin, Rich," he said slowly. Tears began to surface in my eyes, and I embraced my cousin, whispering, "I was just trying to keep anyone

from overhearing that one of my relatives is applying. Of course, I'll put in a good recommendation with the personnel department. Absolutely!" (McGowin, 1993, pp. 19, 20)

One consequence of Diana McGowin's awareness of the fragility of her forgetfulness is that she increasingly feels her "self" diminished each day. And yet, ironically, her entire account gives evidence of an acute awareness of self. On the one hand, the self of the person suffering from Alzheimer's dementia seems to erode, diminish; on the other hand, the experience of self seems highly intensified. For example, the person with Alzheimer's is acutely aware of trying to say something, but the right name or word will not come. An observer may not notice this and only see the silent, non-participatory behavior. Phenomenological research may help us to become more aware of these lived meanings of illness.

On the Structure of Anecdotal Stories

In the various examples of vignette-like or anecdotal stories (throughout this book), there is a certain succinctness in the style of such narratives. The following simple outline describes the methodological narrative structure of the anecdote and suggests that it can be used as a set of guidelines for writing or gathering powerful narrative material or for editing appropriate lived experience descriptions into "exemplary anecdotes" or "phenomenological vignettes."

- An anecdote is a very short and succinct story.
- An anecdote usually describes a single incident or event.
- An anecdote begins close to the central moment of the experience.
- An anecdote includes important concrete experiential details.
- An anecdote often contains several quotes (what was said, done, thought, and so on).
- An anecdote closes quickly after the climax or when the incident has passed.
- An anecdote often has an effective or "punchy" last line: it creates punctum.

Roland Barthes uses the term *punctum* when he poses the question: what it is that distinguishes a photograph from a mere snapshot? He uses the word *studium* to refer to the interest we may have in photographs. Studium is the interest we have when we open a newspaper, for example. We participate in the faces, the gestures, the actions, the events, and the situations that are depicted. The studium is in the order of liking or disliking, but not of loving; it mobilizes a half desire. It is the same interest that one takes in watching people or their clothes and that one may find "all right." To recognize the studium is to recognize the photographer's intentions, of which one may approve or disapprove.

But what breaks or punctures the studium is the punctum. The term punctum means point, sting. Actually, Barthes is not really explaining why an image is compelling, but he draws our attention to the fact that it is so and he wonders why it is so. The difference is this: studium is the interest we invest in or bring to a photograph but punctum is that what disturbs us, what disturbs the studium. "A photograph's punctum is that accident which pricks me (but also bruises me, is poignant to me)" (Barthes, 1981, p. 27). The punctum is what I bring to the photograph and "what is nonetheless already there," says Barthes (1981, p. 55).

The Power of Punctum

A telling example of the "disturbing" nature of punctum in photography is what happened to the famous photographer André Kertész. The editors of *Life* rejected Kertész's photographs when he arrived in the United States in 1937 because, they said, his images "spoke too much"; they made us reflect, suggested a meaning—a different meaning from the literal one. Ultimately, photography is subversive not when it frightens, repels, or even stigmatizes, but when it is pensive, when it thinks. The punctum of a photograph often is a "detail." And certain details of punctum may stir me. If they do, it is doubtless because the photographer has put them there intentionally. But punctum may also appear as a surprise in a photograph. In other words, there is an element of contingency at play in the punctum (and it is significant that Kertész was the first unwitting producer of candid camera).

Digital technology has made it possible to take numerous snaps of things and events in our lives. And many of these pictures are indeed just snapshots. But sometimes it may happen that a picture draws special attention to itself. There is something about it that is compelling to me, the viewer. It has punctum!

The import for phenomenological reflection and writing is that punctum also belongs to language. Thus, a text acquires punctum when an anecdote becomes a compelling narrative "example" and claims the power to stir us and to bring about an understanding that ordinary propositional discourse cannot do. It helps us to "understand" and experience something that we do not know in an intellectual sense.

Indeed, the device of anecdote can be very helpful for phenomenological research and writing. For this purpose, I have collected some additional stories from people who have experienced living with parents who suffer from Alzheimer's. I asked them to write a concrete and particular incident of their experience with their mother or father. Depending on the event and how able people are to describe an experience in detailed, concrete words, the anecdotes will vary in complexity and depth. Some stories are straightforward; other anecdotes are more intriguing.

> When my mother gets hungry she gets up and starts wandering through the house. So yesterday when she appeared hungry, I said to her: "Go to the kitchen and get something to eat from the fridge." "Yes, I will do that," she pronounced in a determined voice. But when fifteen minutes later I got to the kitchen to see how she was doing, she was just standing there. She was standing there, silent, as if sunken in thought. But was she? She did not seem to know why she was there. And yet she seemed to realize that something was wrong—as if she failed at something, as if she was supposed to do something. (RB)

An Alzheimer's sufferer may have forgotten the project, but the sense of lost purpose may linger on. As our memory fails, our projects falter also, and our sense of self fails its realization in our personhood.

My father and mother had just travelled for six hours in a bus to visit our family. And when Dad walked through the door he opened his arms and hugged me. I like it when my father gives me a big hug. I feel that I am still his little girl and that he is protective of me, even though his dementia makes him more withdrawn.

I look at this man who is my father and who has now become so unusually quiet. He almost seems like a stranger. "Hi, Dad," I say, to push off that thought, "Good to see you!" He nods but does not speak. How fragile he seems! With a shudder it strikes me that I no longer really understand my father as I always thought I did. It is as if his forgetfulness of me becomes my forgetting of who he is. Yet, I feel closer to him than ever. (JA)

When the superficialities of life get shattered, we may ironically gain a deepened sense of the self and alterity of the other. Experiential anecdotes like this may make us wonder: what happens to the self or the sense of self of a person who suffers from severe dementia? If selfhood is experienced in the things we do and in the projects in which we are always engaged, then what would selfhood "be" if one no longer has a sense of projects? More concretely, how (or to what extent) does a person suffering from pathological memory loss experience a sense of self? Is the "self" of the person with Alzheimer's who no longer recognizes friends and family members a dissolved self? Has the Alzheimer's sufferer's sense of self narrowed to the extent that projects still exist? For people who are responsible for caring for a parent or spouse with Alzheimer's, it is puzzling to see how something so essential as memory seems to erode.

Editing Experiential Stories into Anecdotes, Vignettes, Sketches

With these discussions I aim to show how phenomenological narrative stories can be powerful texts that function as phenomenological "examples" in describing a phenomenon. But experiential descriptions that are obtained through interview, written submissions, or conversations rarely possess the narrative qualities that make a text evocative, vivid, and experientially resonant. So here are some suggestions for understanding the linguistic structure underlying narrative anecdotes that may assist in making a text insightful and accessible in terms of the phenomenal meanings or themes and understandings:

- Determine sources for experiential narrative material (interviews, observations, conversations, overheard stories, written accounts, and so on) that are "examples" of the meaning aspects of the phenomenon that you study in your phenomenological project.
- After collecting such story-like material, interpret what the significant theme(s) are that seem to emerge from the narrative as you read it against the backdrop of your research question—the "lived experience phenomenon" of your study.
- Edit (rewrite) a promising narrative into a vivid anecdote by deleting extraneous or redundant material and retaining theme-relevant material. (Careful: do not overwrite, change, or distort the text.)

- If possible check or consult with the source (such as interviewee or author) of the narrative to determine iconic validity (but don't confuse iconic validity with empirical or factual validity). Ask: Does this anecdote show what an aspect of your experience is/was like?
- Next, strengthen and refine (edit) the anecdote further into the direction of the phenomenon and its theme(s).
- Ask: "Does this anecdote show what an aspect of meaning of this experience is or was like?"
- Don't forget that good writing is almost always *honing* the text through rewriting.

Finessing the Essence of the Anecdote

Here follows a lived experience description of an Alzheimer's moment. The phenomenological question is: "What is it like to experience Alzheimer's type of dementia in one's relationship with one's father or mother?"

> My father's Alzheimer's has gradually worsened. And it seems that his forgetfulness has gone through a variety of phases. Some of these are more disturbing than others. In the beginning, he often asked me the same questions or he repeated the same comments he had made just a few minutes earlier. For example, I walk into the room and he asks, "How old is Jason now? (Jason is my son, his grandson.) More recently, he started to call me by my brother's name or even by my son's name, Jason. He even seemed to confuse me with some of his old friends. And yet, whenever I visit him, he seemed happy to see me. He always looked at me with a welcoming smile. His eyes lit up when he greeted me even if he called me sometimes by my brother's name. Of course, I didn't mind. So, I joked with him and told him that I had lost some weight so he must confuse me with David, my athletic younger brother who is more handsome than I am. But yesterday, a strange thing happened when I walked in on my father. As I entered his room, he was sitting in his chair in the usual spot at the window. "Hi, Dad," I said. "How are you feeling today?" He turned and looked at me but his eyes did not show any sign of recognition. He just glanced at me. His eyes were, like, empty, you know; he did not seem to realize who I was at all. It made me feel very sad. (MV)

What seems especially striking in this story is the experience of the unrecognized look. Being looked at with empty eyes. Here follows an edited anecdote version of the above experiential account. The anecdote will focus on the look and delete material that is extraneous to this theme:

> Today my father's Alzheimer's dementia seems to have taken a dramatic turn. As I enter his room he is sitting in his usual spot at the window. "Hi, Dad," I say. "How are you today?" He turns, but he does not seem to see me. His face does not light up as it usually does. It is a strange look: with empty eyes. His eyes barely brush me: a glance without recognition. (MV)

When introductory or extraneous material is deleted, the edited anecdote will often be considerably shorter than the original account. But shortening an anecdote may assist in making it more powerful and evocative (rather than drawn out). Putting it in the present tense also helps to make the story more vivid. In a study of Alzheimer's dementia, "the look of non-recognition" could constitute a significant aspect of the Alzheimer's phenomenon. The part of the study dealing with the look does not need to be congested with other empirical details, such as forgetting names or repeating questions and comments. The latter would likely be part of separate sections of the phenomenological research text.

Now, the question could be raised whether "editing" and "rewriting" a transcript or raw text is really changing someone's words and therefore falsifying the account, making it less true. Indeed, it would be falsifying if the pre-edited text had ethnographic or factual relevance. However, what is being done phenomenologically is *fictionalizing* a factual, empirical, or an already fictional account in order to arrive at a more *plausible* description of a *possible* human experience. Indeed, phenomenological research does not aim for empirical generalizations. Rather, phenomenology aims to explore and understand a "possible" human experience, phenomenon, or event.

CHAPTER SIX

Voking Language and Experience

The term *voke* derives from vocare: to call, and from the etymology of voice, sound, language, and tone; it also means to address, to bring to speech. But the voking dimension of phenomenological method is not only to speak and produce text that demonstrates our understanding of something. When we speak, we tend to stop listening to the object about which we speak. And now this object has lost its addressive and enigmatic power. Something can only speak to us if it is listened to, if we can be addressed by it.

The voking features of a text have to do with the recognition that a text can "speak" to us, that we may experience an emotional and ethical responsiveness, that we may know ourselves addressed. There exists a relation between the writing structure of a text and the voking effects that it may have on the reader. The more vocative a text, the more strongly the meaning is embedded within it; hence, the more difficult to paraphrase or summarize the text and the felt understandings embedded within it.

There exist various vocative methods or moments through which meaning gets embodied in phenomenological language, and that causes it to be cemented more firmly in text than it would be in ordinary narrative prose: the methods of tone, lived-throughness, nearness, intensification, appeal, and answerability. It would hardly need stating that these aspects or "methods" are dimensions of writing and not methods in an instrumental sense.

1. The *evocative* function practices a perceptive address to living meaning in the act of writing. It lets the text speak to us in an addressive manner so that its reverberative meanings seduce us to attentive recognition.
2. The *revocative* function aims to bring experience vividly into presence (through the power of experiential anecdote, expressive narrative, or qualitative imagery)—so that the reader can recognize unreflectively (unmediated by reflection or thinking) these experiential possibilities of human life.
3. The *invocative* function intensifies philological aspects of the text so that the words intensify their sense and sensuous sensibility. The term "invoke" derives from invocare: to summon, to call upon, to appeal to, to implore, to conjure, to bring about, to call forth by incantation.
4. The *convocative* function aims for the text to possess the (em)pathic power to appeal—so that its life meaning speaks to, and makes a demand on, the reader.

DOI: 10.4324/9781003228073-7

5. The *provocative* function articulates the kind of ethical predicaments that are suggested in the phenomenon that is being studied, and what are the active normative responses (advice, policies, tactful practices, and so on).

The vocative aspects of phenomenology involve an aesthetic imperative, a poetizing form of writing. Most research we meet in the professional fields is of the type whereby results can be severed from the means by which the results were obtained. Phenomenological research is unlike such research in that the link with the results cannot be broken. And that is why, when you listen to a presentation of a phenomenological nature, you will listen in vain for the "finding," the "result," or the big news. Analogously, to summarize a poem in order to present the result would destroy the result because the poem itself is the result. The poem is the thing. Similarly, phenomenology, not unlike poetry, is a vocative project; it tries an incantative, evocative speaking, a primal telling.

However, phenomenological poetizing is not poetry, a making of verses. Poetizing is thinking on original experience and is thus speaking or expressive writing in a more primal sense. Language that authentically speaks the world rather than abstractly speaking of it is a language that reverberates the world; as Merleau-Ponty (1973) says, a language that sings the world. We must engage language in a primal incantation or poetizing which hearkens back to the silence from which the words emanate. What we must do is discover what lies at the ontological core of our being. So that in the words, or, perhaps better, in spite of the words, we find memories that paradoxically we never thought or felt before.

Evoking Nearness

The *evocative* gives key-words their full value (through metaphor and poetic devices such as repetition and alliteration)—so that layers of meaning get strongly embedded in the text. When concrete things are named in text in which words are evocative, then a peculiar effect may occur: its textual meaning begins to address us. We say: "this poem, this text, speaks to me!" The "speaking" of language gives us the feeling that we are brought "in touch" with something and thus "see" something in a manner that is revealing of its experiential sense. The universalizing or generalizing feature of the text is not empirical or factual but rather it has a stirring quality that involves a sentient or emotional faculty—it establishes a "feeling understanding." What happens is that the feeling understanding communicated through the presencing of language has an augmenting, enlarging effect. It produces a sense of nearness and intimacy with the phenomenon.

The result of the presencing of textual language is quite simply that the meaning becomes more proximal. In other words, the method of evocation brings things into closeness and contact. At the same time, however, the concrete experiential content of the text also renders it sensitive to the unique and the particular. And so, the evocation of meaning works in two parallel directions. The feeling understanding in the word pulls toward a sense of nearness, and the concrete image that is represented in the text pulls toward the particular.

175

The term "evoke" derives from *evocare*, to call forth, to call out—to bring to mind or recollection, to recreate imaginatively through word or image, to bring about (evoking experience through pathic means). Evoking experiential images is the manner in which human science presents data of inquiry. There is no limit to the range of approaches that one can use in bringing experience vividly into presence. But the main aim of evocative inquiry is to listen to the things that are before us, that have a hold on us through the mediating function of the evocative text.

Revoking Lived-Throughness

The term *revoke* means to recall, to bring back, to rescind. Revoking our words is to go back on our word—not to betray them, but to return to those conditions before the word fixed meaning and form to them. To abrogate the cognitive claims that words have made on us, we try to restore our contact with lived life. Gadamer uses the term *vivid* to describe the vocative aspects of language. Intuition is that immediate and imaginative phenomenological grasping or understanding of something when language moves beyond the conceptual:

> Imagination is the general capacity to have an intuition . . . even without the presence of the object . . . .
> We only praise vividness—which sets our intuitive capacities in motion—when it particularly enlivens our "symbolic" or "conceptual" understanding . . . .
> For it is here, in the use of language, in rhetoric and literature, that the concept "vivid" is truly at home: namely, as a special quality of description and narration such that we see "before us," so to speak, what is not as such seen, but is told. (Gadamer, 1986, pp. 158–163)

Through lived experience descriptions, we may bring experience vividly into presence, to fasten a hold on lived-throughness. For example, well-written and well-edited anecdotes may create for the writer and reader the experience of immersion, submersion, entanglement, propinquity, or absorption in place or time.

Invoking Intensification

The *invocative* language of a poem is characterized by *Dichtung*. Poetry, *Dichtung*, means intensification of language. The writer invokes poetic powers of language to have certain effects on the reader. Invocative words become infected or contaminated with the meanings of other words to which they stand in alliterative or repetitive relation. In writing phenomenological texts, we need to discern when and how words do this. We need to be sensitive to the ways that words and expressions may acquire a certain desirable intensity when they are composed with strongly embedded meaning.

The repeating sense of sounds tends to create a spellbinding quality. Just like beat in music, so repetition in text tends to appeal to our embodied sensibility. That is why we may be inclined to use rhythmic gestures when we read language that has recurrent patterns of some sort. In fact, speech itself is gestural in this sense. Think of rap music where words become the percussive elements. Repetition of sensed qualities, through devices such as alliteration, assonance, rhythm, and internal rhyme, contribute an acoustic richness, an audible imagery to the text. The euphonic effect of alliterative, assonant, rhythmic, or rhymed text is that it enhances the reality feeling of its implicit meaning.

As well, the creative and sometimes novel use of certain words and phrases may charge such words with special semantic meaning and mantic weight. For example, Heidegger invokes of the "thinging of things;" Merleau-Ponty speaks of "singing the world" and of the "flesh of the world;" Levinas charges the term "naked face" with significance of alterity; Marion speaks of "self-givenness" of the phenomenon that is "saturated with meaning," and so on. Such *invocative* linguistic devices tend to make words more intense, memorable, and quotable.

Convoking (Em)Pathy

A qualitative text can suddenly open up to a fundamental insight that cannot be reduced to a conceptual phrase or an intellectual statement. Instead, there is a moment of meaningfulness or sense. It is this desire for meaningfulness that is at the core of much human searching and reflection. The term *convoke* derives from *convocare*, to call together, to assemble; a convocation, a convoking—"a call together" (to remind us of what we share as humans). To convoke is to create communal ethical space. Pathic linguistic devices tend to make text more memorable, more worthy, and more capable of memorization. This is also the reason that early Greek epic tales were usually written in memorizable form.

Provoking Epiphany

The term *provoke* derives from *pro-vocare*, to call forward, to challenge; to incite, to stir up, to arouse to a feeling, to quicken, to excite. A strong vocative text tends to provoke actions. It is action sensitive, opening up the realm of the ethical. For example, a phenomenological study may show how children may experience parental divorce, or being neglected or abandoned, or how children experience recognition, and on the basis of this understanding certain actions may be recommended and certain policies may be developed. However, we need to be careful as the general insights yielded by phenomenology may not be applicable in concrete individual situations. People differ in the way they experience things, and phenomenology can only provide plausible insights.

How well do we know the inner lives and experiences of those around us? We probably know best the inner life of the people we live with: spouse, lover, siblings, and friends. And yet, we would often be mistaken if we think we know what the other person is thinking or feeling, or even how this person we know so well would experience certain situations. So, ironically we may know better the inner life of the protagonist of the novel we are reading than the person sitting beside us. Indeed, novels are so attractive because they allow us to experience the inner thoughts and feelings of others, to see what is hidden (but knowable), and also to see what is mysterious (and therefore unknowable in a direct way). To be an

177

author or reader of novels is to concern oneself with the inner worlds of people. Of course, with respect to the exterior world, the protagonist of the story only too often knows more than the reader. And the reverse is also possible, that the reader of the novel possesses crucial knowledge that is unknown to the protagonist. In some sense all narrative texts that are structured as stories depend on the intrigue of inner life and secrecy for the plot and character depiction. Thus, short stories, novels, plays, and films may make us care for the characters and stir secrets to consciousness. If people in everyday life were just an open book to one another, then texts of human narrative might lose much of their appeal.

Phenomenological and Psychological Understanding

From the perspective of professional practitioners or helping lay people (such as family members, friends, and so on), there are always two aspects to a phenomenological interest: on the one hand, there is the experiential meaning of the human phenomenon, and, on the other hand, there is the particular inner experience of this or that individual person or persons. Phenomenology, as a philosophical methodology, cannot help us to know the inner lives of particular persons. As phenomenologists, we can only focus on phenomenological understanding of possible human experiences. And yet, there is always the particular picture of the actual lifeworld where we must deal with the lives of real people.

Health science professionals must deal with the individual experiences of the patients and their families, educators must deal with the individual learning and growth experiences of their students, psychologists must deal with how particular clients experience their personal lives and social relations, and so forth. At the general level, professionals can increase their thoughtfulness by reflecting on the phenomenological meaning and significance of the experiences at stake (such as pain, grief, difficulty, anxiety, loneliness, and so forth); but at the level of everyday thinking and acting, the helping professional or lay person (family member, friend, relative) also needs to know, as well as possible, how this or that child or adult experiences a specific moment or special incident. In concrete and practical relations and situations, these two types of understanding (phenomenology and psychology) cannot really be separated. They are provoked and grasped together—and enacted in the present instant of each moment, as thoughtfulness and tact.

Textual Tone and Aspect Seeing

Texts may carry tone in a variety of forms. Again, this is most readily shown with poetry. A poem that is only read as message does not speak to us, though it may present certain ideas, information, or meaning. But as soon as we read a vocative poem (especially a lyric poem) with a certain interpretive-reflective attentiveness, then another kind of meaning appears to fill its lines. We may call this the inner meaning of a poem as compared to the outer meaning that we gain from reading it for information.

Inner meaning is characteristic of all phenomenological texts. Indeed, when we say that human science method involves eidetic reflection, it is because *eidos* means essence or inner meaning. Thoughtful reflection aims to bring out the inner meaning of something. Interestingly, Heidegger (1977) points out that the Greek term *eidos* originally refers to "the outward aspect" that an object offers to the physical eye. He notes, however, that Plato used the term *eidos* in quite an extraordinary manner to refer not just to the outer but to the inner, nonphysical feature of the object that one perceives. And Heidegger goes a step further by stating that eidos names not only the nonsensuous aspect of what is physically visible: "Aspect names and also is that which constitutes the essence in the audible, the tasteable, the tactile, in everything that is in any way accessible" (1977, p. 301). So, while the terms *eidos* and *aspect* are related to "appearance, face, countenance, presence" (aspect derives from *aspicere*, to look at), on closer inspection what we see in a face or what we find present in a text is less the outward particularities than the dawning experience of recognition that the external appearance makes possible. This dawning of meaning, due to the special textual appearance, is the work of the tone of the text. In passing, what is interesting for us here is that this visual notion of meaning as aspect is perceived as an auditory notion of tonal meaning in a phenomenological text.

Not all texts invite to be read with tone. For example, ordinary newspaper clippings or formal scientific reports are unlikely to contain tone, and it would be silly to try to read a normal piece of information with poetic sensitivity. Tone creates attunement, a heightened sensitivity to the invoked object. So, to be read with tone, a text must have been written in such a manner that it potentially carries tonal qualities. And thus, it happens that when we orient ourselves to the tone of such a text, then it suddenly acquires a meaning that it did not seem to possess before. Moreover, the meaning that is invoked in this reading is not ordinary informational meaning. Here I will call this "poetic meaning" and suggest that it is not necessarily present in all poetry or only in poetry. The poem, after all, is itself a cultural discourse, a literary invention or genre.

The point is that any text that contains poetic meaning shares with poetry that it can "speak" to us in a vocative manner that we experience as particularly striking or thoughtful, though it may be difficult to pin down wherein this thoughtfulness resides. Phenomenological text, too, tends to contain poetic or vocative meanings, and the text as a whole sets itself the task of letting us "see" this implicative meaning in an explicative manner.

Aspect Seeing

Wittgenstein uses the term "aspect" to refer to a special quality of meaning in text. He discusses how something can acquire meaning, and he distinguishes two uses of the word seeing: physical and nonphysical seeing. In addition to simply seeing this or that, says Wittgenstein, it happens that I suddenly "see" the presence of something. For example, I may see a face and notice a resemblance with the face of another person. What happens is that I "see" one person in the face of another: "I contemplate a face, and then suddenly notice its likeness to another. I *see* that it has not changed; and yet I see it differently. I call this experience 'noticing an aspect,'" says Wittgenstein (1968, p. 193e).

The experience of "noticing as aspect" occurs when we suddenly see something new in what we observe or look at. Sometimes we meet someone whom we have not seen for years, but we do not yet know this and simply look at a stranger. But then, suddenly, we realize that we know this person. We see in the unfamiliar face aspects that are familiar, and so we ask: Are you Jan who took a class with me some 15 years ago?

It can also happen that we look at something and then someone points out how this object can be seen differently. Wittgenstein uses the picture of a duck that can also be seen as the image of a rabbit. It seems like a magic trick. Wittgenstein asks: where does this rabbit come from? Yes, to our surprise the duck has changed into a rabbit! We realize that the picture did not change, and yet, suddenly, we are able to see something in it that we did not see before.

Dawning Aspect

Another important point is that with this change something else has changed as well: we have learned to look at this duck as a picture that can be seen in terms of different images. Whereas before we simply saw a duck and did not even think of the duck as "a picture of a duck," now we have become reflectively aware of the interpretive possibilities of this image: of seeing it one way or another (for a clarifying discussion, see Mulhall, 1993). An element of ambiguity has been introduced. And so, when we look at the picture, we cannot help but see a duck and also, upon a slight shift of focus, we see a rabbit. Wittgenstein calls this phenomenon dawning of an aspect. Dawning occurs especially in the cleverly constructed images of psychological projection tests such as the Rorschach. What do you see: a vase or two faces? A young woman or an old woman's face? What do you see in these inkblots?

The interesting fact about the experience of a dawning aspect is that it may disappear when we regard it somewhat longer. For example, I am walking home in the dark evening and suddenly I see a man stand and look at me from ahead down the street. I keep uncomfortably aware of his presence until, as I get closer to the place where he stands, I notice to my relief that it is only the menacing shape of a bush that I mistook for a human figure. Another example of the dawning of aspect is the accidental greeting; the mistake we make in greeting an acquaintance who, upon closer looking, turns out to be a stranger. Somewhat embarrassed we apologize: "I'm sorry; I thought you were someone else."

The question is, how can text acquire meaning that overflows its ordinary informational sense? First, one must expect that the reader is sensitive to the inner meaning that text sometimes acquires. Second, something must be expected of the text as well. For example, Wittgenstein (1968) examines the effects of the pathic or expressive intonation with which words can be read. He focuses especially on the tone in uttering single words. And he focuses on the expressive quality of the sound in giving voice to words. Of course, the experience of dawning of meaning can involve an entire sentence, or a phrase, or a passage, or a stanza, or an entire poem, or story. Moreover, the tone of a text depends on more than the gestural sound quality in terms of which it is expressed.

The tone of a text is influenced by a variety of linguistic factors that can be studied but that cannot always easily be controlled. In addition to the structure of the text, there also is the situational context that affects the tone of texts. All kinds of examples spring to mind: there is the eloquent sermon in the church, the touching eulogy at a funeral, the moving plea of a grieving parent, the memorable proverb that we recall from a grandparent, the seductive allusion whispered by a lover.

Still, the question as to the nature of the phenomenon of dawning remains elusive. Seeing different meaning in an image seems to have to do with what is on the outside (the picture) as well as with what is on the inside (the inner life of the person who looks at the picture). On the one hand, one cannot completely control the dawning experience. The possibility of having a dawning experience seems to be a function of the way one regards something (Mulhall, 1993).

In seeing an aspect, one is neither totally passive nor totally active. Wittgenstein suggests that the imagination is somehow involved. Indeed, we meet people who simply seem to lack the ability to "see" an aspect—they don't seem able to "imagine it." Wittgenstein compares the person who is "aspect blind" to the person who lacks a "musical ear" (1968, p. 214e). Both can "get" one kind of meaning but not another. One is deaf to the tonal qualities of the text, and therefore one is unable to read the text with "meaning." This is true for poetry as well. Most people are able to read the explicit or stated meaning of words, but not all people can or want to "read" poetry. Perhaps some people are insensitive (blind, deaf, indifferent, or numb) to the pathic undertones of a poetic text.

So, the next step is to realize that words, too, carry this possibility of the aspect dawning experience. And Wittgenstein himself uses poetry as an example: "When I read a poem or narrative with feeling, surely something goes on in me which does not go on when I merely skim the lines for information" (1968, p. 214e). When reading with a certain tone, words become completely filled with meaning that transcends the informational content of the text. Wittgenstein, therefore, makes a distinction between what he calls primary and secondary meaning. Most people have little difficulty with the primary meaning of a text, but the secondary meaning is not always easily dealt with. Primary meaning is the informational content that is more or less public and follows the denotative dictionary sense of a text. Secondary meaning can only be grasped when the reader is first of all competent at the level of primary reading, but then an additional competence seems required for grasping inner or secondary meaning.

Aspect Blindness or Meaning Blindness

To reiterate, understanding a text at the level of the secondary meaning first of all requires that one can read the primary meaning of the text. Is it possible that some readers are aspect blind to the special meaning of a poem? In this context Mulhall speaks of "meaning blindness" (Mulhall, 1993, p. 35). But, of course, the blindness toward the inner meaning of a text also has tonal, sentient, and tactile dimensions. Can a poem be understood if one only attends to the informational content of the text? These may be rhetorical questions, and yet they are important because they suggest that it is possible to be "numb" to the transcendent meaning of poetry, and, yes, also, of phenomenological text. To be numb to the poetic meaning of a text implies that one sees no difference between the inner and the outer. But it is always possible that people can be taught how to perceive the tone of the text. Perhaps, when a text is strong enough, it may have the effect of eliciting such perceptiveness. This would be a pedagogical feature of phenomenological text: to sensitize readers to the meanings inherent in the tone of a text. The methodological point is that, in phenomenological writing, one needs to work with both kinds of tonalities: the outer and inner, primary and secondary meaning in texts.

We need to consider something more about tone. For students of English literature, every text has tone: a work may have a tone that is formal, informal, intimate, solemn, somber, playful, serious, ironic, condescending, or any of many possible attitudes. Similarly, a newspaper article tends to have an informative tone, while a textbook might have a didactic tone, and so on. However, our distinction here is somewhat different. We use the notion of tone to distinguish between two kinds of meaning. This is most easily demonstrated with poetry, although it is true for other kinds of text as well.

So, there are two ways of reading a poem: we may read it for its message or read it for its tone. At first, this seems a rather common-sense observation about intonation. Intonation is a function of the inflective sensitivities of "voice and feeling" with which something is read; thus, a good orator can read with tone and also add tone to a text. But even in this common case, tone is not just an acoustic affair; it has to do with meaning and felt experience. And so, when we read with tone in a phenomenological sense, then we read for the tonal meaning that the text must be able to offer. The same is true for writing. When we create text with tone, then we hope that the reader will be affected by it. We experience the tone of text not unlike the way we experience the captivating effect of a compelling musical score or even a catchy tune. Like musical tone, so textual tone may leave visceral and corporeal tracts. We are literally impressed by it and affected by it; we cannot let go of its enchanting quality. In Steiner's words: "we are answerable to the text, to the work of art, to the musical offering, in a very specific sense, at once moral, spiritual, and psychological" (1989, p. 8). The special effect that phenomenological tone aims for is epiphanic; it is meant to touch our understanding of life's meaning that we experience as meaning in life.

Poetic Language: When the Word Becomes Image

So, the phenomenological example (anecdote, story) does not express what one knows but, in an evocative manner, lets one experience what one does not know. When we present an anecdote in a phenomenological text, the sense of the text aspires to become an image. In other words, a phenomenological text aims to *explicate* as well as poetically *invoke* the phenomenological intuition.

In the introduction to *The Poetics of Space*, Bachelard employs the phenomenon of the "poetic image" to refer to that special epiphanic quality of language that brings about, in the reader, what he calls a phenomenological reverberation

(1964a, p. xxiii). The power of phenomenological texts lies precisely in this resonance that the word can affect in our understanding, including those reaches of understanding that are somehow prediscursive and noncognitive, and thus less accessible to conceptual and intellectual thought. In describing the poetic image, Bachelard creates an epiphanic image of image that is phenomenologically subtle and evocative:

> The resonances [of a poetic image] are dispersed on the different planes of our life in the world, while the repercussions invite us to give greater depth to our own existence. In the resonance we hear the poem, in the reverberations we speak it, it is our own. The reverberations bring about a change of being . . . the poem possesses us entirely. This grip that poetry acquires on our very being bears a phenomenological mark that is unmistakable.
>
> After the original reverberation, we are able to experience resonances, sentimental repercussions, reminders of our past. But the image has touched the depths before it stirs the surface [of our being or self]. And this is also true of a simple experience of reading. The image offered us by reading the poem now becomes really our own. It takes roots in us. It has been given us by another, but we begin to have the impression that we could have created it, that we should have created it. It becomes a new being in our language, expressing us by making us what it expresses; in other words, it is at once a becoming of expression, and a becoming of our being. Here expression creates being. (1964a, p. xix)

Bachelard's description of the vocative power of the poetic image speaks to the need for phenomenological writing. In the composing of texts, the creative contingent positioning of words may give rise to invoked images that can move us: inform us by forming us and thus leave an effect on us. Or, as Bachelard puts it, the reverberations bring about a change of being, of our personhood (1964a, p. xviii). In this moment of invocation, language touches us in the soul, says Gadamer (1996). The image presents an intuition: an immediate grasping of something that is presented with poetic vividness.

We only praise vividness—which sets our intuitive capacities in motion—when it particularly enlivens our "symbolic" or "conceptual" understanding.

For it is here, in the use of language, in rhetoric and literature, that the concept "vivid" is truly at home: namely, as a special quality of description and narration such that we see "before us," so to speak, what is not as such seen, but is told (Gadamer, 1986, p. 163).

The Image as a Phenomenological Device

Still, the notion of the image as a phenomenological device is enigmatic and resists clear definition. The essence of image as a phenomenological device is neither some representational figure depicting the likeness or resemblance of something or someone, nor is the image the visual copy of an original to which it is mimetically related. The image that we meet in a vocative phenomenological text is an alluring figure of speech that triggers the imaginary faculty. Image enriches the sense of a text with the depth of meaning that invokes the ineffable quality of lived experience. Thus, when a text images (becomes image), it acquires (in)audibility, (in)visibility, and the (in)sensitivity of touch. If not, the phenomenological text would remain incapable of communicating the concrete lived-throughness of lived experience.

> Sense requires the image in order to emerge from its meagre material, its inaudibility and its invisibility. Sense requires sound, line, and figure, without which it is as abstract and fugitive as the movement of a needle through the stitches of a piece of lace. (Nancy, 2005, p. 67)

The image often possesses aesthetic or poetic significance, as in Bachelard's description. But in everyday experience, the encounter with an image may just be an ordinary experience that has, in spite of its ordinariness, an allusive illusionary quality. For example, I may be walking somewhere and unexpectedly discern a visual image that makes me think of something or someone and that gives me an emotional sensibility of recognition. Or, I may be listening to something or someone, and I feel that I have been captured by a certain feeling or emotion that is somehow evoked, not by the semantic meaning of the words I am hearing, but by their mantic or expressive effects. This mantic meaning of words may present itself when listening to a song whose lyrics are heard not for their content but for their mantic effect. In such case, the words of the singer have become a sound that fuses with the other instruments of the musical piece.

So, it happens that in reading or writing, the propositional or conceptual semantics of a text may rupture so that an image breaks through and touches us with a new kind of knowing or understanding: the word has turned into image. The image is not some picture, but the evocative understanding ignited by the image. When Heidegger reflects on the meaning of Hölderlin's verse phrase "poetically man dwells," he shows how for Hölderlin, poetry provides us with a measure of what it means to dwell on the earth. Of course, the term measure for the poet does not refer to some number or measure in a calculative sense. In Heidegger's words, "the *nature* of measure is no more a quantum than is the *nature* of number. True we can reckon with numbers—but not with the nature of number" (1971a, p. 224). So, measure refers to the awesome sensibility of the experience of the immensity and mystery of the sky above. But this sensibility cannot be contained or expressed in ordinary language. Only when the words turn into image may we imagine the elusive meaning of what is intended.

> But the poet calls all the brightness of the sights of the sky and every sound of its courses and breezes into the singing word and there makes them shine and ring. Yet the poet, if he is a poet, does not describe the mere appearance of sky and earth. The poet calls, in the sights of the sky, that which in the very self-disclosure causes the appearance of that which conceals itself, and indeed *as* that which conceals itself. In the familiar appearances, the poet calls the alien as that to which the invisible imparts itself in order to remain what it is—unknown. (Heidegger, 1971a, p. 225)

This is where Heidegger introduces the notion of image to show that when language has turned into image, the poetic word can make the invisible visible:

> Our current name for the sight and appearance of something is "image." The nature of the image is to let something be seen . . . because poetry takes that mysterious measure, to wit, in the face of the sky, therefore it speaks in "images." This is why poetic images are imaginings in a distinctive sense: not mere fancies and illusions but imaginings that are visible inclusions of the alien in the sight of the familiar. (1971a, p. 226)

Thus, Heidegger speaks of "the poetic saying of images" (2001, p. 226). An "image" presents meaning immediately: we grasp meaning directly by an act of intuition. Language can transform into image if the words assume literary or poetical allusive power.

The Cognitive and the Pathic

The notion of the pathic is useful in understanding how phenomenological text produces a certain kind of noncognitive understanding: pathic knowledge that corresponds to a pathic acting. The etymon of the term pathic is the Latin pathicus. And the etymology (dating back to 1600s) of the noun pathicism and the classical pathicus includes patience and passivity, such as submitting to sexual intercourse, which was used of both men and women. The *Oxford English Dictionary* currently defines pathic as: "Involving feeling, perception, or intuition, rather than cognition or deliberation." In this book the notion of pathic is used to the extent that the act of practice depends on the sense and sensuality of the body: personal presence, relational perceptiveness, tact for knowing what to say and do in contingent situations, thoughtful routines and practices, and other aspects of knowledge that are in part prereflective, and yet thoughtful—full of thought. If we wish to further study and enhance such pathic dimensions of practice, we need a convocative language that can express and communicate these understandings. Pathic texts need to remain oriented to the experiential or lived sensibility of the lifeworld. For example, experiential stories provide opportunities for evoking and reflecting on practice. Eugene Gendlin suggests that this kind of understanding is not cognitive in the usual sense. He says: "It is sensed or felt, rather than thought—and it may not even be sensed or felt directly with attention" (Gendlin, 1988, p. 45).

The term "pathic" implicates forms of expressive understanding that we call empathic and sympathic. Empathy and sympathy are usually discussed as certain types of relational understandings that involve imaginatively placing oneself in someone else's shoes, feeling what the other person feels, understanding the other from a distance (telepathy), or, more generally, to be understandingly engaged in other people's lives. But these relational linguistic notions also open up ways of thinking about expressivity and forms of understanding that are more mantic than semantic. No doubt, there are various forms and modalities of pathic understanding. But the first important point is that the terms empathy and sympathy suggest that this understanding is not primarily gnostic, cognitive, intellectual, technical—but rather that it is, indeed, pathic: involving the emotions, the body, the poetic, the pathetic, and the pathically inspired.

Gnosticism was the belief that reason was the proper device to teach and practice religion; and the gnostic attitude in professional fields holds that professional practice can be defined by rationalistic factors and gnostic knowledge. For example, medical science is the discipline where diagnostic and prognostic knowledge is the dominant knowledge form. Pathic knowledge is more difficult to understand, since it refers to the immediately felt presence of experience. While *gnostic* pertains to knowledge and implies judgment, maxim, and opinion; *pathic* pertains to pathos, meaning the quality that arouses experiential understanding.

The term pathic derives from pathos, meaning "suffering and also passion." Pathic expressiveness is not to be confused with phatic expressiveness. And yet, phatic comes from *phanein*, to show oneself, to appear. So, there is a phenomenological sensibility to phatic expression that present a person's presence to others. The phenomenological notion of pathic and phatic words and expressions raises the question of the limits and possibilities of the communicability of language. Jean-Luc Nancy relates the pathic to the fragment and the secret symbolism of language:

> Thus, it is, for example, that we share the secret of language as something more remote than language itself—but nowhere else than exposed on the flowering surface of language. Or again, for another example, the secret, doubtless inseparable from the preceding one, of the communicability that one would have to call "pathic," communicability by means of "empathy," "sympathy," "pathetic," a secret more remote than all determinate pathos, the secret of pathic ambivalence. (1997, p. 136)

In a larger life context, the pathic refers to the general mood, sensibility, sensuality, and felt sense of being in the world. Alphonso Lingis would say that there is pathic intelligibility in sensual sensibility (Lingis, 1996). The pathically tuned body recognizes itself in its responsiveness to the things of our world and to the others who share our world or break into our world. The pathic sense perceives the world in a feeling or emotive modality of knowing and being. Buytendijk (1970b) draws a close relation between the pathic experience and the mood of the lived body. Similarly, Heidegger uses the notion of *Befindlichkeit* to refer to this sense that we have of ourselves in situations. Literally *Befindlichkeit* means "the way one finds oneself" in the world (Heidegger, 1962, pp. 172–188). We have an implicit, felt understanding of ourselves in situations, even though it is difficult sometimes to put that understanding into words.

A phenomenological text should never be read merely for its explicit meaning. The pathic sense of the text is directly related to the meaning that phenomenology attempts to evoke. The pathognomy of a text refers to its signifying power to express deeper emotive meaning. But the pathognomic aspects of text cannot be explicated in straightforward conceptual terms. Pathic meaning is something that is part of the experience of language in everyday life. We experience the pathic sense of a text when it suddenly "speaks" to us in a manner that validates our experience, when it conveys an evidential understanding or truth that stirs our sensibilities.

It is much easier for us to teach concepts and informational knowledge than it is to bring about pathic understandings. But herein lies the strength of a phenomenology of practice. It is through pathic significations and images, accessible through phenomenological texts that speak to us and make a demand on us, that the more noncognitive dimensions of our professional practice may also be communicated, internalized, and reflected upon. For this we need to develop a phenomenology that is sensitive to the thoughtfulness required in contingent, ethical, and relational situations.

Second, it is much easier to describe the cognitive than the pathic aspects of our world. For the sake of making a somewhat oversimplified distinction, the cognitive aspects are the conceptual, objective, measurable features of something. For example, we may describe an architectural or physical space, such as a school or church, in terms of its dimensional properties and measures. But such spaces also have their atmospheric, sensual, transcendental, spiritual, and felt aspects. Moreover, these pathic qualities are not fixed but subject to change like moods of a landscape. In this sense, we can speak of the pathic sphere of a school, a classroom, an office, a hospital, or any environment where professional practitioners work agogically (in service, teaching, healing, helping, counseling, or ministering relations) with others.

Much research starts from the assumption that knowledge is cognitive, and thus it already passes over other, more pathic forms of knowing that may actually constitute a major dimension of our experience and practice. In the early 1960s, the psychologist Erwin Straus (1966) wrote that in the human and social sciences it has always been the intellectual or cognitive factors and never the pathic facets that have been studied and researched. By pathic he meant the immediate or unmediated and preconceptual relation we have with the things of our world.

Straus himself did not develop or expand on the notion of the pathic. So, it may be worthwhile to do so in this text. While the word *pathic* has rarely, if ever, been systematically explored, certain aspects of meaning underlying pathic knowledge are not new. There has been increased attention given to the phenomenology of the body in human sensibilities, such as Pallasmaa's *The Thinking Hand* (2009) and *The Eyes of the Skin* (2005). From a phenomenological point of view, it can even be argued that the whole body itself is pathic. Thus, "the body knows" how to do things, such that, if we wanted to gain intellectual control of this "knowledge," we might in fact hamper our ability to do the things we are doing—of course, these include routines, habits, motor skills and memories, conventions, rules, and so on.

Merleau-Ponty (1962) describes the body-subject (*corps sujet*) in terms of the access it provides to our world. But it could also be argued that such pathic knowledge does not only inhere in the body but also in the things of our world, in the situation(s) in which we find ourselves, and in the very relations that we maintain with others and the things around us. For example, pathic "knowledge" also expresses itself in the confidence with which we do things, the way that we "feel" the atmosphere of a place, the manner in which we can "read" someone's face, and so forth. Knowledge inheres in the world already in such a way that it enables our embodied practices.

The pathic dimensions of practice are pathic precisely because they reside or resonate in the body, in our relations with others, in the things of our world, and in our very actions. These are the corporeal, relational, temporal, situational, and actional kinds of knowledge that cannot necessarily be translated back or captured into conceptualizations and theoretical representations. In other words, there are modes of knowing that inhere so immediately in our lived practices—in our body, in our relations, and in the things around us—that they seem invisible.

However, knowledge does manifest itself in practical actions. And we may "discover" what we know in how we act and in what we can do, in the things of our world, in our relations with others, in our embodied being, and in the temporal dimensions of our involvements. Even our gestures, the way we smile, the tone of our voice, the tilt of our head, and the way we look the other in the eye are expressive of the ways we know our world and comport ourselves in this world. On the one hand, our actions are sedimented into habituations, routines, kinesthetic memories. We do things in response to the rituals of the situation in which we find ourselves. On the other hand, our actions are sensitive to the contingencies, novelties, and expectancies of our world.

Thus, we may distinguish several modalities of knowing that are noncognitive in a pathic sense. We feel that our knowing resides in our actions, situations, relations, and, of course, our bodies. And phenomenologically that is indeed the case. In our daily living we experience our knowing in how and what to do through our actions, through the situations in which we find ourselves, through our relations with others and the world around us, and through our embodied being or corporeal existence:

1. In actional knowing we feel that our knowledge resides in our actions: knowledge is action. In a sense we discover what we know, in how we act, in what we can do. This actional knowledge is experienced as confidence in acting, as personal style, as practical tact, and also as habituations, routines, kinesthetic memories, and so on.

2. In situational knowing we feel that our knowledge resides in the context of the things of our world. Indeed, we discover what we know and who we are through the things around us and in the things that belong to us and to which we belong. This situational knowledge is experienced as the way we know ourselves through space, the objects, the contingencies of our daily existences. We experience situations by way of recognition, memory, feeling at home, familiar mood, and so on.

3. In relational knowing we feel that our knowledge resides in relations. We discover what we know in our relations with others, for example, as relations of shared experience, trust, recognition, intimacy; as relations of dependence, dominance, equality, expertise, and so forth. In some relations, we feel comfortable, sure of ourselves, and in discussions with others we may surprise ourselves with how much we know, what we can say, and so on. It may also happen that in some relational circumstances, we feel uncomfortable, unsure of ourselves, and awkward. Most of us may have experienced teachers with whom we felt bright and knowledgeable, while with other teachers we felt insecure and stupid.

4. In corporeal knowing we feel that our knowledge resides in our corporeal being. We discover what we know in our immediate corporeal sense of things

and others, and as in our gestures, demeanor, and so on. We trust the body in our daily living and our activities. Thanks to our body knowledge and body memories, we can confidently pick up a hot teapot and pour the drink without spilling. Our body knows how to move around in familiar spaces and places, and how to drive the car in routine traffic. Corporeal knowing also expresses itself in the smell of the city in which we live, the particular smell of the autumn leaves under our feet, the familiar smell of supper in our kitchen at home.

All these modalities of noncognitive or pathic knowing intermingle in our everyday existence. But ordinary cognitive discourses are not well suited to address noncognitive dimensions of professional experience. A pathic language is needed in order to evoke and reflect on pathic meanings. Pathic understanding requires a language that is sensitive to the experiential, moral, emotional, and personal dimensions of professional life (van Manen, 1991).

Protagonists and Practices:
A Tradition of Traditions

CHAPTER SEVEN

On the Way to Phenomenology: Precursors

Each genuinely new phenomenological tradition instigated by an original thought or thinker is made possible by the continuous creativity of phenomenology itself. Phenomenological inquiry is characterized by a tension between order and disorder, system and openness, passivity and activity, and analysis and imagination, which is the single methodological theme inherent in all phenomenologies. Phenomenology is radically dynamic because its methodology is ordered on a radical disorder. The *order* of inquiry is a function of the methodical rigor of the reduction. And the *disorder* of inquiry is caused by the demand of the epoché that seeks to free itself from all constraints and prior presumptions that may contaminate the operation of the reduction. This tension and play between reduction and epoché, order and disorder, carries the imperative of continuous creativity: for phenomenology to constantly and creatively rethink its program and practices. It is this dynamic impulse of continuous creativity that is to blame for the fact that phenomenology as a tradition never has its house in order, so to speak. Phenomenological priorities and practices are constantly being ordered, disordered, and re-ordered.

A new order is formed by new original questions initiated by creative and critical thinkers whose works are subsequently passed down by followers and interpreters. For example, in France, Husserl's thinking was initially introduced by Emmanuel Levinas. But later Levinas himself formulated an entirely new way of pursuing phenomenology that became a Levinassian orientation with numerous followers and interpreters. Sartre also developed his unique existential approach to phenomenology that extended the thinking of Husserl and Heidegger.

While Husserl is generally seen as the founder of modern phenomenology, there are some precursors whose works are critical as a backdrop for understanding certain themes of the practice of phenomenology. These are especially René Descartes, Immanuel Kant, Georg Wilhelm Friedrich Hegel, and Friedrich Nietzsche.

Famous Dreams: René Descartes

René Descartes was born in La Haye, France, in 1596. His mother died when he was barely one year old, so he was brought up by his maternal grandparents. At the age of 11 years, he was sent to a Jesuit college in La Fleche, and at 18 he had completed the usual studies that included a broad range of subjects, such as mathematics, history, philosophy, astronomy, and medicine. Next, Descartes obtained a

DOI: 10.4324/9781003228073-9

law degree and lived in Paris for a few years. Subsequently, he moved to the Netherlands, where his interest in mathematics and science was reawakened. Descartes contributed importantly to a great variety of scientific developments and discoveries. For example, he invented mathematical techniques for calculating geometrical lines and angles that prepared the way for the formation of algebra.

In 1619, Descartes joined the army of Prince (Maurits) Maurice of Nassau, as gentleman soldier—which means that he never really sees battle but takes advantage of the travel. Increasingly he becomes preoccupied with a certain pathos for mathematics, and he wonders how it may be possible to find a basis for any knowledge to be true, certain, and precise. In 1619, he is stationed for the winter in Neuberg, Bavaria. He has a small room where he spends his time. But the questions about truth and science continue to plague him. One November evening, he settles down to find comfort as the room is being heated by a woodstove.

Then it happens. In his preoccupied state of mind, he suddenly is struck by a mental vision: a flash of insight of the unification of all science (all forms of knowledge) founded on indubitable thought. It seems that the many weeks of being haunted by restlessness has yielded to this sudden insight—this pregnant desire of overcoming the scholasticism of his time keeps his mind buzzing for the remaining parts of the evening. But he is still confused. That night, when he finally goes to bed tired, he has three dreams (see Davis and Hirsh, 2005). In the first dream he is caught in a terrible whirlwind while being terrified by phantoms. He feels weak and has great difficulty resisting the push of the wind when all of a sudden, the wind abates and turns quiet—and then he is presented with a melon. In the second dream, he is startled by the booming noises of very loud thunderbolts and by fire sparks flying around his room. He thinks that the sparks are produced by the stove, but when he wakes he finds his room quiet.

When he goes back to sleep, he experiences a third dream that is serene and meditative. He notices an anthology of poetry on the table. As he lifts the cover, it falls open at a verse by Ausonius, "*Quod vitae sectabor iter*" (What path shall I take in life). Then a stranger appears and quotes him a different verse, "*Est et non*" (What is and is not). Descartes becomes agitated and feverishly pages through the book and tries to show the strange visitor the first poem, but he can no longer find it. Instantly, the stranger disappears and Descartes wakes up, disturbed and puzzled.

Now, Descartes tries to interpret the significance of the dreams. He decides that the first dream was centered on an evil genie that tried to deceive him. The thunderbolts of the second dream are evidence of the spirit of truth aiming to awake him to the passion of thinking. The poem of the third dream tells him that he is at a crossroads and must decide what to do with his life. The "*Est et non*" poem shows him that he must separate what is true from what is false in human knowledge. These dreams, together with the flash of insight about a unified science that occurred to him the previous evening, point to the pathos of Descartes' subsequent philosophic quest.

Descartes became most famously known for his pathbreaking work in philosophy and metaphysics that eventually earned him the reputation of being the originator of modern philosophy. In 1637 he published *Discourse on the Method of Rightly Conducting the Reason, and Seeking Truth in the Sciences*. In 1641 he published *The Meditations on First Philosophy*. In 1649, *The Passions of the Soul* was published. Readers who know these texts may have become spellbound by Descartes' seductively compelling style. Note how in the *Method* he starts by charming his readers with a self-deprecating flair before easing them into fascinating trains of thought:

> In my own case, I have never presumed that my mind was in any way more perfect than that of the average person. Indeed, I have often wished that my thoughts were as quick, or my imagination as clear and distinct, or my memory as prompt as some others. (2003, p. 6)

Even people who have never read Descartes know that he coined the famous (or infamous) phrase *"Je pense, donc je suis"* (I think, therefore I exist). He is the thinker who set himself the task of putting aside any belief and any presumption that can be doubted, whether the belief is obtained through sensory observation or through logical deduction. He said, "in order to seek truth, it is necessary once in the course of our life, to doubt, as far as possible, all things" (2003, p. 15). Descartes' methodical doubt began with the resolve to avoid all possible prejudice and precipitancy, and thus:

> never to accept anything as true if I did not know clearly that it was so; that is, carefully to avoid prejudice and jumping to conclusions, and to include nothing in my judgements apart from whatever appeared so clearly and distinctly to my mind that I had no opportunity to cast doubt on it. (2003, p. 16)

Descartes arrives at the conclusion that the only thing he could not doubt is that he was doubting (in other words, thinking). His famous line has turned into a popular proverb: "I think, therefore I am"; in Latin: *cogito ergo sum*.

> Thus, because our senses sometimes deceive us, I decided to assume that nothing was the way the senses made us imagine it. And since there are some people who make mistakes in reasoning and commit logical fallacies, even in the simplest geometrical proofs, and since I thought that I was as subject to mistakes as anyone else, I rejected as false all the arguments that I had previously accepted as demonstrations. Finally, since I thought that we could have all the same thoughts, while asleep, as we have while we are awake, although none of them is true at that time, I decided to pretend that nothing that ever entered my mind was any more true than the illusions of my dreams. But I noticed, immediately afterwards, that while I thus wished to think that everything was false, it was necessarily the case that I, who was thinking this, was something. When I noticed that this truth "I think, therefore I am" was so firm and certain that all the most extravagant assumptions of the sceptics were unable to shake it, I judged that I could accept it without scruple as the first principle of the philosophy for which I was searching. (2003, pp. 24, 25)

So, the starting point for Descartes' method of coming to certain knowledge about his "self" is his own existence: the self is a "thing that thinks." But as he reflects further on whatever is needed for understanding what the self consists of, he realizes that he can imaginatively pretend that he has no body, and similarly he can pretend that there is no world—and still the self would exist as a "thing that thinks," as *res cogitans*.

> Then, when I was examining what I was, I realized that I could pretend that I had no body, and that there was no world nor any place in which I was present, but I could not pretend in the same way that I did not exist. On the contrary, from the very fact that I was thinking of doubting the truth of other things, it followed very evidently and very certainly that I existed; whereas if I merely ceased to think, even if all the rest of what I had ever imagined were true, I would have no reason to believe that I existed. I knew from this that I was a substance, the whole essence or nature of which was to think and which, in order to exist, has no need of any place and does not depend on anything material. Thus, this self—that is, the soul by which I am what I am—is completely distinct from the body and is even easier to know than it, and even if the body did not exist the soul would still be everything that it is. (2003, p. 25)

This thought that the self (soul or mind) is completely distinct from the body has been widely regarded as Descartes fundamental mistake: separating the mind from the body. He is the philosopher who is blamed for the legacy of mind–body dualism—an idea that is now deeply embedded in our everyday sensibility and yet we know is problematic. As his writings were published, there were already objections and questions raised that Descartes was separating the mind from the body. If the mind and body are different substances, then how could it be that in our everyday experiences they seem completely connected, integrated, and interacting?

Now, Descartes was apparently dismayed at this misunderstanding, and he stressed that he was not saying that the body and mind were separate but merely that they were "distinct." Being distinct does not imply separate. Furthermore, in his fascinating reflections on *The Passions of the Soul* (1989), Descartes shows over and over again how body and mind are intricately interconnected and how the state of the body will influence the state of the mind or soul. However, the view that Descartes had attempted to prove the duality of body and mind in his *Discourse on Method* (2003) and *The Principles of Philosophy* (2012) has persisted until the present, though some philosophers have attempted to rescue Descartes from the "excessive interpretation" of his metaphysical dualism by his critics (see, for example, Afloroaei, 2010).

In spite of all the controversy about the mind–body dualism issue, Descartes has had a profound influence on philosophy. And, with respect to phenomenology, he has especially inspired Husserl in the development of his transcendental phenomenology and the method of the epoché and the reduction. What for Descartes was the method of doubt became for Husserl the epoché. But, of course, these notions are nevertheless very different. When Husserl is invited by the Académie Française to present his lectures about his phenomenology in the Amphithéâtre Descartes, at the Sorbonne in Paris, he goes out of his way to acknowledge the importance of the thinking of Descartes:

I have particular reason for being glad that I may talk about transcendental phenomenology in this, the most venerable abode of French science. France's greatest thinker, René Descartes gave transcendental phenomenology new impulses through his *Meditations*; their study acted quite well on the transformation of an already developed phenomenology into a new kind of transcendental phenomenology. Accordingly, one might almost call transcendental phenomenology a neo-Cartesianism, even though it is obliged—and precisely by its radical development of Cartesian motifs—to reject nearly all the well-known doctrinal content of the Cartesian philosophy. (1999 p. 1)

So, it appears that the praise Husserl gave with his left hand, he took back with his right hand. One of Husserl's most pointed criticisms refers to Descartes reification of the ego into a "thing" (that thinks) and Descartes' failure to see that the ego is always already intentionally tied into the world and cannot even be conceived as "distinct" from the world. In Husserl's words: "In these matters Descartes was deficient. It so happens that he stands before the greatest of all discoveries—in a sense he has already made it—yet fails to see its true significance" (Husserl, 1964b, p. 9). However, it seems a bit harsh to accuse Descartes of short-sightedness for not having discovered the significance of the intentionality of consciousness—a discovery that Husserl owes to Brentano more than three centuries later.

Still, there are broadly sustaining themes that give Husserl's project a Cartesian significance (see Martin, 2008). For example, both Descartes and Husserl developed their philosophies in strong reaction against the "science" that was dominant at their time: scholasticism for Descartes and positivism for Husserl. Both Descartes and Husserl were strongly motivated to search for a method that would epistemologically ground their knowledge in apodictic self-evidence and certainty. Both Descartes and Husserl situated the ego (transcendental subjectivity) at the center of their fundamental reflections. And, both Descartes and Husserl were motivated in their search for philosophic thought to become autonomous, emancipatory, and self-responsible (rather than being dependent and owing to doctrinal science, theology, or ideology). While the original doctrines and the fruits of the methodical doubt of Descartes may have been left behind by Husserl's and Heidegger's initial formulations of the project of phenomenology, Descartes is certainly still worth reading by phenomenologists for the originality and daring pathos of his method of doubting, and his thought regarding the originary source and nature of knowledge and meaning.

Appearance and the Thing Itself: Immanuel Kant

Immanuel Kant (1724–1804) is generally regarded as the most influential modern philosopher who was driven by the enlightenment idea that each of us should think for oneself rather than let some authority or others think for you. Kant is also seen as a precursor to phenomenological philosophy. Husserl, Heidegger, and many subsequent phenomenological scholars have taken a deep interest in Kant's works.

In the second edition of the *Kritik der reinen Vernunft* (1787) Kant compares his anthropocentric philosophy with Copernicus' heliocentric revolution in astronomy. Copernicus had proposed that the Earth is not the center of the universe but the Sun is, and that the motion of heavenly bodies arises not from their motions but from the motion of the Earth itself. Analogously, Kant proposes that our thinking, cognition, is not determined by the objects of the sensible world, but that the objects must conform to the constitution of cognition. In other words, the phenomena of human experience depend on the sensory data that are received by consciousness as well as by the active procedures through which consciousness operates and converts data into phenomena (Kant, 1999, p. 113). However, this also means that our cognitive faculty cannot get beyond the possible experiences that are conditioned by consciousness. Famously, therefore, Kant makes a distinction between the things-in-themselves (noumena) that lie beyond the reach and realm of human thinking and the things (phenomena) that we encounter (intuit) in everyday experiences as they appear in consciousness.

Phenomena are the many kinds of sensory things that we come to know in the way they appear through our perceptions of the world around us. But all these things (whether natural or man-made) have a human face in that we can only make sense of them with our human cognitive faculties. What the things themselves "really" look like is beyond our human grasp. Kant termed these unknowables "noumena," even though the meaning of noumenon derives etymologically from the Greek *noumenon*, meaning "thought of," and *nous*, meaning "mind." Kant's noumenon is sometimes synonymous with "*das Ding an sich*," the "thing-in-itself" or otherwise noumenon seems to refer to the existence of the things-in-themselves. But, for Kant, the noumena cannot be directly known by the mind through human categories. Noumena can only be imagined. In this sense, noumena are the unknowable roots of things and the meaning of things.

> We have therefore wanted to say that all our intuition is nothing but the representation of appearance; that the things that we intuit are not in themselves what we intuit them to be, nor are their relations so constituted in themselves as they appear to us; and that if we remove our own subject or even only the subjective constitution of the senses in general, then all constitution, all relations of objects in space and time, indeed space and time themselves would disappear, and as appearances they cannot exist in themselves, but only in us. (Kant, 1999, p. 168)

Things-in-themselves are the noumena and yet, by definition, an object can never be identified as a noumenon—it can be only conceptually imagined by reason, but not experienced experientially through the senses. The distinction of phenomena and noumena is therefore between the world of our senses and the world of understanding.

> The effect of an object on the capacity for representation, insofar as we are affected by it, is *sensation*. That intuition which is related to the object through sensation is called *empirical*. The undetermined object of an empirical intuition is called *appearance*. (Kant, 1999, p 172)

Our knowledge results from intuitions that are gained from direct sensibilities of objects of our world and concepts that are formed through our understanding.

In addition to empirical intuitions, Kant points out that there are a priori intuitions such as space and time. Space and time do not belong to the things, but they make it possible to experience things, or anything at all. A thing, like the computer on which I am preparing this text, I can only empirically intuit because I have an a priori intuition of space and time and the concept of substance, which make it possible to encounter something as a computer. Conversely, we cannot experience time directly. We can only experience time through and in the things of our world. Every moment of our lives we experience as a "now" that constantly changes and moves to the "just now" or the "almost now."

Some commentators have argued that not Husserl, but Kant was the main instigator or founder of the idea of philosophical phenomenology (see Tom Rockmore, 2011). At any rate, it is clear that Kant has been a major influence on the thoughts of major thinkers like Husserl, Heidegger, and Arendt for his methodological focus on the ways things appear as phenomena in everyday life, even though their ultimate reality, as noumena, cannot be fathomed by the human mind.

Words Kill: Georg Wilhelm Friedrich Hegel

Although the emergence of the philosophical tradition of phenomenology is usually identified with the work of Edmund Husserl, the term *phenomenology* was employed already by Johann Heinrich Lampert in his *Cosmological Letters* of 1764 to refer to the study of the existence of phenomena. And phenomenology as a philosophical concept appears famously in Hegel's *Phenomenology of Mind* (1977). Spending a few paragraphs on Hegel does not only show that phenomenology has indeed a long and complex tradition, but it also hints at the fact that in Hegel's early and monumental work there is much that has preoccupied later phenomenologists.

Georg Wilhelm Friedrich Hegel was born in Stuttgart, Germany, on August 27, 1770. In 1788 he studied philosophy and theology in Tübingen. Next, he taught for several years as a private tutor for the children of families in Bern and Frankfurt. In 1799 Hegel received a modest inheritance after his father's death. It allowed him to establish himself as a privatdozent (a professor paid only by students) at the University of Jena. Initially, he had difficulty gaining a fully paid university position, in part, perhaps, because he was apparently a poor and awkward lecturer who would fumble with his notes while speaking. And yet, because of his brilliant mind and ability to penetrate the profound historical and philosophical conditions of human consciousness, he soon became very popular. Through the influence of Goethe, Hegel received a professorial position, but initially it was at a lower rank. Then, when the Napoleonic war broke out in 1806, the University of Jena had to close and Hegel worked as a newspaper editor and next as principal of an academic high school. Finally, in 1816 he received a position of full professor at the University of Heidelberg, and in 1818 he moved to the more prestigious University of Berlin (Pinkard, 2001).

Hegel, who succeeded Kant as the most prominent philosopher of his time, set himself off against Kant's distinction between "phenomena" (objects of human understanding as grasped by the human mind) and "noumena" (the things-in-themselves that cannot be grasped directly by the mind). But in doing so, he also moved away from considering the simple consciousness of sense-experience a proper source for understanding the world. Hegel wanted to explore what form of consciousness constitutes genuine knowledge. He proposed that the things-in-themselves—whatever ultimately exists—do not lie outside of consciousness but are the manifestation of consciousness. "Things" must be studied through examining consciousness from the inside, as it were— as it constructs its world and as it appears to itself. Consciousness constructs human reality. So, to study the things of our world is to study the various modes of consciousness in order to arrive at an increasingly adequate apprehension of the reality of the human world.

One of the critical ideas that can be considered a precursor to later developments of phenomenological thought is Hegel's notion of dialectic—the dialectical progress of the consciousness of freedom. He traces the civilizations of past Chinese, Indian, Persian, Greek, and Roman worlds for the social, legal, and spiritual barriers that hampered human thought to be genuinely harmonious, autonomous, and free from external authority and irrational constraints. Hegel wanted to explore what form of consciousness constitutes genuine or "absolute" knowledge. We can only hope to understand something self-consciously by dealing with all the presumptions, beliefs, and established conventions that give shape to our opinions and that distort a true understanding of the things and world in which we live. When Hegel refers to "absolute knowledge," he does not mean knowing everything absolutely or knowing absolutely everything; rather, it is knowledge of some thing for what this thing really is: its absolute identity.

Famous is Hegel's use of the biblical Adam for explaining the significance of naming in our apprehension of meaning of our reality:

> The first act, by which Adam established his lordship over the animals, is this, that he gave them a name, i.e., he nullified them as beings on their own account, and made them into ideal [entities]. This sign was previously, qua [natural] sign, a "name" which is still something else than "a name" on its own account; it was a thing, and what is signified has its sign outside it, it was not posited as something superseded, so that the sign does not have its meaning in itself, but only in the subject, one must still know specifically what the subject means by it; but the name is in itself, it "persists", without either the thing or the subject. In the name the "self"-subsisting reality of the sign is nullified. (Hegel, 1979, pp. 221, 222)

Simply put, in order to create knowledge of our world, things in their singularity are to be annihilated and replaced by universal concepts. More dramatically put, Hegel seems to say that words kill the very things that they name. However, for Hegel the singularity of things must be sacrificed to the reflective concepts that are constitutive of the knowledge that we build. Reflection distances and separates us from the concrete particularity and the immediacy of our experience. Through reflection, consciousness can step back and take distance from experience and from itself, and thus reflection becomes self-conscious.

Hegel first examines sense-experience, as the simplest form of consciousness. Through sense-experience we come to know things in a manner that gives us access to sense certainty of this or that in the here and now. Hegel's notion of sense certainty is a significant and challenging precursor for phenomenological inquiry. "Sense-certainty appears to be the truest knowledge; for it has yet omitted nothing from the object, but has the object before it in its perfect entirety" (Hegel, 1979, p. 91). For example, I take a bite into an apple I just took from the fruit bowl. Sense certainty is a direct awareness of what is present to us, unmediated by language, conceptual categories, or prior thoughts. Right now, I experience holding and biting into the skin and flesh of the apple. But how can I capture this momentary experience of sense certainty of biting into the apple? The problem is that when we try to capture this primitive sense-experience in words, we inevitably generalize it. When we speak about the things that happen to us or that we do from moment to moment, then we need to express a particularity and yet language can only speak in universals. The purely momentary experience has now been changed into something else—words. All we can really say is that this moment of eating the apple merely "is," says Hegel. At this passive perceptive level of momentary immediacy, "consciousness" is purely existence in all its rich primordial complexity. Consciousness is not yet reflective and active; consciousness does not yet focus on anything—consciousness is simply "being" itself.

Hegel argues that though this particular experiential moment of biting into the apple is immediate (and that means unmediated by concepts or reflective thinking), this moment of existence is nevertheless mediated: it is mediated by the thing of the moment (the apple, the biting, the tasting, the swallowing) and it is mediated by the "I" who experiences the moment.

> But, when we look closely, there is a good deal more implied in that bare pure being, which constitutes the kernel of this form of certainty, and is given out by it as its truth. A concrete actual certainty of sense is not merely this pure immediacy, but an example, an instance, of that immediacy. (1979, p. 150)

Interestingly, Hegel's use of the notion of "example" foreshadows the writings by contemporary philosophers such as Agamben who suggest that the example lets the singular show its singularity. The example lets the singular be seen. But this interest in evoking the singular is not Hegel's project. Still, we should note this important Hegelian predicament: the particulars of the moment cannot be expressed without losing the singularity of this instant. Language always universalizes what it attempts to describe or express. Hegel concludes that the "sense certainty" that we experience in a particular moment of the here and now (right now biting into this particular apple) is so personal and so particular that it can never be grasped as genuine knowledge. Because the pure sense of the moment is beyond language, Hegel (somewhat counter-intuitively perhaps) calls this immediate sense-experience "abstract." It is abstract precisely in the sense that it is ungraspable.

However, from our present post-Hegelian perspective we might point out that language abstracts too. And this realization should be of profound relevance for anyone who engages in qualitative research or inquiry. Language abstracts (and thus distorts or even "kills") the living moments of lived experience it tries to describe. When Adam named the animals and things in the world around him, he killed them (in their singularity and particularity). This must be a sobering thought. And yet, the relation between language and understanding is even more complex. Language may do more than abstract and annihilate. Phenomenologists such as Martin Heidegger, Maurice Blanchot, Emmanuel Levinas, Jacques Derrida, and more recently Michel Serres, Giorgio Agamben, and Jean-Luc Marion have taken up this theme of language–world relation in their radical reflections on notions of singularity, language, meaning, and writing.

Hegel examines two further developments of consciousness: perception and understanding. Through language and concepts, consciousness classifies what it perceives and experiences. So, at a higher level than the certainty of sense-experience, consciousness understands the world through concepts expressed in language. And at still higher levels of the phenomenology of mind or *Geist*, an additional reflectivity occurs. Consciousness does not only construct its reality, it also becomes aware that these constructions or concepts are not things or objects we see, but they are constructs that help us to understand the nature of human reality and world. Thus, at the higher level of knowledge, consciousness becomes self-consciousness.

Self-consciousness is not just some kind of introspective looking into the self: self-consciousness comes into being through what is other than self. We can only see the self through recognition of what is other or not-self. Through being recognized and through recognizing the self in what is not self (other), we dialectically achieve a higher formative self. This process is called formative growth, learning, or becoming. Important for phenomenological methodology is Hegel's notions of the dialectic of identity and difference.

For Hegel, identity means difference and difference means identity, because one cannot think identity without difference. But not all things that are unlike are different in Hegel's sense. Things such as a painting and a hammer are only different in a colloquial and trivial sense. A painting and a hammer are objects that are not really "different" in a comparable sense, but rather they are merely "unlike." Only differences of identities that make a difference permit comparison and are meaningful differences. For example, a painting may be compared with a photograph: a painting is different from a photograph, and what gives a painting its unique identity (difference) may be gleaned by determining its specific differences when it is compared with what gives a photograph its unique identity. In this dialectic process of comparing the identity and difference of a thing, we can see at work what is now a methodological gesture of phenomenological inquiry.

Uncanniness: Friedrich Nietzsche

The work of Friedrich Nietzsche (1844–1900) too has profoundly influenced the thinking of many leading phenomenologists. Heidegger wrote a three-volume study of Nietzsche that is original and penetrating. Nietzsche's writings are often highly provocative, aphoristic, and challenging of established values and ideas of his time. Well-known Nietzschean ideas are that there is no truth, that God is dead, that we are condemned to eternal recurrence, and that humans are governed by the will to power. The death of God is not so much an expression of

Nietzsche's atheism than his conviction that, with the emergence of science and secular values, God and the church can no longer serve as a source for meaning and morality that humans can cling to. Nietzsche's suspicion of religious, scientific, and moral truths was associated with his disdain for human weakness and distrust of human motivations.

Perhaps Nietzsche's most famous essay is "On Truth and Lie in a Nonmoral Sense." In this essay he mocks the human effort to arrive at truth by erecting huge and complex conceptual frameworks and structures of scientific knowledge that in a fundamental sense rests on illusions and self-deception about the nature of reality. According to Nietzsche, humans have a need for lies in order to conquer this reality, this "truth," that is, in order to *live*. That lies are necessary in order to live is itself part of the terrifying and questionable character of existence. "Metaphysics, morality, religion, science . . . these things merit consideration only as various forms of lies; with their help one can have *faith* in life" (Nietzsche, 1968, p. 451). According to Nietzsche, human beings need science, religion, and metaphysics in order to deal (dull ourselves) with the uncertainties and ultimate horror of the realization of the truth that there is no truth. And so, humans create interpretations, generalizations, and principles but then forget that these truths are nothing but their own inventions that have turned into fetish:

> What, then, is truth? A mobile army of metaphors, metonyms, anthropomorphisms— in short, a sum of human relations that have been poetically and rhetorically intensified, translated, and embellished, and that after long use strike a people as fixed, canonical, and binding: truths are illusions of which one has forgotten that they are illusions, metaphors that have become worn-out and deprived of their sensuous force, coins that have lost their imprint and are now no longer seen as coins but as metal. (Nietzsche, 2010, pp. 29, 30)

Nietzsche points out over and over again that all words derive from metaphors, but that these metaphors are already illusory.

> The "thing in itself" (which would be, precisely, pure truth without consequences) is utterly unintelligible, even for the creator of a language, and certainly nothing to strive for, for he designates only the relations of things to human beings and helps himself to the boldest metaphors. First, to transfer a nerve stimulus into an image—first metaphor! Then image again copied into a sound—second metaphor! And each time a complete leap out of one sphere into an entirely new and different one . . . . We think we know something about the things themselves when we speak of trees, colours, snow, and flowers, yet we possess only metaphor of the things, which in no way correspond to the original essences. (Nietzsche, 2010, pp. 26, 27)

Nietzsche was an influential forerunner of the postmodern view that humans have no access to reality as it is in itself. He aimed to unmask the attempt to develop a metaphysic as a sign of existential insecurity and weakness. (However, Heidegger points out that Nietzsche unwittingly still subscribed to a form of metaphysics in his very attempt to overturn it.)

One of Friedrich Nietzsche's provocative claims is that "we possess art lest we perish of the truth" (1968, p. 435). For Nietzsche, truths have lost their value except to keep us comfortable. However, art is not dependent on (ultimately false) concepts and generalizations. In that sense art is honest: art shatters truth and thus is life affirming. Art makes our truths uncanny—strange and thus perhaps unexpectedly truthful. We have art in order not to die of the (false) truth. Nietzsche valued art above science since art is driven not by concepts but by intuition:

> The intuitive man, standing in the midst of a culture, reaps from his intuitions not only a defense against evil but a continuous influx of illumination, cheerfulness, redemption. Of course, when he suffers, he suffers more intensely; he even suffers more often since he does not know how to learn from experience. (Nietzsche, 2010, p. 48)

Nietzsche already observed that experience is always changing and singular. But rather than trying to get at the singularity of things we tend to abstract experiences via metaphors into concepts:

> Only by forgetting that primitive world of metaphor, only by the hardening and the stiffening of a mass of images that originally flowed forth hot and liquid from the primal power of human imagination, only by the unconquerable faith that *this* sun, *this* window, *this* table is a truth in itself—in short, only by man's forgetting himself as subject, indeed as an artificially creative subject, does he live with some degree of peace, security, and consistency . . . [There is] at most an aesthetic comportment, by which I mean a suggestive rendering, a stammering translation into an altogether foreign language. Though even that would require a freely poetic and freely inventive intermediate sphere and mediating force. (Nietzsche, 2010, pp. 36, 37)

According to Nietzsche, human "truths" are fundamental realizations such as, "we all must die alone," "nothing is ever what it seems," "we can only come to know what we love," "human desire can never be fulfilled," "the human being longs for wholeness," "nothing makes us feel more alive than the realization that we must die," "the fundamental truth is that there is no truth." Of course, there are different ways for us to understand truth. And Nietzsche's aphorism that "we have art in order not to die of the truth" can be understood in several ways.

The above quotes should prove inspiring for phenomenologies that understand that human reality cannot be captured with a secure set of procedures and rationality, but that more is required in the sense of a poetic, creative, insightful, and pathic impulse that is the pathos of any depthful phenomenology. No wonder, perhaps, that Heidegger paid extraordinary attention to Nietzsche in his writings.

Inner Duration and Laughter: Henri-Louis Bergson

Henri Bergson (1859–1941) was a highly gifted philosophical thinker and author. Yet, the reputation of Bergson's brilliance was not that he discovered something that we did not already know, but that he revealed something that everyone already knew and yet do not realize or comprehend. Bergson believed that people mostly misunderstand the nature of time, especially people in western cultures who mistake real time for what the clock shows us as the hands move with homogeneous equanimity along the perimeter of the face of the clock. Or as we picture time as a series or sequence of points on a straight line from past to present to future moments along the time-line. Or as we divide time in terms of divisions of the movements of day and night, shades of light and darkness. We regard these manifestations of time as objective time, measurable time. But, actually, the time we live is our experiential reality. It is the inner time we feel with our body as subjective time. Bergson is interested in the inner time that we live through every moment of our lives. He famously proclaimed that our lived or inner time is not abstract or scientific time but it is real time because we live it as duration.

This word "duration" (*durée*) became the central theme in Bergson's thinking. Of course, we all know that time has duration, that time endures. But the question is: do we realize what is implied in this realization? Bergson showed that our understanding of many subjects such as life, matter, space, and subjective or inner experience are entangled with our understanding of time. This inner and durational sense of time is composed of moments that are never quite the same for the person—temporal moments of consciousness are not separate entities but rather streaming and always new, always changing, like consciousness itself. The actual experience of duration is a very different sensibility than our modern portrayal of time presents as absolute time that is manifested by the mechanical vibration of crystal in our watch, or the mechanical movements measured by the pendulum of the wall clock, or the scientific precision of the atomic clock. Duration is the sense of temporality we feel as being alive, as time caries us on through life.

The hands of a clock go around and round. They move unendingly along the circumference of the clockface in a continuous repetition or they move eternally along an infinite line. But that is not how we experience time. While clock time tends to be seen as a steady, external, mechanical, objective movement, in contrast, the movement of subjective time which is the opposite and manifests itself as immediate internal experience is not some kind of stuff like the sand in an hour glass that we can measure. Time is rather an enigmatic cosmic phenomenon that started with the big bang, some 13.8 billion years ago, with the beginning of time. This pure explosive mobility that started the expansion of the universe set in motion the entropic processes of dark energy that seem to be pushing space apart into the ever widening extension of complexities and thus speeding up the growth of the universe as it is known now in time. But it is hard to find words to describe time. Time is not a relation like gravity or an entity like matter. As the cosmologist Sean Carroll says, "we cannot fill a container with a cup of time." And when we say that we have to travel a short or a long time, or when we say that the time it takes to go for a walk or a hike is two hours long, we actually express or describe time in terms of spatial measurements: length, distance, presence or absence as in having no time left.

When we check what time it is, when we look at the time on the screen of our watch, the face of the clock or of some other time piece, we temporarily step out

205

of time. While looking at the clock which tells us that, right now, it is ten minutes past three, we seem to be simultaneously confirming and denying the reality of this "now" moment of time. We have to step outside of time to observe the time (because, ironically, we cannot live it and observe it at the same time).

Henri Bergson became concerned about the fact that we tend to objectify and mechanize all aspects of living, and that we become desensitized to the fact that we experience time as duration. Duration implies that immediate temporal experience is always new and changing. No moment we live is ever quite the same as any other moments in our past or future.

At an immediate subjective or experiential level, we know that time is something that endures, lasts. We know immediately and intuitively with our bodies that time passes. The reason that we feel the passing of time is that our bodies have clocks in them, so to speak. The fact that our heart beats at a certain rate, that we get tired after an activity, that we feel animated during a physical endurance, the manner that we remember things and return to them, the slowing down of time when we feel bored, our perception of the constantly changing world around us, the fact that we often can depend on our body to wake up at a certain time, all this means that we sense time passing—not because we are looking *at* time but because we are *in* time.

According to Bergson, duration is the medium of heterogeneity, symbolized by the god Heraclitus, who represents the flowing form of constantly changing and becoming of life. Being and becoming are the two basic qualities of time, but we do not know how to derive being from becoming or becoming from being. And, when we try to say something about time, for example telling what time it is in the present moment, then we have already distorted the very meaning of temporality. To reiterate, time is not just a string of now-moments strung on a straight string, or a hand moving along the circular line of a clock face, or the repetitive marching of numbers on a digital screen. According to Bergson, reality is pure movement, a continuous stream of change or mobility like the waves in a river.

Phenomenological philosophers Jean-Paul Sartre, Simone de Beauvoir, and Maurice Merleau-Ponty had been fascinated by Bergson's work. His life-goal seemed to have been laying bare the assumptions and penetrating the implications of the immediacy of consciousness and the entanglement of the duration of time, and the materiality and aliveness of temporal reality. His first major publications were *Time and Free Will: An Essay on the Immediate Data of Consciousness* (1889/2001), and *Matter and Memory* (1896/1991). But curiously, at exactly the midpoint of his life in 1900, Bergson published the smaller and surprising book *Laughter: An Essay on the Meaning of the Comic* (2005), originally published as *Le Rire: Essay sur la Signification du Comique*.

The book *Laughter* is somewhat of a surprise since it seemed to have been written as an interceding exercise, as a light-hearted phenomenological examination of a prate preoccupation: a pun about laughter as something to laugh about— laughter as the reaction of the experience of comedy and joking. But this study of the comical and the joke became a bestseller in France and, even though it is no doubt the least philosophically sophisticated, it is likely the most widely read publication by Henri Bergson. It is still worth reading because not only does it give us insights in a common human behavior, it contains some of the major themes of Bergson's works. In his opening paragraph of the book *Laughter* Henri Bergson asks: what is the core meaning of laughter?

> What does laughter mean? What is the basal element in the laughable? What common ground can we find between the grimace of a merry-andrew, a play upon words, an equivocal situation in a burlesque and a scene of high comedy? What method of distillation will yield us invariably the same essence from which so many different products borrow either their obtrusive odour or their delicate perfume? The greatest of thinkers, from Aristotle downwards, have tackled this little problem, which has a knack of baffling every effort, of slipping away and escaping only to bob up again, a pert challenge flung at philosophic speculation. (Bergson, 1911/2005, p. 1)

It is clear, already, from this paragraph that Bergson is not only preoccupied with laughter, he is interested in the phenomenon that is consequential for laughter. He is interested in the comical. Indeed, the subtitle of his book *Laughter* is *An Essay on the Meaning of the Comic*. So, the question is: when does something become comical, a comedy? Bergson immediately gives some advice:

> Now step aside, look upon life as a disinterested spectator: many a drama will turn into a comedy. It is enough for us to stop our ears to the sound of music, in a room where dancing is going on, for the dancers at once to appear ridiculous. (p. 3)

> A man, running along the street, stumbles and falls; the passers-by burst out laughing . . . They laugh because his sitting down is involuntary.
> Consequently, it is not his sudden change of attitude that raises a laugh, but rather the involuntary element in this change,—his clumsiness, in fact. (pp. 4, 5)

Bergson provides many examples of the moment when something becomes comical. And he relates it to the notion of the duration of time. When we experience time as duration then it is enduringly lasting and renewing, always different from the prior moment and from the moment of becoming. This is the nature of the being and becoming of time. It shows that the human reality is always unfolding and in some sense an aspect of our intentionality and freedom of will. But it can happen at any moment as well that something disturbs our intention such as when we stumble and fall.

> What is a comic physiognomy? Where does a ridiculous expression of the face come from? And what is, in this case, the distinction between the comic and the ugly? (p. 11)

> The attitudes, gestures and movements of the human body are laughable in exact proportion as that body reminds us of a mere machine. (p. 15)

And the strange consequence is that onlookers who happen to see us stumble while we walk onto a stage or who watch us sneeze while we are just about to make an important public announcement, they tend to laugh. It is a funny sight when we momentarily look like a mechanical figure or a robot when, for an instant, we seem to have lost control of our actions. In such moments we become thing-like, machine-like, impacted by the pull of gravity or the spectacle of an organic spasm of our body. In such moments we do not belong to the world of human subjects in Kairos time but to the world of material objects in Chronos time. And our behavior becomes mechanical, ruled by the forces of nature. This non-human behavior gives the appearance of being funny and comical. And so, we laugh every time a person gives us the impression of being a thing. Human behavior becomes comical when it becomes a display of a *mécanisation de la vie*, mechanization of life—when expressions, physiognomies, gestures, movements, composures, or entire human situations turn into mechanical manifestations.

Bergson describes laughter as a spontaneous reaction on the inattentive, inflexible, and thus mechanical response. But non-human spectacles can also appear comical and stir laughter when they show excess, indulgence, odd variation, or grotesque exaggeration. For example, animals that look funny because they seem to be caricatures of themselves or other animals. The opposite between the inertness of matter and vivacity of life—living life with *élan vital*—are critical in Bergson's distinction of the comical. Bergson's philosophy reality is not a static state but the opposite: the constant movement of perpetuity, streaming, change, duration (*durée*). Bergson describes this perpetual inclination to self-development of the real as *élan vital*, the urge for life and living, or the life force of temporality. It is problematic when in modern life, the energy of reality and the creative exuberance of freedom turn into insensible mechanical automation. And therefore, public laughter is society's way of correcting us, of drawing attention to situations when human beings display behavior that has become dull, robotic, and mechanical.

Erlebnis, Expression, Understanding: Wilhelm Dilthey

The foundational distinction of "Human" Science versus "Natural" Science is often attributed to Wilhelm Dilthey. Dilthey developed the contrast between the *Naturwissenschaften* (the natural or physical sciences) and the *Geisteswissenschaften* (the sciences of mind) into a methodological program for the latter. For Dilthey the proper subject matter for the *Geisteswissenschaften* is the human world characterized by *Geist*—mind, thoughts, consciousness, values, feelings, emotions, actions, and purposes, which find their objectifications in languages, beliefs, arts, and institutions. Thus, at the risk of oversimplification one might say that the difference between natural science and human science resides in what is being studied. Natural science studies "objects of nature," "things," "natural events," and "the way that objects behave." Human science, in contrast, studies "persons," or beings that have "consciousness" and that "act purposefully" in and on the world by creating objects of "meaning" that are "expressions" of how human beings exist in the world.

Dilthey was born in 1831 in the village of Biebrich on the Rhine River. He studied at Heidelberg University in 1852 and Berlin in the following years. Like several other leading philosophers, before and after him, it was his intention to study theology but he developed an interest in philosophy. He was especially interested in the writings on hermeneutics by Friedrich Schleiermacher, and did his doctoral thesis on *The Principles of Schleiermacher's Ethics* (1864). He was granted his habilitation with a thesis on *Moral Consciousness*. Dilthey studied Immanuel Kant, Georg Wilhelm Friedrich Hegel, and Arthur Schopenhauer and he broadly and deeply immersed himself in history, literature, and the arts. His studies included the works by Goethe, Nietzsche, Shakespeare, Plato, Aristotle, and other early Greek philosophers.

What is "lived experience" (*Erlebnis*)? This is an important question because phenomenological human science begins in lived experience and eventually turns back to it. Dilthey (1985) has suggested that in its most basic form lived experience involves our immediate, prereflective consciousness of life: a reflexive or self-given awareness which is, as awareness, unaware of itself.

Dilthey gave special meaning to the notion of *Erlebnis*, which is translated into English as "lived experience." He suggested that lived experience is to the soul what breath is to the body: "Just as our body needs to breathe, our soul requires the fulfillment and expansion of its existence in the reverberations of emotional life" (1985, p. 59). In German language *leben* is to live and *erleben* can be translated as living through something meaningful. Lived experience is the breathing of meaning. In the flow of life, consciousness breathes meaning in a to-and-fro movement: a constant heaving between the inner and the outer. There is a determinate reality-appreciation in the flow of living and experiencing life's breath. Thus, a lived experience has a certain essence, a "quality" that we recognize in retrospect.

> A lived experience does not confront me as something perceived or represented; it is not given to me, but the reality of lived experience is there-for-me because I have a reflexive awareness of it, because I possess it immediately as belonging to me in some sense. Only in thought does it become objective. (p. 223)

Gadamer (1975) observed that the word "experience" has a condensing and intensifying meaning: "If something is called or considered an experience its meaning rounds it into the unity of a significant whole" (p. 60). What makes an experience unique so that I can reflect on it and talk about it is the particular structural nexus— the motif—that gives this experience its particular quality (central idea or dominant theme). "Lived experiences are related to each other like motifs in the andante of a symphony," said Dilthey (1985, p. 227). He talked of "structure" or "structural nexus" (p. 228) as something that belongs to a particular lived experience (something like a pattern or unit of meaning), which becomes part of a system of contextually related experiences, explicated from it through a process of reflection on its meaning.

The preferred method for natural science, since Galileo, has been detached observation, controlled experiment, and mathematical or quantitative measurement. And when the natural science method has been applied to the behavioral social sciences, it has retained procedures of experimentation and quantitative analysis. In contrast, the preferred method for human science involves description, interpretation, and self-reflective or critical analysis. We explain nature, but human life we must understand, said Dilthey (1976). Whereas natural science tends to *taxonomize* natural phenomena (such as in biology) and causally or probabilistically *explain* the behavior of things (such as in physics), human science aims at *explicating* the meaning of human phenomena (such as in literary or historical studies of texts) and at *understanding* the lived structures of meanings (such as in phenomenological studies of the lifeworld).

Erfahrung is the German word for "life experience." This is the more general term. For example, we may say that a person has had many experiences (*Erfahrungen*) in life. Life experiences (*Lebenserfahrungen*) are more inclusive than lived experiences (*Erlebnisse*). Life experiences are the accumulation of lived experiences and the understandings and sense we may have made of these experiences. Gadamer (1975) showed that certain *Erfahrungen*, for example in the case of aesthetic truth experiences, can have a transformative effect on our being. And thus, we can speak of an "experienced" person when referring to his or her mature wisdom, as a result of life's accumulated experiences, *Erfahrungen*.

Erlebnis is the German word for lived experience—experience as we live through it and recognize it as a particular type of experience. Dilthey (1985) used this term to show that there is a pattern of meaning and a certain unity to experience. Our language can be seen as an immense linguistic map that names the possibilities of human lived experiences.

Hermeneutics is the theory and practice of interpretation. The word derives from the Greek god, Hermes, whose task it was to communicate messages from the gods to the ordinary mortals. Hermeneutics is necessary when there is possibility for misunderstanding, said Schleiermacher (1977). He opened up the idea of hermeneutics as a theory or "technology" of interpretation, especially with respect to the study of sacred (biblical) and classical texts. Schleiermacher's program was critical (as the struggle against misunderstanding) and romantic (in the desire to recover the particularity, or the animating genius or notion of an author's thoughts). His aim was to understand an author as well or even better than he or she understands himself or herself.

Dilthey sought to develop in hermeneutics a methodological basis for the human sciences. According to Dilthey we can grasp the fullness of lived experience by reconstructing or reproducing the meanings of life's expressions found in the products of human effort, work and creativity. The emphasis for Dilthey (1985) was not the fundamental thought of the other person but the "lived experience," of the world itself, which is expressed by the author's text. Dilthey's famous hermeneutic formula was *lived experience*: the starting point and focus of human science; *expression*: the text or artifact as objectification of lived experience; and *understanding*: not a cognitive act but the moment when "life understands itself."

CHAPTER EIGHT

Forming Traditions: Foundational Thinkers

The following sections discuss phenomenological orientations of some of the most prominent and talented foundational phenomenologists. Each provides a brief biographic portrayal of one of these proponents who have made unique contributions to phenomenology. The role of each has been such that a separate phenomenological strand or tradition can be associated with their approach. The intent is not to provide a concise overview of each approach but to identify some selected and significant aspects of the contributions of these proponents to research and writing phenomenologically.

In the early twentieth century, it was Edmund Husserl and Martin Heidegger in particular who launched the modern phenomenological movement. Edith Stein, Hannah Arendt, Max Scheler, and Jan Patočka also count as original thinkers who worked in the wake of the pathbreaking beginnings of Husserl and Heidegger.

Transcendental Phenomenology: Edmund Husserl

Edmund Husserl is generally regarded as the intellectual founder of phenomenological philosophy. His writings are so rich, original, evolving, and detailed that scholars are still grappling to understand his insights and assess the implications and consequences of his work for philosophy, the humanities, and human sciences. Husserl was born into a Jewish family in 1859 in the town of Prossnitz, Moravia (now called Prostějov, in the Czech Republic). Initially, he studied physics, astronomy, and mathematics at Leipzig and Berlin. Next, he turned to mathematics at the University of Vienna, and he obtained his Ph.D. in 1883 with the dissertation *Contributions to the Calculus of Variations*. While at Vienna, and out of curiosity, Husserl attended some lectures on psychology and philosophy by Franz Brentano. Husserl became so fascinated that he decided to make philosophy his life calling. In 1887 he obtained his habilitation with a dissertation *On the Concept of Number*, under the guidance of Carl Stumpf, who was a former student of Brentano. The same year Husserl was appointed as privatdozent at the University of Halle. In 1901, he became full professor in Göttingen, and in 1916 at the University of Freiburg where he remained until his retirement and emeritus in 1928. While his dissertations have not been regarded highly significant, much of his subsequent lifeworks are now considered of immense consequence and magnitude.

Husserl had a Jewish background (the name "Husserl" is possibly derived from the old names "Iserle, Islerin, or Yisrael," meaning Israel). Because of his Jewishness he was eventually banished from Freiberg University by the Nazis as they began to

DOI: 10.4324/9781003228073-10

dominate German society. Husserl died in 1938. As the Nazis would likely destroy his works and possessions, the Belgian Franciscan priest Father Herman Leo van Breda risked his life in 1939, smuggling all of Husserl's manuscripts and extensive personal library to Leuven (Louvain), Belgium, where they are now housed in the Husserl Archives at the Catholic University of Leuven. Van Breda and other scholars worked for many years translating Husserl's posthumous writings. The Archives receives visitors from around the world interested in consulting Husserl's manuscripts, or the extensive Phenomenology Library of the research center.

Husserl was accustomed to sharpen his thoughts with his pen on paper. His phenomenological research was truly a textual labor. He would edit, revise, and rewrite endlessly his fundamental writings. After his death, an astonishing collection of more than 40,000 pages written in shorthand, idiosyncratic stenographic script was found. The study and translation of Husserl's writings are still continuing. Husserl's texts are often dense and difficult, so it is not surprising that there exist many conflicting interpretations and understandings of Husserl's phenomenology. It is not easy to unambiguously highlight some basic themes of Husserl's thoughts that may be helpful for those who wish to apply his methods in a human science research context.

Husserl defines phenomenology as a descriptive philosophy of the essences of pure experiences. He aims to capture experience in its primordial origin or essence, without interpreting, explaining, or theorizing. The essences with which phenomenology concerns itself are *Erlebniswesen*, essences of lived experiences: *concreta*, not *abstracta*. In the *Cartesian Meditations* Husserl begins his exploration by declaring the importance of what he calls "a first methodological principle" (Husserl, 1999, p. 13): only knowledge derived from immediate experiential evidence can be accepted.

> It is plain that I, as someone beginning philosophically, since I am striving toward the presumptive end, genuine science, must neither make nor go on accepting any judgment as scientific *that I have not derived from evidence*, from "experiences" in which the affairs and affair-complexes in question are present to me as "they themselves." (Husserl, 1999, p. 13)

> Any evidence is a grasping of something itself that is, or is thus, a grasping in the mode "it itself," with full certainty of its being, a certainty that accordingly excludes every doubt . . . . An apodictic evidence, however, is not merely certainty of the affairs or affair-complexes (states of affairs) evident in it; rather it discloses itself, to a critical reflection, as having the signal peculiarity of being *at the same time the absolute unimaginableness* (inconceivability) of their *non-being* . . . . Furthermore, the evidence of that critical reflection likewise has the dignity of being apodictic. (Husserl, 1999, pp. 15, 16)

In his early text *Ideas Pertaining to a Pure Phenomenology and to a Phenomenological Philosophy*, Husserl goes to great pains explaining that phenomenology does not concern itself with facts or with realities in the way that psychology does. Rather phenomenology wants to establish itself, "*not as a science of matters of fact, but a science of essences* (as an '*eidetic*' science); it . . . exclusively seeks to ascertain 'cognitions of essences' and *no 'matters of fact' whatever*" (1983, p. xx).

For Husserl phenomenology is the rigorous science of all conceivable transcendental phenomena. His main aim and enduring pathos for phenomenology is to become a rigorous science and thus form as a firm basis for natural science to root itself. Phenomenology must strengthen the weak foundations that paradoxically characterize the sciences. While the sciences are enormously successful, they dismally fail to reflect on the meaning foundations of their own knowledge base.

Researchers who are inspired by Husserl's phenomenological methodology realize that he was motivated to pursue a program that would lead to a science of apodictic (certain or indubitable) knowledge. The pathos that drove Husserl is the question: What is it that can be known without doubt? And, how is this knowledge possible? Thus, to be a follower of Husserl is to enter the quest for certainty, certain knowledge—a quest that Husserl gradually and continually reconceived and that most of his followers no longer believe in. It should be said as well that Husserl's works are extremely complex and that his thinking went through important phases of "maturation," as Merleau-Ponty put it.

Transcendental phenomena are the experiential entities that may become the objects of our reflection in regarding the meaning of objects we encounter in the world. Immanent is what is within us, transcendent is what is outside us. When Husserl discusses how we spatially perceive a thing like a dice, he notes how we always perceive the dice perspectivally. As we look at the dice and its markings from different angles, we perceive adumbrations (profiles) of the dice: the different sides change shape as we regard them from different spatial positions or angles. We cannot visually perceive the dice in its nonpositional cubic essence, from all its infinitely possible aspects or adumbrations at the same time. In other words, we can never be sure of the exact nature of even something as simple as a dice since an infinite number of perspectival adumbrations is possible. Thus, the dice as thing "transcends" (escapes or hides) its ultimate being from our consciousness of it. Transcendental means hidden, but the transcendental character of things is phenomenologically vital for our conscious experience. When Husserl defined the term "transcendental" in his final work, he turns it back to the originary sources of the meaning of experience which is the reflective experiential source of the *I-myself.* So, it sounds a bit like a pun when Husserl uses the I myself to refer to the *I-myself:*

> I myself use the word transcendental *in the broadest sense* for the original motif . . . seeks to come to itself so to speak—seeks to attain the genuine and pure form of its task and its systematic development. It is the motif of inquiring back into the ultimate source of all the formations of knowledge, the motif of the knower's reflecting upon himself and his knowing life in which all the scientific structures that are valid for him occur purposefully, are stored up as acquisitions, and have become and continue to become freely available . . . . This source bears the title *I-myself,* with all of my actual and possible knowing life and, ultimately, my concrete life in general. The whole transcendental set of problems circles around the relation of *this,* my "I"—the "ego"—to what it is at first taken for granted to be—my soul—and, again, around the relation of this ego and my conscious life to the *world* of which I am conscious and whose true being I know through my own cognitive structures. (Husserl, 1970, pp. 97, 98)

Husserl calls this formulation his most general concept of the "transcendental" arrived at through pondering.

The important upshot is that "the experience of an object" is given differently from "the object of an experience." Our experience of the object of the dice is given to us internally with an intuitive certainty that differs from the uncertainty of the external object, the "real" die that is lying in front of us on the table. But the nature of the external die is ultimately uncertain because we can never see it from all sides at once. As we walk around it or turn it in our hand its true reality can never be given with certainty. In contrast, the die that appears to me in consciousness is certainly a true die; if it were not, then we would call it something else.

So, phenomenology does not direct its reflective attention to the external die but to our experience of the die, or better to the way that the die appears in consciousness. And this is a crucial point for Husserlian phenomenology. Put somewhat awkwardly, phenomenology does not study the "what" of our experience but the "experience" of the what—the experience of the intentional object, thing, entity, event as it appears or gives itself in consciousness. Phenomenology is the study of phenomena, and the phenomena are someone's experiences—belonging to someone's stream of consciousness. For Husserlian phenomenological inquiry, experience is the thing and "how" the things of experience appear to consciousness is the intentional focus.

Of course, there are also phenomena that are not derived from perceptions of external objects like die, desks, trees, books, computers, or houses. Other phenomena have to do with thoughts, imaginings, feelings, dreams, moods, and so forth. But Husserl's example of the spatial perception of the die is meant to show that (compared to the spatially external die) whatever appears in consciousness is given in a self-evidential manner. In perceiving a die lying on the floor, I may later doubt that what I saw was in fact a die, but I cannot doubt that I had the experience of seeing a die, even if what I saw turns out to be something else or merely an illusion. Thus, an experience that we had at a certain moment may be wrong (it was not a die) but the internal or immanent experience cannot be denied (I experienced seeing a die). Similarly, when one has the experience of falling in love, one undeniably does experience something that feels like "falling in love"—but perhaps, upon reflection, it was not really love, but merely infatuation, a crush, admiration, or lust.

For Husserl, phenomenology is a rigorous human science precisely because it investigates the way that knowledge comes into being and confronts us with the assumptions upon which all human understandings are grounded. He borrowed the notion of intentionality from Brentano in order to explain the intentional structure of all consciousness. By intentionality he means that all our thinking, feeling, and acting are always "about" things in the world, and thus tie us to the world. Brentano was a scholar who attempted to develop a descriptive psychology that involved the notion of consciousness as inner perception. For Brentano, all mental phenomena are conscious and experienced as "inner perceptions" made up of presentational appearances or presentings. Brentano's contemporaries challenged the idea of consciousness as inner perceptions (for example, we cannot gain access to inner perceptions through introspective accounts). But Husserl spent much effort trying to show how things held by certain sources in consciousness are experienced with various types of evidence.

The methods of the epoché (the suspension or bracketing of the natural or everyday attitude) and the reduction (the constitution of meaning) are two inter-related aspects of phenomenological reflection. First the epoché or transcenden-tal reduction is the moment of withdrawal from the natural attitude and from the everyday world toward the level of the transcendental ego; second, the phenome-nological reduction or the constitution of meaning is the moment of returning to the world as it shows itself in consciousness. As a result, transcendental phenom-enology is also called constitutive phenomenology. In 1933, Fink wrote with the approval of Husserl:

> The "phenomenological reduction" alone is the basic method of Husserl's phe-nomenological philosophy . . . it grants us "access" to transcendental subjectiv-ity and it includes within it all of phenomenology's problems and the particular methods associated with them. (Fink, 1970, pp. 72, 73)

Husserl's phenomenology "is essentially 'constitutive phenomenology'" (Fink, 1970, p. 123), and while it is not subjectivist in a psychological sense, it does keep the transcendental subject at the center of its method of the reduction. Fink speaks of "the moment of receptivity which makes up the inner essence of human experi-ence" (p. 124). Neither the human subject nor a transcendent reality is "absolute"; rather, it is a "transcendental relation," which does not overlook human finitude, frailty, and impotence, that pertains between human and "world-ground" (p. 136).

Now, empiricists argue that the question of how we know the things of our world must find its answer and evidential source in sensory experience. Scientific method such as in medical science finds its origin in the empiricist notion of sen-sory experience. For example, physicians increasingly have sought to base their scientific method on observation and hypothesis testing rather than on estab-lished doctrines of the day. Indeed, contemporary empiricism finds its roots in the ancient Greek Empiric School of Medicine. However, in modern science of Husserl's time, the notion of experience became increasingly identified with sen-sory input and experimental research. Husserl felt that he had to push himself off against his critics, especially the positivistic logical empiricists, who argued that all knowledge must be verifiable through sensory experience.

> The essential fault in empiricistic argumentation consists of identifying or con-fusing the fundamental demand for a return to the "things themselves" with the demand for legitimation of all cognition by experience. With his compre-hensible naturalistic constriction of the limits bounding cognizable "things," the empiricist simply takes experience to be the only act that is presentive of things themselves. But things are not simply mere things belonging to Nature. (Husserl, 1983, pp. 35, 36)

The phrase "back to the things" (*zu den Sachen*) has become a watchword for phenomenology. The phrase occurs in several places in Husserl's writings, and it is not always clear what exactly was meant in it. In the *Logical Investigations* he says, "we can absolutely not rest content with 'mere words.' . . . Meanings inspired only by remote, inauthentic intuitions—if by any intuitions at all—are not enough: we must go back to the 'things themselves'" (Husserl, 1981, p. 196).

Generally, "to the things" seems to mean "to the issues that matter." In his gigantic work the phrase occurs in a variety of forms. At the very least, Husserl urged that a rigorous inquiry of any sort should always radically start from beginnings that can be clear, rather than depart one's inquiry from existing dogmas and unexamined assumptions.

> The impulse to research must proceed not from philosophies but from things and from the problems connected with them. Philosophy, however, is essentially a science of true beginnings, or origins, of *rizomata panton*. The science concerned with what is radical must from every point of view be radical itself in its procedure. Above all it must not rest until it has attained its own absolutely clear beginnings. (Husserl, 1981, p. 196)

Meanwhile, within the context of phenomenology, the phrase "back to the things themselves" has acquired more specific interpretations that align themselves with the very project of phenomenological inquiry. It hints at the central effort of all phenomenology: to somehow return to the world as we originally experience it— to what is given in lived prereflective experience, before we have conceptualized it, before we have even put words or names to it.

> we can absolutely not rest content with "mere words," i.e. with a merely symbolic understanding of words, such as we first have when we reflect on the sense of the laws for "concepts," "judgements," "truths," etc. (together with their manifold specifications) which are set up in pure logic. Meanings inspired only by remote, confused, inauthentic intuitions—if by any intuitions at all—are not enough: we must go back to the "things themselves." (Husserl, 1970, p. 252)

Fink's interpretation of the maxim "to the things themselves" was explicitly endorsed by Husserl's foreword to his text. Fink points out that "*das Ding*" (meaning the thing, but translated by Elveton as "affair") can have different meanings:

> everything which can be brought to the point of manifesting itself as it is, be this real or ideal, a horizon, a meaning, the refusal of meaning, nothingness, and so forth, can be an "affair" [a thing] in the sense maintained by this phenomenological maxim of inquiry. (Fink, 1970, p. 82)

In *Ideas1* Husserl formulates what he calls "the principle of all principles" thusly:

> that every originary presentive intuition is a legitimizing source of cognition, that everything originarily (so to speak, in its "personal" actuality) offered to us in "intuition" is to be accepted simply as what it is presented as being, but also only within the limits in which it is presented there. (Husserl, 1983, p. 44)

216

This fundamental theme of going back to the things themselves, to the living of lived experience, plays through much of the many phenomenologies that have followed in the wake of Husserl's inspiring work: to practice phenomenological reflection is "to go from words and opinions back to the things themselves, to consult them in their self-givenness and to set aside all prejudices alien to them" (Husserl, 1983, p. 35).

From a Husserlian point of view, anything that presents itself to consciousness is potentially of interest to phenomenology, whether the object is real or imagined, empirically measurable or subjectively felt. Consciousness is the only access human beings have to the world. Or, rather, it is by virtue of being conscious that we are always already part of the world. Thus, all we can ever know must present itself to consciousness. Whatever falls outside of consciousness, therefore, falls outside the bounds of our possible human experience. In other words, consciousness is always transitive about something. To be conscious is to be aware, in some sense, of some aspect of the world.

However, it would be misleading to think of consciousness as a mental reservoir that contains our experiences and knowledge and from which we can retrieve our cognitions in the form of memories. So, Husserl warns that one should not be confused but that one should make a distinction between objects of consciousness and psychological or mental content.

> Dazed by the confusion between object and mental content, one forgets that the objects of which we are "conscious" are not simply in consciousness as in a box, so that they can merely be found in it and snatched at in it; but that they are first constituted as being what they are for us, and as what they count as for us, in varying forms of objective intention. (Husserl, 1970, p. 385)

Husserl distinguishes three areas of phenomenological research: phenomenology of hyle (of sense content), phenomenology of the noesis (the experience of acts of consciousness), and phenomenology of the noema (the eidetic content of the intentional object). According to Husserl, the most important part of phenomenology is the analysis of consciousness since it reveals how consciousness constitutes the objectivities.

Yet, consciousness itself cannot be described directly. Such description would reduce human science to the study of consciousness or ideas, committing the fallacy of idealism. Similarly, the world itself, without reference to an experiencing person or consciousness, cannot be described directly either. Such approach would overlook that the real things of the world are always meaningfully constituted by conscious human beings; it would commit the fallacy of realism. So, in cases when consciousness itself is the object of consciousness (when I reflect on my own thinking process), then consciousness is not the same as the act in which it appears. This also demonstrates that true introspection is impossible. A person cannot reflect on lived experience while living through the experience. For example, if one tries to reflect on one's anger while being angry, one finds that the anger has already changed or dissipated. Thus, phenomenological reflection is not introspective but retrospective. Reflection on lived experience is always recollective; it is reflection on experience that is already passed or lived through.

Ontological Phenomenology: Martin Heidegger

Martin Heidegger is widely considered a most important, if not the most significant and gifted philosopher of the twentieth century. He influenced the thinking of virtually all major philosophers, and his thoughts have been formative for developments in the human sciences, arts, humanities, social theory, and theories of technology and computing science.

Martin Heidegger was born in the small south German village of Messkirch on September 26, 1889. His father was a master cooper, a maker of barrels—a man of modest means who also occupied the position of church sexton of the village of Messkirch. Heidegger first went to grammar school where his teacher Gröber (who later became archbishop) gave him a book by Franz Brentano that made a great impression on Heidegger. According to his parents' wishes, Heidegger began to study theology from 1909 to 1911, but after four semesters he turned to the study of philosophy, mathematics, and physics at the University of Heidelberg. In 1913 he was promoted at the University of Freiburg on a doctoral dissertation on the *Study of Judgment and Psychologisms*, and in 1915 he was granted his habilitation.

Heidegger was married to Elfride Petri in 1917. His first son, Jörg, was born in 1919, and Hermann was born a year later, though Heidegger knew that he was not the real father of Hermann. When he was 14, Hermann was told that his biological father was a family friend, doctor Friedel Caesar, but Heidegger raised him like his son. It is known that during his life Heidegger had several lengthy romantic affairs, including with his students Hannah Arendt and Elisabeth Blochmann.

Heidegger died on May 26, 1976, and Hermann was the executor of his will. Hermann, who had become a historian, has been managing Heidegger's writings and publications after his death.

People who attended Heidegger's lectures have commented on his outstanding ability to draw his audience into his thinking. Students described him as a person of unassuming stature, but highly intelligent, with a strong presence and piercing eyes. As a teacher Heidegger carefully prepared his lectures in great detail in writing and even underlined sentences and passages with different colors in order to give proper emphasis and dramatic quality to his oral presentations. He soon became famous and drew scholars from all over Germany, Europe, and beyond to his lectures.

In *The Crisis of the European Sciences* (1936), Husserl had already turned phenomenological analysis away from the transcendental ego and consciousness, toward the prereflective lifeworld of everyday experience. With Heidegger, this turn toward the lived world became an ontological rather than an epistemological project. Instead of asking how the being of things are constituted as intentional objects in consciousness that we can know, Heidegger asked how the being of beings (things) show themselves to us as a revealing of Being itself. Simply put, not the knowledge of phenomena but the meaning of their being became the focus with Heidegger. Still Heidegger, initially employed Husserlian phrases to describe the project of phenomenology:

> Thus, the term "phenomenology" expresses a maxim, which can be formulated as "To the things themselves!" It is opposed to all free-floating constructions

and accidental findings; it is opposed to taking over any conceptions which only seem to have been demonstrated; it is opposed to those pseudo-questions which parade themselves as "problems", often for generations at a time. (Heidegger, 1962, p. 50)

For Heidegger the method of ontology is phenomenology. So, for Heidegger phenomenology requires of its practitioners a heedful attunement to the modes of being of the ways that things are in the world.

> Thus "phenomenology" means—to let that which shows itself be seen from itself in the very way in which it shows itself from itself. This is the formal meaning of that branch of research that calls itself "phenomenology". But here we are expressing nothing else than the maxim . . . "To the things themselves!" (Heidegger, 1962, p. 58)

Much of Heidegger's work is concerned with the question of how philosophy is possible in view of the realization that human life is radically finite and always involved in dynamic change. When we describe a thing, then we tend to assume that this thing has a permanent identity and a permanent presence. However, nothing is ever the same or unchanging. So how then can philosophy describe the things of our world and let life appear to itself? Heidegger is self-consciously aware of the difficulty that is known in philosophy as the problem of thematization.

Phenomenological thematization and description inevitably do violence to lived experience by unwittingly bringing experience to a halt. We cannot really capture experience in its unfolding in time. The problem is that epistemological forms of thematization confuse the nonprimordial (conceptual objectifications) for the primordial (nonconceptual meanings) dimensions of experience as they are lived through. For example, when I look at the clock on my wall and I describe the experience of the clock, I may be inclined to use conceptual terms such as time—hours—minutes—dial—hands—metal—glass—thing. However, these descriptive concepts increasingly thematize and objectify the clock and thereby impoverish the mundane character and experiential meaningfulness of the time-piece as it hangs on my wall. The problem is that the objectifying activity of describing the clock is actually a de-living experience: only leaving a residue of the originally subtle, complex, and rich primordial experience of temporality. Instead, I should try to describe the clock in its own being, as it shows itself to me in lived experience, unmediated by conceptual objectifications and abstractions.

Heidegger asks if it is possible to thematize lived experience without falling into the trap of objectification as it occurs in all positivistic forms of inquiry. He answers in the positive. But the phenomenological task of doing justice to the way we experience the things of our world remains a constant challenge and concern. Heidegger believes that it is possible for language to move beyond the traditional function of thematization, reification, representation, and objectification. For this purpose, Heidegger makes a distinction between traditional (epistemological) objectification as it occurs in social science and formal (ontological) objectification as practiced in phenomenological inquiry. Formal or ontological objectification safeguards the being of beings. The phenomenologist must let ontological objectification be guided or informed by the preontological understanding of being as it is lived in "an unobjective way" (1982, p. 281).

> If being is to become objectified—if the understanding of being is to be possible as a science in the sense of ontology—if there is to be philosophy at all, then that upon which the understanding of being, qua understanding, has already pre-conceptually projected being must become unveiled in an explicit manner. (1982, p. 282)

In inquiring into the meaning of experience, phenomenology inevitably encounters issues of reification and objectification. Husserl had suggested that a phenomenon comes into being when we lift something out of the primordial stream of consciousness. So, phenomenology explores the meaning of phenomena by focusing on something and naming it. However, Heidegger criticizes Husserl for having committed to representational assumptions about being, and thus Husserl's epistemological phenomenology remains stuck in a metaphysics of presence and representation. Husserl assumes that objects of consciousness correspond to transcendental entities, beings. But Heidegger points out that Husserl fails to ask what the being of these beings consists of.

> For us phenomenological reduction means leading phenomenological vision back from the apprehension of a being, whatever may be the character of that apprehension, to the understanding of the being of this being (projecting upon the way it is unconcealed). Like every other scientific method, phenomenological method grows and changes due to the progress made precisely with its help into the subjects under investigation. Scientific method is never a technique. As soon as it becomes one it has fallen away from its own proper nature. (Heidegger, 1982, p. 21)

When Heidegger discusses the method of the reduction, he places it in the context of construction and destruction. Indeed, the notion of "deconstruction" originates not with Derrida (though he made the idea of deconstruction as a method for studying the meaning of things famous), but with Heidegger.

> These three basic components of phenomenological method—reduction, construction, destruction—belong together in their content and must receive grounding in their mutual pertinence. Construction in philosophy is necessarily destruction, that is to say, a de-constructing of traditional concepts carried out in a historical recursion to the tradition. And this is not a negation of the tradition or a condemnation of it as worthless; quite the reverse, it signifies precisely a positive appropriation of tradition. (Heidegger, 1982, p. 23)

Heidegger had already reflected on "the destruction of the problem of lived experience" in a summer course in 1920 at the University of Freiburg. His application of the notion of philosophical destruction will later lead Derrida to launch the notion of deconstruction. As well, Sartre's critique of Husserl's intentionality of the "I" is predated by Heidegger:

220

The "I" as such is not at all an object of consciousness. It is, therefore, not conceptually graspable . . . . It is no possible content of a consciousness but exactly that which is conscious of something . . . .

Although it cannot be forbidden to speak about the "I", that is to objectify it—in fact it even must be done—but it must be just as clear that then it is no longer itself. If it were itself grasped and graspable as the "I", then it would be "at the same time something knowing and something known, at the same time subject and object of one and the same act of knowing." (Heidegger, 2010, p. 95b)

Obviously, the "I" being at once subject and object would be a contradiction. Moreover, the "I" does not appear at the same time as subject and object in lived experience. Heidegger points out that the "I" we refer to when we say "I am hungry" is not really present as such in our living experience. Rather, the "I" is an object of thought: "in thinking alone one becomes conscious of the "I" as such" (Heidegger, 2010, p. 96b).

In *Being and Time*, Heidegger (1962, 2010) distinguishes between two kinds of modalities of things. These modalities are not different aspects or entities of things but different relations that we engage with things. Things that are *zuhanden* are relationally "ready-to-hand" as tools or equipment; things that are *vorhanden* are relationally "present-at-hand" as objects of contemplation or reflection. The difference lies in using a thing versus thinking about a thing. In everyday life we are generally involved with the things of our world in a taken-for-granted manner of ready-to-hand. When I pour a cup of coffee, I am not reflecting on the coffee jar or coffee machine; when I drink from the coffee cup, I am not reflecting about the nature of a cup. But, at times, we are indeed struck by the presence of such things.

Heidegger gives the famous example of a hammer and how we suddenly notice the nature of the hammer when it breaks. Similarly, I may reflect on the existential, cultural, and technical appearance of the jar or the coffee cup made from china or from some other material. And in reflecting on these things, my relation to the thing changes from *zuhanden* to *vorhanden*, from ready-to-hand to present-at-hand. A phenomenology of the things of our world concerns itself with the nearness and distance in the way we position things and they position themselves. But nearness does not just mean close, and distance does not just mean far away. Nearness is the presencing of things in our lives. Only in this positioning of things do they become accessible. Positionality becomes a critical notion in Heidegger's reflections on the way that the meaning of things involves a showing and hiding, a concealing and unconcealing of their meaning and significance.

The requisitioning of positionality places itself before the thing, leaving it unguarded as thing, truthless. Thus, positionality disguises the nearing nearness of the world in the thing. Positionality even disguises this, its disguising, just as the forgetting of something is itself forgotten and drawn away in the wake of forgetfulness. The event of forgetfulness does not only allow a lapse into concealment, but rather this lapsing itself lapses into concealment along with it, which itself even falls away with its fall. (Heidegger, 2012a, p. 71)

Phenomenological insight becomes possible and necessary only in this ontological play of (un)concealment, the showing and hiding of meaning. Nevertheless, says Heidegger, "in all this disguising of positionality, the glimmer of world still lights up, the truth of beying flashes" (Heidegger, 2012a, p. 71).

According to Heidegger, perception is not a process whereby the meaning we experience is constructed through the interpretation of our sensory experiences. We always already are submerged in meaning. Heidegger shows that the ordinary acts of seeing, touching, and hearing are not interpreted sensory acts but already acts of meaning before we can abstract them into sensory moments. What we "first" hear is never noises or complexes of sounds, but the phone, the door, the motorcycle. We hear people walking by, we hear the wind, the woodpecker tapping, a plane flying overhead, the fire crackling, someone talking.

> It requires a very artificial and complicated frame of mind to "hear" a "pure noise". The fact that motor-cycles and wagons are what we proximally hear is the phenomenal evidence that in every case Dasein as Being–in-the-world, already dwells alongside what is ready-to-hand within-the-world; it certainly does not dwell proximally alongside "sensations"; nor would it first have to give shape to the swirl of sensations to provide a springboard from which the subject leaps off and finally arrives at a "world". Dasein, as essentially understanding, is proximally alongside what is understood.
>
> Likewise, when we are explicitly hearing the discourse of another, we proximally understand what is said, or—to put it more exactly—we are already with him, in advance, alongside the entity which the discourse is about.... Even in cases where the speech is indistinct or in a foreign language, what we proximally hear is unintelligible words, and not a multiplicity of tone-data. (Heidegger, 1962, p. 207)

In the decade after the publication of *Being and Time*, Heidegger increasingly focused not on the meaning (being) of Being, but on the originary significance of Being. In his rich, seemingly more fragmentary texts *Contributions to Philosophy* and *The Event*, Heidegger insistently explores the inceptual challenge of reflection that aims to penetrate to the beginning of the meaning of being that he indicates with the older etymological spelling as Beying (*Seyn*). A key term for this later work is "the event" or "enowning," which is impossible to define in English language but that needs to be studied in context and sensitive to subtle German linguisticalities. Some have criticized Heidegger for his mystifying usages of language, but we must recognize that it is only through a rigorous and yet poetic attention to language that Heidegger can creatively evoke understandings that are profound and yet elusive. In Heidegger's words:

> Inceptual speech is always indebted to the beginning for the eventuation of the thoughtful word.
> . . .
> To the indolent, dull, vacant, and stubborn, let it be said: language is in its historical beginning richer, freer, more venturesome, and therefore also always more strange than worn-out ordinary opinion may admit into the precinct of its calculations. The inceptual word thus appears as the disturbance of

an ordinary . . . univocity. Thence the indignation at the supposed play with word-meanings. That which fools consider to be an artificial contrivance, because it opposes their routine, is in essence only the counter-tone of the appropriation which maintains everything proper to beying in the essence of its truth. (2013b, p. 259)

For a phenomenology of practice the question of how to arrive at creative insight has to be a constant concern and challenge. Phenomenological research is the practice of creative insight that has to do with beginnings: the historical-ity of the beginning of beginning where meaning originates. Some of our most cherished personal insights are probably the result of life's inceptualities. And yet, there is more to this enigma. Inception connotes origination, birth, dawn, genesis, beginning, and opening. A phenomenology of "creative" insight would challenge us to find our way back to the beginning—or, as Heidegger says, to inception, the inventive event where thought begins. And, phenomenologists have suggested that the beginning must be sought, not in some fancy abstract theory, but in the primordiality of lived experience.

> The inventive thinking of the saying of the beginning is the thinking appropri-ated by the inceptuality, in the inceptuality, and as the inceptuality . . . . Nowhere does it refer to the "views" of thinkers, to a "doctrine" about beings ("world"). Or to a mere speaking "about" being. Inventive thinking "is" beying, the latter, however, as the appropriating event.
> . . . The inceptuality . . . unfolds the beginning and thus appropriates beginnings . . . whose essence we are starting to surmise. (Heidegger, 2013b, pp. 258, 259)

In his later work, Heidegger increasingly concerns himself with language (1971a, 1971b) and the ability of poetic and expressive language to mediate and reveal the ontologies of life. In various places Heidegger refers to the belonging together of language, being, and thinking. Language is the house of being:

> "Language" is not conceived as speaking and thus not as a mere activity of the human, but rather as house, i.e., as protection, as relationship.
> The relationship is repeatedly pointed to by another citation, which says: lan-guage speaks and not the human.
> . . . that language speaks, is the indication that the essence of language itself is playful, though it thereby does not get tangled up in itself, but releases itself into the free space of that inceptual freedom that is determined by itself alone. (2012a, pp. 158, 159)

The act of speaking and talking itself can be rather meaningless. Mere speaking happens in the chatter of everyday life. But the essence of language, says Heideg-ger, lies in "saying" (*Sagen*), because the inception of meaning occurs in saying. Heidegger points out that the verbs speaking and talking can be used intransitively (someone is speaking or talking), but in saying there constantly lies a relation to something to be said and to what is said. Even silence can be a form of saying. So, when we say, "silence speaks," then we really mean that something is said—there is saying in the speaking of silence:

> only in saying does the whole essence of language come to appearance .... One speaks. Someone talks .... He rattles on perhaps because he has nothing to say. And one speaks endlessly and it all says nothing. Contrariwise, one can be silent and in such a way say much, while there is no silence that speaks. Even the speechless gesture, precisely this, resonates in saying, not because there is a language of gestures and forms, but because the essence of language lies in saying. (2012a, p. 159)

One of the most provocative and contested issues that Heidegger raises is contained in his thinking about technology and ontotheology. In *The Question Concerning Technology*, Heidegger shows that technology should not just be simply interpreted as the tools and techniques that we use to produce things. He famously says, there is nothing technological about technology. Rather, we need to see that technology has become the ontotheology of our modern existence. Technology makes the world appear to us as standing reserve that we can exploit and use for our consuming wants and desires. Heidegger speaks of the danger of technology and that we need to understand how it has profoundly shaped our spiritual, social, and physical existence. Philosophers of technology such as Feenberg (1999) have critiqued Heidegger for exaggerating the threats that technology poses for human existence. More positively oriented critics, such as Iain Thomson (2000), show how Heidegger's phenomenology of technology contains many profound insights that are worth studying and heeding and that require our thoughtful response.

Personalistic and Value Phenomenology: Max Scheler

For Max Scheler, phenomenology does not hinge on a method as so painstakingly elaborated by Husserl, but on an attitude, and "the manner in which I understand and execute this attitude" (Scheler, 1973, p. xix). Scheler was an admired philosophical phenomenologist and a very successful author; during his lifetime, he drew many scholars to his work on personalism, value ethics, community, solidarity, sympathy, love, and religious experience.

Max Scheler was born in 1874 in Munich, Germany. His Jewish mother taught him the Jewish way of life, but when he was 11 years old he was baptized into the Roman Catholic Church. As a student he was introduced to Wilhelm Dilthey in Berlin, but in 1901 he met Husserl and, after reading the *Logical Investigations*, Scheler became a phenomenologist. He was a student and assistant with Husserl and started teaching in Jena and then in Munich in 1907.

However, due to a messy divorce and some rumored scandals involving affairs, he was fired in 1910; he spent the next nine years in Berlin writing, giving talks, and working for newspapers. He also collaborated with Husserl in editing the journal *Jahrbuch für Philosophie und phänomenologische Forschung*. But gradually, as Husserl was still in the early stage of his work, Scheler chose his own direction that was different from Husserl. In 1919 he was appointed professor in philosophy and sociology at the new University of Köln. But when in 1922 Scheler left the church, went through another divorce, and started a third marriage, he was fired again. Perhaps not ironically, Scheler emphasized in the Preface to the second edition of his book *Formalism in Ethics* (1921) that:

> It is precisely because I place all care for the community and its forms in the living *center of the individual person* that I may be allowed to reject most emphatically every direction in an ethos that makes the value of the person originally and essentially dependent on his relation to a community ... (1973, p. xxiv)

Scheler declares that a person-value is higher than all values of things, organizations, and community. Even a spiritual ground of the world, whatever else it may be, deserves to be called "God" only to the extent that it is "personal" (p. xxiv).

In 1927 Scheler read Heidegger's *Being and Time*, and he was very impressed. The next spring, he was appointed professor of philosophy in Frankfurt, where he joined the famous scholars Ernst Cassirer, Max Horkheimer, and Theodor Adorno. But before he had time to start his work, he died of a heart attack in May 1928. Heidegger declared later that phenomenology would not have become what it is if it was not for the work and influence of Max Scheler.

While Scheler was strongly inspired by Husserl's initial work, he also became one of the first critics. Scheler's phenomenological approach was to orient directly to the insights that a phenomenological attitude should yield. A "method" should not block or stand in the way of gaining such phenomenological insights directly from the attitude that enables the phenomenological experience. He states, "I owe to the significant works of Edmund Husserl the methodological consciousness of the unity and sense of the phenomenological attitude," but he also makes clear that Husserl and he were "men who otherwise vastly differ both in world view and on philosophical matters" (Scheler, 1973, p. xix).

In *Formalism in Ethics*, Scheler aims to show that human values such as pleasure, happiness, love, and solidarity are not just ethical categories as in Kantian philosophy, but they belong to a domain of values that are actually experienced in our daily lives, and that we also experience them variously as higher and lower values. Values are not like goods that belong to objects, rather

> they belong in essence to the sphere of the person (and act-being). For neither the person nor acts can ever be given to us as "objects." As soon as we tend to "objectify" a human being in any way, the bearer of moral values disappears of necessity. (Scheler, 1973, p. 86)

So, for Scheler ethical values are phenomenologically given in lived experience—and they are given in the totality of a singular order, an "order of ranks," even though the height of a value may not be felt as such, or preferred, one over the other.

Scheler's most famous phenomenology is contained in *The Nature of Sympathy* (1970)—his study on the ethics and nature of sympathy. The second part of the book is concerned with love and hatred.

Scheler's work is proof that phenomenology does not need to be practiced as a rigorous method in the sense of Husserl. Yet, he carefully and brilliantly explores phenomenological distinctions by means of the "method" of the phenomenological attitude and reflections for direct insights. Scheler's intent is to show that the ethical is already contained in the shared feelings we experience with others. For him ethics is already deeply embedded in our living with others and not just something added. The phenomenological challenge is to determine the essence of the shared feeling of sympathy or fellow-feeling (*Mitgefühl*) by distinguishing it from other feelings.

In his initial examination of the phenomenon of fellow-feeling, Scheler makes distinctions among four kinds of relationships: (1) immediate community of feeling, e.g., of one and the same sorrow, "with someone"; (2) fellow-feeling "about something," rejoicing in his joy and commiseration with his sorrow; (3) mere emotional infection; and (4) true emotional identification.

First, Scheler describes the phenomenon of "community of feeling" (*Miteinanderfühlen*) by using the moment of parental grief as an example:

Two parents stand beside the dead body of a beloved child. They feel in common the "same" sorrow, the "same" anguish. It is not that A feels this sorrow and B feels it also, and moreover that they both know they are feeling it. No, it is a *feeling-in-common*. A's sorrow is in no way an "external" matter for B here, as it is, e.g., for their friend G, who joins them, and commiserates "with them" or "upon their sorrow." On the contrary, they feel it together, in the sense that they feel and experience in common, not only the self-same value-situation, but also the same keenness of emotion in regards to it. (Scheler, 1970, p. 13)

In the case of community of feeling, there is no experienced separation of feelings and emotions. Now, Scheler shows that "fellow-feeling" (*Mitgefühl*) or sympathy differs from "community of feeling" in two important respects:

All fellow-feeling involves *intentional reference* of the feeling of joy or sorrow to the other person's experience. [But] *my* commiseration and *his* suffering are phenomenologically *two different facts*, not *one* fact, as in the first case [of community of feeling]. (1970, p. 13)

Fellow-feeling occurs when there is an orientation toward the other's feeling or pain as well as a sympathetic feeling for the other. In fellow-feeling we not only feel vicariously what it is like to have a certain pleasant or unpleasant experience, we also feel for the other person who has this pleasant or unpleasant experience. Scheler speaks of vicariously visualized feelings in which we participate as we would in the vicarious experience of reading a novel. In contrast, a cruel person who tortures another may experience the vicariously visualized feelings, but does not feel for the other person. Thus,

Fellow-feeling proper, actual "participation" presents itself in the very phenomenon as a *re-action* to the state and value of the other's feelings—as these are "visualized" in vicarious feeling.... [T]he two functions of *vicariously visualized* feeling, and *participation* in feeling are separately given and must be sharply distinguished. (1970, p. 14)

Scheler continues to use the phenomenological method of comparison to distinguish "emotional" infection (*Gefühlsansteckung*), which can be easily confused with fellow-feeling:

> We all know how the cheerful atmosphere in a "pub" or at a party may "infect" the newcomers, who may even have been depressed beforehand, so that they are "swept up" into the prevailing gaiety . . . . It is the same when laughter proves "catching," as can happen especially with children . . . . The same thing occurs when a group is infected by the mournful tone of one of its members . . . . Naturally this has nothing whatever to do with pity. Here there is neither a *directing* of feeling towards the other's joy or suffering, nor any participation in her experience. On the contrary, it is characteristic of emotional infection that it occurs only as a transference of the *state* of feeling, and does *not* presuppose any sort of *knowledge* of the joy which others feel. Thus, one may only notice afterwards that a mourning feeling, encountered in oneself, is traceable to infection from a group one has visited some hours before. (1970, p. 15)

In the emotional infection, the person gets lost in a certain celebratory, joyous, grieving, or moody psychological atmosphere with others without really being conscious of this process. We share certain feelings with others in an atmosphere of togetherness or we-ness. In such situations, we may become different from the way we felt before or the way we usually are.

Next, Scheler discusses emotional identification (*Einsfühlung*), which happens when we identify so strongly with another person that we take on their life, as it were. We literally feel "one" (*eins*) and unified with this person:

> The true *sense of emotional unity*, the act of identifying one's own self with that of another, is only a heightened form, a limiting case as it were, of infection. It represents a limit in that here is not only the separate process of feeling in another that is unconsciously taken as one's own, but his self (in all its basic attitudes), that is identified with one's own self . . .
>
> Thus, identification can come about in *one* way through the total eclipse and absorption of another self by one's own, it being thus, as it were, completely dispossessed and deprived of all rights in its conscious existence and character. It can also come about the other way, where "I" (the formal subject) am so overwhelmed and hypnotically bound and fettered by the other "I" (the concrete individual), that my formal status as a subject is usurped by the other's personality, with all *its* characteristic aspects; in such a case, I live, not in "myself," but entirely in "him," the other person—(in and through him, as it were). (1970, p. 18)

Scheler spends a major part of his fellow-feeling study on the phenomenon of love. How is love different from fellow-feeling?

> Love is above all a *spontaneous* act, and remains so even when given in response, whatever the grounds for this may be. Fellow-feeling, on the other

hand, is always a *reactive* condition. Thus, one can only have fellow-feeling for that which is *subject to feeling*, whereas love is altogether free from this limitation.

Admittedly . . . all fellow-feeling is *based* upon love of some sort and vanishes when love is altogether absent . . . . [T]he act of fellow-feeling, if it is to amount to more than mere understanding or vicarious emotion, must be rooted in an enveloping act of love. (1970, p. 142)

Scheler was a contemporary of Husserl but, ultimately, not really a student of Husserl. He read Husserl's first major work of the *Logical Investigations* and thereafter declared himself a phenomenologist. Inspired by Husserl, but not really committed to the latter's epistemological preoccupations and methods, Scheler shows how he begins his own phenomenological explorations, such as the experience of fellow-feeling and love, through insightful reflections on the lived experience of fellow-feeling and on related and opposite phenomena. Scheler provides an inventive and creative example of doing phenomenology by adopting a thoughtful phenomenological attitude toward the phenomena he is studying. Husserl himself was still at the beginning of his career, and though he was initially encouraged by Scheler's interest, he increasingly felt that Scheler was offering his admiring readers "fool's gold" rather than the real precious matter resulting from rigorous scientific excavations and cultivations.

In contrast, Scheler already seemed to see the shortcomings of a purely intellectual approach to the logic of phenomenology: "The heart possesses, within its own realm, a strict analogon of logic, which it does not, however, borrow from the logic of the intellect" (1970, p. xii). He believed that phenomenology could only be practiced through the sense of wonder and a direct and loving participation in the world. Scheler's phenomenology can be seen as a very early alternative to a strictly cognitive or intellectual method. From then on, this injection of ethical and pathic elements into the very process of inquiry and reflection gradually becomes a sustaining theme throughout the methodological developments of subsequent phenomenologies for an explication of the phenomenological attitude.

Empathic and Faith Phenomenology: Edith Stein

Edith Stein describes herself as: "I, Edith Stein, was born on October 12, 1891 in Breslau, the daughter of the deceased merchant Siegfried Stein and his wife Auguste, née Courant. I am a Prussian citizen and Jewish" (Stein, 1917/1989, p. 119). She was the youngest of 11 children. After grammar school she studied philosophy, psychology, history, and German philology at the University of Breslau. There she also joined the women's suffrage movement. In 1913 she transferred to the University of Göttingen, where she became the student of Edmund Husserl and also studied with Adolf Reinach and Max Scheler. Stein was one of the first scholars to study with Husserl and apply his phenomenology to the study of empathy.

During World War I Stein broke off her studies and briefly worked for the Red Cross and then as a substitute teacher at the girls' secondary school where she had been a student four years earlier. In 1916 she followed Husserl to Freiburg where she became a member of the faculty and worked with Heidegger, editing Husserl's publications. In 1916, she passed her doctorate, with *summa cum laude* honor, on a dissertation, published in 1917, *The Empathy Problem as it Developed Historically and Considered Phenomenologically*. Her dissertation is a fine example of what a Husserlian phenomenological study looks like. She completed this brilliant study when she was scarcely 25 years old.

Husserl recommended Stein for a professorship in 1919, but she was refused an appointment (her habilitation thesis was rejected because she was a woman). For a few years she continued to work on Husserl's projects while she also wrote several papers that were published by Husserl in a journal he edited. During some holiday travels, Stein had profound conversion experiences and joined the Catholic faith. In 1922, she broke off her assistantship with Husserl and started to teach at a Dominican girls' school for the next ten years. There, she translated Thomas Aquinas' *De Veritate* (On Truth). In 1929 she visited Husserl and Heidegger and, for a while, dedicated herself again to philosophy with a book relating the scholastic writings of Thomas Aquinas to the work of Husserl, entitled *Potency and Act* (1931). She briefly became a lecturer at the Munich Institute for Pedagogy. But because of her Jewish background, she was forced by the anti-Semitic bureaucracy to resign in 1933.

Stein criticized the Nazi policies and, in a letter, she asked Pope Pius XI to openly denounce the regime. By the early thirties she joined the Carmelite Convent and after her investiture adopted the name Sister Teresia Benedicta a Cruce. She wrote several philosophical and theological studies, but as the Nazi threat increased in 1938, she had to escape to the Netherlands, where she entered the Echt Convent. Unfortunately, in retaliation against the Dutch Roman Catholic Bishops, who had written an open letter of protest against the deportations of Jews, she, with many other converts from the Jewish faith were arrested by the Gestapo. She was deported to Auschwitz on August 7, 1942, where she died two days later in the gas chambers. On May 1, 1987, Edith Stein was honored and beatified by Pope John Paul II.

Stein was Husserl's first assistant and graduate student. And Husserl was the supervisor of Stein's dissertation, *On the Problem of Empathy*. The German word for empathy is *Einfühlung*, literally "in-feeling" or "feeling with." She benefited from Husserl's manuscript *Ideas I*, but she had submitted her dissertation just prior to the publication of Husserl's *Ideas II*, in which he addresses the notion of empathy and intersubjectivity more extensively. She explained that she would have had to do additional work if she could have read *Ideas II* before finishing her study. Still, in her dissertation Stein demonstrates original insights that also critically depart from the writings on empathy by Theodor Lipps, Adolf Reinach, Max Scheler, and Husserl himself.

At the outset, Stein states her intent to do a phenomenology of empathy, not a psychology of empathy. She wants to describe what it is that is experienced in the act of empathy, and she starts with an anecdotal example:

A friend tells me that he has lost his brother and I become aware of his pain. What kind of an awareness is this? I am not concerned here with going into the basis on which I infer the pain. Perhaps his face is pale and disturbed, his voice toneless and strained. Perhaps he also expresses his pain in words. Naturally, these things can all be investigated, but they are not my concern here. I would like to know, not how I arrive at this awareness, but what it itself is. (Stein, 1989, p. 6)

Stein immediately points out that, in spite of the physical countenance or expressions, there is no outer perception of the pain. The friend's facial changes may be empathically grasped as an expression of pain, but the pain is not primordially given to her. By primordial, Stein means the present experience of the now that one lives through: "All our own present experiences are primordial. What could be more primordial than experience itself?" (1989, p. 7). But not all experiences are primordially given or primordial in their content. For example, memories may bring back experiences that point to a past primordiality—and this past has the character of a former "now." With these observations, Edith Stein wants to reflect on the question of whether we can empathically grasp the meaning of a primordial experience (such as joy) of another person that is not our own primordial experience.

> While I am living in the other's joy, I do not feel primordial joy. It does not issue live from my "I." Neither does it have the character of once having lived like remembered joy. But still much less is it merely fantasized without actual life. This other subject is primordial although I do not experience it as primordial. In my non-primordial experience I feel, as it were, led by a primordial one not experienced by me but still there, manifesting itself in my nonprimordial experience. (Stein, 1989, p. 11)

In the opening sections of her dissertation, Stein discusses and criticizes the various theories of empathy that were current at her time (and that perhaps are still held by many today). While she finds many insights developed by thinkers, such as Lipps and Scheler, that are helpful for the understanding of empathy, she also identifies a variety of problems. Specifically, by using anecdotal experiential examples, she shows that the empathic experience of another person's experience is not some kind of outer or inner perception, or the imitation experience of someone else's gestures associated with a certain feeling. It is true that the moods and feelings of those who are close to us may influence and affect our feelings and mood. If my spouse is in a bad mood, it may affect my mood too. Feelings and moods are contagious. Similarly, when a baby hears another baby cry, she may also start crying. But, Stein points out, these are not empathic acts. As well, she raises interesting questions about the nature of negative empathy:

> Negative empathy: the case in which the tendency of the empathic experience to become a primordial experience of my own cannot be realized because "something in me" opposes it. This may either be a momentary experience of my own or my kind of personality. (Stein, 1989, p. 15)

She gives the example of being completely filled with grief over a bereavement at the same moment that a friend tells some joyful news. So, there are several possibilities for empathy to be frustrated or yet to be fulfilled under certain conditions. Stein also explores the phenomenon of "background experiences" that may have latent but unpredictable consequences for later experiences.

Stein's dissertation is helpful for phenomenological researchers and students of phenomenology—not only for the insights it provides into the phenomenology of empathy but also for the manner in which this dissertation, under the supervision of Husserl himself, was conducted. Ironically, professional philosophers criticize and argue about Stein's explications of empathy but they pay little attention to the way that she approaches and conducts Husserl's methodology. But this is precisely the concern of this book. From a methodological point of view, we can see how Stein first aims to show how the various "theories" of empathy fall short of a phenomenological understanding of what the empathic experience actually is like.

> Thus, we conclude from our critical excursions that none of the current genetic theories can account for empathy. Of course, we can guess why this is so. Before one can delineate the genesis of something, one must know what it is. (Stein, 1989, p. 27)

Only after carefully showing that the meaning of the primordial experience of empathy is lacking does she determinedly engage her phenomenological study. Stein carefully and painstakingly examines the meaning of empathy in relation to physical causes and psychological motives. For example, we may understand that someone's mood may have changed drastically as a result of the use of alcohol or a psychotropic drug. The behavioral causes and the mental effects of alcohol or drugs may be explainable through medical science, but physiological changes cannot be grasped through empathy. In contrast, the feelings of joy or sadness that accompanies this use of alcohol or drugs may be a proper object for empathic understanding. But Stein also shows that the interaction between physiological and psychic or spiritual processes may be complicated.

Most striking are several seemingly obvious, but original distinctions that Stein makes that anticipate later insights by Maurice Merleau-Ponty about the role of the body in the understanding of perception and intersubjectivity. For example, Stein shows the importance of sensual empathy in our understanding of the mood of another person who sits at the table with us.

> The hand resting on the table does not lie there like the book beside it. It "presses" against the table more or less strongly; it lies there limpid or stretched; and I "see" these sensations of pressure and tension in a co-primordial way. If I follow out the tendencies to fulfilment in this "co-comprehension," my hand is moved (not in reality, but "as if") to the place of the foreign one. It is moved into it and occupies its position and attitude, now feeling its sensations, though not primordially and not as being its own. Rather, my own hand feels the foreign hand's sensation "with," precisely through the empathy whose nature we earlier differentiated from our own experience and every other kind of representation. During this projection, the foreign hand is continually perceived as belonging to the foreign physical body so that the empathized sensations are continually brought into relief as foreign in contrast with our own sensations. This is so even when I am not turned toward this contrast in the manner of awareness. (Stein, 1989, p. 58)

Edith Stein shows how what I sense nonprimordially in someone else can coincide with the other's primordial sensation. But it is also possible that for persons who are very different from us, their primordial experiences are not given to us in this empathic manner. In her later writings, Stein (1994, 2000) shows how empathic processes lie at the base of the possibility of forming community with others—communities that enrich our lives and to which we also contribute through the valuations of our own lives (Sawicki, 1998). Thus, as singular persons we can only become who we are through community: the community of family, neighborhood, workplace, volunteer activities, political associations, and so on.

Personal Practice Phenomenology: Jan Patočka

When Jan Patočka spent his Christmas Eve of 1935 at the home of the Husserls in Kappel, he was surprised with a gift from his mentor. It was a wood-carved desktop lectern that Husserl himself had received as a gift half a century earlier, in 1878, from his mentor Tomáš Garrigue Masaryk. In recounting this event, many years later, Jan Patočka said, "And so I became the heir of a tradition." Three years after Patočka received the gift, Husserl died. But Patočka himself can also be seen as contributing to a tradition that built on the diverting orientations of Husserl and Heidegger. Many of his publications are based on lecture notes kept by his students and that were disseminated after his death. His work influenced the thinking of Derrida, Ricoeur, and others.

Patočka was born in 1907 in Czechoslovakia. His early writings concern the thinking of Comenius (Ján Amos Komenský) and the philosophic and political thoughts of Tomáš Garrigue Masaryk. Patočka studied with Husserl and Heidegger in the 1930s, and he was also influenced by Eugen Fink, Henri Bergson, Emmanuel Levinas, Hannah Arendt, and Maurice Merleau-Ponty. For many years Patočka was banned from teaching in communist Czechoslovakia. He was a spokesman for the human rights movement in Czechoslovakia and participated in giving lectures at a so-called underground university, dedicated to a free and uncensored education. He was frequently subjected to questioning by the secret police and died in 1977 after an 11-hour-long interrogation.

Patočka was probably the first to show that Husserlian explication of the reduction is not as clear and unambiguous as Husserl had presumed. He saw the limits of Husserlian phenomenological reflection that is based on an intellectual interpretation of consciousness. He turned to Heidegger's *Being and Time*, which starts from the practical horizon of being in the world. Heidegger's notion of *Dasein* is based on the idea of self-understanding in the situated "here" (*Da* of *Dasein*). Both Husserl and Heidegger place the project of self-understanding at the heart of their phenomenological philosophy. But Patočka argues that Husserl's interpretation of the ego as consciousness is still too abstract, and Heidegger's notion of *Dasein* is too impersonal. Patočka stresses the corporeal and situated nature of our personal being. We are not just situated in the world; we are our situatedness. We are our personal being in our purposes, projects, and possibilities.

Patočka's thinking is of interest for the notion of a phenomenology of practice, since he was probably the first one who spoke of the primacy of practice. He developed an approach to phenomenology that may be termed a personal practice phenomenology. According to Patočka, it is within the practical, embodied, and situated horizons of our personal everyday lives that the structures of the phenomena of lived experience are most clearly seen:

We understand practically: that is, we are able to, we are familiar with, we know how to deal with. That is the original meaning of "to understand." That is how we first understand ourselves and things. That is how a child begins to understand a spoon, a saucer—as it begins to know how to deal with them.

...

In Heidegger's conception, consciousness—if we can ask about it at all—is something that first arises in the primordial clarity of a being that must accomplish its being, that is preoccupied with its own being. The point is the essential primacy of practice. At the very protofoundation of consciousness, of thought, of the subject, there is acting, not mere seeing. That explains why there is so much opaque, obscure, in our clarity. (Patočka, 1998, pp. 96, 97)

Patočka says that phenomenology needs to "bring out the originary personal experience. The experience of the way we live situationally, the way we are personal beings in space" (Patočka, 1998, p. 172). He praises Husserl's immense courage to put the power of reflection in service of a drive toward cognitive clarity, moral autonomy, and human (self-)responsibility. But he also notes that Husserl was "an antipragmatist, and antipracticist" and therefore forgetful of the concrete and situated nature of personal being in the lifeworld. This can lead to a disinterest of the consequences for the practice of human living.

Modern humanism thrives on the idea that humans are in some sense the heirs of the absolute, an absolute conceived along the lines of Christianity (from which our humanism grew), that they have a license to subjugate all reality, to appropriate it and to exploit it with no obligation to give anything in return, constraining and disciplining themselves. (Patočka, 1998, p. 178)

Phenomenological reflection and consciousness involve an inevitable distanciation from the objects of reflection. But the embodied nature of our practical existence also reminds us from moment to moment that we *are* our bodies and that we *are* the situatedness and the things of and in our world. "On the basis of their corporeity humans are not only the beings of distance but also the beings of proximity, rooted beings, not only innerworldly beings but also beings in the world" (Patočka, 1998, p. 178).

Political Phenomenology: Hannah Arendt

Hannah Arendt was born in Linden, Germany, near Hannover, in 1906. She grew up in Königsberg and studied philosophy and theology with Martin Heidegger and Edmund Husserl at the University of Marburg and Freiburg. Heidegger had become famous for his spellbinding lectures that drew students and academics near and far. Hannah Arendt found in him a fascinating teacher who could revive real thinking at the German university, and more: she had a stormy romantic relation with Heidegger. To avoid embarrassment, Heidegger suggested she submit her dissertation, on the concept of love in the thought of Saint Augustine, for promotion with Karl Jaspers. She did so and remained a strong family friend with Jasper and his wife for the rest of their lives.

After being briefly arrested by the Gestapo she fled to Paris in 1933—there she met other German refugees such as Walter Benjamin. In 1940 she managed to obtain a visa and traveled with her husband and mother to the United States. She initially worked as an editor and wrote many articles on political-philosophical issues such as freedom, power, authoritarianism, civil disobedience, and educational policy.

Arendt taught at several American universities, and from 1967 to 1975 she held a professorship at the New School for Social Research in New York. Her major works include *The Origins of Totalitarianism* (1951), *The Human Condition* (1958b), and *The Life of the Mind* (1978). Arendt drew attention to the issue of the source and meaning of evil in a world that had just witnessed the horrors of the Holocaust. When the German Nazi Adolf Eichmann, who had been responsible for deporting thousands of Jews to extermination camps, was standing trial for crimes against humanity in 1960, the world of public opinion depicted him as an evil monster. But Arendt coined the phrase the "banality of evil" to describe the case of Eichmann. People do not seem to realize what profound interpretation of the phenomenological epoché lies at the reversal of Arendt's notion of the banality of evil. She argued that it is too easy to consider Eichmann a monster and unlike any of us. The problem is that many people are capable of executing evil acts when they are placed in situations where immoral things are expected of them. There is a danger of getting caught up in submitting to the program of any political movement. That is why Arendt spent much of her philosophical career explaining the philosophical intricacies of learning to think critically and independently about any contingent situation in which we may find ourselves.

In *The Human Condition*, Arendt develops a phenomenological political account of action that is provocative and of practical import. She makes a distinction between a hierarchy of human activity (vita active) labor, work, and action. Labor is the most basic human activity that serves human survival; work involves the making and construing of useful and beautiful objects to make life convenient and enjoyable; action is the communal practice of creating a common social world. Action presupposes the acknowledgment that we live in a plural world that is made possible by the value of the public space. According to Arendt, political action should never be placed in the service of limited political aims and goals (however laudable they may seem at first), but rather that political action should be seen as participating in the public sphere of a free and plural shared world. Predetermined political goals turn thinking and acting into instrumental processes—always and inevitably leading to forms of totalitarianism and authoritarianism. In *Between Past and Future*, Arendt argues that political opinions and judgments are best formed in specific and concrete contexts—not guided by some grand narrative or abstract principle, but guided by concrete examples: human stories that express some truth.

In the two-volume set *The Life of the Mind* (1978), Arendt analyzes the notions of thinking and willing. The third volume was planned to be about judging, but she died before she could complete it. The first volume, *Thinking*, is largely influenced by the thoughts of Aristotle, Heidegger, and Kant. Arendt examines the relation between appearance and being, truth and meaning, and the relation between thinking and language. In particular, the role of metaphor in language may carry notable significance for phenomenological inquiry and writing. It is very tempting to use metaphor in phenomenological and hermeneutic studies, but we need to see its limitations as well.

A metaphor is a figure of speech that creates an analogy between two objects, by using one word or image to clarify another. Creative use of metaphor may help to discover new meanings about something. In philosophy, too, metaphor helps us to perceive one idea in terms of something else and thus may create new insights or new meaning about the original idea. Arendt examines how it is that ultimately all philosophic and poetic thought is metaphoric in origin, and what that means for inquiry or thinking.

> All philosophic terms are metaphors, frozen analogies, as it were, whose true meaning discloses itself when we dissolve the term into the original context, which must have been vividly in the mind of the first philosopher to use it. When Plato introduced the everyday words "soul" and "idea" into philosophical language . . . he still must have heard the words as they were used in ordinary pre-philosophic language. *Psyche* is "the breath of life" exhaled by the dying, and idea or *eidos* is the shape or blueprint [of] the craftsman. (1978, p. 104)

Arendt points out that "metaphor itself is poetic rather than philosophical in origin" (p. 105).

> If the language of thinking is essentially metaphorical, it follows that the world of appearances inserts itself into thought . . . . Language, by lending itself to metaphorical usage, enables us to think, that is, to have traffic with non-sensory matters, because it permits a carrying-over, *metapherein*, of our sense experiences. There are not two worlds [of being and appearing] because metaphor unites them. (p. 110)

Arendt warns that when metaphors intrude, as is their tendency, into reflective thought, then they may be used and misused to provide plausible evidence and insights into matters that are really undemonstrable. She cites the example of using the iceberg metaphor for the notion of the unconscious. There may be an unfortunate tendency to infer or draw all kinds of additional conclusions about the unconscious that are really features of the iceberg—such as the huge size of the part of the iceberg that is below water, what happens when an underwater section of the iceberg breaks off and shoots to the surface, and so forth.

The poetic and philosophic use of metaphor is such that the metaphor cannot be reversed. The role of metaphor is to illuminate an "invisible" phenomenon given by non-sensory experience by means of a "visible" or concrete or sensory image. Thus, a phenomenon that cannot be directly described may be indirectly evoked. Arendt's discussion of metaphor may be seen as a term of reflection in her approach to the role of story in political thinking, and the notion of example in the heuristic process of making the invisible visible and graspable.

So, the phenomenologist should be informed by Arendt's interpretation of the use of metaphor in thinking. Both Nietzsche and Arendt point out that all language, all words, originate in metaphor, but that the original creative act tends to be converted into deceptive illusions when we think that we understand something more deeply by covering it with a metaphor. We need to recall Nietzsche's profound reflections on the danger of using metaphors and believing that we now understand a phenomenon better because we have traded one metaphor for another. And it is even more dangerous when we continue to exploit a metaphor by extending its meaning and applications. These are important concerns to keep in mind when using metaphor as a methodological phenomenological device.

Some of Arendt's other engaged writings are collected in *Between Past and Future* (1958a). For example, her observations of the issues of pedagogical responsibility are very astute and they remain highly relevant for our times:

> Education can play no part in politics, because in politics we always have to deal with those who are already educated. Whoever wants to educate adults really wants to act as their guardian and prevent them from political activity. Since one cannot educate adults, the word "education" has an evil sound in politics; there is a pretense of education, when the real purpose is coercion without the use of force. (Arendt, 1958a, p. 177)

> If we remove authority from political and public life, it may mean that from now on an equal responsibility for the course of the world is to be required of everyone. But it may also mean that the claims of the world and the requirements of order in it are being consciously or unconsciously repudiated; all responsibility for the world is being rejected, the responsibility for giving orders no less than for obeying them. There is no doubt that in the modern loss of authority both intentions play a part and have often been simultaneously and inextricably at work together.
>
> In education, on the contrary, there can be no such ambiguity in regard to the present-day loss of authority. Children cannot throw off educational authority, as though they were in a position of oppression by an adult majority, though even this absurdity of treating children as an oppressed minority in need of liberation has actually been tried out in modern educational practice. Authority has been discarded by the adults, and this can mean only one thing: that the adults refuse to assume responsibility for the world into which they have brought the children. (p. 190)

The pedagogy of Hannah Arendt is highly relevant in our present time when adults seem incapable to realize what possible futures, worth living, they are robbing from the young.

Chapter Nine

Phenomenological Orientations: Protagonists

The authors described in this chapter belong to the community of scholarship that pushed phenomenology in a variety of productive directions. Many of these scholars are now deceased, but their work is very much alive and remains a constant and rich source for methodological and substantive insights that may serve various phenomenological research interests. We can learn from these original thinkers why to do phenomenology and how to engage in phenomenological projects.

By focusing on selective aspects of the works of distinguished phenomenologists, we discover that there are indeed a variety of phenomenologies that may guide our inquiries. In this chapter, a selection of scholars is presented who have made original and creative contributions to phenomenology. Each phenomenologist is profiled in terms of ideas that contributed to a new inventive phenomenological orientation. The various phenomenologies are sampled for substantive and methodological insights and/or practical implications for research. Other than indicating the birthplace and study contexts of the individual phenomenologists no attempt is made to present a full biographic and publishing output of their work. Rather, the attempt is made to offer and discuss exemplary citations from these selected scholars and thus give the reader an impression of their narrative voices. In other words, the objective of making brief visits with some of the most original, creative, and eloquent phenomenological minds in the following pages is simply to show some examples of how phenomenology is done. No attempt is made to give general introductions or summaries of their work. But my hope is that the reader will be quite fascinated with and moved by the profound insights and personal journeys and commitments of these unusually talented authors and thinkers.

So, in the following sections I provide only glimpses of mesmerizing and alluring aspects of the works by these fascinating thinkers. One should read the following segments as confidentially shared portrayals. Each focuses on something unique that makes the writings of this person worth reading, especially if the portrayal happens to mention a characteristic or a theme that happens to be a fascinating subject matter to pursue for you, the reader.

So, my intent is modest. I aim to show that each of the original thinkers in the sections below offers examples of how phenomenology may be practiced as a reflective form of inquiry about the meaningfulness of the world. And my hope is that the reader will be inspired to explore further the *original* texts of these scholars, to find out for themselves how to pursue phenomenology.

DOI: 10.4324/9781003228073-11

For the reader it would be helpful to ask: how might Alphonso Lingis, Michel Serres, Bernard Stiegler, or Jean-Luc Nancy (or any one of the other major authors) address a question in which I am interested? How is their style of reflecting and writing an example for my own thinking about the topics and concerns that fascinate me? For this reason, I have focused in the following pages on the texts of recognized scholars and original thinkers in the phenomenological tradition, rather than on the exegetical writings of their numerous interpreters, critics, and commentators. People frequently ask, "Who and what should I read?" As much as possible I try to point them to authors and texts as cited below for reasons as described below. But surely the author list could easily have been longer.

It is against the backdrop of these writings that we may discover an innovative approach, a productive process, a certain style, a way with language, a rhetorical manner that characterizes the work of great phenomenologists such as Maurice Merleau-Ponty, Jean-Paul Sartre, Michel Serres, Hélène Cixous, Alphonso Lingis, or Jean-Luc Nancy, and the more practitioner and clinical oriented phenomenologists such as Martinus Langeveld, Jan van den Berg, Frederik Buytendijk, and Johannes Linschoten. This does not mean that we should try to imitate that unique approach, that personal style, or that distinguished linguistic facility. But attentiveness to the personal signature that characterizes the work of outstanding phenomenologists may help us to develop an approach that enhances our own strength.

The attempt is made in this chapter to thematize the various phenomenological orientations associated with the proponents who might be identified with these thematic phenomenologies and whose writings may speak to the possible resourcefulness that these phenomenologies may offer to interested followers or students of phenomenology. Thus, each "phenomenology" orientation is indicated with a suggested adjective, such as Levinas' ethical phenomenology, that speaks to the particular work.

Ethical Phenomenology: Emmanuel Levinas

Emmanuel Levinas was born in Kovno, Russia (now Lithuania) on January 12, 1906. He began his studies of philosophy at the University of Strasbourg in 1924, where he started a lifelong friendship with Maurice Blanchot in 1926. Subsequently, he studied phenomenology for a year under Husserl at the University of Freiburg where he also discovered Heidegger in 1929. Levinas was the first to introduce the work of Husserl and Heidegger to France.

After his university studies, Levinas became a teacher and the director of a Jewish teachers' college in 1946. A year later he published *Existence and Existents*. Though he had translated and written critical works on Husserl and Heidegger, Levinas did not really acquire international academic recognition until he was in his late 50s. He wrote the impressive work *Totality and Infinity* in the evenings, in his spare time, as director of the teachers' college. He wrote it in the same living space where his wife and son spent their time and studied the piano. His doctoral dissertation was published in 1961. His second major work, *Otherwise than Being or Beyond Essence*, appeared in 1971. These two scholarly texts have become classics.

238

Levinas received a position at the University of Poitiers in 1964; next he moved to Nanterre University (Paris campus) in 1967; subsequently he was appointed at the Sorbonne in 1973. He wrote many influential articles that have been published in a variety of collected works. After his retirement he was given a position at the University of Fribourg in Switzerland. He is now considered one of the most profound and influential philosophers of the twentieth century.

Levinas died on December 25, 1995, at the age of 89. The early work of Levinas addresses the origin of consciousness: primal reality, presence, the instant of the moment, and the core being of the self. In *Existence and Existent* Levinas discusses Husserl's notion of primal impressional consciousness. As shown above, this is Husserl's term for describing the lived presence of the now that lies at the basis of our everyday existence. But Levinas emphasizes that time is not a succession of instants flying by before an I. "The 'present', the 'I' and an 'instant' are moments of one and the same event" (Levinas, 2001, p. 80).

For Husserl, the primal impressions of our prereflective existence are the originary source of consciousness. Primal impressional consciousness is a pre-consciousness, not yet differentiated and not yet intentional—and yet this primal consciousness announces the becoming of the "I" and the formation of the consciousness of an autonomous individual. However, the primal impression is still ambiguously passive while it is at the same time the birth of the activity of spontaneity.

For Husserl the simultaneity of passivity and spontaneity are a sensory blending of the felt and feeling. Primal impressional consciousness is the substrate of our existence from which our intentional awareness of the things in our world arises. The living source of primal impressions produces retentions and protentions in the temporal bow and wake of the stream of consciousness—and these constitute the elements from which sprout our awareness of, for example, melody and rhythm in music, which was Husserl's focus for his discussion of the phenomenology of temporality and internal time consciousness. But if Husserl's famous concept of primal impressional consciousness possesses phenomenological plausibility, then all lived experience arises from it: human conversations, the reading of a text, the enjoyment of a meal, our interest in an unexpected event, indeed any human experience finds its source in this realm of primal intentional consciousness.

In his own thinking, Levinas, increasingly felt uncomfortable with the primacy of intentionality and ontology in the works of Husserl and Heidegger. He asked the question how the focus of inquiry could shift more radically beyond being, beyond self, and beyond sameness toward what is other than being: otherness or alterity. In *Totality and Infinity* (1961/1979), Levinas points out that in relation to the face we come closer to the other. At the same time, it is the face that makes the distance between the self and other irreducible, infinite. In caringly worrying for a person, I cannot reduce this care-as-worry to the care of the self, as described, for example, by Foucault (1988). Indeed, it is especially the face that takes on caring-meaning for us. Many will recognize this phenomenon in their own lives. What is meaningful in the face is the command to responsibility. But what is the phenomenology of the encounter with the face of the other person we meet?

Do we "look" the person in the face? Or do we experience the face of the other more immediately? Levinas ponders:

> I wonder if one can speak of a look turned toward the face, for the look is knowledge, perception. I think rather that access to the face is straightaway ethical. You turn yourself toward the Other as toward an object when you see a nose, eyes, a forehead, a chin, and you can describe them. The best way of encountering the Other is not even to notice the colour of the eyes! When one observes the colour of the eyes one is not in social relationship with the Other. The relation with the face can surely be dominated by perception, but what is specifically the face is what cannot be reduced to that.
>
> There is first the very uprightness of the face, its upright exposure, without defence. The skin of the face is that which stays most naked, most destitute. It is the most naked, though with a decent nudity. It is the most destitute also: there is an essential poverty in the face: the proof of this is that one tries to mask this poverty by putting on poses, by taking on a countenance. The face is exposed, menaced, as if inviting us to an act of violence. At the same time, the face is what forbids us to kill. (Levinas, 1985, pp. 85, 86)

In a deeper sense, we are taken hostage by the face of the other. We are taken hostage by the enigma of love and our ethical responsibility.

> [T]he responsibility for the other is the fundamental moment of love. It's not at first a state of mind. It isn't a sentiment but a duty. The human is as a first duty. Every feeling as a state of mind presupposes being a hostage! It is false that this responsibility for the other isn't a burden for me, but it isn't only a burden. People have always asked how Kant could have considered love as a duty. Love is a duty before the face of the other. (Levinas in Rötzer, 1995, p. 60)

In experiencing this response to the face of the other we have experienced our response-ability. This is what Levinas talks about as being addressed by the otherness of the other. In this experience, I do not encounter the other as a self who is in a mutual relation with me as a self. Rather, I pass over myself and meet the other in his or her true alterity, an otherness that is irreducible to me or to my own interests in the world.

Levinas' notion of alterity has inspired many subsequent phenomenologists. For example, Jean-Luc Nancy sees the otherness of the other as the originary source of all meaning. He playfully suggests that there is a deeper truth in the common saying, that people are strange:

> The other origin is incomparable or inassimilable, not because it is simply "other" but because it is an origin and touch of meaning. Or rather, the alterity of the other is its originary contiguity with the "proper" origin. You are absolutely strange because the world begins *its turn with you*. We say "people are strange." This phrase is one of our most constant and rudimentary ontological attestations. (Nancy, 2000, p. 6)

Levinas (1979) describes the event of being addressed and the phenomenon of the involuntary experience of ethical responsibility as fundamental, not only to the experience of human relationship but also to the experience of the self. This kind of experience alludes to the originary ethical encounter. And according to Levinas (1981), in this addressive event thought comes too late. What happens is that this person in distress, this child in need, has made an appeal on me already. I cannot help but feel responsible even before I may *want* to feel responsible. For Levinas (1979, pp. 187–253), to meet the other, to see this person's face, is to hear a voice summoning me. This is the call of the Other. A demand has been made on me, and I know myself as a person responsible for this unique other. This relation with the other is nonreciprocal; in some sense, it is a nonrelational relation. Levinas states this predicament even more provocatively. He says that the other is not only someone I happen to meet, but this person takes me hostage, and in this gesture I have experienced also my own uniqueness because this voice did not just call. I do not need to look around to see if it was meant for me. The point is that I felt responsive, I am the one, the voice called *me*, and thus took *me* hostage:

> I believe . . . that politics must be controlled by ethics: the other concerns me. I have a completely modern expression for this: I am hostage to the other. I am hostage to *my* other. One acknowledges the other to the extent that one considers oneself hostage. What's important is that I'm the hostage. This is connected with the fact, which is very important to me and which wasn't seen by German Idealism, that the "I" is without reciprocity. You can't say we are Is in the world. The I-ness of my I is something entirely unique in the world. Therefore, I'm responsible and may not ensure that the other is responsible for me. The human in the high, strong sense of the word is without reciprocity. I didn't invent this, Dostoevsky said it—it's his great truth. We're all guilty of everything in relation to the other, and I more than all others. (Levinas in Rötzer, 1995, p. 59)

Levinas suggests that hostage is not just an exaggerated and metaphorical way of speaking. Not if we recognize this experience in our own life: is this not precisely what happens to us when we are claimed by our sick child or by someone in need? The strange thing is that here is this vulnerable child who exercises power over me. And I, the big and strong adult, I am being held hostage by this small and weak person who relies on me. If, as a parent, I am careless (meaning: free of worry), then I may inadvertently expose the child to risks and dangers. For example, I fail to keep my eye on my child when he or she wanders astray. Thus, the paradox is that a careless parent or teacher is not necessarily uncaring but unworrying. It should be noted that the experience of feeling the appeal of an other is not necessarily indicative of a traumatic occurrence. Seeing a newly born, seeing my healthy child, or meeting my friend or my neighbor all can be events wherein I experience the appeal of the other. In fact, some have extended Levinas' notion of alterity by applying it to animals or even nonliving things for which I experience a special responsibility. Thus, I may experience the encounter with a felled tree, a clear-cut forest, a polluted lake, or a special object or piece of art as addressing me or making an appeal to me.

241

More succinctly put, in the experience of the appeal of the other we may distinguish several thematic aspects. What happens in the event where I experience the appeal or summons of the other is this: (1) In the encounter with the other, I have felt an appeal that was directed *at me*. (2) The appeal orients me *to the other* who addresses me. (3) My response to the appeal is *unmediated* by my intentions or thinking. (4) My response is *passively felt* and noncognitive, in the sense that I did not ask for the experience of feeling addressed. (5) The appeal touches me and converts my immediate response into a realization of undeniable responsibility. (6) Feeling "moved" by the appeal moves me into action; I must do something; often I have already acted before thinking what to do. (7) I experience my responsibility to act as an appeal for doing something good for the other. (8) This goodness is not self-centered or measurable in terms of utility; in the words of Levinas, "only goodness is good."

Levinas' notion of goodness is admittedly open to interpretation. If someone skids on a slippery walk, I may have spontaneously used my hand to prevent the other from falling. This action is so immediate that it had not even been registered in consciousness until afterwards. But sometimes the appeal of the other is more complex and confronts me with the question of how to make a decision to act. In this case the appeal that I experience as responsibility to act has to be interpreted. How do I decide what action is appropriate for the person who makes an appeal to me, but who needs or asks for something I cannot provide? And what do I do if several people have made an appeal to me but I cannot respond to each and all? These are the kinds of questions that ethicists and commentators like Derrida have raised. So what role does the ethics of responsibility of Levinas play in situations where we are confronted with conflicting values or difficult dilemmas?

Levinas argues that in situations where a course of action is challenging or where a third person(s) enters the picture, then ethics turns into the moral. For Levinas, ethics differs from morality in that the ethical is absolute while the moral is relative. The ethical experience of responsibility in the face of the other is absolute and prior to consciousness and our intentional relation to the world. Moral decision-making is always at some level conscious—moral issues and decisions must be interpreted, weighed, and reasoned according to certain principles, conflicting values, norms, codes of conduct, or the regulation of rules.

Even so, practical decision-making in the ethical sphere of Levinas always takes its departure from an appeal that the other makes to me. I experience this appeal as having been addressed to me by the other who now has decentered my world. But, of course, I can only be receptive to the appeal of the other when I have taken care of my own physical well-being, health, and spiritual balance in life. If I am too self-centered, preoccupied with my own agendas, indifferent to the world, or in a state of depression or desperation, then I am unavailable to the other who makes an appeal to me. That is why Levinas says that I am responsible to take care of myself so that I can act responsibly for the other.

When the appeal the other makes to me throws me into doubt or an unsolvable predicament, then I must interpret how I can responsibly respond to the other in a manner that is in the best interest of this other, while not harming a third person or party. But in trying to have regard for the good of third persons, I may be confronted with situations where I cannot be equally just, graciously generous, or unconditionally available in terms of my time, resources, and competencies. Moreover, I may not necessarily know with sufficient confidence what is the best course of action from alternative actions that are available or open to me.

Existential Phenomenology: Jean-Paul Sartre

Jean-Paul Sartre was born on June 21, 1905, in Paris. His father died in 1906, and so Sartre grew up with his mother and maternal grandparents. When Jean-Paul was 11 years old, his mother remarried. And many years later, in his autobiographical *Les Mots*, Sartre describes the subsequent years as the most miserable of his life.

In 1924 Sartre studied psychology and philosophy at the École Normale Supérieure. There, he was a student alongside Maurice Merleau-Ponty, who was three years younger than Sartre. In 1929 he met Simone de Beauvoir, and they both graduated with doctorates in philosophy in that same year. For the rest of their lives Sartre and de Beauvoir were very close and their "relationship" was unique, as it was consciously open and not possessive. They discussed marriage, but never married; probably because de Beauvoir felt that Sartre really remained hesitant.

For almost his entire life, Sartre lived in a Parisian hotel, and, aside from his clothes and wallet, he lived without the trappings of private property and personal possessions. As he became increasingly famous, he hired an assistant and kept an office to deal with the many people who sought to interview or meet him. Sartre spent much of his social and writing life in Parisian cafés. In these cafés he met regularly with friends and colleagues. Just as the image of Heidegger cannot be separated from the famous hut (cabin) in the German Black Forest, so Sartre cannot be understood out of context from the urban life of the Parisian café.

Sartre explained that he was drawn to phenomenology because it provided a philosophy of realism, the concrete and ordinary things of everyday life. At the École Normale he had read Bergson's philosophical essay on the immediate data of consciousness, which partially deals with the concreteness of existence. But, initially, Sartre considered himself only a mediocre student of philosophy. And de Beauvoir advised him against spending too much time on philosophy, saying "If you haven't a talent for it, don't waste your time on it" (1978, p. 28).

But, one day in 1933, their friend Raymond Aron told Sartre and de Beauvoir enthusiastically about the new sensational German philosopher Edmund Husserl, who could look at an ordinary object like the glass of beer they had on the table in front of them (or apricot cocktail, as de Beauvoir remembers it) and could talk about it in such a manner that it became pure philosophy. "Well," Sartre confessed, "I can tell you that knocked me out. I said to myself: 'Now here at long last is a philosophy.' We thought a great deal about one thing: the concrete" (1978, p. 26). The significance of the story about the glass of beer or apricot cocktail is that it attracted Sartre to phenomenology and its attentiveness to the ordinary, the quotidian: to concrete things and common affairs of human existence. To create philosophy from a glass of beer!

Aron had spent the previous year in Berlin. So, Sartre promptly decided to go and also study in Berlin, where Husserl was appointed professor of philosophy. Immediately after Aron talked about Husserl, Sartre read Emmanuel Levinas' dissertation *Theory of Intuition in Husserl's Phenomenology*, which helped him to write a funding application for studying in Berlin for a year. Sartre recounts that in Berlin he read Husserl's "*Ideen* and nothing but *Ideen*. For me, you know, who doesn't read very fast, a year was just about right for reading his *Ideen*" (1978, pp. 29, 30). Sartre never met Husserl in person. Ironically perhaps, just before he left for Berlin, Levinas had invited Husserl to the Sorbonne in Paris, where Husserl presented a series of lectures on Descartes. Levinas translated these *Cartesian Meditations* into French.

Though, in the early years, Sartre hesitated between dedicating himself to philosophy or literature, he became both a philosopher and a literary author. When studying in Berlin in 1933, his writing routine was in the morning to read Husserl and to work on *The Transcendence of the Ego*, and in the late afternoon to work on the novel *Nausea*. *The Transcendence of the Ego* was published in 1934. *The Imaginary*, a phenomenological investigation into the imagination, was published in 1936 and his *Theory of Emotions* in 1938. In the same year he published his first philosophically inspired novel, *Nausea*. These texts brought Sartre early recognition. A year earlier he had already published a bundle of collected stories entitled *The Wall*.

In the postwar period, Sartre's novels, stories, and plays were very popular with the reading public. They reflected the existential sensibility of the times and prompted people to wonder about the meaning of human existence: Are we truly condemned to freedom? Is there any meaning outside of what we make of life? Is it possible to love and be loved? How to make sense of the absurdity of life? Sartre's fictional writings and plays can indeed be seen to exemplify the phenomenological intuitions that are elaborated in his philosophical works (see Cox, 2009).

During World War II Sartre was briefly retained in a military prisoner of war camp; upon his release he actively joined the underground liberation movement. Sartre remained politically engaged for his entire life. Like many of his contemporary intellectuals in France, Sartre was increasingly sympathetic to Marxism, but he equally denounced Russian Stalinism and American imperialism. He was frequently severely criticized by the French communists and radicals of the political left. Sartre's strongest writings probably consist of his many essays in existentialism, and his analyses, expressions, and evocative presentations of the phenomenology of everyday life situations and events.

During the war years, Sartre wrote his magnum opus, *Being and Nothingness* (1956). The first part of this title echoes Heidegger's influential work *Being and Time*. The second part shows the influence of Descartes, who wrote in his *Meditations* that human beings are situated between God and nothingness, between supreme being and non-being. To distinguish *Being and Nothingness* from Husserl's epistemological work, Sartre subtitled it *An Essay on Phenomenological Ontology*.

From a methodological perspective, it is instructive to observe how Sartre makes use of fictional examples at two levels or in two variations: through his novels and through the many fictional anecdotes in his phenomenological and philosophical explications and essays. For example, in his novel *Nausea*, Sartre describes a moment when the protagonist, Roquentin, is overcome by the unsettling enigma of the thingness of the thing:

I lean my hand on the seat but pull it back hurriedly: it exists. This thing I'm sitting on, leaning my hand on, is called a seat.... I murmur: "It's a seat," a little like an exorcism. But the word stays on my lips: it refuses to go and put itself on the thing. It stays what it is.... Things are divorced from their names. They are there, grotesque, headstrong, gigantic and it seems ridiculous to call them seats or say anything at all about them: I am in the midst of things, nameless things. Alone, without words, defenceless, they surround me, are beneath me. They demand nothing, they don't impose themselves: they are there. (Sartre, 2007, p. 125)

In his philosophical writings, Sartre also often used vivid concrete experiential stories (fictional or real) from observations he made about life around him in the Parisian streets and cafés. Sartre had only one functioning eye, and with one eye he had no depth perception. So, it is perhaps not surprising that many examples from *Being and Nothingness* describe incidents that take place within a field of vision that is limited to a mere few meters. His world consisted of his favorite Parisian cafés, and many of his philosophical examples are no doubt created from observing this world. He owned no personal assets, and he was very careless and generous with his money. So, he watched the waiters and customers in the café, looked at passers-by, flirted with female admirers, and talked with his philosopher and artist friends.

In *Being and Nothingness*, there are many examples that could have been inspired by the life in the Parisian café. The examples are instructive for Sartre's approach to phenomenological reflection and writing: existential description and analysis.

I have an appointment with Pierre at four o'clock. I arrive at the café a quarter of an hour late. Pierre is always punctual. Will he have waited for me? I look at the room, the patrons, and I say, "He is not here." Is there an intuition of Pierre's absence, or does negation indeed enter in only with judgment? At first sight it seems absurd to speak here of intuition since to be exact there could not be an intuition of *nothing* and since the absence of Pierre is this nothing. Popular consciousness, however, bears witness to this intuition. Do we not say, for example, "I suddenly saw that he was not there." Is this just a matter of misplacing the negation? Let us look a little closer.

...

It is certain that the café by itself with its patrons, its tables, its booths, its mirrors, its light, its smoky atmosphere, and the sounds of voices, rattling saucers, and footsteps which fill it—the café is a fullness of being.... We seem to have found fullness everywhere. (Sartre, 1956, p. 9)

In the next pages, Sartre does a careful analysis of his experiential description of Pierre's absence. He shows that in spite of the fullness of the café it is Pierre's absence that he sees against the backdrop of all the faces and the motion that goes on in the café.

This figure which slips constantly between my look and the solid, real objects of the café is precisely a perpetual disappearance; it is Pierre raising himself as nothingness on the ground of the nihilation of the café. So that what is offered to intuition is a flickering of nothingness; it is the nothingness of the ground, the nihilation of which summons and demands the appearance of the figure, and it is the figure—the nothingness which slips as a *nothing* to the surface of the ground. (Sartre, 1956, p. 10)

In his early writing, Sartre is especially compelled by one central idea of Husserl: the notion of intentionality. Husserl had shown that intentionality means that consciousness is not anything itself, but rather that consciousness is oriented externally, to the things of the world outside of itself. For example, when someone asks what I am doing, I say that "I am watching a movie or listening to music, or reading a book." However, Sartre points out that when we are engaged in something, then there is no "I" that is present.

> There is no *I* on the unreflective level. When I run after a streetcar, when I look at the time, when I am absorbed in contemplating a portrait, there is no *I*. There is consciousness of *the streetcar-having-to-be-overtaken*, etc . . . . [but] I have disappeared; I have annihilated myself. There is no place for *me* on this level. And this is not a matter of chance, due to a momentary lapse of attention, but happens because of the very nature of consciousness. (Sartre, 1991, p. 45)

When I say, "I am reading a novel," the "I" is not the "I" who was reading. Rather, in saying "I . . . " we objectify something that was not there in our experience of the story of the novel. The moment that we focus and reflect on the "I," the living experience of the novel, the movie, or the music has disappeared. Thus, in his early and provocative essay *The Transcendence of the Ego*, Sartre radicalizes Husserl's account of the ego's intentionality and argues that the ego or self is really not a subject but an object of consciousness. More accurately, the ego or self is a thing!

> In the act of reflecting I pass judgment on the consciousness reflected-on; I am ashamed of it, I am proud of it, I will it, I deny it, etc. The immediate consciousness, which I have of perceiving does not permit me either to judge or to will or to be ashamed. It does not *know* my perception, does not *posit* it; all that there is of intention in my actual consciousness is directed toward the outside, toward the world. In turn, this spontaneous consciousness of my perception is *constitutive* of my perceptive consciousness. In other words, every positional consciousness of an object is at the same time a non-positional consciousness of itself . . . . Thus, reflection has no kind of primacy over the consciousness reflected-on. It is not reflection which reveals the consciousness reflected-on to itself. Quite the contrary, it is the non-reflective consciousness which renders the reflection possible; there is a pre-reflective cogito which is the condition of the Cartesian cogito. (Sartre, 1956, p. liii)

When the self becomes the object of consciousness, the "I" has become an object, a thing, not unlike the book I hold in my hand or the table or chair I sit on. Intentionality implies that consciousness is directed toward some object—but consciousness is not a tool or an instrument directing us to something, rather consciousness is directedness itself.

Sartre terms the ontological region of things like rocks and books as *être-en-soi* (being-in-itself) and the region of consciousness *être-pour-soi* (being-for-itself). When I look at an object or thing like a book or a rock, I can say that this thing "is" here in front of me. The thing simply is. A thing is a being without consciousness that "is" in-itself (*en-soi*). But consciousness is not a thing. It is a no-thing, nothing-ness. Consciousness is not a being that is, but a being that has existence; it exists for-itself (*pour-soi*) as a project in the world. Unlike the in-itself, the for-itself can reflect, take distance from itself.

When we see someone walking down the street and we admire the person's beauty or we notice something peculiar, we may be regarding this other person's body as an object, as an in-itself. Similarly, I may feel objectified by the other's look—as in Sartre's example of being caught spying on someone. But such is not the case when we are in charge of ourselves in daily existence. According to Sartre, I am my body: "I am not a relation to my hand in the same utilizing attitude as I am in relation to the pen; I am my hand" (Sartre, 1956, 323). In contrast, a thing, like a rock or a chair, has to be what it is. A book may be lying on top of a rock but neither the rock nor the book are conscious of each other. As things they simply are. But the human body is a thing that is everywhere:

> My body is everywhere: the bomb that destroys my house also damages my body in so far as the house was already an indication of my body. This is why the body always extends across the tool which it utilizes: it is at the end of the cane on which I lean and against the earth; it is at the end of the telescope which shows me the stars; it is on the chair, in the whole house; for it is my adaption to these tools. (Sartre, 1956, p. 325)

A thing's being is its essence. Sartre's famous pronouncement is existence is prior to essence. A human being creates his or her own essence by making certain choices and commitments in life. So, Dasein exists for-itself and must determine its own essence through the project of its existence. And to exist means to continually transcend oneself.

Some of Sartre's expressions have become fashionably famous in the interpretation of actions in everyday life circumstances. For example, we commit to an act of "bad faith" when we say that we could not help ourselves doing something that we really did not want to do (1993, pp. 147–186), or we demonstrate "false joy" in feigning happiness when we receive a gift that we do not really like (1993, p. 237). And there is the existentialist distinction between authentic and inauthentic behavior, as in the roles we play in social situations:

> Let us consider this waiter in the café. His movement is quick and forward, a little too precise, a little too rapid. He comes toward the patrons with a step a little too quick. He bends forward a little too eagerly; his voice, his eyes express an interest a little too solicitous for the order of the customer. Finally he returns, trying to imitate in his walk the inflexible stiffness of some kind of automaton while carrying his tray with the recklessness of a tight-rope-walker by putting it in a perpetually unstable, perpetually broken equilibrium which he perpetually reestablishes by a light movement of the arm and hand. All his behavior seems

to us a game . . . . He is playing, he is amusing himself. But what is he playing? We need not watch long before we can explain it; he is playing at being a waiter in a café. (Sartre, 1956, p. 59)

The waiter may be happy or unhappy with his or her job. But if the waiter in Sartre's café were to say, "I am just a waiter," then Sartre would say, "Yes, but you have the freedom to change. You are not a waiter like a rock is a rock."

> Yet there is no doubt that I am in a sense a café waiter—otherwise could I not just as well call myself a diplomat or a reporter? But if I am one, this cannot be in the mode of being in-itself. I am a waiter in the mode of *being what I am not."* (Sartre, 1956, p. 60)

Sartre's famous phrase expresses well the nature of the for-itself and consciousness: it is what it is not, and is not what it is. Translated it means that the human being is consciousness and not simply a being that is (like a thing). Properly speaking, *Dasein* (the human existent) has no essence, except insofar as we may sometimes feel that we are who we are and we cannot really change ourselves. Again, this kind of existence Sartre calls "bad faith" or deceiving oneself. A person who acts in bad faith denies his or her freedom and tries to escape from the condition that we are indeed condemned to freedom. Even refusing to make a choice is really to make the choice not to choose. For Sartre to identify oneself as someone who is forgetful or who doesn't like books or as someone who is thrifty are instances of bad faith and a denial of personal freedom. To assume a certain identity is to behave as if one is an in-itself—a thing that is what it is.

Thus, Sartre develops a powerful phenomenology of ontology that interprets and understands reality from this dialectic of negation: being and nothingness. The for-itself is not an entity that has an identity. Interestingly, for Sartre there is no identity at the core of human existence—that must always be what it is not. So, to reiterate, consciousness is not some-"thing" but rather a no-thing. Consciousness is characterized by its dynamic no-thing-ness; it manifests itself ontologically as nothingness. If consciousness were a thing, then the human being would be an in-itself. So, more precisely, consciousness is an *event* that *happens* to Being. To reiterate, Sartre's formulation of the human being: It is something which is what it is not and which is not what it is—implies that the human being cannot be defined in terms of his or her present character, factual being, or existence. The human is always able to transcend his or her situation, and that constitutes the existential of human freedom.

As we can see from the above examples, Sartre's phenomenology has two main methodological dimensions: (1) existential description, and (2) reality analysis. Sartre was incredibly adept at providing vivid and plausible descriptions of everyday observations and experiences while making increasingly analytic phenomenological sense of these social realities at multiple levels of meaning that would ultimately be referenced to his philosophical concepts such as the for-itself (our subjective self) and the in-itself (the self as object), the notions of being and nothingness, and so on.

Gender Phenomenology: Simone de Beauvoir

Simone de Beauvoir was born on Boulevard Raspail, Montparnasse, Paris, on January 9, 1908. Her father worked at a law firm, but he was interested in culture and the arts and spent his leisure time acting in theater. Her mother was a Catholic from a bourgeois family of stiff religious beliefs. As a child, de Beauvoir felt isolated from her peers but developed a lifelong close relationship with her sister, Poupette. At 21 de Beauvoir studied philosophy at the Sorbonne in Paris and lived with her grandmother. At the Sorbonne she met Jean-Paul Sartre and Maurice Merleau-Ponty. Sartre became her best friend and intellectual partner for life. De Beauvoir taught at the Lycée and she became a regular among a circle of friends that included Albert Camus, Pablo Picasso, Georges Bataille, and other artists and intellectuals. They would visit the Parisian cafés to discuss existential and philosophical issues and to write. She died on April 14, 1986.

De Beauvoir's novels, essays and philosophical works reflect a sustained and critical concern with the art of living and how to self-consciously live a life of personal choices that fully face the challenges and consequences of individual freedom, responsibility, and authenticity. Her authorial openness about her personal life and relationships often challenged the social norms of her time. Her lifelong relationship with Sartre has been regarded as the romance of the century. De Beauvoir made of her life and work an exemplary work of art. She is seen as the first and original literary voice of French feminism and of women's emancipation in general.

Sartre was de Beauvoir's steady companion, and they were always interested in each other's thoughts and work. Their relationship became renowned for the two vows that they made to each other: to remain free and available to love other people; and to remain completely open to tell each other about everything they felt, thought, and did. They decided that there would be no secrets between them. It is told that, a few times, Sartre proposed to de Beauvoir. She declined. But, from de Beauvoir's later writings it is obvious that she experienced conflicting emotions in her ongoing relationship with Sartre. Still, her personal and philosophical aim was to live her life as a woman who was free and self-responsible. Indeed, she lived fully and passionately with many lovers of both sexes. In spite of her independence, her relationship with Sartre endured. Simone de Beauvoir used to say that Sartre was the philosopher and that she was the writer. But more recently her work has been treated as part of the existential philosophical tradition.

In her first novel, *She Came to Stay*, de Beauvoir describes the dramatic intrigues of a triangular relation between a man and two women (ostensibly Sartre, herself, and the young woman, Olga, who used to be her student). In this study of the relationship between self and other, the older woman experiences a devaluing sense of exclusion and objectification that leads to terrible consequences. De Beauvoir saw life as a process of personal becoming and acquiring identity through possible choices that gradually close down other possibilities. Her work shows especially the influence of the philosopher Henri Bergson, who was much admired and who wrote *Time and Free Will: An Essay on the Immediate Data of Consciousness* (2001). Bergson also wrote on matter and memory, and on the phenomenology of laughter.

De Beauvoir's novels and autobiographic writings focus on women who take responsibility for themselves by making life-altering decisions. She explains that, "far from suffering from being a woman, I have on the contrary, from the age 21, accumulated the advantages of both sexes." Her writings became an influential force for feminism around the world.

De Beauvoir's famous book, *The Second Sex* (2011), was the first major study of gender politics. The book was received as scandalous and placed on the *Index Librorum Prohibitorum* (list of prohibited books) by the Vatican Catholic Church. De Beauvoir was described as vulgar, frustrated, obsessed with sex, a nymphomaniac. In *The Second Sex* she traced the nature of male oppression through historical, literary, and mythical sources. She attributes the oppression of women to a systematic objectification of the female as "Other." Men have regarded themselves as "subject" and woman the "Other" in society by putting a false aura of "mystery" around the woman. This gendered image of women as mysterious could be used as an excuse for claiming not being able to understand women and their problems and for not treating women as equals. She explains:

> [A] husband looks for himself in his wife, a lover in his mistress, in the guise of a stone statue; he seeks in her the myth of his virility, his sovereignty, his unmediated reality .... But he himself is a slave to his double: what an effort to build up an image in which he is always in danger! After all, it is founded on the capricious freedom of women: it must constantly be made favourable; man is consumed by the concern to appear male, important, superior; he playacts so that others will playact with him; he is also aggressive and nervous; he feels hostility for women because he is afraid of them, he is afraid of them because he is afraid of the character with whom he is assimilated. What time and energy he wastes in getting rid of, idealizing, and transposing complexes, in speaking about women, seducing, and fearing them! He would be liberated with their liberation. But that is exactly what he fears. And he persists in the mystification meant to maintain woman in her chains. (de Beauvoir, 2011, p. 756)

De Beauvoir's study of female oppression by males became the lens through which the domination and subjugation of the powerless by the powerful could be understood: the oppression of blacks by whites, the colonized by the colonizer, the poor by the rich, and so on. It is hard for those who dominate to acknowledge their privileged position and to relinquish in their individual and social lives the overt and covert power policies of control. In *The Phenomenology of Ambiguity*, de Beauvoir writes:

> A freedom which is occupied in denying freedom is itself so outrageous that the outrageousness of the violence which one practices against it is almost cancelled out: hatred, indignation, and anger ... wipe out all scruples. But the oppressor would not be so strong if he did not have accomplices among the oppressed themselves; mystification is one of the forms of oppression; ignorance is a situation in which man may be enclosed as narrowly as in a prison; as we have already said, every individual may practice his freedom inside his world, but not everyone has the means of rejecting, even by doubt, the values, taboos, and

prescriptions by which he is surrounded; doubtless, respectful minds take the object of their respect for their own; in this sense they are responsible for it, as they are responsible for their presence in the world: but they are not guilty if their adhesion is not a resignation of their freedom. When a young sixteen-year old Nazi died crying, "Heil Hitler!" he was not guilty, and it was not he whom we hated but his masters. The desirable thing would be to re-educate this misled youth; it would be necessary to expose the mystification and to put the men who are its victims in the presence of their freedom. But the urgency of the struggle forbids this slow labor. We are obliged to destroy not only the oppressor but also those who serve him, whether they do so out of ignorance or out of constraint. (de Beauvoir, 1967, pp. 97, 98)

De Beauvoir was engaged politically, not through political meetings and social actions but through writing. In her study of the phenomenology of choice and freedom, the *Ethics of Ambiguity*, she describes the personal and political contradictions that arise in life. She also argues that nothing is simple. Those who see life as absurd deny that it can ever be given meaning. But to say that it is ambiguous is to assert that its meaning is never fixed, that it must be constantly won (de Beauvoir, 1967, p. 129).

Throughout her many personal relationships with men and women, de Beauvoir maintained her close friendship with Sartre. She stayed with him when he fell ill, until he died in 1980. Their relationship has become famous for the attempt of two brilliant thinkers to remain equal and authentic to each other. Both Sartre's and de Beauvoir's philosophical and fictional writings benefited from each other's critical influence and contributions. De Beauvoir wrote about her life with Sartre in *Adieux: a Farewell to Sartre* (de Beauvoir, 1985).

Embodiment Phenomenology: Maurice Merleau-Ponty

Maurice Merleau-Ponty was born in Rochefort-Sur-Mer on March 14, 1908. He passed the agrégation in philosophy from the École Normale Supérieure in 1930—where a year earlier his fellow student Jean-Paul Sartre had preceded him also with a doctorate in philosophy. After teaching at Chartres, the École Normale Supérieure, and the University of Lyon, Merleau-Ponty was offered a position in psychology and pedagogy at the famous Sorbonne. In 1952 he was the youngest academic ever to be awarded the prestigious Chair of Philosophy at the Collège de France, which he held until his untimely death. Merleau-Ponty suffered a fatal stroke on May 3, 1961, at the age of 53.

Merleau-Ponty is known as a cautious and tentative Socratic philosopher. His writings are rich, expressive, evocative, and profound. Often his texts possess the textual sensibility of a constant probing wondering and questioning. The Preface to his influential study *Phenomenology of Perception* (1962, 2012) is one of the most lucid and evocatively written introductions to the question of the meaning of phenomenology. In this Preface, Merleau-Ponty does a sympathetic and creative reading of Husserl's work. He interprets Husserl's transcendental phenomenology with its emphasis on the investigation of consciousness and essences into an existential phenomenology that posits that the world is always already there. Merleau-Ponty's orientation is existential in that he aims for phenomenology to put Husserl's essences "back into existence" (1962, p. vii). Phenomenology engages a radical, primal, or hyper-reflection: it reflects on what is prior to reflection—lived experience. To do phenomenology one must always begin with lived experience. Merleau-Ponty often reflectively expressed himself in uncannily evocative metaphoric language:

> Husserl's essences are destined to bring back all the living relationships of experience, as the fisherman's net draws up from the depths of the ocean quivering fish and seaweed. Jean Wahl is therefore wrong in saying that "Husserl separates essences from existence." The separated essences are those of language. It is the office of language to cause essences to exist in a state of separation, which is in fact merely apparent, since through language they still rest upon the ante-predicative life of consciousness. In the silence of primary consciousness can be seen appearing not only what words mean but also what things mean: the core of primary meaning round which the acts of naming and expression take shape. (1962, p. iv)

The program that Merleau-Ponty articulated in his reading of Husserl's texts has inspired many phenomenologists. He describes phenomenological "seeing" as making contact with our prereflective experience:

> To return to things themselves is to return to that world which precedes knowledge, of which knowledge always speaks, and in relation to which every scientific schematization is an abstract and derivative sign-language, as is geography in relation to the country-side in which we have learnt beforehand what a forest, a prairie or a river is. (1962, p. ix)

> To return to the world of actual experience . . . since it is in it that we shall be able to . . . restore to things their concrete physiognomy . . . to rediscover phenomena, the layer of living experience through which other people and things are first given to us. (1962, p. 57)

In developing a more existential phenomenology Merleau-Ponty suggests that we must begin by reawakening the basic experience of the world and by practicing a "direct description" of this world:

> All the efforts [of phenomenology] are concentrated upon re-achieving a direct and primitive contact with the world . . . it also offers an account of space, time and the world as we "live" them. It tries to give a direct description of our experience as it is, without taking into account of its psychological origin and the causal explanations which the scientist, the historian or the sociologist may be able to provide. (1962, p. vii)

In "Eye and Mind," Merleau-Ponty urges science to become thoughtful again of its source,

Scientific thinking, a thinking which looks on from above, and thinks of the object-in-general, must return to the "there is" which precedes it; to the site, the soil the sensible and humanly modified world such as it is in our lives and for our bodies—not that possible body which we may legitimately think of as an information machine but this actual body I call mine, this sentinel standing quietly at the command of my words and my acts. Further, associated bodies must be revived along with my body— "others," not merely as my congeners, as the zoologist says, but others who haunt me and whom I haunt; "others" along with whom I haunt a single, present, and actual Being as no animal ever haunted those of his own species, territory, or habitat. In this primordial historicity, science's agile and improvisatory thought will learn to ground itself upon things themselves and upon itself, and will once more become philosophy. (Merleau-Ponty, 1964a, pp. 160, 161)

For Merleau-Ponty the original human relation to the world is a relation of perception. But this perception takes place at a primal, corporeal, and preconscious level. The body-subject is already interlaced with the flesh of the world before having reflective knowledge of it. Or, to say it differently, our knowledge of the world—of others and things—is corporeal, rather than intellectual. We know the world bodily and through our embodied actions. And in some sense this is a preknowing knowing: we know our world first of all through our embodied being rather than immediately in a disembodied intellectual manner. That is why Merleau-Ponty can say that we do not really know what we see. Most of the time, we act and do things apparently unthinkingly—it is as if the body already knows what to do and how to do it. And that is indeed the case.

Many years later, these phenomenological observations of the functioning of the unconscious and the conscious by Merleau-Ponty have been physiologically supported and explained by neuroscientists studying the structures and systems of the brain (see, for example, Damasio, 2010; Eagleman, 2011). We now know that the human brain's 86 billion neurons are constantly interactively probing, testing, and combining the trillions of connections of the synapses that produce the internal mental models that the brain forms of the external worlds we inhabit and experience. The brain is a complex organ that controls thinking and deciding, speech and language, memorizing and predicting, affect and emotion, perception and sensing, touch and motor skills, heart rate and sleep, breathing and temperature, hunger and thirst and every function and process that regulates our body. Yet, the constantly active intertwining parts of the brain's complicated networks are mostly "automatic" and thus unconscious, preconscious, or nonconscious.

But it is phenomenology that explores the lived and living meaningfulness associated with the wondrous workings of the neural networks of the brain and that make it possible for each of us to ask, "Who am I?" "What is the significance of my experience?" The human brain is not only constantly and predictively probing its internal and external world, it is also interactively connected to the neural networks of others. Merleau-Ponty was not aware of the future discoveries if neuro science but he already understood the existential reality at the phenomenological level.

It is through my relation to others, and also "through my relation to 'things' that I know myself," says Merleau-Ponty (1962, p. 383). The relation between human and world is ontological: the subject is as much affected by the other as by the object or thing; just as the other and the thing are affected by the subject. In fact, the Cartesian subject–object distinction is not very helpful to understand the original interwovenness of human and world. Perception, in its fullest, most complex, and most subtle sense, is the preconscious or prereflective act of existence. Reflection is only possible because our existence is first of all and always prereflectively entwined into the world.

With respect to language, Merleau-Ponty describes how body and consciousness are meaningfully involved in each other. "Language bears the meaning of thought as a footprint signifies the movement and effort of a body" (1964b, p. 44). Word and thought cannot really be separated. So, some authors who argue that the mind and body have to be reunited are already making a mistaken philosophical assumption. Only intellectually can we make a Cartesian separation. Experientially, body and mind are always already inextricably intertwined. When we say or write something, then we do not experience a thought with an available vocabulary of words that our voice or hands must exteriorize and express. Merleau-Ponty criticizes the naive view that speaking means putting thoughts into words. Rather, thought and feeling is present *in* the word. Just as we cannot separate body from mind, so word and thought or feeling are inseparable.

> To speak is not to put a word under each thought. We need to rid ourselves of the idea that our language is the translation or cipher of an original text; then we also see that the idea of *complete* expression is nonsensical, and that "all language is indirect or allusive. (1964b, pp. 43, 44)

We know this inseparability when we have a hard time talking or writing of something determinate as long as we cannot find the words for it. So, when I hear myself speak, I hear myself think. Or better, my speaking is my thinking.

Just as body and consciousness are dialectically related, so word and thought stand in a dialectical relation. The word does not only present itself in speaking but also through gestures, physiognomy, and tone by which the words are uttered and expressed. That is why Merleau-Ponty refers to language and words as gestures. When we have a conversation, then we understand the speaking of the other person immediately and directly, through mimesis, rather than through intellectual interpretation.

> Mimesis is the ensnaring of me by the other, the invasion of me by the other; it is that attitude whereby I assume the gestures, the conducts, the favourite words, the ways of doing things of those whom I confront . . . . It is a manifestation of a unique system which unites my body, the other's body, and the other himself. (1964a, p. 145)

Literally, the word is thought's body. This close tie between body and thought raises interesting questions for understanding how human proximity and mutual understanding is achieved in technologically mediated contexts such as online writing and texting.

So, it is in relation with the other that thought finds itself. In conversation with the other I may find that I am thinking thoughts that I did not know I had. "There is a 'languagely' [*langagière*] meaning of language which effects the mediation between my as yet unspeaking intention and words in such a way that my spoken words surprise me myself and teach me my thought" (1964b, p. 88). It is not necessarily that the other shares or gives these thoughts to me but that the other can draw thoughts from me—thoughts that I had no idea I possessed. The other is lending me thoughts, which make me think in ways that I did not necessarily expect and, thus, may surprise me myself. So, it may happen in a conversation that I say something in response to something the other said, and as I utter those words I am surprised at my own thinking, my own words: Did I say that? Hmm that is good!

Merleau-Ponty is known as the philosopher of ambiguity. In his phenomenology there is no truth that can be written and established once and for all and always. Knowledge and understanding are ambivalent and ambiguous. Truth and falsehood do not stand in relation of opposition to each other, but they are aspects of a constantly changing and shifting dynamic of primal human reality. In his later (posthumously published) work *The Visible and the Invisible*, Merleau-Ponty explores the reversibilities of seeing and the seen, speaking and the spoken. Douglas Low (2000) has attempted to complete the unfinished parts of *The Visible and the Invisible*.

Thought is not external to language but the other side of language. Word and meaning are reversible. The reversibility of language means also that not only humans speak but things too speak to and with us. Thus, with Merleau-Ponty language and understanding, world and meaning, become truly pathic in an ontological and noncognitive sense. Merleau-Ponty underscores Husserl's basic idea of the project of phenomenology that can be understood as a project of language:

> In a sense, the whole of philosophy, as Husserl says, consists in restoring a power to signify, a birth of meaning, or a wild meaning, an expression of experience by experience, which in particular clarifies the special domain of language. And in a sense . . . and as Valéry said, "language is everything, since it is the voice of no one, since it is the very voice of things, the waves, and the forests." (Merleau-Ponty, 1968, p. 155)

Merleau-Ponty makes extensive use of the pathic power of poetic language in his writing. It is no accident that, in his introductory discussion of phenomenology (in the Preface to *The Phenomenology of Perception*), he concludes by comparing the sensitivity and sensibility of phenomenological inquiry to the artistic process:

> Phenomenology is as painstaking as the works of Balzac, Proust, Valéry or Cézanne— through the same kind of attention and wonder, the same demand for awareness, the same will to grasp the sense of the world or of history in its nascent state. As such, phenomenology merges with the effort of modern thought. (2012, p. lxxxv)

Practical examples of Merleau-Ponty's philosophical reflections are always cradled in his efforts of showing how we perceive things. An early example is his 1949 essay "Cézanne's Doubt" (Merleau-Ponty, 1964c, pp. 9–24) which describes how Cézanne's seeing, and his distorted but inspired manner of experimenting with his paint media, is instructive for understanding how things and objects appear to us as visual experiences: the phenomenology of appearance.

Also insightful are his reflections into the everyday experience of touch and the relation between reflection and touch: being touched by others and things, reflections as touch, and the paradox of self-touch.

> There is a rigorous simultaneity (not in any sense a causality) between the body and this reflection. We said: The body touching and seeing what it touches, seeing itself in the midst of touching the things, seeing itself in the midst of touching them and being touched, the sensible and the sensing body is not the stand-in of an already total reflection, it is reflection in figural form, the inner of what is outer. (2003, p. 273)

The self as subject and object, the self of reflection and the self of self-reflection, are the enigmas of the phenomenologies of touch.

> To touch is to touch oneself (to touch oneself = touched touching). They do not coincide in the body: the touching is never exactly the touched. This does not mean that they coincide "in the mind" or at the level of "consciousness." Something else than the body is needed for the junction to be made: it takes place in the untouchable. That of the other which I will never touch either, no privilege of oneself over the other here, it is therefore not the consciousness that is the untouchable. (1968, p. 254)

Merleau-Ponty returns again and again in his various texts to the enigma of touch. His is a true phenomenological work that is complete in its incompleteness, enabling others to creatively extend and deepen his thoughts and writings and engage them in projects and queries that is a phenomenology of phenomenology:

> [I]f no work is ever absolutely completed and done with, still each creation changes, alters, enlightens, deepens, confirms, exalts, re-creates or creates in advance all the others. If creations are not a possession, it is not only that, like all things, they pass away; it is also that they have almost all their life still before them. (1964a, p. 190)

In his final writing of *The Visible and the Invisible*, Merleau-Ponty strongly questioned the rationality of Husserl's project of describing the essences of consciousness. He stresses that ultimately it is primal lived experience, wild being, that must be interrogated while realizing that interrogation can only express this brute or wild being—it can never capture it in descriptions of essences. In his own writing Merleau-Ponty increasingly demonstrates how lived experience needs to be interrogated by adopting an expressive vocative style in his ontological phenomenology of embodiment.

Hermeneutic Phenomenology: Hans-Georg Gadamer

Hans-Georg Gadamer was born in Marburg on February 11, 1900, as the son of a chemistry professor. He lived for the entire twentieth century, and died on March 14, 2002, at the age of 102. Gadamer and Ricoeur are among the foremost representatives of hermeneutic phenomenology. Phenomenology becomes hermeneutical when its method is taken to be essentially interpretive and primarily oriented to the explication of texts (rather than directly oriented to lived experience). Gadamer studied under Nicolai Hartmann and under Martin Heidegger at the University of Freiburg, alongside Leo Strauss and Hannah Arendt. Apparently, Gadamer strongly felt the presence of Heidegger as a paralyzing obstacle for his own writing. He felt that Heidegger was always reading over his shoulder, as it were. Therefore, he chose to develop philosophical hermeneutics and focus on classical philology and on the early Greek philosophers to open up a field for himself.

Gadamer and Heidegger became close, though Gadamer did not join the Nazi Party and did not become politically active; thus, he was not appointed to a university position during the Nazi years. After studying under Heidegger, he continued with the development of a philosophical hermeneutics as a phenomenology of human understanding. Gadamer's magnum opus *Truth and Method* appeared in 1960, only a few years before his official retirement. In it, he explicates, in a phenomenological manner, the hermeneutic method as it had been originally developed by theologian-philosopher Friedrich Schleiermacher (1768–1834), and subsequently by Wilhelm Dilthey and Heidegger himself. Schleiermacher applied hermeneutics to the reading of texts. According to Schleiermacher, a text should be read with an open mind while keeping the larger significance of the text in view—rather than criticizing some narrow and selected statements. As well, one must take into consideration the historical temporality and rationality of the text. For Schleiermacher hermeneutics deals with the reconstruction of the past.

Gadamer praised but also criticized the hermeneutic program of Schleiermacher to reconstruct the past. Gadamer agreed that one must approach a text with openness and sensitivity to the historical tradition and interpretive horizon of the text. But he argued that placing oneself in the original reconstructed historical context would be impossibly complex. In contrast, hermeneutics means to place the interpretation of the ancient text in the context of one's own social-historical existence. Gadamer applies the textual hermeneutics also to human experience and life in general. He carefully explores the role of language, the nature of questioning, the phenomenology of human conversation, the significance of prejudice, the meaning of truth in art, the human ontology of play, and the importance of tradition in the project of human understanding. Tradition is the historical authority that infuses and influences our thinking and acting.

Gadamer taught at the universities of Marburg and Leipzig. In 1949 he accepted a position at Heidelberg, where he remained until his retirement. He wrote several texts that speak to the meaning of human understanding in professional practices. For example, in *The Enigma of Health* he examines what it means to speak of health and healing. Gadamer rarely talks about Husserl but when he mentions Husserl, it is for passing credit to him for coining the notion of *Lebenswelt*, lifeworld—the world in which we live in the natural attitude of everyday life. The notion of the *Lebenswelt* was popularized by Husserl. The phenomenological idea of the lifeworld is the ground of all knowledge in lived experience, and has to remind us of all the presuppositions that underlie scientific and technical knowledge.

An important notion is Gadamer's explication of prejudice as human understanding. According to him, all knowledge consists of prejudice, really prejudgments. However, in modern scientific context prejudice is seen as the opposite of sound judgment. The significant difference between prejudice and judgment is that prejudice cannot be traced back to a single source—prejudices are deeply embedded in historical consciousness. This means as well that human understanding cannot really be controlled through the use of a method or by means of rules. Rather all human understanding occurs as dialogue. In other words, human existence cannot really be approached as a methodical problem. Indeed, there is the irony that the title of Gadamer's *Truth and Method* seems to promise a method to truth. But he says:

> My revival of the expression "hermeneutics," with its long tradition, has apparently led to some misunderstandings. I did not intend to produce an art or technique of understanding, in the manner of the earlier hermeneutics. I did not wish to elaborate a system of rules to describe, let alone direct, the methodical procedures of the human sciences. Nor was it my aim to investigate the theoretical foundations of work in these fields in order to put my findings to practical ends. (Gadamer, 1975, p. xvi)

Actually, methods cannot be considered a guarantee for human truth and understanding. This is of course, a significant observation for all human science research. There is no method to truth. This is also an important reminder to those who think that they can find a procedural hermeneutic method in Gadamer's work.

Gadamer's hermeneutics of truth in art may be considered a major theme in the practice of phenomenological human science. Gadamer reaches back to the time before Kant, when the notion of taste still was connected to the idea of knowledge and truth. With Kant, the appreciation of art became a matter of aesthetic experience. Thus, whether an art object was considered beautiful was the result of an immediate private sense of personal taste. Just as some people immediately like the taste of a certain food, while other people have an immediate reaction of repulsion, so the viewing of a painting or the hearing of a musical melody may elicit an immediate positive or negative personal response. Thus, aesthetic judgment has nothing to do with knowledge or ethics. However, Gadamer wants to restore the original idea of taste as the application of an educated judgment. While it may be true that we have immediate personal preferences about things, taste is the expression of overcoming such immediate inclinations.

With Kant aesthetic experiences can be seen as located outside one's everyday reality and outside the domain of knowledge, but Gadamer wants to show that art actually provides us with experiences that are formative of new ways of understanding the world. If we can see the relation and place of art in one's own social, historical, and cultural life context, then this means that an aesthetic encounter may provide us with an experience of truth. For Gadamer, a critical notion in the understanding of art is the idea of play, not in a metaphorical but in an experiential sense. Play is the mode of being of the work of art. And for the human being to play is always to be played. In a work of art, we may recognize ourselves or our existential situation. But this kind of recognition is never simply a repeated "re"-cognizing. What we recognize in a worthwhile work of art is always a human truth that we come to know in a deeper, formative, and transformative manner.

Critical Phenomenology: Paul Ricoeur

Paul Ricoeur was born in Valence in 1913; he died in 2005. He experienced much sadness in his life. His mother died shortly after his birth, and his father lost his life as a soldier when Paul was only two years old. He and his older sister were brought up by his grandparents and later by his aunt. As a child, Paul was very close to his sister, who died young from tuberculosis. At 18, he married his sister's friend, whom he had known and played with since he was eight years old.

Ricoeur studied in Germany but after the outbreak of World War II he joined the French army. He was taken prisoner and spent five years in a German prisoner of war camp. Early in his career, Ricoeur became the Dean of the new Paris University of Nanterre. He attempted to install a very progressive administration of student and staff democratic participation in university affairs; however, the radical students involved in the revolt of 1968 totally ignored the fact that he was on their side and made his position impossible. Ricoeur disappointedly stepped down from his post and left France for several years—teaching in Belgium and the United States. Later, he experienced the additional trauma of his son committing suicide. So, it is not surprising perhaps that Ricoeur, who was brought up in a strong Protestant milieu, developed an interest in the phenomenology of evil (Ricoeur, 1969).

During his time in the German prisoner of war camp Ricoeur had translated Husserl's *Ideas of a Pure Phenomenology* into French. Since he had no paper to write on, he translated Husserl's book in the margins of the book pages in minuscule tiny letters. After the war he completed the French translation which was published in 1950, and translated into English as *A Key to Husserl's Ideas I*. Paul Ricoeur is generally known as a phenomenologist who began his studies with Husserl but who was also deeply steeped in all areas of philosophy, literary theory, theology, hermeneutics, critical theory, and the human sciences such as history, linguistics, politics, and psychology.

In his early work, Ricoeur developed a phenomenology of the human will, published as *Freedom and Nature: The Voluntary and the Involuntary* (1966). The study of the will is divided into three parts: deciding, acting, and consenting. Ricoeur applied Husserl's method of pure description to the will. When we say, "I will" we mean, I decide, I act or move my body, and I consent. These are the three modalities of the will that are carefully explored in the text. But Ricoeur also shows that the phenomenon of the will seems to elude the grasp of Husserlian descriptive method. The voluntary seems always already contaminated with the involuntary. Decision and choice are conditioned by motivation, hesitation, and the corporeal involuntary. Acting and moving are conditioned by the forces of bodily spontaneity and effort. And consenting is understood through experienced necessity and refusal.

These conditions of the voluntary are in turn related to modes of the involuntary: deciding is constrained by motives, values, needs; acting is held back by preformed skills, emotions, and habits; and consenting is restrained by character, the unconscious, and life. Max Scheler had already developed a phenomenology of feeling, and Maurice Merleau-Ponty and Gabriel Marcel (1949, 1950) had shown how consciousness is always already incarnated in our concrete embodied existence. Similarly, Ricoeur finds that the will (the voluntary) and the involuntary also find their roots and expression in the affect and situated existence of the body-subject. And though the will seems to be a function of agency, action, and freedom, it also seems to be mingled with passivity.

The first mode of willing is deciding. Sometimes decisions are made in a deliberative manner but often everyday decisions are "made" from moment to moment. Both deliberated decisions and the decisions of everyday existence are always somehow rooted in the involuntary. In fact, everyday decisions are rarely performed in a rational and calculative manner by weighing alternatives and their consequences. For example, the active voluntary will of choosing (I decide that I'll make a cheese sandwich) is initiated by the passive involuntary will of desire or bodily want (feeling like eating something or feeling thirsty and looking for something in the fridge or food cupboard). Or my sudden desire to have something to eat is actually a function of the fact that I am tired of sitting at my desk and so I get up from my chair and turn to the fridge for some solace. The question is how this passivity of the involuntary can be described and understood when it is not directly given as a phenomenon in consciousness. According to Ricoeur, this is where the clarity of Husserlian description needs to be supplemented with the ambiguity of interpretation.

> I must always decide amid an impenetrable obscurity. Decision brings to a halt, more or less arbitrarily and violently, a course of thought which is incapable of definitive clarity. A decision is never more than an islet of clarity in an obscure, moving sea of unknown potentialities. (Ricoeur, 1966, p. 342)

For example, Ricoeur shows how the will often involves hesitation and requires attentiveness and choice. The will to choose requires that we focus our attention on something. Attention helps to limit our range of choice to the matter at hand. But I may hesitate about my choice and hesitation has the function of opening up alternative possibilities. And in this process of making up one's mind, says Ricoeur, we actually are involved in processes of self-determination, formation of the self, and personal becoming.

The second mode of willing is action or moving the body. Decision and choice have to result in action for their fulfillment. "I do" is the declarative action that seals the decision to marry the person we have chosen to be our life partner. Action is practical intentionality. Again, action can be correlated with conscious choice, or it can be correlated with habituated or involuntary movement. For example, I am in the kitchen and open the fridge. But I may have opened the fridge before I actually decided that I wanted something to eat or drink. In a manner of speaking, my body felt like something and had opened the fridge before I intellectually agreed to do so. In "feeling like something" the body often seems to "know better" than our intellect what we need or want. So, while, "wanting" or "feeling like" something is an expression of my will, it seems that when, in our everyday circumstances, we "decide" this or we "agree" on that, we first of all do so at the level of the involuntary. I have an itch on my head and my hand has already started to scratch before I am consciously aware of the itch. Even our ethical responses to situations are usually already caught up in dispositions that have become part of our habits and emotions. Because actions involve body movement, this mode of the will is even more subject to the involuntary. It would be strange if after having lived for decades as a vegetarian, I find myself accidentally eating a piece of meat and having to remind myself that I am a vegetarian. The voluntary is always in some respect inseparable from the involuntary.

The third mode of the phenomenon of the will in Ricoeur's study is consent or acquiescence. The involuntary correlate of consent is the absolute involuntary condition of character, the unconscious, and the personal circumstances of life itself. As we move from the modes of willing (decision to action to consent), the role of the involuntary gets increasingly stronger. We can only consent or refuse our consent. In consent there is the recognition of experienced necessity. But it is also in consent that we can experience our human freedom. For Ricoeur, a phenomenology of the will (deciding, acting, consenting) has pedagogical significance in the sense of self-formation.

> In effect, for a responsible being, that is, a being who *commits himself* in the project of an action which he at the same time recognizes as his, determining *oneself* is still one with determining his gesture *in the world*. We can thus search out what possibility of *myself* is simultaneous with the possibility of *action* opened up by the project. (1966, p. 63)

Whereas Ricoeur's phenomenology of the will is defined in terms of an intention or a project in which an individual is engaged, his later phenomenology of action is explored in a more complex context of personal or narrative identity. Action is now seen as text-like and thus requires interpretation like narrative texts. In *Oneself as Another*, Ricoeur (1992) focuses on selfhood and personal identity. He asks a series of "who" questions: Who is speaking? Who is acting? Who is the narrator? And, who is the subject of moral action?

Ricoeur states that phenomenology remains the unsurpassable presupposition of hermeneutics. While the interpretive element became gradually more central in Ricoeur's work, for him critical hermeneutics remains in service of phenomenology. Ricoeur is a committed phenomenologist in all his work, but he explains that from the very beginning the claim to description in Husserl's method is compromised with interpretation. Husserl argued that phenomenology consists of describing what appears in consciousness. However, Ricoeur shows that, according to Husserl's own accounts, whatever appears in consciousness is already the work of the constituting ego (i.e., subjectivity). And in this constitution process, the interpretive is already at work.

The central claim of Husserl is that all transcendence is doubtful; ultimately, we never have a complete or full view of the object we observe. We only ever see a thing from a certain side, orientation, or perspective. Only immanence (what is directly given through intuition in consciousness) is not doubtful since it is not given through profiles and adumbrations (see the section on Husserl above). While Husserl insists that phenomenology must always return to intuition, Ricoeur argues that, in fact, Husserl cannot avoid that his description of the matter of consciousness is mediated by interpretation. In his text "Phenomenology and Hermeneutics," Ricoeur painstakingly analyzes Husserl's *Cartesian Meditations* and shows how Husserl himself describes the complicated process of the reduction as an *auslegung* (explication). But by investing subjectivity with such a crucial role of explication, Husserl's phenomenology constantly stands in danger of slipping toward a psychology of consciousness, rather than a phenomenology of what is given in the world. Heidegger and Gadamer already pointed out that *Dasein*'s or the human being's experience of meaning always occurs in the world in which one finds oneself—rather than in the abstract entity or realm that Husserl calls consciousness.

Husserl does not really remain faithful to his discovery (via Brentano) of the importance of the phenomenological notion of intentionality—that the meaning of consciousness lies outside itself in the intentional relation to the "things" in the world. Instead the idealist constitution of meaning in consciousness has the effect of culminating in the hypostasis of subjectivity. And this, in turn, has the effect of confusing the project of phenomenology with psychology. Perhaps Ricoeur's analysis of the interpretive underpinnings of Husserl's claim to a descriptive phenomenology sheds light on how human science scholars such as Amedeo Giorgi (2009) seem to remain committed to psychologistic (Husserlian) suppositions and the tendency to shift from a phenomenological into a psychological method of describing what supposedly is held in consciousness through the construction and analysis of introspectively written protocols.

To reconcile the interpretive hermeneutics-phenomenology issues, Ricoeur introduces his notion of *distanciation* into his method:

> Hermeneutics comes back to phenomenology . . . by its recourse to distanciation at the very heart of the experience of belonging. Hermeneutical distanciation is not unrelated to the phenomenological *epoché*, that is, to an *epoché* interpreted in a nonidealist sense as an aspect of the intentional movement of consciousness towards meaning. For all consciousness of meaning involves a moment of distanciation, a distancing from "lived experience" as purely and simply adhered to. Phenomenology begins when, not content to "live" or "relive", we interrupt lived experience in order to signify it. Thus, the *epoché* and the meaning-intention [*visée de sens*] are closely linked. (Ricoeur, 1983, p. 116)

Ricoeur's preoccupation with interpretation and the conflicts between interpretations is given by his interest in the written nature of phenomenological texts. "The reference of the linguistic order back to the structure of experience (which comes to language in the assertion) constitutes, in my view, the most important phenomenological presupposition of hermeneutics" (Ricoeur, 1983, p. 118). It is important to realize that Ricoeur inserts a methodologically significant part to the textual nature of all experience and all expressions of experience such as art, monuments, and events. Yet, he concedes that there is a complication between the nonlingual and the textual nature of experience:

> Even if it is true that all experience has a "lingual dimension" and that this *Sprachlichkeit* imprints and pervades all experience, nevertheless it is not with *Sprachlichkeit* that hermeneutic philosophy must begin. It is necessary to say first what comes to language. Hence hermeneutic philosophy begins with the experience of art, which is not necessarily linguistic.... Texts, documents and monuments represent only one mediation among others, however exemplary it may be. (Ricoeur, 1983, p. 117)

Ricoeur (1992) makes a distinction between two interpretations of the meaning of identity: self-sameness (*identité du meme*, in Latin *idem identity*) and self-hood (*identité du soi*, in Latin *ipse identity*). The identity of one-self (*soi-meme*) differs from the identity of the self (*le soi*). Ricoeur appears to be saying that the continuity of self is not the same as the sameness of self. Moreover, the two senses of identity relate differently to temporality and personal history. The identity of the self as *memeté* changes over time on the inside as well as on the outside. On the inside, we become more mature, more knowledgeable, less impulsive, and hopefully wiser, and on the outside we also grow older and maybe heavier, greyer, and physically changed. Thus, our identity changes. Yet, all the while, the identity of the self as *ipséité* has not really changed. In other words, the identity of the self is not dependent on an unchanging core of personal being.

In order to unify both senses of self-identity, Ricoeur introduces the notion of narration. The identity of a person lies in the story that self narrates. In other words, we do not need to choose between, on the one hand, a stable core of self that remains identical over time and, on the other hand, the fragmenting plurality of ever-changing shards of selves that lack the recognizable quality of identity. This contradiction may be partially resolved through Ricoeur's notion of self as involved in constant reinterpretation of the past (the narrative self reinterpreting memory of itself through creative imagination such as through story) or recategorization of its identity (the biographic self seeking a sense of order or unity). Thus, the notion of inner self depends on the possibility of a self-generating subjectivity. And yet, the inner self needs an Other to affirm its sense of continuity and identity.

While Ricoeur opens up for us the possibility to think of the emergence and meaning of the phenomenon of self and of inwardness as, for example, tied into a narrative understanding of self-identity, it would be misleading to suggest that this has resulted in a conclusive phenomenology of inwardness and self-identity. The phenomenon of the self remains interestingly ambiguous, as suggested in the thinking of other scholars.

Literary Phenomenology: Maurice Blanchot

Maurice Blanchot was born in 1907, in the village of Quain, Bourgogne, France. He died at the age of 95 in 2003. Blanchot is an enigmatic figure, who has exercised enormous influence on the thinking and work of scholars such as Emmanuel Levinas, Jacques Derrida, Hélène Cixous, and Alain Badiou. Michel Foucault is reported to have said that he would have wanted to be Blanchot. However, Blanchot's influence stands in stark contrast to his fame. He is little known in the scholarly community and little is known about his life. Most of his life he kept a withdrawn existence. For ten years he lived in the beautiful medieval Èze village in the south of France, and later in Paris. He participated in several journals such as *Les Temps Modernes*, edited by Sartre and Merleau-Ponty, and *Critique*, edited by Georges Bataille. He rarely appeared in public, never gave interviews, and did not allow himself to be photographed. Blanchot was friends with Bataille and especially with Levinas with whom he shared philosophical views.

Blanchot wrote a variety of genres such as novels, essays, and texts that feature a unique fragmentary philosophical style. He wrote extensively and profoundly on the philosophical thoughts of Hegel and Heidegger, yet he rarely explicitly quoted from their work. The main question that preoccupied Blanchot much of his life concerns the meaning of literature, writing, death, and ultimately the phenomenology of language and truth. It is said that usually he acted as if he were already dead and said that his books were posthumous.

Blanchot's texts tend to be obscure and challenging for readers who have just discovered him. And it is not easy to interpret his writings in a straightforward manner. But that should not deter us from making an effort to try and sense what he means by the phenomenon of writing and language, and how words may turn into images just like artistic objects that lack semantic clarity and yet provide us with fundamental insights into the nature of the real, life, and the mystery of being and meaning. In Blanchot's writing about writing, one is constantly brushing against the mysterious veils of the expressivity of existence that surrounds us and haunts us.

> To write is to make oneself the echo of what cannot cease speaking—and since it cannot, in order to become its echo, I have, in a way, to silence it . . . . I make *perceptible*, by my silent mediation, the uninterrupted affirmation, the giant murmuring upon which language opens and thus becomes image, becomes imaginary, becomes a speaking depth, an indistinct plenitude which is empty. (Blanchot, 1989, p. 27)

Language has the power to make contact with things, though this contact is so immediate and fatal that in its fusion it burns up what it lights up. Commenting on Levinas's thought, Blanchot writes:

> When Levinas defines language as contact, he defines it as immediacy, and this has grave consequences. For immediacy is absolute presence—which undermines and overturns everything. Immediacy is the infinite, neither close nor distant, and no longer the desired or demanded, but violent abduction—the ravishment of mystical fusion. Immediacy not only rules out all mediation; it is the infiniteness of a presence such that it can no longer be spoken of, for the relation itself, be it ethical or ontological, has burned up all at once in a night bereft of darkness. In this night there are no longer any terms, there is no longer

a relation, no longer a beyond—in this night God himself has annulled himself. Or, one must manage somehow to understand the immediate in the past tense. This renders the paradox practically unbearable. (Blanchot, 1986, p. 24)

Blanchot's provocative writings sometimes appear to be reversals of Heidegger's pronouncements, and this has been interpreted as a rejection of these notions (Massie, 2007). For instance, Heidegger terms death the ultimate possibility of impossibility. Blanchot terms death the impossibility of possibility. Telling is also the reversal of the light of the day and the dark of the night. Blanchot insists that truth can only be perceived in the darkness of "the night," which contrasts with Heidegger's notion of truth that occurs in the clearing of being.

Blanchot (1981) uses the allegory of Orpheus to allude to the significance of the night and what happens in the act of writing. The story of Orpheus, son of Apollo and the muse Calliope, is well known (Holme, 1979). It happened that shortly after their marriage, Orpheus' wife, Eurydice, dies from the poison of a snake bite. The grieving Orpheus descends into the dark caverns of the underworld to implore the gods with his songs to reunite him with Eurydice and allow him to take her back to the daylight world of the living. This is a classic story about the seductive power of the artist. Orpheus enchants the ferryman Charon, the hellish three-headed dog Cerberes, and the monstrous Erinyen. "When Orpheus descends toward Eurydice, art is the power by which night opens," says Blanchot (1989, p. 171). His songs are so moving and so stirring of the soul that finally Hades and Persephone grant his wish to take Eurydice with him from the realm of the dead, but on one condition: that he will not turn around to look at her until they should have reached the upper air of daylight.

Orpheus, whose poetic eloquence has wrestled his love from the underworld, now becomes strangely silent in her presence. He turns mute. Why? Because by uttering even a single word he would have shattered her being. She would be vanished, killed by the very words intent to confirm her existence. So, they proceed in total silence, he leading and she following, through passages dark and steep, until they nearly reach the cheerful and bright upper world. Just then, it is said, in a moment of forgetfulness, as if to assure himself that she was still following him, Orpheus casts a quick glance behind. At that very instant she is borne away. Eurydice is snatched from him so fast that their stretched-out hands for a last embrace fail to reach each other. Orpheus grasps only the fleeting air of her gesture, and her last words of farewell recede with such speed that they barely reach his ears. He has lost her for a second time, and now this loss is forever. In Ovid's *Metamorphoses* we read the inherited interpretation of Orpheus' fatal act:

> he turned his eyes so he could gaze
> upon her. Instantly she slipped away.
> He stretched out to her his despairing arms,
> eager to rescue her, or feel her form,
> but could hold nothing save the yielding air.
> Dying the second time, she could not say
> a word of censure of her husband's fault;
> what had she to complain of—his great love?
> Her last word spoken was, "Farewell!" which he

could barely hear, and with no further sound
she fell from him again to Hades.

(Ovid, 2000, lines 97–107)

All that Orpheus is left with is the image of that fleeting gaze that he saw of Eurydice. This is the way the story is usually told: "when in fear he might again lose her, and anxious for another look at her, he turned his eyes so he could gaze upon her" (Ovid, 2000, lines 95–98). But Blanchot suggests a different reading. Orpheus was not forgetful at all.

According to Blanchot the ambiguous gaze of Orpheus was no accident. He does not subscribe to the romantic view according to which Orpheus tragically forgot his promise in a moment of anxious unguardedness. The gaze was motivated by desire, says Blanchot. This story is not primarily about retrieving a lost love, but perceiving perfect love as lost. Orpheus desired to cast a glance at Eurydice in her immortal perfection, before she would resume her imperfect mortal state as they approached the light of day.

> Orpheus wants Eurydice in her nocturnal obscurity, in her remoteness, her body inaccessible and her face inscrutable; he wants to see her, not when she is visible, but when she is invisible, and not as in the intimacy of normal life, but as in the strangeness of that which excludes any intimacy, not to make her live, but to have in her the fullness of her death. (Blanchot, 1982, Preface)

Love had drawn Orpheus into the dark. But what lies on the other side belongs to the great silence, to a "night" that is not human. So, the gaze of Orpheus expresses a desire that can never be completely fulfilled: to see the true being of love, to see Eurydice in her pure invisibility. That alone is what Orpheus came to seek in the Underworld. He came "to look in the night at what night is concealing" (Blanchot, 1981, p. 100). It is about a mortal gaining a vision of what is essentially invisible: Love? Death? The Secret? He wanted to touch Eurydice with his eyes in her perfection—not as she exists as a mortal woman but as she visits the night of death in her perfection of love itself. Thus, Blanchot suggests that the search for literary-philosophic truth cannot really be fulfilled—though it must be attempted through the work of writing.

> [I]t is certainly true that by turning around to look at Eurydice, Orpheus ruins the work, the work immediately falls apart, and Eurydice returns to the shadow; under his gaze, the essence of the night reveals itself to be inessential. He thus betrays the work and Eurydice and the night. But if he did not turn around to look at Eurydice, he still would be betraying, being disloyal to, the boundless and imprudent force of his impulse, which does not demand Eurydice in her diurnal truth and her everyday charm, but in her nocturnal darkness, in her distance, her body closed, her face sealed, which wants to see her not when she is visible, but when she is invisible, and not as the intimacy of a familiar life, but as the strangeness which excludes all intimacy; it does not want to make her live, but to have the fullness of her death living in her. (Blanchot, 1981, p. 100)

266

Orpheus' mistake, then, was not a mistake at all, but a willful desire: the desire that leads him to "see" Eurydice and to possess her through the words of his song. As a poet he is destined only to sing about his desire for his love. "He is only Orpheus in his writerly song and his compulsion is to reach the unreachable, the perfection of love itself. Orpheus could have no relationship with Eurydice except within the hymn" (Blanchot, 1981, p. 101). Through the words and lyrics of his song, his work, Orpheus descends into the depth of the night in his desire to approach this "point" (as Blanchot calls it) that the work tries to bring up to the light of day.

> To look at Eurydice without concern for the song, in the impatience and imprudence of a desire which forgets the law—this is inspiration . . .
> His inspired and forbidden gaze dooms Orpheus to lose everything—not only himself, not only the gravity of the day, but also the essence of the night: this much is certain, inevitable. (1981, pp. 100, 101)

This interpretation of inspiration and the careless gaze of the writer sounds rather alarming and forbidding. Why would one want to be inspired? But Blanchot sees inspiration as some kind of blessed compulsion, a gift and sacrifice that has been accepted before it could be refused. It is a sacrificial grace that makes the text, the writerly work, possible, even though it inevitably fails to live up to the desired object of the gaze. The work always fails, though that does not mean that its demand can be ignored.

> The work is everything to Orpheus, everything except that desired gaze in which the work is lost, so that it is also only in this gaze that the work can go beyond itself, unite with its origin and establish itself in impossibility.
> Orpheus' gaze is Orpheus' ultimate gift to the work, a gift in which he rejects the work, in which he sacrifices it by moving towards its origin in the boundless impulse of desire, and in which he unknowingly still moves towards the work, towards the origin of the work. (Blanchot, 1981, pp. 102, 103)

Blanchot provides his readers with a most insightful and most compelling image of the phenomenological project: of what it means to inquire into the meaning of things through writing. His many books offer us a treasure of eloquent, often enigmatic, writings about writing, and about the relation between language and truth. His phenomenological gaze is like a sacred addiction; it cannot be resisted by those who have been graced by this gift. And the gift that Blanchot gives us is a sense of the pathos that compels and inspires the writer to write and aim for the gift of insight—it is the phenomenological pathos and inspiration to write.

It would be remiss not to mention that Orpheus received a terrible punishment for his desire and attempt to see the perfect femininity of the feminine. After his failure to capture Eurydice in her absolute truth with his gaze, he had sworn off mortal love altogether. Melancholically, he could now only sing of his longing for the perfection of love itself. His punishment came in the form of the mad fury of enraged women. The Maenads, the female followers of Bacchus, killed him by tearing his body to pieces. Thus, the inspired songs and words of Orpheus fell silent. Ovid describes how the wild creatures cried for the poet, the birds lamented his death, the trees shed their leaves in mourning, the rivers were swollen in their own tears, no longer to be able to hear Orpheus' enchanting tones. But, in his death, the ghost of Orpheus was now united with Eurydice:

> The ghost of Orpheus sank under the earth, and recognised all those places it had seen before; and, searching the fields of the Blessed, he found his wife again and held her eagerly in his arms. There they walk together side by side; now she goes in front, and he follows her; now he leads, and looks back as he can do, in safety now, at his Eurydice. (Ovid, 2000, Bk XI: 1–66)

The writer's problem is that the Orphean gaze unwittingly destroys what it tries to "rescue." In this sense, every word kills and becomes the death of the object it tries to represent. The word becomes the substitution of the object. Even the subtlest poem destroys what it names. For this reason, Blanchot says that the perfect book would have no words. The perfect book would be "blank" since it tries to preserve what it can only destroy if it tried to represent it in language. Perhaps this is why writing can be so difficult. The author becomes tacitly aware that language kills whatever it touches. The result is the terrible realization that it is impossible to truly "say" something. The writer desires to capture meaning in words. But the words constantly substitute themselves, destroy the things that they are meant to bring into presence.

And yet, at times, in a moment of transcendental bliss, the writer may experience the privilege of the gaze of Orpheus: the gaze that has penetrated the dark and momentarily has glanced to the other side. Writing that searches for the inception of meaning, therefore, can be a profoundly unsettling experience. In the space of the text we witness the birth of meaning and the death of meaning—or perhaps inceptual meaning becomes indistinguishable from the dark.

Oneiric-Poetic Phenomenology: Gaston Bachelard

Gaston Bachelard was born in Bar-sur-Aube on June 27, 1884, where he became a postmaster before studying physics. Later he became interested in philosophy and in the relation between the poetic image and language, memory, and dream as presented in *The Psychoanalysis of Fire* (1964b), *Water and Dreams* (1983), *Air and Dreams* (1988), *The Poetics of Space* (1964a), and *The Poetics of Reverie* (1969). He died in 1962.

In his evocative text *The Poetics of Space*, Gaston Bachelard employs the notion of the "poetic image" to refer to that special epiphanic oneiric quality of language that brings about in the reader a vocative response. The power of a phenomenological text resides in this resonance that the word can affect in our understanding—including those reaches of understanding that are more pathic and thus less accessible to conceptual and intellectual rationality. The creative contingent positioning of words may give rise to evoked images that can move us: inform us by forming us and thus leave an effect on us. When this happens, says Gadamer

(1996), then language touches us in the soul. Or, as Bachelard puts it, the reverberations bring about a change of being, of our personhood:

> The resonances [of a poetic image] are dispersed on the different planes of our life in the world, while the repercussions invite us to give greater depth to our own existence. In the resonance we hear the poem, in the reverberations we speak it, it is our own. The reverberations bring about a change of being . . . . [T]he poem possesses us entirely. This grip that poetry acquires on our very being bears a phenomenological mark that is unmistakable. (1964a, p. xviii)

> After the original reverberation, we are able to experience resonances, sentimental repercussions, reminders of our past. But the image has touched the depths before it stirs the surface [of our being or soul]. And this is also true of a simple experience of reading. The image offered us by reading the poem now becomes really our own. It takes roots in us. It has been given us by another, but we begin to have the impression that we could have created it, that we should have created it. It becomes a new being in our language, expressing us by making us what it expresses; in other words, it is at once a becoming of expression, and a becoming of our being. Here expression creates being. (1964a, p. xix)

Perhaps a phenomenological text is ultimately successful only to the extent that we, its readers, feel addressed by it—in the totality or unity of our being. The text must reverberate with our ordinary experience of life as well as with our primordial sense of life's meaning. This does not necessarily mean that one must feel entertained by a phenomenological text or that it has to be an "easy read." Sometimes reading a phenomenological study is truly laborious. And yet, if we are willing to make the effort, then we may be able to say that the text speaks to us not unlike the way in which a work of art may speak to us even when it requires interpretive attentiveness.

In *The Poetics of Space* Bachelard explores a whole series of images that he characterizes as primal images: "images that bring out the primitiveness in us" (1964a, p. 91). He starts with the image of our home:

> It is striking that even in our homes, where there is light, our consciousness of well-being should call for comparison with animals in their shelters. An example may be found in the following lines by the painter, Vlaminck, who, when he wrote them, was living quietly in the country: "The well-being I feel, seated in front of my fire, while bad weather rages out-of-doors, is entirely animal. A rat in its hole, a rabbit in its burrow, cows in the stable, must all feel the same contentment that I feel." Thus, well-being takes us back to the primitiveness of the refuge. Physically, the creature endowed with a sense of refuge, huddles up to itself, takes to cover, hides away, lies snug, concealed. (1964a, p. 91)

The various chapters of *The Poetics of Space* are entitled "Drawers," "Nests," "Shells," "Corners," "Immense Intimacy," and so on. For example, Gaston Bachelard shows how a human being likes to withdraw into his or her corner and experiences physical pleasure in such spaces.

269

To reiterate, we may say that a phenomenology of practice operates in the space of the formative relations between who we are and who we may become, between how we think or feel and how we act. And these formative relations have pedagogical consequence for professional and everyday practical life. Phenomenological reflection—reading and writing of phenomenological texts—can contribute to the formative dimensions of a phenomenology of practice. By varying the prefixes of the derivatives of "the formative," the *various* formative relations may become manifest. Phenomenology formatively informs, reforms, transforms, performs, and preforms the relation between being and practice. In-formatively, phenomenological studies make possible more thoughtful advice and consultation. Re-formatively, phenomenological texts make a demand on us, changing us into what we may become. Trans-formatively, phenomenology has practical value in that it reaches into the depth of our being, prompting a new becoming. Per-formatively, phenomenological reflection contributes to the practice of tact. And pre-formatively, phenomenological experience gives significance to the meanings that influence us before we are even aware of their formative value.

In *The Poetics of Reverie* Bachelard explores the power of poetic language to evoke understandings that occur in daydreams, dreams, and that stir the imagination. "I justify not being able to read poets except by dreaming" (1969, p. 67). Bachelard is skeptical of human science scholars and philosophers who make an effort to tell, in a precise and stable language what is being observed objectively. For them words do not dream, says Bachelard (p. 57). Reverie can help us know language and what can be done with words.

> I am a dreamer of words, of written words. I think I am reading; a word stops me. I leave the page. The syllables of the word begin to move around. Stressed accents begin to invert. The word abandons its meaning like an overload which is too heavy and prevents dreaming. Then words take on other meanings as if they had the right to be young. And the words wander away, looking in the nooks and crannies of vocabulary for new company, bad company . . .
>
> And it is worse, when, instead of reading, I begin to write. Under the pen, the anatomy of syllables slowly unfolds . . . . A word is a bud attempting to become a twig. How can one not dream while writing? It is the pen which dreams. The blank page gives the right to dream. (Bachelard, 1969, p. 17)

Gaston Bachelard makes us aware that phenomenological methodology needs to embrace the full pathic power of words and language. The real phenomenologist must make it a point not to be immodestly systematic but to be systematically modest (Bachelard, 1964a, p. xxi). The oneiric text must make of the reader a phenomenologist. Literature, poetry, anecdotal portrayals, vignettes, philosophic fragments, and images all play a part in the oneiric pathic power of the words. At times, words think for us, submerging us into their oneiric spheres of meaning.

Sociological Phenomenology: Alfred Schutz

Alfred Schutz (1899–1959) studied sociology, law, and business at the University of Vienna. Initially, he was greatly influenced by figures such as the economist-

270

philosopher Ludwig von Mises and the sociologist Max Weber. Schutz studied Bergson's philosophy of consciousness and inner time, but subsequently he discovered Husserl's phenomenology of internal time consciousness and he became an ardent social phenomenologist. Although he did not attend lectures by Husserl, Schutz made a careful study of Husserl's writings, which led to his *The Phenomenology of the Social World* (1932/1972), a book that was highly regarded by Husserl. In 1927 Schutz was appointed as executive officer of the Viennese bank Reitler and Company, which led Husserl to call Schutz "a banker by day and a philosopher by night." In 1939, Schutz moved to the United States and from 1943 he taught at the New School for Social Research at Columbia University in New York.

In North America, phenomenology was introduced importantly through the sociological work of Alfred Schutz, rather than directly into professional philosophy. The introduction of Schutz's work in American sociology became a creative source for phenomenologically oriented approaches in the social sciences. Phenomenology evolved in part alongside the emergence and evolution of specific awarenesses with respect to the diversity of human experiences and the diversity of ontologies underlying these experiences as recognized in the social science disciplines of symbolic interactionism, the new ethnography, and ethnomethodology. Schutz's work provided an impetus for these developments. His many phenomenological papers have been collected in a three-volume set: *The Problem of Social Reality* (1973); *Studies in Social Theory* (1974) *and Studies in Phenomenological Philosophy* (1970). As well, there have been co-authored and edited posthumous publications such as *The Structures of the Life-World* (with Thomas Luckmann) (1973) and *On Phenomenology and Social Relations* (with Helmut Wagner) (1970).

The phenomenological sociology and social science of Alfred Schutz is significant for its contribution to a phenomenology of social action, the lifeworld, the notion of multiple realities, the idea of taken-for-grantedness of everyday life practices, and so forth. His work was the inspiration for entire new waves in North American social science and the spread of phenomenological philosophy. In the late 1960s, when the counter-culture and the New Left were forming and making an impact on North American and European campuses, there was an emergent sense of the failure of traditional forms of social inquiry. This failure was diagnosed by such authors as Alvin Gouldner, Erwin Goffman, Jack Douglas, and C. Wright Mills as a paradigm crisis in the social sciences. Some sociologists, such as Peter Berger and Jack Douglas, adopted an existentialist approach to the study of social phenomena focusing on notions like love, intimacy, deviance, and other everyday life topics. Others looked toward symbolic interactionism, ethnography, and ethnomethodology for models of inquiry that would be concerned, not with behaviors, but with social psychological, cultural, and social meanings and meaning structures. The work of Schutz provided the impetus for these developments.

Although existential sociology, ethnography, and ethnomethodology are characterized by their own distinct methodologies and epistemological assumptions, these disciplines in turn contributed in part to prepare the way for a wider reception of phenomenological inquiry in philosophy and professional academic fields in North America. Ethnography offered ways of examining how subjects construct their own meanings and cultural reality. Ethnomethodology enabled the social sciences to study the practices of everyday life and the meanings associated with those practices. At first, the rise of these qualitative approaches encountered considerable opposition. The root of the commotion was the challenge to traditional social science regarding their taken-for-granted assumptions about everyday life. In particular, the more radically reflective approaches, such as the ethnomethodological studies of Harold Garfinkel, asserted that the participation of the researcher had to be examined as part of the research data.

Phenomenology is the study of "meaning," but what is meaning?

> Meaning is not a quality inherent in certain experiences emerging within our stream of consciousness but the result of an interpretation of a past experience looked at from the present Now with the reflective attitude. As long as I live *in* my acts, directed toward the objects of these acts, the acts do not have any meaning. They become meaningful if I grasp them as well-circumscribed experiences of the past and, therefore, in retrospection. Only experiences which can be recollected beyond their actuality and which can be questioned about their constitution are, therefore, subjectively meaningful. (Schutz, 1973, Vol. 1, p. 210)

Schutz (1973) proposes that we can contrast empirical phenomenology with eidetic phenomenology, but that this opposition has nothing to do with the interest in mundane topics of everyday life, nor with the fact that a phenomenon may be an empirical entity (such as a chair) or an imagined or mental entity (such as fear). The point is that eidetic phenomenology aims to understand the invariant meaning of a phenomenon (object or experience) by the eidetic method of "variation in imagination" rather than by using the method of comparing "various empirical examples."

In his transcendental approach, Husserl often practiced a purely eidetic phenomenology but in the social sciences his followers have used the idea of eidetic more broadly to include empirical examples. Thus, virtually all phenomenology since Husserl could be called an empirical phenomenology. Ultimately the phenomenological interest lies in understanding the experiential meaning structure of a phenomenon that makes it meaningful and distinguishable from other phenomena. Most other qualitative and social sciences take these meanings for granted, but Schutz (1973) developed a phenomenological sociology that focused on the phenomenological structures of the lifeworld. As well, some of his studies such as "The Stranger," "The Homecomer," and "Making Music Together" (1971) are perfect examples for how one can study the social and cultural world phenomenologically.

Postcolonial Phenomenology: Frantz Fanon

Frantz Omar Fanon was born on the Caribbean island of Martinique. He spent his student years in Lyon, France, where he studied medicine and psychiatry as well as literature and philosophy. He also attended lectures by Maurice Merleau-Ponty. Fanon worked as a physician and psychiatrist in the French colony of Martinique. His aim was to write an emancipatory work: "What we are striving for is to liberate the black man from the arsenal of complexes that germinated in a colonial situation" (p. 14). It is anti-colonial, black consciousness in search for a style and a method that can disalienate.

Black Skin, White Masks is probably Frantz Fanon's most famous and widely read book. It is also the text that is most phenomenological in its approach. Especially Chapter 5, entitled "The Lived Experience of the Black Man," appears written from a phenomenological orientation. It starts with concrete examples of how phenomenology focuses on a phenomenon. But Fanon employs several textual genres that seduce the reader to feel addressed and brought to indignation and reflection. For example, Fanon hears people throwing comments at him and about him: "'Dirty Nigger!' Or simply 'Look a Negro!'" (2008, p. 89). This is what it is like to walk down the street. It is the daily experience of knowing and feeling talked about as a black person. Why? Because of one's black skin.

Chapter 5 of *Black Skin, White Masks*, which starts with these words, is written from the perspective of a phenomenologically reflective attitude. It reflects on the meaning and significance of a consciousness that is self-aware of the experiential pathology of racism suffered by the black man. Interestingly, Fanon almost always uses the expression "the black man" and very rarely he will say, "the black woman." It is likely that Fanon felt that black women's experience of their black skin was not the same as black men.

The phenomenology of Frantz Fanon is highly personal but also universal. His book *Black Skin, White Masks* is written with a biographic and psychological flair that is often painfully personal. At the same time, Fanon insists to his black readers that the racial denigration of the black skin as inferior to the white is due to the fact that the black man suffers from a universal double consciousness. He experiences himself as wanting to be a full and authentic human being, but he experiences himself as inferior, in need of the disalienation of racism. Ironically, racism is the invention of the white European: "Inferiorization is the native correlative to the European's feeling of superiority. Let us have the courage to say: *It is the racist who creates the inferiorized*" (Fanon, 2008, p. 73).

Fanon submitted the manuscript of *Black Skin, White Masks* as the dissertation for his doctoral study while completing his degree in medicine and psychiatry at the University of Lyon in France. But the dissertation was refused, so he sent the manuscript to a book publisher. The book editor Francis Jeanson, a left-wing philosopher, recalls that he had invited Fanon for an editorial discussion of the submitted manuscript. Fanon appeared nervous during this first meeting in Jeanson's office. And when Jeanson praised the manuscript, Fanon interrupted him and remarked sarcastically: "Not bad for a nigger, is it?" Jeanson became annoyed, and suggested Fanon should leave his office. The latter had presumptively racialized their relation. However, in spite of this awkward beginning Jeanson and Fanon apparently reconciled and became close and lifelong friends. Jeanson believed that his response to Fanon's rudeness actually had earned him Fanon's respect. And Fanon realized that Jeanson's suggestion that his book be entitled *Black Skin, White Masks* reflected Jeanson's empathic and depthful understanding of black psychopathic consciousness to experience the desirable white world from the position of a culturally imposed, racial disorder of inferiority.

Fanon had originally entitled his dissertation manuscript *Black Skin, White Masks* as "Essay on the Disalienation of the Black." It reveals the painful truth that the white racist gaze is a profoundly alienating experience for the consciousness and self-identity of the black person. The alienation is like a sickness. But the psychiatrist Fanon argued that helping the black man achieve disalienation is a necessary but difficult psychiatric, political, and personal process.

The black person cannot help but personally have to go through the racist-induced feelings of inferiority because even though being black is a feature shared with others, still, for each person it is one's own body and one cannot help but experience it as one's sense of self-identity. This black skin is no one else's but mine, my own body, the black person says. This highly personal existential predicament is rarely acknowledged in the radical literature of racism. Even though Fanon clearly understands that racism is a collective and cultural phenomenon, it is equally clear that black people experience the racist indignity in their own private and personal personhood. At the fundamental experiential level, the damage is utterly existential.

In his battle against racism and colonialism Fanon does not engage traditional Marxist arguments that have to do with the *asymmetric mode of production* and that lead to conditions of exploitation and poverty. Rather he turns to politico-cultural factors that generate *asymmetric modes of being* such as the felt relational inferiority that becomes culturally associated with the black skin. Indeed, it is not *the mode of production* but *the mode of being* that is mainly investigated and explicated in Fanon's work. The black skin is the display of an inferior mode of being which is culturally imposed on people of color.

Sartre's analysis of the Jewish cause is a relevant insight cultivator for Fanon. Sartre begins his Preface to *Black Orpheus* (1948/1976) with these words:

> What would you expect to find, when the muzzle that has silenced the voices of black men is removed? That they would thunder your praise? When these heads that our fathers have forced to the very ground are risen, do you expect to read admiration in their eyes? Here, in this anthology, are black men standing, black men who examine us; and I want you to feel, as I, the sensation of being seen. For the white man has enjoyed for three thousand years the privilege of seeing without being seen. (1948/1976, p. 7)

From a phenomenological point of view, racism must not only be structurally explained, it must also be understood in its experiential reality. In the words of Jean Wahl:

> At a time when attempts to explain things on the basis of historical conditions, class, race, and psychological complexes are proliferating, phenomenology has thereby shown that our concern should be less with explanation than with beholden the rootedness of our affirmations and our lives in a foundation that is itself life and that pre-exists affirmation. (Wahl, 2017, p. 257)

Fanon uses his own experiences as examples of showing racist practices. He says, "What is essential to us is not to accumulate facts and behaviour, but to bring out their meaning" (2008, p. 146). Commentators have praised Fanon's evocative writing mode. At times his linguistic approach is lyrical and seductive and other times it is journalistic and factual. This is his voice as psychiatric phenomenologist, emancipatory critic, radical activist, and post-colonial theorist:

This work represents seven years of experiments and observations. Whatever the field we studied, we were struck by the fact that both the black man, slave to his inferiority, and the white man, slave to his superiority, behave along neurotic lines. As a consequence, we have been led to consider their alienation with reference to psycho-analytic descriptions. The black man's behaviour is similar to an obsessional neurosis, or, if you prefer, he places himself in the very thick situational neurosis. (Fanon, 2008, pp. 41, 42)

"Look how handsome that Negro is."
"The handsome Negro says, 'Fuck you,' madame."
Her face coloured with shame. At last I was freed from my rumination. I realized two things at once: I had identified the enemy and created a scandal. Overjoyed. We could now have some fun. (Fanon, 2008, p. 94)

Still on the genital level, isn't the white man who hates blacks prompted by a feeling of impotence or sexual inferiority? . . . doesn't he have a feeling of inadequacy in relation to the black man, who is viewed as a penis symbol? (Fanon, 2008, p. 137)

If we want to understand the racial situation psycho-analytically, not from a universal viewpoint, but as it is experienced by individual consciousnesses, considerable importance must be given to sexual phenomena. Regarding the Jew, we think of money and its derivatives. Regarding the black man, we think of sex. (Fanon, 2008, p. 138)

Before embarking on a positive voice, freedom needs to make an effort at disalienation. At the start of his life, a man is always congested, drowned in contingency. The misfortune of man is that he was once a child. (Fanon, 2008, p. 206)

Why is it a misfortune to have been a child? Because it acknowledges that our psychological problems in adulthood are inherited in a Freudian fashion from our earlier childhood. In his writing, Fanon used methods of psychoanalysis and psychotherapy, narrative description and autobiography, and he used the existentially rich phenomenological works, such as by Sartre.

In *Anti-Semite and Jew* Sartre writes: "They [the Jews] have allowed themselves to be poisoned by the stereotype that others have of them, and they live in fear that their acts will correspond to this stereotype . . . We may say that their conduct is perpetually overdetermined from the inside." (Fanon, 2008 p. 95)

We see how Fanon weaves Sartre's evocative explications into his own quote within quote: "The Jewishness of the Jew, however, can go unnoticed. He is not integrally what he is. We can but hope and wait. His acts and behaviour are the determining factor" (Fanon, 2008, p. 95).

Fanon refers to Shakespeare's Prospero and Sartre's famous phenomenological saying of the human being not being wholly what he is. Prospero is a fictional character and the protagonist of William Shakespeare's play *The Tempest*. Fanon

275

favorably compares the Jewish curse of love of money with the more devastating curse of the black skin. The point is that the Jew can be unknown in his Jewishness. He is not wholly what he is. But the black skin cannot go unnoticed.

With the last line on the last page of *Black Skin, White Masks*, Franz Fanon movingly expresses his most intimate desire:

> My final prayer:
> O my body, make of me always a man who questions! (Fanon, 2008, p. 206)

Material Phenomenology: Michel Henry

Michel Henry was born in Hai Phong, Vietnam, January 10, 1922. After his father died in a car accident, his mother returned to France to their family home in Lille and later to Paris, where Henry went to university. From 1943 to 1945 Henry joined the French resistance. After the war he studied under Jean Wahl, Jean Hyppolyte, and Paul Ricoeur. From 1960 onward Michel Henry was a professor of philosophy at the University of Montpellier. During his career he received several invitations to be appointed at the Sorbonne, but he preferred the quieter academic life at Montpellier, where he could dedicate himself to research and writing. His publications include *The Essence of Manifestation* (1963), *Philosophy and Phenomenology of the Body* (1965), *Marx: A Philosophy of Human Being* (1976), *Seeing the Invisible: On Kandinsky* (1988), *Material Phenomenology* (1990), *I Am the Truth: Toward a Philosophy of Christianity* (1996), and *Incarnation: A Philosophy of the Flesh* (2000)—the publication dates are the French books. He also wrote four novels. He died in 2002.

Henry's material phenomenology is a phenomenology of immanence: the immanence or interiority of subjectivity. For him phenomenology is a science of true beginnings. More so than most of his predecessors and contemporaries, Henry has made it his project to search for the very beginnings where meaning originates. To that end, he turns to Husserl's phenomenology of internal time consciousness: the primal impressionality of consciousness. It is here where the question of origin is raised by Husserl, in a manner that Henry finds truly compelling:

> It is in the *Lectures on the Internal Consciousness of Time* (1905) that, for the first and last time, phenomenology attempts to elucidate the givenness of the impression in a rigorous way. In this extraordinary text, which is certainly the most beautiful of twentieth century philosophy, there is a huge confrontation in which a hyletic phenomenology in the radical sense of the term attempts to clear a path through the sediment of the tradition. This struggle results in a remarkably profound philosophy of archi-constitution that renews many of the aspects of classical thought yet does so at the cost of losing the essential and hyletic phenomenology itself. (Henry, 2008, p. 21)

In spite of his extraordinary praise of Husserl's famous text, Henry nevertheless complains that Husserl has never truly managed to disclose the true interiority of subjectivity in a sufficiently radical and pure manner. But what does one find when one tries to step back in order to gain access to whatever it is that gives itself to us, prior to consciousness and prior to the impressional affectivities or the originary source of human experience? Henry comes forth with (for lack of a better word) "Life" itself. It is the affectivity of life that we can sometimes feel as it surges through our existence. This affectivity is not caused by life, but it is the auto-affectivity of life itself. At the level of life there are no intentionalities, no real or transcendental objects, things or events to be observed. Therefore, Henry says, life is not a phenomenon. Life cannot be approached by way of the Husserlian eidetic reduction. And yet, life lies at the very foundation of everything. The key idea for Henry is the notion of revelation:

> Life is the original appearing that from now on we are going to designate with the word "revelation." ...
> The first feature of the revelation of life is that it is accomplished as a self-revelation. Life revealing itself means that it experiences itself. (Henry, 1999, p. 351)

The hyletic refers to the raw material from which consciousness, thought, and memory are shaped. But rather than use the term *hyletic*, Henry calls his approach a *material* phenomenology to indicate the interest in the originary source of the material of consciousness that is not (yet) formed into phenomena, not (yet) tied to the things of the world in a manner that is referred to as the intentionality of consciousness. Henry wants to explore the deepest roots of the affectivities of human experience and feeling about which we can only say that it feels its own feeling. Life feels its life in the affective pathos of its aliveness. This may sound confusing, but upon willing reflection it may actually resonate with our sense of existence.

For Henry absolute subjectivity cannot be objectified or brought in an intentional relation with consciousness. His is a nonintentional phenomenology. The immanence of subjectivity is not a phenomenon that "appears," and thus it remains invisible to the phenomenological gaze. Without resorting to a foundationalist twist, Henry uses the notion of foundation to point toward an immanent revelation that can only be an interior presence to its own interiority:

> That which permits something to be in itself manifesting, is what we call a foundation . . . . The foundation is not something obscure, neither is it light which becomes perceivable only when it shines upon the thing which bathes in its light, nor is it the thing itself as a "transcendent phenomenon," but it is an immanent revelation which is a presence to itself, even though such a presence remains "invisible." (Henry, 1973, pp. 40, 41)

According to Henry, life can never be seen from the exterior, since it never appears in the exteriority of the world. Life feels itself and experiences itself in its invisible interiority and in its radical immanence. In the world we never see life itself, but only living beings or living organisms. We cannot see life in them. Just as it is impossible to see, hear, or touch the soul of others with our sensory organs or to discover it by opening the physical body, so life cannot be seen by observing or opening up beings that we think of as alive with life.

277

The genuine object of phenomenology is phenomenality, because phenomenality constitutes our access to the phenomenon; in its very phenomenalization, phenomenality opens the path which leads right up to the phenomenon. Now, in its ultimate possibility, the method is nothing other than this openness of a path leading to the phenomenon; it allows us to apprehend the phenomenon and to know it. (Henry, 1999, p. 344)

Michel Henry offers a radical phenomenology and what is important in a radical phenomenology is the phenomenological essence of this self-relation. Every relation which does not stand out against the horizon of the world and which does not render the world manifest in its way draws its possibility from pathos. Pathos designates the mode of phenomenalization according to which life phenomenalizes in its originary self-revelation; it designates the phenomenological material out of which this self-donation (self-givenness) is made, its flesh: a transcendental and pure affectivity in which everything experiencing itself finds its concrete, phenomenological actualization. In this pathos, the "how" of revelation becomes its content; its *Wie* (who) is a *Was* (what). If life originally reveals nothing but its own reality, this is solely because its mode of revelation is pathos, which is this essence entirely concerned with itself, this plenitude of a flesh immersed in the self-affection of its suffering and joy. In the immanence of its own pathos, this reality of life is then not any life whatsoever. It is everything except what contemporary thought will turn it into; that is, some impersonal, anonymous, blind, mute essence. In itself, the reality of life bears necessarily this pathetic self-generation, this Self that reveals itself only in life as the proper self-revelation of this life—that is, as its logos. "That which is felt without the intermediary of any sense whatsoever is in its essence affectivity," says Henry (1973, p. 462).

The material phenomenology of Michel Henry exercises in complete lucidity the power to think *après coup*, to meditate on life. This power to think is capable of founding the phenomenological method by proceeding to its radical critique. Husserl wanted to see and grasp—*Sehen und Fassen*—life in apodictic evidence. Unfortunately, there is no possible evidence of transcendental subjectivity because in the language of the world, all life vanishes. Paradoxically, there is no direct phenomenological access to life because one would need to reduce life to something else to do so. And yet, it would seem that the only access to the meaning of life is direct since life manifests itself in us as the primordiality of existence.

Henry's phenomenology of life sees meaning as an immediate feeling of one's own existence. Life feels itself as living. Life is both visible and invisible. It is visible because it can be seen in all that is alive; it is invisible because it can only be seen indirectly. It is not surprising that some have accused Henry of a phenomenology of mystical theology, especially since he wrote on themes of Christianity, such as his book *I Am the Truth: Toward a Philosophy of Christianity* (2003). But if one remains open-minded toward his radical phenomenology, then one may be persuaded to grasp his project by the way that Henry develops a painstaking study of seeing the invisible in painting. He turns to the abstract paintings of Kandinsky to convey how the unity of form, composition, and color conveys the invisible intensity of life itself.

278

If, despite the diverse impressions that stitch it together into an uninterrupted framework, the world is one, it must be one because the different senses providing our access to the world are themselves one, one and the same unique power with a plurality of modes of fulfilment. This single power is our body. What does its unity consist of? What makes seeing, hearing, touching and feeling the same, in spite of the variety of distinct experiences? It is their subjectivity. There is no seeing that does not experience its seeing, no hearing that does not experience its hearing, no touching that does not immediately experience itself and does not coincide with itself in the very act by which it touches anything whatsoever. On the basis of their radical subjectivity, all of these powers are one; one and the same force sees, hears and touches. Because our true body is a subjective body, it is the unity of all the powers and all the senses comprising it. Because all these senses that offer the world are one, the world, in turn, is only one and the same world. (2009, pp. 111, 112)

For Henry life can never be studied as an object. So, he asks, "How is life then present in art?" And, he says, abstraction is the answer to this question in the sense that life is never present in terms of what we see or seem to see in a painting "but only in terms of what we feel within ourselves when this seeing happens: the painting's composition of the tones and tonalities of colours and forms" (2009, p. 121). Their invisible unity. When Henry says, "but only in terms of what we feel within ourselves when this seeing happens," he is echoing Rilke, who writes about the moving moment of poetic in-seeing as "a divine seeing into the heart of things" and he is also virtually translating Kandinsky's famous line: "Everything has a secret soul, which is silent more often than it speaks" (1977, p. 3).

Deconstruction Phenomenology: Jacques Derrida

Jacques Derrida was born to Jewish parents in 1930, in the town El Biar, in the French colony of Algeria. He excelled at sports in school, but as he grew older he became intrigued by the influential figure of writer-philosopher Jean-Paul Sartre. He decided to try to pursue an academic career in literature and philosophy, though his admiration for Sartre eventually waned. Initially his career did not unfold smoothly. But he managed to gain a position at the Sorbonne teaching philosophy and logic. In Paris he immersed himself in the study of phenomenology and structuralism: especially Husserl, Heidegger, Levinas, and Blanchot. His creative thought and his eventual immense productivity announced itself without warning: in 1967 he suddenly published three major books that brought him instant fame: *Speech and Phenomena* (a study of Husserl), *Of Grammatology* (perhaps his magnus opus), and *Writing and Difference* (a series of essays). By the time he died at the age of 74 in Paris in 2004, he had written about 70 books that have been published in numerous languages.

Derrida is now considered one of the most original thinkers, if not the most influential thinker of his time. His development of the idea of deconstruction, his critical reading of classical philosophic texts, and his provocative take on a wide range of issues and topics have influenced scholars in virtually all countries and continents across the humanities, social sciences, philosophy, architectural disciplines, and the arts.

Derrida became famous for a new way of reading classical philosophic texts, and indeed a provocative way of reinterpreting the entire history of philosophy. He is regarded as being foremost responsible for the so-called French linguistic turn—with colleagues such as Julia Kristeva (1980) and Hélène Cixous (1976, 1997). Derrida aims to show that meaning is always primarily linguistic, though any pronouncement about his work is bound to be overly simplistic or downright wrong. In his famous text *Of Grammatology*, he begins a preoccupation with the notion of writing that has somehow governed virtually his entire oeuvre. He has argued that western thought is dominated by logocentrism and that commonly accepted ideas such as immediacy, presence, absence, identity, and proximity are misleading the logic of our thinking or simply untenable. For Derrida language includes the full complexities of human expression and signification: literature, cinema, visual art, sculpture, and so on. His famous claim that there is "nothing outside of the text" refers, on the one hand, to the notion that the meaning of a text can never be fixed (is always different and deferred), and, on the other hand, that this linguistic predicament is symptomatic of every human situation and experience.

In an interview, contained in *A Taste for the Secret*, Derrida (2001) offers some insights into his life as author, such as his reasons for writing, his initial resistance to being photographed, and so on. The curious reader might ask, but are personal secrets revealed? The title would lead one to expect not. Yet, Derrida shares some inner thoughts. On clarity: "my own experience of writing leads me to think that one does not always write with a desire to be understood—there is a paradoxical desire not to be understood" (2001, p. 30). On school: "even though I have always been in school I was never good at school. I failed a lot of examinations, was held back" (2001, p. 40). On grammar: "I detest grammatical mistakes. Even when I take liberties that some people find provocative, I do so with the feeling—justifiable or not—that I do in fact know the rules. A transgression should always know what it transgresses" (2001, p. 43). On death: "I think about nothing but death, I think about it all the time, ten seconds don't go by without the imminence of the thing being there" (2001, p. 88). On afterlife: "I do not believe that one lives on *post mortem*" (2001, p. 88).

The concern with the meaning and place of writing and secrecy recurs throughout Derrida's work. In *A Taste for the Secret*, Derrida explains how the condition for sharing, thematizing, or objectifying something implies that there be something non-shareable, nonthematizable, nonobjectifiable. And this something is the absolute secret—we speak of it but we cannot say it, we evoke it but we cannot write it. The secret is absolute because it is detached, cut off (*ab-solutus*) or separated (*secrete*) from that to which it belongs. What is the significance of this unconditional and absolute secret? Dwelling in the secret forces the recognition of the irreducibility of things. It reminds of the singularity of experience and of existence in its relation to language and inquiry. The reader may agree that we must not only have a taste for the secret, but we must cultivate the care for the secret.

Having a taste for the secret has personal significance for Derrida. He relates it to his childhood in Algeria, his Jewishness, his sense of a mother tongue, and his contested status in the Academy. All of this has made him prefer the secret to the non-secret: "it clearly has to do with not-belonging," he says. And he explains that ultimately, there inheres a kind of terror in the demands made by the public and political space. It leaves no room for the secret. If the right to the secret is not maintained, we are in a totalitarian space.

Derrida (1995a) shows that the uniqueness of each person comes into sharp relief against the fact of his or her individual mortality. Ironically, we are given this mortality right at birth. Therefore, Derrida calls this "the gift of death" since it is our own mortality that belongs to each of us more uniquely than anything else imaginable. Whatever can be taken away from us, there is one thing that belongs to us so essentially that nobody can take it away and that is our own death. I may give my death in sacrifice to someone else, and yet even that supreme gift cannot be substituted for his or her own death. Thus, it is the non-substitutional uniqueness of the other that I must preserve, and not kill, by betraying it to the general. And yet, says Derrida, this is precisely what we do every day. He points at Kierkegaard's recounting of the story of Abraham and his son Isaac. He tries to understand how it is that we can seemingly forget our responsibility to care for the one we love most. And yet, says, Derrida, we are all indicted with this irresponsible responsibility.

> By preferring my work, simply by giving it my time and attention, by preferring my activity as a citizen or as a professorial and professional philosopher, writing and speaking here in a public language . . . I am perhaps fulfilling my duty. But I am sacrificing and betraying at every moment all my other obligations: my obligations to the other others whom I know or don't know . . . also those I love in private, my own, my family, my son, each of whom is the only son I sacrifice to the other, every one being sacrificed to every one else in this land of Moriah that is our habitat every second of every day. (Derrida, 1995a, p. 69)

It seems that the call of caring responsibility is constantly betrayed in our efforts to be caring in a general sense of duty, as in our professional practice that can also mean a caring for the self. In other words, by writing about caring (even by writing about caring for my children), I am forsaking the real call that my children make on me. Derrida articulates the dilemma in such a way that his confession of failing to be responsive to the call of his own son becomes an unsolvable predicament. He says,

> what can be said about Abraham's relation to God can be said about my relation without relation to *every other (one) as every (bit) other [tout autre comme tout autre]*, in particular my relation to my neighbour or my loved ones who are inaccessible to me, as secret and transcendent as Yahweh . . . . Translated into this extraordinary story, the truth is shown to possess the very structure of what occurs every day. Through its paradox it speaks of the responsibility required at every moment for every man and woman. (Derrida, 1995a, p. 78)

In a way Derrida seems to let us off the hook in our unique responsibility to care for the other as other. On one hand, he suggests that we need to heed this call, and yet, on the other hand, his deconstructionist strategy aims to show that we must constantly fail since we cannot possibly be responsive to every other who is out there and also makes an appeal to our caring responsibility. Since we can only worry about one thing at a time, we cannot worry about everyone and everything.

Indeed, even as a teacher, as nurse, as physician, as therapist, one would have to agree with Derrida. We cannot really see how we could worry for each child, for each patient in our charge. Does that mean that we flee into the ethical domain of professional responsibility that says that we must subsume our caring behaviors under a general moral code? The problem with Derrida's approach is that he has already fled into language and ethics when he deconstructs reflectively the pre-reflective occurrence of the caring encounter. The point is that in everyday life, the experience of the call of the other, of care-as-worry, is always contingent and particular. It is the singularity of this person who addresses me in my singularity.

For Derrida intersubjectivity is therefore intertextuality. In contrast to Husserl's search for an indubitable ground of human understanding in the cogito, Derrida points out the essentially unstable and undecidable character of the nature of signs, language, and meaning. Through the method of deconstruction Derrida aims to demonstrate not the invariance of human phenomena but the essential variance, the "*différance*," destabilizing all meaningful distinctions and discernible identities. Conventionally we take identity to mean that something differs uniquely from other things that may seem the same. Phenomenology may indeed be conceived as the study of identity and difference. The phenomenological question is, what makes a thing what it is and not something else?

Perhaps it is important to realize as well that Derrida's deconstruction is aimed at texts rather than at the lived experiences that may lie at the origin of words, phrases, and texts. True, from a phenomenological point of view, no experience is ever the same. Even my own experience is different from a similar experience prior or subsequent to it. For example, the notion of "keeping a secret" may have a certain phenomenal identity that we may try to elucidate, but the experience of keeping a certain secret from a certain person may not be experienced as exactly the same as keeping a secret on a different occasion, even with the same person. In other words, one does not need Derrida's notion of *différance* to realize that the particular meaning of the lived experience of "keeping a secret" is never finally settled. Every iteration is a reiteration. However, phenomenologically we focus on capturing the essence of a certain experience (what something "is" in its "isness" or essence) by means of the device of the phenomenological universal. Even genetic phenomenology aims to reclaim the stability of presence in the temporality of the constantly changing now of the not-now or of the no-longer-now.

Deconstruction is hard to define because it rejects the validity of any sense of "is-ness," including, of course, the notion of deconstruction. Even the meaning of deconstruction is deconstructed by rejecting the authority of any positive definition. This is a consequence of the point that everything is text for Derrida. Phenomenology begins with lived experience, proceeds through language, and ends in phenomenality. But deconstruction begins with language, shows the impossibly unstable state of every linguistic entity, and ends in the realization of the iterability of deconstructed language. It might be argued that phenomenology escapes linguistic deconstruction by turning back to experience as lived, in the sense of turning back to the world as experienced (rather than the world in words).

282

In his many essays, Derrida is a master of aporias, showing how our ordinary intentions and actions involve us in paradoxes, insoluble contradictions, and impasses. He calls these predicaments undecidables. For example, when we are hospitable or give someone a gift, we may think that we are doing so with no strings attached. We are giving this gift out of the goodness of our heart. But Derrida shows how things are not so simple. The conditions of possibility are at the same time the conditions of impossibility. We cannot give a gift without receiving something in return, if only gratitude or the inner satisfaction that we have done good. Gifts create debts. So, is it really possible to give a gift? Or is gift giving ultimately always some kind of exchange? It seems indeed as if authentic giving or hospitality is an undecidable: neither possible nor impossible.

Feminine Phenomenology: Hélène Cixous

Hélène Cixous was born in 1937 in Oran, Algeria. In 1968, she became a professor of English literature at Université de Paris VIII–Vincennes. During her entire career Cixous was very close to Jacques Derrida who often wrote texts together with her. Hélène Cixous is especially known for her notion of *écriture féminine*, feminine writing. Many have tried to break the secret of *écriture féminine*. How does one write as a woman and not as a man? But, in *The Laugh of the Medusa* (1976), Cixous claims that *écriture féminine* cannot be captured in a definition or even a philosophy. It is not possible since "it will always surpass the discourse that regulates the phallocentric system" that aims to theorize or enclose it (1976, p. 883).

Cixous repeatedly expresses her wariness of reductive language that would simplify her practice of *écriture féminine*. Still, she makes clear that she wishes to offer new ways of writing and speaking, and that she writes to women:

> I write this as a woman, towards women. When I say "woman," I'm speaking of woman in her inevitable struggle against conventional man; and of a universal woman subject who must bring women to their senses and to their meaning in history. (1976, p. 875).

To do so, she emphasizes the fictional and poetic elements in her writing. She says that, for her, what is most true is poetic writing and what is most true is seeing life naked:

> What is most true is poetic. What is most true is naked life. I can only attain this mode of seeing with the aid of poetic writing. I apply myself to "seeing" the world nude, that is almost e-nu-merating the world, with the naked, obstinate, defenceless eye of my nearsightedness. And while looking very very closely, I copy. The world written nude is poetic. (1997, p. 3)

Cixousian writing is constantly bent back onto itself and thus may seem confusing since it is not ordinary prosaic prose but already poetic, and thus (seeming unwittingly) showing what it is about. She uses neologisms, metaphors, puns, parodies, jests, and alliterations in multilayered self-reflexive texts. When Cixous says, poetically, that what is most true is poetic, she may mean that there may be other kinds of writing that are more or less true but not most true. If so, what is most true than most true? And when she says that she applies herself to "seeing" the world nude, one wonders: what is the interpretive intent of this mode of seeing? Of course, many phenomenological authors and thinkers would say about their work that it cannot be captured in definitional terms, and that it must be approached and read in their entirety, and not as arguments or summaries.

The phenomenological reader might suggest that Cixous seems to practice the epoché with her expression of seeing the world naked. Seeing the world naked would be the perfect epoché since it means seeing without overlays, distortions, projections, or impositions. It means seeing in the kind of way that Rilke talks of as poetic "in-seeing into the heart of things." And it can refer to the kind of seeing that Levinas describes as seeing the naked face of the other.

Levinas too contrasts this naked seeing as opposed to seeing with the "possessive" eye that wants to own the world. According to Levinas seeing the nakedness of the face shows the irreducibility of the otherness of the other.

Hélène Cixous writes:

It is impossible to define a feminine practice of writing, and this is an impossibility that will remain, for this practice can never be theorized, enclosed, coded—which doesn't mean that it doesn't exist. But it will always surpass the discourse that regulates the phallocentric system; it does and will take place in areas other than those subordinated to philosophico-theoretical domination. (1976, p. 83)

Cixous only rarely refers explicitly to "phenomenology" and yet her frequent autobiographic, poetic, and feminine writing seems playfully driven by a pathos that we may recognize as phenomenological evocation that rids the world of untruths, by stripping what is in the way of seeing the beautiful truth of things nude. To see the essence of truth nude, it has to be stripped naked.

Like other phenomenological thinkers and authors, Cixous turns to the ancient mythology of Prometheus, or rather the female version of Promethea, to reveal hidden aspects of the human condition—such as to pursue the idea of feminine writing as love writing, animated by *jouissance*, sexual pleasure.

The Laugh of the Medusa (1976) is an appropriate text to engage with the fundamental contexts of Cixous's liberating feminist and literary feminine writing style. Famously, Cixous refers to the story of Medusa who was originally a beautiful maiden, but when Poseidon seduced her in the temple of Athena, the goddess Minerva punished Medusa by transforming her beautiful hair in terrifying phallic snakes. This caused great disturbance among the deities. Perseus was charged to find Medusa and cut off her monstrous head. Perseus was the noble son of Zeus and Danaë, a princess. He had to fulfill this task to save his mother. During that period of conspiring, Medusa was pregnant by Poseidon. So, it appears that Medusa was being punished for her predicament, even though Poseidon was the male sexual aggressor and father of the unborn.

Perseus was warned not to look straight at Medusa because of her potent eyes. He was armed with a mirrored shield by Athena, gold-winged sandals by Hermes, and a sword by Hephaestus, god of the underworld. Perseus searched and found Medusa and approached her, while not looking at her straight on but via the reflection from the mirrored shield he had received from Athena. Of course, the very idea of the male not looking the woman straight in her eyes betrays the unequal gendered encounter between the powerfully armed Perseus and the pregnant Medusa.

Perseus beheads Medusa. Her body perishes but now her head becomes even more powerfully potent: her eyes can turn into stone anyone who looks at Medusa's head which has been transformed into a terrifying beauty in spite of the snakes—though many thought her ugly. Whatever Medusa's potent eyes stare at turns into stone. However, Medusa never turns any women into stone, only men, who fear the potency of the deadly female spirit inside the head of Medusa. Typically, men fail to see the original beauty and profoundly mysterious femininity of the maiden Medusa for fear that her look may turn them weak and impotent. After the slaying of Medusa, Athena attaches Medusa's head to her own battle shield.

In short, the ancient story of Medusa is of a man-hero, Perseus, who kills the pregnant woman whose hair and head has turned ugly and deadly dangerous with snakes as punishment for her affair with Poseidon. But Cixous says:

> You only have to look at the Medusa straight on to see her. And she's not deadly. She's beautiful and she's laughing.
>
> Men say that there are two unrepresentable things: death and the feminine sex. That's because they need femininity to be associated with death; it's the jitters that gives them a hard-on! for themselves! They need to be afraid of us. Look at the trembling Perseuses moving backward toward us, clad in apotropes. What lovely backs! Not another minute to lose. Let's get out of here.
>
> . . .
>
> Almost everything is yet to be written by women about femininity: about their sexuality, that is, its infinite and mobile complexity, about their eroticization, sudden turn-ons of a certain miniscule-immense area of their bodies; not about destiny, but about the adventure of such and such a drive, about trips, crossings, trudges, abrupt and gradual awakenings, discoveries of a zone at one time timorous and soon to be forth-right. (1976, p. 885)

The only way to understand Cixous's call for *écriture feminine* seems to let her write for herself. The apotropaic face of Medusa wards off evil and should be understood as the radical feature of writing. There is no better way than to catch the evocative and provocative tone that determines the partially autobiographic writing of Cixous when she exhorts to herself:

> why don't you write? Write! Writing is for you, you are for you; your body is yours, take it. I know why you haven't written. (And why I didn't write before the age of twenty-seven.) Because writing is at once too high, too great for you, it's reserved for the great-that is, for "great men"; and it's "silly." Besides, you've written a little, but in secret. (1976, p. 876)

In part, Hélène Cixous thematizes her program of feminine writing through a focus on sexuality:

> Men still have everything to say about their sexuality, and everything to write. For what they have said so far, for the most part, stems from the opposition activity/passivity, from the power relation between a fantasized obligatory virility meant to invade, to colonize, and the consequential phantasm of woman as a "dark continent" to penetrate and to "pacify." (We know what "pacify" means in terms of scotomizing the other and mis- recognizing the self.) Conquering her, they've made haste to depart from her borders, to get out of sight, out of body. The way man has of getting out of himself and into her whom he takes not for the other but for his own, deprives him, he knows, of his own bodily territory. One can understand how man, confusing himself with his penis and rushing in for the attack, might feel resentment and fear of being "taken" by the woman, of being lost in her, absorbed, or alone. (1976, p. 877)

Cixous makes clear that the critical consequences of the man's writing are serious for the woman:

> Men have committed the greatest crime against women. Insidiously, violently, they have led them to hate women, to be their own enemies, to mobilize their immense strength against themselves, to be the executants of their virile needs. They have made for women an antinarcissism! A narcissism which loves itself only to be loved for what women haven't got! They have constructed the infamous logic of antilove. (1976, p. 878)

So, Hélène Cixous calls women to arms, meaning she calls them to write, because women have not written for and of women:

> I say that we must, for, with a few rare exceptions, there has not yet been any writing that inscribes femininity; exceptions so rare, in fact, that, after plowing through literature across languages, cultures, and ages, one can only be startled at this vain scouting mission. (1976, p. 878)

Woman must write the self to liberate herself.

> Write your self. Your body must be heard. Only then will the immense resources of the unconscious spring forth.
>
> . . .
>
> To write. An act which will not only "realize" the decensored relation of woman to her sexuality, to her womanly being, giving her access to her native strength; it will give her back her goods, her pleasures, her organs, her immense bodily territories which have been kept under seal; it will tear her away from the superegoized structure in which she has always occupied the place reserved for the guilty (guilty of everything, guilty at every turn: for having desires, for not having any; for being frigid, for being "too hot"; for not being both at once; for being too motherly and not enough; for having children and for not having any; for nursing and for not nursing . . .) (1976, p. 880)

Cixous's strongly poetic and phenomenological work has been influenced by several German, British, and French philosophers and authors, including Martin Heidegger and Jacques Derrida. In *La Venue à l'Écriture* (1977), a strongly Derridean work, Cixous advances the position that *écriture feminine* is not necessarily writing by a woman; rather, it is feminine writing likewise practiced by certain male authors, such as James Joyce, Clarice Lispector, and Jean Genet. Feminine writing should stand as an alternative to mainstream writing, which is shaped by a libidinal, cultural, political, and masculine economy. Again, according to Cixous, this practice cannot really be defined or described, and trying to do so would result in distorted oversimplification.

Hélène Cixous shows how phenomenology can offer the grammar and creative vocabulary of a feminist feminine discourse that does not convince primarily through its logic and argument, but rather that enlists and seduces through its radical and poetic *écriture feminine*. Jacques Derrida said:

> I have often declared my admiration for Hélène Cixous, for the person and for the work: immense, powerful, so multiple but unique in this century. I have even written, I believe, that Hélène Cixous is in my eyes, today, the greatest writer in the French language. (Cixous, 1998, p. ix)

And Derrida added: "I am weighing my words as I say that. For a great writer must be a poet-thinker, very much a poet and a very thinking poet."

Technoscience Postphenomenology: Don Ihde

Don Ihde was born in 1934. He coined the term *postphenomenology* to seek a new program to replace what he calls *classical phenomenology* and to describe the coupling of phenomenology with pragmatism (of figures like William James and John Dewey). He sees this coupling as opening up a future for phenomenology that has been referred to as empirical or material phenomenology, contributing to a new vision of the phenomenology of technology. Ihde adopts the nomenclature of empirical and material phenomenology in part from Dutch philosophers of technology such as Hans Achterhuis and Peter-Paul Verbeek, who had taken some of their cues from Ihde himself. Ihde is clearly impatient with the continuing reputation of the great minds such as Husserl, Heidegger, and Merleau-Ponty.

> I do not consider myself "above" phenomenology, but I do consider postphenomenology to be "past" and different than classical phenomenology as a development from phenomenology. Besides, I do not see why one has to forever reverence the godfathers—surely there can be developments past classical phenomenology and postphenomenology is but one. Too much of so-called continental philosophy acts as if the last words were said by the godfathers, but surely there can be development in new directions? Some would "naturalize" phenomenology, others do "hetero-phenomenology," so I do postphenomenology. I certainly acknowledge my debts to Husserl, Heidegger, Merleau-Ponty—and also the hermeneutic traditions which add Gadamer and Ricoeur to the tradition. But I am also critical of the "subjectivism" associated with Husserl, the "romanticism" associated with Heidegger, and the "linguisticism" associated with the hermeneuts. Moreover, philosophy of technology—better technoscience studies in my

term—must be sensitive to materiality. Husserl had very little to say about technologies; Heidegger had lots to say but retained a nostalgic romanticism over simple technologies; and Merleau-Ponty, often insightful, usually was indirect about technologies. (Ihde, 2010)

Ihde argues that "technologies must be understood phenomenologically, i.e., as belonging in different ways to our experience and use of technologies, as a human–technology relation, rather than abstractly conceiving of them as mere objects" (1993, p. 34). He distinguishes four types of human–technology relations: embodiment, hermeneutic, alterity, and background relations.

The embodiment relation pertains to technological artifacts that have become part of our body experience. For example, our glasses, clothes, shoes, the blind person's cane, and the walker of the senior citizen are examples of technologies that have become integrated with our bodily being, functioning, and acting. So, technology can be an extension (extender and/or magnifier) of the body. The technology itself tends to become relatively transparent, unnoticed. With the cane in my hand, the end of the stick becomes my fingertip. I can feel the texture of the world. The car becomes an extension of the body. I say, "I cannot go through there; I had a flat." Technology can alienate, but can it also enhance the richness of our bodily experience?

The hermeneutic relation applies where technology is used to interpret and read the world in which we dwell. Examples of the hermeneutic relation are the microscope, the thermometer, the road map, and street signs. These are technologies that possess graphic, alphabetic, or other instrumental languages to read interior and exterior meaning aspects of our environment. In hermeneutic relations the technology is not so much experienced-through as experienced-with. In hermeneutic relations the technology is more text-like. The television brings me the world interpreted, the scientific equipment lets me "read" nature. Just as the scientist actually perceives the subatomic reality, which in a modernist view of science was in principle imperceptible, so the computer user may actually experience the presence of the other who emails or communicates with us via the Internet.

Alterity relations between humans and technologies occur when the technologies that we use assume anthropomorphic or alterity significance. For example, we may treat our car, computer, or mobile as if they have personalities. In alterity relations, the computer is experienced as quasi-other. There are two aspects of the human computer relation that tend to anthropomorphize the computer. In an alterity relation, the technology appears as quasi-other with whom we converse. The experience is focused upon and directed to the technology equipment. (Think of the supercomputer HAL in the movie *2001: A Space Odyssey.*) Because the computer mimics linguistic interpretive activity, there is the tendency to take the computer as a simulacrum. Some feel that there is no difference between a face-to-face conversational encounter and an online chat. The computer as writing technology "helps" me in a way that the pen does not. It remembers for me, calls my attention, prompts me, corrects me, even annoys me. But is the meaning and significance of other as other reduced?

Finally, *background relations* exist between us and our technological environment that have become so taken for granted that they recede into the background.

For example, the heating, electrical, or plumbing technologies of our house main-tain such nearly invisible relations. In background relations technology is expe-rienced as part of the things and furniture of our world with which we interact instrumentally, aesthetically, and practically such as with the appliances in our house. Some of this relational experience (such as with the thermostat and heating system in the house) is unnoticed, at the back, as it were of our daily activities. Other relational experiences are similar to the way we deal with the various natural or man-made objects around us (technologies such as the fridge, the microwave oven, or the washing machine).

Ihde's phenomenology of technology is helpful in examining our professional relations with equipment and their technological consequences in the practice of medical care, nursing, teaching, and so on. While his interest is in technology, Ihde also has commented on the expressive dimension of phenomenology. He suggests that while "phenomenology, particularly in its Husserlian form, may be seen to reciprocate with the analytic philosophies of language with respect to reference, its deeper concern lies with the other tendency [of] expression" (1983, p. 167). The difference between the designative, referential, semantic functions of language and the expressive, transcendent, poetic functions of a text is not simply an issue of interpretability. Both designative and expressive meaning involve interpretation, though in a different manner and to a different degree.

Learning Phenomenology: Hubert Dreyfus

Hubert Dreyfus was born in Terre Haute, Indiana, in 1929. He earned his Ph.D. at Harvard and taught at various universities, but mostly at the Massachusetts Institute of Technology and the University of California, Berkeley. Dreyfus has been a main interpreter of Husserl, Foucault, and especially Heidegger. His own original work concerns the meaning and significance of technology for human thinking, interacting, and learning. While at MIT Dreyfus wrote *What Comput-ers Can't Do: The Limits of Artificial Intelligence* (1972), which was updated and revised in 1979 and again in 1992 as *What Computers Still Can't Do: A Critique of Artificial Reason*. Dreyfus argues that technologists tend to think of the brain as computer hardware and cognition processes as software programs. Artificial intelligence optimists hold out a future when our bodies no longer grow old or get diseased. Our brains will be hooked up to digitized machines that will trans-form our cognitive selves into disembodied information-processing intelligences. But Dreyfus points out that this optimism rests on a history of first-step fallacies that assumes that just because we have been able to climb an incline we think that we can actually scale the mountain behind it (Dreyfus, 2012).

In 1980 the brothers Stuart Dreyfus and Hubert Dreyfus pursued a project on human learning. They described the development of human skill acquisition as a five-stage process, from novice to mastery (Dreyfus and Dreyfus, 1980). Later, they refined and renamed the five stages somewhat from novice, to advanced beginner, to proficiency, to competence, and to expertise. And they applied the model toward the phenomenology of ethical expertise (Dreyfus, 1991). The novice learns to deal with situations by relying on rules; the advanced beginner is able to recognize rele-vant contexts for acting; the competent learner is able to make strategic plans; the proficient person has learned to internalize a repertoire of types of situations and positions; and the expert is able to improvise and spontaneously act intuitively in challenging situations. Patricia Benner (1984) and other researchers in the health sciences have used this "novice to expert" model to study how nurses progress in their development of professional skills and expertise.

Dreyfus criticizes the technological rationalization of human practices (interactions and relations). Even social practices that are by their very nature communicative fall under the sway of a strange liaison between technological and critical rationality. For example, friendship is becoming increasingly rationalized. More so than before people seem to make friends not because of the inherent quality of the experience of friendship, but because they hope that being friends and playing golf with the boss will get them ahead in life. Moreover, psychologists are proposing that friendship is healthy for a more relaxed and longer life. Love and marriage too are thought to add years to one's life. In discussing Michel Foucault and the notion of "marginal practices," Dreyfus sees a technological twist:

> Marginal practices always risk being taken over by technological rational understanding and made efficient and productive . . . . As soon as you have friends for your health or for your career you've got some new kind of friendship, which is of a technological-rational kind . . . . This new kind of friendship could replace the other kind of friendship. People wouldn't even know anymore what real friendship was. (Dreyfus in Flyvbjerg, 1991, p. 7)

It would seem that these reflections on the meaning of friendship and intimacy in technological contexts of social media and social networking environments such as Facebook, Twitter, and blogs are increasingly relevant.

Sense Phenomenology: Michel Serres

Michel Serres was born in Lot-et-Garonne, France, in 1930. He was a naval officer in his youth. He is knowledgeable of the physical sciences and mathematics, and he is steeped in literary, artistic, ancient, and contemporary philosophical traditions. Serres' writings are philosophically rigorous but also, at times, highly lyrical and vocative. He has written across an incredibly wide range of topics, phenomena, and concerns. Serres argues that the sciences and scientific languages are valuable but that they have veiled our sensuous perceptions of the world. "Sense and sensibility" is not only the title of one of his main texts, it also names the underlying theme of his reflective interests. As an author, he uses wordplay, mythologies, proverbs, paintings, architecture, and poetry as resource for his phenomenological explorations.

Serres takes on ethical issues of global pollution, politics, and questions such as how to educate the young. He asks, what do we do when we raise a child, teach a student, or educate a person as a member of society? And he urges the young:

> Depart. Go out. Allow yourself to be seduced one day. Become many, brave the outside world, split off somewhere else. These are the three foreign things, the three varieties of alterity, the three initial means of being exposed. For there is no learning without exposure, often dangerous, to the other. I will never again

know what I am, where I am, from where I'm from, where I'm going, through where to pass. I am exposed to others, to foreign things. (Serres, 1997, p. 8)

For Serres, pedagogy requires risky but necessary departures from home and challenging encounters with others and otherness. Against the background of his own youthful adventures at sea, Serres likens learning to a voyage from the familiar to the foreign. "No learning can avoid the voyage . . . . Learning launches wandering" (1997, p. 8). In his book *The Five Senses: A Philosophy of Mingled Bodies*, Michel Serres (2008) explores the language of the senses and how our senses can let us experience what language does not know.

Philosophers such as Maurice Blanchot and Jean-Luc Marion have used the myth of Orpheus and Eurydice to explain the Orphean gaze as the desire to see the invisible. But Serres tells the Orphean myth in his own compelling manner. The insight that Serres is aiming for has to do with the enigmatic nature of language that transcends description and evokes evocations. Serres wants to show how the lyrical and sonorous qualities of language can bring about understandings that ordinary propositional discourse is unable to achieve.

As we read Serres' text we begin to wonder: how does the word relate to being, naming to existence, poetic description to truth, the finite to the infinite? Through his phenomenological rewriting of the myth, which is both philosophical and poetical, Serres lets Orpheus bring Eurydice back to life. The word had kept her captive in death, but now the vocative voice of Orpheus has to affect the opposite and draw her back into her mortality.

> She leaves the word. Arises from her name. Frees herself from the cartouche.
> Removes herself from representation. Rediscovers movement, solidity, her dissolved flesh and vanished radiance, the material volume of her body, the delicate, satiny texture of her skin, the variable, clear, coloured light of her gaze, the horizontal agility of her gait as it adapts to the ground, the weight of her chest, hips, shoulders and neck, her hard skeleton. She steps softly out of the shadow, image and word. The word is made flesh.
> Evocation: something, flesh, emerges from voice.
> Orpheus invokes, his voice and strings tremble, he calls out, shouts, sings, chants. He composes both music and Eurydice. (2008, p. 132)

We begin to wonder: how does the word evoke body, create flesh, give voice to being? In this text, written before the personal computer had taken hold, Serres already plays with language and notions such as software, the virtual, softness, and hardness in his retelling of the original poetic text of Ovid's *Metamorphoses*.

> The ghost-woman reawakens, she follows her vocation.
> Voice makes the name flesh, delivers words from death, light dispels the darkness, music adds flesh, hardens what is soft: how far does incarnation go?
> Just as the hard beasts trail softly behind the lyre's harmonies, just as the dark forests soften their sharp thorns and needles, in concert, so does the soft evocation Eurydice follow her husband in hardness through the complex maze of creation and birth towards the propylaea which it is forbidden to cross in this

way. Eurydice hardens. As the lion advances towards the cithara it becomes image, shadow, phantom, it is more verbal and nominal. Eurydice's progress, on the other hand, becomes flesh and blood, her name finds voice, her voice finds harmony, harmony a throat, her throat a head, head and flowing hair emerge from her shoulders, she springs forth from evocation, torso, armpits, waist and breasts rising out of darkness as Aphrodite once emerged from the sea, as each of us did from the uterine black box, from sensorial virginity and ignorance, as each of us emerges from the cold. Light and warmth soften skin wrinkled by frozen darkness. Orpheus composes, constructs a living Eurydice, piece by piece and sense by sense. Stand up and walk! Go, speak!

The length of the labyrinth shows how much patience is required to achieve incarnation. Creation emerges from the Underworld where words, concepts, images, names and shadows flit about, it incorporates them through enchantment or by summoning them; frigid, drugged, the nominal awakens. Construction. Each book is released from the library, the deadliest of traps. (2008, p. 132)

But, of course, we know already that the word fails and, thus, Michel Serres continues:

Orpheus sets himself the most difficult of tasks . . . . But he fails in his attempt to drag Eurydice to the very top of the incline, in the very last act of making flesh; his lover collapses back into her own shadow: head into throat and throat into harmony and harmony into voice and voice into name, instantaneous involution, reversion to epitaph. The supreme achievement, rare and grandiose, is giving life to speech; the banal everyday gesture, the easy one, is substituting a word for a thing. Creation tries to break through to the world itself . . . (but) Nothing is quite as easy as naming, describing, conceiving. (2008, p. 133)

Now this last line is especially significant. Here Serres is criticizing method, theory, conceptualization, and representational discourse.

These magnificently composed inceptual lines are from a chapter of reflecting on what words can and cannot do. Serres proposes and shows that words that evocate can create. Serres shows this through his own poetically evocative narration. This reflective writing is true phenomenological analysis. The analysis is the writing. In the act of evocation, phenomenological writing can turn inceptual: it lets us glimpse what is originary. Through his text Serres lets us see what cannot be seen directly, lets us hear in the vocative silence of the poetic word what cannot be heard in prosaic parlance—to paraphrase Cixous: that what is most profound is poetic.

Sensual Phenomenology: Alphonso Lingis

Alphonso Lingis was born in 1933 in Crete, Illinois. He grew up on a Pennsylvania farm. His parents were Lithuanian. In the late fifties, Lingis studied at the University of Louvain in Belgium (where the Husserl Archives are kept). There he wrote his dissertation under Alphonse de Waelhens, a Lacanian philosopher. But Lingis achieved his initial fame as expert translator of key works of Merleau-Ponty and Levinas:

PHENOMENOLOGICAL ORIENTATIONS: PROTAGONISTS

I wrote my dissertation on Sartre and Merleau-Ponty and soon after that Merleau-Ponty died, leaving *The Visible and the Invisible*, and I had felt that I had really learned philosophy in writing my dissertation. In courses you get acquainted with things but in a dissertation you try to think it through yourself as far as you can and as hard as you can. So, I really felt that he had taught me, he had brought me into philosophy. I wanted to translate this out of gratitude, I had a very strong sense of gratitude towards him. So, I translated *The Visible and the Invisible*, and then in my first year of teaching (at Duquesne University), Ricoeur came to the United States and I arranged that he would speak at my school. I asked him what's happening this year in France and he said the big event was that Levinas had published *Totality and Infinity*, so I discovered this book and then the editor of my University Press suggested that I translate it. I love this book, I love it very much. (Lingis, 1997, p. 29)

Lingis subsequently also translated Levinas' *Otherwise than Being or Beyond Essence*, as well as *Existence and Existents*, and he edited and translated the *Collected Philosophical Papers* by Levinas. Alphonso Lingis is considered one of the most relevant and original philosophers alive. He has written formal philosophical texts such as *Libido: The French Existential Theories* (1986a) and *Phenomenological Explanations* (1986b). Lingis' analytical style in these early texts is technical and contrasts sharply with the almost lyrical style of most of his later works. For example, *Libido* is a phenomenological examination of sexuality in the works of Sartre, Merleau-Ponty, Levinas, and others. It is a subject much avoided by mainstream philosophers, but Eros becomes a dominant theme in the later writings of Lingis. Here he describes the sensuality and sexuality of the hand and the eyes:

The movements of sexual desire are caresses. The hand, which is not only an apparatus for grasping and taking, an instrument for discovering and feeling, a sense organ, and a contrivance for gesturing, an expressive organ, is also an organ for caressing, a sex organ. The eyes are not only organs for penetrating, exposing, or discovering, sense organs, and organs for approaching, having, and inhabiting, organs of appropriation. For there are also looks that caress. Even the least dexterous and blindest parts of the body—belly, thighs, breasts, buttocks—are organs for caressing; they are indeed specially so. (Lingis, 1986a, p. 22)

Major themes in the works of Lingis are community, ecology, ethics, and the cultural other, sensuality and alterity. Levinas' influence is especially noticeable in *The Community of Those Who Have Nothing in Common* (1994), *The Imperative* (1998), and, *Sensation: Intelligibility in Sensibility* (1996). In addition, Lingis has written a series of unusual phenomenological studies that look like travel writings but really are fundamental reflections on human existence and the human condition and what it means to encounter others in forgotten, sometimes destitute, sometimes exotic places. These writings originate from his travel experiences all over the world. In an interview he explained:

I always went away. As soon as I got a job any week I wasn't required to be in the United States I left the country, I've done that every year since I started

293

teaching. I don't know if I had any special project in mind, I just wanted to see the world. I wanted to live in the world. It wasn't exactly a kind of planned philosophical project. I wanted to do a lot of different things and see a lot of different places. I don't exactly travel, I've never thought of myself as a traveller. What I used to do for many years was just go to one place, very often by accident. I had a French friend who had been to a lot of places, a guy I admired a lot. He wasn't an academic but he went everywhere. I used to go to Paris first when my term was over and visit him. And I had for a number of years this private rule that the first place he would mention, I would go there for the rest of the summer. And this went on for a number of years, and in this way, unbeknownst to himself, he sent me to Istanbul, to Prague, to all sorts of spectacular places, until one year the first place he mentioned was Berlin and I changed the rule. (1997, p. 28)

The reason that Lingis was drawn to Sartre and Merleau-Ponty for his dissertation may make understandable why Lingis eventually developed a way of writing and doing philosophy that is so uniquely analytical, lyrical, eloquent, and literary. Sartre is known as a philosopher and as a novelist. Especially during his lifetime, Sartre was most celebrated for his existential novels and plays. In these literary works Sartre experimented with phenomenological themes from his philosophical texts.

Lingis differs from Sartre in that he does not attempt to find the sources for his writing in Paris, in his own social milieu and place of residence. Rather, he gathers his material far away from his desk, in ever-changing foreign and remote locations. These writings include books entitled *Excesses: Eros and Culture* (1983), *Abuses* (2001), *Dangerous Emotions* (2000), *The Imperative* (1998), *Violence and Splendor* (2011), and *Irrevocable: A Philosophy of Mortality* (2018). In interviews, Lingis explains that these works were initially ignored because they were not considered philosophy.

With Lingis, the narratives are not fictional but expressive of his experiences of meeting real people: ordinary villagers, temple priests, beggars, prostitutes, prisoners, carnival queens, drug addicts, urban ghetto dwellers, and so forth. He writes about friendships, being among strangers in the back quarters of Bangkok, receiving help when sick, being moved by the misery and suffering he sees among the destitute and the outcast, feeling gratitude for the kindness of strangers. But his stories are not journalistic tales. His reflective and ethical concerns in these written encounters are expressed in numerous phenomenological themes such as violence, the face, excesses, lust, the voices of things, and inner space.

Philosophically animated by the works of especially Emmanuel Levinas, Maurice Merleau-Ponty, Edmund Husserl, and Martin Heidegger, and in dialogue with authors such as Jacques Derrida, Georges Bataille, Jacques Lacan, Slavoj Žižek, Gilles Deleuze, and Clifford Geertz, Lingis has created a profound and provocative richness of phenomenological texts. His writings have been described as philosophical works of art. They inaugurate a way of doing research that is highly original, as in this reflection on limit moments, such as when one is called to the deathbed of a parent:

The nurses say, "I am so glad you have come!" They know you can do, must do, something they cannot do—say something to the dying one. What can one say? Anything one tries to say sounds vacuous and absurd in one's mouth. It seems to you that the problem is not simply that you do not have the skills in speaking or that you cannot come up with the right things to say because you have no experience in this kind of situation, but that language itself does not have the powers. There is not, in the words and the combinatory possibilities of language, the power to say what has to be said. Yet you have to be there, and you have to say something. You have never been more clear about anything. There are those who do not go, to the bedside of the dying one, demoralized by the terrible impotence of language to say anything. It seems to them that, in their speechlessness, they are carried away already into the region of death and silence with the other. But if you somehow find the courage to go, you are sure you have to be there and have to say something. What is imperative is that you be there and speak; what you say, in the end, hardly matters. You end up saying—"It'll be alright, Mom" which you know is a stupid thing to say, even an insult to her intelligence; she knows she is dying and is more brave than you. She does not reproach you for what you said; in the end it doesn't matter, what was imperative was only that you say something, anything. That your hand and your voice extend to her in accompaniment to the nowhere she is drifting on to, that the warmth and the tone of your voice come to her as her own breath gives way, and that the light of your eyes meet hers that are turned to where there is nothing to see. (Lingis, 1994, pp. 108, 109)

Language is the human device that allows us to say what we say in conversations and relations. But, sometimes it is not a matter of *what* we say, but *that* we say something, and *how* we speak. Lingis invokes such limit-situations through powerful pathic examples that show something universal in the singularity of the story. He shows through example how it is when you have to say something that language cannot say. "It is the saying that is imperative" (1994, p. 113). Saying what cannot be said. Yet Lingis shows how this paradox is overcome in words: through the language of the phenomenological example.

Lingis proposes that we cannot regard the world as a mere spectacle to be absorbed and understood; rather, we are inextricably part of and bound ethically to the world by virtue of our sensual, living contact with it. In his view, responsibility is coextensive with our sensibility; in our sensibility we are exposed to the outside, to the world's being, in such a way that we are bound to answer for it.

In his public lectures Lingis has courted the scorn of mainstream philosophers who do not understand his pathic mode and manner of presenting his work. He is known to engage his audience in performance presentation that is highly original and evocative of sensual sensibilities. His aim seems to be to make strange and to create an atmosphere of the exotic required for understanding his poetic prose. Here is a personal observation:

The auditorium is filled. The professors and graduate students who have come to listen to Alphonso Lingis' lecture "Love Junkies" are quieted by the darkness.

It is not common that a speaker starts in complete darkness. And besides, Lingis is yet not to be seen. Some are looking expectantly behind them, to the entrance of the auditorium. But all is dark while the last visitors slip through the doors. Then suddenly, without warning, a loud rocking song shakes up the auditorium. And simultaneously a projector throws abstract and fluid silhouettes of erotically moving bodies onto a large screen. The audience is spellbound while the music pours over them and the carnal lyrics are matched by the sensually moving figures on the screen. Not until the sound and last lyrics are dying down do the lights partially go up, and the voice of Lingis is heard. He had entered the auditorium, and now slowly walks to the front in the semi-darkness of the auditorium. What the members of the audience see is a man whose face and partially exposed shoulders and chest are smeared with white chalk. His clothes are ragged and evoke an exotic image of an alien singularity, reading his script "Love Junkies" in a gentle but compelling voice. It is a story about a touching love affair between Wayne and Cheryl, a transsexual—two outcasts who share a cell in prison. Both are drug addicts, and both are dying from AIDS. As Lingis slowly walks up and down the aisles, reading his lecture from a handful of pages, each of which he tosses over his shoulder, one page after the other as he finishes with them.

This is the lecture by Alphonso Lingis, as I remember it, when he visited the University of Alberta, September, 2008. His reading of "Love Junkies" was accompanied by video images, a soundtrack, and, of course, Lingis himself clothed in rags covered with white chalk and white face paint. In the lecture Lingis evoked an image of love, sensual and violate closeness, between two sadly outcast figures. The audience was confronted by the challenge to grasp the extreme and ecstatic experiences of love between two persons, singularities, the kinds of people they may likely never encounter in their personal lives.

With Lingis, the Levinassian face of the other is concrete and unique, as he describes descending from a bus in a third world city:

> Pushing our way through the crowd we feel something, look down: a beggar child touches us . . .
>
> To face another is to touch with the eyes . . . . It is to soil our eyes . . . with the sweat and the grime, the toxins and microbes . . . . The suffering of another is felt in our eyes . . .
>
> Then the one exposed to my eyes and purposes turns and faces me. In the contact the torment of another afflicts me as an appeal, presses upon me with the urgency of a demand.
>
> The homeless woman, in looking to me, appeals for the image of what my eyes have seen. (Lingis, 1998, p. 131)

In a real sense it is others and things that use my eyes to look at themselves. As Lingis says, what the look desires to see is ultimately not the things but the look itself. The only thing the eye cannot see is itself seeing. Perhaps that is why the look desires the look.

When one descends into the deep, regresses to the depths, the eye detached from the grasping hand, the mobilizing posture, is detached from its look, moved now by its own voluptuous desire. The voluptuous eye . . . caresses, is caressed by the surface effects of an alien domain. It is seeking the invisible. The invisible that the eroticized eye seeks is no longer the substances, the principles, the causes of the alien; it is the alien look.

The look . . . looks for the other. And the voluptuous eye, that finds it does not have a look of one's own, is seeking in the other for a look, the look of the other. (Lingis, 1983, p. 13)

More perhaps than any other phenomenologist, Alphonso Lingis has a sensual sensitivity for what kinds of subject matter deserve contemplative phenomenological reflection. In his book *Irrevocable* (2018) the essay titles include "The Weight of Reality," "Return of the First Person Singular," "Angels with Guns," "The Future of Torture," "Irrevocable Loss," and other topics. In this recent book Lingis shares with all who happen to be transitioning into old age the question of the meaning and significance of mortality. What does the death of the other have to do with our own death? How do we experience the imminence of death? Lingis starts his phenomenological reflection on the philosophy of mortality with a glance to Socrates:

Socrates made learning how to die the subject matter of philosophy and made philosophy the daily practice of dying. He speaks of the relief he will feel when the opacity of his body will be broken. His last words, "Crito, we owe a cock to Asclepius," say that life is the sickness for which death is the cure. Did not Socrates here claim to know things that he did not know: what death is—that death is relief—and what life is—that life is sickness? (2018, p. 161)

For Heidegger anxiety regards death to be associated with nothingness. But is that how we experience the sense of the irrevocableness of death, as it stalks us, ready to strike us any time at all? Right now, while reading this line. So, Lingis probes his vocative reflections on phenomenological themes of death, such as "knowing nothingness," "longing for nothingness," and "the corpse I am becoming." The sense of my death is the sense of ending definitively and irrevocably, says Lingis. And he wonders how the dead are present to us and how we may feel tormented by them:

The dead also torment us. The voice of a parent who in words or without words said to us from childhood, "I do not love you," curses us still today, twenty years after he or she died. When our mother or our child dies, we are tormented by all the things that we failed to say. (2018, p. 169)

While Lingis writes in a manner that has been termed lyrical, poetic, expressive, eloquent, evocative, and powerful, it should be understood that his textual practice is the quotidian essence of phenomenological analysis. While many philosophers theorize and write abstractly about phenomenology, Alphonso Lingis writes phenomenology. His is the concrete turning to the things themselves.

In all his books Lingis includes his photographic images of people, things, and places he has encountered and visited. Many of these images possess Roland Barthes' (1981) power of "punctum." They touch us, prick us, move us, as only true photographs can do. Just as phenomenological "examples" make the singular knowable and visible, so Lingis' photographs possess existential and eidetic addressiveness and sensuosity that make the invisible visible in a pathic manner.

Fragmentary Phenomenology: Jean-Luc Nancy

Jean-Luc Nancy was born in 1940 near Bordeaux, France. In 1973, he was granted a Ph.D. with a study on Immanuel Kant under the supervision of Paul Ricoeur. Nancy has been associated as a professor of philosophy with the University of Strasbourg throughout his academic career, and he has been a visiting professor of philosophy at many other universities such as the Freie Universität in Berlin and the University of California. Major influences in his work are René Descartes, Georg Wilhelm Friedrich Hegel, Immanuel Kant, Friedrich Nietzsche, Martin Heidegger, Jean-Paul Sartre, Georges Bataille, Maurice Blanchot, and Jacques Derrida. Together with his friend Philippe Lacoue-Labarthe, he wrote a study of Jacques Lacan. Nancy has been critical of Freudian and Lacanian theory in most of his writings. He served as a member in several cultural delegations of the French Ministry of External Affairs to Eastern Europe, Great Britain, and the United States. In 1987, Jean-Luc Nancy was elected docteur d'état (doctor of state) in Toulouse with a dissertation entitled *The Experience of Freedom*, focusing on the notion of freedom in the work of Kant, Schelling, Sartre, and Heidegger, and exploring the meaning and possibility of nonsubjective freedom.

Jean-Luc Nancy has written more than 50 books and hundreds of articles. Major themes in Nancy's work are the philosophical notions of community and topics of contemporary politics such as justice, responsibility, and the ontological contingency of "naked existence" as a moral concern. Nancy's writings are extremely diverse as reflected in the titles of some of his books *The Inoperative Community* (1991), *The Birth of Presence* (1993), *The Muses* (1997b), *The Sense of the World* (1997b), *Being Singular Plural* (2000), *The Ground of the Image* (2005), *Listening* (2007c), *L'Evidence du Film* (2007a), *Corpus* (2008), and *The Fall of Sleep* (2007b). Nancy frequently uses the texts of other thinkers to work out his own reflection on the topics at issue. For example, his book *The Inoperative Community* (1991) is a further rethinking of community in the writings of Bataille and Blanchot. This, in turn, led to Blanchot's book *The Unavowable Community* (1988). A provocative theme in Nancy's reflection on the meaning of community is that community is not something that can be produced, as is often supposed by social theorists and political communitarians.

> Community occupies a singular place: it assumes the impossibility of its own immanence, the impossibility of a communitarian being in the form of a subject. In a certain sense community acknowledges and inscribes—this is its peculiar gesture—the impossibility of community. A community is not a project of fusion, or in some general way a productive or operative project—nor is it a project at all. (1991, p. 15)

Nancy survived a lengthy struggle with cancer and the trauma of a heart transplant, but he never stopped writing. His writing about his illness was made into a movie, *L'Intrus: The Intruder*. Nancy's work is remarkable for its creative originality, literary scope, intellectual rigor, and often poetic style. Reading Nancy, one cannot help but wonder if and how the mortality perspective of illness may have been the source for the immortality of creative genius in Nancy. While his topics at times may seem challenging, they nevertheless are approached concretely with a phenomenological quotidian sensitivity. This is doing phenomenology directly on the things or on an eventful moment. For example, here is Nancy writing about what it is like to listen to music:

> Music is the art of the hope for resonance: a sense that does not make sense except because of its resounding in itself. It calls to itself and recalls itself, reminding itself and by itself, each time, of the birth of music, that is to say, the opening of a world in resonance, a world taken away from the arrangements of objects and subjects, brought back to its own amplitude and making sense or else having its truth only in the affirmation that modulates this amplitude. (Nancy, 2007c, p. 67)

When Nancy reflects on the event of listening to music he wonders what a person hears who is musically unsophisticated. There is a difference between hearing music and listening to music. One may hear music but be unable to interpret it or to make sense of its composition and execution. No matter: it is the work in its totality and all its parts that listens to itself. Nancy's text at times seems to emulate Heidegger's ontological sensibility. For sure, he does not abstract or argue in a traditional philosophical manner. He listens to the things and events with which he keeps a phenomenological relation. Or better, when Nancy describes what it is like to listen then the thing of listening listens to itself.

> It is not a hearer [*auditeur*], then, who listens, and it matters little whether or not he is musical. Listening is musical when it is music that listens to itself. It returns to itself, it reminds itself of itself, and it feels itself as resonance itself: a relationship to self deprived, stripped of all egoism and all ipseity. Not "itself," or the other, or identity, or difference, but alteration and variation, the modulation of the present that changes it in expectation of its own eternity, always imminent and always deferred, since it is not in any time. (Nancy, 2007c, p. 67)

Nancy's paragraphs, like the above, often read like fragments. Ian James caught the unique style of thinking, expression, and writing of Nancy with the title of his book *The Fragmentary Demand* (2006). He says:

> Nancy's thinking always emerges in a contingent practice of writing which traces diverse paths and traverses a multiplicity of specific philosophical contexts, primarily and most obviously those of speculative idealism and existential phenomenology . . . . Nancy's thinking maintains itself as fragmentary, as a practice of thought which unfolds as a plurality of singular gestures or exposure to/ at the limits of thought. (James, 2006, pp. 231, 232)

From a phenomenological methodological perspective, Nancy's use of the notions of sense and fragment are suggestive for stimulating creative insight. For example, the table of contents of *The Sense of the World* (1997b) consists of a fragmentary list of texts that are each only four or five pages in length—fragments that offer, in expressive philosophical language, radically reflective responses to the fragmentary demand of thinking on notions such as "The Sense of the World"; "The End of the World"; "Suspended Step"; "Sense and Truth"; "Touching"; "*Spanne*"; "Someone"; "Political Writing"; and "Sense that Senses Itself."

In his lengthier essays, Nancy reflects on some of the critical themes of phenomenology. In his *Being Singular Plural* he explains how singularity is not the same as individuality or the particular. There is always an inescapable contingency associated with the encounter of the singular.

> "Someone" here is understood in the way a person might say "it's him all right" about a photo, expressing by this "all right" the covering over of a gap, making adequate what is inadequate, capable of relating only to the "instantaneous" grasping of an instant that is precisely its own gap .... As for singular differences, they are not only "individual" but infraindividual. It is never the case that I have met Pierre or Marie per se, but I have met him or her in such and such a "form," in such and such a "state," in such and such a "mood," and so on. (Nancy, 2000, p. 8)

Singularity is access to the world:

> "Strangeness" refers to the fact that each singularity is another access to the world .... In the singularity that he exposes, each child that is born has already concealed the access that he is "for himself" and in which he will conceal himself "within himself," Just as he will one day hide under the final expression of a dead face. This is why we scrutinize these faces with such curiosity, in search of identification, looking to see whom the child looks like, and to see if death looks like itself. What we are looking for there, like in the photographs, is not an image; it is an access. (Nancy, 2000, p. 14)

Nancy finds the source of "origin" in the "being-with" of our existence with others. The origin is not some ancient mythical source; rather, it lies in the ever-renewing beginning of our being with others.

> To reach the origin is not to miss it; it is to be properly exposed to it. Since it is not another thing (an *aliud*), the origin is neither "missable" nor appropriable (penetrable, absorbable). It does not obey this logic. It is the plural singularity of the Being of being. We reach it to the extent that we are in touch with *ourselves* and in touch with the rest of beings. We are in touch with ourselves insofar as we exist. Being in touch with ourselves is what makes us "us," and there is no other secret to discover buried behind this very touching, behind the "with" of coexistence. (Nancy, 2000, p. 13)

To do phenomenology does not mean to trace the meaning of existence back to some mythical inceptual origin. The originary is right there in the singular

300

modalities of our everyday existence, but it requires of us that we are in touch with ourselves and with life as we live it. Of course, this "being in touch" can be a challenging prerequisite that may mean that we are capable of experiencing and expressing insights into the singular meanings of the pluralities of existence. Nancy radicalizes Heidegger's notion of *Dasein* by showing how the singular of the everyday cannot be approached as an undifferentiated generality.

> Heidegger confuses the everyday with the undifferentiated, the anonymous, and the statistical. These are no less important, but they can only constitute themselves in relation to the differentiated singularity that the everyday already is by itself: each day, each time, day to day. One cannot affirm that the meaning of Being must express itself starting from everydayness and then begin by neglecting the general differentiation of the everyday, its constantly renewed rupture, its relief and its variety. A "day" is not simply a unit for counting; it is the turning of the world—each time singular. And days, indeed every day, could not be similar if they were not first different, difference itself. (Nancy, 2000, p. 9)

It is obvious that the singular in Nancy's work acquires singular significance. Every singular is always singular. He often uses the strategy of showing how inside and outside, difference and sameness, the infinite and finitude, singularity and plurality construct and deconstruct each other. The plurality of phenomena and events that we experience in everyday life are made up of singularities, each different and original in their singularity.

Merleau-Ponty's notion of hyper-reflection would be quite applicable to the authorial style of Nancy. He practices a kind of reflection that continually reflects on itself, resulting in expositions of constantly shifting paradoxes. For example, how can we think the origins of meanings of phenomena of everyday experience when the originary is veiled by the taken-for-granted ordinariness of ordinary experience? For Nancy the origin of the singular lies in the singular plural itself.

> This very humble layer of our everyday experience contains another rudimentary ontological attestation: what we receive (rather than what we perceive) with singularities is the discreet passage of other origins of the world. What occurs there, what bends, leans, twists, addresses, denies—from the newborn to the corpse—is neither primarily "someone close," nor an "other," nor a "stranger," nor "someone similar." It is an origin; it is an affirmation of the world, and we know that the world has no other origin than the singular multiplicity of origins.
>
> . . .
> The "ordinary" is always exceptional, however little we understand its character as origin. What we receive most communally as "strange" is that the ordinary itself is originary. With existence laid open in this way and the meaning of the world being what it is, the exception is the rule. (Nancy, 2000, pp. 8–10)

From the early eighties, Nancy developed close intellectual bonds with Jacques Derrida. Derrida's approach is clearly evident in Nancy's thinking, but he also seems to push beyond deconstruction in a direction that shows surprising insights.

Derrida was obviously intensely engaged with Nancy as well; Derrida (2005) wrote a highly readable and fascinating text, *On Touching—Jean-Luc Nancy*, that further explores, in turn, major themes that appear in Nancy's phenomenology. This text not only gives access to Nancy's thinking, it also provides an example of Derrida's most lucid writings—here the reflection of one original mind is augmented by the radical reflectivity of an other. *On Touching—Jean-Luc Nancy* is a genre of phenomenological philosophical thinking that transposes the apparent exegetical style of interpreting Nancy's texts to a level of originality and fascination that does not only clarify but also (re)invent.

Religious Phenomenology: Jean-Louis Chrétien

Jean-Louis Chrétien was born in 1952. He is a philosopher, theologian, and poet, and he teaches philosophy at the University of Paris. His translated publications include *The Unforgettable and the Unhoped For* (2002), *Hand to Hand: Listening to the Work of Art* (2003), *The Call and the Response* (2004b), and *The Ark of Speech* (2004a). In his work, Chrétien draws on both phenomenological and theological sources for his reflections on the main theme "the call and the response" and related themes such as prayer, hospitality, the unforgettable, the irresistible, and silence.

In his various books Chrétien sets out to show how humans live by responding to the call—the call of experience. For Chrétien the theme of call and response moves phenomenology into a domain where, as Ricoeur points out, experience may not be immediately given. And, therefore, Chrétien is being seen as a prime proponent of the French movement responsible for the theological turn in phenomenology. Dominique Janicaud (2000, 2005a, 2005b) leads the critique of this theological turn in the work of Emmanuel Levinas, Michel Henry, Jean-Louis Chrétien, and Jean-Luc Marion. Janicaud (2000, 2005a) points out that theology compromises phenomenology since it is based, not on immanent experience, but on transcendent elements such as faith that cannot be approached with the reduction. He argues for a return to a "minimalist phenomenology."

While Levinas and Marion have denied that their works can be reduced to theology, Chrétien seems to be indifferent to the "accusation." Instead, he is intent to broaden phenomenological method to address possible human experiences that may lie within the broad domain of faith. To advance his phenomenology of religion, Chrétien reflects on the meaning of prayer, because "prayer is the religious phenomenon par excellence . . . . With prayer, the religious appears and disappears" (2000, p. 147). While some people may never pray, never experience praying, Chrétien argues that prayer is a *possible* human experience. And the possibility of a phenomenology of prayer implies the possibility of a phenomenology of religious experience. And, of course, a phenomenology of religious experience is a highly relevant human concern.

So, the question for Chrétien is what happens in the moment of praying? He is not interested in the ethnography of prayer: how prayer is conducted in different religions and cultures. Rather he approaches prayer as a universal "speech act" and his guiding question is with regard to the phenomenology of the *voice* in this act, whether the voice is audible or silent. How to describe the lived experience of the voice in the prayer? Chrétien observes that "a first description of prayer can situate it in an act of presence to the invisible" (2000, p. 149). The praying voice places the person in the presence of some power, and it exposes the self of the praying person to the otherness that may be called God or Allah or Jaweh or some other divinity.

> The invisible can range from radical invisibility of the Spirit to the inward sacredness of power of a being visible by itself, like a mountain, a star, or a statue .... The being before God of the one praying is an active self-manifestation to God. All the modalities of praying are forms of this self-manifestation, be it individual or collective. (2000, p. 150)

When we see someone praying, we may see the lips of the person move as if speaking alone. But Chrétien points out that the speaking alone of praying is very different from speaking to oneself in pure soliloquy, or addressing someone else who is absent to the senses.

> The first function speech performs in prayer is therefore a self-manifestation before the invisible other, a manifestation that becomes a manifestation of self to self through the other, and where the presence of self to the other and of the other to self cannot be separated, as in the invisible poem of respiration evoked by Rilke. This manifestation does not merely bring to light what was there before it; it has its own light: that of an event, the event wherein what is invisible to myself illuminates me in a fashion phenomenologically different from a conversation with myself or an examination of consciousness. (2000, p. 154)

In *The Call and the Response*, Chrétien models the existential structure of call–response on Heidegger's notion of the call of thinking and the call of language. Chrétien's own language is increasingly poetic and evocative of voice:

> How must we think the call that makes us speak? How must we think the speech that responds and hears only by responding? How must we think the voice in which, and through which, alone both call and response become incarnate? ...
> Each time a voice initiates speech for the sake of saying what is, there is at its core, like a force momentum carrying it forth or like a promise keeping it, the whole sonorous profusion of all that it answers. We speak only for having been called, called by what there is to say, and yet we learn and hear what there is to say only in speech itself. We shatter silence only along its own hidden fault lines, or rather silence shatters of its own accord and resonates in our voice .... We always speak to the world, we are always already in the act of speaking always in the world still .... Between my voice as it speaks and my voice as I hear it vibrates the whole thickness of the world whose meaning my voice attempts to say, meaning that has gripped it and swallowed it up, as it were, from time immemorial. (Chrétien, 2004b, p. 1)

In *The Ark of Speech* (2004a), Chrétien explores the interplay of speech and silence in the experience of hospitality. His phenomenological texts at times acquire extraordinary evocative power.

The most spiritual contact is expressed and described by all that is most sensual and most fleshy in the loving encounter between human beings. Only love can signify something beyond itself in this way. This silence at once clear and secretive arises from a mutual presence, in which those who are silent give themselves to each other, bearing their gifts at the tip of their intimacy, reinforcing and deepening this intimacy with the very gifts that they exchange. (Chrétien, 2004a, p. 60)

As shown above, it is argued that Chrétien's phenomenological reflection at times turns into a theological hermeneutic. The theological element is especially suggestive with respect to the phenomenon of gift and giving, which is strongly present in Jean-Luc Marion's texts as well. But according to Marion, radical phenomenology should never be confused with theology. Meanwhile, Chrétien writes finely attuned texts that are persuasively reasoned, while being highly thoughtful, poetic, and evocative.

Philological Phenomenology: Giorgio Agamben

Giorgio Agamben was born in Rome on April 22, 1942. He studied law and philosophy at the University of Rome, where he wrote a dissertation on the political life of Simone Weil. At the early age of 24, Agamben was invited to join a select group of philosophers attending Heidegger's Le Thor seminars in 1966–1968. At the time Heidegger was 77 years old. The series of small seminars was formative in Agamben's decision to make philosophy his vocation. He has taught at the Iuav University of Venice, the Collège Internationale de Paris, and the European Graduate School. He has been a visiting professor at various universities in the United States and was appointed distinguished professor at the New School in New York.

Agamben's philosophical and phenomenological writings are very diverse and range from philology, aesthetics, poetics, to politics (2005). Major influences on Agamben's work are Heidegger, Hegel, and especially Walter Benjamin—Agamben was the editor of the collected works of Benjamin in Italian. As well, Agamben is steeped in Aristotle, Plato, Greek and Roman law, and Jewish and Christian biblical texts; he engages the critical and literary works of Edmund Husserl, Ludwig Wittgenstein, Jacques Derrida, Gilles Deleuze, Michel Foucault, Friedrich Hölderlin, Franz Kafka, Fernando Pessoa, and many others. Agamben actively participates in political commentary and radical critique on modern life and nation-state policies.

Several disparate themes in Agamben's work recursively emerge in his numerous books: potentiality and actuality, the experience of language and metaphysics, the relation between the prose of philosophy and poetry, the philologically inspired notion of community, political being and the state of exception, the idea of bare life as opposed to qualified life, and the exemplary and paradigm.

Agamben's discourse is often difficult, dense and depthful, penetratingly precise, and exegetically demanding. But some of his texts pose a different challenge, as they are written in the puzzling prose of fable, fragment, aphorism, anecdote, riddle, parable, epigram, and short story. From the perspective of phenomenological research and writing, Agamben's reflections on the experience of language, prose, the paradigm, and the example are especially noteworthy. Difficult but delightful, Agamben's stories strive to capture the ineffables of living that the explanatory prose of philosophy is unable to express. For example, in his *Idea of Prose*, Agamben offers several dozen "Ideas" such as Matter, Prose, Caesura, Vocation, the Unique, Dictation, and Truth. Some of these reflections are a couple of pages, others only a few sentences. The Idea of Love is two sentences long:

> The Idea of Love: To live in intimacy with a stranger, not in order to draw him closer, or to make him known, but rather to keep him strange, remote: unapparent—so unapparent that his name contains him entirely. And, even in discomfort, to be nothing else, day after day, than the ever open place, the unwaning light in which that one being, that thing, remains forever exposed and sealed off. (1995a, p. 61)

"Apparent" is a common word, meaning clearly seen or understood, and seeming real, but not necessarily so. Phenomenology concerns itself with appearance, how something shows itself in experience or consciousness. But, Agamben says, Love appears as unapparent. His felicitous use of the word "unapparent" turns Love into something enigmatically mysterious and reverses its reality ever more ambiguous. The remainder of this fragment resonates with our experience of love, or perhaps as filled with images and sentiments of how we should experience love or how we experience the Idea of Love. Even a careful reading of Agamben's text may leave one stranded or submerged in evocative significations that may only be hinted at by poetic equivocations and confirmed by private reminiscent reverberations. In these fragmentary texts Agamben seduces us compellingly into reflections on the eidetic secrets of our experiences (he calls "Ideas") that are essentially beyond the pure prose of philosophy.

Agamben continues his reflective explorations of the experience of language in his stylistic small book *The Coming Community* (1993). It is a reflective examination of philological phenomena such as Whatever, Example, Halos, Pseudonyms, Homonyms, and the Irreparable. In particular, his brief reflection on Example may be instructive for thinking about the nature of phenomenological meaning and phenomenological writing. Agamben has continued his reflections on exemplarity in his 2002 lecture "What Is a Paradigm?"

Although Agamben states that he is not interested in epistemology or method, his reflections on paradigm engage him in examining what it means to use a paradigm in philosophy, in the human sciences, or even in art and other humanities. He traces the philosophical discussions of the meaning and significance of paradigm back to Aristotle, to Kant, to Victor Goldschmidt's study of Plato, and to Walter Benjamin. Agamben points out that Aristotle showed how paradigm is neither a universal nor a particular, neither general nor individual:

> Aristotle says that the paradigm, the example, does not concern a part with respect to the whole, nor the whole with respect to the part, it concerns a part with respect to the part. This is a very interesting definition. This means that the paradigm does not move from the particular to the universal, nor from the universal to the particular, but from the particular to the particular. In other words, we first have deduction which goes from the universal to the particular, we have induction which goes from the particular to the universal and then the

third we have the paradigm and the analogy which go from the particular to the particular. (Agamben, 2002)

Agamben notes that the etymological meaning of the Greek paradigm is "what shows itself (para) beside." Paradigm means simply example—a single phenomenon, a singularity. What makes a paradigm so interesting is that it does what concepts, generalizations, ordinary analogies, or metaphors cannot do: makes the singular knowable (Agamben, 2002).

In relating the paradigm to Plato's Dialectics, Agamben shows how the paradigm makes a new relation possible, especially the relation between the Idea and the Phenomenon. Sometimes the Idea acts as a paradigm for sensible things, but sometimes it is the sensible thing that acts as a paradigm for the Idea:

> The paradigmatic relation does not occur between a plurality of singular objects or between a singular object and the general principle or law which is exterior to it, the paradigm is not already given, but instead the singularity becomes a paradigm—Plato says it becomes a paradigm by being shown beside the others. Thus, the paradigmatic relationship takes place between the single phenomenon and its intelligibility. The paradigm is a singularity considered in the medium of its knowability. What makes something intelligible is the paradigmatic exhibition of its own knowability. Aristotle said the example is "more knowable." So, the relation that an example and an object have in common is the exhibition of this knowability. (Agamben, 2002)

The example is an example of what it exemplifies. Its significance lies not in its factuality or in some kind of presupposed principle. Its significance lies in the fact that it makes the singular knowable. This is a critical insight for the project of phenomenology. Phenomenology is oriented to the singular, the phenomenality of the phenomenon made knowable through the example.

> [T]o show a phenomenon in its original paradigmatic character means to exhibit it in the medium of its knowability. You have no presupposed principle, it is the phenomenon itself which is original. No more origin, but an original phenomenon. (Agamben, 2002)

While concepts are linguistic generalizations and thus forgo the singular, examples and paradigms are the singularities that lie at the heart of the eidos. Of course, a paradigm must possess a certain rhetorical power in order to function as a paradigm or example in a text. Agamben's texts like *Idea of Prose* may be seen as consisting of experimental paradigms (Ideas) that make the phenomenality of sensible things (phenomena) intelligible and knowable.

Radical Phenomenology: Jean-Luc Marion

Jean-Luc Marion was born in Meudon, France, in 1946. He studied at the University of Nanterre and the Sorbonne and undertook graduate work in philosophy at the École Normale Supérieure in Paris, where he studied with Jacques Derrida.

306

Marion's early work consisted of detailed studies of Descartes, Husserl, and Heidegger. His doctoral dissertation is entitled *Descartes's Grey Ontology*, wherein he situates Descartes within the history of the Aristotelian discourse on thing and being. First, Marion received a philosophy appointment at the University of Poitiers. Next, he taught at the University of Nanterre. In 1996, he became Professor of Philosophy at the Sorbonne, University of Paris. Since 1994, Marion has also been teaching as a visiting professor of philosophy at the University of Chicago, where he now holds the chair of John Nuveen Visiting Professor in the School of Divinity. Marion is currently considered one of the most original and influential living philosophers. Some of his leading texts are *Being Given: Toward a Phenomenology of Givenness* (2002a), *In Excess: Studies of Saturated Phenomena* (2002b), *Prolegomena to Charity* (2002c), and *The Visible and the Revealed* (2008).

More radically than any other recent phenomenologist, Marion addresses the issue of what is meant by the originary phenomenological principle "how things show or give themselves." He points out that things do not show themselves because we turn to them—when things show themselves, they can only do so because they have already given themselves to us. His is a phenomenology of *donation*, givenness. Therefore, Marion's phenomenology challenges the primacy of the subject and its intentional relation to the world, and he rejects the constituting or meaning-making function of consciousness.

Marion argues that a third reduction is needed. Whereas Husserl's transcendental reduction concerns the intentional objects of consciousness, and whereas Heidegger's existential reduction concerns the being of what shows itself, Marion's phenomenological reduction seeks to understand the appearing of a phenomenon in the way that it gives itself as a self: "Philosophy today has become, essentially, phenomenology; yet phenomenology no longer pretends to return to the things themselves, because it has undertaken the task of seeing what gives itself—what gives" (Marion, 2004, p. ix). This statement is actually somewhat ambiguous because what is unique about Marion's phenomenology of givenness is that he attempts to provide a more radical account of things-in-themselves than originally formulated by Husserl and Heidegger. In exploring the consequences of this radical phenomenology of "being given," Marion advances the notions of excess and saturated phenomena. Marion asks, what happens when a phenomenon is so saturated with intuition (sensed meaning) that it exceeds and overwhelms any intentionality? He shows that when reflecting on a saturated phenomenon, the lived experiences are so paradoxically "given" that no systematic phenomenological description is possible.

Marion offers several examples of familiar saturated phenomena: the event, the flesh, the idol, the icon, and, more enigmatically, the revelation. Such phenomena cannot be adequately grasped and described with traditional phenomenological method that remains faithful to the Husserlian and Heideggerian notions of the reduction. In his text, *In Excess*, Marion uses the four guiding Kantian categories of quantity, quality, relation, and modality to describe the excess of meaning of these saturated phenomena. He says that saturated phenomena may be invisible according to quantity (the event), according to quality that the look cannot bear (the idol and the painting), according to relation of absolute phenomena because they defy any analogy (like flesh), and according to modality phenomena that cannot be looked at, that escape all relation (like the icon of the other person) (Marion, 2002b).

For example, what gives itself in the look of the other? Marion points out that we cannot look at the look. So, we must look where the look gives itself, in the face:

> The look of the other person remains unable to be looked at. Further still: what do we look at in the face of the other person? Not his or her mouth, nevertheless more expressive of the intentions than other parts of the body, but the eyes—or more exactly the empty pupils of the person's eyes, their black holes open on the sombre ocular hollow. In other words, in the face we fix on the sole place where precisely nothing can be seen. Thus, in the face of the other person we see precisely the point at which all visible spectacle happens to be impossible, where there is nothing to see, where intuition can give nothing [of the] visible. (Marion, 2002b, p. 115)

Marion asks, how to reach a phenomenon that owes all its phenomenality to givenness? He formulates the principle "so much reduction, so much givenness" meaning, the more the reduction is able to remove the constraints and conditions imposed on a phenomenon, the more a phenomenon will appear in its pure givenness. In other words, the reduction needs to transcend the (Husserlian) objectness and the (Heideggerian) beingness of a phenomenon.

Marion gives the example of the gaze of two lovers who look each other in the eyes. We can only see the look by objectifying it. We try to make the invisibility of the look visible by making it into an object. But there is no object to be seen, and only the lovers can see the Orphean gaze of love:

> consider the phenomenological determination of love: two definitively invisible gazes . . . cross one another, and thus together trace a cross that is invisible to every other gaze other than theirs alone . . . . Two gazes, definitively invisible, cross and, in this crossing, renounce their invisibility. They consent to let themselves be seen without seeing . . . the two gazes, invisible forever, expose themselves each to the other in the crossing of their reciprocal aims. Loving no longer consists trivially in seeing or in being seen, nor in desiring or inciting desire, but in experiencing the crossing of the gazes within, first, the crossing of aims. (Marion, 2002c, p. 87)

Husserl's basic maxim is that phenomenology must return back to the things themselves and describe how phenomena or meanings are constituted in consciousness. For Marion, this is not radical enough. The notion of the self of the thing itself refers back to what the thing is, not as an object or a being, but rather as an event that appears in the "being given." A phenomenon is never really a static object but rather as Heidegger says the thinging of the thing. It is this thinging that is given in the event of the appearance of the phenomenon. What is so attractive in Jean-Luc Marion's phenomenology of "being given" is that the thing is returned to its originary significance that lies beyond the metaphysics of the being of beings or things.

If appearing implies showing *itself*, as showing *itself* implies giving *itself*, both imply a *self* of the phenomenon. Such a *self*, supposing it could be reached, would in no way be equivalent to the *in-itself* of the object or the thing . . . . The *self* of the phenomenon is marked by its determination as event. It comes, does its thing, and leaves on its own; showing *itself*, it also shows the *self* that takes (or removes) the initiative of giving *itself*. The event, I can wait for it (though most often, it surprises me), I can remember it (or forget it), but I cannot make it, produce it, or provoke it. Let us describe the event, where the phenomenon gives *itself*, to the point of showing itself *itself*. (Marion, 2002a, p. 159)

Marion discusses the meaning of the myth of Orpheus and Eurydice in order to raise the question of how in a painting something may show itself that is really invisible to the eye. The eye only sees paint on a canvas or color on a screen. So how does that which shows itself in a painting give itself? Blanchot had already made the bold assertion that Orpheus' turning gaze was no mistake. That Orpheus wanted to see Eurydice in the perfection of her immortality. The desire to see the truth of Eurydice is really the desire of the writer. But, of course, the opposite happens: Orpheus' gaze objectifies Eurydice and fails to see her in her essence, her invisibility (except perhaps in that fleeting moment of the turn). Marion also suggests that the very glance of Orpheus already destroys what it is trying to see.

> As soon as Orpheus wants to see Eurydice, he transforms her into an object and thereby disqualifies her as beloved. He makes her disappear because he does not admit her as invisible. Only the object is visible, and the entrance into visibility qualifies an object as such. (Marion, 2002c, p. 80)

Blanchot said that the act of writing begins with Orpheus' gaze (Blanchot, 1981, p. 104). Orpheus was not only a singer but a writer. Without mentioning Blanchot, Marion works on Blanchot's theme of the gaze of Orpheus, but he uses not the metaphor of writing but of painting. Marion says, "Orpheus did not sing; he painted. Or better, he saw in the unseen what the shroud of darkness could not hide" (2004, pp. 26, 27). So, for Marion the origin of meaning, of givenness does not lie in the glance of Orpheus (the transcendental subject) but in the self of the phenomenon: in its self-givenness:

> [T]he origin of givenness remains the "self" of the phenomenon, with no other principle or origin besides itself. "Self-givenness, *Selbstgebung, donation de soi*" indicates that the phenomenon is given in person, but also and especially that it is given of itself and starting from itself. Only this givenness, having originated in itself, can give the self of the phenomenon and invest evidence with the dignified rank of guardian of phenomenality. (Marion, 2002a, p. 20)

> [T]o give the gift, the giving must withdraw "in favor of the gift." The giving (*Geben*) is held back from the gift (*Gabe*), from its visibility and its availability, precisely because in giving it it undoes itself and withdraws from it, therefore turns itself away from the gift and abandons it to itself. By an inescapable consequence, the giving can never appear *with*, or still less *as* the gift given by it, since to give it not only does it leave it behind: it also differs from it. (Marion, 2002a, p. 35)

This is indeed a radical phenomenology that focuses entirely on the phenomenon itself as it gives itself without the mediating act of the subject or consciousness. In *The Erotic Phenomenon* Marion (2007) shows how he applies his phenomenology to the fundamental human phenomenon of love. The Cartesian pronouncement, "I love therefore I am" is compelling but ambiguous. How should the erotic phenomenon be approached? Can I love first? Am I loved by another? Is the capacity to love conditional upon knowing oneself already loved? Marion's phenomenology of love no doubt illuminates the experiences readers will have had with love. He discusses the eroticization of the face, the arousal of the flesh, erotic pleasure and joy, jealousy and hatred, and so on. Marion explains that he wants the erotic phenomenon to show itself without getting bogged down in the tradition of philosophy. So, he starts and stays with his own experience while trusting that it is the experience of others.

> I will say I started from and in view of the erotic phenomenon within me and for me—*my own*. I would thus be lying in claiming a surface neutrality: it will be necessary that I and no other speak of this erotic phenomenon that I know, and as I know it . . .
>
> Of course, I am going to speak of that which I barely understand—starting from that which I know badly—my own amorous history . . . . Nevertheless, I will keep within me the memory, new at each instant, of those who have loved me, who still love me, and whom I would like to be able to love, one day, as they should be loved—without measure. They will recognize themselves in my grateful recognition of them. (2007, p. 10)

I am partially quoting these lines because they seem to contradict Marion's phenomenology of self-givenness that should not rely on the constituting consciousness or the intentional subject (of the author). He says, "one must speak of love in the same way as one must love—in the first person . . . Loving puts in play my identity, my ipseity, those resources of mine that are more inward to me than myself" (p. 9). And yet, he says, "we must attempt to do the impossible: to produce what we will show starting from itself" (p. 9). The point that Marion seems to make is that the resources for phenomenological reflection lie in the memories of our lived experiences—and the lived experiences that others (the readers) recognize in themselves, but the erotic reduction must let the erotic phenomenon show itself as it gives itself in its self-givenness. This givenness plays out intriguingly in the mutual givenness of the eroticized "flesh" which transcends the intentional object of the body. In other words, the "flesh" in the erotic encounter can neither be described by means of the intentionality of the epistemic reduction of Husserl, nor Dasein's being of the ontological reduction of Heidegger. For Marion, the eroticized "flesh" is neither the body-object that we possess nor the body being that we are.

> The other gives me to myself for the first time, because she takes the initiative to give me my own flesh for the first time. She awakens me, because she eroticizes me . . .
>
> The eroticization that gives rise to the flesh does not result from a touch that is simply less possessive, groping, or predatory than another . . . [there is] the

indistinction between my flesh's feeling and its feeling itself feeling, for my flesh feels not only reciprocal feeling, but also the other flesh's feeling of itself. (2007, pp. 119, 120)

The eroticized flesh transcends our intentional experience of the other and the world. Marion explains that the book *The Erotic Phenomenon* has no quotes, no bibliography, and no references. He wants to describe the erotic phenomenon as it gives itself, without him getting caught up in philosophical debates. Still, some of his main themes such as "My Flesh and the Other's" and "Eroticization as Far as the Face" call upon echoes of the thinking of Emmanuel Levinas and Maurice Merleau-Ponty. In the introductory chapter Marion makes a statement that he would want to be programmatic for all his work: "We very much desire to know rather than not to know, and yet this desire does not bear upon what we know, but rather upon us, we who know" (2007, p. 12).

Technogenetic Phenomenology: Bernard Stiegler

Bernard Stiegler was born on April 1, 1952, in Seine-et-Oise, near Paris, France. He died in 2020. When he was 26, Stiegler was arrested for a series of armed bank robberies and jailed for five years, until 1983. During his incarceration Bernard Stiegler developed a passionate interest in philosophy. He studied philosophy by correspondence with Gérard Granel (who translated Husserl, Heidegger, and Wittgenstein into French). After leaving prison, Stiegler studied with Derrida. He completed his dissertation at the School for Advanced Studies in the Social Sciences, Paris, in 1992; and subsequently started teaching at the Collège International de Philosophie. This Collège was co-founded by Derrida in order to free the teaching of philosophy from the interferences by government authorities. Stiegler has occupied several leading positions at French academic and cultural institutions. He started his own school of philosophy in the small village of Épineuil-le-Fleuriel in central France in 2010.

From the mid-nineties Stiegler became known through a series of articles, books, and interviews for his writings on digital technology, individuation, consumer capitalism, youth, and his work on the audiovisual project Isler, a study of Heidegger. He describes his transformation in prison in a book, aptly entitled *Acting Out*. His trilogy *Technics and Time* has brought him recognition as a most provocative and profound phenomenologist for his original thoughts on the relation of humanness and technology.

Stiegler is so provocative because he is more emphatic than any of his predecessors about technology as the ontology of human existence. Stiegler uses the ancient myth of Prometheus and Epimetheus to show that from the very beginning human evolution has been intertwined with the evolution of technics. If humanity failed to see that it has always been emerged in the ontology of technics, it is because like the proverbial fish in the water, humans did not see that their aquatic world was technics. Without technics humanity would not have come into existence and without humanity technics would not have been possible.

The myth of Prometheus really tells the creation of the human. When Zeus felt it was time to create mortals, he charged Prometheus to go about and blow life into the forms he had made: the created creatures—animals and other mortal life forms that Zeus had fashioned from earth. As Stiegler retells the myth, Epimetheus begged his brother to let him do the task that Zeus had given to Prometheus. The latter was so fond of his brother Epimetheus that he let him do the job. So, Epimetheus was given the task to bring the creatures to life and bestow them with qualities and properties that would ensure their thriving and surviving. For example, slow and tall creatures like giraffes, he gave gentleness and long necks so they could eat greenery from the top of tree; to ferocious creatures like lions, he gave power and strong teeth to catch and devour their prey; to creatures like antelopes, he gave speed and observance to flee from the predatory cats; and to other creatures, he gave large wings and sharp eyes to glide through the sky, or smaller wings for quick flights.

However, after doling out all these critical qualities to the creatures, Epimetheus came upon the humans and realized that he had nothing left to give. This was a big problem because obviously the human creatures were naked and dependent at birth. Now, this predicament was not totally surprising. Epimetheus was known to be slow and dumb witted. He is portrayed in ancient mythology as living in the present and not possessing the intelligence of foresight. In Greek mythology, Epimetheus means "hindsight," literally "afterthought," and Prometheus means "foresight," literally "forethought." Epimetheus can only learn from experience by reflecting on past mistakes made. In desperation, for having no qualities left to bestow on humans, Epimetheus went to his brother Prometheus who was supposed to oversee the whole creation process. Prometheus is considered the smart brother who has foresight. He realized that humans were doomed to perish without help. They could not possibly keep themselves warm and safe. Prometheus saw that he needed to do something, and so he stole the fire from the immortal gods and gave it to the humans. In essence, he gave them the beginning of technology. Now they could build heated places to keep warm and use the fire to make tools.

So, according to Stiegler's reading of the Prometheus myth, the human condition is that it was characterized by an original lack, a default of being. Their creation lacked determinacy and a real beginning like the other creatures. Due to the fault of Epimetheus, humans lack an original property and therefore an essence. The human being is originally without an origin (Stiegler, 1998, p. 19). The default means that from the beginning, humans have been dependent on fashioning artificial means (i.e., technology) to survive and make a living. They had to invent their own prostheses, artificial body parts or tools. Indeed, humans are prosthetic beings—cyborgs. Stiegler reinterprets the Prometheus myth to show that tools and fire were not something discovered and acquired by the early humans as a useful adoption, but to show that humans could not have come into existence as humans without the primordial gift of technics (the use of fire). According to Stiegler, humanity thanks its coming into being to a double fault: the fault and stupidity of Epimetheus who had nothing left to fix them up, and the fault of Prometheus who had to steal fire from the gods for the humans. Thus, humans are neither immortals (gods) nor mere mortals like animals, who do not know of their mortality until death strikes them. The ontology of technics has placed human beings between the gods who live forever and the animals who only live in a closed presence. With technics comes time, and with time memory—the awareness that we are born and must die someday.

Cyborgs are beings with organic and inorganic parts. Human cyborgs are humans equipped with mechanical, electronic, and robotic parts. But from a Stieglerian technics point of view, cyborgs should not be seen as humans outfitted with technological contraptions—caricatures of human ontology. Rather, technology is the condition of human evolution and existence. So, humans have always been cyborgs in the sense of being wound up with technology. But humans are organic and inorganic in an even more profoundly evolutionary sense. Humans do not just create technology; they are in turn created by technology. Their evolving biology and intelligence are creations of technology just as much as technology is their own creation. Therefore, Stiegler wants to correct Heidegger. It is not just the being of being that has been forgotten by philosophy, but the technics of being: technics is the fundamental ontology of humans.

Stiegler describes the human condition as primordial idiocy, the origin of which lies in the Epimethean forgetfulness. However, this Epimethean bane is also the source of human freedom and of the singularity of the humanness of human beings. According to Stiegler, the human being is originally a prosthetic, technical-accidental being. Anthropogenesis (human becoming) is in essence technogenesis. And technogenesis is a process of the technological exteriorization of life: biologically, socially, and psychologically human beings evolve and develop historically and culturally through their technological nature.

In *Taking Care of Youth and the Generations*, Stiegler (2010) turns his insights into technics and life to the meaning and pedagogical significance of attention in the contemporary technological world. Technics, space, and temporality are closely interwoven. What does taking care of youth and the generations have to do with time? Stiegler starts with some simple questions:

> What do these children deserve; what do "our" children deserve; what do children deserve, who(so)ever they are? Do they not deserve, at least, to have fathers, grandfathers, and a family (which is fundamentally always adoptive) within which they can play, and through doing so learn to respect, that is, to love, and not merely to fear? What does it mean to play with one's daughter or grandson? It means to laugh and to "forget about time" with them—to give them one's time, and to give it not merely to their brains but to the formation of their nascent attention by concentrating one's adult attention on their juvenility—as imagination. (Stiegler, 2010, p. 14)

In *Taking Care of Youth*, Stiegler offers gradually an extensive and detailed phenomenological examination of the meaning of attention, starting simply with Husserl's primal impressional consciousness and its retentional and protentional structure:

> The formation of attention always consists of the psychotechnical accumulation or re-tentions and pro-tentions. Attention is the flow of consciousness, which is temporal and, as such, is created initially by what Husserl analyses as "primary" retentions— "primary" because they consist of apparent (present) objects

313

whose shapes I retain as though they were themselves present. This retention, called "primary" precisely because it occurs in perception, is then "conditioned" by "secondary" retentions, as the past of the attentive consciousness—as its "experience." Linking certain primary retentions with secondary retentions, consciousness projects protentions, as anticipation. The constitution of attention results from accumulation of both primary and secondary retentions, and the projection of protentions as anticipation. (Stiegler, 2010, p. 18)

Next, he discusses the development of technologies of cognition and the convergence of audiovisual, informatics, and telecommunications techniques with cultural technologies through new media. Stiegler focuses on numerous societal issues in linking the phenomenology of technics, with the microeconomy of attention, to a critique of the capitalist apparatus, and the nihilism of the societal caretakers and I-don't-give-a-damn-ers before the ungovernable populace. He warns against the threat of the destruction of young people's attention by technical industries that need to capture the attention and intelligence of the young and steer it away from their parents and educators toward their commercial purposes.

Objectivity Phenomenology: Günter Figal

Günter Figal studied philosophy in Heidelberg, and received his habilitation in 1987. He currently holds the Husserl and Heidegger Chair at the University of Freiburg, Germany. Figal's work may be of interest to human science scholars as he aims to shed new light on the phenomenology of objects, the thingworld, and on the Husserlian question of what it means to turn to the things themselves. Figal agrees with Ricoeur that hermeneutics started in phenomenology and turns back to phenomenology. The older hermeneutics of Schleiermacher and Dilthey aimed to establish a human science based on understanding, *Verstehen*, rather than causally explaining human phenomena. Their hermeneutics was an epistemological project concerned with the question of how to understand the mind (spirit, genius, subjectivity) of an author or artist through the expressions (texts, art, and so on) created by the author or artist. The test of hermeneutics was to understand the meaning of a text or art object better than the author did himself or herself.

Figal points out that the new hermeneutics (of Heidegger, Gadamer, and Ricoeur) is not aimed at the epistemological issue of understanding the mind (intentions, thoughts, feelings, subjectivity) of the author of a text, but rather at the more ontological question of interpreting possible worlds that are presented by the text—regardless of the author. Understanding a text is thus more a form of self-understanding.

The universality of philosophical hermeneutics, as put forth by Hans-Georg Gadamer, rests upon the conviction that every understanding is "ultimately self-understanding" ... understanding is self-knowledge within the inscrutability of one's proper—yet never fully appropriable—being .... Gadamer too, just like Heidegger before him, takes Aristotle's "practical wisdom," as the paradigm of understanding. As self-understanding, it is the luminosity of a situation in

314

which one must comport oneself even though it may never be fully illuminated. (Figal, 2004, pp. 21, 22)

Normally, when we are engaged with things, they become transparent, disappear, or lose the independence of their thingliness (Figal, 2010, p. 111). For example, while typing on this keyboard and looking at the computer screen, the keyboard and screen are no longer seen as things-in-themselves. Only by stepping back and giving an account of them do they become visible to the interpretive gaze. Figal calls this stepping back of distanciation the objective turn of hermeneutic phenomenology. He emphasizes the "autonomy of things" and the "primordiality of the thingworld," which cannot be reduced to the lifeworld (Figal, 2012, p. 504). Phenomenology does not constitute the thing but lets it appear as it is in its objective self through the reflective act of distanciation. Phenomenological understanding of the objectivity of a thing is not necessarily a function of closeness but rather remoteness (Figal, 2012, p. 505). Interpreting is stepping back to let the text or the phenomenon show itself. Figal points out that interpretation is not understanding but presentation. It does not consist of giving one's subjective view or one's personal perception of something. Rather, like an actor on a stage, it means "being absent oneself when letting the objective show or present itself from itself" (Figal, 2012, p. 506).

The German term for object is *Gegenstand* and objectivity is *Gegenständlichkeit*. These terms express both the objectness of the object as well as the sense that the object confronts us from the outside: it stands in a certain tension over and against us. When this is applied to hermeneutic interpretive practice, it means that the text or object that is interpreted stands in a heightened or intense relation to the interpreter. In other words, rather than start from the subject or the self, Figal wants to start from the objectivity of the object that confronts us and makes a demand on us. Interpretation arises in response to objects of our world as they interpose, interrupt, intersect, and intervene the normal steady state of our interactions, enactments, and activities. In this sense, texts too are encountered as exterior objects that require being recognized for their objective status and their potential significance.

For the practice of interpretation Figal assigns exemplary significance to models. Models are like phenomenological examples. So, to reflect in a hermeneutic phenomenological manner on the meaning of some object is to examine it as an originary model. Some models are more appropriate or better suited to get at the originary meaning of objects. And so, models must be well chosen as interpretive examples because the essence of the object has to be in the model. "Models must prove themselves as models by allowing the matter whose models they are to be recognized" (2010, p. 29). For Figal, models let their inceptive originariness of meaning be shown with special clarity. "Models are supposed to be distinguished by their pregnancy; they must prove themselves as such by really letting something be shown in them" (Figal, 2010, p. 30).

Only some objects we encounter in our daily lives require a hermeneutic response. Figal distinguishes between hermeneutic objects and mere objects. Hermeneutic objects are true externals in that they confront us and ask to be interpreted. "Works of art, the classical texts of philosophy, as well as the sacred texts of religions are hermeneutic objects par excellence. They are an ever driving impetus for interpreting, the promise of meaning" (Figal, 2004, p. 29). Mere objects, says Figal, are no longer true externals, but rather only the external of the internal:

> [T]hey are interiors, the intended furnishings of consciousness fixed in a determination that is transplanted into exteriority—as if what is grasped in the concept were actually given. Mere objects are immanent to consciousness, and this includes the exteriority attributed to them. Yet this exteriority cannot be explained solely on the basis of the immanence of consciousness; that there are externals can be traced back to another experience, namely, the experience of hermeneutic objectivity. The knowing of mere objects pre-supposes the understanding of hermeneutic objects. Thus, the mere object wears a borrowed exteriority. (Figal, 2004, p. 30)

True objects and mere objects constitute our world: they include the human world of meanings, values, and norms as well as the physical world of things. The hermeneutical space of our world is marked by three existential dimensions: freedom, language, and time (Figal, 2010). Figal derives these three dimensions from the historical philosophical literature. He sees them as the fundamental, persistent, and interrelated themes of our existence.

Ecstatic-Poetic Phenomenology: Jennifer Anna Gosetti-Ferencei

Jennifer Anna Gosetti-Ferencei studied at Columbia University, where she obtained a Master of Fine Arts in poetry; at Villanova University, where she gained an M.A. and Ph.D. in Philosophy; and at Oxford University, where she was granted a Doctor of Philosophy in German Literature and a Master of Studies in European Literature. Her extensive and varied background is evident in the wide range of sources she cites and discusses from philosophy, phenomenology, the fine arts, and languages. She translated (with Matthias Fritsch) Heidegger's *Phenomenology of Religious Life* (2004). She published a selection of her own poetry, *After the Palace Burns: Poems* (2003), for which she won the Paris Review Prize in poetry. Gosetti-Ferencei has a special interest in the phenomenology and philosophy of literature and aesthetics. Her several books include *Heidegger, Hölderlin, and the Subject of Poetic Language* (2004), *The Ecstatic Quotidian: Phenomenological Sightings in Modern Art and Literature* (2007), and *Exotic Spaces in German Modernism* (2011).

Gosetti-Ferencei is especially relevant for human science and the humanities in that she explores the crossings between phenomenology and the media of poetry and painting. In particular, she explores the creative significance of poetic language and the vocative for phenomenological understanding. In *The Ecstatic Quotidian* Gosetti-Ferencei proposes that phenomenology is like art in that it tends to be interested in the ordinary and in everydayness: the quotidian. And, of course, the whole point of phenomenology is to help us grasp the meaning of the world as we live it in everyday experience. The everydayness of the world and its taken-for-grantedness makes phenomenology not only desirable but also possible.

But Gosetti-Ferencei shows how, in both phenomenology and the arts, the attentive and aesthetic gaze at the ordinary inevitably causes the ordinary to shift toward the extraordinary, which she terms the *ecstatic*.

Now, this shift from the ordinary (the quotidian) to what lies outside the ordinary (the ecstatic quotidian) is suggestive of the moment of phenomenological seeing. What happens when we "see" an ordinary phenomenon phenomenologically? We need to acknowledge that this phenomenological seeing is a reflective seeing through the refractional lens of the phenomenological method of stepping outside of oneself: the epoché (bracketing) and the reduction (returning or leading back to experience as lived). This "stepping outside of oneself" of *Ekstasis* is experienced as a deranged astonishment or distracted wonder: re-seeing the world ecstatically through the (re)turning and refocusing of the phenomenological glance to the world as lived. In describing this moment of wonder, Heidegger suggests that what we now see is not really the extraordinariness of the ordinary, but rather it is the very ordinariness of the ordinary that is yielded in this ecstatic experience.

Gosetti-Ferencei advances methodological and ontological discussions that had already begun by the proponents of the phenomenologies of ordinary life at the University of Utrecht in the 1940s and 1950s. Martinus Langeveld spoke of the "home-garden-kitchen" interest of phenomenology. Langeveld and his colleagues employed an artful approach in their sensitive explications of everyday phenomena such as the conversation, the smile, at homeness, the hotel room, the secret place, things, and so on. This focus on the ordinary or the quotidian was fused with literary and poetic styles that made descriptions of everyday life phenomena recognizable.

Indeed, Frederik Buytendijk spoke of the "phenomenological nod" that occurs when recognizing the subtle and nuanced experiential meanings that only a phenomenological description can evoke through descriptive and evocative means. And that is why he proposes that a phenomenological association with literature and the arts can provide insights into the psychology, the everyday motivations, and the deep dramas of human life—insights that the discipline of psychology itself is incapable of producing. Buytendijk explicates this reflection on the value of literary and poetic text in his 1962 book *De Psychologie van de Roman* (The Psychology of the Novel)—a phenomenological study of the novel's power and potential for understanding human phenomena through Fyodor Dostoevsky's *The Brothers Karamazov*.

So, Gosetti-Ferencei's project is not new (see van Manen's 2013 review of Gosetti-Ferencei's ecstatic-poetic phenomenology). But Gosetti-Ferencei pushes the envelope so to speak by contrasting purely poetic with purely (Husserlian) phenomenological texts. In *The Ecstatic Quotidian*, she provocatively plays on this tension between poetic seeing and phenomenological seeing. Both seem to spin around the pivot of recognition of Husserlian essence in the singular. But, while Husserlian phenomenology aims at direct description in the act of intuitive seeing, literary description makes use of indirectness. Gosetti-Ferencei examines Husserl's phenomenological seeing of the essence of something side by side—Rilke's poetic seeing—and she notes that the indirect poetic phenomenology of Rilke results in an immediate or pathic grasping of meaning.

317

But what Rilke's poetry achieves is a noncognitive grasp that works the registers of intuition and feeling so that the specificity of that which speaks to the poetic gaze can be preserved there. Rilke's grasp at essences occurs only through the performance of language, which for Husserl would have to be restricted to a function of expressing the phenomenologist's findings. Rilke's poem does not represent, it enacts the capacities of poetic recognition. (Gosetti-Ferencei, 2007, p. 113)

And, she writes:

What the phenomenologist accomplishes in reflective study of the structure of phenomena, the poet accomplishes only through an indirect approach. We may speak of the common aim of grasping essences, but this means something different to the Husserlian phenomenologist than it does to the speaker of Rilke's poem. (Gosetti-Ferencei, 2007, p. 115)

Thus, Gosetti-Ferencei proposes or implies that there are two kinds of phenomenologies: the eidetic Husserlian approach that aims to capture the essence of a phenomenon, and the literary poetic approach that is able to capture a more subtle and noncognitive essence that only poetry is able to express.

An early theme in Gosetti-Ferencei's *The Ecstatic Quotidian* is her attempt to return to childhood reminiscence and childhood consciousness as a source for regaining an innocent view of the ordinariness of everydayness life. Gosetti-Ferencei aims to use childhood consciousness to access the quotidian dimension of phenomenological experience. She says, "It might turn out that the naïve attitude of childhood as reflected upon is more like phenomenological reflection than it resembles the natural attitude" (2007, p. 77).

Gosetti-Ferencei's theme of recovering one's sense of self and the world through reminiscing on our childhood is a pervasive theme in our culture and literature. She quotes extensively from the poets Rilke, Frost, and Wordsworth and the novelist Proust. The question is whether childhood consciousness can be regained and whether our remembrances of seeing the world as child have a recognizable structure. In "Quite Early One Morning," Dylan Thomas publishes two slightly different versions of a brief text "Reminiscences of Childhood." His descriptions contain sensuous, vivid, and pungent reminiscences of his hometown and childhood world. Was it ever like this?

The recollections of childhood have no order; of all those every-coloured and shifting scented shoals that move below the surface of the moment of recollection, one, two, indiscriminately, suddenly, dart up out of their revolving waters into the present air: immortal flying-fish. (Thomas, 1954, p. 6)

The second version of "Reminiscences of Childhood" is only slightly but tellingly revised. The last line of the text now reads: "The memories of childhood have no order and no end" (Thomas, 1954, p. 14).

The memories of childhood have no order (reminiscing is fragmentary) and no end (one narrates and re-narrates one's childhood in order to make a home in it).

It is indeed strange how our memories of childhood appear so arbitrary and contingent. Why can I remember in such vivid and sensuous ways seemingly trivial incidents, while more important moments seem to be erased from memory? As with remembering and forgetting names of people we meet, there seems no order to our remembrance and forgetfulness of things from childhood. Sometimes we unexpectedly catch glimpses of images that present themselves to us from a past. And in these glimpses we may recognize that what we see belongs deeply to us and defines who we are—children still. Or that is what we may hope: to recover something that we have lost. Is the attempt to see like a child a romanticist project? These are issues that should be addressed in Gosetti-Ferencei's work.

The most significant theme of Gosetti-Ferencei's work is probably her exploration of the power of literary phenomenology and of literature, poetics, and the arts for phenomenological grasping of ordinary life phenomena. She says, "While Husserl maintained a scientific approach to lived experience, the technical determination of which may have put its real vitality out of reach, other phenomenologists have turned to art and literature to grasp the original quality of the world" (2007, p. 41). Nobody would disagree with Gosetti-Ferencei that traditional philosophical argument is a different genre from poetic expression, each working and playing on their own linguistic registers. And as long as the comparison is maintained between Husserlian eidetic texts and literary-poetic textualities, it seems appropriate to extend the reach of phenomenology beyond the limited eidetic analysis that Husserlian phenomenology permits.

Gosetti-Ferencei strongly implies that Husserlian phenomenology needs to be more sensitive to the subtle nuances of the richness and depth of human experience. At the same time, she suggests provocatively that Rilke's poetry is a poetic phenomenology that needs to be placed and acknowledged side by side with the classic Husserlian phenomenology. But it is not entirely clear why Gosetti-Ferencei does not acknowledge that a notable number of phenomenologists since Husserl have increasingly realized the expressive value of literary and poetic elements in their phenomenological reflections and writing.

Gosetti-Ferencei extensively discusses the beginning of this poetic theme in the texts of the later Heidegger and she frequently cites Sartre, Merleau-Ponty, Bachelard, and Blanchot, all of whom have made the literary form thematic for their philosophical and phenomenological project and writings. And constantly, she keeps falling back on Husserlian phenomenology when she is establishing a dialogue between phenomenology and modern art.

The relationship between phenomenology and literature is a vital and complex one, and while literature assists in the imaginative variation of the phenomenologist, phenomenology often helps to explain the particular operations of modern literature as it transforms everyday perceptions into what writers hope to be truer, more intense forms of recognition. (2007, p. 111)

Yet, in *The Ecstatic Quotidian* she does not mention phenomenological philosophers such as Alphonso Lingis, Jean-Luc Nancy, Giorgio Agamben, Michel Henry, and Jean-Luc Marion, who all exemplify in different ways literary styles, attention to the image, and the use of paintings in their phenomenological writings. By insistently using Husserl's consciousness phenomenology as her exemplary template, Gosetti-Ferencei does not create the opportunity to acknowledge that post-Husserlian phenomenology has evolved toward a rich philological fusing of phenomenological reflection with poetic and literary forms. So, strangely Gosetti-Ferencei's case seems somewhat overdrawn. Still, her detailed probing into the power of the literary and poetic forms is enlightening and seductive.

To reiterate, Gosetti-Ferencei is a most intriguing author who has already contributed in an original manner to the international scene of phenomenology. In her various publications, she displays an extensive familiarity and detailed knowledge of a great variety of artists, poets, literary authors, and phenomenologists, and their work. She makes a strong and nuanced case for the methodological relevance of literature and the arts for phenomenological understanding. Gosetti-Ferencei's contribution consists in part of her explorations into the intricacies of the relationship between phenomenology and visual art, literature, and poetics. She searches exhaustively for the commonalities and distinctiveness of visual seeing of the image in paintings and poetic seeing of the image in literary texts, and then she urgently relates poetic recognition of the image to phenomenological recognition of essences.

Evential Phenomenology: Claude Romano

Claude Romano, born in 1967, is a graduate of the École Normale Supérieure of the rue d'Ulm, where he obtained a doctor of philosophy. He has been teaching at the University of Paris-Sorbonne since 2000 and is a member of the Husserl Archives in Paris. In 2010 he received the Moron Grand Prix of the French Academy for *L'Événement et le Temps* (1999) and *Event and World* (2009).

Quite commonly the terms "phenomenon" and "event" are uttered in one breath. Phenomenology focuses on the phenomenon or the event in the investigation of the meaning of lived experience. But the term "event" is less commonly focused upon and that is, in part, why the work of Claude Romano is so fascinating. An event is the process of something happening to us, opening the world to us, and opening us to the world, in ways that we may not anticipate. For example, a talk is something that we can plan for as we promise a friend to meet at a certain time. But it can happen that our meeting actually turns out to be a surprise as our get-together is unexpectedly eventful. In the latter case, Claude Romano would rather say that our meeting possesses a meaningful evential sense.

Claude Romano uses the term *advenant* (becoming) and the neologism *evential* (meaningful event) to investigate this meaning of the happening of an eventful and meaningful event. He throws new light on a familiar feature of experience: there is a difference between an experience as factum and an experience as event. For example, we may talk by phone or email with a friend we have not seen for a while and agree to meet and have coffee together. Our meeting is arranged and the fact of our meeting materializes when we sit together over a cup of coffee. This is the event as factum, as something that happens and that was predictable. The event as factum is usually plannable, explainable, and predictable. But the actual event may contain surprise elements that we had not foreseen when planning the meeting. This is the eventiality of an event which is not explainable and interpretable in the factual sense. In fact, this unplannable aspect to an event may be its unexperience-able character in the moment of its happening. Claude Romano offers a detailed exploration of the etymological and phenomenological meanings of *experience* in his *Event and World* (2009, pp. 143–212). Not until later, in the latency of the event may we realize what the experienced encounter meant for us and will mean for us in its future effect and unfolding.

> For a genuine encounter can never be reduced to its actualization as a fact; it always happens in the secret and suspense of its latency such that we are never contemporary with it and never realize it until later, "too late," according to the essential—transcendental—a posteriori of a necessary retrospection, when the event of an encounter has *already* happened, has already reconfig-ured all our possibilities and the world. (Romano, 2009, p. 123)

Indeed, the experience of meeting this old friend may turn out more meaningful than just the factual situation. Romano also gives the example of a *dating* experi-ence. He first of all points out the impossibility of a dating event as such. When exactly does such event happen?

> Because it never appears to one who experiences it until it has already taken place, so that the first moment, the beginning of a love, the start of a friend-ship, are already "lost": once an event "is brought about," it is already too late; we are never contemporaries of its actualization and can only experience it when it has already taken place, and this is why an event, in its eventness, happens only according to the secret of its latency. An encounter is not the datable fact of the meeting of two beings but rather that which lies in reserve in this meeting and which gives it its future-loading: it is the silent upending that the other introduces into my own world. Reconfiguring my possibilities from the outside, before any projection of an autonomous potentiality-for-being. (Romano, 2009, p. 47)

The experience of the event of our meeting may leave one profoundly stirred. The point is that our talk together became an event that only afterwards can be seen for its significance. The event of the talk may transfigure how I feel about myself and my life. In this sense, the event has an unpredictable quality and in some real sense the event is enigmatic, ungraspable in its meaning and consequence. Before we realize what has happened to us, an event may have "already upended who we were," says Romano. What cannot be experienced and yet, by this very disparity, this intimate being out of step, comes and touches us, wounds us, and, by address-ing itself to us, by prescribing that we undergo it, gives us the possibility of receiv-ing it [*l'accuellir*] by being transformed (Romano, 2009, p. 49).

Romano describes four phenomenological traits of events: (1) events single us out, in that I am at play in my selfhood; (2) events configure new worlds; (3) events are an-archic in that they are inexplicable and yet make sense; (4) events are not datable in time but they open up time (2009, p. 49).

Experience of the ungraspable is therefore expressed in being caught by surprise. Poets have strongly and beautifully expressed the mix of almost sacred terror and astonishment that characterize it.... Horror and wonder, the appalling and the mystifying, astonishment and terror: all are experiences of being grasped by what cannot be grasped, by what, like surprise, overtakes us and suspends any grip, is never at our disposal, but has us at its disposal by exposing us to what cannot be experienced. For a genuine encounter can never be reduced to its actualization as a fact; it always happens in the secret and suspense of its latency such that we are never contemporary with it and never realize it until later, "too late," according to the essential—transcendental—a posteriori of a necessary retrospection, when the event of an encounter has already happened, has already reconfigured all our possibilities and the world. (Romano, 2009, p. 123)

The notion of latency has also been discussed by Husserl in reference to the idea of *habitus*—a term made famous by Pierre Bourdieu (1985). Husserl says,

lived experience itself, and the objective moment constituted in it, may become "forgotten"; but for all this, it in no way disappears without a trace; it has merely become latent. With regard to what has been constituted in it, it is a *possession in the form of a habitus*, ready at any time to be awakened anew by an active association.... The object has incorporated into itself the forms of sense originally constituted in the acts of explication by virtue of a *knowledge in the form of a habitus*. (Husserl, 1973, p. 122)

Romano explores the primary phenomenological meaning of experience as undergoing what cannot be experienced in the common sense of "having experiences." An event cannot be experienced in its eventiality. Commonly we can tell, if asked, what experience we were having just now. But an event cannot so easily be grasped.

But must not events at the same time be "experienced" in some way or other by the one to whom they occur? Is the empiricist concept of "experience," in terms of which events cannot be experienced, the only possible concept of "experience"? *In other words, is there not an experience that does justice to events in the evential sense?* Is there not, paradoxically, a nonempirical undergoing of what is, in itself, unable to be experienced? And, if so, how is this to be conceived? (Romano, 2009, p. 143)

The implication of Romano's work for phenomenological researchers is that at times, certain phenomena are best studied as events, and that events should be grasped as evential—and in their latency rather than in their factual occurrence.

Chapter Ten

Phenomenology and the Professions: Practitioners

As the philosophers—Edmund Husserl, Martin Heidegger, Max Scheler, Edith Stein, Jan Patočka—developed the foundational elements of phenomenology there were scholars in the clinical professions who were attracted to this emerging discipline. Even before phenomenology became widespread among philosophers it formed a movement among professional practitioners such as Adolf Reinach, Ludwig Binswanger, Karl Jaspers, and Eugene Minkowski.

For example, Adolf Reinach had studied law and his professional interest was juris prudence, but Reinach also became deeply interested in phenomenological philosophy and was one of Husserl's first and highly gifted students. Adolf Reinach was one of the first clinical professionals who took up phenomenological philosophy in a unique non-traditional manner. For example, in a talk on the phenomenology of law at Marburg in 1914 Reinach proclaimed: "I have not set myself the task of telling you what Phenomenology is. Rather, I would like to try to think with you in the phenomenological manner." Instead of theorizing about the meaning and method of phenomenology, Reinach started with concrete examples that are of concrete concern to the practice of criminal law.

Soon after the appearance of *Logical Investigations* in 1901, and the second major work on the *Ideas* in 1913, Husserl gained the interest of many western philosophers. But he also became a major influence on the thinking of clinical professionals in the area of psychology and psychiatry, medicine, and pedagogy. The Swiss psychiatrist Ludwig Binswanger (1881–1966) was one of the first professional practitioners who aimed to adopt the perspective and method of Heidegger's phenomenology to his clinical work in existential psychotherapy and psychiatry.

A few decades later, in North America, phenomenology seeped further into the professional fields, in part via ethnomethodology, ethnography, interpretive sociology, and other such social science streams that had been inspired especially by the phenomenological sociology of Alfred Schutz. Some scholars such as the psychologists Adrian van Kaam and Amedeo Giorgi had developed contact with Dutch proponents at the University of Utrecht. To distinguish the professional interest in phenomenology from the purely philosophical interest, the notion of "human science phenomenology" became current. Phenomenological movements inspired by developments in the human sciences and humanities combined with philosophical phenomenologies and with more empirically based movements imported from the social sciences formed a dynamic ever-changing field.

DOI: 10.4324/9781003228073-12

Juris Prudence and Phenomenology

Phenomenology of Law: Adolf Bernhard Philipp Reinach

Adolf Reinach (1883–1917) was one of Husserl's earliest and most brilliant students. He was born into a prominent Jewish family in Mainz, Germany, on December 23, 1883. In 1905 Reinach completed his studies in law at Munich and then continued in 1906–1907 at the University of Tübingen where he attended lectures and seminars on penal law.

At the outbreak of World War I, Reinach served in the army. He was decorated with the award of the Iron Cross for his courage, but killed by a bullet on November 16, 1917. He was only 34 years old.

Adolf Reinach starts his monograph containing his public lecture "On Phenomenology" (*Über Phänomenologie*) with these words: "I have not set myself the task of telling you what Phenomenology is. Rather, I would like to try to think with you in the phenomenological manner." This pedagogical invitation by Adolf Reinach in 1914 to come to an understanding of phenomenology by thinking phenomenologically is highly felicitous. Reinach continues:

> To talk about phenomenology is the most useless thing in the world so long as that is lacking which alone can give any talk concrete fullness and intuitiveness: the phenomenological *way of seeing* and the phenomenological *attitude*. For the essential point is this, that phenomenology is not a matter of a system of philosophical propositions and truths—a system of propositions in which all who call themselves "Phenomenologists" must believe. (Reinach, 1968 p. 194)

The requirement of involving his participants in a way of thinking of concrete fullness and intuitiveness shows how Reinach is already operating on the principle that phenomenology must start not with theoretic abstractions but with concrete experience and that is guided by the phenomenological attitude and includes the act of phenomenological seeing. However, Reinach's extensive discussion of Kant's notion of the apriori still is a carefully argued critique that he sets up to advance his own juris prudential apriori explication.

According to Reinach, phenomenology is not a systematic philosophical doctrine that one must commit to. Rather, to understand phenomenology one must practice its way of seeing and adopt its phenomenological attitude. Indeed, years later, Merleau-Ponty, one of the most outstanding phenomenologists who also set himself the task of asking, what is phenomenology, comes to a similar starting point: If you want to understand phenomenology then you must do it! Thinking in a phenomenological manner means engaging the phenomenological *way of seeing* and the phenomenological *attitude*. Reinach presented his essay on thinking phenomenologically at Marburg in 1914, to an audience of early phenomenologists.

Since those early days scores of philosophers have tried to define what phenomenology is but it seems that no definition has ever found unanimous consent. So, in the early years of phenomenology, about one hundred years ago, Reinach suggested that the best way of proceeding is to in practice phenomenological thinking and the phenomenological attitude. Already, his phenomenology immediately took a more realistic turn than Husserl's work. In opening the chapter on "The Apriori Foundations of the Civil Law" which develops a phenomenology of "claims and promises," Reinach starts with a concrete example:

> One man makes a promise to another. A curious effect proceeds from this event, an effect quite different from the effect of one man informing another of something, or making a request of him. The promising produces a unique bond between the two persons in virtue of which the one person—to express it for the time being very roughly can claim something and the other is obliged to perform it or to grant it. This bond presents itself as a result, as a product (so to speak) of the promising. It can, according to its essence, last ever so long, but on the other hand it seems to have an inherent tendency towards meeting an end and a dissolution. We can conceive of different ways which can lead to such a dissolution. The thing promised is performed; in this way the bond seems to find its natural end. The promisee waives; the promisor revokes. Even in this way, though it seems to us less natural, a dissolving of the promise can sometimes occur. (Reinach, 1983, p. 8)

Actually, Reinach's description of the experience of promising is perfectly transparent and a perfect example of a phenomenological description. But the promise is not just a lived inner experience, it also is a social act. In the next paragraphs Reinach explicates how the social act involves turning to another subject.

> Experiences which need not turn without, can unfold without being in any way externally expressed. But the social acts have an inner and an outer side, as it were a soul and a body. The body of social acts can widely vary while the soul remains the same. A command can be expressed in mien, gestures, words. One should not confuse the utterance (*Ausserung*) of social acts with the involuntary way in which all kinds of inner experiences such as shame, anger, or love can be externally reflected. This utterance is rather completely subject to our voluntariness and can be chosen with the greatest deliberation and circumspection, according to the ability of the addressee to understand it. On the other hand, it should not be confused with statements about experiences which are now taking place or have just taken place. If I say, "I am afraid," or "I do not want to do that," this is an utterance about experiences which would have occurred without any such utterance. But a social act, as it is performed between human beings, is not divided into an independent act and a statement about it which might or might not be made; it rather forms an inner unity of voluntary act and voluntary utterance. For the inner experience here is not possible without the utterance. (Reinach, 1983, p. 20)

If we put ourselves in the position of the promisor, we see that a genuine promise can be performed and expressed, yet without reaching the subject to whom it is directed. As long as this does not happen, there can be no question of claim and obligation. It is also not enough that the promisee perceive the external signs, for instance hear the words, without understanding them. He must grasp through them that which is expressed in them, he must take cognizance of the act of promising itself, he must, as we would put it somewhat more exactly, consciously take in the promising (*des Verprechens innewerden*). (Reinach, 1983, p. 28)

In these short quoted paragraphs (selected from the careful and lengthy studies of the apriori papers) we can see how the context of the promise becomes critical for civil law situations and contestations. Clearly, we see, how phenomenology becomes the medium for understanding the originary meaning and significance of social acts such as the promise. But it is also clear how the phenomenology of the promise is not only clarifying of legal civil law, it also helps clarify the phenomenology of making promises in everyday life. The work of Reinach is important because it shows that early phenomenology was not only of interest to philosophers, in fact it was especially significant for professionals in fields such as law, health science, psychology, and pedagogy who were interested in the reality demands of the clinical professions.

The monograph "The Apriori Foundations of the Civil Law" has been greatly admired as a perfect case of phenomenological analysis. It shows Reinach's discovery of the social acts and his ability to respect what is given in experience, to let things "show themselves from themselves" as Heidegger had described the act of phenomenological thinking. John Crosby, the translator of Reinach's text, said that Reinach understood phenomenology as a philosophical realism, and while Husserl was developing his transcendental phenomenology, Reinach was developing a very different, concrete phenomenology. Apparently, Reinach was deeply disappointed by Husserl's first major work in transcendental phenomenology. But, fortunately, for present-day phenomenologists he provided a brilliant example of doing phenomenology on the concrete phenomena.

Reinach was not only a professional lawyer who uniquely approached his legal practice and interest in a phenomenological manner, he is credited also for the initiation of an early version of a speech act theory as was subsequently developed by Austin and Searle. It is called, *The Apriori Foundations of Civil Law* (*Die apriorischen Grundlagen des bürgerlichen Rechtes*) and was a systematic treatment of social acts as performative utterances and "apriori foundations" of civil law. Husserl greatly admired Reinach's thinking and explained Reinach's notion of apriori principles in his obituary for Reinach as follows:

[They] are apriori in exactly the sense of the basic axioms of arithmetic and logic, that is, they are truths which are grasped in intellectual insight as being valid without any possible exception, and they are prior to all experience . . . . Reinach's apriori principles are simply expressions of absolutely valid truths which are grounded in the essential meaning of these concepts. What is utterly original in this essay of Reinach's, which is in every respect masterful is the idea that we have to distinguish this apriori which belongs to the proper nature of any legal order, from the other apriori which is related to positive law as something normative and as a principle of evaluation: for all law can and must be subjected to the idea of "right law"—"right" from the point of view of morality or of some objective purpose. (Husserl 1919 obituary, in Reinach 1983, p. xiii).

Psychopathology and Psychiatry and Phenomenology

Adolf Reinach was not the only early professional practitioner who turned to phenomenology in order to enrich insights into the meaning of phenomena of clinical practice. Henri-Louis Bergson (1859–1941), Ludwig Binswanger (1881–1966), Eugène Minkowski (1885–1972), and Karl Jaspers (1883–1969) were among the first well-known clinicians who turned to phenomenology. Binswanger, Jaspers, and Minkowski also decided that phenomenology could be especially relevant for the practice of psychopathology and psychiatry. But while Reinach unfortunately died very young and could only have limited influence on the development of a phenomenology that could address concrete phenomena these three psychiatrists became influential especially for psychology and the health sciences. In fact, their influence was felt also among philosopher-phenomenologists who used psychiatry to develop their philosophical interests even though, humorously perhaps, most professional philosophers had no training or background in medicine and certainly no clinical experience either in psychiatry, psychology, counseling or psychotherapy.

Phenomenology and Psychoanalysis:
Ludwig Binswanger

Ludwig Binswanger (1881–1966) was one of the first physician-psychiatrist who turned to phenomenology in order to enhance his understanding and clinical practice of psychopathology. He studied the early work of Husserl and became especially involved in Heidegger's thinking and work on existential analysis. In other words, Binswanger focused on the methods of phenomenology in order to apply them to the clinical methods of psychiatry. Thus, Binswanger became a founder of the existential school of psychiatry as he ventured to apply philosophical ideas of Heidegger to the psychological understanding and treatment of psychiatric patients. According to the interpretation of Binswanger's clinical work by Nassir Ghaemi, a later colleague of one of his most compelling case histories, Binswanger made great efforts to understand the subjectivity of his most famous patient, Ellen West—her schizophrenic ways of being in the world by using his new Heidegerrian existentials of temporality, spatiality, corporeality, social relationships, and own world, world with others, and surrounding world:

> He began a discussion of her *"Eigenwelt"* the "own world" of her subjective purely personal experience, compared with her *"Mitwelt"* the "with world" of interpersonal relationships, and her *"Umwelt"* the "surrounding world" of natural objects, including our bodies, existing independently of us. He held that Ellen West's mode of existence was marked by a withdrawal during childhood into her *Eigenwelt* from her *Umwelt* and her *Mitwelt*. "The *Eigenwelt* does not go trustingly over into the *Umwelt* and *Mitwelt*, to let itself be carried, nourished, and fulfilled by it, but separates itself sharply from it." (Ghaemi, 2001, p. 61)

Interestingly, Binswanger proposed that there are different modes of existence and that every human being has control over their mode(s) of existence such as being a business person, being a romantic, being an artist, and being a parent. As well human beings can transcend their worldly existence by falling in love, by committing to a life of care and service for others, and so forth. Thus, there is the primary mode of being-in-the-world and the transformed mode of being-beyond-the-world according to one's striving.

The *Eigenwelt* (self-world) refers to a person's relationship to themselves and to a person's own subjective existence. It would seem that Binswanger's psychiatry had two operational dimensions: an existential psychological and an ontological phenomenological dimension. For example, Binswanger diagnosed psychologically and psychoanalytically that his patient Ellen West's particular psychological case was classified as schizophrenia (though other psychiatrists did not necessarily agree with Binswanger's analysis) and from a philosophical Heideggerian perspective he wrote fascinating phenomenological accounts of the meaning and significance of the condition of schizophrenia.

Phenomenology and General Psychopathology: Karl Jaspers

Karl Jaspers (1883–1969) was quite fascinated by the mystic Christian traditions of Meister Eckhart and Nicolas de Cusa which would seem to lead him into some oddly conflicting directions. As psychiatrist, Karl Jaspers believed that patients who suffer from primary delusions would effectively be "un-understandable" and therefore untreatable in a therapeutic manner for the psychiatrist, since there are no rational coherent processes that shaped their views and their way sense-making of their world (Jaspers, 1997, pp. 98–104).

However, the fifteenth-century monk Nicolas de Cusa became famous in the way that he converted disbelievers into God-fearing believers. By appealing to their experiences of religious icons such as a portrait of the Holy Mary or the Holy Jesus, he brought people to accept miraculous acts. For example, de Cusa demonstrated iconically how God can see everyone, always, everywhere. And Jaspers made unwittingly use of the fact that de Cusa would play dramatically on the idea of the "un-understandable" that yet could persuade and seduce his congregation. In his written letters de Cusa presented the dramatic rehearsal of his test of faith with the following inveigling words, meant for his colleagues, monks and bishops, to apply and entice their communal members.

> I will now show you, dearest brethren, as I promised you, an easy path unto mystical theology . . . And first I pray the Almighty to give me utterance, and the heavenly Word who alone can express Himself, that I may be able, as ye can receive it, to relate the marvels of revelation, which are beyond all sight of our eyes, our reason, and our understanding. I will endeavour by a very simple and commonplace method to lead you by experience into the divine darkness; wherein while ye abide ye shall perceive present withy you the light inaccessible, and shall each endeavour, in the measure that God shall grant him, to draw ever nearer thereunto, and to partake, here, by a sweetest Foretaste, of that feast of everlasting bliss, whereunto we are called in the word of life, through the gospel of Christ, who is blessed for ever. (de Cusa, 1960, pp. 1, 2)

But instead of just preaching his message, de Cusa engaged his listeners in bold bodily exercises so that their beliefs were not just mentally communicated but they were made to feel in their bodies and with the proof of their own eyes how the omnivoyant divine eyes of God were always looking upon them and taking note of their sins and unkindly acts.

> If I strive in human fashion to transport you to things divine, I must needs use a comparison of some kind. Now among men's works I have found no image better suited to our purpose than that of an image which is omnivoyant—its face, by the painter's cunning art, being made to appear as though looking on all around it . . . lest ye should fail in the exercise, which requireth a figure of this description to be looked upon, I send for your indulgence such a picture as I have been able to procure, setting forth the figure of an omnivoyant, and this I call the icon of God. This picture, brethren, ye shall set up in some place, let us say, on a north wall, shall stand round it, a little way off, and look upon it. And each of you shall find that, whatsoever quarter he regardeth it, it looketh upon him as if it looked on none other. And it shall seem to a brother standing to eastward as if that face looketh toward the east, while one to southward shall think it looketh toward the south, and one to westward, toward the west. First, then, ye will marvel how it can be that the face should look on all and each at the same time. For the imagination of him standing to eastward cannot conceive the gaze of the icon to be turned unto any other quarter, such as west or south. Then let the brother who stood to eastward place himself to westward and he will find its gaze fastened on him in the west just as it was afore in the east. And, as he knoweth the icon to be fixed and unmoved, he will marvel at the motion of its immoveable gaze. If now, while fixing his eye on the icon, he walks from west to east, he will find that its gaze continuously goeth along with him, and if he returns from east to west, in like manner it will not leave him. Then will he marvel how, being motionless, it moveth, nor will his imagination be able to conceive that it should also move in like manner with one going in a contrary direction to himself. (de Cusa, 1960, pp. 3–5)

The idea that the inner life of a delusional individual could be un-understandable seems like a self-defeating approach to psychopathology. But Jaspers was a brilliant scholar who became increasingly interested in philosophy and less concerned with his psychiatric career. He declared that clinical practice became less attractive to him than the philosophical theories that he admirably articulated in his professional practice.

> Close contemplation of an individual case often teaches us of phenomena common to countless others. What we have once grasped in this way is usually encountered again. It is not so much the number of cases seen that matter in phenomenology but the extent of the inner exploration of the individual case, which needs to be carried to the furthest limit. (Jaspers, 1997, p. 56)

So, by the time Jaspers became 38, he had traded his university position from medicine and psychiatry to being a full-time philosopher. Actually, it was not uncommon at European universities for philosophers to be partially prepared and responsible for an academic program in psychology or psychotherapy.

But more often it was and it is still the case that philosophers who lack any credits in psychiatry, medicine, or psychology at all try to apply their philosophical skills to such practical fields in which they have no legitimate grounding. Usually it is quite obvious when a philosopher tries to present himself as a researcher with a focus on concerns of psychiatry or neonatology though it usually shows in the excessive amount of abstract theorizing. At any rate, with Karl Jaspers this condition was reversed with much professional conviction and success.

Phenomenology and Psychopathology: Eugène Minkowski

In his essay entitled "Death," Eugène Minkowski (1885–1972) begins his phenomenological question about the meaning of death as follows:

> A shadow falls on becoming. Death soars above the triumphal march of life like a bird of prey. Anguished, we see it approach. We are such children . . . Could we therefore live without dying? (2019, p. 130)

Next Minkowski eloquently proposes that we have a need of death in order to live. What could life be without death? He says that he would almost like to say that we would look for death even if it did not exist. So, "what is death?" (p. 131) and what do I experience when in the presence of death? In life, death is a necessary part of the stage play: it replaces the curtain and marks the end" (p. 132).

But Minkowski points out that death not only interrupts a life, as if it were a play—the presence of death also makes us see the whole of that life play as a single unity. So, death marks the end of life, yes, but this does not just imply a destruction; rather, death creates "a" life. But, of course, this is a life that is just finished. And we now make sense of it as a whole life which is partly known and which remains partly forever mysterious, so that we let our imagination fill in. So, death finishes a life and thereby makes the idea of "a" life appear. It does so in putting an end to that life. Again, one should not just see death as a destruction of life but as a creation of "a" life. When death ends a living then "a" life takes shape. We may now honor this life (but differently from when the person was still alive): "it is death, and death alone, that brings to us the notion of *a* life. Death, insofar as it is destruction, engenders a becoming, not a being" (p. 133). It should be noted that Minkowski italicizes the indefinite article "*a*" in these passages—emphasizing indefiniteness. According to the *Oxford English Dictionary* the article "*a*" is used to denote an individualized quality or state. Minkowski transforms the meaning of death and what comes after death:

> [Death] transforms the order and texture of the events of life into *a* life. It is not in being born but in dying that one becomes a whole, a [wo]man. When it is a question of staking out a road, pickets are set, one after another, until the last. Here it is only the last one that counts; and when it is put in place, all the others rise up from the earth as if enchanted and stake out the whole road that has been travelled.

> Death is an essentially individual phenomenon, not because it attacks only individuals but because it completes the idea of an individual. Life does not become exhausted. It is only the living being who dies; and in order to be a living being, that is, a being having lived, having a life behind him [or her], it is necessary to be mortal. (p. 133)

Minkowski asks rhetorically, "what will I be when I am no longer" (p. 143). "A life is achieved not by its works—with those one is never finished—but by death" (p. 134). Minkowski says, "It is not my own death but simply my mortality that I witness in the presence of the death of someone else (p. 144). Every human being knows that death is inescapable. We all must die. We all have a date with death. But as long as we do not know the precise date or dwell on it, we can live with the knowledge of death.

> if we knew the [precise] date of our death in advance, we probably would not be able to continue to live at all. Like those obsessed, we would pass our time checking our watches, calculating the time that yet remained for us to live. The date of death ought to be ignored in life. Nevertheless, it is true that death furnishes us with a fundamental given, to wit, that something precise must necessarily happen in the future. (p. 145)

Minkowski suggests that somehow we feel that we will leave "a" life behind.

> Death exists for me only because there is an "after it" in me, and I feel so bound to this after that my life draws all its meaning from it . . . every life draws its inspiration from this "after death" and cannot exist without it.
> . . .
> The "after" of death is given to me much more primitively that death itself and all that precedes it. It is the first given of life in general, insofar as life is oriented toward the future. I participate in this much more intimately than in the present and in the past. It is from this that I draw all my force, and it is it that illuminates my soul. (p. 146)

Minkowski's essay on the phenomenology of death in his book *Lived Time* is quite remarkable (1933/2019). This is indeed the interesting phenomenological insight of Minkowski who applies the epoché and the reduction by bracketing our common understanding of death and turning it upside down, by showing that death is the beginning of the phenomenon of "a" life.

THE UTRECHT TRADITION OF PHENOMENOLOGY

In the 1940s, various academics from professional faculties at Dutch universities had begun to approach their fields in a phenomenological manner. The phenomenology of Edmund Husserl, Martin Heidegger, Eugène Minkowski, Jean-Paul Sartre, and Maurice Merleau-Ponty had become an inspiration for academics in the professional disciplines to approach their own professional interests in new and exciting perspectives. Scholars such as the clinical psychologist and pedagogue

331

Martinus Langeveld (1983a, 1983b), the medical doctor Frederik Buytendijk (1970a, 1970b), the psychiatrist Jan Hendrik van den Berg (1966, 1972), the pediatrician Nicolaas Beets (1975), the psychologists Johannes Linschoten (1987), the psychiatrist Henricus Rümke and others, integrated phenomenological themes into the very languages and structures of their professional disciplines. Yet, they largely avoided discussing theoretical, methodological, and technical philosophical issues.

As Langeveld declared emphatically, they were primarily interested in phenomenology as a practical and reflective enterprise, but not necessarily in phenomenology as theoretical philosophy. Some had participated in seminars with Edmund Husserl and Martin Heidegger, and many of these proponents found inspiration in the works of Henri Bergson, Ludwig Binswanger, Karl Jaspers, Wilhelm Dilthey and maintained correspondence with phenomenologists such as Max Scheler, Jean-Paul Sartre, Simone de Beauvoir, Romano Guardini, Helmuth Plessner, Albert Camus, Maurice Merleau-Ponty, Eugène Minkowski, Georges Gusdorf, and Paul Ricoeur.

The young Franciscan priest Herman Leo van Breda traveled to Freiburg in 1938 to study Husserl's work and prepare for his Ph.D. dissertation. Husserl had died in the same year of 1938 after he had become ill from a fall. Herman van Breda found the legacy of thousands of pages written by Husserl in Gabelsberger stenographic script, and he was afraid that all these unpublished materials were in danger of being confiscated and destroyed by the Nazis. Van Breda hurriedly contacted the Belgian prime minister, Paul-Henri Spaak, and the rector of the University of Leuven, and with their approval he smuggled in 1939 Husserl's manuscripts (40,000 pages), his private research library, and even his desk from Husserl's home and from the University of Freiburg to Louvain (Belgium). Subsequently, Herman van Breda established the Husserl Archives at the Higher Institute of Philosophy of the Université catholique de Louvain.

Van Breda became a professor at Leuven and stayed in charge of the Husserl Archives his entire career. As well, van Breda sought and received collaboration from Husserl's former assistants Eugen Fink and Ludwig Landgrebe and assistance from others like Stephen Strasser to start translating and editing the documents which became the basis for the Husserliana, the complete works of Edmund Husserl.

Unfortunately, the Université de Louvain library burned down to ashes on May 17, 1940. But fortuitously van Breda had cautiously decided to move Husserl's documents to the Higher Institute of Philosophy during the prior week of May 7, which amazingly saved the entire Husserlian archive. It is largely due to the efforts of van Breda that the enormous wealth of Husserl's work is still in existence today.

It should be noted, however, that the Belgian and Dutch phenomenological scholars played a key role in rescuing and preserving the Husserlian phenomenological archives. Early phenomenologists already formed a movement that later would become known as the Utrecht or Dutch School. One of the first to apply phenomenological method in the Netherlands was the philosopher and linguist Hendrick J. Pos (1898–1955). He invited Husserl in 1928 to give the so-called *Amsterdamer Vorträge* (Amsterdam Lectures) on phenomenological psychology. But it was not until after World War II that phenomenology became more deeply established in Dutch and Belgian philosophy. The primary sway of influence now came from the south, from France. Heidegger's influence was important, but it was especially the French existentialists such as Jean-Paul Sartre, Simone de Beauvoir, Albert Camus, Gabriel Marcel, Emmanuel Levinas, and in particular Maurice Merleau-Ponty who dominated the philosophical scene in the Netherlands and Belgium (for a more detailed account see Levering and van Manen, 2002).

It is not accidental that Sartre's *L'Existentialisme est un Humanisme* (1946) is echoed in the title of William A. Luypen's 1959/1960 text *Phenomenology and Humanism*, subtitled *A Primer in Existential Phenomenology*. Luypen's book became a bestseller and was being translated into many languages and reprinted numerous times. It departs from the "primitive fact" of existential phenomenology by emphasizing Husserl's notion of the lifeworld and his credo "*Zu den Sachen selbst,*" interpreted as "back to original experience," as well as the primacy of intentionality and the nature of phenomenological knowledge. The purpose of Luypen's point of departure was to work through a phenomenology of freedom and intersubjectivity by thematizing lifeworld phenomena such as the experience of ethics, liberation, work, hatred, indifference, love, and justice. Luypen did not merely want to translate but also to reinterpret and rethink philosophically the phenomenological influence.

An early sign of the Dutch clinical interest in phenomenology was the publication *Persoon en Wereld* (Person and World) (1953) edited by the psychiatrist van den Berg and the psychologist Linschoten. It contained articles such as "The Secret Place in the Life of the Child" (Langeveld), "The Conversation" (van den Berg), "Driving a Car" (van Lennep), "The Hotel Room" (van Lennep), "Face and Character" (Kouwer), and "Aspects of Sexual Incarnation" (Linschoten). In the Preface to *Persoon en Wereld* (1953), van den Berg presents the program of existential or phenomenological psychology as a new "psychology" ("psychology" was also the term for general phenomenological studies of human phenomena). He explains how this psychology refuses both introspection and extraspection. The refusal of introspective psychology means the refusal to study the other by studying oneself. The refusal of extraspection was the refusal to adopt the objectifying attitude of naturalistic scientific psychology. Instead, these phenomenological scholars were interested in the meaning of immediate experience and exploring the relation of the human being to his or her world.

The various figures that are commonly considered to belong to the Utrecht Circle did not really form a close-knit group. They did not even refer to themselves as the Utrecht School. And some were associated with different universities. The first mention of the Utrecht School is probably on the back cover of *Persoon en Wereld* (1953) by van den Berg and Linschoten, which states, "one could say that in the fifties at Utrecht University a phenomenological school had emerged under the leadership of F.J.J. Buytendijk." Buytendijk has written major phenomenological texts on physiology (1974), medical topics such as obsessive compulsive behavior (1970a), and other phenomenological texts (1962, 1970b). So, historically, this development came to be known as "the Utrecht School" or "the Dutch School" of phenomenology. And in hindsight, this Utrecht School of phenomenology may be considered an original Dutch contribution to the international formation of a phenomenology of practice in the professions.

In *Person and World*, the editors, van den Berg and Linschoten announce programmatically that the phenomenologist resolves to stay as close as possible to the ordinary events of everyday life. Indeed, Langeveld spoke of the "home, street, and kitchen approach" in practicing phenomenology to emphasize this quotidian interest in ordinary life topics, even as these topics often were born in the life-world contexts of clinical professional practices. The interest in the ordinary and the everyday was simultaneously expressed in the work of the philosopher Henri Lefebvre, who was said to have "discovered" the "quotidian" at about the same time (Ross, 1997, p. 19).

A short digression on the background of the quotidian in art may be instructive for understanding the cultural-historical context of the Dutch school of phenomenology. In her book *The Art of Describing: Dutch Art in the Seventeenth Century*, Svetlana Alpers (1983) shows, in passing, that the interest in the quotidian has deep roots in the culture of the lowlands in the seventeenth century. She discusses the difference between Italian art and Dutch art of the seventeenth century. Italian painting had traditionally set the standards for composition and interpretive themes in terms of which art in more northern countries was judged. And many northern artists made the compulsory pilgrimage to Italy and from thereon painted local subjects against Italian landscapes. The great themes in Italian art were often taken from biblical and Greek mythology sources. Alpers points out that to understand the grand Italian Renaissance paintings presumed an interpretive knowledge of these spiritual sources as they were symbolically composed. But in the northern countries, some painters became differently motivated. Pieter Bruegel the Elder is well known for painting scenes such as the "Harvest" and "Children's Games" that can now be studied as a sociology of ordinary lives of peasant villagers and children's play. Jan Steen, Hendrick Avercamp, Gabriel Metsu, Johannes Vermeer, and Gerard Terborch began painting ordinary life scenes in a manner that was utterly unique to art at that time.

So, compared to Italian art, seventeenth-century Dutch and Flemish art was oriented to the ordinary, to uniqueness, and to singularity. Even in Dutch portraits it is striking how artists brought out the individuality and uniqueness of the person portrayed. Alpers argues that Dutch art was (and still is) connected to "a desire to preserve the identity of each person and each thing in the world" (1983, p. 78). These painters begin to explore everyday life scenes rather than idealized, spiritual scenes, and they attend to these scenes descriptively rather than symbolically—depicting them in an experiential, concrete, and down-to-earth manner. The artists are attentive to ordinary objects and subjects not normally attended to. For example, painters like Gabriel Metsu, Gerard Terborch, and Johannes Vermeer have painted epistolary scenes of letters-written and letters-read by lovers. In one instance, Metsu creates two paintings hanging side by side of lovers writing and reading love letters. The man and woman are separated by the frames of their respective depictions, reminding us that love letters are necessitated by physical separation. This way of using paired paintings to create the tension of absence had not been done by anyone else at the time. Because there is a gap in time between writing the letter and receiving the letter, the present time for the writer of the letter is the past time for the addressee. When the writer is writing, he or she is usually writing to the moment, speaking to the addressee as if he or she were present. Thus, it is uncanny how in the quotidian interest of the seventeenth-century painters the phenomenological studies of the Utrecht School find early precedents in the artistic tradition of the cultural past. Furthermore, we find that the phenomenology of ordinary life of the Dutch school turned to expressive artistic (literary, poetic, and visual) media to enhance the quotidian quality of their phenomenological writings.

In the Postscript to the book *Persoon en Wereld* (1953a), Linschoten explains why phenomenological psychology was interested in artistic sources and why a sharp distinction must be made between poetics and science. Linschoten argues that vivid description has the function of bringing the things of our lifeworld into nearness. Literary material can be used as a resource. But according to Linschoten, phenomenology starts where the novel or poem stops. Phenomenological portrayal is an explication of meaning that proceeds in a hermeneutic circle. Novels, poems, cinematography, and the arts may bring us back to the prepredicative spheres of lived experience, but phenomenology wants to capture this prepredicative sphere in predicative or textual forms.

In the introductory chapter to *Phenomenological Psychology: The Dutch School*, which contains several articles from *Persoon and Wereld*, Kockelmans (1987) also observes how the phenomenologists of the Utrecht School frequently make use of poetry and literature. He cites three reasons: (1) Many "great poets and novelists have seen something very important and have spoken of it in a remarkably adequate way" that is useful for phenomenological explication; (2) phenomenologists may use literary sources "to illustrate a point on which the phenomenologists wishes to focus attention"; and (3) most importantly perhaps, "poetic language . . . is able to refer beyond the realm of what can be said 'clearly and distinctly'" (Kockelmans, 1987, pp. viii, ix). Kockelmans adds that it is important to note that no author he includes in his collection from the Dutch School has used literary work as a substitute for the work that the author has tried to accomplish. Poems and novels do not prove anything, says Kockelmans, but "both can be enormously helpful in bringing certain phenomena closer to us and . . . helping us to understand ourselves and the world in which we live" (1987, p. ix).

So, the Dutch Circle consisted of an assortment of phenomenologically oriented academics in professional fields such as psychology, education, pedagogy, pediatrics, law, psychiatry, and general medicine. They formed a loose association of like-minded academic and professional practitioners (see Levering and van Manen, 2002). What made their work unique is that (1) these individuals approached phenomenology not from a purely philosophical but from a practical professional interest; (2) they rarely thought about or bothered to develop methodological explications of their phenomenological research practices; (3) in addition to philosophical and phenomenological sources, they used a variety of literary and artistic ingredients in their phenomenological studies; (4) their practical phenomenological writings demonstrate a vivid narrative quality that appealed to the professional readership but that was not self-consciously discussed (though occasionally criticized by some commentators).

On the whole, the various scholars of the Universities of Utrecht Leiden, Amsterdam, and Groningen (and some other universities in Belgium and Germany) seemed especially interested in *doing* phenomenology in service of their professional disciplines or more generally for the purpose of understanding the practices of everyday life. What they did do—each in their unique way—was to produce often compellingly insightful portrayals of concrete human phenomena or concerns. This quotidian interest is evident in phenomenological writings on down-to-earth, and yet professionally relevant topics such as "falling asleep and suffering from insomnia" (Linschoten), "the phenomenology of child play" (Vermeer), "suffering from obsessive compulsions" (Buytendijk), "the phenomenology of paediatric diagnosis" (Beets), "the pedagogical atmosphere" (Bollnow), and so on.

To reiterate, the name "The Utrecht (Dutch) School" became the informal labels by which the work of these phenomenologists became known. But during the mid-sixties there was already a falling out among some of the Utrecht School colleagues, and several main figures had reached retirement. Linschoten wrote a book entitled *Idolen van de Psycholoog* (Idols of the Psychologist), a title that hints at Bacon's *Organon*. In this book Linschoten is seemingly critical of the phenomenological psychology of his mentors and colleagues such as Frederik Buytendijk and Benjamin Kouwer. A positivistic line from his book goes like this: "All sciences measure. Psychology follows the same route when it submits experimental subjects to critical experiments in determining measures and other properties" (1964, p. 67).

Some saw Linschoten's publication as driving the nails in the coffin of the demise of the Utrecht human science experiment with a practical phenomenology. Others were convinced that Linschoten never meant to divorce himself from phenomenology, but that he recognized that psychology could and should be pursued in both an experimental (quantitative) as well as a phenomenological (qualitative) manner—even though these basic approaches may not be commensurable (see van Hezewijk and Stam, 2008). Unfortunately, Linschoten died in the same year that *Idolen van de Psycholoog* was published, and those who had an interest in interpreting his book as a critique of the waning reputation of the Utrecht movement in the early seventies had the ammunition to push social science policies in directions that favored academics who were engaged with more empirical analytic and quantitative research agendas, modeled on the way that quantitative research was done in the United States.

Phenomenology of Physiology: Frederik J. Buytendijk

Frederik J. Buytendijk (1887–1974) completed his medical studies in 1909 and was promoted in 1918 on a dissertation entitled *Proeven over Gewoontevorming in Dieren* (Experiments of Habit Formation in Animals). In 1921, he was named Chair in Physiology at the University of Amsterdam, and in 1929 he was appointed at Groningen University. In 1946, he received the assignment of Chair in Theoretical Psychology at the University of Utrecht, as well as appointments in Nijmegen and Leuven. After 1957, he remained as emeritus at Utrecht and returned for two more years as chair after the death in 1964 of his student and successor, Johannes Linschoten.

The medical doctor Buytendijk was unique in that his philosophical starting point was the healthy human being rather than the ill person. In his wide range of health science publications, Buytendijk preoccupied himself only rarely with methodological issues. A seeming discussion of methodology is contained in his *De Psychologie van de Roman* (Psychology of the Novel) (1962), in which he argues that one can only really understand what one cares about. He speaks of "the objectivity of love," and in reflectively analyzing novels by Fyodor Dostoevsky, he shows how literature might provide especially relevant insights for psychological understanding. He also provides fascinating insights into the phenomenology of reading fiction. In discussing Dostoevsky's *The Brothers Karamazov*, he likens the narrating voice of the text to that of the lover or the mother. In the presence of such pure love, there is the experience of solid ground, of deep trust that pervades the words as well as the silence about the words. "We must *believe* in the novel," says Buytendijk, "more than a child in a fairytale and only thus do we, as readers, enter a new world as virtual reality and discover a life and meaningful relationship of an order different than the one given to us in our own existence" (1962, p. 37).

In his chapter "Husserl's Phenomenology and Its Significance for Contemporary Psychology" (in Kockelmans, 1987) Buytendijk shows how phenomenological method can be applied to those modes of existence that belong to the praxis of the lifeworld. This text can be seen as a foundation for the work of the Utrecht phenomenology movement, though it is rarely quoted.

Buytendijk's phenomenological program required that knowledge of human existence be gathered by observations of everyday life situations and events. He argued that the obvious features of a lifeworld that we interpret linguistically must become questionable and enigmatic. The book *Persoon en Wereld* (Person and World) (1953) is a collection of now classic phenomenological lifeworld studies. In this programmatic publication, the editors van den Berg and Linschoten use the following epigram by Buytendijk:

> We want to understand human beings from the meaningful ground structures of that totality of situations, events, and cultural values to which we are oriented and about which we have consciousness, and to which all our actions, thoughts, and feelings are related—this is the world in which we exist as persons, where we encounter each other in the course of our personal histories that we shape through the meanings that we construct and assign to everything. Human beings are not "entities" with properties, but initiatives of relations to a world that they choose and by which they are chosen. (Buytendijk in van den Berg and Linschoten, 1953, title page)

According to Buytendijk, to understand human existence, one does not start from the simple or from the bottom but from the complex and from the top. Similarly, animal psychology is best understood from the higher orders down. That approach is characteristic of all his work, from his *Psychology of Animals* to *Prolegomena of an Anthropological Physiology* (1965). For example, in the latter book, he employs considerations about the idea of an anthropological physiology and aspects of human embodiment and psycho-physical problems to introduce a comprehensive study of exemplary modes of human existence and physiological regulatory systems. He describes in detail modes of being such as being awake and asleep, being tired, being hungry, and being emotional, as well as regulatory aspects such as posture, respiration, and circulation.

In addition to his lengthy studies in physiology, Buytendijk wrote many smaller studies on topics such as innerliness and obsessive compulsiveness. For example, in his text "The first smile of the child," he uses physiology and phenomenology to explore this pedagogical human phenomenon:

> Phenomenology discovers that there exists a secret alliance between animated corporeality and spiritual existence. This alliance is uniquely present in every function and observable expression, but nowhere is it so evident as where animated movement becomes the expression of what is most human in human beings: the joy of being in the world. (1988, p. 15)

He points out that we should not assume that the smile of the child can be compared with the smile of an adult. As well, the smile possesses a different phenomenological significance than laughter.

> In searching for an adequate explication of the first smile of the infant there are two reasons to be extra careful. First, it is quite possible that during the first few months after birth the human impulse in the infant still slumbers in a latent state. At the time when the first smile appears, the child may still function in a state, which may not be animalistic but which is, nevertheless, a physiologically closed existence—an existence as yet without an inner life. If this were the case then we could not really compare the crying and smiling of the infant with our adult expressions. (1988, p. 15)

Buytendijk cautiously and tentatively explores various kinds of smiling and mimic responses, as well as how smiles are often enigmatic and not so easily recognizable in their expressiveness. Still, the smile seems to externalize a sunny, silent surrender by a broadening of the face, by the expression of the eyes, and by the closed lips, everything that the encounter contains as possibility.

He describes the smile in the friendly encounter as something that opens a space between people. The smile of the friendly encounter wells up, as it were, from an atmosphere of quiet well-being. This inner sense of well-being increases as a warmth that irradiates us as a flood inundating our being. Finally, he points to the significance of the smile in the human becoming of the infant:

> The smile is the expression of an emerging quality of humanness in the first hesitant, sympathetic encounter, and thus it is an answer in which a sense of self-being is being constituted. But it is also the beginning growth of an awareness of being shy with oneself, now that this small child enters as a vital self the threshold of the tender unity with the other: This happens when the child is being called by the mother who is the matrix of pure love.

The child reveals his or her human nature through smiling—the child who movingly moves while still caught in the involuntary strictures of the organism, but then overcomes it in the smile; the child who is caught in the stream of unselfconsciousness, but then overcomes it by the ontic participation in the awakening awareness of a felt security. Something awakens in the child from a slumber, like a bird wakens in the morning, welling up from his or her deep innerliness and radiating as a recollection of this origin and as a sign of a certain destiny. (1988, p. 23)

Buytendijk published his pedagogical ideas in *Erziehung zur Demut: Betrachtungen über einige pädagogische Ideen* (Educating toward Humility: Some Reflections on Pedagogical Ideas). During the war, he wrote his study *Pain* (1973), which still offers a relevant contemporary critique of the search for a life without suffering.

Nowadays people regard pain merely as an unpleasant fact that, like every other evil, one must try to get rid of. To accomplish this, people generally assume that there is no need for any reflection about the phenomenon of pain itself.... We tend to be irritated by things that older generations simply accepted with equanimity. Modern individuals are irritated by old age, long illness, and even by death; above all they are annoyed by pain. Pain simply should not occur. Modern society demands that all possible means be used to combat and prevent pain, everywhere and for everybody. Advances in diagnosis and therapy are expected to produce more and more such pain-killing methods.... The consequence is an excessive state of *algophobia* (fear of pain) that is itself an evil and places a seal of apprehensiveness on the whole of human life . . . . Medicine, the competent authority for discovering remedies, has been largely successful in reducing pain ... [but has not] had the hoped-for effect of ridding us of the fear of pain. (Buytendijk, 1973, p. 15)

The invention of opioids, the many decades of near indiscriminate use of prescription medication of opioids, the millions of cases of recreational use of opioids, and the huge addiction crises and dependency on opioids attests to the mindless approach to pain.

While pain as suffering carries mostly negative connotations in today's world, Buytendijk points out that pain forces us to reflect and to give it a place and meaning in our lives.

Phenomenology of Pedagogy: Martinus J. Langeveld

Martinus J. Langeveld (1905–1989) was born in Haarlem, the Netherlands. He studied at the University of Amsterdam and received his Ph.D. on a dissertation entitled, *Language and Thinking*. He was a teacher in Dutch language at the Lyceum from 1931 to 1938; next, he was appointed as professor of pedagogy at the University of Utrecht. As part of his academic work, he founded the Institute for Clinical Pedagogy, where he practiced clinical pedagogy, helping children with learning and psychological problems, as well as their parents.

The pathos that drove the work of the proponents of the Utrecht School was a preoccupation with the ordinary—intriguingly, the enigma of the quotidian. For example, in his text "The Secret Place in the Life of the Child," Langeveld gives the reader a resonating understanding of the felt meaning of that special place that young children at times seem to seek out. The "secret place" is the place where the child withdraws from the presence of others. Langeveld sensitively describes what it is like for a child to quietly sit in this place to which the adult does not pay attention. This special space experience does not involve the child in activities such as hide and seek, spying on others, doing mischief, or playing with toys. Rather, what we see is that the child just sits there, while perhaps gazing dreamingly into the distance. What is going on here? Langeveld describes this space experience as a place of growth.

The child may find such space experience under a table, behind a heavy curtain, inside a discarded box, or wherever there is a corner where he or she can withdraw. This is where the child may come to "self-understanding," as it were. As a clinical child-psychologist and pedagogue, Langeveld's intention is to show the formative pedagogical value of the experience of the secret place for the growing child. He describes it as normally an unthreatening place for the young child to withdraw. Langeveld says things like: "the actual experience of the secret place is always grounded in a mood of tranquillity, peacefulness: It is a place where we can feel sheltered, safe, and close to that with which we are intimate and deeply familiar" (1983a, p. 13). He portrays the various modalities in terms of which the secret place may be experienced. Of course, sometimes children may experience certain spaces such as the dark cellar, the spooky attic, the mysterious closet as uncomfortable, as looming danger:

> The phenomenological analysis of the secret place of the child shows us that the distinctions between the outer and inner world melt into a single, unique, personal world. Space, emptiness, and also darkness reside in the same realm where the soul dwells. They unfold in this realm and give form and sense to it by bringing this domain to life. But sometimes this space around us looks at us with hollow eyes of disappointment; here we experience the dialogue with nothingness; we are sucked into the spell of emptiness, and we experience the loss of a sense of self. This is also where we experience fear and anxiety. The mysterious stillness of the cellar, the enigmatic body of the closed door, the deep blackness of the cave, the stairway, and the spying window which is placed too high to look through, all these lead to the experience of anxiety. They may seem to guard or cover an entry-way or passage. The endless stairway, the curtains which move by themselves, the door which is suspiciously ajar, or the door which slowly opens, the strange silhouette at the windows are all symbols of fear. In them we discover the humanness of our fears. (1983a, p. 16)

But during the fourth and fifth year of life the "I" gradually begins to assert itself against the world, the anxieties disappear in degrees. These are the beginnings of the initial developments of a unique human personality in which the first opposition between world and "I" becomes conscious and in which the world is experienced as "other," says Langeveld. Now the secret space becomes invitational:

The indeterminate empty space speaks to us, as it were. In a sense, it makes itself available to us. It offers itself, in that it opens itself. It looks at us in spite of the fact and because of the fact that it is empty. This call and this offering of availability are an appeal to the abilities of the child to make the impersonal space into his very own, very special place. And the secrecy of this place is first of all experienced as the secrecy of "my-own-ness." Thus, in this void, in this availability, the child encounters the "world." Such an encounter the child may have experienced before in different situations. But this time he or she encounters the world in a more addressable form—everything that can occur in this openness and in this availability, the child must actively fashion or at least actively allow as a possibility. (1983a, p. 17)

In spite of quoting these sentences from Langeveld, it is quite inadequate to summarize or paraphrase Langeveld's text, since it is precisely the quality of the entire text that leads one to recognize reflectively what the experience may be like for a child. In "The Secret Place in the Life of the Child" we can also observe how Langeveld locates the normative in the phenomenological account of the experience of the secret place. He shows not only what the experience is like, but also how it is a pedagogically appropriate experience for the child:

In the secret place the child can find solitude. This is also a good pedagogical reason to permit the child his secret place . . . something positive grows out of the secret place as well, something which springs from the inner spiritual life of the child. That is why the child may actively long for the secret place.

During all the stages leading to adulthood, the secret place remains an asylum in which the personality can mature; this self-creating process of this standing apart from others, this experiment, this growing self-awareness, this creative peace and absolute intimacy demand it—for they are only possible in aloneness. (1983a, p. 17)

Langeveld argues that it is inevitable to see how the normative is intimately linked to our understanding of children's experiences, since we are always confronted with real-life situations wherein we must act: we must always do what is appropriate in our interactions with children. We could say that a phenomenology of practice sponsors a pedagogical sensitivity that expresses itself in thoughtfulness and tactfulness on the part of the adult (van Manen, 1991, 2012).

The best way to explore the essential meaning of a certain phenomenon, such as the secret place, is by showing what it is not. Langeveld presents counter-examples of the secret place and space experiences such as the child's experience of a lookout from a tree, a tower, or a window. From a lookout, the child experiences the tension between distance and nearness. Langeveld shows how the lookout experience differs from the eidos of the secret place experience. With additional examples of counter-experiences, he shows that the secret place does not involve the child in activities such as hide and seek, spying on others, doing mischief, going into forbidden places, or even simply playing with toys. In other words, by drawing us near the phenomenon of the secret place and by imaginatively varying the example and comparing the secret place with the lookout place, the spying place, the hideout, etc., we discover, in part, the unique meaning of the secret place. Rather than see the child involved in spying or hiding activities, what we see is that the child may just "be" in that special place, while perhaps gazing dreamingly into the distance (Langeveld, 1983a, 1983b).

Some may feel uncomfortable with the way in which phenomenologists like Langeveld seem to reach deeply into the stylistic realms of the humanities. Often the texts by proponents of the Utrecht School are not only insightful but also evocative. The texts not only analyze and probe the lived experience, they "speak" to us and they may stir our pedagogical, psychological, or professional sensibilities.

Phenomenology of Psychiatry: Jan Hendrik van den Berg

Jan Hendrik van den Berg (1914–2012) attended medical school and specialized in psychiatry. He completed his doctoral work under Henricus Rümke with a dissertation on phenomenological existential schizophrenic psychosis entitled *De Betekenis van de Phaenomenologische of Existentiële Antropologie in de Psychiatrie* (The Significance of Phenomenological or Existential Anthropology in Psychiatry). Van den Berg lived in France and Switzerland, where he studied the phenomenology of Heidegger, Sartre, and Merleau-Ponty. He received a lectorate in psychopathology in 1948 at the University of Utrecht and later at Amsterdam University. In 1954, he was appointed Chair of Phenomenological Methods and Conflict Psychology at the University of Leiden. Van den Berg's writings made an important contribution to the reputation of the Utrecht School. His publications have been widely translated into various languages. His book *Het Ziekbed* (1952) was published in English as *The Psychology of the Sickbed* (1966). *The Phenomenological Approach to Psychiatry* (1955) was reissued as *A Different Existence* (1974), which still is an excellent introduction to the phenomenological approach. In addition to numerous phenomenological studies in psychology and psychiatry, he also wrote several lucid general lifeworld studies, such as *Zien: Verstaan en Verklaring in de Visuele Waarneming* (Seeing: Understanding and Interpretation in Visual Perception) (1972).

Van den Berg became especially known for the development and application of a phenomenological historical approach that he termed the *metabletical method*. "Metabletica" is a word derived from the Greek meaning "change." His book *Metabletica: Principles of a Historical Psychology* (published in English in 1961 as *The Changing Nature of Man*) describes the changing historical relation between adults and children. It appeared several years before a similar work by the French historian Phillippe Ariès. Van den Berg describes the process of the infantilization of adulthood and the appearance of puberty as a historical and cultural phenomenon. The special feature of the metabletical method is that it approaches its object of study not diachronically, as development through time, but synchronically, from within a meaningful constitution of relations among different events during the same shared sociohistorical period. For example, in *Divided Existence* (1974), van den Berg provides a concrete portrayal and a surprisingly early postmodern interpretation of the development of the human psyche by connecting it with a variety of simultaneous developments in the surrounding culture, showing how the sense of self-identity is increasingly fragmented, divided, and impacted by externals. If we want to understand someone's world we should look, not inside the person, but to his or her world. In fact, this is also the method of van den Berg's phenomenology: to understand a phenomenon like love or grief, you need to see what the lover's or grieving person's world looks like. "The phenomenologist should not direct his glance "inwardly" but "outwardly." Expressed paradoxically, true introspection is effected by means of the physical sense of sight: "we are seeing ourselves when we observe the world" (van den Berg, 1972, p. 130).

Van den Berg was especially conscious of the historical and cultural embeddedness of phenomenological psychology. In fact, he was far ahead of the later postmodern critique of the dangers of foundationalism, essentialism, and historical and cultural universalism. He argues that the very project of all phenomenology was contextualized by limits of language, culture, time, and place. According to van den Berg, phenomenological psychology does not claim to have found a universally valid approach to human phenomena; rather, it is always self-conscious of its anthropological starting point. Therefore, it is futile to speak of a general phenomenology of perception since people from different cultures "see" differently, and people see and understand their worlds differently from the ways that their close and distant forebears did, just as their own children will perceive the world differently. As an example, van den Berg criticizes such studies as the Kinsey report *Sexual Behavior of the Human Male*. He suggests that while this report might be characteristic of the North American male, it says virtually nothing about, for example, the European male.

Van den Berg begins his discussion about the phenomenology of conversation with an anecdote (as he often does in his writings) about the evening visit of Tennyson with his friend Carlyle. The story goes that the two friends were sharing their evening in front of a burning fireplace while mostly steeped in silence, sipping their wine without really engaged in much discussion, occasionally uttering a thought perhaps. Van den Berg says:

> We will start with an anecdote of a remarkable conversation to present a remarkable characteristic of all conversations.
> There is a story about Tennyson visiting Carlyle at his home. Both sat the entire evening in silence at the fireplace. When the guest was about to depart Carlyle closed the evening with these words: "We had a grand evening, please do come back very soon." (van den Berg, 1953, p. 137)

Van den Berg points out that these friends apparently hardly spoke together that evening. Yet Tennyson, the poet for whom words constitute the meaning of his poetic existence, felt that he did have a grand togetherness. So, did these two friends really have a conversation in some sense?

Van den Berg is fascinated with this situation, and he wonders if this was not such perfectly shared togetherness that it was actually a conversation without words—words were not necessary. Can one have a conversation without words spoken? In a somewhat Heideggerian fashion, van den Berg helps us wonder: What is really at the heart of a conversation? What is it that makes a conversation a unique and peculiar human experience?

> Nobody would want to defend that these two friends were involved in an animated conversation. Not a word was spoken! And yet, something must have happened during that evening that is closely related to a true conversation. Why would otherwise Carlyle have urged so sincerely for another evening like that?
>
> It seems to me that the remarkable anecdote needs to be interpreted in the following manner. The main condition for any true conversation was optimally fulfilled so that the spoken word became totally unnecessary and could be left out. What was this condition? It would be no mistake to observe that both experienced a certain kind of togetherness. There was a being-together that could have permitted any kind of conversation, but also a being-together that allowed words to go on a silent retreat, and yet that could have accommodated all kinds of conversational language. This togetherness was so special that the spoken word might have disturbed the shared enjoyment of the intimate quiet at the open fire. (van den Berg, 2021, 31)

Common sense seems to say that a conversation consists of talk, words spoken, and no doubt this is superficially true. But van den Berg suggests that words are not the defining feature of a conversational relation. More essentially, it is a certain mode of togetherness, a certain way of sharing a world, of experiencing a shared sphere and each other's company, that makes a conversation what it is. Van den Berg explores the phenomenological features of this conversational space. He suggests that we may all know this kind of togetherness where we feel so well understood that our words are given a true holiday. We can speak or we can be silent because we feel totally comfortable in this shared conversational space.

Note that van den Berg is using the anecdote for letting us grasp the experiential sensibility of a conversational togetherness that would be very difficult to explain in objectifying language. And his reflection on the short anecdote is part of a subsequent phenomenological analysis that consists of the sensitive writing of a text. The analyzing occurs in the writing, and the writing is the analyzing. At a superficial level, we might take it for granted that the essence of a conversation is of course the speaking together. But van den Berg shows that at a deeper level a conversation is indeed an enigmatic phenomenon: a true conversation may not need any words. The Carlyle anecdote functions as an incept that lets us grasp the (ungraspable) meaning of a conversation by going to the very source of its meaning.

Phenomenology of Pedagogical Atmosphere: Otto F. Bollnow

Otto Friedrich Bollnow (1903–1991) gained a doctorate in mathematics and physics under the author and publisher Max Brod (executor of Franz Kafka's literary estate). Bollnow taught at Göttingen, Giessen, Kiel, and Mainz and eventually became a chair in philosophy, pedagogy, and ethics at the University of Tübingen. He authored some 40 books and hundreds of articles on philosophy of life, pedagogy, adult education, philosophical anthropology, and gerontagogy, mostly from a hermeneutic phenomenological perspective. An effective introduction to Bollnow's thinking and writing might be citing a range of topics from the various tables of contents of his books. They show that his phenomenological approach was very much dedicated to reflecting on the meaningfulness of concrete, professionally critical, and existentially relevant topics of everyday living. His texts consist of making fine and subtle existential distinctions of the meaning of the practice of pedagogy and the broad range of topics of a cultural hermeneutics. He wrote studies on Dilthey and Heidegger. However, it is noteworthy that Heidegger accused Bollnow of misinterpretation of *Being and Time* (2014, pp. 216, 217).

One of Bollnow's best-known hermeneutic phenomenological texts is "The Pedagogical Atmosphere" (1988). While the term "pedagogical relation" is a well-known and well-discussed concept, especially in the German theoretical educational literature, interestingly the term has become taken for granted and rather unclear. Bollnow wonders what it really means to speak of a relation. He points out that he prefers to substitute the concept of pedagogical relation with the notion of pedagogical atmosphere. "I take the term pedagogical atmosphere to mean all those fundamental emotional conditions and sentient human qualities that exist between the educator and the child and which form the basis for every pedagogical relationship" (1988, p. 5). Bollnow is concerned that his study is not confused with the self-help child psychology literature which spells out what one should and should not do as a good parent. Rather he reaches for the deeper and more meaningful preconditions of pedagogy:

What we are most concerned with here is examining and describing those affective conditions and qualities which are necessary for the raising or educating of children to be possible or successful. And we mean this to be taken in a most fundamental sense, for we do not merely want to describe those prerequisites which foster and enhance childrearing, or alternatively those conditions which create difficulties and which we can do without; rather, we mean to describe the conditions which must be supposed to exist before there can even be something like childrearing for education to be possible. (1988, p. 5)

Bollnow suggests that from the perspective of the child, the foremost precondition for a pedagogical atmosphere is the existence of a sheltering environment of the home, the family, and the community from which the supportive feelings of security and safety can radiate (1988. p. 12). Bollnow provides phenomenologically descriptive analyses of the meaning of trust and confidence as qualitative conditions in the pedagogical atmosphere between the adult and the child. He suggests that the experiential distinction between trust and confidence is not sharp, though one experiences a certain difference. We may feel confident that a coach has the skill and ability to teach our child the necessary skills of a certain athletic practice, but we may not feel that we should completely trust this person.

Trust seems to be a more complex notion than confidence. And confidence acts as the less complicated preform of real trust. Confidence refers to a certain ability and performative skill on the part of the person in whom we have (or like to have) confidence. "Confidence always relates to a distinct ability. As a rule it is meant in a positive sense. It means one is convinced that someone has the ability to perform well this or that task" (1988, p. 38).

Bollnow seems to be resorting to a language analysis of the core meanings of confidence and trust. Still, if a person is aware of our confidence and admiration in an outstanding skill then this may encourage and even improve this person's special ability. But confidence can also remain a one-sided relation. I may have confidence in someone's ability to do a certain task, but the person may not be concerned about my confidence. For example, if a carpenter is highly skilled in building a cabinet then my feeling of admiration and confidence in the carpenter's skill may not really matter to the carpenter who is confident in his or her own ability and knows that he or she is highly competent.

It is true, however, that my confidence in a carpenter who is actually aware of my admiration may be experienced as encouraging or inspiring. Even though in the case of an excellent artisan that is not really necessary. Competence and self-confidence are independent from a person's reaction to our confidence. Another example is the medical surgeon who will perform an operation on my body or on the body of my child. I would feel that it is very important that I can have confidence that the surgeon can competently and expertly perform the operation, even if there are reasons that I may not entirely trust the honesty of this medical professional when I am engaged in a financial transaction about the surgery. Ultimately, the surgeon–patient confidence relation is one-sided.

In contrast, trust is not a one-sided but a reciprocal relationship. If I entrust my child to a certain teacher then I want to be sure that this person is indeed worthy of this trust. It is important to me as a parent that the teacher can be trusted because trust is a moral affair. Of course, I would like to have confidence that the teacher of my child is instructionally competent and expert in his or her curricular domain of knowledge, values, and skills. But, ultimately, it is less important that I can have confidence in the teacher's expertise than that the teacher can be trusted to be good and right in his or her interactions and intentions with my child's educational development. This is why the notion of trust in the pedagogical atmosphere has a two-sided relevance.

What was initially experienced in the pedagogical atmosphere as the unlimited trust which the child feels toward one special person (usually a mother, father, family member, or a teacher) and which later is gradually replaced by a less absolute sense of trust in the sphere of the lifeworld. In other words, the original trust invested in a single person has now become a more generalized sense of trust in the world. Children who grow up while visited by frequent anxiety may never develop a sense of trust in life. Conversely, Bollnow points out that doting love of a parent or a relative for a child is not to be mistaken for pedagogical trust. The trust of doting love does not offer educational benefit and can even be damaging to the child.

True pedagogic trust is neither blind nor stupid. Some of the qualities that matter in the pedagogical atmosphere are carefully investigated and described by

Bollnow: patience, hope, serenity, believing in the child, and humor as the ability to lighten things that weigh too heavily on a child.

For example, children may value the special attention and a supportive presence in the company of a teacher who happens to be blessed with a quality that Bollnow refers to as serenity. This is the teacher who inspires the child because the serene way of standing in life is admired by the child and worthy of imitation. The child wants to "be" like the exemplary teacher or mentor.

> Serenity must constantly renew itself against the temptations which make life in schools difficult and against the sober seriousness to which teachers often feel obliged, and especially against the moroseness and joyless sullen tone which can easily take over in classrooms, thus suffocating any kind of happy willingness to learn. (1988, p. 57)

The phenomenology of teacher qualities such as serenity that can positively establish, shape, and create a trusting and secure pedagogical atmosphere are rarely mentioned in contemporary literature on teaching and educational practices. These are qualities and virtues that seem to have lost their relevance in the more behavioristic, consumer oriented, and objectifying practices of modern schooling.

Similarly, patience is a virtue or quality of the pedagogical atmosphere that is rarely focused on. Bollnow brackets the notion of patience by distinguishing pedagogical patience from producing oriented patience that is concerned with making. Producing patience has to be controlled and properly paced to secure the value of the product. A lack of producing patience by educators is often manifested as haste that diminishes the value of the work due to mistakes and other mishaps and thus the success of the student. Second, Bollnow brackets the patience required of the farmer, grower, or gardener. The processes and rates of growth in plants are often almost invisible. This is a patience that cannot be hastened or hurried but must attend to the organic processes and limits of growth.

True pedagogical patience differs from producing patience and growing patience because it must be sensitive to the child's unique development and abilities. And yet it is often much more difficult for the educator to patiently wait until a child is ready for learning certain knowledge and skills. Much depends on the willingness and attitude of the child and the ability of the educator to show patience and yet motivate positively the learning process. Pedagogical patience is as far from premature haste as it is from inattentively missing the right moment, when the child's development goes through certain phases and when the educator's intervention may be required.

Phenomenology of Pediatrics: Nicolaas Beets

Nicolaas Beets was a pediatrician who produced several phenomenological studies about the Dutch child in the fifties. In a 1952 text that examines the relation between medical and pedagogical thought, Beets provides a discussion about the question of why physicians and psychologists, who play a professional pedagogical part in the lives of children, should refrain from turning immediately or primarily to diagnostic theories and psychological models in trying to understand children and in deciding how to deal with difficulties and problems experienced by these young people and their parents or guardians. Beets aims to make clear what is characteristic about phenomenological pedagogy as a mode of thinking that differs from clinical psychological and medical science ways of thinking. Thus, he performs a phenomenological analysis of the pedagogical pediatric diagnosis as compared with the medical diagnosis.

When Nicolaas Beets compares the approach of the medical practitioner with the pedagogical approach, he provides extensive examples from his own pediatric practice. The children he describes had frequently been referred to him because they had experienced traumas, abuse, or they seemed to display disturbed behavior at home or at school. In dealing with these young people, Beets found that often a diagnostic (medical or psychotherapeutic) approach was quite inadequate for understanding and helping these children. In fact, it is the diagnostic way of thinking that he considered in conflict with the pedagogical attitude and with pedagogical work with young people. So, in order to create clarity about the difference between medical-therapeutic thinking and pedagogical thinking, he examines the two approaches, by setting them side by side, in their "pure" form.

Beets shows that medical diagnostic thinking first of all searches for symptomatic clues and causal factors. One looks for developmental patterns, for difficulties surrounding the birth, psychological, physical, and genetic abnormalities in parents, grandparents, and other close family members. He points out that psychological clinical thought operates in a similar manner: one does psychological analyses, administers diagnostic instruments, and applies intelligence tests, personality inventories, and other measuring devices. One searches for disease patterns *by looking back* into personal and family histories.

Thus, the medical mode of thinking leads to a certain idea of the meaning of therapy: to locate the pathology and then to "cut out" the intrusion that has been festering there for days, weeks, or even years. Just as one frees someone surgically from his or her diseased appendix, so one searches for and removes the "problem" by "cutting it out" of people's lives. Therapy means to liberate someone from a piece of the past, a pathology that hinders present unencumbered "normal" living. Implicit in the diagnostic idea of pathology is the (almost moral) idea of the (statistical) average or normal pattern. Developmental and stage models of psychological counseling also tend to work on this basic assumption. For example, grief counseling is aimed at assisting the client to engage in grief work (working through stages of grief) in order to rid oneself eventually of the source of pain and remove the obstacle to make possible more normal activities and feelings.

The main effort of diagnostic thinking is aimed at forming an interpretive picture, an explanatory representation of the child, by looking back, says Beets. He provides several concrete examples of young children whom he has encountered and who have been under medical-psychological treatment. Often, says Beets, when a diagnostic judgment is made, medication is prescribed and expert advice is given to the parent, the teacher, the school principal, or school counselor; then the child is sent home and people are left to do whatever they think is best. Beets admits that he paints the picture of a pure diagnostic approach, but in his days (the 1950s) this was not an unusual medical-therapeutic routine in dealing with problem children.

How then does pedagogical thinking differ from medical diagnostic thinking? The difference is this: pedagogical thinking turns itself immediately and directly to the child himself or herself in his or her particular situation at home, at school, and in the way that the child spends his or her time and relates to others in everyday life. The pedagogue wants to meet this concrete child without reducing him or her to a diagnostic picture, a psychological type, a set of factors on a scale, or a theoretical category.

What is pedagogically much more compelling, Beets says, is the way in which any particular child fails to match preconceived theoretical distinctions, how a particular child constantly refuses to fit explanatory formulations and definitions, how this child defies diagnostic judgment, how that child is always different from our assessment.

This constant "defying difference" is what makes the child who he or she is—which is never the same as the diagnostic portrait that the expert constructs. The human being always falls "outside" of the dossier, the diagnosis, the report; instead, the child is "inside" relations with others. For example, there is Hans, a child who has been diagnosed as schizophrenic, among other things. Beets describes how his first encounter with the boy left him worried, how he could not help but see the picture of schizophrenia in the child's strange behavior. But soon, and for a period of regular visits, Beets was able to reach the child, Hans, himself, with all his personal idiosyncrasies and life circumstances. Nicolaas Beets says:

> Hans is who he is in his daily interactions with his parents, friends, teachers, and me. That is first of all who he is. Further—but that is the "marginal sphere" or "background" for me—it is possible that Hans might fit the category of schizophrenia, but my fear with regards to that diagnosis diminishes in my continued interaction and relation with him. (1952/1975, p. 61)

Thus, Beets makes a strong distinction between diagnostic psychotherapy and pedagogical help. He does not deny that therapy and pedagogy can flow into each other. But to the extent that the therapist orients to preconceived interpretive patterns or to causal relations between diagnosis and treatment, the expert remains stuck in a medical way of thinking; and to this extent it is impossible to maintain a genuine pedagogical relation with the child.

Again, Beets does not just argue his case abstractly. He continuously gives examples of the manner that children are treated or dealt with in different settings: pediatrics, psychotherapy, and pedagogy. He shows how, within a medical model (whether as therapist or pediatrician), an adequate treatment can only be started or recommended once a diagnosis has been made—to think in terms of diagnosis and treatment means that therapy logically flows from a diagnosis.

Of course, this usually works excellently in medicine. In contrast, the pedagogical encounter is always personal, particular, concrete, tentative, and more open toward an uncertain future.

Phenomenology of Idolatry: Johannes Linschoten

Johannes Linschoten was born in Utrecht and attended secondary school in Bandung, Indonesia (a Dutch colony at the time). Like others, he fought in World War II. And he spent three years in a Japanese prison camp. He finished his education back in the Netherlands in Bilthoven, in 1946. Linschoten studied psychology in Utrecht beginning in 1946 under the supervision of Frederik Buytendijk and Martinus Langeveld, before being appointed as a professor in 1949. Linschoten's oeuvre is interesting in that he engaged in both experimental and phenomenological research.

Already in the early 1950s, Linschoten published insightful phenomenological studies on concrete phenomena such as *Over de Humor* (On Humor) (1951/2021), and *Over het Inslapen* (On Falling Asleep) (1952/1987). These are excellent and interesting examples of doing phenomenology on quotidian topics. Together with Jan van den Berg, Johannes Linschoten edited a *liber amicorum* in dedication to Buytendijk on his 65th birthday, entitled *Persoon en Wereld* (Person and World) (1953). It was the first collection of phenomenological studies that became known as the work of the Utrecht School. The volume was unusual in that it featured phenomenological studies that were not written by professional philosophers, but by professional clinicians and practitioners in psychology, medicine, law, pedagogy, and related professions. The book, written in Dutch, received many reprints. Linschoten contributed *Aspecten van de Sexuele Incarnatie* (Aspects of the Sexual Incarnation) to the volume. The phenomenological essay explores the body and world as a condition for the phenomenon of sexuality.

In 1954, Linschoten authored a study on William James, *On the Way toward a Phenomenological Psychology: The Psychology of William James.* He discussed William James' writings as a North American approach to phenomenology. He focused on the tension in James' work between a phenomenological appreciation of experience and an explanatory account of experience in physiological terms.

Upon his return to the Netherlands, he was appointed at the University of Utrecht, but his tenure as chair was brief. He died at the age of 38 while working in his laboratory in Utrecht. His last publication, *Idolen van de Psycholoog* (Idols of the Psychologist), appeared posthumously in 1964, the year of his death.

Much has been written and probably overstated that Linschoten "converted" away from phenomenology (see, for example, Terwee, 1990). However, the phenomenologist Langeveld wrote in his "In Memoriam" (1964) that Linschoten did not abandon phenomenology, as both personal conversations and the 1963 essay *The Inevitability of Phenomenology* (published in 1979) seem to make clear. Langeveld remembers Johannes Linschoten (1925–1964) as a highly gifted and talented scholar who was frantically driven in his work. Linschoten was admired by friends and colleagues for his penetrative insights, brilliant studies, and intense dedication to his experimental as well as phenomenological research. But unfortunately, Linschoten's early death made the assessment of the intent of his last work ambiguous and subject to conflicting interpretations.

Phenomenology of Ministering: Anthony (Ton) Beekman

Anthony (Ton) Beekman was born in The Hague in 1926. He studied philosophy and theology among the Franciscans, and pedagogy at the University of Utrecht. In 1972 Beekman completed a dissertation entitled *Dienstbaar Inzicht* (*Ministering Insight*, 1975) under the supervision of Martinus Langeveld. He was appointed to a position in theoretical pedagogy at the University of Utrecht by Langeveld, and he became responsible for the methodological study of phenomenological pedagogy from 1972 to 1986. Langeveld hoped that Beekman's appointment would serve as a counterweight to the increasingly dominant empirical-analytical research models that arrived from North America.

In collaboration with his students Karel Mulderij and Hans Bleeker, Ton Beekman devised a practical method for phenomenological pedagogy (Beekman, et al., 1984) by injecting a reflective phenomenological approach to the lifeworld with participant-observation types of methods based on the work of the ethnographers James Spradley and David McCurdy (1972). Bleeker and Mulderij studied children's experiences of urban living spaces and playgrounds, and physically handicapped children's experiences of their bodies and wheelchairs.

However, Beekman does point out that phenomenology is different from the typical ethnographic approach. Ethnographic studies focus on cultural or subcultural meanings. They aim at taxonomies, inventories of cultural meanings: for instance, how lunch time and the staffroom for teachers at a particular school may have important social meanings for them because these are times of meeting, planning, gossiping, and sharing stories about students. Instead phenomenology is concerned with existential meanings of human phenomena that are not specific to certain groups of people and cultural contexts.

When the main thrust of the phenomenologies of the Utrecht-style scholars lost their impetus in the seventies, Ton Beekman made an effort to rescue phenomenology from the eroding tradition of the so-called Utrecht intellectual movement by making it more accessible to beginning researchers in education, pedagogy, and psychology. His methodological reflections possess an attractive anarchic-creative quality, such as his *Het Wilde Denken* (Wild Thinking) (2001). As well, he made visits to the United States and Canada, where he assisted in initiating phenomenology workshops and human science programs.

PHENOMENOLOGY OF PRACTICE PROJECTS

The phrase "phenomenology of practice" (as presented in this book) was adopted by Max van Manen to describe the development and articulation of meaning-giving methods of phenomenology on the basis of the practical examples that can be discerned in the primary literature of phenomenology.

A phenomenology of practice not only wants to be sensitive to the concerns of professional practices in professional fields, but also to the personal and social practices of everyday living. In this way phenomenology of practice distinguishes itself from the more orthodox and strictly philosophical exegetical phenomenologies that focus more on meta-theoretical and technical philosophical issues. As well, phenomenology of practice is sensitive to the realization that life as we live and experience it is not only rational and logical, and thus in part transparent to reflection—it is also subtle, enigmatic, contradictory, mysterious, inexhaustible, and saturated with existential and transcendent meaning that can only be accessed through poetic, aesthetic, and ethical means and languages.

At the University of Alberta, the program associated with the "phenomenology of practice project" has produced graduate research papers, doctoral dissertations, and books that aim to make contributions to phenomenological professional practices in education, pedagogy, psychology, nursing, medicine, the arts, as well as practices of everyday life. A sample of graduate seminar research papers can be found in *Writing in the Dark: Phenomenological Studies in Interpretive Inquiry* (van Manen, 2001).

Samples of doctoral research studies of a phenomenological orientation engaged at the University of Alberta phenomenology of Practice seminar include the following:

PEDAGOGY: *Wonder and the Agencies of Retreat* by Philo Hove (1999); *Understanding Lifeworlds of Special Needs Children* by Chizuko Fujita-Maeda (1990/**2021**); *Risk and the Playground* by Stephen Smith (1989/**1998**); *Sublimity and the Image: A Phenomenological Study* by Erika Goble (2014/**2020**); *Seeing Disability Pedagogically* by Tone Saevi (2005);

MEDICINE: *Phenomenology of Neonatology* by Michael van Manen (2013/**2019**).

PSYCHOLOGY: *Phenomenology of Adolescent Love* by Wendy Austin (1997/**1999**); *The Experience of Loneliness in Young Children* by Anna Kirova (1996); *Phenomenology of Grief Counseling* by Graeme Clark (1994); *The Language of Home and the Home of Language: A Qualitative Study of Immigrant Experience* by Anne Winning (1991).

HEALTH SCIENCE: *The Phenomenology of Diagnosis of Mental Illness* by Yvonne Hayne (2001); *Living with Illness* by Carol Olson (1986/**1993**); *The Phenomenology of Woman to Mother: The Transformative Experience of Childbirth* by Vangie Bergum (1986/**1989**).

FINE ARTS: *The Phenomenology of Drawing from Observation* by Rose Montgomery-Whicher (1997/**2022**).

EDUCATION: *Teaching Outside the School* by Andrew Foran (2006); *In Search of a Living Literacy* by Patrick Howard (2006); *On the Pedagogy of Examinations in Students in China* by Shuying Li (2005); *A Traveler's Tale: The Experience of Study in a Foreign Language* by Keun Ho Lee (2005); *Asking After Lived Experiences of and with Difficulty in Physical Activity from the Life-Worlds of Children and Young People* by Maureen Connolly (1990); *Ministrative Insight: Educational Administration as Pedagogic Practice* by Rodney Evans (1989/**2013**).

NURSING: *The Lived Experience of Obsessive Compulsive Disorder* by Mary Haase (2003); *Phenomenology of the Nursing Relation* by Brenda Cameron (1998).

TECHNOLOGY: *PowerPoint and the Pedagogy of Digital Media Technology* by Catherine Adams (2008b); *The Pedagogical Significance of the Computer–Student Relation* by Norm Friesen (2003/**2005**); *Technology, Computer Use and the Pedagogy of Writing,* by Stefan Baldursson (1989).

Methods, Research, Writing

CHAPTER ELEVEN

Philosophical Methods: Epoché and Reduction

How can phenomenology gain access to the prereflective experiences as they occur in the taken-for-granted spheres of our everyday lifeworld? Normally we rarely reflect on the living sensibilities of our experiences, since we already experience the meanings immanent in our everyday practices through our bodies, language, habits, things, social interactions, and physical environments. Phenomenology is the method to break through this taken-for-grantedness and get to the raw meaning structures of our experiences. This basic method is called the epoché and reduction. It consists of two opposing moves that simultaneously complement each other. First, the *epoché-reduction* goes out to access the phenomenon and set aside assumptions and bracket beliefs to create openness—this move is called the epoché. Second, and yet simultaneously, the *epoché-reduction* turns back to the phenomenon to reflect on its eidos—this move is called the reduction (Taminiaux, 1991, p. 34). So, the *epoché* is necessary for the *reduction-proper* to be possible.

The epoché should ensure that the phenomenon to be examined can be described exactly as is experienced, or intended. The Greek word *epoché* means bracketing, to set aside. Ancient skeptics used the term to indicate the suspension of belief. Thus, Husserl adopted the term *epoché* to indicate the act by which the taken-for-granted beliefs of the natural attitude are suspended. He used the term *bracketing* as an analogy with mathematics where what is done within the brackets can be kept separate from the operations outside of them. Bracketing means parenthesizing, putting into holds the various assumptions that might stand in the way from opening up access to the originary or the living meaning of a phenomenon. The term *reduction* derives from *re-ducere*, to lead back. The meaning of the word reduction can be misleading since the phenomenological reduction is ironically directed against reductionism (abstracting, codifying, and shortening).

The Basic Method: Phenomenological Reduction

The epoché and the reduction are the great finds of Husserl's phenomenology. Eugen Fink who was Husserl's long-time assistant, said that "The 'phenomenological reduction' alone is the basic method of Husserl's phenomenological philosophy" (1970, p. 72). But the reduction is not easy to explain or describe. From the time that the reduction appears in the publication of *Ideas*, Husserl kept reintroducing it, making further refinements and distinctions. The twin methods of the epoché and the reduction are the way to gain access to the meaning structures of a phenomenon, a lived experience or event. But Husserl distinguished several modes

DOI: 10.4324/9781003228073-14

and forms of the reduction. In *Cartesian Meditations* he describes the epoché and reduction in Cartesian terms as the suspension of belief, and in *The Crisis of the European Sciences* he describes the reduction as transcendental access to the life-world. Also, at different points in his expansive writings, Husserl distinguished various kinds of reduction, such as the psychological reduction, the eidetic reduction, the epistemological reduction, and the transcendental reduction. Part of the difficulty of understanding the Husserlian reduction is that Husserl's writings are difficult, seemingly convoluted and abstracted. When Husserl uses examples to describe the reduction and related methodological moves, they tend to be rather simple perceptual experiences such as seeing a die, a tree, a sheet of paper, or a house. Of course, we would like to know how the reduction applies to more complex human phenomena and events.

So, with a nod to Jan van den Berg (1961), I will venture a fitting example at the hand of a not uncommon experience of the remembrance of childhood and try to show what Husserl means by the reduction:

> It is fall time and I am walking home from my university office. As I turn the corner to walk through the park that takes me to my house, I notice that the autumn leaves have fallen in thick layers on the path. I keep walking while the leaves rustle and crunch under my shoes. And then a strange sensation occurs: it is as if I am back in time, walking among the trees in the forest near my childhood home in the Netherlands. When I lift my eyes from the leaves on the ground to the path, I almost expect to see outlines of the woods that I have not thought about or seen for many decades. As my feet kick up the leaves that crunch under my shoes, I realize that the feel and smell of the rotting leaves suddenly stir a powerful childhood memory. Indeed, this experience of walking through these leaves in this Canadian city has transported me into a vivid memory of the world of my childhood on a different continent. And strangely, I suddenly remember things that I would have been unable to do if I had just tried to recall them without this actual moment of walking through this park. I now remember the curve of the path in the woods where a dense grove of ancient trees had left the ground covered with heavy layers of fallen and decaying leaves. I remember the early childhood friend with whom I used to play in these mysterious woods, how we built a hidden hut and what secret treasures we stashed there . . .

I think what happened is this: the feel of the dried and fallen leaves and the sensory smell of their qualities have triggered a memory. But I could also provide some other possible explanations: perhaps I was in a state of nostalgia that made me remember my childhood, or it is the physiological stimulus of the senses (olfactory and kinesthetic) that triggered a memory response. Psychology might present me with even more authoritative explanations of how this memory was extracted from my brain. But none of these cognitions would help me with a phenomenological understanding.

Phenomenologically, I need to open myself (the epoché) and try to bracket my presumptions, common understandings, and scientific explanations; at the same time, I need to regard the phenomenon that was given in my experience (the reduction) and observe how the remembrance emerged as it were from the leaves under my shoes. Thus, I need to describe how my feet literally kicked the memories up from the layer of leaves on my walk through the field. How strange that memories were held captive in those leaves and how my feet were able to dislodge them merely by treading right through them. What is it about memories that they can be released this way? Of course, I am familiar with the neural network explanations of the wiring of the brain. But even these sophisticated physiological complexities do not really make the meaningfulness of memories transparent. I must suspend my scientific knowledge of how memories work and I apply the epoché by opening myself simply to the experience of that moment. The reduction gives me this insight: a factual or empirical incident of walking through these leaves on this October afternoon has given me a thematic insight into the nature of childhood remembrance. I say, "These leaves released a childhood memory. They brought back a sense of my self-identity as a child. The memories let me experience in the present the way I was in times past."

The inceptual significance of the childhood memory does not just lie in its empirical factuality, it lies in the originary primordialities of its experiential occurrence. In this childhood memory I am transported into a reality that resonates with inarticulated significances: my sense of self as child, the wondrous sensibility of self-identity: the self touching itself as it was, as it is, and as it is becoming. My skin and eyes and ears feeling, sensing, and hearing the brittleness of the leaves under my feet. The past and present intermingle in the sensation of the crumbly leaves under my feet: the awareness that my life and my being are exactly this brittleness. Of course, the phenomenological eidos of that experience of walking through the leaves is not the particular experience of the leaves, because someone else may have a different sensory experience that may evoke certain forgotten childhood memories. *The eidos is the phenomenological insight that we may sometimes find, to our surprise, memories in the things around us, in the things and events of our world.*

However, this eidetic reduction is still incomplete since it is still only an expression of a factual-empirical incident. And Husserl insists that the phenomenological reduction is not a function of facts but rather of essences. And so, I need to move from the factuality of the psychological reduction to the reduction-proper. To do this I need to bracket my self, and at the level of intersubjectivity ask, "How does childhood remembrance appear in consciousness or show itself in intentional experience?" And I will have to observe that this memory is contained or held in the "things" (in this case, my experience of the autumn leaves), and I need to realize that memories are released by sensory organs and limbs (touch, sound, smell, vision). In other words, when I ask, "where and how do childhood memories show themselves?" then I have to describe how "the memories are experienced in the things and the spatial contexts of our world, and we may release them with our bodies. However, this is a contingent event."

Now this is an odd observation because I know full well that memories are not contained in things, but rather in the billions of neurons and synaptic connections in the cerebrum of the brain. Or are they? This assumption is exactly what is wrong with my stance. I wonder even about this strange phenomenon of rich childhood memories to be lodged in organic bits of neural connections inside my skull. I have to suspend my "knowledge" of science. This suspension is what the phenomenological epoché wants us to accomplish—and thus to gain insights into the prereflective meanings that may show themselves in an ordinary experience such as "walking through the rustling autumn leaves." If I was merely trying to explain the miraculous memory incident, then a neuroscience explication might actually "solve" the miracle. Miracles are undone when we think we understand their miraculous causations. But the wonder of this moment cannot be solved. And it is truly wondrous how a childhood memory hidden in the things around us may be released by an accidental gesture of our bodies: a certain touch, brush, kick, whiff, glance, or sound.

Indeed, many people may have had this kind of experience: perhaps a childhood remembrance occurred when listening late at night to a distant church bell, when hearing a parade go by, happening upon an old toy, or when hearing children play in a park. The phenomenology of remembrances that are elicited from the things in our lifeworld (leaves, bells, a band, an image, a playground) are not necessarily under our control. For example, I look at a childhood photograph that hangs on my wall, but it may not elicit any unusual memories. Similarly, if the next day I walk through the leaves again, they may not yield memories any longer—in Heidegger's language the things are not thinging. The way a memory gives itself cannot be likened to turning on a computer and opening a data file on a memory drive. In contrast, there is a temporality, and contingency, and gift-quality of a remembrance that is part of its phenomenological sense and essence. And, I am reminded of Jean-Luc Marion's distinction of the saturated phenomenon (that overflows with meaning) and Claude Romano's notion of the eventiality of the event (that also has contingency and latency and cannot be fathomed now for its future significance).

We need to notice as well that in the above example a remembrance is probably only granted when we happen to be in a certain disposition that prefigures the epoché and the reduction. Without openness to the things of my world, I would not have become aware of the inceptive childhood remembrance in the first place. As I walked I was not preoccupied with any problems; I did not think of anything in particular. I was just walking home through the autumn leaves. So here we may find that the epoché and the reduction can already occur in everyday contexts of ordinary life. Phenomenological reflection and analysis are a logic of neither deduction (the reduction is not based on general inference) nor induction (the reduction is not based on empirical generalization)—phenomenological reflection involves the reduction (seeing the essence of something).

To reiterate, the reduction is not a technical procedure, rule, tactic, strategy, or a determinate set of steps that we should apply to the phenomenon that is being researched. Rather, the reduction is an attentive turning to the world and seeing the uniqueness or singularity of something when in an open state of mind, effectuated by the epoché. It is because of this openness that the essential insight may occur that remembrances or memories are "held in the things around us," and that memories may be released through sensory contact, even though these occurrences are not really predictable or under our control.

In his *Ideas Pertaining to a Pure Phenomenology and to a Phenomenological Philosophy*, published in 1913, Husserl already offered the epoché and the reduction as the central method for practicing the method of phenomenological seeing.

How does it become possible, thanks to the epoché, this subjectivity in its accomplishment, in its transcendental "conscious life," extending into hidden subsoils, in the distinct manners in which it "brings about," within itself, the world as ontic meaning? How can we bring this to light with self-evidence, not inventing or mythically constructing? (Husserl, 1983, p. 153)

This early questioning formulation of the epoché and reduction has been understood in a variety of ways by Husserl's interpreters. And Husserl himself constantly kept revising and reworking the meaning and functioning of the transcendental epoché and the transcendental reduction until his last published work *The Crisis of the European Sciences and Transcendental Phenomenology* (1970) published originally in 1936.

What must be shown in particular and above all is that through the epoché a new way of experiencing, of thinking, of theorizing, is opened to the philosopher; here, situated *above* his own natural being and *above* the natural world, he loses nothing of their being and their objective truths and likewise nothing at all of the spiritual acquisitions of his world-life or those of the whole historical communal life; he simply forbids himself—as a philosopher, in the uniqueness of his direction of interest—to continue the whole natural performance of his world-life; that is, he forbids himself to ask questions which rest upon the ground of the world at hand, questions of being, questions of value, practical questions, questions about being or not-being, about being valuable, being useful, being beautiful, being good, etc. All natural interests are put out of play. But the world, exactly as it was for me earlier and still is, as my world, our world, humanity's world, having validity in its various subjective ways, has not disappeared; it is just that, during the consistently carried-out epoché, it is under our gaze purely as the correlate of the subjectivity which gives it ontic meaning, through whose validities the world "is" at all.

This is not a "view," an "interpretation" bestowed upon the world. Every view about . . . every opinion about "the" world, has its ground in the pregiven world. It is from this very ground that I have freed myself through the epoché; I stand *above* the world, which has now become for me, in a quite peculiar sense, a *phenomenon*. (Husserl, 1970, p. 152)

And even though the reduction (with Heidegger, Levinas, Merleau-Ponty, Derrida, Chrétien, and Marion) has increasingly gained interpretive, linguistic, and material complexity and significance, it is still considered the principle "method" of phenomenology. Even phenomenologists who have criticized or disavowed Husserl's method of the reduction can be seen to be practicing it in some form.

Heidegger, too, underscored the significance of the reduction for phenomenological method:

We call this basic component of phenomenological method—the leading back or reduction of investigative vision from a naively apprehended being to being *phenomenological reduction*. We are thus adopting a central term of Husserl's phenomenology in its literal wording though not in its substantive intent. *For*

Husserl the phenomenological reduction, which he worked out for the first time expressly in the *Ideas Toward a Pure Phenomenology and Phenomenological Philosophy* (1913), is the method of leading phenomenological vision from the natural attitude of the human being whose life is involved in the world of things and persons back to the transcendental life of consciousness and its noetic-noematic experiences, in which objects are constituted as correlates of consciousness. For us phenomenological reduction means leading phenomenological vision back from the apprehension of a being, whatever may be the character of that apprehension, to the understanding of the being of this being (projecting upon the way it is unconcealed). Like every other scientific method, phenomenological method grows and changes due to the progress made precisely with its help into the subjects under investigation. Scientific method is never a technique. As soon as it becomes one it has fallen away from its own proper nature. (Heidegger, 1982, p. 21)

Heidegger's description of the reduction seems still tied to Husserl's original formulation except that he shifts the emphasis from understanding the invariant meaning (eidos, essence) of something to understanding the mode of being of something. While Husserl steps out of the world to grasp the meaning from above, Heidegger stays in the world of beings to understand their modes of being from within the world. While Husserl discusses the reduction as if it were a philosophical technique (which is not a technique in the procedural sense), Heidegger offers the significant advice that the reduction cannot even become a technique. Husserl proposes epistemologically that the reduction could produce transparent knowledge of a phenomenon (though with some phenomena this knowledge would be more probabilistic); Heidegger proposes ontologically that the reduction is always incomplete and that eidetic meaning of phenomena can only partially be brought to unconcealment. As part of the methodological reduction, we need to suspend the inclination to rely on a set of rules, a schema of steps, or a series of steps. Rather each phenomenon requires its own unique approach and unique application of the epoché and reduction.

The epoché describes the ways that we need to open ourselves to the world as we experience it and free ourselves from presuppositions. The reduction is generally the methodological term that describes the phenomenological gesture that permits us to rediscover what Merleau-Ponty (1962) calls "the spontaneous surge of the lifeworld" and the way that the phenomena give and show themselves in their uniqueness or essence. The aim of the reduction is to re-achieve a direct and primitive contact with the world as we experience it or as it shows itself—rather than as we conceptualize it. But, we need to realize as well that in some sense nothing is "simply given." The phenomenological attitude is sustained by wonder, attentiveness, and a desire for meaning. At the very least, humans have to be open or receptive to what gives itself in their own lives.

Jean-Luc Marion radicalizes the idea of self-givenness. But in his study *The Erotic Phenomenon*, too, the reduction spirals outward and upward through successive layers of meaning from the singularity of the self to the phenomenological universal. Of course, there tend to be certain imperatives in the way that things are given or how we perceive things—logically, orderly, emotionally, (in)consistently, and so on. Nevertheless, the reduction aims at removing any barriers, assumptions, suppositions, projections, and linguisticalities that prevent the phenomena and events of the lifeworld to appear or show themselves as they give themselves. So, we need to engage in the reduction in order to let that which gives itself show itself.

But the discovery of the prereflective lifeworld by means of the reduction always transcends the lifeworld. The "direct and primitive contact" of which Merleau-Ponty speaks is perhaps experienced as a moment (of understanding) of lived meaning, of meaningfulness. So, the method of the reduction is meant to bring the hidden, invisible, originary aspects of meaning that belong to the prereflective phenomena of our lifeworld into visibility or nearness. Again, the practice of human science is never simply a matter of procedure. Rather, the reduction refers to a certain attitude of attentiveness and style of thinking. If we want to come to an understanding of the meaning and significance of something, we need to reflect on it by practicing a thoughtful attentiveness to their singular uniqueness.

How then is reflection supposed to emulate lived meaning or prereflective experience? Of course, the emulator is language, and the phenomenological process of emulating is performed through writing. The intent of writing is to produce textual "portrayals" that resonate and make intelligible the kinds of meanings that we seem to recognize in life as we live it. There is an entire separate form of reduction that comes into play in the experience of reflective writing: the vocative.

Especially in the work of the more recent French phenomenologists, such as Michel Serres and Jean-Luc Nancy, the vocative aspects of the philological reduction are strongly expressed. While the linguistic meaning structures of reflective experience can never fully imitate lived experience from which they were reduced, nevertheless, the more vocative a text is "constructed," the more the "invisible" or ambiguous aspects of human existence seem to come within reach. Phenomenological lived experience description moves through layers of thematic analysis, spiraling into an unfolding of the phenomenological universal, the *eidos*.

The *eidos* (essence) is a phenomenological universal that can be described through a study of the structure that governs the instances or particular manifestations of the essence of that phenomenon. In other words, phenomenology is the attempt to uncover and describe the *eidetic* structures, the internal meaning structures, of lived experience. A universal or essence may only be intuited or grasped through a study of the particulars or instances as they are encountered in lived experience. And yet, this is not a deductive or inductive logic. For Husserl, to intuit the meaning of a phenomenon means *Wesenschau*—to *schau* (see) the *Wesen* (essence or *eidos*) of the phenomenon.

So, the reduction is a complex reflective attentiveness that must be practiced for phenomenological understanding to occur, of the meaning of a phenomenon or event. This practice is inevitably tied into the linguistic or philological forms of meaningful reflective writing through sources and media of aesthetic and ethical expressivity. Therefore, the reduction is not simply a research method, it also describes the phenomenological attitude and the reflective gestures of the vocative that must be adopted by anyone who wishes to participate in the questions that a certain project requires. In other words, phenomenological meaning and understanding have to be produced constantly anew by the writers and the readers of phenomenological texts and other media. In any confusion surrounding the reduction, it is helpful to keep in mind the underlying idea and purpose of the reduction: to gain access, via the epoché and the vocative, to the world of prereflective experience-as-lived in order to mine its meanings.

The Insight-Sensitive Attitude: Epoché Reduction

Before providing a more detailed sketch of the epoché and the reduction, it should be reiterated that insightful phenomenological researchers and authors do not use the epoché and the reduction instrumentally as tools but rather approach their investigations with an attentive and a talented phenomenological attitude that helps them to arrive at phenomenological insights that form as a result of a way of phenomenological reflecting and seeing rather than through some sort of technical employment of tool-like instrumentalities. Having acquired a body of basic informational knowledge of philosophical phenomenological methodology and literature does not make one a phenomenologist. But engaging the "phenomenological attitude" means to surrender to a certain pathos that creates an openness and sensitivity to the world and a wondering attentiveness that is the trigger for phenomenological insight. But that pathos still has to be disciplined to become productive phenomenological reflection.

Phenomenology does not just pose a problem to be solved or a question to be answered. A good phenomenological study almost always passes through a phase of wonder. Heidegger suggests that phenomenological thinking compels us into the basic disposition of wonder. What does this mean? Wonder has a dis-positional effect: it dis-locates and dis-places us. Wonder is not to be confused with amazement, marveling, admiration, curiosity, or fascination. For example, amazement is the inability to explain something that is unusual. An explanation can reduce the amazement. Curiosity tends to be superficial and passing. In contrast, wonder is deep. Fascination is being struck with an object of awe. And astonishment comes close to the experience of wonder. But, says Heidegger, "even astonishment does not fulfill what we intend with the word 'wonder' and what we are trying to understand as the basic disposition, the one that transports us into the beginning of genuine thinking" (1994, p. 143).

There is no natural transition from a moment of wondering to a moment of questioning. Wonder does not rely on method and cannot simply be caused as when asking for answers in questioning. Just as inspiration may be the antecedent to writing poetry, so wonder may be the antecedent to inquiry. But just as between inspiration and poetry there lies the poetic talent and writing ability of the poet, so there lies insightfulness, knowledge, and narrative ability between wonder and phenomenological questioning.

The idea of the phenomenological attitude is evident already in the foundational explications of phenomenology by Heidegger (1962), Merleau-Ponty (1962), Henry (2008), and others. According to Heidegger, Husserl's teaching took the form of practicing phenomenological seeing. Merleau-Ponty (1962) described phenomenology as a "manner or style of thinking" (p. viii). In addition, Henry (2008) put that the "transcendental possibility of experience is the original phenomenalizing of the phenomenality of the phenomenon" (p. 104), which is opening the path to the meaning of a phenomenon. None of these methodological characterizations refer to the application of a technical or scientific set of procedural steps. The practice of phenomenological "seeing" is an internalized, perception-based, and sensitive serendipitous act. Furthermore, the methods of the epoché and the reduction are involved, in a broad sense, as the distinguishing critical feature and essence of the phenomenological attitude.

While Husserl (1970) characterized the practice of the epoché and the reduction in many different ways (he mentions the transcendental, phenomenological, skeptical, vocational, and psychological epoché and reduction), a key feature is that it makes possible a transformation of the natural attitude. It is hard to fully realize and recognize the depth, pervasiveness, and taken-for-grantedness of the objectivism, naturalism, positivism, and shallow distractionism that shapes our way of looking at ourselves and the world around us and how this has affected the ecology of the planet and human civilizations. Even expressing our naturalistic predicament like this betrays a blindness to the fact that we always already immediately see the things around us as objects and objective forces.

Etymologically, the term "attitude" refers to the disposedness, disposition, posture, and fittedness of the comportment of a certain way of seeing, feeling, and acting, according to the online *Oxford English Dictionary*. An attitude regarding an object of thought can be deliberately or even unwittingly adopted. And an attitude can also be purposefully altered or disposed. This is a key idea for Husserl's phenomenology as it is the taken-for-grantedness of the natural attitude that prevents us from seeing the so-called hidden meanings of phenomena. He defines an "attitude" (*Einstellung*)

> as a habitually fixed style of willing life comprising directions of the will or interests that are prescribed by this style, comprising the ultimate ends, the cultural accomplishments whose total style is thereby determined . . . Humanity always lives under some attitude or other. (Husserl, 1970, p. 280)

The point of the epoché and the reduction is that one aims to be sensitive to whatever it is that instils the phenomenological attitude.

Serendipitous "Method"

Insights do not happen when we are busy with all kinds of things such as multitasking or distractedly looking at our mobile for messages every ten minutes. But strangely, insights may occur when we truly do nothing. So, what is it like to do nothing? Well, merely experiencing an empty moment. Just listening to some music. Indulging in boredom. Submitting to a mood of openness. Withdrawing from others (the they). Letting go or letting be. Giving over to active passivity. Being caught in a Kairos timeless moment of the now. Or going for a lone walk. Aristotle, Socrates, and Heidegger were the great philosophers who are famous for their liking to walk. They were peripatetic thinkers who felt that walking leads to deep discussion and deep learning.

The school of "peripatetics" was founded by Aristotle and named after the cloister, *peripatos*. The followers were brilliant research students. Socrates used to walk around the squares and market place where he mused on the truth of things. Some more recent thinkers too confess that they need to walk to think. Heidegger used to hike along the wood paths of his cabin in the woods. He even describes the moments of coming upon a sunny clearing in the woods of the Black Forest as a metaphoric experience of *alethea*, truth, the bright clearing of an insight.

Only when we actively surrender to a mood of passivity and ready ourselves for a chance meeting with Kairos—while refusing to be distracted by everyday business around us, then we may seize an insight by letting it seize us or by being seized by it. And yet, if we are not searching it will not find us. Insights will not come if we do not read and reflect, write and rewrite. Jacques Derrida pointed out (Derrida and Ferraris, 2001) that even before we sit down and write we were already writing—even when seemingly doing nothing. So, we must always be attentive and prepared to write, even when we do not have a writing instrument at hand or when are not sitting behind the keyboard. Insights may come to us in various surprising situations and contexts. This means that insights still may happen when we are in a state of active passivity. Sometimes an insight comes when we are just about to fall asleep. If that happens then better write it down. Indeed, an insight may tend to occur as a fleeting evanescent Kairos moment (Hermsen, 2014). Or an insight may come to us serendipitously, as if by coincidence, luck, playful providence—not necessarily through straightforward systematic analysis—but as if through the backdoor.

In the next section the phenomenological meanings of the epoché and the reduction are presented as methods for doing phenomenology. But, as suggested above, these methodical concepts are best understood as attitudinal methods and as serendipitous ways of approaching phenomenological topics and questions.

The Abstemious Epoché-Reduction: Invitations to Openness

The phenomenological idea of the epoché and the reduction is to return to the world as we live it. The various aspects and methodical gestures of the epoché serve this purpose: to open oneself to experience as lived—how certain phenomena and events are constituted and give themselves in lived experience. Phenomenological reflection on lived experience is neither inductive nor deductive. It does not try to develop conceptual schemes or prove preconceived ideas. Rather, the epoché-reduction tries to make contact with experience as we live it. And the attempt to make contact with the world as we experience it requires that one places oneself in the open. The philosophical literature contains many philosophical investigations and explications that can make the precise meanings of the epoché and reduction complex and confusing. And that is not surprising, in view of the fact that the project of phenomenology can be understood in a variety of ways. For the purpose of an eclectic phenomenology of practice (as presented in this book), some common distinctions may be made. Several levels of the epoché (bracketing or suspension of belief) and the reduction (reflection on essence) can be distinguished for their heuristic value and methodological usefulness. In the following sections I distinguish several aspects of the epoché as it is entwined with the reduction.

The basic idea of the reduction is already at the heart of my opening paragraph of the phenomenological method: phenomenology is a method of abstemious reflection on the basic structures of the lived experience of human existence—abstemious in the sense that reflecting on experience must, as much as possible, be open and abstain from theoretical, polemical, suppositional, and emotional intoxications. Lived experience means that phenomenology reflects on the experiential prepredicative and prereflective life of everyday existence. So, I distinguish among the following methodical moments of the epoché-reduction: the heuristic reduction, the hermeneutic reduction, the experiential reduction, and the methodological reduction. In the process of inquiry these "methods" are practiced as if more or less in concert. But we can also deal with them separately while keeping the integrity of the larger phenomenological project in view.

The heuristic, hermeneutic, experiential, and methodological variations of the epoché-reduction are the general preparatory elements of the reduction-proper. The distinguishing feature of these preparatory moments of the reduction lies in the emphasis on the epoché: to position oneself into openness. This openness is achieved through the suspension of our taken-for-granted beliefs and the suspension of our natural attitude and beliefs. So, the general reduction is first presented as four aspects of the epoché as it belongs to the general reduction. Next the reduction-proper is presented as five varieties: the eidetic, ontological, ethical, radical, and originary reduction.

The Heuristic Epoché-Reduction: Wonder

The heuristic epoché-reduction consists of the epoché of bracketing (disturbing, shattering) the attitude of taken-for-grantedness. It aims to awaken a profound sense of wonder about the phenomenon or event in which one is interested—the heuristic moment occurs in the disposition of wonder. Wonder overwhelms, but wonder should not be confused with curiosity, fascination, or admiration.

In his "Preface" to the *Phenomenology of Perception*, Merleau-Ponty suggests that the best formulation of the reduction is probably that given by Eugen Fink (Husserl's assistant), when he spoke of "wonder" in the face of the world (Merleau-Ponty, 1962, p. xiii). What does this mean? Wonder is the unwilled willingness to meet what is utterly strange in what is most familiar. Wonder is the stepping back and let things speak to us, an active–passive receptivity to let the things of the world present themselves on their own terms. The reduction in the gesture of wonder does not want to break its contact with the world. Rather, it only steps back far enough "to watch the forms of transcendence fly up like sparks from a fire; it slackens the intentional threads which attach us to the world and thus brings them to our notice" (Merleau-Ponty, 1962, p. xiii). Indeed, at the most basic level the phenomenological epoché-reduction consists of the attitude or mood of wonder.

When we are struck with wonder, we seem to have evaporated momentarily our present preoccupations. The mind is cleared of garbage, so to speak (this is again an aspect of the epoché). We are struck by the strangeness of this thing, this phenomenon. Momentarily, we are speechless as when the mouth hangs open while being taken in by the wonder of something. Perhaps it is strange to speak of wonder as a method. But if we understand method as *methodos*, as path or way, then we may indeed consider wonder an important motive in human science inquiry. The "way" to knowledge and understanding begins in wonder. So methodologically the heuristic reduction requires "discovering" the miraculous moment of wonder (though wonder is not due to a miracle), and in this moment a question may emerge that both addresses us and is addressed by us. This fundamental wonder may animate one's questioning of the meaning of the lived experience of the world.

In *Basic Questions of Philosophy*, Heidegger explains that wonder is a disposition (a state of being dis-placed) that is compelled by the need of primordial thinking. He shows how wonder differs importantly from related notions such as amazement, marveling, astonishment, awe, and admiration. In wonder we see the unusual in the usual, the extraordinary in the ordinary. But Heidegger makes a fine point that the problem is that the ordinary tends to be passed over in favor of the extraordinary—however, wonder concerns itself with the ordinary itself, and so everything that belongs to the ordinary is therefore extraordinary. And Heidegger warns that the experience of wonder should not turn into "a vague and empty wallowing in 'feelings'" (1994, p. 149).

To reiterate, in terms of the particular research project in which one is engaged the heuristic reduction challenges the researcher to be receptive and awakened to a profound sense of wonder. But it also challenges the researcher to inquire and write in such a manner that the reader of the phenomenological text is similarly struck by or stirred to the same sense of wondering attentiveness to the topic under investigation. Phenomenological inquiry continually edifies a wondering disposition of attentiveness to the world, "because it reveals that world as strange and paradoxical" (Merleau-Ponty, 1962, p. xiii). Wonder is not just a stepwise procedure of phenomenological method, but rather the *disposition* of wonder should remain as part of the phenomenological attitude in the total inquiry process.

The Hermeneutic Epoché-Reduction: Self-Awareness

The hermeneutic epoché-reduction consists of the epoché of bracketing all interpretation and explicating reflectively whatever assumptions seem to need attention in writing the research text.

One needs to be aware of one's own constant inclination to be led by preunderstandings, frameworks, and theories regarding the (psychological, political, and ideological) motivation and the nature of the phenomenological question. The hermeneutic reduction consists of a search for radical reflectivity in one's relation with the phenomenon. One needs to overcome one's subjective or private feelings, preferences, inclinations, or expectations that may seduce or tempt one to come to premature, wishful, or one-sided understandings of an experience that would prevent one from understanding the phenomenon as it is lived through.

On the one hand, this means that one needs to practice a critical self-awareness with respect to the assumptions that prevent one from being as open as possible to the sense and significance of the phenomenon. We need to forget as it were our vested interests and preunderstandings, and practice a radical openness to the phenomenon. On the other hand, it means that one needs to realize that forgetting one's preunderstandings is not really possible, and therefore these various assumptions and interests may need to be explicated so as to exorcise them in an attempt to let speak that which wishes to speak.

Practically, the hermeneutic reduction consists of reflectively examining and turning over in one's textual labor the various preunderstandings that seem to impinge on the reflective gaze. This does not mean that one must hope to arrive at some kind of pure vantage point, as if such a pure gaze were possible. But it requires that the various dimensions of lived meaning of some selected human experience are investigated for their various sources and layers of meaning, rather than being overlaid with a particular frame of meaning. Phenomenological inquiry continually is open to questioning assumptions and preunderstanding—this radical self-awareness and explicating assumptions is part of the phenomenological reflection itself.

The Experiential Epoché-Reduction: Concreteness

The experiential epoché-reduction consists of the epoché of bracketing all theory or theoretical meaning, all belief in what is (un)real. The experiential reduction aims at explicating concrete or lived meaning. It suspends abstraction in favor of quotidian common place or every dayness.

Phenomenology is a method to reveal lived meanings of possible human experiences. But what do we mean by experience? On the one hand, this seems a silly question. Experience is simply everything that we feel, live through, become aware of. On the other hand, there are many confounding questions associated with this simple notion. How do we know what we experience, feel, sense, and what we live through? Can we have experiences that we are not aware of? What role does reflection and language play in having experiences? Is all experience linguistic? Or can we have experiences for which we do not have language? How is the body involved in everyday experience? Is all experience meaningful?

It seems that the notion of experience opens up a container filled to the brim with philosophical questions and problems. But perhaps it is possible to make some minimal assumptions about human experience and leave the philosophical problems aside for now, even if some of these assumptions are contradictory.

In existential terms we may say that experience is where and how we are in time and place as time and place; experience is also how we are corporeally and relationally in the world as embodied and relational beings. Phenomenologically we are interested in the *ti estin*, in the whatness of where and how we are in the world. What then is experience? Experience is the name for that what presents itself directly as consciousness. So, is experience identical with consciousness or awareness? Does experience present itself immediately, unmediated by subsequent thought, image, or language?

And yet, it would seem that experience can only be accessed through thought, image, or language. What is important about this way of describing human experience is that there is a sense of immediacy associated with experience. Experience seems to be a kind of immediate awareness that is not (yet) aware of itself. Even experiences that involve reflecting, imagining, speaking, or writing are in this sense direct, immediate, unmediated by thought, image, or language. Indeed, when we read or write a text, then the experience of reading or writing presents itself to us immediately, prelinguistically. In other words, the experience of the space and time of text is as immediate as experience outside of this textorium. But if we try to

369

describe how reading or writing are experienced, then we tend to try to "capture" such experiences through concepts, aesthetic images, or by way of cognitive or expressive language.

So, phenomenology focuses on lived experience, but phenomenological reflection only begins in earnest when it tries to grasp reflectively the lived meanings of this prereflective experience. In the words of Ricoeur: "Phenomenology begins when, not content to 'live' or 'relive,' we interrupt lived experience in order to signify it" (1983, p. 116). Phenomenological human science is the study of lived or existential meanings; it attempts to describe and interpret these meanings to a certain degree of depth and richness. The experiential reduction requires that one avoids all abstraction, all theorizing, all generalization, even all belief in the existence of what we call real or not real (for example, the experience of a dream can be just as real as the experience of an actual event).

Of course, any research project should examine the available theories and discuss the body of knowledge about the topic being investigated. From a phenomenological perspective, theories need to be reviewed for the extent to which they speak to concrete experience and the extent to which they fail to do so. Most theories contain some phenomenological material, or they are built on certain intuitions that presume phenomenological understandings. But in the end scientific theories are abstractive and so they are less sensitive to the concrete. Thus, in the experiential reduction, one needs to strip away the theoretical or scientific conceptions and thematizations that overlay the phenomenon one wishes to study and that prevent one from seeing the phenomenon in a non-abstracting manner.

The way in which to bracket theoretical meaning is not to ignore it but to examine it for possibilities of extracting phenomenological sensibilities. It is helpful to examine how the theories or conceptualizations gloss or hide the experiential reality upon which they ultimately must be based. Theories tend to explain phenomena that are not necessarily understood in a lived or concrete sense. So, one must ask: how is this topic actually experienced? Phenomenological inquiry is continually oriented to the beginning, to experience as lived.

The Methodological Epoché-Reduction: Approach

The methodological epoché-reduction consists of the epoché of bracketing all conventional techniques and seeks or invents an approach that might fit most appropriately the phenomenological topic under study. Phenomenology engages a radical or hyper-reflection by including its own reflectivity in its reflective investigations.

Phenomenological method is challenging since it can be argued that any particular line of inquiry constantly has to be invented anew and cannot be reduced to a general set of strategies or research techniques. Repeating past approaches prevents and stultifies original thinking. Heidegger stated: "When a method is genuine and provides access to the objects, it is precisely then that the progress made by following it . . . will cause the very method that was used to become necessarily obsolete" (1982, p. 328). Phenomenological inquiry is often difficult since it requires sensitive interpretive skills and creative talents from the researcher. Methodologically speaking, every notion has to be examined in terms of its assumptions, even the idea of method itself. Moreover, it is difficult to describe phenomenological research methods since even within the field of phenomenology itself "there is no such thing as one phenomenology, and if there could be such a thing it would never become anything like a philosophical technique" (Heidegger, 1982, p. 328).

A flexible rationality is required that is able to invent an approach for investigating a selected phenomenon in a scholarly, creative, and original manner. One needs to employ a flexible narrative rationality that can make phenomenological meanings in textual forms "re-cognizable" or feelingly knowable. Therefore, one must experiment with a methodologically informed inventiveness that fuses the reflective and the prereflective life of consciousness. Generally speaking, the reduction is not an end in itself—rather, the reduction is a means to an end: to be able to return to the world as lived in an enriched and deepened fashion.

In trying out different forms of writing and different ways of organizing the phenomenological text, one needs to be aware of the factor of contingency that makes a strong phenomenological text fragile and vulnerable (and more evocative). It is ironic that the stronger the meaning is embedded in a text, the more easily can it be damaged or destroyed by carelessness with respect to its rhetorical style and content. Still, it can be helpful to examine exemplary phenomenological studies. Ask: What makes this text strong and insightful? How would this work with a different topic? How would this phenomenologist have approached such topic? And how might that phenomenologist have treated this question?

The phenomenological challenge is to create a text that is in some sense iconic in its entirety. This also means that the writer needs to become aware of the potential effects of the text on different readers. How should the basic phenomenological question be opened up? How is it possible to maintain a sense of wonder about the phenomenon? How to bring about the proper tension between the concrete and the universal dimensions of the text? How to bring the text to a deepened sense of meaning? This context provides also the opportunity to address two chronic ailments of phenomenological human science: the issue of subjectivism and the issue of objectivism.

First, methodological subjectivism is the expectation that phenomenology can give us access to the private and inner lives of particular individuals so that we may know what and how they feel and experience in a particular situation and at a particular moment in time. It is true that empirical procedures of phenomenological method (such as interviewing and writing lived experience descriptions) seek to obtain experiential accounts of individual persons, but these accounts should not be used to explore the psychological life of this or that particular person. Rather, any particular experiential account is solely studied as a concrete plausible example of a possible human experience.

An experiential text—whether as a real empirical account or as fictional literary text of a novel, may become the source and provide access to a reflective understanding of a phenomenological topic. But no claims are made that this research gives us valid insights into the personal life and biographic world of this or that particular person. Phenomenology is not analytic or therapeutic psychology. Thus, phenomenology cannot determine if a particular person, John, actually suffers from loneliness (rather than grief, loss, or some other existential anxiety), but a phenomenology of loneliness can help us understand more thoughtfully John's experience if (psychologically or existentially) he seems to suffer from loneliness.

371

Second, methodological objectivism is the expectation that definable methods and procedures can produce valid phenomenological research results. In the natural and behavioral sciences, the specific methods and procedures are spelled out in advance of the research in the expectation of producing a certain kind of knowledge base. For example, carefully prepared experimental designs or survey methods will almost certainly lead to a research "outcome," even if the outcome is in conflict with theoretical speculation. But in the more phenomenological human sciences, the methods and procedures that may be discussed in advance do not give any guarantees about the successful production of knowledge. In fact, it could be argued that method (as technique) does not give access to lived experience. But, unfortunately perhaps, it is precisely the technology of a method that makes it so seductive to some researchers. Rather, one should adopt a phenomenological attitude that entails heuristic attentiveness, creative insight, interpretive sensibility, linguistic sensitivity, and scholarly preparedness and tact.

The Reduction-Proper: Meaning-Giving Sources of Meaning

The epoché-reduction, as presented above, is the preparatory phase of the phenomenological method that involves opening up and freeing oneself from obstacles that would make it difficult to study phenomena and events of our lifeworld. The reduction-proper, as presented below, engages the reflective phenomenological attitude. In order to make the phase of the reduction-proper more accessible it is discussed in terms of five dimensions, even though the reduction should be understood as a singular methodological entity. Anyway, the five distinctions are the eidetic, ontological, ethical, radical, and originary dimensions of the reduction-proper as we may encounter it in the literature. The idea of the "reduction proper" dates back to Husserl, who reformulated and revised it numerous times. The reduction-proper should be seen as the opposite move of the reductional epoché as discussed above.

The Eidetic Reduction: Eidos or Whatness

The eidetic reduction consists of grasping insight(s) in determining and testing the essential meaning of a phenomenon or event. This is done through the process of "variation in imagination" or by comparing the phenomenon with comparative examples. When an imagined, fictive, or empirical variation does not conflict or change the essence of a phenomenon, then this can be considered an invariant. But if the comparison fails to hold and changes the nature of the phenomenon than that comparison should be considered as a variant. For example, keeping a secret is not the same as lying because in lying there is deception, and secrecy does not necessarily involve deception. Also, keeping a secret is not the same as remaining private because secrets always involve others from whom we keep secrets or with whom we share but privacy is essentially a nonrelational experience. So, lying and privacy are variants of the phenomenon of secrecy. But if we keep someone in confidence about something then confidentiality is likely an invariant relation of secrecy.

The eidetic reduction seeks to describe *what* it is that shows itself in experience or consciousness and *how* something shows itself. The eidetic reduction focuses

372

on what is distinct or unique in a phenomenon. The eidetic reduction may not be a universally accepted or valued feature of phenomenological inquiry. But for many philosophers who consider phenomenology to be grounded in Husserlian methodology, the eidetic reduction is at the heart of phenomenological reflection.

The eidetic reduction is less or not really interested in the factual status of particular instances: whether something actually happened, how often it tends to happen, or how the occurrence of an experience is related to the prevalence of other conditions or events. For example, phenomenology does not ask, how do these Canadian people experience travel? But it asks, what is the eidetic nature of the experience of travel (so that I can now better understand what this particular experience may be like for these Canadian people)? So, the phenomenological *eidos* of a phenomenon or event, such as being a traveler (rather than a refugee, or just a tourist), has been adequately described if the description reawakens, evokes, or shows us reflectively the lived meaning and significance of the prereflective experience of travel, in a fuller or deeper manner.

Eidetic reduction aims to somehow express in language what is experienced prior to reflection on the experience. In Merleau-Ponty's words: "The eidetic reduction . . . is the ambition to make reflection emulate the unreflective life of consciousness . . . . The world is not what I think, but what I live through" (1962, p. xviii). In the eidetic reduction one needs to see past or through the particularity of lived experience toward the eidos that lies on the other side or at the heart of the concreteness of lived meaning. The idea of phenomenological eidos does not refer to some immutable universal or generalization about human nature of human life. This would be committing the fallacy of essentialism. The first important reminder is that phenomenological inquiry is only concerned with "possible" human experiences—not with experiences that are presumed to be empirically or culturally universal or shared by all humans irrespective of time, culture, gender, or other circumstance. The second important reminder is that phenomenological determination of meaning is always indeterminate, always tentative, always incomplete, always inclined to question assumptions by returning again and again to lived experience itself, the beginnings of phenomenological inquiry.

The eidetic reduction is partially accomplished by comparing the phenomenon with other related but different phenomena. For example, in exploring the phenomenology of keeping a secret, one would practice the eidetic technique of "variation in imagination." How is the experience of secrecy different from the experience of privacy or the experience of reserve? What makes keeping a secret different from being deceptive? Are there different kinds of secrecy? How is keeping a secret different from lying? What are concrete examples of this experience? (See van Manen and Levering, 1996, on the phenomenology of secrecy.)

In the eidetic reduction it seems that patterns of meaning are emerging. Some thematic meanings that appear to belong to this particular phenomenon may suggest themselves. These are not thematizations in the sense of theoretical or conceptual abstractions. In other words, these themes do not belong to existing theories, taxonomies, genres, paradigms, philosophies, or conceptual frameworks. Rather, phenomenological themes correlate with the findings of the reduction— they are the working material for phenomenological writing (reflective inquiry).

The eidetic reduction differs from concept analysis in that the reduction does not claim to clarify linguistically the boundaries of a phenomenon or how a concept is being used in different contexts. Rather, the reduction attempts to offer exemplary images of the phenomenon—intimations of meaningfulness. The eidetic reduction asks: Does this piece of text bring the experience into view? Does this phrase resonate with our prereflective sensibilities? Are these portrayals of lived meaning recognizable? Do they evoke something unique about this human experience?

So, the eidetic reduction is not a simplification, fixation, or contraction of the world into a system of eidetic concepts—rather, it is the exact opposite: the eidetic reduction makes the world appear as it precedes every cognitive construction or conceptualization: in its full ambiguity, irreducibility, contingency, mystery, and ultimate indeterminacy. Phenomenological inquiry continually asks: does this textual portrayal of the eidos of this phenomenon or event point at a difference that makes a meaningful difference?

The Ontological Reduction: Ways of Being

The ontological reduction consists of explicating the mode or ways of being that belong to or are proper to something. The ontic meaning of something is the mode of being in the world of that something or someone. Heidegger did not quite accept Husserl's notion of the reduction as the grasping of the essence (eidos) of a phenomenon as constituted in consciousness. In contrast, Heidegger explains that the reduction should be understood as going back to the world as lived—which can never be brought to full unconcealment. Heidegger shifts to focus from ontic meaning (whatness of being) to ontological meaning (mode of being). To understand a phenomenon is aiming to understand the ontological mode of being of the being (meaning) of that phenomenon. But for Heidegger this understanding was not a Husserlian epistemological problem but an ontological concern: every way of being in the world is a way of understanding the world as an event of being. So, for example, the experience of "keeping a secret" is already a certain mode of being in the world (the mode and mood of secrecy) and understanding the things of the world as manifestations of their secret being. For example, Derrida speaks of the "absolute secret" as the ontology of secrecy: the secret of its secrecy.

Heidegger's hermeneutic-ontological phenomenology is a profound and truly inexhaustible source for what it means to think, reflect, inquire, and do phenomenological research. Yet, Heidegger would have been surprised at (and would probably have abhorred) how some contemporary researchers are trying to use his texts for constructing practical research programs and interpretive procedures. There is no Heideggerian procedural method that one can follow, step by step, for conducting research into specific lifeworld phenomena. However, the researcher can aim and aspire to cultivate his or her inquiry program and practice by attentively attending to Heidegger's thinking.

In his later ontological writings on *The Visible and the Invisible*, Merleau-Ponty suggests that the essence of a phenomenon will always elude us: we can ultimately only sense what is *not* essential to a phenomenon. And Jean-Luc Marion has suggested that the more interesting phenomena in life—such as sacrifice, painting, love—are so saturated with meaning that they can never be fully grasped in their eidos. Still, this does not prevent Marion in his book *The Erotic Phenomenon* from writing a fascinating phenomenological reflection on the saturated phenomenon of "love" as a way of being.

The Ethical Reduction: Alterity

The ethical reduction consists of going beyond the eidetic reduction of Husserl and beyond the ontological reduction of Heidegger. The early Husserl is a cognitive phenomenologist in that he does not accept that there could be anything outside of consciousness. For Husserl, primal impressionality is the beginning of consciousness, but for Levinas it precedes consciousness. Levinas does not agree with Husserl's view that primal impressionality is already a consciousness. And he criticizes Heidegger's ontological phenomenology for placing central *Dasein* and the being of beings. Heidegger's ontology cannot deal with the question of what lies beyond being, or the meaning of what is other than being. There is (or should be) a difference in the way that we approach and apprehend the being of a person or thing (their whatness or mode of being) from the way we approach the singular otherness of a person or thing (their alterity).

The Husserlian focus on the essence of the whatness of things, and Heidegger's preoccupation with the modalities of being in the world, both are manifestations of the primacy of being. When we inquire into the being of some thing or phenomenon, then we want to know what that thing or phenomenon "is" in its *quiddity*, uniqueness, or identity. Thus, Levinas says that the interest underlying the phenomenologies of Husserl and Heidegger are directed at sameness. Indeed, Heidegger wrote "any *Dasein* whatsoever is characterized by mineness" (1962, p. 32). This mineness in Heidegger's ontological phenomenology revolves around being or presence, which really means the "self." But Levinas suggests that for a truly profound understanding of human existence, one must not only ask for the meaning of being, self, or presence, but also for the meaning of what is not self: otherwise than being, *alterity*.

Levinas finds the phenomenological power of this question about ethics and alterity in the encounter with the face of the other that makes an appeal to us. In the vulnerability of the face of the other, says Levinas, we experience an appeal: we are being called, addressed. In this call we experience the otherness of the other. And our response to the vulnerability of the other is experienced as a response-ability. This is an ethical experience, an ethical phenomenology. When we truly look the other person in the eyes, we may have the experience of a realization of the enigma of the other. Ultimately, I can never really know this other person. What I do, when I speak about the other person, is reduce this person to my own categories and my own terms. But the otherness of the other is irreducible to myself. Thus, I have to leave behind the epistemological reduction of Husserl and the ontological reduction of Heidegger and acknowledge that in the experience of alterity I am addressed in my ethical responsibility to this other person who makes an appeal on me.

Levinas has shown that it is only in the direct and unmediated encounter with the other that we can gain a glimpse of the meaning of the ethical impulse that he describes as the human responsiveness to the appeal of the otherness of the other, which calls for my care. Usually we think of other people as selves who are in the world just as we are in the world as selves. And so, we are cohabitants, fellow human beings who live in reciprocal relationships. In these relations, each of us cannot help but see others as objects of our personal perception and thinking. But this is not the only possibility. It also may happen that the other person bursts upon my world and makes a claim on me outside of my own intentional cognitive orientation. In other words, it is also possible to experience the other in the vocative: as an appeal, as someone who stirs and touches me. This is especially true of situations where we meet the other in his or her vulnerability, as when we happen to be handed a hurt and helpless child or when we suddenly see a person hurt in front of us.

The strange thing is that the more I care for this other, the more I worry and the stronger my desire to care. By desire Levinas does not mean a personal want or need. Wants and needs differ from desire. I may always have wanted to buy a fast fancy sports car, and now that I finally am able to afford my dream, I feel satisfied; or I may find that I am disappointed and that my want was not as worthwhile as I thought. At any rate, my want has been stilled. But desire that lives in my relation of care reaches beyond anything that might bring satisfaction and thus acquiesce to the desire. For example, love is desire in this sense. Think of the lover who asks his or her loved one, "Do you love me?" And the love one says, "Yes, you are my love and only love." The question is: What happens to desire? Chances are that a week later, a day later, or maybe even five minutes later the lover may again feel the desire to ask and say, "Yes, but do you *really* love me?" And again, his or her love responds, "Yes, my love, I really do love you." This example illustrates that true desire cannot be stilled. No answer can forever satisfy. In fact, desire feeds on itself and fans itself—think of the great love tragedies. Similarly, caring responsibility increases in proportion to the measure that it is assumed. The more I care for this person, the more I worry, and the more I worry, the stronger my desire to care. Many of not most parents have experienced this care for their child.

What is also peculiar about this ethical experience of caring responsibility is that it singles me out. It addresses each person uniquely. When the voice calls, then it is no use to look around to see if it was meant for someone else. No, here is this child in front of me, and I look this child in the face. Before I can even think about it, I already have experienced my responsiveness. I "know" this child calls upon *me*. It is undeniable: I have experienced the appeal. And this experience is a form of knowing (though not in the usual cognitive sense). I know I am called. I am being addressed: I am the one who is charged with responsibility (Levinas, 2003). What makes Levinas' insights so unique is that he is the only philosopher who offers us an ethics of responsibility that is not founded in a theory of ethics. That is why Levinas calls it pure ethics. It is a primal ethics. Or, in a deeper sense, this is not yet ethics, not yet philosophy, not yet politics, not yet religion, not yet a moral judgment. Levinas (2008) shows us that in the encounter with the other, in this greeting, in this face, we experience primal ethics, the purely ethical before we have involved ourselves in general ethics as a form of thinking, reflecting, theorizing, and moral reasoning.

The Radical Reduction: Self-Givenness

The radical reduction consists of focusing on the way that a phenomenon gives itself as itself, while applying the epoché to all senses of subjectivity or agency.

The radical reduction censures out consciousness, subjectivity, or the person that constitutes the meaning of the world by focusing only on the self that gives itself. Jean-Luc Marion regards Husserl's eidetic reduction as the first form, Heidegger's ontological reduction as the second form, and his self-givenness as the third form of the reduction-proper, a radical reduction. Phenomenology should not depend on any constituting or sense-making subject or agency and solely attend to the self-givenness of phenomena.

Marion argues that the classical "first principle" of phenomenology—to return to the things themselves—is not radical enough because the Husserlian phenomena are ultimately intentional objects that originate in the subjectivity (consciousness) of the subject, or in the intersubjective agency of the transcendental ego. Similarly, for Heidegger, at the core of Dasein's thrownness and Dasein's task of constituting its world remains the "I" or the "self." Marion aims to move beyond intentionality. He repeatedly returns to Husserl and Heidegger and notes how both remain infected with traces of Kantian/Cartesian themes that Marion aims to overcome or erase. He suggests that phenomenology cannot accept the authority of some constituting source of the subject or agent. The first principle of phenomenology should focus solely on the self-givenness of things. "What *shows itself* first *gives itself*—this is my one and only theme," says Marion (2002a, p. 5).

Intentionality means that to be conscious is to be conscious of something. Intentionality describes how humans are always tied to the world by constituting their world. Therefore, the radical reduction of Marion and his colleagues does not take into consideration the constituting role of intentionality. The radical reduction is nonintentional: it cannot be reduced to the consciousness of the subject. The radical reduction is also evident in the work of, for example, Michel Henry and Jean-Louis Chrétien. Michel Henry says, "The question of phenomenology . . . is no longer concerned with the phenomena but the mode of their givenness, their phenomenality, not with what appears but with appearing" (Henry, 2008, p. 2). Indeed, for some phenomena the phenomenologist may want to focus the inquiry not on the whatness, but on the howness, of phenomenality. For example, in his discussion of the meaning of the "event" Claude Romano shows how the eidetic meaning of "event" lies in the self-giving and dynamic manner in which it shows itself. We might say, the eidos or whatness of the eventual nature of the event lies in the how: the giving of self-givenness. Thus, the meaning of the event lies not primarily in what happens at present but rather in the significance the event acquires in the unfolding of its latency. In other words, the meaning is not its whatness (the fact that I had had a good talk with an old friend I met for coffee) but its latent consequence (the things my friend talked about now keep haunting me). The event gives itself as lingering self-giving.

Some phenomenologists, such as Dominique Janicaud (2000, 2005a, 2005b), have questioned Marion, Henry, and Chrétien on a suspected theological inspiration of this notion of self-givenness. Marion admits a deep interest in the divine and he addresses religious themes such as charity and revelation in his writings. However, he strongly denies that his phenomenology can be reduced to theological foundations.

Phenomenology, Marion says, can only accept the being given. When something shows itself, then it is the "self" of the givenness of the thing that shows and gives itself. The thing that shows itself appears in its givenness rather than as constituted in or by consciousness in one way or another. The thing appears as a phenomenon that gives itself of itself. So, it is not the self of the subject (the transcendental ego, consciousness, or *Dasein*) that constitutes or constructs the phenomenon, but it is the self of the thing (the given) itself that is the giving source of its givenness. The researcher who wishes to practice Marion's third reduction should aim at describing how something gives itself while refraining from engaging a perspective that remains committed to a constructivist subject. Examples of this approach to a radical reduction can be seen especially in the writings of Jean-Luc Marion (2002a, 2002b, 2006), Michel Henry (1973, 1999, 2008), and Jean-Louis Chrétien (2002, 2004a, 2004b). The radical epoché and reduction mean that one aims to extricate oneself as much as possible from the meaning-giving process. That does not mean that the subject or person is denied to exist in the phenomenology of self-giving, but that the subject is largely passive and open to whatever gives itself.

The Originary Reduction: Inception or Originary Meaning

The originary or inceptual reduction consists of orienting to the originary beginning of the phenomenon. The method of the originary reduction is to open oneself and thus experience openings (the epoché) where the originary meanings of a phenomenon may be discerned. Heidegger speaks of a flash of insight that may happen as an appropriative event. For Heidegger this appropriative event occurs when the truth of "beying" reveals itself. In the flash of insight we not only gain a phenomenological understanding of some object or thing, we also gain an original sight of ourselves as humans. This goes to the very origin and core of the beginning of the meaning of being, for which Heidegger reserves the archaic spelling of "Seyn" ("beying"). Heidegger formulated his radically innovative notion of inception already in the 1930s, in his *Contributions to Philosophy* (1999, 2012b) that he wrote after *Being and Time*. But *Contributions* as well as related texts such as *The Event* (2013b) and the *Bremen and Freiburg Lectures* (2012a) were translated only recently into English.

When Heidegger refers to inceptual thinking (*anfängliche Denken*), then he tends to have in mind those rare historical events when human understanding took a different turn—for example, when the idea of truth-as-unconcealment emerged in ancient Greek culture. But, more down to earth, we may also use the notion of inception to reflect on the manner that a sudden insight reveals a truth about a phenomenon. Most precise perhaps is the formulation that inception is the essential event or happening of "being" itself as appropriation—which is *Ereignen* (commonly translated enowning, a neologism which means, making into one's own). Heidegger sees the grounding attunement of the first beginning as deep wonder or deep awe but in this context marked by a shock: being taken aback.

To reiterate, Husserlian phenomenology focuses on the eidetic meanings of phenomena. The eidetic reduction is often considered at the core of phenomenological analysis. But, post-Husserlian phenomenology of thinkers such as Jean-Luc Nancy and Michel Serres are ultimately interested in the originary reduction that aims at tracing the meaning of a phenomenon to its originary character, its source, the beginning of its beginning, or *rizomata panton*. While the eidetic reduction focuses primarily on the whatness of meaning of a phenomenon, the originary reduction focuses primordially on the emergent meanings and how a phenomenon originates and comes into being.

From a phenomenological perspective the occurrence of a flash of insight is more intriguing than understanding it as a creative act or experience. In a creative act, the subject is the creator, the agent of the creation, the creative production. But inception does not depend on my creative agency; rather, an inceptual thought may happen to me as a gift, a grace—an event that I could neither plan nor foresee. That is why Heidegger describes the inceptual experience in terms of appropriative event or happening. In a manner, the inception may be regarded as the birth of meaning. Indeed, for the phenomenologist, there is that most momentous moment in the struggle of phenomenological inquiry when an intuitive understanding is sparked: catching a reflective insight, suddenly "seeing" the phenomenal meaning of something, discerning a truth in an instant of writing, being struck by an incisive thought (where did it come from?).

> Insight into that which is, is the appropriative event itself, as which the truth of beying relates itself to unguarded beying and stands by it.... At first and almost to the very end it appeared as though "insight into that which is" signified only a glance that we humans cast forth from ourselves to that which is. "That which is" one customarily takes as a particular being, for indeed the "is" is said of beings. But now everything has turned. Insight does not name our inspection of the being, insight as flashing entry is the appropriative event of the constellation of the turn in the essence of beying itself in the epoch of positionality. (Heidegger, 2012a, pp. 70, 71)

The problem for phenomenological researchers is that this event or happening of an original insight cannot be secured by a planned method, even though original insight is supposedly the aim of the method of the reduction. There are no technicalities, procedures, schemes, packages, programs, or computer apps (applications) that will somehow produce or capture an original thought or creative insight. Instead, a phenomenology of the happening or emergence of meaning challenges us to find our way back to the beginning—or as Heidegger says: to inception, the inventive event where thought and meaning begins, where something shows itself, or where that what gives itself gives itself. This beginning must be sought, not in some abstract edifice or theory, but in the primordiality of lived experience.

So, what are the inceptualities of the lived experience of original insights? And how are inceptual moments experienced? Inception connotes origination, birth, dawn, genesis, beginning, and opening. Heidegger already mused how we need to open inceptual space and place ourselves at the beginning of this beginning, and thus witness the birth of meaning. Do we need to prepare and ready ourselves for them? Or do they happen to us when least expected, as if by a granting gesture of grace? The event of inception is confounding. But perhaps, the ontological epistemology of inception may be described as follows:

(1) Inception is that fragile moment of a heuristic event: of the coming upon, being struck by, or suddenly grasping an original idea, experiencing a fundamental insight, realizing the depthful meaning of something. For example, we may have the experience of a sudden understanding of the significance of a question we are pursuing.

And the sudden thought may come as a surprise at a moment when we were not even thinking of these things. Heidegger says that these moments occur in a flash of beying and are fragile and delicate: "When insight takes place then the humans are struck to their essence by the lightning flash of beying. The humans are what is caught sight of in the insight" (Heidegger, 2012a, p. 71).

(2) Inceptual thinking is not the same as conceptual thinking: inceptual thinking involves ingrasping, coming upon an inceptual thought. Heidegger makes a distinction between *Begriff* and *Inbegriff. Begriff* means concept, but *Inbegriff* cannot easily be translated. A concept is an abstract representation that is given precise meaning in theories and scientific reports. But the dictionary describes *Inbegriff* to mean epitome, essence, quintessence. An *Inbegriff* can mean "exemplary example" (see the section on the vocative). An *inbegriff* evokes the richness and uniqueness of the particularity of meaning. So, while the concept generalizes from particulars to abstraction, the *Inbegriff* singularizes.

In their translation of Heidegger's *Contributions to Philosophy*, Parvis Emad and Kenneth Maly translate *Inbegriff* as ingrasping (Heidegger, 1999, p. 45). In contrast, in their new translation of *Contributions to Philosophy*, Richard Rojcei-wcz and Daniela Vallega-Neu translate *Inbegriff* with the term "epitome" (2012b, p. 52). In *The Emergency of Being: On Heidegger's Contributions to Philosophy*, Richard Polt suggests that the best approximation of the term *Inbegriff* may be the word "incept" (Polt, 2006, pp. 115–128). Incepts cannot be methodized or secured by systematic action or manipulation. An inceptual moment happens like a sudden twist or turn. The significance of epitome or incept "lies in the grasping of the turning itself" like a radical turn in our thought: an abrupt and unmediated grasping of "what is essential in the sense of the original-unique" (Heidegger, 2012a, p. 52).

In the turn there suddenly lights up the illuminated clearing of the essence of beying. This sudden self-lighting is the lightning flash. It brings itself into the brightness proper to it, a brightness it brought in with itself... when the truth of beying flashes, the essence of beying lights up; the truth of the essence of beying enters. In taking place, toward what does the entrance [*Einkehr*] turn? Toward nothing other than beying itself, essencing as yet in the forgetfulness of its truth. (Heidegger, 2012a, p. 69)

(3) An inceptual thought tends to come to us indirectly, as if through the backdoor. Perhaps we were musing or thinking about something else when the sudden insight strikes us. No planning, systematic method, or carefully constructed program will get us to the place where inceptual thought dwells. But even though inception cannot be forced; nevertheless, there exist relations of significance between inception and the pathos of thinking and reflecting.

Phenomenologists know that the more intensely the researcher is preoccupied and troubled by that irresistible query that drives the inquiry, the more likely that an original thought will suddenly strike—though often at the least expected moment. It is as if our deepest frustrations and desperate doubts prepare that very fertile small plot where an inceptual thought may sprout and take root. Inception does not happen in an area where we are not residing; it only will happen there where our attentive searching and pregnant desires for the inquiry of our compulsive interest dwell.

(4) We cannot find an inceptual thought; rather, it finds us. The original thought or idea is not something we find by willful action or deliberate efforts. This also implies that we cannot hire others to do the searching for us. Phenomenological inquiry may benefit from cooperative reflection, but the more fundamental inceptual insights are not so easily gained from others or in concert with others. They tend to require personal struggles, private pain, and intimate commitments.

> The inventive thinking of the saying of the beginning is the thinking appropriated by the inceptuality, in the inceptuality, and as the inceptuality.... Nowhere does it refer to the "views" of thinkers, to a "doctrine" about beings ("world"). Or to a mere speaking "about" being. Inventive thinking "is" beying, the latter, however, as the appropriating event....
>
> The inceptuality . . . unfolds the beginning and thus appropriates beginnings . . . whose essence we are starting to surmise. (Heidegger, 2012b, p. 258)

We seize an inceptual thought by letting it seize us or by being seized by it. And yet, paradoxically, if we are not searching, it will not find us. This means that inception is most likely to happen when we are in a state of active passivity.

(5) We know we may have "touched truth" when inceptuality resonates with the call of our quest, the project of our existence. Just as the sudden welling up of a poetic expression may deeply move the poet from whose mind or fingers the words grew into written image (or were the poet's fingers merely the automatic tools?), so an inceptive thought may strike a person with a powerful sensation of having witnessed a momentous moment even though it may only have presented itself in a split second, the blink of an eye.

In sum, phenomenological reflection, analysis, and the generation of insights regarding a phenomenon may indeed require a certain emergent emergency (see Polt, 2006). The emergency is the pregnancy and affective gestation period and condition necessary for an inceptive happening to happen. Only if we are seriously and obsessively thinking about the meaning of a phenomenon (by reflecting on experiences, anecdotes, vignettes, related readings, and so on) can it happen in an unguarded moment that we are suddenly struck or visited by an inceptive insight. But this emergence still assumes a certain struggle and state of emergency, even if the struggle at the time seems in vain or hopeless. Thus, being unable to "see" significances in one's material and being unable to write may actually be a critical state of mind. The frustration and condition of emergency may be necessary mental and physical requisites for inventive insight.

These interpretations of Heidegger's writings on inception are obviously a simplification and a bold translation of Heideggerian originary thinking onto the plane of the quotidian concerns of everyday life. He is concerned with the profound occurrence of inception that opens the space to pure being. He speaks of this originary inception and then the "other inception" that is made possible by it. And even the "other inception" that Heidegger speaks of is an ambiguous notion, though highly suggestive for thinking about originariness of meaning in ordinary experiences that become elevated to phenomenal phenomena. Richard

Polt suggests that if "we manage to think inceptively about our own lives, we will remedy some of the remoteness of [Heidegger's difficult text of] the *Contributions*" (2006, p. 253). Günter Figal says something similar:

> The . . . moments of philosophy that are understood as originary also arise in the everyday world. Peaceful pausing, being present [*Dasein*] and being-withdrawn [*Entzogensein*], the characteristically substantive meaning of a word, as well as doubt, the experience of the "as a whole," and the question of what something is, may be experienced in the everyday. (Figal, 2010, p. 43)

Finally, the originary event of thought and meaning is sometimes described with the concept of "creativity." But Heidegger warns that this would be a shallow understanding of inception. For one thing, inception is often characterized as something that happens to us and that should be understood as an incept (*Inbegriff*), not as a concept (*Begriff*). Similar to the radical reduction, the originary reduction places less emphasis on the activity of the subject: subjectivity tends to be understood in a different, perhaps more passive modality. The challenge for inceptual or originary thought is to find nonconceptual and nontheoretical access to the realm where understandings are evoked through more indirect, poetic, and vocative means. It requires on the part of the researcher patience and a willingness to surrender to the grace of serendipity, even if that means to be frustrated and exasperated when phenomenological insights just do not seem to come.

Inversion—From Meaning to Method

Commonly, writings that deal with phenomenological methodology focus on the thematic understandings that the text may offer the reader. The focus on the thematic aspect of the text is primarily concerned with what the text says, its "semantic" meaning and significance. In contrast, when we focus on the "mantic" aspect of the text, we try to capture how the text speaks, how the text divines and inspirits our understanding. Both forms of meaning are methodologically of critical rhetorical importance to hermeneutic phenomenological inquiry.

We may benefit from the writings of numerous authors who have inspired phenomenology to creatively branch in different directions. Moreover, contemporary phenomenological studies may have different intents and may be contextualized by changed social and methodological frames. So, what do we see when we examine exemplary phenomenological texts? How do we gain a view of how they are constructed?

To investigate how phenomenological texts speak, I examine two fine examples of quotidian phenomenological writing and ask: What do these text look like? How have these works been constructed? What methodological insights are to be gleaned from working backwards, as it were, not from method to meaning but from meaning to method? The point of method is not to claim that, above others, there is one correct or superior mode of inquiry to discover and ascertain the truth or the true meaning of something. There is no single method, just as there is no uncontested truth. Rather, the reason for reflecting on method is to discover the rhetorical approaches and philosophical suppositions that may hold promise in rendering human experience intelligible, interpretable, and understandable in our present time and place. So, the expectation is not to arrive at a recipe, a fool-proof set of techniques and know-hows that are guaranteed to produce repeatable scientific results; rather, the aim of this section is to become sensitive toward some of the vocativities that have been outlined in this chapter. These vocative elements contribute importantly to the phenomenological (cognitive and noncognitive) understanding of the text.

I will focus on the text "On Falling Asleep" by Johannes Linschoten and (to a lesser extent) on *The Fall of Sleep* by Jean-Luc Nancy. Both texts reflect on the experience of falling asleep; both texts are compelling examples of phenomenological insight and writing. Neither Linschoten nor Nancy ever address the process of phenomenological reflection in a technical or procedural manner, but they both use reflective devices and evocative figures.

At first the topic of falling asleep may seem poorly chosen. Why not select a less banal and more scholarly theme to illustrate issues of phenomenological method? But when considering the phenomenon of sleep, the philosopher Gadamer is struck by the mystery of its occurrence:

> This is one of the greatest enigmas we experience in our lives. Think of the deepness of sleep, of sudden awakening and the loss of all sense of time so that we do not know if we have slept for a couple of hours or the whole night. These are extraordinary things. The ability to fall asleep is one of the most inspired discoveries of nature or of God, this gradual drifting away so that one can never actually say, "Now I am sleeping." (1996, p. 114)

Gadamer suggests that reflections on sleep could "help us recognize in the hidden character of health the mystery of our nature as human beings" (1996, p. 115). He cites Plato, who says "it is impossible to heal the body without knowing something about the soul, indeed without knowing something about the nature of the 'whole'" (Gadamer, 1996, p. 115). The term "whole" is meant here not as a methodological catchword, says Gadamer; rather, it refers to "the unity of being itself," to our place in the world and to the way we are in the world because this unity of being is at stake when we concern ourselves with illness and health.

In this speculative formulation of Gadamer's we already gain a measure of the challenge of phenomenological method to make explicit meaning that is felt and grasped at the core of our being. Sleep is such an ordinary fact of our existence that it seems strange that a great philosopher would run out of words in his attempt to describe it. That is why we need, in addition to our conceptual propositional discourse, a vocative expressive language of poetic reach to get beyond the realm of what can be described clearly and unambiguously. So, in a sense, this example of two phenomenological texts about falling asleep is less about the topic of falling asleep than about the methodological feature of vocative expressibility of phenomenological texts.

Kockelmans (the translator of Linschoten's text) makes a comment that is a good starting point for reflecting on some distinct aspects of these vocative texts. When he introduces the selection of texts by Dutch and German phenomenologists in his edited book, he makes a passing remark about how this work makes much use of poetry and literature. Some may feel uncomfortable with the way in which these European phenomenologists, even in their own writing, seem to reach deeply into the stylistic realms of the humanities. In accounting for this poetic feature of phenomenological works Kockelmans says:

> Often an appeal to poetry and literature is almost unavoidable in that poetic language with its use of symbolism is able to refer beyond the realm of what can be said "clearly and distinctly." In other words, ... in human reality there are certain phenomena which reach so deeply into a man's life and the world in which he lives that poetic language is the only adequate way through which to point to and to make present a meaning which we are unable to express clearly in any other way. (1987, p. ix)

Kockelmans adds, however, that poems and literature cannot function as a substitute, because, he says, "poems and novels do not 'prove' anything" (1987, p. ix). He places the term "prove" in quotation marks, as if to indicate that we should not take this idea too narrowly. Kockelmans does not elaborate why it is that phenomenological texts often seem to require the special language of novels and poetry to do their work. And so, he leaves us to wonder, in what sense does the inclusion of poetic imagery play a part in the "seeing" of meaning and in the power of the text to show, present, and clarify meaning?

From the first moment we read Linschoten's article, we immediately recognize how prominent this poetic aspect of phenomenological writing is by simply taking note of the frequent quotes from literature. In the text "On Falling Asleep" we encounter lines, stanzas, and paragraphs from folk-poems and from the writings of authors such as Wordsworth, Rilke, Gide, Baudelaire, Nietzsche, Poe, and Proust. As well, Linschoten (1987) gives us interpretive insights by drawing from the relevant works of phenomenologists such as Sartre, Merleau-Ponty, Bergson, Bachelard, Buytendijk, van den Berg, and Bollnow.

The point is that these philosophers, poets, and novelists are not simply included for purpose of embellishment, mere rhetoric, or illustration; no, the poetic material is there for reasons inherent to the logic of phenomenological inquiry. We might never discover this logic if we insist on sticking to the philosopher's mountain peak and on developing an approach to phenomenological research and writing that proceeds from epistemology to application, from method to meaning. It tends to overlook the imaginal play of language that is exemplified in the more concrete and practical examples of actual lifeworld studies. To reiterate, in this case I examine the phenomenological structures of Linschoten and Nancy's texts—not by going from method to meaning, but by going from meaning to method. I ask the question: what methodical features did Linschoten and Nancy ostensibly employ to do their phenomenological inquiry, to write their texts on falling asleep? What might we find when we ask how these texts seem to have been written? I will be especially attentive to vocative elements in the texts.

Linchoten's article originally appeared in a Dutch philosophical journal in 1952. It was published in English in the 1987 compilation of Dutch and German phenomenological studies translated by the philosopher Joseph Kockelmans. This book, *Phenomenological Psychology: The Dutch School*, contains several articles dating from the 1950s and 1960s (see van den Berg and Linschoten, 1953)—a fine set of samples of phenomenological texts associated with the Utrecht School of Phenomenology.

Jean-Luc Nancy's *The Fall of Sleep* was published in French in 2007; it is separated from Linschoten's article by more than half a century. Nancy's text appears in an English translation in 2009. It is probably one of the most readable examples of Nancy's reflective writing. Nancy also makes frequent use of poets and novelists in his writings, though in *The Fall of Sleep* he only uses Shakespeare, Foster, and Baudelaire. But, interestingly, Nancy's own writing is even more lyrically evocative than Linschoten's writing. Both authors create a wondering sensibility that helps to create an intrigue in the question of the meaning of falling asleep. Linschoten immediately asks what it is like to fall asleep by comparing it to insomnia. In contrast, Nancy starts out by asking what kind of falling it is that happens in falling asleep by comparing it to other kinds of falling.

Now, in the following sections I will examine the tonal features that will be discerned in these texts. I will show how these are the vocative elements or methods of concreteness, nearness, intensification, appeal, and epiphany that are already initiated in Chapter 6. While it is possible to separately discuss these mantic figures they often are visible only as aspects of the text as a whole.

Lived-Throughness: The Revocative Value of a Text

Lived-throughness is the *revocative* quality of a text that brings an experience vividly in our presence. This sense of lived-throughness may be accomplished through the use of experiential descriptions, concrete imagery, and poetic or narrative examples. Linschoten begins his 38-page article about falling asleep with an epigram. He issues an appeal to our concrete sense of the problem of sleeplessness with the aid of a stanza from a poem by Wordsworth:

> A flock of sheep that leisurely pass by,
> One after one; the sound of rain and bees
> Murmuring; the fall of rivers, wind and seas,
> Smooth fields, white sheets of water, and pure sky;
> I have thought of all by turns, and yet do lie
> Sleepless! . . .

> (In Linschoten, 1987, p. 79)

Linschoten uses Wordsworth's poem about an insomniac to introduce the topic of falling asleep. He says:

> These words of a desperate poet unable to get to sleep plunge us immediately into the midst of the problematic which will interest us here: the question of falling asleep. All of us know of the conflicts and exasperations which surround not being able to fall asleep. (1987, p. 79)

Less than a half page further, Linschoten uses another poem, an old German folk rhyme, to further describe the experience of falling asleep. He asks the methodological question whether it is possible to reflect on falling asleep since sleep, as a life phenomenon, is evidently unreflexive. Here is the translated German rhyme:

> I would like to know how one falls asleep
> Over and over I press myself in the pillow
> And thereby think: "Now I will pay attention,"
> But before I have really reflected,
> It is already morning already,
> And I have again awakened.
>
> (In Linschoten, 1987, p. 80)

Linschoten poses his phenomenological question concretely through the use of poetry. The experience of falling asleep is not a theoretical issue but a concern that is an aspect of everyday life. Folk-poems are evidence that concrete interests in falling asleep are passed on from one generation to the next.

Sleep does not always come when desired. Linschoten continues his appeal to our common experience by adopting a style of concrete particulars:

> We all remember those nights when we tried everything but without success; on the contrary, the more we exerted ourselves the more awake we became. The insomniac tosses and turns in his bed, continually changes position, sighs, squeezes his eyes shut, stops the ticking of the clock that is two rooms away, puts plugs in his ears, is warm and cold in turns, listens to his heartbeat, tries all the well-known tricks without success—and then in an unguarded moment falls asleep. (Linschoten, 1987, p. 79)

As a reader of Linschoten text I do indeed recall those nights of wakefulness myself; but even more vividly, I recall the numerous times that my son would come to our bedside when he was still elementary school age:

> "Papa, I can't sleep!"
> "What do you mean, you can't sleep?"
> "I dunno. I'm trying. I'm trying. I'm trying really hard, but, you know, I just can't sleep. It makes me mad! What should I do?"

There were many nights that I would attempt to give my son advice. But advice does not seem to work well for combating sleeplessness. So, I told stories in the hope that the soporific effect would make him doze off somewhere in the middle. But, to no avail. I tried to help him by patiently probing and listening to any unresolved problems or anxieties that I thought might prevent him from doing what his brother did so easily. The latter would be in a deep slumber almost as soon as his head hits the pillow. What makes it difficult for sleep to come for one child when it comes so easily for another? And what could I do? Is it possible to help a child deal with insomnia? Does it help to count sheep? What do you do for a child who is too old for lullabies, too young for sleeping pills, and too big to continue the habit of crawling in bed with his parents?

As adults we may have trouble sleeping because we are doing shift-work, or we must try to nap during an unbearably uncomfortable plane flight. Or, we cannot sleep because we cannot stop worrying about some things or someone. Patients, especially, may have difficulty sleeping in a strange hospital bed. They may not sleep because they worry about upcoming surgery, or they may be roomed with people they don't know. Perhaps they are used to sleeping under heavy bedding and now they are covered by a meager hospital blanket, or they are used to sleeping unencumbered and now they must lie in bed dressed in pajamas or in a hospital gown that cuts into the neck. Nurses tell that physicians routinely place a standing order for bedtime sedation to help patients "sleep," but this is medically manipulated sleep.

Linschoten (1987) provides concrete portrayals of falling asleep and of insomnia, so that as readers we may find continuity between these concrete examples and the particulars of our own lives. Concreteness of text places us right in the midst of lived reality where a phenomenon such as falling asleep can be a felt concern. And, if we are able to alert the reader to the interest of the concrete question, then they may be set up well for phenomenological attentiveness.

Jean-Luc Nancy uses different opening lines, making us wonder what it means to say that we fall in falling asleep:

> I'm falling asleep. I'm falling into sleep and I'm falling there by the power of sleep. Just as I drop from boredom. As I fall on hard times. As I fall, in general. Sleep sums up all these falls, it gathers them together. Sleep is proclaimed and symbolized by the sign of the fall, the more or less swift descent or sagging, faintness. (2007a, p. 1)

Nearness: The Vivid Evocation of Experience

Evocation means that experience is brought vividly into presence, so that we can phenomenologically reflect on it. Linschoten not only grounds his writing in the concrete lifeworld, his selecting from poetic and literary sources and his own anecdotal portrayals are often vivid and sensuous. I would like to note that this is not always the case in human science texts. A description may be concrete, situated in the lifeworld, but not every concrete description is vivid. Vividness or aliveness is sometimes used as an evaluative category to appraise phenomenological texts positively. However, vividness is not an aim in itself. Vividness becomes functional when it acquires the power of realization, of fastening a hold upon nearness. A vivid experiential description is methodologically valuable because it creates the experience of nearness or presence—"only by evoking it are we able to make something present," says Linschoten (1987, p. 99). Evocation calls forth, or brings to immediate presence, images and sensibilities that are so crisp and real that they in turn evoke reflective responses such as wondering, questioning, understanding. Therefore, Gadamer says, "We praise vividness—because it sets our intuitive capacities in motion" (1986, p. 162). Phenomenological texts aim to enchant, to turn mundaneness into transcendence, familiarity into strangeness.

Let me give another example of which a personal reading of Linschoten may remind us. The short story "The Guest" by Albert Camus (1957) plays in a small Algerian town. Daru has been assigned the task of escorting an Arab murderer into custody. He must first spend one night in his secluded room alone with the prisoner before accompanying him to the authorities in the neighboring village. Daru is a school teacher and it is not surprising that he is uncomfortable with the situation.

> In the middle of the night, Daru was still not asleep. He had gone to bed after undressing completely; he generally slept naked. But when he suddenly realized that he had nothing on, he wondered. He felt vulnerable and the temptation came to him to put his clothes back on. Then he shrugged his shoulders; after all, he wasn't a child and, if it came to that, he could break his adversary in two. (Camus, 1980, p. 79)

For a while Daru remains alert because he has the distinct impression that his prisoner only pretends to be asleep. As he lies awake, he becomes aware of all the country sounds around him. He listens to his guest's breathing, which finally has turned regular and heavy; the Arab now seems asleep. But still, Daru cannot sleep, and he remains preoccupied with his circumstances: sharing a room with a perfect stranger with whom he now seems to share a bond. When unexpectedly, he hears the man stir, Daru stiffens because he suddenly realizes that his revolver is still on the desk in the next room. This man, after all, is a self-confessed murderer. Yet, Daru does nothing but quietly observe the Arab, who silently gets to his feet and walks out of the room.

> Daru had not stirred. "He is running away," he merely thought. "Good riddance!" yet he listened attentively. The hens were not fluttering; the guest must be on the plateau. A faint sound of water reached him, and he didn't know what it was until the Arab again stood framed in the doorway, closed the door carefully, and came back to bed without a sound. Then Daru turned his back on him and fell asleep. Still later he seemed, from the depths of his sleep, to hear furtive steps around the schoolhouse. "I'm dreaming! I'm dreaming!" he repeated to himself. And he went on sleeping. (Camus, 1980, pp. 80, 81)

Of course, the story of Daru is only important here in that it confronts us with an immediate sense of the phenomenon of going to sleep, sleeplessness, and dream-sleeping while still being aware of things happening. We may recognize the uncomfortableness of going to bed naked in the presence of a stranger. We may feel the impossibility of going to sleep when the world around us keeps calling upon us; we may sense how it is possible to keep on sleeping even though the pilot light of our awareness seems to be registering certain goings on. Camus gives us vivid examples of the difficulties of sleeping and of sleeping in spite of difficulties; he brings these experiences into present nearness so that we can "know" them cognitively while "feeling" them noncognitively. But, of course, Camus offers us a story and not a phenomenological study, and so there is no analysis, no reflection, no attempt to bring to language the possible meaning structures of the phenomenon as such.

Yet, what makes Camus' story phenomenologically attractive is that it not only provides a concrete description, but the description in turn evokes vivid images and associations that prompt our thoughtful reflection. We might wonder, what made falling asleep for Daru initially impossible and what allowed him to fall asleep when he did? Can one be truly asleep and yet hear things? Are we still attuned to the world when we sleep? What makes us wake up to one sound but not another? More fundamentally, what is sleep anyway? Indeed, these are the evoked wonderings that lead to phenomenological reflections. We might say that in Linschoten text the reflections are tied to the evocations. When the phenomenologist strives for vividness, it is not for the sake of vividness itself, but for the precise aim of evoking particular images that call forth and bring into presence relevant aspects of the experience in which we are interested, so that we can reflect on the meanings that inhere in them.

Intensification: Invocative Value of Key-words

Intensification means that we must give key-words their *invocative* value, so that layers of phenomenological meaning become strongly embedded in the text. Let us again pay attention to Linschoten's method of writing. We can see that he not only borrows from poets and novelists in order to explore concrete experience, he not only writes in a manner that is vivid and that evokes images that become available for reflection—he also makes use of poetic devices such as repetition and alliteration in order to produce certain poetic effects and understandings.

Linchoten's text becomes quite differentiated and complex in its exploration of the various dimensions of falling asleep. But I can only give one simple example. Linschoten makes a distinction between two kinds of silence: a silence that prevents one from sleeping and a silence that is conducive to sleep. But to convince us, he cannot just state this or use a conceptual definition (as I do here); rather, he needs to evoke our felt understanding. He writes:

> The silence we need in order to sleep is not merely the *absence of noise*, but the *meaningless, stilling* silence. The ticking of the clock, a speech which is boring, the creaking of the bed, noise made by streetcars and cars, and even a lively conversation around us do not keep us from falling asleep provided they are meaningless and worthless; however, a low soft conversation in the room next door, or an alarming drip from a leaking roof, or the irregular breathing of your spouse can be enough to deprive you of all sleep. That is because they address themselves to us and we have to answer to their appeal. (Linschoten, 1987, p. 90)

The silence, which is stilling, announces a changed intentional relation with the world. Linschoten's phenomenological writing often works so well, not only because he grounds his description concretely in the lifeworld, and not only because his language evokes vivid images but also because he works poetically with language so that felt understandings that lie beyond language come within reach. Linschoten text is phenomenologically convincing because he writes in a sober-minded manner and yet he is sensitive to the poetic. The alliterative phrase *stilling silence* is an example of that kind of intensification of language that resembles the thickening and compressing effect of poetry. This "thickening" is, of course, the thickening of meaning that we experience in the contingent often unpredictable moment of happening on the right words and the right combination of words in our attempt to say something just right. If we were to alter the text by paraphrasing or summarizing, then we would most likely experience some loss of meaning. The silence that stills the world makes the things of the world withdraw just as the settling darkness makes the world of the visible recede and surrender its pull on our attentiveness. But silence and darkness in themselves do not induce sleep. In fact, some people need light, and others a chime, or the sound, perhaps, of distant traffic.

Thus, we could speak of the sounds of silence that have a stilling effect on the world, and indeed this stilling is precisely the experience of the phenomenon of sleepiness. To experience stilling silence is to feel sleepy. But, says Linschoten, the moment that we encounter "the dark" or "silence" itself, then sleep becomes impossible. When silence no longer means the gradual dissolving of our conversational relation with the world, but becomes, instead, substantial and acquires the significance of a charged stillness that may be broken at any moment, then silence turns threatening or frightening. This kind of silence, substantial silence, issues an appeal to us from which we cannot escape. For example, a suspicious rustle in the house may hardly qualify as noise, but it can alarm us and keep us awake. We wonder: Is there someone moving around down there? A burglar perhaps? In other words, we hear some noise and wonder what it could mean. Linschoten observes that it is also possible that the voice of silence that addresses us is emotionally encouraging, sexually stimulating, or intellectually challenging as in the case when we are unable to sleep because we cannot let go of certain desires or problems that preoccupy us.

In examining how we experience falling asleep, Linschoten constantly contrasts it with opposite experiences such as insomnia or the inclination to wake up when disturbed—this, of course, is the "phenomenological variation in imagination" or the eidetic reduction. He questions the popular view that sleep can be brought about by blocking out stimuli and darkening the environment. He says that he wants to "defend the thesis" that there is no necessary relation between the absence of stimuli and our falling asleep. But, while he develops a thesis-like argument about the role of noise and darkness in falling asleep, the overall logical structure of his discourse is less a scientific reasoning than a reflective experiential showing. At the hand of evocative descriptions, he brings us to understand in a feeling and emotive manner how "darkness and absence of noise can motivate our falling asleep, but they cannot cause it" (1987, p. 89).

Let us examine some of the eidetic reduction types of statements that appear in Linschoten text. Some of the thematic claims that Linschoten makes aim at calling into question common (mis)conceptions. For example, he shows that the art of falling asleep by boring oneself through slowly counting or through endlessly reciting short sentences such as "when the flowers grow" may indeed be effective but not because one becomes bored. Linschoten states that (i) falling asleep means that the world falls asleep and wraps itself in stilling silence; (ii) sleep is a meditation of the body that surrenders and relaxes its hold on the world; (iii) boredom does not precede sleep but is the inability to sleep; (iv) insomnia is the sign of an insecurity or uncertainty that makes it impossible to "leave" the world.

People who do phenomenological research like to discover and list themes. But thesis-like or thematic types of statements communicate primarily conceptual meaning, and this conceptual meaning does not need to involve a "felt" or more deeply sensed understanding. Therefore, these themes must constantly be "mantically massaged" as it were. We must discover the nodal points and the nerve endings of sensory sense; we must discern where a certain pressure or compressure may suddenly bring about linguistic liveliness. This working of the text with experiential accounts, evocative constructions, intensified language, and thoughtful reflections embeds and converts thematic claims into a narrative text that contains and safeguards phenomenological meaning.

Moreover, the silences in texts also have meaning; not only the words themselves but also the spaces between the words and between passages can be charged with special meaning as a result of intensification. It is clear that one cannot easily fiddle with the words of a text that possesses a high degree of intensification. Indeed, when we change the words by trying to paraphrase or summarize a poetic text, then the secondary meanings tend to seep away. That is why Burms and de Dijn (1990) suggest that meaning may be differently incarnated or embedded in different types of text. In poetic text, meaning tends to be strongly embedded, while in informational text, meaning tends to be weakly embedded. To say that meaning is strongly incarnated means that the relational tension between words and passages is compressed and tightly woven and would be disturbed if interfered with.

It is no accident that the Dutch and German word for poem is *gedicht* and *Dichtung*; writing poetically means *dichten*, "to make dense, to thicken, to intensify." Poetry is the thickening of language. The author tries to intensify complexities and subtleties of meaning through poetic or rhetoric devices and through a careful weighing of words and word combinations while remaining attuned to the usage of words and to the possible augmenting and distorting effects that words may have on each other when they are composed and composted, placed side by side, and commingled in fertile combinations. Moreover, repetition of sensed qualities, through devices such as alliteration, assonance, consonance, diction, sentence structure, repetition, and imagery, contribute an acoustic richness, an audible imagery to the text. The euphonic effect of alliterative, assonant, rhythmic, or rhymed text is that it enhances the reality feeling of its implicit meaning.

Indeed, the phenomenon of strongly embedded meaning seems to hold true for an alliterative phrase such as "stilling silence." Linschoten describes the stilling silence as the world that falls asleep: the world "becomes still and wraps itself in silence" (p. 91). He says that we need to experience this positive quality of silence in order to be able to rest and sleep. Linschoten seems to use just the right words in his attempt to evoke the phenomenological sensibility and sensuousness of the nature of this silence. The stilling effect of this silence is experienced as something unique, "namely, that silent enveloping something which we do not have to answer because it does not say or ask anything." It is "the gradual becoming silent of the conversation . . . the dialogue between me and my world" (p. 91). By carefully quoting the lines from Linschoten text, I try to avoid having to paraphrase his explications. Why? Because decompressing strongly embedded meaning through annotations, paraphrasing, and summations cannot be done without loss of meaning.

(Em)Pathic: The Convocative Effect of Text

The tone of the text has to do with its convocative pathic quality. With the image of the darkening world and the felicitous phrase "stilling silence," Linschoten shows that falling asleep is not so much a result of certain activity, but rather the abandonment of activity. In going to bed and readying ourselves for the night we must *convoke* a world, which falls asleep and stops appealing to us. By letting go of our wide awakeness, by closing down our dialogue with the world in which we live and of which we are a part, we seem to evoke sleep itself, says Linschoten. We conjure sleep by imitating it as an attitude. Linschoten cites Merleau-Ponty, not in order to appeal to his authority but to use the evocative tone by means of which Merleau-Ponty, in his *Phenomenology of Perception*, describes this experiential moment. He makes us feel, as it were, what it is to physically evoke sleep through imitation:

> I lie down in bed, on my left side, with my knees drawn up; I close my eyes, breathe slowly, and distance myself from my projects. But this is where the power of my will or consciousness ends. Just as the faithful in Dionysian mysteries, invoke the god by imitating the scenes of his life. I too call forth the visitation of sleep by imitating the breathing and posture of the sleeper ...
>
> Sleep "arrives" at a particular moment, it settles upon this imitation of itself that I offered it, and I succeeded in becoming what I pretended to be: that unseeing and nearly unthinking mass, confined to a point in space and no longer in the world except through the anonymous vigilance of the senses. (2012, pp. 166, 167)

Linschoten elaborates Merleau-Ponty's description by showing through concrete examples that falling asleep is not an activity performed by us, such as grasping or thinking, and that the simultaneous conjuring and overpowering effect of sleep is already suggested in the figure of the Sandman. In Dutch language, sleep (*slaap*) is personified as a mysterious man. All Dutch children have heard of the Sandman, Klaas Vaak, who sprinkles magic sand in your eyes and in doing so makes you sleep. In the morning your mother may look at your eyes, wipe them clean and say: "Yes, I can see that the Sandman has visited you." Many Dutch children have attempted at one time or another to catch Klaas Vaak (the Sandman) in the act, only to find that he is always too clever. He surprises you before you can actually see him. But the evidence—sand in your eyes—is there again in the morning.

Epiphany: The Provocative Quality of Text

Epiphany means that a text has a *provocative* quality, so that its deeper meaning may exercise and provoke a transformative effect on the self of the reader. Epiphany refers to the sudden perception or intuitive grasp of the life meaning of something. This experience is so strong or striking that it may stir us at the core of our being.

Now, with respect to Linschoten (1987) text on falling asleep, it, too, is successful only to the extent that we, its readers, feel addressed by it—in the totality or unity of our being. Linschoten text must resonate with our ordinary experience of life as well as with our sense of life's meaning. This does not necessarily mean that one must feel entertained by Linschoten text or that it has to be an "easy read." In fact, reading a phenomenological study may be a truly laborious effort. And yet, if we are willing to make the effort, then we may be able to say that the text provokes us not unlike the way in which a work of art may provoke us even when it gives itself to us and thus gives us to ourselves, as Marion would say.

To get at the epiphanic dimension of meaning, Linschoten again resorts to literature: to the writings of Proust and Baudelaire. Marcel Proust tells of an incident that many of us may recognize from childhood. He is waiting for his mother to come to his bed and say good night but she is not coming.

> I had cut myself off from the possibility of going to sleep until I actually had seen her, and my heart began to beat more and more painfully as I increased my agitation by ordering myself to keep calm and to acquiesce in my ill fortune. Then, suddenly, my anxiety subsided, a feeling of intense happiness coursed through me, as when a strong medicine begins to take effect and one's pain vanishes: I had found a resolution to abandon all attempt to go to sleep without seeing Mamma. (Linschoten, 1987, p. 113)

The young Marcel longs so much for his mother to come that he cannot sleep. He wants to sleep, but he cannot. Like an insomniac, he simply cannot leave the world. Perhaps his mother's absence represents the feeling of Marcel's insecurity. "He desires to sleep in order to escape from being awake; but this desire precisely keeps him awake," says Linschoten (1987, p. 114). To reflect is to be engaged in a conversation with the world. The one who reflects stays wakeful. So rather than sleeping, Marcel Proust cannot stop waking and reflecting on his predicament. And, as Linschoten shows, nobody is more caught up in reflection than he or she who tries to escape it.

Perhaps that is why the poet Baudelaire conjured up the ideal of sleep—not really to sleep but to live in his dreamworld, says Linschoten. Baudelaire desired to live in a world where he would be conscious but not reflexive. Thus, he sought the blissful nothingness of sleep. In Baudelaire's words: "to know nothing, to learn nothing, to feel nothing, to sleep and to sleep again and again, that is my only wish" (Linschoten, 1987, p. 95). Not to have to think, to will, to linger with things, but simply to drift in the stream of one's experiences. The dreamer feels that it is reflection that spoils experience, and it is this reflection from which the poet Baudelaire tries to flee. "What is the characteristic of reflection which so horrifies the dreamers?" asks Linschoten. And he answers, "It is to be found in the fact, that it [reflection] cannot comprehend itself, that it alienates itself from the experience, and yet is presupposed for the possibility of letting oneself go in the stream of experience" (1987, p. 95). Nancy also cites Baudelaire at the end of his text on *The Fall of Sleep*. Baudelaire confesses to be afraid of sleep "as one fears a huge hole" (in Nancy, 2009, p. 47). But then he also seems to long for the blissful nothingness of sleep: "a numb feeling yearning for nothingness" (p. 47). Perhaps Baudelaire is playing on Friedrich Nietzsche's reflections on that state of dreamlike unconscious consciousness that seems to characterize the contented lives of animals who can simply dwell in the present, conscious but not thinking.

Consider the herd grazing before you. These animals do not know what yesterday and today are but leap about, eat, rest, digest and leap again; and so, from morning to night and from day to day, only briefly concerned with their pleasure and displeasure, enthralled by the moment and for that reason neither melancholy nor bored. It is hard for a man to see this, for he is proud of being human and not an animal and yet regards its happiness with envy because he wants nothing other than to live like the animal, neither bored nor in pain, yet wants it in vain because he does not want it like the animal . . .

Man may well ask the animal: why do you not speak to me of your happiness but only look at me? The animal does want to answer and say: because I always immediately forget what I wanted to say—but then it already forgot this answer and remained silent: so that man could only wonder. (Nietzsche, 1981, p. 8)

But one should wonder even more how it is that we cannot learn to forget, that we always remain attached to the past. Nietzsche's reflections on the temporality of the moment foreshadow Husserl's notion of primal impressional consciousness. The moment of the now is always still and already attached to the retentional and protentional consciousness of the just now and the now to come. However, Nietzsche does not yet see that we are attached to the past through a preconscious and a conscious memory chain: retentional memories as well as the memorable memories that we can actually recall.

It is astonishing: the moment, here in a wink, gone in a wink, nothing before and nothing after, returns nevertheless as a spectre to disturb the calm of a later moment. Again, and again a page loosens in the scroll of time, drops out, and flutters away—and suddenly flutters back again into man's lap. Then man says "I remember" and envies the animal which immediately forgets and sees each moment really die, sink back into deep night extinguished for ever. In this way the animal lives *unhistorically*. (1981, pp. 8, 9)

Some would envy the animal who can exist in the unconscious consciousness of the pure present. Why can we not just live blissfully in the present! But Nietzsche points out that it is not really possible to live in the moment, in the present of the now, and not be burdened with the histories of our past and the futures to come.

he is moved, as though he remembered a lost paradise, when he sees a grazing herd, or, in more intimate proximity, sees a child, which as yet has nothing past to deny, playing between the fences of past and future in blissful blindness. And yet the child's play must be disturbed: only too soon will it be called out of its forgetfulness. (1981, p. 9)

Both Linschoten and Nancy arrive at some profound realizations about sleep, wakefulness, and the longing as well as the horror that the dreamlike state of sleep may confront us with. These are the epiphanic qualities of their texts that provoke the reader to read the texts as a writer: to read is to rewrite. And obviously phenomenological text should never be read merely for its surface message. The epiphanic sense of the text is directly related to the lived meaning that phenomenology attempts to evoke. On the one hand, this is a somewhat difficult point to make since the epiphanic power of text cannot be presented in straightforward conceptual terms. On the other hand, epiphany is something that is part of the experience of language in everyday life. We experience an epiphanic moment when a text suddenly addresses us in a manner that validates our experience, when it conveys a life understanding that stirs our sensibilities, when it pulls the strings of unity of our being. A phenomenological text makes us "think," and it makes the world address us and call upon us to think our feeling in the broadest and deepest sense of the term. It moves us to experience reflectively life's meaning at the level of sensory and prereflective awareness as well as at the level of reflective meaning that concerns our place in life.

Linschoten ends his lengthy article by making an important epistemological comment about the nature of phenomenological writing and texts. He reminds the reader that "the essence of falling asleep is not contained in the terms of this analysis." Rather, his text has reached its goal only if the reader is "continuously confronted with the phenomenon" (1987, p. 115). This is also true for the writer. I quoted George Steiner earlier when he says that "the genuine writer is a self-reader" (1989, p. 126). To write is to stir the self as reader. As writers, we know that we have achieved epiphany when we have managed to stir our own self. Of course, there is always the danger that we are merely enchanted by the superficial haunt of shallow sentimentality or catchy formulations; that is why it is good practice to check again the effect of the text several days after writing it. It is tempting to simply conceive of the pathic or mantic meaning of a text as the emotive or feeling dimension of language, but it is a mistake to distinguish too strongly between feelings and understandings, ideas and emotions. It is apt to paraphrase a line from a prose poem by the poet Karl Shapiro (1968) and say that phenomenological understandings are what ideas feel like. Perhaps I should offer the stanza from which this is taken in its entirety, since what Shapiro says about poets seems true also of phenomenologists:

As you say (not without sadness), poets don't see, they feel. And that's why people who have turned to feelers seem like poets. Why children seem poetic. Why when the sap rises in the adolescent heart the young write poetry. Why great catastrophes are stated in verse. Why lunatics are named for the moon. Yet poetry isn't feeling with the hands. A poem is not a kiss. Poems are what ideas feel like. Ideas on Sunday, thoughts on vacation. (Shapiro, 1968, p. 257)

A text that is thoughtful—which reflects on life while reflecting life—does not necessarily need to include borrowings from poets or novelists. In thoughtful phenomenological texts, the distinction between poetic and narrative is hard to draw. The researcher-as-author is challenged to construct a phenomenological text that possesses concreteness, evocativeness, intensity, tone, and epiphany.

CHAPTER TWELVE

Human Science Methods: Empirical and Reflective Activities

Phenomenological philosophers rarely employ empirical methods derived from the social sciences. And, yet, many phenomenological studies are rich in experiential empirical material. For example, the texts by Sartre contain concrete stories of events that he observed in situations around him, such as in the Parisian cafés that he frequented. Lingis' phenomenological travel texts are extremely rich with observations and interactive conversations with people he encounters. Blanchot, Merleau-Ponty, Cixous, Marion, and Derrida frequently use experiential materials from myths and literature. In offering pedagogical advice to the young, Serres uses many stories from his personal life. And as we have seen, many other phenomenological authors use incidents from personal life, from history, the news media, fictional stories, novels, and artistic sources. In this way the rich grounds and experiential soils of human existence are being mined, plowed, and seeded for phenomenological insights.

Especially phenomenological researchers who are not professional philosophical phenomenologists have turned to the empirical methods of the social sciences (1) to gather more systematically experiential material, (2) to use reflective methods to thematize the meanings embedded in the experiential material, (3) to pursue the significance of thematic aspects of phenomena and events for human existence. Indeed, this is the main reason for phenomenology to turn to social science methods: to gain experiential material for the purpose of phenomenological reflection and existential insights into the practices of the lifeworld. When social science methods are adopted to do phenomenology, then it is common practice to speak of "human science phenomenology."

First, it is important to realize that data-gathering methods borrowed from the social sciences—like the interview, observation, participation—for the purpose of phenomenological inquiry differ critically from those methods as practiced in social science disciplines such as ethnography, narrative inquiry, critical theory, biography, and so on. The difference is that the phenomenological interview and related methods primarily deal with prereflective experiential accounts. It should be noted as well that phenomenological interviewing and observing need to be conducted while the researcher has adopted the phenomenological attitude as described under the reduction.

Second, the reflective methods of thematizing and meaning analysis must be integrated with the method of the epoché and the reduction. From a Husserlian perspective, reflective human science methods are concerned with identifying the major and minor eidetic meanings and insights that belong to the phenomena or

DOI: 10.4324/9781003228073-15

events that are being studied in a phenomenological research project. But from a broader phenomenological perspective, too, the reflective process of analyzing and thematizing meaning needs to remain informed by the understanding and adoption of the various forms of the reduction. In analyzing texts, we ask of each textual fragment: "How does this speak to the phenomenal meaning?" These reflective methods of thematization are an interim part of the larger reflective process that eventually must prove itself in the phenomenological research-writing project. Phenomenological themes are like creative short-hands that are supposed to help with the process of carefully spinning out a detailed phenomenological text. Themes should become helpful guides in the writing of the meaningful and significant phenomenalities of the phenomenological text.

So, as the phenomenological research approach is imported into professional disciplines such as psychology, education, pedagogy, nursing, and medicine, its methodological resources begin to include research methods and tools that belong to the social sciences, but those were rarely employed by professional philosophers (until quite recently). First, phenomenological human science adopted empirical data-gathering methods, and, second, it adopted reflective methods and techniques.

Empirical methods describe the various kinds of research activities that provide the researcher with experiential material. They may include personal descriptions of experiences, gathering written experiences from others, interviewing for experiential accounts, observing experiences, identifying fictional experiences, and exploring imaginal experiences from other aesthetic sources.

Reflective methods describe certain forms of analysis or phenomenological reflection in keeping with the reduction-proper. We may distinguish thematic reflection, such as collaborative reflection, linguistic reflection, etymological reflection, conceptual reflection, exegetical reflection, and hermeneutic interview reflection. In any research project, the selection and usage of empirical (experiential) and reflective (reductional) methods and approaches depend upon the context and the nature of the study. The important point is that these methods are especially adapted for the purpose of phenomenological inquiry (see also van Manen, 1997).

Empirical Methods of Gathering Lived Experience Descriptions

So, the main purpose of the empirical methods is to explore examples and varieties of lived experiences, especially in the form of narratives, vignettes, anecdotes, stories, and other experiential accounts. The lifeworld, the world of everyday lived experience, is both the source and the object of *phenomenology of practice* research. And so, we may search anywhere in the lifeworld for material: through interview, observation, language analysis, fictional accounts, and so on. We need to realize, of course, that experiential accounts or lived experience descriptions are never truly identical to the prereflective lived experiences themselves. All recollections of experiences, reflections on experiences, descriptions of experiences, recorded interviews of experiences, or transcribed conversations about experiences are already transformations of those experiences. Even life captured directly by audio-recorder or camera is already selected or transformed at the moment it is captured. Without this dramatic elusive element of lived meaning for our reflective attention, phenomenology would not be necessary. The upshot is that we need to find access to life's living dimensions while hoping that the meanings we bring to the surface have not entirely lost some of the natural quiver of their undisturbed existence, as Merleau-Ponty might say.

One method of phenomenological research is to "borrow" other people's experiences. *We gather and borrow other people's experiences because these allow us, in a vicarious sort of way, to become more experienced ourselves.* We are interested in the particular experiences of this child, this adolescent, or this adult man or woman since they allow us to become "informed," enriched by this experience so as to be able to render the full significance of its meaning. Traditionally, social and human science techniques are used to obtain "data" from "subjects" by way of interviewing, eliciting written responses, participatory observing, and so forth. Phenomenological research may proceed along similar lines, but with some important qualifications. From a phenomenological point of view, we are not primarily interested in the experiences of our so-called subjects or informants for the sake of being able to report on how this or that particular person (or group of people) experiences or perceives something. Rather, the aim is to collect examples of *possible human experiences* in order to reflect on the meanings that may inhere in them.

Personal experience is often a good starting point for phenomenological inquiry. To be aware of the structure of one's own experience of a phenomenon may provide the researcher with clues for orienting to the phenomenon and thus to all the other dimensions of phenomenological research. Our personal life experiences are immediately accessible to us in a way that no one else's experiences are. However, the phenomenologist does not necessarily want to trouble the reader with purely private, autobiographical facticities of his or her own life (unless that is the specific intent). In drawing up personal descriptions of lived experiences, the phenomenologist knows that the patterns of meaning of one's own experiences are also the possible experiences of others and therefore may be recognizable by others.

To conduct a personal description of a lived experience, I try to describe my experience as much as possible in experiential terms, focusing on a particular situation or event. I try, as Merleau-Ponty says, to give a "direct description" of my experience as it is, without offering causal explanations or interpretive generalizations of my experience. It is to the extent that *my* experiences could be *our* or *your* experiences that the phenomenologist wants to be reflectively aware of certain experiential aspects. In phenomenological descriptions, one often notices that the author uses the "I" form or the "we" form of the personal pronoun. This is done not only to enhance the evocative value of a truth experience expressed in this way, but also to show that the author recognizes both that one's own experiences are the possible experiences of others and also that the experiences of others are the possible experiences of oneself.

The "data" of human science and humanities research are human experiences. It seems obvious, therefore, that if we wish to investigate the meaning dimensions of a certain experience (phenomenon), the most straightforward way to go about our research is to ask selected individuals to write their experiences down. To gain access to other people's experiences, we may request them to write a personal experience: this is called a *lived experience description* (LED):

- Describe the experience as much as possible as you live(d) through it. Avoid causal explanations, justifications, generalizations, or interpretations.
- Describe the experience from the inside, as it were—almost like a state of mind: the feelings, the mood, the emotions, and so on.
- Focus on a particular example or incident of the object of experience: describe specific events, an adventure, a happening, a particular experience.
- Try to focus on an example of the experience that stands out for its vividness, or as it was the first or last time; describe exactly what happened, how it felt, at that particular moment.
- Attend to how the body feels, how things smell(ed), how they sound(ed), and so on.
- If possible, write the experience in the present tense rather than in the past tense. (It enhances the reality sense.)
- Avoid trying to beautify your account with fancy phrases or flowery terminology.

When asking people to provide a lived experience description, it is important to realize that it is not of great concern whether this experience actually happened in exactly that way. Phenomenology is less concerned with the *factual* accuracy than with the *plausibility* of an account—it needs to be "true" to our living sense of it.

Practical Phenomenological Interview Points

The phenomenological interview is used as a means for exploring and gathering experiential material. The interview first of all serves the very specific purpose of exploring and gathering experiential narrative material, stories, vignettes, or anecdotes that may serve as a resource for phenomenological reflection and thus develop a richer and deeper understanding of a human phenomenon.

But that is much more difficult than it may sound. The phenomenological interview aims for prereflective experiential accounts—not for cultural narratives, socio-psychological opinions, personal views, perceptions, perspectives, explanations or interpretations. Sometimes, interviewers overestimate the ease with which one can get people to tell or share "lived experiences" in story or narrative form.

Unfortunately, authors who write about qualitative interview methods for qualitative researchers tend to seriously underestimate the unique challenge of the phenomenological interview. It is often difficult to get interviewees to actually tell an experiential account in prereflective terms. It is much easier to get a person to tell *about* an experience than to tell an experience as lived through. Generally, it is much easier for an interviewee to share his or her views, interpretations, or opinions about something than to give a detailed experiential account of an event or moment as it happened at a particular time in a particular place.

What are some of the things to keep in mind in conducting phenomenological interviews? Where would be an appropriate place for the interview? What is the interactional sphere that contributes to an interview? When is the optimal time for doing an interview? What attitude is conducive for a successful interview? How should the interviewer conduct himself or herself? Here are some pointers:

Where? Interviews are not always best conducted in formal settings such as university offices or interview rooms. People are more inclined to remember and tell life stories when the surroundings are conducive to thinking about these experiences. Interviews with patients about their illness experience may or may not be most productively done while still in the hospital or in home settings. Some interviews are best performed at the kitchen table, in a coffee shop, or in any other setting that feels right.

Who? The researcher should be personable in order to win the trust of the interviewee, especially if the phenomenon being studied touches on fragile matters. So, it is often important to develop a relationship of personal sharing, closeness, or friendliness before seriously opening up the topic of research. Ask yourself: which persons could tell us personal life stories (anecdotes, stories, experiences, incidents, and so on)? Who has rich experiences in the matter that is being studied? Is this person articulate or eloquent? Is it better to interview or is it more appropriate to try to gain written accounts? Indeed, sometimes it is easier to talk than to write about a personal experience, because writing forces the person into a more reflective attitude, which may make it more difficult to stay close to an experience as it is (was) immediately lived through.

When? Try to arrange for an interview that needs not to be rushed. Having a coffee or a meal together creates the atmosphere as well as the time-space to explore the experience. It usually takes a bit of time before one may then ease into a more focused questioning. In the beginning, one should not worry if the responses are short—good interviews take time. Perhaps it is better to think of the interview as a conversation than as "interview." Conversations require the right kind of atmosphere and tone. Some conversational interviews are better done in the evening than early in the morning.

Why? It is important to keep the focus on the kind of experience that one wishes to investigate. The phenomenological question should instill in the researcher a sort of wonder and openness to the phenomenon, and this wonder should infect and animate the conversation.

How? If possible one should collect accounts of personal experiences by means of recorded conversations. Sometimes language can get in the way. For example, if one is interested in the experience of "hope," then it might be that this word is so laden with meaning or with shallow associations that it is difficult for the interviewee to know what kind of life experience the interviewer is trying to study. Sometimes it is helpful for the interviewer himself or herself to share a story or an instance of an experience or to circumscribe the topic with personal examples or to use illustrations from life, a book, or a movie.

What? First, it is important for the interviewer to keep the main research question in mind (even if this is too difficult to fully share with the interviewee). Constantly remain alert to the emergence of stories. Second, it cannot be overemphasized that the aim of the interview conversation for phenomenological inquiry is first of all to gain experiential material that is rich and detailed. As we interview people about their experience of a certain phenomenon, it is imperative to stay close to experience as lived. As we ask what an experience is like, it may be helpful to remain very concrete. Ask the person to think of a specific instance, situation, person, or event. When exactly did this happen? What were you doing? Who said what? And what did you say then? What happened next? How did it feel? What else do you remember about the event? (Do not ask for interpretations, explanations, generalizations, speculations, or for anything that may get away from telling the experience as lived through.) In other words, explore the whole experience (story, anecdote, vignette, sketch) to the fullest!

Whatever? Often, it is not necessary to ask many questions. Patience or silence may be a more tactful way of prompting the other to gather recollections and proceed with a story. Whatever happens, do not be afraid of silences. And if there seems to be a block, then it is often enough to repeat the last sentence or thought in a questioning sort of tone and thus trigger the other to continue. "So, you say you felt uncomfortable . . . ?" And whenever it seems that the person being interviewed begins to generalize about the experience, you can insert a question that turns the discourse back to the level of concrete experience: "Can you give an example?" "Do you remember a particular incident?" and so on.

Two Interview Reminders

Here are two reminders for a productive interview of experiential material:

(1) *Keep the phenomenological intent of the interview clearly in mind.* It is important to be mentally prepared before starting out on an interview itinerary. Too often a beginning researcher enthusiastically goes about "interviewing subjects" using the so-called unstructured or open-ended interview method without first carefully considering what interest the interview is to serve. What experiential phenomenon are you aiming to explore? What would be examples of such experience? What experiences may provide opposite examples? Sometimes it happens that a researcher is confused about his or her real interest or research question, and then the interview is somehow expected to bring about that clarity. Usually, this is an idle hope. If the interviewer does not remain attentive to the need to gain lived experience material, then he or she may end up with material that consists of many short (too short) responses to short, long-winded, or leading questions by the researcher. It is better to gain a limited number of detailed and concrete stories than many hours of interviews that contain very little experiential material. The researcher may end up with an unmanageable quantity of tapes or transcripts and yet little of it is of interpretive value.

(2) *Try to obtain concrete stories of particular situations or events.* Interview material that is skimpy and that lacks sufficient concreteness—in the form of stories, anecdotes, examples of experiences—may be quite useless, tempting the researcher to indulge in overinterpretations, speculations, or an overreliance on personal opinions. Similarly, an overabundance of poorly managed interviews may lead either to total despair and confusion (what do I do now? what method can I use for analyzing all these hundreds of transcript pages?) or to a chaotic quest for meaning (there's so much here!

401

what do I include? exclude?). The important lesson is that one does not want to get in this kind of predicament in the first place.

The Hermeneutic Interview

The hermeneutic interview serves different purposes from the phenomenological interview. The hermeneutic interview aims at exploring the ways that fundamental phenomenological meanings and methods can be interpreted and understood. This kind of interview should not be confused with, for example, psychological or ethnographic interviews that aim at exploring biographic meanings, personal or cultural, or gender-based perceptions.

One may distinguish between two kinds of hermeneutic interviews: the data-interpreting interview and the method-interpreting interview.

The data-interpreting interview seeks assistance in the interpretation of the empirical data (lived experience accounts) gained through phenomenological interviews, observations, and other data-gathering methods. Sometimes, the hermeneutic interview can be used as a follow-up from the phenomenological interview. However, it should not be assumed that those who have shared their experiences should have the expertise and insights to interpret their own experiences. The data-interpreting interview may also be productively performed by asking others of their interpretive insights regarding poems, photographs, art objects, myths, historical and cultural events, short stories, and other narratives. For example, a professional practitioner such as a teacher, nurse, or physician could be consulted for his or her interpretive insights of a special narrative, art object, or movie that lies within the range of their professional experience.

The methodology-interpreting interview is typically concerned with the interpretive insights sought from phenomenologists regarding their approach to phenomenological assumptions, themes, and methods. Some phenomenologists are more lucid in their interpretations of the practice of phenomenological inquiry than they are in their writings. For example, phenomenologists such as Emmanuel Levinas, Jacques Derrida, and Bernard Stiegler may require serious intellectual stamina on the part of the reader who is trying to understand the basic philosophical concepts and scholarly intents of these authors. Introductions to their work are sometimes more easily gained through published interviews with these authors. Often such interviews are available in printed form in books and journals, as audio podcasts through broadcast stations, or as videos accessible online through YouTube; sometimes one may be lucky to conduct such an interview oneself.

Observing Lived Experiences

Observation or close observation is a more indirect method of collecting experiential material from others. For example, with young children or very ill people, it is often difficult to generate written descriptions or to engage in conversational interviewing. "Close observation" is exactly what the phrase suggests. In contrast to the more experimental or behavioral observational research techniques, close observation tries to break through the distance often created by observational methods. The best way to enter a person's lifeworld is to participate in it. For example, to gain access to the experience of young children, it may be important to play with them, talk with them, listen to them, interact face to face, puppeteer, paint, draw, or follow them into their play spaces and into the things they do while remaining attentively aware of the way it is for children.

Naturally it is not only in situations with young children that close observation may be the preferred approach. "Close observation," in the way that this term is used here, generates different forms of experiential material than we tend to obtain with the written or the interview approach. However, as soon as this is said, we should be cautious of a too simplistic interpretation of close observation as a variation of participant observation. Close observation involves an attitude of assuming a relation that is as close as possible while retaining a hermeneutic alertness to situations that allows us to constantly step back and reflect on the meaning of those situations. It is similar to the attitude of the fiction writer or novelist who is always on the lookout for stories or incidents to become part of the novel. The method of close observation requires that one be a participant and an observer at the same time, that one maintains a certain orientation of reflectivity while guarding against the more manipulative and artificial attitude that a reflective attitude tends to insert in a social situation and relation.

Borrowing from Fiction

Fictional literature, such as novels and short stories, can be excellent sources for experiential material. The phenomenological value of a novel, for example, is determined by what may be called the perceptiveness and the intuitive sensitivity of the author. Phenomena such as love, grief, illness, faith, success, fear, death, hope, struggle, or loss are the stuff of which novels are made. The titles of some celebrated works, such as *Crime and Punishment*, *Nausea*, *The Trial*, and *Remembrance of Things Past*, announce fundamental life experiences that are available to our interpretive reading.

For example, in reading Sartre's *Nausea*, we cannot help but feel invaded by the same mood that inhabits Roquentin. And so, as readers, we find the experience of everyday life irresistibly shifted to the world of the novel where such fundamental life experiences are lived through vicariously. As we identify ourselves with the protagonist of a story, *we live his or her feelings and actions without having to act ourselves*. Thus, we may be able to experience life situations, events, and emotions that we would normally not have. Through an evocative novel, we are given the chance of living through an experience that provides us with the opportunity of gaining insight into certain aspects of the phenomenon or event that we have chosen to study.

Tracing Etymological Sources

The first thing that often strikes us about any phenomenon is that the words we use to refer to the phenomenon have lost some of their original experiential meaning. Words that once could reverberate with lived meaning and reveal a living world now have become lame, limp, mute, emptied, and forgetful of their past power. Gusdorf (1965) asked: what can still be conveyed by words such as "earth" or "water," "happiness" or "hope"? How flat words like "parent" or "teacher," "home" or "school," "knowledge" or "care" have become. Note, for example, how nowadays the word "caring" is being overused by social work, medical, legal, educational, and counseling professionals. And this occurs at a time when we no longer seem to know what it means to care. We speak of medicare, day-care, legal care, health care, after-school care, and so on. We hope to meet caring doctors and caring teachers for our children. But do we still know how to connect these social service professionals with the original deeper meanings of "care" as sorrow? Of course, retrieving or recalling the essence of caring is not a matter of simple etymological analysis or explication of the usage of the word. Rather, it is the reconstruction of a way of life: a willingness to live the language of our lives more deeply, to become more truly who we are when we refer to ourselves, for example, as caring teachers or parents.

Being attentive to the etymological origins of words may sometimes put us in touch with an original form of life where the terms still had living ties to the lived experiences from which they originally sprang. It can be shown, for example, that the words "parent," "child," "baby," "womb," and "birth" are all closely related to the verb "to bear" as in the experience of pregnancy, childbirth, as well as in the very experience of parenting as providing spaces that bear children, spaces in which children live and exist as children. The etymology of the word "parenting" refers both to giving birth and bringing forth; it has connotations of origin or source. To parent (*parere*) is to originate, to be the source, the origin from which something springs. How is this sense of source maintained in the experience of parenting? I may feel pride at the recognition of having brought this child into the world, but at the same time I know a deeper recognition: that it was not I who helped produce this child but rather something other and "larger" than me that made it possible for me to have this child in the first place. And so my experience of pride, as new father or mother, is tempered by the strange sense that I much less produced this child than that it came to me as a gift. My pride is then really a pride of being worthy of this gift that comes as if it were I who brought the child into being. And here is the theme of the effect which, in a deep sense, the child has on the mother and the father. The child is not simply received as a gift for which we make room in our lives. As Marcel (1978) expressed it, the truth is much more, that the gift is a call to which we have to make a response. Parents bring forth children, but the child must be born in the dual sense of bearing and birth, bringing and awakening to the world. The English word "child" can be traced to the Gothic "*kilthe*," meaning womb. Similarly, words akin to the term "baby" are translatable as the borne one, the one who is carried in the womb. An old word for child is still preserved in the Lowland Scots "bairn," cognate with Anglo-Saxon "bearn," meaning bearing and born. In my native Dutch language the word for womb is "*baarmoeder*," literally "mother who bears," mother who holds, carries the child. So, both childbearing and giving birth are aspects of the same verb "to bear."

In these persistent etymological references to bearing and safekeeping of the child, we may find clues to the meaning of parenting and of teaching as *in loco parentis*. In providing bearing for their children, parents give and teach the very young something without which growing up or even the living of a life becomes quite impossible. Parents who bear, give bearing to children, make available space and ground for being. They teach their children that the world can be experienced as home, a place for safe dwelling, a habitat in which human beings can "be," where we can be ourselves, where we can have habits: ways of being and doing things. So to bear children is, in a broad sense, to provide place and space for them to live, to be. The child is carried, borne inside the womb at first, then it is born into the world where it remains, for a while at least, most helpless, dependent, in need of nurture, warmth, caresses, holding fast, and safe outside the womb. Conversely, it is in the fact of the worldly experience of separateness, lostness, without a bearing, without the security of safe ground that the primordial nature of parenting can be intuited.

Searching Idiomatic Phrases

It is sometimes surprising how didactic language itself is if we allow ourselves to be attentive to even the most common of expressions associated with the phenomenon we wish to pursue. The reason is that idiomatic phrases largely proceed phenomenologically: they are born out of lived experience. For example, we say, "every child needs a home." In the concept of home or dwelling, there is a strong sense of watching over something, preserving a space in which the human being can feel sheltered, protected, and what is thus preserved in the idea of a house with its wall and fences is a safekeeping, holding, or bearing of something that needs to be watched over. This caring modality of parenting, this nurturing, sheltering, and providing protective ground for the child is not something theoretical that needs to be proven or tested as our response to the child's experiences of fear and being afraid. Rather, it is something primordial which defies literal language and precise definition.

Ordinary language is in some sense a huge reservoir in which the incredible variety of richness of human experience is deposited. The problem often is that these deposits have silted, crusted, or fossilized in such a way that the original contact with our primordial experiences is broken. For example, of the reading experience we say of someone that she is "lost in a book." But what does this expression reveal? Is the reader truly lost? While absorbed in a book a reader may lose her sense of time, place, body, etc. Who has not had the experience of showing up late for supper, an appointment, or missing a bus stop because of being lost in a book? But in another sense, the reader who is lost in a story is not lost at all. We may be temporarily "absorbed" in a different world from that of the one who made the remark, but the reader lacks nothing, misses nothing, needs nothing; that is why the reading experience is so absorbing. The person who is much more nearly lost is the person who made the remark. Indeed, when someone says of his companion that she is lost in a book, then he is the one who experiences a loss, namely the attentive presence of his companion. The expression "she is absorbed in a book" can show us more clues of the nature of the reading experience. It raises the question of the meaning of the sense of spatiality that belongs to the text. What is the nature of reading space? And how is the experience of this space related to the experience of the space where we see the reader sitting while submerged in the book? What is it about a space that makes it a good place to read? And what is the nature of the time experience and the experience of one's body in those different dimensions?

Similarly, with respect to the phenomenon of parenting, what other expression might provide helpful occasions for phenomenological reflection on the lived experiences from which the expressions derive their meaning? This search of etymological sources can be an important (but often neglected) aspect of phenomenological "data collecting."

We say "like mother, like daughter" or "like father, like son." What could be the experiential significance of this phrase? The word mother is associated with a variety of expressions: "mother earth," "mother language," "mother tongue," etc. We speak of "fatherland," "forefathers," etc. And the word "parenting" is often used to connote "creating," "originating," "begetting," "to be the source of something." The point is not that one blindly collects a multitude of linguistic items associated in some way with the phenomenon, but that one reflectively holds on to the verbal manifestations that appear to possess interpretive significance for the actual phenomenological description. For idiomatic language (as well as the language of writers and poets) is an inexhaustible source for phenomenological analysis.

Themes and Theme Analysis

In qualitative research models such as grounded theory, ethnography, and concept analysis, the idea of theme and theme analysis possess different meanings from the way that "theme" is used in phenomenological inquiry. In grounded theory, thematic analysis is seen as an effort to codify and develop theory; ethnographic thematic analysis aims at discovering the categories that identify and describe cultural groups and practices. In contrast, content analysis actually preselects the themes that it is looking for in empirical data. Content analysis may examine transcripts for the recurrence of certain thematic terms that would show, for example, the existence of gender bias in texts. Grounded theory and ethnography use techniques for letting the themes "emerge" from the data as it were. "Emerge" means looking for thematic similarities and differences at the hand of *constant comparison* of people's narratives. Thematic analysis in these qualitative methodologies is sometimes facilitated with special computer software. But these are not the ways of doing phenomenology!

It should be clear that codifications, conceptual abstractions, or empirical generalizations can never adequately produce phenomenological descriptions, understandings, and insights as described in this book. None of the work of the leading proponents (see Section Two) of the phenomenological tradition would be commensurate with abstracting, coding, and procedural approaches; developing taxonomies; looking for recurring concepts or themes; and so on. When we examine a paper or a dissertation that claims to have used a phenomenological method, it may be helpful to ask: does this "look like" any of the phenomenological studies that one encounters in the more primary literature? This does not mean that one has to test oneself against the great texts of the original thinkers, but one should be able to recognize the presence of a phenomenological attitude and the presentation of phenomenological insights in a study.

Approaches to Thematic Reading and Analysis

Thematic analysis refers to the process of recovering structures of meanings that are embodied and dramatized in human experience represented in a text.

In human science research, the notion of theme may best be understood by examining its methodological and philosophical character. Unfortunately, theme analysis is sometimes defined as an unambiguous and fairly mechanical application of some frequency count or coding of significant terms in transcripts or texts, or some other breakdown of the content of protocol or documentary material. But "analyzing" thematic meanings of a phenomenon (a lived experience) is a complex and creative process of insightful invention, discovery, and disclosure. Grasping and formulating a thematic understanding is not a rule-bound process but a free act of "seeing" meaning that is driven by the epoché and the reduction.

In exploring and discovering phenomenological themes, we can read texts as sources of meaning at different levels: the whole or entire text; the selective or separate paragraph; and at the detailed level of the sentence, phrase, expression, or single word.

(1) In the holistic reading approach we attend to the text as a whole and ask, "How can the eidetic, originary, or phenomenological meaning or main significance of the text as a whole be captured?" We then try to express that meaning by formulating such a phrase.

(2) In the selective reading approach, we listen to or read a text several times and ask, "What statement(s) or phrase(s) seem particularly essential or revealing about the phenomenon or experience being described?" These statements we then select. Next we may try to capture these phenomenological meanings in thematic expressions or through longer reflective descriptive-interpretive paragraphs. Some phrases that occur in the text may be particularly evocative, or possess a sense of punctum. These phrases should be treated as possible rhetorical "gems" for developing and writing the phenomenological text.

(3) In the detailed reading approach, we look at every single sentence or sentence cluster and ask, "What may this sentence or sentence cluster be seen to reveal about the phenomenon or experience being described?" Again, we try to identify and capture thematic expressions, phrases, or narrative paragraphs that increasingly let the phenomenological meaning of the experience show or give itself in the text. If the whole experiential account is particularly powerful then we try to lift it out as an exemplary story or anecdote.

Existentials: Guides for Thematic Reflection

Often phenomenological research studies focus on the meaning dimensions of a selected phenomenon or event. For example, the opening chapter of this book offered explorations and explications of phenomena such as care and worry, boredom, eye contact, touching and being touched, and the clock to tell time. Obviously, the number of phenomena and events that could become topics of phenomenological inquiry and research is virtually limitless. The possibilities of life experiences are rich and numerous beyond belief, from the tiniest and commonest phenomenon to the most complex. It is easy to get lost in these inquiries or to get stuck on some aspect of it. One possible way to assist in a balanced reflective inquiry process is to employ the idea of lifeworld "existentials." Existentials are in a manner of speaking universal human lifeworld phenomena. But since the phenomena of body, time, space, human relation, technics, and materiality are universal to all human existence, I have suggested that the term "existentials" may be appropriately coined for this purpose.

In other words, when exploring the meaning aspects of a phenomenon or event, the existentials of lived world (existentiality), lived relation (relationality), lived body (corporeality), lived space (spatiality), lived time (temporality), lived things (materiality) and lived technics (technology) can be used to explore the phenomenon in a heuristic manner. They are existentials in the sense that they belong to everyone's lifeworld—they are universal themes of all human life. Actually, it was Merleau-Ponty's *Phenomenology of Perception* (1962, 2012) that prompted for me the idea of existentials as guides for phenomenological reflection that I started in my early phenomenology workshops. Merleau-Ponty's *Phenomenology of Perception* is organized in major sections on body, spatiality, things or world, others or relations, and temporality. And these existential themes clearly are systematically explored and belabored in the various chapters. In fact, gradually these fundamental existentials occur repeatedly in the phenomenological literature. We all experience our world and our reality through these existentials.

Of course, we can even distinguish additional existentials such as death (dying), language (linguisticality), and mood (modality). The point is that existentials are helpful universal "themes" of human existence to explore meaning aspects of our lifeworld and of the particular phenomena that we may be studying.

All phenomenological human science research efforts are really explorations into the structure of the human lifeworld, the lived world as experienced in everyday situations and relations. Our lived experiences and the structures of meanings (themes) in terms of which these lived experiences can be described and interpreted constitute the immense complexity of the lifeworld. And, of course, we can even speak of the multiple and different lifeworlds that belong to different human existences and realities. We know that the lifeworld of the child has different experiential qualities from the lifeworld of the adult. Similarly, there are the lifeworlds of the teacher, the parent, the researcher, the administrator, and so forth. And each of us may be seen to inhabit different lifeworlds at different times of the day, such as the lived world of work and the lived world of the home.

As we remain at the most general level of the lifeworld we may find that this grounding level of human existence may also be studied in its fundamental thematic structure. For example, fundamental existential themes such as "life," "death," "being," "otherness," "meaning," and "mystery" have occurred in the phenomenological human science literature. In the following paragraphs we identify six such fundamental existential themes that probably pervade the lifeworlds of all human beings, regardless of their historical, cultural or social situatedness. In order not to confuse these fundamental lifeworld themes with the more particular themes of certain human phenomena, such as parenting or teaching, that we want to study, I shall coin these fundamental lifeworld themes with the term "existentials." There are several existentials that may prove helpful as guides for reflection in the research process, such as lived space (spatiality), lived body (corporeality), lived time (temporality), lived human relation (relationality or communality), materiality (lived things), and technicality (lived technics).

These fundamental lifeworld existentials may be seen to belong to the existential ground by way of which all human beings experience the world, although not all in the same modality of course. In the phenomenological literature these six existential categories have been considered as belonging to the fundamental structure of the lifeworld. This is not difficult to understand, since about any experience we can always ask fundamental questions that correspond to these lifeworld existentials. Therefore, spatiality, corporeality, temporality, relationality, materiality, and technicality are productive categories for the process of phenomenological question posing, reflecting, and writing.

Existentiality—Lived World

The term "existentiality" refers to human existence and to the person's existential world in which he or she lives their freedom and responsibility. The psychiatrist Binswanger suggested that to understand another person we have to consider three existential modes of that person's worldly existence: *Umwelt* (the surrounding world in which we live), *Mitwelt* (our shared world with others), and *Eigenwelt* (the self-world in which we know ourselves as who we are).

Our *Umwelt* in which we exist, and that exist in us, shapes our way of being. Van den Berg gives the example of an anthropologist who took an inhabitant of the not yet contacted isolated villages and regions of Papua New Guinea to the modern city of Singapore. They walked around the busy streets and afterwards the anthropologist asked his companion what had impressed him most about the big city. He expected that the man would tell him about the cars, the tall buildings, and the airplanes overhead. But instead the Papua villager expressed his amazement about a man who could carry that many bananas and fruit. He had seen the city vendor pulling his wagon with produce. Carrying produce such as bananas was familiar to him. The visitor to the big city saw what his *Umwelt*, or his internal (mental) model in neural system language, prompted and enabled him to see. Of course, many of us live in an *Umwelt* that differs from other people we meet and who live in a world that differs in some significant respect from ours. For example, to understand a child we have to understand the child's world, to understand the drug addict we have to understand the *Umwelt* of living as an addict. In sum, the existential of lived world can generate many thematic questions to explore the phenomena and or events that interest us.

Relationality—Lived Self-Other

The existential theme of *Mitwelt* and relationality may guide our reflection to ask how self and others are experienced with respect to the phenomenon that is being studied. To explore relational aspects of a phenomenon is to ask: How are people or things connected? What meaning of community? What ethics of being together? The etymological meaning of relation includes reference to what people return to. Therefore, we speak of family as relations: the intimacies that draw us to return and reunite. How is the self experienced in relation? In what ways is the subject–object relation constituted? Is the other experienced as object or in his or her otherness (alterity)? We may even experience the other in a nonre-lational relation such as when the self is erased from the relation in experiences of sacrifice, total dedication, or service. Phenomena such as love and friendship can be examined for their relational qualities and significance. How is contact online experienced differently from real-life contact in our encounters with oth-ers? Some phenomenological authors regard relation as the fundamental motif of their understanding of human phenomena. For example, Dominic Pettman (2006) examines love and eros as technological relations. For Jean-Luc Nancy, the pervasive theme is the relational couplet of singular-plural and the centrality of community. Emmanuel Levinas is the philosopher-phenomenologist of the ethical relation of alterity: the experience of the otherness of the other. These are possible sources for examining the existential theme of relation as a guide for reflection on a phenomenon that interests us.

Now, with respect to the discussion of secrecy in the above mentioned stories, the question of relationality may help to gain certain insights. How are relations experienced in these stories? All secrecy stories show how secrecy is fundamen-tally a relational experience, even though the parents may or may not seem aware of the child's keeping a secret. Without this relation of parental norms and expec-tations, the secret could simply not exist. The stories also show how the child may experience a sense of separation (*secrete* means to separate) from the mother and/or the father. For a child to hide something or to keep a secret from the parents is to experience (discover) privacy, mask, persona. By keeping a secret, the child learns to become invisible, as it were, even though some parents seem to be able to look right through their children's pretenses. In the hunting story the boy begins to experience an inner world, and a tension between the inner world and the outer world he shares with his parents. He realizes that he is different from the others, and this difference is his *Eigenwelt*, the self-world. He feels different from others who do not seem to feel the cruelty he has experienced in the silence of the forest. In the birthday story we can see the tensions experienced in the relations between the child and the father and mother.

We can also see that in some situations secrecy and lying are close cousins, though not really the same phenomenon. The bedroom story shows how a secret understanding may complicate relationships, and yet the relation seems enriched. In the breakfast story, the girl seems to experience a deep relation with an imagined other: the secret self of her own inner life. Asking the question of how secrecy is an experience of relation makes us aware that keeping or sharing secrets is indeed always relational. Sharing a secret enhances the sense of shared intimacy; keeping a secret breaks or places a certain tension on the intimacy.

Corporeality—Lived Body

The existential theme of corporeality may guide our reflection to ask how the body is experienced with respect to the phenomenon that is being studied. As object? As subject? Sartre has shown that, in ordinary life the body tends to be experi-enced as passed-over-in-silence (*passé sous silence*). While we are bodily engaged in the world, we do not really pay attention to the body. How and when do we become aware of our bodies? How do our desires, fears, cheerfulness, anxieties incarnate themselves in the world in which we dwell? How is the phenomenon we study perceived, sensed, touched by the body? We may look at our own body in the same appraising manner as we may look at someone else's body—however, this look is not the same, since we perceive our own body with our own body. So, how is the body of self and other perceived differently? Similarly, how do we experience being touched by some thing or by a person? How do we experience the body in online activities? Some phenomenological authors regard body, corporeality, or embodiment as the fundamental motif of their understanding of human phenomena. Merleau-Ponty (2012) is the phenomenologist of the body. Richard Zaner (1971) wrote an early text on the phenomenology of embodiment that is still relevant. And Donn Welton (1999) has edited classic and contemporary readings on the phenomenology of the body.

Now, with respect to the discussion of secrecy, the question of corporeality may help to gain certain insights. How is the body experienced in these stories? Or how does a body experience secrecy? In the hunting story the boy is trying to pretend normalcy and not show his sense of sadness. Secrecy may make one aware of the corporeal possibilities and limits of acting normally. In the birthday story, too, there is a strong fear of becoming exposed by the betrayal signs of the body under the inquisitive eyes of the mother. The whole body is involved in hiding a secret. Why? Because the body could be the place of hiding, betrayal, exposure. Keeping a secret is felt in the body, in one's gestures, the look of the eyes, and so on. The body can also be the very subject of the secret. The girl who reads her parents' book on sexuality is literally learning secrets that are budding in her own body. And the girl who sees the Shadow Man on the door sees the secret shadow body with the sensitive sensuality of her own body. All these various themes can be further phenomenologically elaborated (analyzed).

Spatiality—Lived Space

The existential theme of spatiality may guide our reflection to ask how space is experienced with respect to the phenomenon that is being studied. How do we experience interiorities differently from exteriorities? For example, how is space in a cathedral experienced differently from a small church? What effect do high ceilings have on us? How do we shape space and how does space shape us? For example, how do we experience the bed and bedroom differently when we are healthy from when we are sick? How is space experienced differently from place? How do we experience the worldly or unworldly moods of certain places? How do we enter, dwell, and exit virtual spaces or places of novels, films, or the computer screen? How do we experience the dimensions of cyberspace? Some phenomenological authors regard space and place as the fundamental motifs of their understanding of human phenomena such as Bollnow (1960). Bachelard (1964a) describes the poetics of space, and Casey (1997) describes the historical significances of the phenomenologies of place and space.

Now, with respect to the discussion of secrecy, the question of spatiality may help to gain certain insights. Once children learn to keep secrets, they will henceforth live in two worlds: an inner and an outer world. This is strongly felt by the boy in the hunting story. One no longer shares the same world with the others who are unaware of the secret feelings of pity of the boy for the killed animal. As well the spell of the silent space of the forest is broken by the event of the shooting, and this sphere corresponds to the inner space of the child. There is also the problem of where secret objects can be hidden. The secret space under the mattress is a poor hiding place. The girl in the Shadow Man story seems to dwell in another visual space dimension. The Shadow Man may be imaginary, yet, in an undeniable way, he is experienced as real. In this story, the child's senses are very much alive. The Shadow Man lives in a realm that is perceptible only through the senses, but one must be especially attentive to see him. Could we say that secrets dwell in the shadows of everyday life? Or is the shadow play on the door a manifestation of the restless shadows dwelling in the deeper reaches of the soul? Are these the secrets that live within, invisible, and yet are seen out there in vivid outlines contextured by the familiar things of the world?

Temporality—Lived Time

The existential theme of temporality may guide our reflection to ask how time is experienced with respect to the phenomenon that is being studied. Everyone knows the difference between objective (cosmic) time and subjective (lived) time, clock time, and phenomenological time. We experience the time of waiting differently from when we are actively involved in something. For example, when we travel by car for a three-hour drive to another city, it may feel that some stretches of the road are longer than other parts, even though they are objectively the same length. It may just feel that it takes longer to do, for example, the first 50 miles than the last 50 miles. This experience also shows that lived space and lived time are mingled. Space is an aspect of time, and time is experienced as space. That is why we speak of the "length" of time it takes to do something. Even the clock has a lived sensibility to the passing of time. Note, for example, that a number display on a digital time piece shows time differently from an analogue time piece with hour, minute, and second hands. A clock or watch with an analogue face shows time as movement in space, when the hands slowly but determinately sweep across the dial. We tell what time it is by glancing how far the hands of the clock still have to go for lunch time to start. Lived time is also experienced as telos: the wishes, plans, and goals we strive for in life. Our sense of identity is experienced in terms of the times of our childhood, the periods of our working or love life, and so forth. Some phenomenological authors regard temporality or time as the fundamental motifs of their understanding of human phenomena. For example, Heidegger's *Being and Time* (1962) describes being as time, since without time there would not be being.

Now, with respect to the discussion of secrecy, the question of temporality may help to gain certain insights: the boy in the hunting story is becoming aware of how the temporality of excitement of the hunt conflicts with the time he grieves for the deer. The phenomenon of secrecy also may mark a significant spiritual development. Secrets makes possible the experience of the hidden, the beyond, otherness, mystery, depth—something meaningful or even spiritual. Temporality is shown in the hiding of secrecy as a sign of maturation and growth! The child who bought a birthday present for his mother is learning how secrets can be played with in the relationship of the father with the mother. The secret birthday present will be

412

revealed on the birthday. This, too, is the experience of lived time. Keeping and sharing secrets is also important in that we learn to negotiate in our interactions with others what secrets to share and what not to share and for what purpose. The girl who hides the book on adult sexuality is learning things that have to do with her own future and becoming a grown-up woman like her mother. There is also the wonderful temporal atmosphere of the girl who sees the Shadow Man. He is only visible when the light plays on the door at a certain moment of breakfast time. But during this time, she is deeply immersed in the temporality of the encounter.

Materiality—Lived Things

The existential theme of materiality may guide our reflection to ask how things are experienced with respect to the phenomenon that is being studied. It would be diffi-cult to overestimate the significance of "things" in our lives. The things are our world in its material thinglike reality. With almost any research topic we can ask, how are "things" experienced and how do the experiences of things and world contribute to the essential meaning of the phenomenon? In a real way, we see and recognize ourselves in the things of our world. And the things tell me who I am. How do they do this? How are things extensions of our bodies and minds? How can things be experienced as intimate or strange? Things can disappoint us or reflect our disap-pointment back to us. And they can remind us of our responsibilities. Some authors such as Bruno Latour (1992, 2007) and Peter-Paul Verbeek (2005, 2011) suggest that things, especially in their technics state, have agency just as human persons do. Thus, in our encounter with things, we experience the moral force they exert on and in our lives. Of course, things present themselves at different scales. Do we actually experience micro-objects at the nano-level, even if that falls outside of our immedi-ate sensory possibilities? And how do hyper-objects form part of our experiences of phenomena that we are interested in? Hyper-objects are massive things like climate (the phenomenon of global warming) and other ecological objects of vast propor-tions as described by Timothy Morton (2013). We can use the term *hyper-things* to point to complex, difficult, and elusive aspects of "things," such as the "atmosphere" of a city, the "horror" of a war, and the "spectacle" of a grand vista. Even immaterial things possess a certain materiality.

Now, with respect to the discussion of secrecy, the question of materiality may help to gain certain insights: Material reflection asks how things are experienced. Secret things can be objects or personal items that are being stashed. But secret things can also be thoughts, deeds, experiences, events, and discoveries, as in the hunting story where the secret thing is an eventful memory. The above experiential stories show that the thing hidden or stashed in secret cannot be separated from the self. Indeed, in hiding the book on sexuality, the girl is hiding herself. In the book story (it is not just about a book), mother and daughter now seem to share something meaningful: the secret of a secret. So, the secret itself has become a "thing" that is being kept: the secret of an unacknowledged, and yet known, secret between mother and daughter. The Shadow Man is a thing of an entirely different order. He is a secret manifestation made possible by the interaction of all kinds of things: the door, the streaming light, the breakfast table and things, perhaps the body figure of the father, the shadow as thing, and so on.

Technology—Lived Technics

The existential theme of techné is touched upon in the relation to especially Heidegger, Ihde, and Stiegler. It may be helpful to add some additional thoughts to the existential theme of technology. I will distinguish here among five kinds of lived cyborg relations in the human experience of the existential of things and technology:

Technology as taken-for-granted is the attitude that most of us take toward technology in our lives as tools and techniques. Our lifeworld is increasingly changed through ever-newer forms of technology that make life more comfortable for those who can take advantage of new technologies, but also more cumbersome for those who are less inclined to keep up with the latest gadgets and media. Fans of technology tend to think that technology is all good and cannot do wrong. It enhances our health, work, learning, and productivity and adds joy and interest to living. Are we taking our cyborgian existence for granted? How?

Scholars like Don Ihde, Hubert Dreyfus, and Hans Achterhuis have been trying to determine how the various digital technologies, such as computers and handheld devices, and features, such as the Internet and online activities, can be understood. Achterhuis had published an edited work entitled, in Dutch, *From Steam Engine to Cyborg*, where each of his Dutch colleagues discusses the work of a philosopher whose work they consider to be part of an empirical turn in the phenomenology of technology. Ihde was so taken with this book that he had it translated under the title *American Philosophy of Technology: The Empirical Turn* (2001). Achterhuis speaks of the "empirical turn" in phenomenological technology that yields "concrete empirical manifestations of different technologies" (2001, p. 3).

According to Achterhuis and colleagues, the classical philosophy of technology of Heidegger and other continental philosophers had been profound but too far removed from everyday life concerns. This is not a surprising development, as Hans Achterhuis had been a student at the University of Utrecht where, in the 1950s and 1960s, these sentiments of a phenomenological concern with down-to-earth topics of everyday living had already been advanced by scholars such as Buytendijk, Langeveld, van den Berg, Linschoten, Beets, and others (see the section on the Utrecht School in this book). With respect to the computer, several experiential relations may be distinguished that the person maintains with this empirical or ontic dimension of technology (see, especially, Ihde, 1990). In what ways are we cyborgs?

Behind all the recent developments in phenomenologies of technology looms Heidegger's fundamental thinking about the danger and saving power of technology as ontotheology, which defines our historical being and fate, the ruinous consequences of which we may not be able to escape. "Technology is a way of revealing," says Heidegger in *The Question Concerning Technology*. Technology reveals beings as resources available for our use. Technologies (as techné) always modify and transform the worlds that are revealed (experienced) through them. The ontic meaning of technology is "a means to an end," or "a human activity," making things, but while this is "correct," says Heidegger, "it is not yet true." For that, we need to move from the ontic to the ontological. Technology as techné lets things reveal themselves; therefore, it belongs to aletheia: the revealing of cyborgian existence and things as self-showing.

For Heidegger, the essence of technology is *Gestell* (frame-enframing) to order the self-revealing as standing reserve, as a field of energy or power that can be used or stored. In this sense, the world becomes a resource; people, too, become mere resources. Ontologically, technology is a civilizational variant or mode of revealing that serves as a set of possibilities by which technology ontically appears. Thomson (2005) provides a discussion of the danger and promise of technology, especially in the context of education, in his text *Heidegger on Ontotheology*.

With the notion of technics, Bernard Stiegler brings the cyborgian nature of being human to consciousness. Stiegler does not reject Heidegger's insights into the significance of technology as a way of experiencing contemporary life. Rather, he seeks to develop a more complex phenomenology that tries to understand the various relations that humans maintain with technology, with implications for ethics and politics, as well as the pedagogy of youth who are caught up in the latest technological innovations.

In *Art and Its Shadow* (2004a) and *The Sex Appeal of the Inorganic* (2004b), Mario Perniola argues that contemporary sensibility is transforming the relations between humans and things or technology. Perniola's work explores the role of eros, desire, and sexuality in today's experience of the aesthetic of things and the experience of technology. How is technology overcoming the constraints of the physical body? What does it mean to feel things as in the cyborgian experience of the body increasingly consisting of organic and inorganic parts? How do humans identify with or become extensions of computerized technologies? Can we speak of things as having feelings? Perniola suggest that humans may experience themselves as "things that feel." For example, on the Internet, a substitute sexuality is sought as cybersex leading to moments of the person giving him- or herself as a virtual thing and as technological being.

The phenomenology of technology is no doubt an increasingly important field of study. For example, Dominic Pettman, in *Love and Other Technologies: Retrofitting Eros for the Information Age* (2006), makes use of Stiegler, Heidegger, Nancy, and Agamben to develop a highly original study of love and language as technologies of self, community, pornography, identity, and desire. Cathy Adams (2006, 2012) shows how a phenomenology of technology and things throws new light on the changing pedagogy of teacher–student relations, as educators adapt to the new media of PowerPoint, Smart Boards, and so forth. Michael van Manen (2012a, 2012c, 2021) is also inspired by Stiegler in showing how the increasing technologizing of medicine impacts the ethics of health science practices and the experiences of patients and their families in intensive care units such as the neonatal intensive care unit environment. We may increasingly ask, how our existence is being shaped as a cyborgian reality. In some sense we are all sometimes naive or sometimes more sophisticated cyborgs. But as a theme of the existential of technology, reflecting on the cyborgian nature of our work, love, and leisure life may help us understand more pointedly the accidental humanness of being human.

In the above reflections, I have playfully named some themes that may occur when we let ourselves be led by the guiding questions of the existentials. Many more insights and thematic understandings about the child's experience of secrecy could be articulated. These insights will have to begin to animate a reflective analysis of the reduction and simultaneously a writing process articulating the phenomenology of childhood secrecy. The text exploring the phenomenology of the secrecy experience could indeed be organized and developed by means of these existentials, but that is just one option.

What Is a Phenomenological Question?

Obviously a phenomenological study should be guided by a phenomenological question. But questions that are abstract, theoretical, conceptual, or that ask for explanations, perceptions, views, factual information, or interpretations will not lend themselves to conduct phenomenological exploration and reflection. As well, phenomenological inquiry often begins with a question that comprises an element of wonder: discovering the extraordinary in the ordinary, the *strange* in the taken for granted. A phenomenological inquiry asks what is given in immediate experience and how it is given or appears to us.

For example: As a parent I noticed that when my children were around five or six years of age, they began to become interested in secrets and to keep and share secrets. As a parent I did not think that I should pry into my children's secrets but I became interested in the pedagogical issue of the meaning and significance of secrets in children's lives. Are secrets a positive developmental phenomenon or are secrets unhealthy? Some parents were very adamant that they did not like their children to have secrets and they declared resolutely that in their family people value transparency and do not like that secrets might disturb honest and open relations. Other parents had not really thought about secrets or they considered secrecy an innocent childhood phenomenon. Some parents were aware that some children grow up with family secrets that can be quite toxic for children's sense of identity and their relations to others.

We can see that a study of adult secrecy and childhood secrecy can have a phenomenological significance and a personal or psychological significance. The phenomenology of secrecy focuses on the existential experiential meaning of secrecy, the personal and psychology of secrecy focuses on the meaning of secrecy in the lives of particular adults or individual children. It follows that research questions can focus on the phenomenology of secrecy and/or on the psychology of secrecy. But generally, it would be helpful to understand the phenomenology of secrecy if one would try to understand the role of secrecy in the lives of particular individuals.

It is worth reiterating the point that a phenomenology of secrecy asks phenomenological questions: A phenomenological question does not aim for empirical or descriptive generalizations; it does not formulate a social scientific law of how some things or some people behave under certain circumstances; it does not test a hypothesis; it does not ask for people's opinions, views, perceptions, or interpretations of an issue or phenomenon; it does not aim at psychological, gender-based, ethnographic, or other types of explanation; it does not aim for theory development; it does not ask for moral judgments; it does not describe specific (empirical) ethnic, cultural, or social groups of people; it does not anticipate codified categories for analysis. So, it is important that the research question is phenomenologically appropriate, and it is important for phenomenological inquiry that the phenomenological question stays at the heart of all phases and moments of the inquiry.

416

When doing interviews, it is often helpful to elicit a specific experience. This can be done by asking when and how this experience occurred—what was it like the first time? The most recent time? The most memorable moment? And so on.

For example, a good focus for pursuing the question of the phenomenology of secrecy may be in trying to elicit the beginning of the experience of secrecy in a person's life—in childhood. So, a helpful simple question could be: try to recall and describe the first time that you kept a secret from your mother, father, brother, sister, or friend.

To help the phenomenological interview along, more detailed questions may be posed, such as:

- Can you remember the earliest time when you began to keep a secret from your father or mother? Think back to these early years and try to remember a particular incident or moment.
- What did you hide? A thought? An object? Something you did? Try to remember a single instance or event.
- Did you have a secret place where you hid or stashed things? Can you describe that place?
- How did this experience of keeping something secret make you feel? For example, how did your body feel? How did you feel toward your mother or father? Please give examples.
- What did you do? What did you say? What did you think? What happened?

It is helpful to keep the question focused on a single and concrete moment that the experience was lived through or took place.

Second, it follows from the above explication of the proper phenomenological question that phenomenological analysis can only be conducted on prereflective or experiential narratives. It cannot be performed on data that consist of views, opinions, beliefs, perceptions, interpretations, and explanations of experiences. In other words, one should not confuse *concrete* experiential accounts with *interpreted* experiential accounts. The best materials for conducting phenomenological analysis are direct descriptions of the experience, rather than accounts *about* the experience. So, lived experience descriptions of "keeping or sharing a secret" should not be confused with how we judge people or the act of "keeping or sharing a secret." Opinions, perceptions, or beliefs are only helpful to the extent that they lead or give access to the lived experiences that lie behind these opinions, perceptions, or beliefs.

The Interview Transcript

Here is an example of a poor interview transcript that contains a person's views, interpretations, and perceptions of the experience of secrecy (rather than the experience itself):

I don't like keeping secrets because it is really a form of lying. Sometimes I notice that someone is keeping something secret from me and then I instantly begin to distrust this person. If people cannot be honest and open with me, then I would rather not associate with them. For example, I could never love someone who keeps secrets from me, and I would not really love someone if I would do the same. Most secrets that people keep have to do with things that are morally reprehensible. And so, when someone is telling me something that I am supposed to keep a secret, then I know that I am either going to hear some bad stuff or gossip about someone else, or, if the secret is about the person him or herself, then I will hear something sordid that I would rather not know. (AN)

This transcript lacks experiential detail. We can learn something about the opinions of the interviewee and how the interviewee thinks about and feels about keeping secrets. But this transcript does not describe what it is like to keep a secret. The interviewee merely talks *about* it. The transcript is not a lived experience description in that it does not make a lived-through experience of secrecy accessible.

Next, follow a few examples of interview and written transcripts that capture moments of secrecy in more experiential terms. I call these "lived experience descriptions" turned into anecdotes:

As an indigenous child I loved going out on hunting and fishing trips with my dad or grandpa. The freshness of the forest was a delight to all my senses—the pungent aroma of fall, the warm tones and hues as the earth blended toward an ash-blue sky, the early morning bite of coolness on my cheeks and the silence of the woods as we waited.

This day of memories was all these things until it happened.

The silence was fractured by the invading crack of a rifle: a deer was killed. I was five.

When we returned home, I ran to my grandmother and, caught up in the excitement of the event, exclaimed, "Bang, down goes the deer and blood comes out of it!" I was supposed to rejoice with the rest of the family about this great happening, but in my deepest soul I knew I could not share in it. I pretended to be happy, but I was sickened. Why was I so different? Why did I grieve for the deer and the forest and the silence?

Perhaps this is the conscious moment of my knowing of the profound schism between myself and the men in my immediate family. This would remain my secret until my adolescence. (JF)

Here is a second example:

When I was about six years old, my father and I went to purchase a birthday present for my mother. As we were driving home, my father turned to me and said that I was to tell no one what we had done. "Why?" I asked, not understanding. "Because if we keep Mom's present a secret, we can surprise her when her birthday comes," he replied.

As we drove up to our house, my father turned to me once again, and said rather sternly, "Now remember not a word; we don't want to let Mom know our secret." Something passed between us. I felt very strange and I could not look my father in the eye. It was as if I had already done something wrong.

"We're home," I casually announced. Then my mother inquired as to what we had been up to and my father calmly replied that we had been looking for a birthday gift. "Dad!" I burst out. My mother looked at me, and I froze. I looked toward my father for help. "We were looking for a birthday present," my father said again, as he peered into a pot on the stove, "but we didn't find anything interesting." I turned away and hurried outside. My father had just told a lie!

At supper I ate quietly waiting for my Dad and me to be exposed. All I could see was my plate. My parents' voices sounded distant and muffled, as if I were listening to them with my head underwater in the bathtub.

That night I lay in bed thinking: nothing happened; my Dad and I still had our secret. I felt fine, almost smug. Almost. (EL)

Here is another anecdote that shows good experiential detail:

I always looked forward to the times when Mom had to be out of the house. It was then that I could go through the drawers and closets of my parents' bedroom. How curious I was about what my mother was like when she was younger. How I loved to experiment with her lipstick, jewelry, and clothing. Of course, I was always careful to put everything back exactly as I had found it. Somehow, I knew it wasn't quite right to snoop or I would have done so while she was at home. But the contents of those drawers were irresistible to me, holding hints of the past and my future.

One day, when exploring a closet, I came across a book with the title *Normal Adult Male and Female Sexual Functioning*. Never had I seen anything quite so graphic. There were detailed descriptions of intercourse, complete with pictures. With a pounding heart I tucked the book between the mattress and the box spring of my own bed. Whenever I could, I pored over the contents of the book.

The thought of returning the book to its original storage space hadn't occurred to me until the day I walked into my bedroom. To my horror, there it was, in broad view, lying on top of my bed. I had failed to anticipate the inadequacy of my hiding place when it came to the time when Mom changed the bedding. I quickly put the book back where it belonged, hoping, perhaps, that she might come to believe that she had only imagined the whole thing. When I saw my Mom, much to my relief, there was no demand for an explanation. She probably read the panic in my eyes. Not a word was spoken, but the look that passed between us said, "I know that you know, and you know that I know." But the ever so slight smile upon her lips told me that it was all right. (CA)

And here is one more example:

I distinctly remember the atmosphere of breakfast time in my childhood home: eggs on a blue plate, oozing yellow yolk, toast. These are the familiar things of breakfast time. I loved the gleaming of the forks and spoons on the red and white checked tablecloth, the hum of the refrigerator, purring like some great white cat.

My father was a big brown man, bringing forkfuls to a high sagging face. His hands were cracked; I could feel the grease on those mechanic's hands. He

419

talked and talked. Mother talked, too. Their words would hang in the air, wrapping me like a blanket. My sister was there, too, sipping juice, tiny sips like a small brown bird.

The kitchen walls were yellow, and the far one, with the door, rippled with light and shade. The door on this wall was usually closed and on it, out of the shifting shadows and light, would appear: The Man on the Door. He was older than my father. He sat on a high-backed chair, sideways to me. I could not see his features or his clothes. He was the Shadow Man who sits and sits.

I can still recall this strange presence as if he is right here: He knows of me and of whom I know; we share this. Still, he never turns his face to me; he is simply there, always in profile, light streaming on the door and wall around him. And although I am not at all frightened, I am awed by this person, who appears only to me, with whom I talk without talking, who never looks but sees me. I cannot exactly call him a friend, but he is as natural and as inevitable as the green crown of maple leaves rustling at the edge of our neighbor's yard, as real as the pop bottles I find in the tall grass on the way to school, or the pebbles I cast at telephone poles. Mother and father continue talking. I hardly hear them, absorbed as I am in the secret manifestation of the Shadow Man. Outside, a loud car passes and the sound fades away toward the next block. The shadows cast by the glasses on the table shorten and change shape. The Man on the Door flickers, momentarily fades, returns, flickers once more, and then slides away, dissolves. And with his disappearance, my family returns. I can hear my parents' conversation, and my eyes return from the yellow wall to the yellow egg yolks on my plate. I finish my breakfast. (RM-W)

These four transcripts contain rich and subtle experiential detail. From an analysis of these experiential examples, we can learn how moments of secrecy may actually be experienced. The challenging part of the phenomenological research process is working out the phenomenological descriptions and interpretations in a narrative text. Obviously, the phenomenological work is not completed with the identification of themes. The themes are only abstractions of the interpretive descriptions that must be constructed at the hand of the themes.

An Example of a Thematic Reading

Here follows a brief example of thematic analysis of a lived experience description provided from a memory by an adult of an early experience of "childhood secrecy." The experience is presented as (i) a lived experience description; (ii) converted into an anecdote; (iii) submitted to the holistic, selective, and line-by-line thematizations; and (iv) themes used for some exemplary phenomenological reflective writing.

(i) We start with an experiential description (LED) collected from an adult who was asked to recall an early secrecy experience from childhood. We could either do a thematic reading of this entire transcript or first edit the transcript into a shorter anecdote or story by deleting excess material.

When I was about 11 or 12 years old, I went around with a bunch of boys from the neighborhood. They were not bad boys, and we were not really behaving like a youth gang. However, we would get into trouble every now and then. For example, we had several secret parties in the woods behind our village. During those parties we drank some alcohol and smoked cigarettes if we could get our hands on them. At the time we wanted to feel "grown up." One day, I was charged with getting a bottle of liquor by bribing a cousin of mine who would buy it for me. I had to hide the bottle of liquor outside under a wood stack for two days until the party that was planned for the weekend. But I was absolutely terrified at the thought that my father would discover the bottle. I considered getting rid of it, but how? During the day at school I could not get the stashed bottle out of my mind. I remember feeling self-conscious in front of my parents but trying to act normally. I constantly felt that my parents might already know what I was up to and suddenly confront me. I had difficulty looking my mother straight in the eyes. I felt as if she could look right through me and read my secret thoughts from my face. Those two nights I could hardly sleep . . . I am sure my father would have killed me if he had discovered the bottle. Toward my mother I felt guilty and sort of as if I was betraying her. I am sure she would have felt disappointed in me if she would have found out. To this day, I have never told her about this childhood secret that happened some thirty years ago.

(ii) I decide to convert the LED into an anecdote for the sake of this example. Next, this transcript has been edited in a manner described in the chapter about writing anecdotes and anecdote editing. In converting the LED, the transcript was edited toward the theme of this line: "I am sure she would have felt disappointed in me if she would have found out."

I must have been about 12 when I hid a bottle of liquor outside under a fire-wood stack for a get-together some kids were organizing. I had to keep the bottle stashed for two days under the wood stack, but I was absolutely terrified at the thought that my parents would discover it. I considered getting rid of it, but how?

During the day, at school, I could not get the secret bottle out of my mind.

I remember trying to act normally at home, like nonchalantly whistling a tune and such, but feeling very self-conscious. I constantly felt that my parents might already know and suddenly confront me. I had difficulty looking my mother straight in the eyes. I am sure my father would have killed me if he had discovered the bottle. Toward my mother I felt guilty and, sort of, as if I was betraying her. I knew she would have felt disappointed in me if she were to have found out.

(iii) Thematization-oriented reading:

Holistic reading: An overall theme for this experiential description may be: When we hide something in secret—even if it is just an object—we are actually hiding our "self."

Selective reading: One sentence that seems especially significant is the last one of the anecdote. One could ask, "Found out what?" And the answer would likely be: "My mother would have felt disappointed if she found out *who I really am.*" In this line we can see how the experience of secrecy has to do with the emergence of a sense of (self-)identity in the young person.

Detailed reading: Next, I do a line-by-line reading of the anecdote. For every sentence I ask: "What does this sentence say about the experience of a secret for a child?"

1. I must have been about 12 when I hid a bottle of liquor outside under a firewood stack for a get-together some kids were organizing.
2. I had to keep the bottle stashed for two days under the wood stack, but I was absolutely terrified at the thought that my parents would discover it.
3. I considered getting rid of it, but how?
4. During the day, at school, I could not get the secret bottle out of my mind.
5. I remember trying to act normally at home, like nonchalantly whistling a tune and such, but feeling very self-conscious.
6. I constantly felt that my parents might already know and suddenly confront me.
7. I had difficulty looking my mother straight in the eyes.
8. I am sure my father would have killed me if he had discovered the bottle.
9. Toward my mother I felt guilty and, sort of, as if I was betraying her.
10. I knew she would have felt disappointed in me if she were to have found out.

For every line I ask: "What does this sentence say about the experience of a secret for a child?"

1. Secrecy involves hiding something.
2. Secrecy may be experienced as fear of being found out, discovered.
3. A secret may be hard to bear, or keep, or resolve.
4. The inner weight of the secret may take over the outer being.
5. One may try to cover up the secret by artificial nonchalant behavior.
6. Young children may experience as if the parent can look right through them.
7. One may betray the secret through the face and the eyes.
8. Keeping secrets can be dangerous.
9. A certain transparency or openness is transgressed in the child.
10. Hiding some "thing" is hiding the "self," involving self-identity.

(iv) Reflective writing on the themes is discussed here. On the basis of these themes, as well as some of the themes that emerged in the discussion of the existentials, with respect to childhood secrecy, one can start experimenting with writing a tentative text that aims at exploring how children begin to experience the phenomenon of secrecy. This is just a beginning, but it should be seen how the reflections on secrecy above make these writing practices possible. Of course, one would want to extrapolate the themes even further, use side headings for more explicit organization of the reduction that produces the reflective phenomenological themes, and add material that would supplement the text:

> Children younger than about four or five years old may not fully know what secrets are. They may still think that their parents can look right through them and read their thoughts. As they get older, children gradually come to the

awareness that they can keep something inside. Some secrets deal with things that are personal; some have to do with family; other secrets exist among siblings, friends, or in the peer group.

The experience of secrecy is the experience of showing and hiding, concealing and revealing. There are nice secrets, deep secrets, intimate secrets, social secrets, but also there are terrible secrets, embarrassing secrets, dreadful secrets, spooky secrets, and reluctant secrets. We experience secret desires, secret pleasures, secret fears. Feelings of power, punishment, shame, guilt, care, love, and hate may all be associated with the realms of secrecy. Some secrets that children keep are "nice" secrets. And children may seek out secret places when hiding under the covers of the bed. Other secrets tend to be concerned with things that are forbidden, and that have to do with things for which one can receive punishment. It is quite a remarkable discovery for a child to realize that one can keep things "inside" and thus keep hidden from the mother or the father. In the beginning there is still a sense of uncertainty. A parent may say, "I can see that you are not telling me everything because it is written right on your forehead," or "I can see it in your face." The child may actually look in the mirror for signs of betrayal because he or she is still unsure whether mother or father can "read" what the child is thinking. And, of course, in a way, the child may have a guilty look on his or her face, or betray not being open or transparent. So, there is truth to the tale that the mother or father can "read" the secret. Even adults may have trouble hiding their thoughts, and, therefore, people tend to become adept at manipulating their physiognomy such as keeping a cool face, wearing sunglasses, looking away, and so on. Gradually the growing child will discover that there is something like an interior space, an inner self, that is different from the outer or public self, and that one can keep hidden even from one's parents. The term "secret" literally means to *separate*. The significance for understanding children is that this split between an inner world and an outer world also marks a new turn of growth toward independence and separation from the intimate relations of parents. By keeping thoughts inside, the child can make a part of the self invisible. This also means that a child can now discover that he or she may have feelings or thoughts that are quite different from his or her mother or father—the beginning of an awareness of self-identity.

(v) Some (in)variant themes of the experience of secrecy by a child based on additional experiential material could be:

- Encountering secrecy is the experience of something withheld from oneself, of being excluded (from community).
- Encountering secrecy creates distance, may alienate intimacy, disturb closeness.
- For a child to hide something or to keep a secret from one's parents is to discover inwardness, privacy, mask, persona, inner invisibility.
- Something is shown in the child's hiding of secrecy: growth toward autonomy, independency?
- When something is hidden or kept secret from someone, "self" is concealed somehow.

- In keeping a secret the child begins to experience and form a sense of personal identity.
- A certain transparency, mutuality, or openness is transgressed in the child's secrecy/hiding from the parent.
- A relational emotion is experienced by the child: maybe disapproval, guilt, or excitement—being "bad."
- There is a sense of risk of discovery, of being found out (who you really are!).
- By "having a secret" and "keeping a secret space" the child separates self (the soul) from family (community). Etymologically the word secret means "separated, divided, set apart."
- Secrecy makes possible the experience of depth, the beyond, otherness, mystery—something "forgotten."

(vi) The next phase may be to focus further on the essence of secrecy by distinguishing secrecy from privacy, lying, snubbing, gossiping, telltale, and so forth (see van Manen and Levering, 1996). I reiterate that it is important to distinguish the psychology from the phenomenology of secrecy. The psychology of secrecy is concerned with the empirical or inner lives of particular people. The phenomenology of secrecy speaks to the existential meaning and significance of secrecy. But obviously the phenomenology can inform (enrich, deepen) the psychology of secrecy.

Insight Cultivators (Applied to the Theme of Illness and Health)

Sometimes we may have a hard time understanding a certain phenomenon or event but then we unexpectedly may get an insight when we happen to see or read an entirely different text or source. It is as if this different text has cultivated a new insight for us. And we exclaim, "Oh now I see!" Insight cultivators are interpretive sources for gaining thematic insights when studying a phenomenon or event. Insight cultivators may be gleaned from philosophic and other sources in the humanities and human sciences. Insight cultivators are often engaged in metaphoric reading for meaning. They aid in the reflective interpretive process of gaining insights when reading the reflective writings of philosophers and other scholars of the arts, humanities, and human sciences. Therefore, insight cultivators may give us the sense of, "Oh, now 'I see!'" They help us to interpret our lived experiences, recall experiences that seem to exemplify these insight cultivators, and stimulate further creative insights and understandings with respect to our phenomenon under investigation.

Usually insight cultivators are found in careful readings of related literature. The work of other phenomenologists may turn into sources of insights for our own project. Naturally, we should not assume that we must uncritically accept or integrate those insights into our study. Insight cultivators allow us to see and reflect on new possibilities as well as limits, or to transcend the limits of our interpretive sensibilities. A researcher may benefit from studying how other human science scholars have addressed and brought to text their understandings of selected phenomenological topics. In this way, a phenomenological study of a topic of our interest may suggest different ways of looking at a phenomenon, or reveal dimensions of meaning that we had hitherto not considered. We may find that literature, biography, and other artistic sources may provide us with powerful examples of vicarious lived experiences and insights normally out of range of the scope of our personal everyday experiences. Sometimes, a source may provide us with a helpful insight for our research method.

For example, the book *Classic Writings for a Phenomenology of Practice* (by Michael and Max van Manen, 2021) contains several exemplary studies that show how a phenomenological study of a professional, clinical, or everyday life topic may be pursued. This book offers six studies that exemplify doing phenomenology directly on phenomena. They were created by proponents of the fields of psychiatry (Jan H. van den Berg, "The Phenomenology of the Conversation"), health science (Frederik J.J. Buytendijk, "The First Smile of the Child" and "Experiencing a Compulsive Disorder"), pedagogy (Martinus J. Langeveld, "The Secret Place in the world of the Child" and "The Thing in the Life of the Child"), and psychology (Johannes Linschoten, "The Experience of Humor"). These selected and professionally situated phenomena are explicated in a phenomenological manner that might serve as insight cultivators for other studies. The writings are examples of what Herbert Spiegelberg (1975) later called "doing phenomenology on the phenomena."

Especially the writings by van den Berg may show students of phenomenology how phenomenological topics can be productively pursued. In his now classic texts *The Psychology of the Sickbed* (1966) and *A Different Existence* (1972) and in his book *Things* (1970) van den Berg employs very clearly the method of starting with a lived experience description or an anecdote or vignette followed by phenomenological reflections on the experiential details of this description or story. In this sense, van den Berg's helpfully accessible phenomenological texts may serve as "methodological insight cultivators" for other researchers in very different fields of study.

Sometimes we stumble on or over an insight cultivator. We may gain surprisingly profound insights in the most unlikely places or in the most contingent moments. While searching for one particular item on the Internet, in the library, or the bookstore, the title of another text or object catches my attention. I peruse the text, and a passage in it gives me an entirely new insight into the material that has been preoccupying me in my research project. While waiting at the airport, I read an article about an unrelated matter, but this article gives me a new way of looking at my research question. Or, as I listen to the radio, a story told by someone interviewed gives me a wonderful example of a situation that I have been wondering about for my paper. By remaining open to unexpected sources of insight cultivators, helpful ideas, and other ways of looking at a question, new understanding may occur to us.

Sometimes etymology and lexicology can provide insight cultivators. Etymology may give us insights into the root meanings of words: how certain words came into existence and how some words may have lost some of the original meaning that still echo in the present meanings of these words (see, for example, the essay about the language and experience of care-as-worry in Chapter 2). Similarly, lexicology reminds us to look for semantic relations between words that may enlighten meaning aspects of the phenomenon that we are studying.

How do we experience our body in illness or health? This is a question that can easily comprise a book-length study. In the following sections, some basic distinctions are explored that may be especially appropriate for pursuing the phenomenon of the body in illness and health and the significance of insight cultivators. Increasingly, the health science professional is becoming aware that people require not only health-care assistance, surgical intervention, or pharmaceutical treatment, but that the professional also must be involved in the way that people experience and live with their problems in a different, sometimes deeply personal and unique manner. It is argued that the caring aspects of medicine and nursing especially are involved in helping the patient, the elderly, the disabled, or the person who for reasons of circumstance is out of step with the body, *to recover a livable relation with his or her psycho-physical being.*

So, on the basis of textual insight cultivators I shall distinguish five phenomenological aspects of body experience that occur in the literature of leading phenomenologists and that seem to resonate with life as we recognize it in experiences of illness and health. I am certainly not suggesting that these five experiential aspects are exhaustive dimensions of body experience. Inevitably, these are selective thematic simplifications. I have aimed to be observant of distinctions that have implications for discussions of illness and health. Not included in these distinctions are the ways we might experience the dead body of a loved one, the body as (re)constituted by gendered awareness, self-body experience as related to LGBTQ issues, and so forth. But such extensions and reflections obviously could be put in dialogue with a broader phenomenological thematic of gender identity. For the purpose of showing how insight cultivators might help in discovering and finessing distinctions in the thematic of body experience in illness and health the following brief distinctions and examples are offered:

1. The body experienced as an aspect of the world
2. The body experienced as reflective
3. The body experienced as observed
4. The body experienced as focus of appreciation
5. The body experienced as call.

Each of these dimensions may be further divided into two modalities with respect to the question of whether they concern one's own body experience or one's experience of the other's body. These different modes of experiencing our bodies are not offered as theoretical concepts; rather, these distinctions aim to describe and frame some common aspects of some possible human experiences that one may be able to recognize in one's own life. The phenomenological approach asks of us that we constantly measure our understandings and insights against the lived reality of our concrete experiences, which, of course, are always more complex than any particular description and interpretation can portray.

It should be reiterated that these experiential distinctions leave out many other possible experiential qualities that we may discern in the experience of our bodies and the bodies of others. For example, body experiences that tend to be more gendered and body experiences that may be unique to female as compared to male sexuality are not pursued here, as are the variations of body experience of people who identify with LGBTQ cultures and lifestyles. As well, it is quite possible that in various cultures and subcultures, different and distinct nuances of body experience are at play.

In making the following distinctions I orient myself primarily to the literature of the phenomenology of the body as we may find it in the classic works of Sartre (1956), van den Berg (1953), Rümke (1988), Merleau-Ponty (1962), Levinas (1981), and so on. Yet, life is always more complex than any description or interpretation that we may attempt. Phenomenologists like the ones mentioned here did not necessarily ask themselves how the body experiences of women, men, children, elderly people, transvestites, fashion models, ballet artists, athletes, performers, physically challenged, or other groups of people may possess unique and different qualities.

For example, the objectifying body may acquire different value in the gendered look, in the predatory gaze, in the lover's glance, or in the artist's eyes. The distinctions made here are introductory. The attempt is to consult the larger literature with the aim of showing how phenomenological inquiry importantly depends on cultivating insights provided by sources that may sometimes lie in entirely different domains. "Insight cultivators" are distinctions that help us explore or deepen our understanding of a certain experience, a phenomenon. It is hoped that in the following paragraphs these insight cultivators resonate especially with health-care providers who need to be aware of how the body is experienced in various modes of wellness or illness, comfort or discomfort.

The Body of Self, Experienced as an Aspect of the World

The most common manner of experiencing the body is as nonpositional consciousness, in the mode of near self-forgetfulness. Sartre speaks of the body as "what is passed over in silence" or "passed-by-in-silence," *le passé sous silence,* because we do not ordinarily notice the body much while we are walking, reading, driving a car, teaching a class of students, preparing supper, and generally conducting ourselves in a normal or healthful state. And even this is too general a statement to describe our lived experience, because when I am walking it is not the act of walking that keeps me preoccupied. Rather, I am walking to my classroom from my office, or walking to the bathroom from the living room, or walking down the street for shopping at the corner store. The neurosciences have shown how many, or most, of our daily activities have become automated and that our brain has formed complex interior models of the many sites and worlds that we live and inhabit. The complexities of the 86 billion neurons in our brains is a fascinating field of study and we are learning dizzying new facts of the capacities of our brain and physiological organisms. However, we should acknowledge that neuroscience cannot provide us with experiential understandings of the phenomenology of the realities of our lifeworlds as they are doubtless controlled by the functions of the brain. Still, some of the earlier insights into human consciousness, and gained through the science of phenomenology, are now supported and even more complexified by the neurosciences. But the phenomena of consciousness, human meaning, and related topics remain ultimately a mystery at the existential level, even though the insights by Sartre are fascinating.

Sartre distinguished between nonpositional or nonthetic (implicit or passed by) and positional or thetic (explicit or positive) consciousness. Nonpositional consciousness is the prereflective consciousness that is always presumed to underlie consciousness of everyday experience, and without which consciousness could not become conscious of things in the world and of itself. In much of our daily existence, we live in a prereflective mode, but by suddenly focusing on our consciousness of something or by focusing on consciousness itself we are capable of thetic consciousness or thetic self-consciousness. In Sartre's words:

> There is on the level of unreflective consciousness no consciousness of the body. The body belongs then to the structures of the non-thetic self-consciousness . . . . Non-positional consciousness is consciousness (of the) body as being that which it surmounts and nihilates by making itself consciousness—i.e., as being something which consciousness is without having to be it and which it passes over in order to be what it has to be . . . . the body is the neglected, the "passed by in silence." And yet the body is what this consciousness is; it is not even anything except body. The rest is nothingness and silence. (Sartre, 1956, p. 330)

Positional consciousness means that when we are explicitly conscious of something, we are always conscious by being in a certain position or perspective we take in such moments. So, in daily life I may rarely think about my body. I go about my business by being preoccupied with the things of my world. But sometimes I may feel a sudden pain, or I can consciously focus on my body and notice that I am out of breath from walking quickly, or I may feel cold and look for my coat to cover myself, or I am about to go out to a party and examine my body in the mirror for its aesthetic appeal, and so forth.

It is not the physical movement of walking itself but the meaning this walking acquires in my daily projects that makes a stroll along the river valley with a friend different from a walk to the corner store, or a walk down the hall in a strange school or hospital. Of course, this does not mean that we are completely unaware of the body or that we cannot recall particular aspects of the body in its silent modality. When we speak of our body as an aspect of our world, then our sense of it is a kind of unaware awareness; indeed, our primary occupation is in the world and with the world: with our projects, purposes, relations with others, and the places we travel or inhabit.

Disease too shows itself not always directly or only as a body sensation but also as a changed physiognomy of the world. When I feel the dulling sensations of the flu, then my whole world seems to turn dull. We may first discover that we are ill, not because we feel body symptoms, but because we notice how changed aspects of the outside world become symptomatic of something that must be wrong within us. The food looks less appetizing, the radio is too loud, the sunshine too bright, or the overcast sky too depressing. Everything seems to become too much, too difficult, too cumbersome. Quite literally, the world has become sick. And so, when in the morning I drop everything I touch, I may say to my spouse: "Everything is falling down; maybe I'm coming down with something. I wish I could go back to bed."

Insight cultivator: Sartre's phenomenology of the body passed-over-in-silence is a powerful insight cultivator for the experience of illness that has not yet fully unfolded itself. Interestingly, the world becomes ill before we notice that we have become ill.

The Experience of the Other's Body as an Aspect of the World

When we meet other people in everyday life, we first of all meet them through their bodies: a welcoming smile, an outstretched hand, a reluctant gesture, or a shy look. And yet, while the body seems to press itself to the forefront and while we are no doubt aware of the other person's embodied state of being, we rarely think of the other person's body; instead we engage in a discussion or work on a shared project. So, just as we bypass our own body in favor of the things in which we are involved, so we may bypass the body of the other person, who is similarly engaged in the world.

Sometimes, when we are less engaged and more observant of another person, we become aware of how that person is immersed in his or her world. I observed this incident when my son was still a teenager: I saw my son riding his bike down the street, on the wrong side of the road. He did not notice me, but I saw how aptly he steered his bike around parked cars while his hands were not even on the handle bars of his bike but in his coat pockets. I know what that feels like. I have ridden the bike like that myself when I was young and lived in the Netherlands. My son was totally absorbed by the road while avoiding the curb and the potholes and he did not seem to realize himself how marvelously he was using his feet, legs, and upper body to keep his balance. In a sense, he had to forget his body, which I saw, in order to ride on his bike down the street while avoiding oncoming traffic and without crashing into parked cars. I could not help but admire his physical skill. Simultaneously, I was struck by how much he had grown in the past year, and it occurred to me that he was in great need of a haircut. This was my experience of his body.

We participate so much with the other person's embodied existence that their words become our words, their gestures our gestures. Therefore, it is not surprising that we may even catch another person's mood or feeling of routine as it may be expressed in a sympathetic feeling how to ride this bike home and accompanied by an empathic understanding, as articulated by Edith Stein (1989). In other words, seeing my son riding his bike was also an empathic act of my own body.

It may also happen that in the company of a person we meet, we feel how tired we are while previously we seemed to feel fine. We may even feel the beginning of an illness of the other person's body in our own body. Indeed, later we hear how the person we met earlier had become ill with a virus.

Insight cultivator: the insight of Edith Stein about our empathic experience of the other person's illness is an insight cultivator of how our own body seems to detect the state of ill-health of the other person while they seem to feel fine (still).

The Body of Self, Experienced as Encumbered

It is exactly because a person's well-being is disturbed that he or she can no longer live in a self-forgetful, passed-over relation to the body, and to all other dimensions of his or her world. Serious illness changes everything: our sense of time and priorities, our experience of space, our felt relations with others, and our sense of self and of the body. At the moment when our wellness is disturbed, then we discover, as it were, our own body. We might say the body reflects on itself as body. We discover the object-like nature of our body when the unity of our existence in the world is broken. This happens when we notice something that is conspicuous such that we begin to reflect on it. A painful sensation in the abdomen, a suspicious lump under the arm, a discoloration of the skin, a strange tightness in the chest. The conspicuous disturbance always possesses the character of an encumbrance, something that confronts us, something that stands before us as it were, and hence the experience of object, the disease as intruder, as described by Nancy (2008). It is the encumbered body. When we sense something conspicuous, then we tend to worry. It is when this relation remains disturbed in a disquieting manner that we exist in a protracted state of "dis-ease," literally un-easiness.

Sometimes, only a reassuring explanation is required to appease us and to help us to resume or rebuild an unbroken relation with the body and thus with the world. The power of explanation is quite amazing. A woman experienced for several years unsettling body sensations: partial paralysis, discomfort, and fatigue. She was submitted to a multitude of examinations: bronchoscopy, CAT scan, MRI, and many other unpleasant tests. At one point, she was sent to yet another specialist. He asked her simply to make a piano movement with the fingers of one hand, which she did easily, and then with the fingers of her other hand. But the fingers would not cooperate. "Well," he said, "it is quite clear: you have multiple sclerosis."

The woman promptly broke down in tears—but not from fright or distress. No, she said, she cried from relief. Finally, after all these years, someone had named her illness. Even though the verdict was terrible, she experienced this diagnosis as an alleviation. She said, "When I now feel disturbing symptoms, I can tell myself: 'This is what it is. This is what I have to live with.' It allows me to give the disease a place in my life."

Explaining can heal, in the sense that it prompts us to a less anxious, more reflective relation with our body. Many people now and then experience something that is worrisome, but usually the diagnosis is reassuring. The physician explains that it is the flu or a bladder infection; and, along with some medication, the explanation is often already enough to make the person feel somewhat better. We soon continue to go about our everyday business, forgetful of our body.

If, for reason of physical discomfort or pain, we had to keep reflectively focusing on our body's state of being while teaching a class of students or while having a conversation with someone, then we would notice how difficult it becomes to continue in these activities. We would probably experience the situation as unbearable, unnatural, artificial, or forced. It is significant that it is much more difficult to describe the experience of health than the experience of illness; see, for example, Gadamer's *On the Enigma of Health* (1996). People who are trying to study health or well-being rather than illness discover that the elusiveness of the phenomenon of health parallels the elusiveness of the ordinary experience of the body in its "natural" taken-for-granted or silent modality. As long as we are healthy, we may not have reason to take notice of our corporeal being. Unlike a healthy marriage relationship, which is threatened by the taken-for-grantedness of its partners, a healthy body relation thrives on the smoothness of forgetfulness.

But the body is never completely out of our field of awareness. The body is experienced as passed-over or passed-by-in-silence; nevertheless, the silent body is prereflectively at the center of our existence and, thus, in a mode of unaware awareness, it remains the source of all our activities and feelings. This is true for health-care professionals as well as for the patients with whom they must deal. The significance of the recognition of the body as passed-by-in-silence for health care is that we must learn how to teach the patient, and also the patient's family, to reclaim or reconstitute as best as possible this dimension of the body in its wholly or partially unencumbered state. This self-forgetful state is what the health science professional must help the patient to recover.

Insight cultivator: Jean-Luc Nancy describes the illness as an intruder that invades our body and makes us aware of its encumbered state. The illness is like a prowler, a terrorist, that threatens our comfortable existence.

The Experience of the Other's Body as Encumbrance

While we must, in a sense, "forget" our body in order to be able to focus attention and awareness toward the projects in the world in which we are engaged, someone else may quietly observe our body and study the manner in which we accomplish things. This then is the body in the fourth modality, as it comes into being under the eyes of someone else. In other words, the body of the other whom I observe becomes my experience.

In *The Life of Illness* Carol Olson gives witness to the intricate involvements of the way we may experience the other's body as it is encumbered by illness. Carol has been on dialysis for several decades, but what she remembers most from the time in 1971 (when, like her brothers and sisters, she, too, was diagnosed with genetic kidney failure) are tales of the body. She had ample opportunity to observe how the disease ravaged the people around her. For example, she recalls waiting in the dimly lit hall of the dialysis unit when she noticed Jim, another dialysis patient. In Olson's words:

> I saw Jim leaning against the wall, gasping for air. He was hunchbacked and barrel-chested with bone disease. I could see the pain vibrating in him, burning him. And darkly, the fatigue encircled his eyes. Staring at him, I feared my pain. (1993, p. 169)

What Carol saw was somebody's body—a diseased object. And she saw his body with her own body, knowing that his fate was her fate. In a way she already experienced her own body as reflectively engaged in the diseased guise of another's body. But the next moment Jim returned her glance, and Carol knew herself as looked at. She says:

> Then he smiled at me. And in his eyes, I saw how strong was this suffering man; how strong his kindness towards me, how strong his dignity. I believed if he could live, so could I. I came away from this encounter with new courage. (1993, p. 170)

In this relational regard of the body, Olson found the strength to accept her own diseased body and the life of illness that was in store for her.

It can happen that I meet a friend and that I notice something unusual: he is leaning heavily on a table and he is straining his eyes. "Is something wrong?" I ask, "Are you feeling all right?" My friend may be quite surprised by my question. "Yes, I'm fine. Why do you ask?" Only when I insist that he seems out of sorts may the self-awareness of feeling unwell actually announce itself. Thus, one person may detect in the body of the other person one's state of well-being from the manner in which he or she is in the world.

Some experienced medical practitioners have developed an uncanny ability to sense a patient's state of health. The color of the skin, the body's composure, an overly cautious gait—all these may be signs of an oncoming illness or emerging handicap that has not yet fully revealed itself to the person. Similarly, experienced nurses may have an uncanny ability to sense a patient's critical state or level of comfort or discomfort. A post-operative patient may discover with grateful relief how a small adjustment to the tubing can make breathing easier or swallowing less painful. An experienced nurse may have developed a perceptive eye that can spot trouble in the state of being of a patient even if the nurse is not able to give explicit reasons for her knowledge and understanding of the patient's condition.

The implication of our experience of the *other's* body as object for *our* scrutiny is that this modality also makes possible the objectifying medical look and the detached scientific attitude towards the object-body. The health-care professional, the doctor or nurse, meets a person, a patient, who stands in an encumbered relation to the body. And when an illness has manifested itself, then it is clear that the sick person cannot, is not allowed to forget his or her body.

Insight cultivator: The patient, Carol Olsen, observes with an objectifying glance of her own body the suffering of the other patient's body, which shows her the subjective suffering that lies in store for her as she is about to start the objective procedures on the same dialysis machine.

The Body of Self, Experienced as Self-Observed

But, just as we can see the body of the other in its external dimensions, so the person himself or herself can also do this. For example, we may look in the mirror and observe the shape of our body. Or we can focus on a part of our body and regard this hand or this leg with an almost detached curiosity. We may even feel a kind of existential amazement that this hand, this curious object is a part of our body. This, then, is a third experiential modality, when one's own body becomes an object for one's own scrutiny—and this occurs especially when the body is rebellious and unreliable.

When we feel sick or we are injured, but we need to climb the stairs or participate in an activity, then the body rebels and refuses to cooperate. When the rebellious body does not want to do, or objects to doing what *you* want to do, then it announces itself in its objectness. My body lets me know that I am unable, disabled—"unable" means literally that I "cannot easily handle," that I "cannot keep a hold" on things. It is telling that the term ability is related to *habilitas*, habit or silent routine—as in the silent body. The body has become unreliable, and if I persist in my effort, then it may fail me. I become unsteady, slip, let go of my grasp. Or my body protests by acting up and turning overly sensitive and painful. The painful body is not a body constantly in pain; rather, it pains when I try to do something that I am unable to do. And, thus, I become sensitive to my sensitive body.

But even in a situation of health, one's body may play unexpected tricks. I turn again to the incident of my teenage son on his bike: almost as soon as my son saw me, he fell off his bike, whereupon he examined his wounded knee just as he examined his bike to determine if either needed some repair. Both the body and the bike were evaluated for their functionality, not unlike many an athlete examines the foot as well as the footgear for its instrumental functionality. We are never totally objectified. But it is true that each of us can objectify our own body and manipulate aspects of its appearance or physical condition.

Nevertheless, our own body is an object different from all other objects. Merleau-Ponty (1962) has shown this well in pointing at our special relation with our own body. If I am unhappy with the way I look, or if I worry about my physical health, then I can try to ignore or suppress the demands my body makes on me, yet I cannot hide from my body. While I can hide my body and thus myself from the view of others, I cannot separate my body from my sense of self. I can never study my body, be separated from my body, or leave behind my own body in the same way as I can do with other objects. I cannot even see my body in the same way that I can see other bodies or objects. Rather, my body makes it possible that I can see, hear, feel, and sense other things in the world. Because I have a body, I can explore the things of the world. But I do not have a body by means of which I can explore my own body; rather, my own body is such that all other bodies can be there for me and for themselves.

The health-care profession is acutely aware of the modern complaint that some physicians, medical technicians, and even nursing staff suffer from a dichotomizing Cartesian blindness. They sometimes forget that, in a manner of speaking, there is a person attached to the body. After separating the body from the mind, they only have an eye for the body. Recently the health-care profession has become more aware that illness, disease, healing, and health cannot really be properly understood when the physical is divorced from the spiritual. Reflectively and prereflectively we experience our selves as embodied beings in an inspirited world that confronts us in its materiality, but of which material we are also made. The flesh of the world is our flesh, says Merleau-Ponty (1962). The *corps-sujet* (body-subject) is that materiality through which we incarnate our understandings, moods, fears, anxieties, loves, and desires. Both body and mind should be viewed as complex aspects of the indivisible being of the person as he or she exists in his or her world.

Nevertheless, the health-care professional must regard the body-person, at times, in an objectifying body–mind (di)vision. We must observe as well that it is the patient who constantly invites the medical doctor to think in a Cartesian manner. The point is that the patient himself or herself cannot help but think this way when consulting the physician with a complaint about some conspicuous physical disturbance. I have begun to notice an irregularity about my body and I become suspicious: is this a sign of some terrible disease? For example, I may feel numb in my arm and I may see it as an oncoming cardiac event or as a sure sign of a stroke. In earlier times, one might have suspected the presence of evil spirits giving rise to a debilitating paralysis. Or an affliction was interpreted as a punishment for sins committed. But the modern person lives in a scientized culture and cannot help but adopt the diagnostic attitude of medical science.

So, I ask the physician to do what I do and examine my body to determine what is wrong with it. Now, the complaints "I feel sick" or "I feel a pain in my abdomen," require an abstraction, a cognitive objectification of the body sense. The feeling of unwellness has become an awareness of an entity that is a disease. I feel as if something is affecting me, and I say: "I have come down with something" or "I've got something." Accordingly, for a physician to adopt an objectifying view of a patient's body is in itself a proper professional activity. Indeed, the many modalities of body experience I mention here all speak to the complexity and miraculous nature of human existence.

In everyday Dutch and German language, there exists a common distinction between *lichaam* and *lijf*, *Körper* and *Leib*. In English, this distinction can only be made somewhat awkwardly using the concepts physical body and lived body. The (objectifying physical) body is an aspect of the lived body, not necessarily its opposite, as is often suggested with the distinction object-body and subject-body. Rather, the physical body is the form in which our lived body can show itself as object. It is only when the relation between physical body and lived body is broken that we may speak of an alienated corporeal existence.

Insight cultivator: Merleau-Ponty shows how our own body is an object different from all other objects. Why? Because it is the body of self that self-observes itself.

The Experience of the Other's Body by the Glance My Body

Coming back to the story of my son on his bike, what happened is that my son has suddenly seen me. Immediately, he cheerfully calls me and maneuvers an agile turnabout. This is the fourth experienced modality of the body that happens when the person becomes aware that someone else is watching him or her. As Sartre remarks, "I see *myself* because *somebody* sees me" (1956, p. 260). My son caught my admiring glance and he felt himself confirmed in my eyes. Sometimes he loves to show off for his father! But when, the next moment, he also noticed my grim face and realized my annoyance at his irresponsible biking style, he hesitated, tried to pull his hands from his pockets, lost his concentration, swung wildly off balance, and crashed against the curb. In the space of just a split second, he found out what Sartre says: that when someone watches you, his or her look can be experienced as confirming or as criticizing, positive or negative, subjectifying or objectfying—actually, Sartre only had an eye for the negative consequences of the objectifying look, and in this case my son would have agreed with him.

Sartre could be criticized in that he focused mainly on the manner in which the look of the other may rob us of our subjectivity and make us feel like an object. It is indeed a painful experience when, as a patient, one feels as if the sick body has become a thing at the disposal of the medical workers rather than a thing that is meaningfully integrated in one's own life projects. This is how one may feel when one is moved about, fed intravenously, ignored while tested, discussed by others, or placed in waiting in the dental chair or in anticipation of treatment, lab work, surgery, or simple recovery.

However, the experience of one's own body can be qualified by the look of the other in several ways. First, if the other person looks at me in a way that partakes in whatever it is that I am doing, then this look allows my body the transparency of *passé sous silence*. For example, when I am speaking up in the group, or when I am a student demonstrating my skill at a mathematics problem in front of the class on the board, then the participatory look of the others allows me to forget my body and I can focus on my task. This is possible because the look of the others, the teacher and the students, is engaged with me at the blackboard. And if the situation is routine and things go well, then I will feel confident, complete my job, and return to my seat. In other words, the participatory look produces the passed by, self-forgetful body.

But if the look of the other does *not* center in my landscape but stops in my body, then this look can do two things: either it objectifies and makes my body into a thing—an object—or the look may in fact intensify my subjectivity and give me the exceptional right to be myself as someone who has this body. Almost every school child learns the experience of the objectifying critical, mocking, disapproving look with which other kids may sometimes regard him or her. It is the look that produces body image nicknames, such as fatty, skinny, sticks, red, chunk, pimple farm, zit face, crater face, thunder thighs, flab, buns, pecks, pipes (these are some names my kids could rattle off when they were younger). The problem is that self-consciousness produced by the objectifying look of others makes it very difficult to focus one's attention to the things or the task in which one is engaged.

It sometimes happens that you are doing something or talking with somebody and suddenly you realize that the other person is no longer just listening and responding to you, but is now observing your hands, your gestures, or some other aspect of your body. Teachers, lawyers, psychologists, and therapists may make the mistake of regarding the other with such a scrutinizing look that their glance hinders the conversational relation that is essential for mutual understanding to occur.

And, of course, women know how the look of the male may reduce their sense of self to a mere body as sexual object. Similarly, the child in the wheelchair or the person with physical deformities may experience his or her body as conspicuous in certain social situations. The sexually objectified body or the disfigured conspicuous body is the self-conscious body that knows itself as being looked at with curiosity, aversion, or badly disguised disgust. But, of course, the opposite is also possible. The look of the other may actually enhance my feeling of self and subjectivity as in the affirming look of lovers or as in the experience of the child who calls out, "Look at me, Dad! Look at me, Mom!" It shows that this modality of the body is established in a relational sphere; in this relation, the body can be experienced either as justified or as denied by the glance of the other.

Insight cultivator: Sartre implicitly shows us the difference between the subjectifying and the objectifying look of the other who I experience as seeing me and who makes me see myself.

The Body of Self, Experienced as Appreciation

When I become aware of my graying hair, the aging shape of my own body, the medical condition that changes the way I am used to doing things, or the sudden

435

invasive illness that threatens my health, then I may feel regret at my lost youthfulness or I may feel betrayed by the deceptive disease that has so radically changed my relationship to my body and to those parts of my body that are so much my own and so thoroughly familiar to me.

For the person who suffers from severe arthritis, the illness is visible in the gnarled strange yet familiar hand. Illness is situated in the experience of cherished parts of one's own body that are familiar and yet may feel strange. Even the general body can be experienced as unacceptable, as in the extreme case of anorexia nervosa (starvation) or bulimia (binging and purging).

The primary appreciation of one's own body may be easily disturbed when we are in the company of others who make us aware of the idiosyncrasies of our gestures. I may notice how, while talking with someone, this person seems to be noticing something strange or unusual about the way I talk, the way I look, or the way I use my hands. The self-consciousness created by this appraising look may turn embarrassing or troublesome when I sense that the person seems to be making a negative or disconcerting judgment about me. So, I cannot help but wonder: Do I look sick? Am I making a fool of myself? But it is also possible that the other person suddenly says something flattering. Experiences like this may eventually have certain lasting effects on the nature and quality of the intimate appreciation of one's own embodied being.

Body image dissatisfaction is quite common among young women and increasingly among young men, leading to feelings of low self-respect. Many people seem to live in peace with the shape and nature of some parts of their body but in a certain discord with other parts. The phenomenological psychiatrist Henricus Rümke (1953) discusses the experience of repulsion of one's own nose, an issue rarely discussed in the medical literature, though plastic surgeons continue to profit from people's negative appreciation of aspects of their nasal appearance. No doubt, there are cultural and gender dimensions to this phenomenology of body appreciation. It can also happen that one experiences hate, sorrow, or sympathy for some part of one's body. And, in contrast, a part of our body that does not meet with our own approval may contribute to an unexpectedly experienced justification of well-being of the whole body: for example, when being touched, when caressed, or when making love.

The patient in pain, the woman in childbirth, or the person recovering from surgery may experience such total sense of surrender to the care of the other that this other is not experienced any longer as a person who may hold judgment about me, who may criticize my awkward behavior, who may objectify parts of my exposed body. For a patient in such condition it may not matter any longer that under normal circumstances he or she is quite modest or bashful, quite reluctant to undress in public, or embarrassed to be dressed in clothes that are revealing of body shape. He or she may feel ashamed of being overly fat, thin, or ill-shaped. And yet, this person—made vulnerable by a medical emergency, the painful labor of childbirth, physical trauma of an accident—now has totally surrendered his or her body to the trust of the caring other.

Insight cultivator: Henricus Rümke shows how we can experience aspects of our own diseased body as unacceptable or even with downright disgust.

The Experience of the Other's Body as Appreciation

It is also possible, and even common, that we develop an affective response toward the body or toward certain body parts of the other person. Kouwer (1953) has pointed out that one may cherish an immediate and inexplicable positive or negative appreciation for another person's face, hands, mouth, hair, neck, or his or her general body appearance. Moreover, the experienced physiognomy of the body seems to express aspects of people's character. One's own body is probably always involved in some manner in this affective appreciation of the other person's embodied being. And so, some people see obesity or excessive thinness in others as cause for strong feelings of disgust or admiration, feelings of erotic attraction or rejection.

Sometimes, a negative appreciation is associated with disfigurement or owed to a certain gesture that makes the other person's body become unacceptable. For example, when I see young people who have engaged in the increasingly common practice of having rings or pins inserted through their noses, or other body parts, I am not yet able to disregard the almost physical sympathic sense that this piercing of a sensitive body part seems to evoke in my own body—it almost physically hurts me. The repulsiveness of certain parts or diseased aspects of the patient's body may carry negative appreciative meaning. And the now routine measure of putting on protective gloves before touching any part of the patient's body may stimulate in the patient an ambiguous sense of those covered-over hands as well as a negative sense of one's own body as possibly uncouth, repulsive, or offensive. One might ask in what ways these subtle experiences of body appreciation may interfere with the need to establish a positive relation to one's own body.

Beverley, a nurse, described to me how, when working on a children's burn unit, she often felt strangely uncomfortable when a child, finally healed from terrible burns, left the unit to go back home. The child who initially was horribly disfigured had improved tremendously through delicate plastic surgery, to the delight of all medical doctors and nursing staff. Even the child was pleased, when looking in the mirror again, to see how skin grafts can improve one's appearance. However, Beverley felt ambivalent, because she also knew that when the child would leave to join the outside world again, a terrible shock would usually await for which neither the physician nor the nurse had appropriately prepared the young patient. Beverley and her colleagues had provided care and comfort. Yet, she said that she felt discomfort that the child may have been ill-served by inappropriate comfort. What does it mean to have a healed body if one is incapable of living with this body in the experiential modalities that make ordinary life livable?

Insight cultivator: Kouwer shows how people may feel a strong negative reaction when they see some illness symptom in the body presence of some other who suffers from a debilitating disease.

The Body of Self, Experienced as Call

The modality of the body experienced as call introduces an existential and moral element into the distinctions made thus far. Again, I am not trying to make artificial conceptual-theoretical distinctions; rather, I aim to evoke experiences of the body-person that one may recognize in one's own life. When we meet a friend, we greet with "How are you?" Indeed, this reference to "how we are" may make us aware of the general sense of being that we feel "in a knowing kind of way" as a certain mood. And so, rather than routinely responding with "Fine," we may actually comment on the way we sense ourselves to be in the "How are you?" "Gee, today I had an off day; I don't know why I am so down!" or "Really wonderful, I just went to this movie that I must tell you about!"

Life and living with others can be experienced as pleasurable, meaningful, satisfying, loving, secure, joyful; conversely, we may experience our existence as alienating, empty, threatening, meaningless, without purpose. These fundamental life-feelings are very much tied up in our body experience.

Even the simple knowledge of a disease that we do not feel yet can profoundly impact our pervasive life-feelings. In *The Psychology of the Sickbed*, van den Berg (1966) recounts a disarming illustration from Robert Louis Stevenson's tale "The Bottle Imp." It is worth retelling since it could be a metaphor for an ordinary life too. It is the story of a man who had experienced exceptional fortune in his life:

With the help of a magical power, which lives in a bottle, he had become rich. He buys himself a wonderful house on one of the sunny islands of the Pacific. He has it furnished to his taste, sparing neither money nor trouble. And he marries a beautiful and charming woman who fits exactly into these surroundings. When he wakes up in the morning he sings as he gets out of bed, and, singing, he washes his healthy body. On a certain morning his wife hears the singing suddenly stop. Surprised by the silence she goes to investigate. She discovers her husband in a state of silent consternation. As an explanation he points at a small insignificant pale spot on his body. He has leprosy. At the discovery of this seemingly insignificant change, his whole existence is ruined. It is no longer of any interest to him that he is a rich man, the owner of one of the most wonderful houses in the world. No longer has he an eye for the beauty of his island; this beauty has disappeared; at the most it is an accentuation of his despair. If he thought of the happiness of his marriage just a moment ago, now his wife belongs to the caste of the healthy, inaccessible to him from now on. (van den Berg, 1966, pp. 35, 36)

Each and every day there are thousands of people for whom a hitherto untroubled or even pleasurable existence is profoundly put into question by a sudden indication of cancer, a positive fatal disease, or a suspicious sign of Alzheimer's syndrome. For many of these people life, being itself, has become "dis-eased."

Insight cultivator: The medical doctor and psychiatrist van den Berg gives us a reminder that a fatal illness can strike any of us on any day. How do we live with this knowledge? Every disease has a prognostic profile and path and yet we do not know how it may strike us fatally or how it may impose an (un)liveable chronic existence of illness.

438

The Experience of the Other's Body as Call by the Other

What the previous distinctions of body experience have in common is that they are experiences of "the body of self" and "other selves," which, as such, are always self-referential. I see the other from my vantage point (bodily or corporeally), and so I understand the other and even my own body ultimately in a mode of being that has my own corporeal existence somehow at the center. Even my own body can thus be experienced as if it were an alter ego, another self. For example, we sometimes say that "part of me" wanted to do this and "another part of me" wanted to do that.

What many people find is that seeking pleasure in work, play, sex, or food is ultimately experienced as unsatisfying. It is difficult to find meaning and purpose completely within the self, in one's own embodied self. This is why self-discovery, self-exploration, and other self-referential activities in the end do not always gratify.

While this fundamental way of self-referentially orienting to the world may be the most common, it is not the only way of experiencing the body. It is also possible to experience the other's body in a manner that precedes any kind of self-referential interest. Levinas (1981) uses the expression "face to face" as a way of describing the nature of this experience. In this relational encounter, I do not experience the other as my alter ego, as another self with whom I fuse into seamless intersubjective intercorporeality as in Merleau-Ponty's (1962) description of a shared conversation or a shared landscape. Neither is the other a person whom I meaningfully constitute or construct as a member of my social world. Rather, it can happen sometimes that I have a fundamental sense that I do not know who this other is, but I experience him or her as an ethical call or appeal—this is an experience of otherness that does not occur in the self-referential attitude.

With Alphonso Lingis, the Levinassian face of the other is concrete and unique, as he describes descending from a bus in a third world city:

> Pushing our way through the crowd we feel something, look down: a beggar child touches us . . .
>
> To face another is to touch with the eyes . . . . It is to soil our eyes . . . with the sweat and the grime, the toxins and microbes . . . . The suffering of another is felt in our eyes . . .
>
> Then the one exposed to my eyes and purposes turns and faces me. In the contact the torment of another afflicts me as an appeal, presses upon me with the urgency of a demand.
>
> The homeless woman, in looking to me, appeals for the image of what my eyes have seen. (Lingis, 1998, p. 131)

In a real sense it is others and things that use my eyes to look at themselves. As Lingis says, what the look desires to see is ultimately not the things but the look itself. The only thing the eye cannot see is itself seeing. Perhaps that is why the look desires the look.

Intersubjectivity, such as the nurse–patient relation, may thus be experienced ethically as relational subjectivity that is penetrated by the other. Nurses speak of moral distress when describing the sense of being unable to shake their sense of grief and guilt when thinking about a patient in agony, who they had to leave in the hospital when going home. The ethical in this sense is not an abstraction, requiring moral theorizing or philosophy of ethics; rather, the ethical experience of the call of the other is always in the concrete, in the situation in which this vulnerable other bursts upon my world. Intersubjectivity in this sense is not something that one creates or gives shape to through some kind of decision to be personally responsive in one's own body awareness. Rather, the other is already given to me as an ethical event in the immediate recognition of his or her vulnerability or weakness. I meet a person who has just been hurt in an accident, I see a child suffering from severe pain, I find an elderly woman sobbing at the loss of her husband. I simply cannot help but feel that this person, this child, that old woman, has made a claim on me. I have experienced a call. As this person looks me in the face, I know and feel that I am responsible. And now the question becomes: what am I going to do about this call?

This is where ethical reflection may come in. See, for example, "On ethical (in)decisions experienced by parents of infants in NICU" by Michael van Manen (2014). He shows how the body of the newborn child may speak a language of its own and has already appealed to us when painful decisions must be weighed by the parents and the neonatal intensive care unit staff. Decisions have become impossible and yet one must act. And so, the indecisions fall back to the presence of the newborn.

Insight cultivator: A phenomenological text can show how the body can speak and appeal to us. In a real sense it is others and things that use my eyes to look at themselves. As Alphonso Lingis says, what the look desires to see is ultimately not the things but the look itself. Yet, the only thing the eye cannot see is itself seeing. Perhaps that is why the look desires the look.

Insight Cultivators Can Mobilize Phenomenological Insights

For Levinas and Lingis, the existential or experiential fact of our responsibility resides first of all in the significance of the face of the other who looks at me—the face that I recognize as my responsibility for the other. That is why it is so difficult to hurt the other when I am face to face with him or her and why it is easier to joke about the patient whose body lies anesthetized and covered on the operating table. Responsibility is experienced as "being there" for the other. And this ethical situation cannot be theorized, cannot be conceptually understood as situation in its contingency; rather, it is a kind of moral experience that simply happens to you and that you can validate experientially in your own body knowledge.

Somehow this self-forgetful experience of the vulnerability of the other may have healing consequences for the self. A cardiac patient recounts how, in the memory of his suffering father, he found the strength to endure and overcome his own suffering.

> It was my long-dead father who, the night before my surgery, provided me with support when I needed it. While I was undergoing all sorts of uncomfortable prep procedures, I unexpectedly began to have vivid images of my father who

had passed away many years ago when I was still a young man. This was strange since the thought of him occurred to me so seldom. But now I saw him again as he was in my youth, and how he had to endure incredible physical insults and indignities as a result of severe illness. I felt a profound sense of sorrow for him. He must have experienced great pain from circulatory problems and from out of control insulin reactions; he even had to suffer amputations. As a boy, I had seen in him what I thought was a superhuman capability to endure and still love others in such endurance. I realized with a shock that he had been younger than I am now. It was at the thought of his unbelievable love and suffering that I somehow received the courage and support from my memories of him. (TN)

Moreover, Levinas shows us that this experience has a fundamental ethical structure—as in what may happen when we meet a child playing in the street who greets and smiles at us or as we sit at the bedside of our own sick son or daughter. The very moment that we turn to this child's face, we feel already addressed in our fundamental responsibility, says Levinas. This is *feelingly knowing*. And now we are no longer the same from the moment before. We are decentered toward the other. This event is prior to reflection, prior to perception even, and prior to understanding the world or even to understanding this particular person who belongs to this face. The ethical experience of the other occurs in the situation in which this vulnerable other bursts upon my world. One nurse said:

> You never ever forget a child who you have nursed for a long time and who has died. Whether you like it or not, such a child has placed a claim on you. One time I became so overwhelmed that the parents said, "please, cry with us." But I did not want to do that since I had to go on functioning. I went to the washroom and had a drink of water. And then I returned because I had to support the parents as much as I could. I had to listen to their grieving stories and make sure that they did not have to go home all by themselves. But I heard the heart-rending sobbing of the parents for many weeks afterwards. (BC)

Of course, we must not confuse the parent–child with the nurse–child relation. For the nurse the child remains a patient. And yet such moments are ambiguous. Another nurse explained it like this:

> The first week I worked in the emergency unit, I had to deal with a child who had almost drowned. When I saw a piece of his hair sticking out from under the sheet, I got a terrible shock. For a moment I thought that I had recognized my son. He still had not learned to swim. I completely lost control of myself and had difficulty with my work for the remainder of the day. I always thought that I gave my all to my patients. But then I learned that I am involved differently with patients at an emotional and relational level. (JC)

At times, the nursing relation is a relation beyond relation. This means that it is a relation of self–other where self is erased (passed by) in the ethical experience of the vulnerability of the other. Here, caring is experienced as an ethical encounter that is beyond relation. Levinas does not speak of "relation beyond relation," although this notion is somehow implied in his discussion of otherness as "beyond" being. According to Levinas, the ethical experience of the other is always located in the person who experiences the other as an appeal to his or her responsibility.

It may be tempting to reject Levinas' notion of the face, the other, and the ethical experience as too idealistic, too self-effacing, and too sacrificial. Can physicians and nurses continue to feel this sense of responsibility without traumatizing and losing themselves, and without becoming so emotionally drained and distraught that they simply cannot keep their lives in control? Or must they, at least in their professional functioning self, become partly detached, partly self-protective, or inevitably somewhat jaded even toward human suffering? Of course, these are all possibilities. In addition to dealing with the emotions of patients, family members, and colleagues, health-care professionals must come to terms with their own emotional lives; in doing so they also differ just as their jobs, personalities, and backgrounds differ.

Health science professionals—such as medical practitioners, specialist physicians, nurses, physical therapists, midwives, and paramedics—are all in different ways involved in helping the patient, the elderly, the disabled, or the person who for reasons of circumstance is out of step with the body, to recover a livable relation with his or her psycho-physical being. Some people have to learn to live with chronic ailments or pain or permanent handicaps, others with the aftermath of surgery, some with bodies that crave drugs or alcohol, and again others with the knowledge that a degenerative disease has set in or that death is imminent.

Increasingly, the health science professional is becoming aware that people require more than just health-care assistance, surgical intervention, or pharmaceutical treatment, and that the professional must be more involved in the way that people experience and live with their problems in a different, sometimes deeply personal and unique manner. Different patients who have received a same diagnosis may experience their illness in fundamentally different ways. The clinical path of any particular disease may have different consequences and significance for different individuals. Even this cursory investigation into the various modalities of body experience shows that we may encounter our own body and the bodies of others in complex relational dimensions. None of these dimensions are alien to human existence, and yet we may feel alienated in our embodied being if body experience and situated experience are in conflict or disharmony. For example, if I visit my physician with a complaint, then I am quite prepared to objectify my body and submit it to medical scrutiny. However, if the physician only has regard for my body as object and forgets that I am the person who *is* this body, then I may experience alienation: alienation from human relation and alienation from lived body relation.

Similarly, if I suffer from a chronically severe pain or from a crippling disability but am unable to suppress this consuming pain, or if I am unable to give this pain or disability a place and meaning in my life, then I must suffer from disintegrative existence: because in our everyday life, we regularly must be able to forget our bodies in order to be attentive to the things of the world in which we are involved.

Every person is challenged to develop a livable relation with his or body in the world. This means that he or she must know that to live means to *be* a body and to *have* a body. A yogi who aims for a harmonious body–mind integrative state of being may objectify aspects of the body through focused meditative exercise in order to subjectify his or her embodied and spiritual existence. But it is unlikely that anyone will ever achieve lasting wholeness or harmonious integration of body-object and body-subject, or that anyone can ever appreciate in a totally positive and permanent manner every aspect of his or her physical existence, or that body-self and body-other can ever be truly reconciled. More likely, we must constantly be reflectively engaged in questioning how to live in contextually appropriate relationships with the body and how to acknowledge the ultimately mysterious nature of our embodied being such that a possible inspirited body relation may be brought into view. The health science professional can help to bring about reflective awareness of what modalities of body experience are disturbed and what may be done to develop meaningful, worthwhile, and livable relations between the physical body and the lived body, between the embodied being and the world.

CHAPTER THIRTEEN

Methodological Issues

Some researchers, who are newcomers to phenomenology, run into problems when they present their work to others who are not familiar with the methodology of phenomenology. It is difficult to deal with questions that arise from confusing the methodology of phenomenology with other social or human science methodologies that are based upon very different methodological, epistemological, and ontological assumptions. This chapter reviews some common conceptions and misconceptions.

Conceptual Analysis

Concept analysis is a philosophical technique for specifying differences of meaning. It is the process of breaking up a complex conceptual or linguistic entity into its most basic semantic constituents. Conceptual analysis is sometimes confused with phenomenological analysis. But a concept is generally considered a theoretical notion while a phenomenon is an experiential notion. Another assumption of conceptual analysis is that the meaning of a concept lies largely in its usage. For example, in comparing two related concepts such as secrecy and lying, a conceptual analyst might ask: In what ways is the concept of "secrecy" used in everyday life? And in what situations and circumstances is the concept of "lying" used? Are there situations where these concepts are interchangeable? Getting at the most basic meanings of a concept is accomplished by tracing its usages in different settings, contexts, and in different domains of life.

While phenomenology differs from conceptual or language analysis, conceptual analysis can be a helpful tool for phenomenology because concepts can reveal how human beings understand their world. For example, with respect to the concepts of secrecy and lying, we may note differences in intent as well as moral value. The intent of lying is usually to deceive but the intent of keeping a secret is usually to keep something hidden for personal reasons. People may keep some things secret from others for reasons of discretion, privacy, or modesty. We simply do not like other people to know things that are very personal. Many of us probably tell small lies throughout the day. For example, someone greets you and says "How are you?" and you say, "Fine." However, you do not really feel fine.

The point is that lying generally tends to be seen as morally wrong; that is why an innocent lie is sometimes called a "white lie." Small children cannot yet differentiate between the concepts of truth and falsehood, and therefore cannot be blamed for telling lies. Interestingly, adults tend to use different words for the untruths that

DOI: 10.4324/9781003228073-16

small children commit. Instead of saying, "You are lying, aren't you?" the adult says to the young child, "You are telling a story, aren't you?" And as the child grows a bit older the adult may say that the child is "fibbing" or "telling tales." Clearly, with our ordinary language, we show that we sense that lying carries a moral weight that cannot yet be applied to a small child as long as the child does not yet possess an understanding of truth, falsehood, or deception.

Concept analysis and concept clarification is a helpful philosophical technique and cognitive aid, since it enables us to "grasp" things and "know" the things that the concept names. But, from a phenomenological point of view, concepts are also risky abstractions. As Buytendijk says, a concept is like a leash that enables us to keep the dog. However, the danger is that we begin to confuse the leash with the dog, and we call this science (Buytendijk, 1961, p. 93). Trying to capture and understand the meaning of lived experience conceptually inevitably robs the experience of its rich, subtle, complex, and depthful character. For example, to understand the lived experience of keeping and sharing secrets it is not enough to treat secrecy as a concept. Rather, the lived experience of secrecy must be explored in its manifold of living meanings and significations. It is not enough to simply "overlay" it with a concept and describe how the concept is used. Phenomenology will sensitively explore the lived life that belongs to its living self.

Truth as Veritas and Aletheia

In his discussion of the *Parmenides* Heidegger (1998) makes a distinction between two notions of truth: *veritas* and *aletheia*. *Veritas* is the Roman word for truth based on the idea of justice and requiring an agent to apply some law or reason in order to make a clear distinction between the true and the false, between what is the case and what is not the case. The Romans borrowed the word *falsum* from the Greek *sphallo*, meaning "to bring to a downfall." But in the Greek language the word *sphallo* is not really the counter-concept for *aletheia*. Heidegger argues that the Roman word *falsum* is linked with militaristic associations of victory, decisiveness, will to power, and domination over another. These terms *veritas* and *falsum* are the words that we inherited in the social and human sciences.

According to Heidegger, in the western world *veritas* is the correspondence theory of truth—*veritas* brings certainty and provides a sense of what is righteous and just (1998, p. 53). He also argues that truth as *veritas* is pragmatic, technical, and bureaucratic. It relies on controlled and controllable methods and instrumental procedures. Social and human sciences that are driven by *veritas* have the implicit mission of conquering the "real" by means of discourses of representation and theories of cognition.

In contrast, *aletheia* is the ancient Greek term that means disclosure, unconcealment, withdrawal, and openness. *Aletheia* is the movement of truth that does not rely on an adjudication between the true and the false in terms of fixed principles. Instead, the truth of *aletheia* is derived from the study of meaning and meaningfulness. Reflection or inquiry that is governed by *aletheia* involves a heedful attunement to the things that present themselves to us in order to let them reveal themselves in their self-showing. The unconcealed (the *alethes*) reveals its presence to us as something that simultaneously withdraws, separating the essence from the counter-essence (1998, p. 132). Thus, the truth of something is not an all-or-nothing affair, but rather a complex and constant interplay between showing and hiding.

Aletheia as disclosure is not just something opening up, so that we can see it (like the contents of a box). Rather, the disclosing is like a sunset or fireworks that show truth in the disclosure but at the same time guards, shelters, and preserves this truth in its withdrawal (1998, p. 133). Heidegger and Gadamer propose that art is a way to truth as *aletheia*, providing us with an experience of truth—not as something that conquers or kills us—but truth as the constant play of showing and hiding, self-showing and concealment.

The fundamental project of art is, according to Levinas, that it substitutes the image for the concept. That is why art is not epistemological; it is not really a form of knowledge in the usual conceptual sense. When art is broken off from its object, then it becomes nonconceptual, inceptual, lyrical (like music that tells no story). When people "regard" art, they often turn silent. Why? Are they struck with wonder? Are they wondering if they are "getting it"? (Perhaps there is nothing to get.) Or do they have difficulty opening themselves to some truth? To that what is truly other? Art may let us experience the uncanny: it brings into presence in a pathic, performative, nonrepresentational modality what we may fear and what fascinates us at the same time.

For example, in a phenomenological reflection on the phenomenon of laughter, Jean-Luc Nancy discusses a prose poem by Baudelaire. Baudelaire paints in words his desire to paint the laughter in the laughing face of a beautiful woman:

> this disturbing countenance, where quivering nostrils breathe the unknown and the impossible, burst, with inexpressive grace, the laughter of a wide mouth, red and white and alluring, that makes one dream of the miracle of a superb flower blooming on a volcanic soil. (Nancy, 1993, p. 370)

Nancy shows how the phenomenality of desire and of laughter cannot be captured by means of propositional discourse. "We read this poem in prose as a presentation of laughter, as nothing but this presentation—or: we read it as a presence of laughter," says Nancy (1993, p. 370). Baudelaire speaks of his deep desire to paint this encounter with the laughter of beauty, and Nancy suggests that the truth of laughter cannot be represented but only presented. While laughter may be seen as a banality in ordinary life, this meaning is not banal:

> The desire to paint paints art, absolutely. And this would, in the end, be banal, if the painting weren't laughing.
>
> The painting is the poem, and it is into the painting that the artist sinks—and is fulfilled. The poem here is thus no longer a painting as image or representation. It is rather representation passing beyond itself, to its truth, which cannot be represented. But this truth is presented: it is the presentation of the artist's desire, which knows itself to be the desire to die in the presence of what surpasses all representation. Such a truth is none other than what tradition has called the "sublime": presentation of the impossible presence, beauty beyond

beauty. Not something like "sublime painting," but painting of the sublime itself. (1993, pp. 377, 378)

Nancy's text is enlightening, because it shows how phenomenological meaning can be made accessible through art and artistic devices. Some insights, such as the phenomenon of the sublime, have no clear reference or intentional object. They can only be gained through immediate nonintentional presentative language rather than through representational discourse. Phenomenological truth operates largely as presentational *aletheia* rather than as representational *veritas*.

The Reduction, Preduction, and Abduction

It may be helpful to distinguish the reduction from preduction and abduction. As we have seen in earlier chapters, the reduction is philosophically the critical Husserlian method in phenomenology. But from an epistemological or logical point of view, we may additionally distinguish the various forms of deduction, induction, preduction, seduction, production, and abduction. It is not an accident that these various pre-positions of the root word "duce" are methodologically significant. What do these notions mean with reference to phenomenological reflection and analysis? Of course, it should be acknowledged that deductive and inductive reasoning are part of all rational explication, including phenomenology. A deductive discourse is logically rational in that it remains clear about its assumptions; an inductive discourse is rational in that it develops its concepts in keeping with the detail of its empirical material.

However, even though a phenomenological text requires deductive and inductive consistency and clarity, the actual methodology of phenomenological inquiry hinges neither on deductive conclusions nor on inductive generalizations. The basic philosophical method of phenomenology is the reduction, which aims not at logically valid deductive conclusions or inductive theory development, but at the production of plausible insight into the primal or inceptive meaning structures of prereflective or lived experiences.

The production of phenomenological insights through the epoché and the reduction has been described in the previous chapters as a method of phenomenological reflection on prereflective experience that involves reflective analysis and writing.

In addition, the great challenge of any attempt at authoring a phenomenological research text implies, in part, the mobilization of the heuristic moves of preduction and abduction. To import the seductive notions of preduction and abduction into this discussion is not just a linguistic digression. Abduction describes the moment when a sudden leap occurs that makes insight possible. Preduction describes the state of active passivity that is often required for the creativity of abduction to be triggered. Therefore, we may regard abduction as closely related to inception. Phenomenological inquiry does indeed importantly require a certain heuristics and creative impetus, and the researcher has to be seduced, as it were, into a readying state of preduction for the sake of production: to produce phenomenological insights through the inceptive and heuristic process of abduction.

Validity, Reliability

The term validity derives etymologically from the Latin *validus*, meaning strong. The criterion of strength can indeed be used to assess the phenomenological acceptability and convincibility of a study. For example, the phenomenological method of the eidetic reduction is commonly accompanied by the epoché, which involves suspending one's presuppositions, biases, and taken-for-granted assumptions regarding the phenomenon that one is researching. And so, a phenomenological study may be assessed on the criteria of its suspension of personal or systemic bias, its originality of insight, and its scholarly treatment of sources. Such validation criteria presume an informed and scholarly competence on the part of the reader and reviewer of the phenomenological study and text.

It should be clear from the earlier chapters that measures such as content validity, criterion-related validity, and construct validity apply to tests and measures that are not compatible with phenomenological methodology. It should also be clear that phenomenology differs from concept analysis, grounded theory method, and similar qualitative methodologies that make use of coding, labeling, and classifying types of procedures.

A common problem for phenomenological researchers is to be challenged in defending their research in terms of references that do not belong to the methodology of phenomenology. This is especially challenging when external concepts of validation, such as sample size, sampling selection criteria, members' checking, and empirical generalization are applied to phenomenology. These are concepts that belong to the languages of different qualitative methodologies. Qualitative research is not well served by validation schemes that are naively applied across various incommensurable methodologies.

Conversely, if a notion such as "lived experience" is used across different social or human science methods, such as ethnography, narrative inquiry, and phenomenology, it needs to be acknowledged that it will not carry the same meaning. Alfred Schutz points out that the mixing of concepts that belong to different methods is apt to lead to problems. He warns that mixing, for example, objectifying and phenomenological methods, may result in misinterpretations and misunderstandings if it is not realized that concepts will change with the change of method. He says,

> choose the scheme of reference adequate to the problem you are interested in, consider its limits and possibilities, make its terms compatible and consistent with one another, and having once accepted it, stick to it! If, on the other hand, the ramifications of your problem lead you in the progress of your work to the acceptance of other schemes of reference and interpretation, do not forget that with the change in the scheme all terms in the formerly used scheme necessarily undergo a shift of meaning. To preserve the consistency of your thought you have to see to it that the "subscript" of all terms and concepts you use is the same! (Schutz, 1970, p. 270)

By "subscript" Schutz means the methodological underpinnings that characterize different kinds of inquiry. A phenomenological study does not describe

448

an event in the same sense that, for instance, an ethnographic study describes an event. For example, when an ethnographer describes the secret codes and secret behavior of a particular street gang or a certain motorcycle club, the description of these cultural secret norms is expected to exhibit a certain degree of reality validity for the way this particular street-gang culture or that particular motorcycle club is operated and experienced by the members who belong to this gang or club, as well as the kinds of talk and cultural expressions that belong to that (sub)culture. It follows that the methodical procedure of members' checking can be applied when validating an ethnographic portrayal of the secret behaviors of the members of such particular group. In performing a members' check, the ethnographer wants to ascertain that indeed the members of this group agree that the words used, the terminologies, and the secret codes that are described in the ethnographic study are practiced as they are described and portrayed.

In contrast, phenomenology cannot be applied to a particular culture or specific subculture. Phenomenology describes not the *factual* empirical but the *existential* empirical meaning structures of a certain phenomenon or event. Thus, a phenomenological study of secrecy does not focus on a particular culture or specific social group. Instead, phenomenology studies the existential meaning structures of the phenomenon of secrecy.

Now, it certainly is methodologically and ethically commendable to ask persons who have provided experiential descriptions (through interviews, written accounts, and so on) whether the examples or anecdotes derived from these experiential materials are resonant with their original experiences. But validating the quality of the experiential accounts or anecdotes does not validate the quality of the phenomenological study as a whole. The more important and difficult issue is whether the phenomenological interpretations of the underlying meaning structures of these descriptions are valid and executed in a scholarly manner, and whether the phenomenological themes and insights emerging from the descriptions are appropriate and original. For these questions, no procedural method will be adequate to ascertain the value, strength, originality, and significance of a phenomenological study.

The validity of a phenomenological study has to be sought in the appraisal of the originality of insights and the soundness of interpretive processes demonstrated in the study. No predetermined procedure such as "members' check" or "triangulation of multiple methods" can fulfill such demand for validating a phenomenological study. If there were such a validation procedure, then it would have to validate itself, in turn, by the underlying methodological justification of such validation criteria. Indeed, there is a price to be paid for insisting on a procedure that would validate a phenomenological study (see van Manen, 1997). Barthes expressed this warning eloquently:

> Some people speak of method greedily, demandingly; what they want in work is method; to them it never seems rigorous enough, formal enough. Method becomes a Law . . . the invariable fact is that a work which constantly proclaims its will-to-method is ultimately sterile: everything has been put into the method, nothing remains for the writing; the researcher insists that his text will be methodological, but this text never comes: no surer way to kill a piece of research

and send it to join the great scrap heap of abandoned projects than Method. (Barthes, 1986, p. 318)

An interesting case of validity critique is contained in the scornful criticism by Stephen Strasser who once referred to Jean-Paul Sartre's famous account of the objectifying look as "phenomenological impressionism" (1974, pp. 295–302). In his account of "the look" Sartre shows how the glance of the other can be experienced by us as objectifying and as robbing us of our own sense of agency and subjectivity. The other's objectifying look takes away our world and enslaves us to the other. But Strasser accused Sartre of getting carried away with literary style and of failing to see that a more differentiated phenomenological analysis would show that the look can be experienced positively as well as negatively—that the look of the other can enhance our sense of self and even make intimacy possible (Strasser, 1974, p. 298). He says,

> the desire arises in our phenomenologists, usually in an unconscious way, to embellish his descriptions by using an artistic style. The "well-written" work of such a phenomenologist assumes a literary character. He feels encouraged in this because precisely in our time prominent thinkers have drawn attention to the truth concealed in the work of art. (1974, p. 299)

Strasser's criticism overtly addresses Sartre's suggestive and artistic style, but really his critique is just as much aimed at his Dutch and German colleagues who, at the time, were widely admired for the brilliant and eloquent manner in which they brought phenomenology down to earth by means of insightful as well as evocative textual writings. Psychiatrists such as van den Berg (1972, 1987) and Rümke (1988), educationists like Langeveld (1979) and Bollnow (1988), medical doctors like Buytendijk (1988) and Beets (1952), and clinical psychologists such as van Lennep (1987a, 1987b) and Linschoten (1987) were writing practical studies that were meant to speak to our everyday experience, as well as to the lifeworld and concerns of the professional practitioner.

These authors shied away from technical philosophical issues and they openly admitted that they were primarily interested in phenomenology as a reflective method, not in phenomenology as a rigorous form of professional philosophy. On the whole these phenomenologists were more interested in actually applying phenomenology to their professional practices than in asking whether doing phenomenology was possible, or even in the question of whether it would be possible to prepare a research methodology that would describe how they were doing phenomenology in the first place. What they did do was produce insightful studies of concrete human phenomena in professional fields of medicine, psychology, pedagogy, jurisprudence, and so forth.

Strasser's critique of Sartre (and all others who use literary material in their phenomenological studies) is that Sartre did not acknowledge or see that the look, in both its objectifying as well as in its subjectifying forms, may actually be encouraging, admiring, praising. For example, an athlete may feel strengthened by the look of the onlookers, and this positive look may stimulate even greater athletic feats. Similarly, a loved one may feel enhanced in his or her physical appearance by the complimentary glance of the lover. And a child on a climbing apparatus may feel admired and praised by the parental look of recognition on the playground.

In his defense, however, Sartre would probably say that he was describing the phenomenology of the "objectifying look." And, thus, he would deflect the validation critique of someone like Strasser. Indeed, the "subjectifying look" or the "look that strengthens and encourages" could be explored as a different phenomenological topic. Strasser tried to argue that the use of literary material in a phenomenological study is responsible for biased or one-sided phenomenological studies. However, Strasser's validity critique is methodologically not sustainable. In fact, the use of literary material and narrative examples is now widespread and common in the works of philosophical and human science phenomenologists such as Heidegger, Serres, Lingis, Nancy, and many others.

Reliability issues tend to arise with questions of the repeatability of a study. For example, a test is reliable if it produces the same result each time it is administered. However, it is unlikely that a phenomenological study would be involved in measurement schemes such as interrater reliability by having different judges rate, measure, or evaluate a certain outcome. The point is that phenomenological studies of the same "phenomenon" or "event" can be very different in their results. Compare, for example, Linschoten and Nancy in their studies of the phenomenon of falling asleep. A phenomenologist may study a phenomenon that has already been addressed repeatedly in the literature, but strive for new and surprising insights.

The topic of bias, misinterpretation, or overinterpretation in research expresses a concern with the validity of a study—for example, the validity of whether a research instrument measures what it claims to measure, whether a research procedure yields accurate results, whether the logical or argumentative structure of a research program is correct, or whether the practice of a study produces insights that are acceptable. Notions such as measurement bias and confounding bias are obviously more appropriate in the assessment of the soundness of quantitative research programs and outcomes than in qualitative research. The epoché is the critical phenomenological device that should defeat bias that occurs from unexamined assumptions, personal or systematic prejudices, closed-mindedness, and so on. But it should be acknowledged as well that all understanding presumes preunderstandings. That is why Gadamer argued that prejudices are not only unavoidable, they are necessary, as long as they are self-reflectively aware or acknowledged.

Data Analysis, Coding

Present-day qualitative method uses the language of "data collection, data coding, data analysis, data capture," and so forth. However, strictly speaking, phenomenology is ill-served with such usage of the term "data." The Latin term *datum* or *data*, as a general concept, refers to the idea that certain kinds of information are represented in forms fitting for processing: decoding, interpreting, sequencing, sorting, counting, and so forth. The *Oxford English Dictionary* refers to data as "items of (chiefly numerical) information considered collectively, typically obtained by scientific work and used for reference, analysis, or calculation" and "operations performed by computer programs" (online *OED*). But such usage of the term data is incompatible with the program and assumptions of phenomenological inquiry.

No doubt, the words "data" and "data analysis" are terms of a discourse that may be attractive to the ear of those qualitative researchers who like to believe that their procedures ensure solid measured outcomes. Data analysis converts data into figures, visuals, graphs, concepts, or lists of objectivistic themes. However, it is actually somewhat bizarre to use the objectifying term "data" for phenomenological inquiry as phenomenology is concerned with meaning and meaningfulness rather than "informational" content. Phenomenology deals with descriptions, narratives, stories, poetry, anecdotes, sayings—not with codes or objectivistic data. Some phenomenologists such as Amedeo Giorgi (1970, 2009, 2011) use terms such as "meaning units" that are more appropriate than the nomenclature of "data" and "codes" as they still retain the sense of meaning and meaningfulness.

There is a certain irony in the fact that etymologically the meaning of the term "data" expresses "givenness," what is "given." In this etymological sense, the term "data" should be well suited for qualitative phenomenological methodology. But it requires a cautious reconceptualization of the idea of data. Phenomenology is the study of what "gives itself" in human lived experience or consciousness (Marion, 2002a). And yet, methodologically speaking, phenomenology does not rely on (numerical, coded, or objectifying) data but rather on data as "phenomenological descriptions and explications."

Evidence and Intuition

We must distinguish empirical evidence (e.g., "I saw it happening with my own eyes," or "we can generalize that this medicine is safe on the basis of repeatable pharmaceutical studies") from intuitive-based evidence ("I experience intimacy when I share a personal secret with my loved one"). Phenomenological evidence has to do with interior intuitive understanding and is meaning-based and based on the logic of eidetic reduction. In contrast, empirical evidence has to do with exterior knowledge and is based on the logic of generalization of observation and quantifiability.

Phenomenological evidence has to do with grasping the meaning of a phenomenon or event. However, phenomenological evidence is ultimately ambiguous and never complete. Therefore, Heidegger and Merleau-Ponty criticized Husserl's claim that the intentionality of a phenomenon can be apodictically grasped through the eidetic reduction. If we are concerned with "evidence-based practice," then we have to distinguish between (a) specific practical situations where "best action" can be supported by empirical (hopefully generalizable) evidence that seems most relevant and applicable under the circumstance and (b) practical situations where thoughtful sensitivity, tactfulness, and meaningful understanding play a critical role. In the latter situation, phenomenological understanding and insight into a certain phenomenon may lead to more appropriate action.

An example for contrasting empirical evidence-based practice and phenomenological intuitive evidence-based practice may be provided with obsessive compulsive disorders (OCDs). There is a strong medical science-based body of evidence for using certain drugs in treating OCDs. And there is also a need to understand how obsessive actions are actually experienced. OCD experiences are quite complex: the strange contradiction of wanting and not wanting to do something (Buytendijk, 1970a). Phenomenological understanding of obsessions may help to deal with the disorder in a more relational and conversational manner. However, the evidence for such understanding is meaning-based and oriented to understanding the prereflective dimensions of the life world of the person living with obsessive thoughts and inclinations.

Intentionality

Husserl adopted the notion of intentionality from Franz Brentano (1874/1995), to refer to the worldly structure of consciousness. Intentionality describes the ways we are "attached" to the world and how consciousness is always being *conscious of* something. All our thinking, feeling, and acting are "oriented to" or "with" the things in the world. This also means that we can never step out of the world and view it from some detached vista. We are *au monde*, meaning simultaneously "in" and "of" the world.

The intentionality of always being in the midst of things also means that the things around us always present themselves partially, perspectivally, seen from this side or with that aspect. When we hear, see, or touch something or someone, or when we think of something, then our experience of this thing, object, person, being, or subject is always as it is given or as it appears to us (in experience or in consciousness), rather than as it is in its unity or wholeness. So, we have to make a distinction between the object and our lived experience of the object. When I look at the book on the table, or when I take the book in my hand, I always only see one part of the book at a time: I see the cover, or the open page, or the spine, or the back side, or the printed title. In fact, I never see the thing, book, exactly from the same angle, distance, or perspective. No experience of this or that book (or any "thing" whatsoever) is ever exactly the same.

And yet, what I "see" in each act of perception is the book. In my *experience* of the book, I see the book in its unity or wholeness—and not necessarily as an object that looks like a book and that has different sides or adumbrations, some of which are hidden from my view. Indeed, the object I see may turn out to be a dummy book or just the image of a book on a poster. And yet my "experience of having seen a book" cannot be doubted, even if afterwards the factuality of having seen a book turns out erroneous or false.

As well, when I see this book, I see my interest in the book. Or, rather, the book gives itself in a certain modality, depending in part on my look. For example, the book presents itself as an invitation to pick it up and continue reading it. Or the book reminds me of certain things I experienced while reading it. Or I may be struck by the aesthetics of the cover of the book. Or the book tells me that I need to take it back to the library or return it to the friend who lent it to me. Or I reach for the book as a backing for a piece of paper on which I am writing a grocery list. Or, perhaps, the book belonged to my great-grandparents and I realize that it was read by other people before I was even born.

So, there are certain intentional relations between the thing (the book as object of consciousness that we can observe in its various adumbrations) and the thing-in-itself (the book as-it-shows-itself to us in consciousness) (not in the sense of Kant but in the sense of Sartre). This does not mean that there are two kinds of books: the real book in the external world and the mental book in the internal realm of consciousness. According to Sartre, consciousness and the world are immediately given together: the world, essentially external to consciousness, is essentially related to it. When we focus our reflective awareness on our experience of the book, then we adopt a phenomenological attitude and we approach the book as a phenomenon.

This thing-in-itself-as-it-shows-itself in consciousness is a phenomenon. And every distinct phenomenon is characterized by its phenomenality: the intentional ways that the phenomenon gives itself, shows itself, or appears in consciousness. And, of course, there are various modalities in which the phenomenality of a phenomenon may appear or give itself. It may give itself in a different intentionality to you or to me, to an adult or a child, to a woman or a man, to a sick person or a healthy person, to a teacher or a student, and so on. Phenomenology is the study of the phenomenality of a phenomenon—of a possible human experience.

However, the notion of intentionality has acquired different interpretations in the more recent so-called radical phenomenologies of authors such as Emmanuel Levinas, Michel Henry, Jean-Louis Chrétien, and Jean-Luc Marion. Marion used the adjective *radical* to describe the phenomenological method that aims to assign the givenness of the phenomenon not to the self of the intentional subject (consciousness or *Dasein*) but to "the self of the phenomenon" (Marion, 2002a, p. 20). This is radical because it forces the intentionality of the phenomenological focus to disappear, to be reconceived, or to shift away from the self of the subject to the self of the phenomenon itself.

In the traditional phenomenology of Husserl, the reduction ultimately reverts to the intentional subject or consciousness responsible for constituting the phenomenon in the first place. But what happens when the intentional relation between "I" and the world is disregarded or denied its constituting function? In that case, the very sense of the "I" or subject and subjectivity is required to be rethought. Thus, phenomenologies of alterity, self-givenness, donation, and life pose a challenge to the primacy of the "I" (the subject, self, ego, consciousness) and its intentionality.

In a chapter on "nonintentional consciousness," Levinas (1998) points out that intentionality always focuses on what can be thought, felt, perceived, and become the object of emotions. Intentionality reveals the world as it can be comprehended, grasped, or appropriated. Thinking is always grasping, appropriating, reducing what is other to the self, the same: "Thought, qua learning [*apprendre*], requires a taking [*prendre*], a seizure, a grip on what is learned, and a possession" (1998, p. 125). Thus, intentionality places consciousness, self, or presence at the center of our world. But there are experiences that have a nonintentional structure. These are the immediate experiences prior to reflection and prior to thematization. And Levinas shows that the experience of alterity (experiencing the otherness of the other) is also essentially a nonintentional phenomenon.

454

Phenomenological analysis that involves nonintentional meaning will be guided by vocative elements of language. They evoke meaning that is felt immediately but not grasped as knowledge or concepts. It would appear, therefore, that the vocative methods as described in this book introduce forms of "knowing" and "grasping" that are noncognitive and nonappropriative.

The question is what interpretation of subjectivity should be understood as the (non)intentional measure for what can be experienced by the self. For example, Marion argued that a phenomenon such as "a baby's birth" has obvious phenomenological meaning, and yet the subjectivity of this lived meaning experienced by the newly born cannot be accessed via the reduction. Also, there are phenomena or events, such as a significant conversation or a meaningful talk, that are so "saturated with meaning" (Marion, 2002b) or that have "evential latency" (Romano, 2009) that their lived meaning can only partially be discerned now and perhaps gradually more later.

To reiterate, for Husserl it is consciousness (the transcendental ego) that constitutes the phenomena and thus lets them appear, give, or show themselves. But in the work of Levinas, the emergence of meaning does not start from and with the intentional self (ontology or being), but from the other or the otherness of the other (alterity). In the writings of Marion the self is bypassed so that its intentional relation to the world cannot contaminate the phenomenological research into the meaning of phenomena. Similarly, the phenomenologies of Michel Henry and Jean-Louis Chrétien reduce the self to a passive nonintentional rather than an active intentional role. Thus, the radical phenomenologies of these authors contain a sense of the subject or the self that is more passive or passively receptive— the subject lacks agency and active intentionality. It might even be argued that the constitution of meaning in these methodologies is initiated, not by the subject or the ego, but by the intentionality of the things or objects that call upon us to respond, as in the writings of Jean-Louis Chrétien (2004b) and, in a more hermeneutic manner, in the work of Günter Figal (2010). The suggestion that "things" and "objects" have agency, subjectivity, or even ethical or moral agency is further found in the writings of authors such as Peter-Paul Verbeek (2005, 2011) and Sylvia Benso (2000).

Generalization, Bias, and Prejudice

Phenomenological generalizations should not be confused with empirical or quantitative generalizations that draw conclusions of validity of observation from a sample of a population to the general population. Empirical generalizations are factual, and, of course, empirical or quantitative generalizations are extremely important in the social and the human sciences. But empirical generalizations cannot be drawn from phenomenological studies.

Many qualitative inquiries try to arrive at generalized understandings. Phenomenology is a form of inquiry that does not yield generalizations in the usual empirical sense. The only generalization allowed in phenomenological inquiry is "never generalize." And yet, in some way we could speak of phenomenological understandings as generalized. So, we could ask, how is phenomenological generalization possible while respecting singularity and uniqueness? For example, how can we keep a focus on the singularity of a phenomenon while still being able to arrive at some type of universal or generalized insight into this phenomenon?

We may distinguish two kinds of phenomenological generalizations: existential and singular generalization. First, existential generalization orients to eidetic or essential understanding—to what is universal or essential about a phenomenon in an existential sense. Existential generalizations make it possible to recognize recurring aspects of the meaning of a certain phenomenon (for example, the phenomenology of keeping or sharing a secret). Second, singular generalization orients to what is singular or unique. Phenomenological examples (such as Sartre's particular story of the incidence of the objectifying look) may be considered singular generalizations that make it possible to recognize what is universal about a phenomenon.

Within phenomenological methodology, the term *sample* should not refer to an empirical sample as a subset of a population. This use of the notion of sampling presupposes that one aims at empirical generalization, and that is impossible within a phenomenological methodology. But the term "sample" can be related back to the French root word "*example*," which has paradigmatic significance, as has been pointed out with reference to Buytendijk, Agamben, Figal, and others. To reiterate, it is important to emphasize that phenomenological inquiry cannot strive for empirical generalization—from a sample to a population. And so, it does not make much sense to ask how large the sample of interviewees, participants, or subjects should be, or how a sample should be composed and proportioned in terms of gender, ethnicity, or other selective considerations.

The notion of purposive sampling is sometimes used to indicate that interviewees or participants are selected on the basis of their knowledge and verbal eloquence to describe a group or (sub)culture to which they belong. This is helpful for ethnographic-type studies, but, of course, phenomenology is not ethnography. However, it may indeed be wise to gather and explore experiential descriptions from individuals who are capable of putting their own experiences in oral or written words. If it is necessary to use the notion of "sample" or "sampling," then it is best to do so with reference to the attempt to gain "examples" of experientially rich descriptions.

So, the more important question to ask is, "How many examples of concrete experiential descriptions would be appropriate for this study in order to explore the phenomenological meanings of this or that phenomenon?" The answer does not depend on some logarithm or statistical criterion or on some formula of data saturation. Data saturation presumes that the researcher is looking for what is characteristic or the same about a social group of people or an ethnic culture. The researcher keeps collecting data until the analysis no longer reveals anything new or different about the group. But phenomenology looks not for sameness or repetitive patterns. Rather, phenomenology aims at what is singular and a singular theme or notion may only be seen once in experiential data. For example, a phenomenologist does not look for how many times a certain word is used by informants or how often a similar idea is expressed. In contrast, a phenomenologist may actually look for that instant when an insight arises that is totally unique to a certain example (sample) of a lived experience description.

Still, for many researchers, the questions arise: "How many people should I interview? How many interviews should I conduct with each interviewee?" Depending on the nature of the phenomenological study, the response will vary. Some more "theoretical" studies will be done without any empirical data collection whatsoever; other studies will benefit from a few or a great many interviews or experiential data sources. Too many transcripts may ironically encourage shallow reflection. Again, depending on the phenomenological question, the general aim should be to gather enough experientially rich accounts that make possible the figuration of powerful experiential examples or anecdotes that help to make contact with life as it is lived. In the end, the outcome of the study should contain just the right amount of experiential material (whether in single sentence or story form) that creates a scholarly and reflective phenomenological text.

Interpretive Psychological Analysis versus Phenomenological Analysis

A common issue of logic in the qualitative methodology of phenomenology would be: Is this a psychological or a phenomenological study or question? Or, more precisely put: Is this interpretive psychological analysis or is this interpretive phenomenological analysis? By way of example, we will compare topics of psychological studies with phenomenological studies of children's experience of secrecy. First, we might find that some parents do not like their children to have secrets; other people say that they do not trust people who keep secrets—secrets are like lies. Some people may hate secrets while others are curious. And individuals who do not like secrets may feel that we should be open and transparent with each other. Some say that they never keep secrets. Psychological investigations foreseeably could lead to such psychological themes as (dis)trust, deception, distance, friendship, and so forth. And, of course, we might be interested in the psychological reasons that some people are secretive while others tend to be more open with their inner lives.

Some researchers might be interested in questions of whether younger people are more or less secretive than older people? Are females more inclined to keep secrets in some cultures that males in different cultures? These are indeed psychological and socio-psychological studies. These psychological studies tend to involve empirical, qualitative, and quantitative methodologies. Other researchers may be more interested in the meaning of secrecy. Jacques Derrida (Derrida and Ferraris, 2001) explains how the condition for sharing, thematizing, or objectifying something implies that there be something nonsharable, nonthematizable, nonobjectifiable. And this something is the absolute secret—we speak of it, but we cannot say it; we evoke it, but we cannot write it. Here we see how secrets are ultimately enigmatic phenomena that shape our existence. These intuitively given and grasped themes are very different from psychological feelings, opinions, or interpretations. Rather, this is the fascination of phenomenology.

Phenomenological reflections would try to discover what are the structural existential features of the experience of keeping and sharing secrets. These intuitively grasped meanings are very different from psychological themes. For example, phenomenological themes may include meaning insights such as: when we hide a secret (thing or thought), we hide our self. Secrets separate the self from others (secrete means to separate). Secrecy is the experience of inwardness, inner and outer self. When children begin to keep and share secrets, they double their reality: they now live in an inner and an outer world. Children discover that secrets can make them invisible: we experience inner invisibility. To keep a secret from your parent means that you have or know something they do not. Secrets kept may create and also disturb relations of intimacy. Secrets shared may create relations of intimacy. The experience of secrets may be seen in people's physiognomy and behavior; and so forth.

The upshot of confusing psychological with phenomenological analysis is that the focus of psychology is on the psychic states, motivations, feelings, and behaviors of particular people or groups of people, while the focus of phenomenology is on the originary, phenomenal, and essential meaning structures of human experience and consciousness. If a person has acquired intuitive meaning insights into the phenomenology of a certain phenomenon or event (such as the meaning of secrecy) then this should enable that person to think and act with increased thoughtfulness and tact in empirical contexts and situations where secrecy might be at stake.

Bacon's Idols

In his *New Organon*, Francis Bacon (1561–1626) presents the "idols" that are his warnings about fallacious thinking or misdirected interpretation. It may be relevant to stay cognizant of Bacon's considerations. Bacon used the title *Organon* to refer to the intellectual tools for interpreting or understanding the truth of nature. He describes four kinds of "idols" (images or phantoms) to explain the human frailty of making self-serving judgments or prejudicial observations. These idols may still serve us as warnings for unwittingly going astray in our efforts to gain insights—not only into the nature of nature's physics, but also into the structures and meanings of the human lifeworld.

First, there is the *idola tribus*: the idols of the tribe ensue from an all-too-human tendency to read one's own desires and needs into things, and to oversimplify, overgeneralize, overinterpret, or to be struck by novelty. Just because a certain issue, topic, idea, or theory is the latest to hit the fashion-conscious academic market does not mean that it is truer or more worthwhile than earlier ideas or perspectives.

Second, there is the *idola specus*: the idols of the cave are situated in our personal and idiosyncratic sentiments and preoccupations. Academics tend to form their understandings based on their favored authorities. And, not infrequently, the knowledge and views of academics are influenced and shaped by factors that lie in the personal and political sphere reigned by envy, jealousy, resentment, likes, and dislikes.

Third, there is the *idola fori*: the idols of the marketplace are caused by language. The danger of scientific or theoretic languages is that they cannot capture the more subtle and complex aspects of human existence. Therefore, human science must ultimately be understandable in the ordinary language of the lifeworld. Of course, the problem with ordinary language is that we all have somewhat different under-standings of terms, and different languages are not fully capable of capturing the different forms of knowledge and subtleties of meaning.

Fourth, there is the *idola theatri*: philosophical schools of thought, politicized, gendered, and ethnocentric perspectives may prevent us from arriving at simple and modest insights. This is when a professionalized discourse becomes polemi-cal: the researcher's perspective turns into an accusatory screen that can only see its own vision as valid. Therefore, we must be aware of the false authority of received theories, of the pretentiousness of exotic perspectives, and of fanciful interpreta-tions and abstractions that seem appealing. Some philosophers who seem to feel especially entitled do not get this: they preach that phenomenology should be rel-evant and understandable but they do not or cannot practice it.

CHAPTER FOURTEEN

The Desire to Write

Writing (whether with pen, keyboard, or virtual tools) is an odd activity. We may even ask if it is really an activity at all. The activities of a carpenter, cook, painter, athlete, salesperson, and so forth can be observed and described. But writing is unlike most human activities in that there is little to be observed in the experience. How would one determine the process of writing? Does it happen in the moment that a finger hits the keyboard? Or would certain thoughts have to be externalized as visible words? Could writing be performed silently before sitting down with the tools of writing? If someone is entering words on paper or on the computer screen, but nothing of consequence is being produced, is this writing? Merleau-Ponty and Marion remark that if one looks too closely at a painting one will only see paint, pigment, and canvas; instead one must look at it as a whole and orient to what is seen *in this view* which is almost totally incommensurable with the close-up. The same is true of written text.

As I stare out of the window into the dark evening, I barely notice the mountains in the distance, across the wide waterways. In fact, I am musing and scarcely aware that I am looking out of the window, until my wife casually walks into the room. "What are you up to?" she queries. Awoken, as if from a daydream, I say, "I am writing." "Oh no, you aren't. You are just looking out of the window." She laughs, teasingly, and leaves.

It is true. I was staring out of the window. And yet, while I may have been observing the ocean, following some distant ship with my eyes, I did not really see that. My thoughts were elsewhere. More accurately, I was elsewhere. Where? One way to say it is that I was caught up in the words that I was contemplating, silently chewing them and then spitting them via the keyboard, onto the computer screen. But is this writing? Am I writing? Well, yes and no. I am producing words, a text even. Yet, these are just words. This is not really writing. So, my wife was right. But when could I say that I am actually writing? I wonder if there is such a moment that I can say: "Now. Now I am writing."

What then is the phenomenon of writing anyway? I try to recollect an experience of writing. It is hard to think of a specific instance but I do have a sense of a certain space or mood. I am vaguely aware that in the experience of writing (or trying to write) something happens to me. I seem to be seeking a certain space. A writerly space. In this space I am no longer quite myself. Just as in reading a compelling story, the self of the reader seems to have slipped away, so in the act of writing the "self" has become partially erased. It is like falling into a twilight zone, where things are no longer recognizably the same, where words are displaced, where you

460

DOI: 10.4324/9781003228073-17

can lose your orientation, where anything can happen. Is this what makes writing difficult: this sense of erasure of the self? Should I actively and reflectively seek to write? Or should I seek to surrender myself to that special reflective mood? I type, "phenomenological reflecting is already like writing in the sense that we withdraw from the world." I am sitting at my keyboard, mulling over these last words. I think that Derrida said something like that.

Often writing is best done in special places that we seek out. The physical environment has to be conducive to writing. The public office may not be the best place. Too many interruptions. Sometimes a quiet coffee shop is not bad. I look at my present space. This den in my home. This desk. This is where I work best! This is where I write. So, is this then the space of writing? Yes and no. When I am actually typing on the keyboard or staring out of the window, then I still seem to be somewhere else. Where am I then? One might answer: inside your thoughts. The writer dwells in an inner space, inside the self. Indeed, this is a popular way of spatially envisioning the self: an inner self and an outer self. But phenomenologically it is probably just as plausible to say that the writer dwells in the textorium: the virtual space that the words open up.

The practice of writing is not unlike reading. When I am not at home and I feel like reading a novel, I first have to find a space that is good for reading. It must be a space that is comfortable for the body, but not too comfortable. It does not need to be quiet as long as the sounds or people do not draw attention to themselves. Once I have found this physical space conducive to reading, I am ready, so to speak, to enter that virtual reality, the textorium, the space of the words that transports me away from my everyday reality to the reality of the novel. When I have entered this world of the text, then I am somewhere else. So, there is a doubling of space experience here. The physical space of reading or writing allows me to pass through it into the world opened up by the words, the space of the text.

But is this not a misleading way of speaking? After all, the space opened up by the text is not a "real" physical dimensional space. Is the idea of textual space not just a metaphor and therefore a gloss for how we actually experience the process of reading and writing? This seems to be true. We are using a spatial/temporal phenomenology. Interestingly, the term "space" itself possesses rich semantic meanings. Etymologically the word "space" does not just refer to physical extension and perspective. Space possesses the meaning of lapse or duration in time as well as distance; it carries the meaning of temporal and physical expanse as well as the time spent in an experience.

When we enter this space of the text, we indeed seem to enjoy a temporal experience in a world evoked by the words of the text. And we always enter this world alone. To write is a solitary experience, a solitary and self-forgetful submersion in textual reality. For the writer this is where insights occur, where words may acquire a depth of meaning. But this is also the place where writing shows its difficulties, where we find out what language really is, where writing may become impossible, where language ironically seems to rob us of the ability to say anything worth saying, or saying what we want to say. Strangely, in the space of the text, our experience of language seems to vacillate between transparency and impenetrability. One moment I am totally and self-forgetfully entering this text—which opens up a world. The next moment the entrance seems blocked, or, perhaps, I am re-entering the text with an acute awareness of its linguistic obscurity and darkness.

But the self is affected in an even more fundamental way in writing. A peculiar change takes place in the person who starts to write and enters the text: the self retreats or steps back, as it were, without completely stepping out of his or her social, historical, biographic being. This is similar to what happens when we read a story. One traverses a world that is not one's own. Here everything is undetermined. Everything is possible. Just as one is no longer oneself when one loses oneself in a novel, so the writer who writes is no longer this or that personal self. In the words of Blanchot, the writer becomes depersonalized, an "it" or neutral self—a self who produces scripture.

To reiterate, writing is similar to reading in that we take leave of the ordinary world that we share with others. We step out of one world, the ordinary world of daylight, and enter another, the textorium, the world of the text. In this world of shadows and darkness one traverses the landscapes of language. One develops a special relation to language, a reflective relation, which disturbs its taken-for-grantedness. In fact, it may happen that in the attempt to write one loses one's very sense of language: one finds it impossible to write. And yet one must write. One is drawn to write. One writes. One has become "one" who writes.

Reading the Writing

Something peculiar may happen when, at a research conference, a phenomenological text is read aloud. The audience responds with silence. It is as if nobody has anything to say. There is nothing to say. But this sudden silence is not so strange if one reflects on what is actually happening: the listeners have been drawn into textual meaning and they are struck with perplexity, the silence of wonder. This experience is well known to readers. When a text is successful, and when the reader is open to it, then the text may have an effect that is almost inexplicable. The words literally take the reader or listener into a wondrous landscape, evoking a feeling of disorientation, causing confusion that tends to accompany the experience of strangeness, of being struck with wonder. This effect of the text is contingent not only on the text itself, it may also be contingent on the reader, the mood, or the context within which it is encountered.

So, what happens when writing begins? One peculiar feature of writing is that (just as in reading) the words draw us in. As Nancy says, "one has to understand reading as something other than decipherment. Rather, as touching, as being touched. Writing, reading: matters of tact" (Nancy, 1993, p. 198). Writing is reading. As author I am the first reader of my text. So, to write is to touch and to self-touch. Words affect us with the touch of tact, in-touchness. How strange words can do this! And it does not matter whether the words are presented on paper or on the computer screen. These scribed traces have the effect of mesmerizing consciousness. Evoking worlds, insights, emotions, understandings. Even our own words, especially our own words, can have this mesmerizing effect. We are writing these words and as they stare back at us they pull us in, carrying us to a special region. The etymology of "draw" does have associations with pulling, bearing, and carrying (Klein, 1979, p. 228). As words draw us and carry us away, they seem to open up a space: a temporal dwelling space where we may have reality experiences, "realizations" that we never imagined possible.

Textualizing Orality and Oralizing Written Text

Writing is not just putting into language the spoken word. Speaking and writing differ in spatial, temporal, and relational ways. Conversational relational space has a quality of immediacy. In normal discussions we are physically immediately present to the other person's speaking. The telephone, too, retains a sense of this immediacy. This temporal-spatial immediacy also means that the speaker cannot erase what has been said. One cannot restart a conversation in the way that one can restart a written text. One cannot edit out a phrase and replace it with a more appropriate one. One cannot step back reflectively from one's spoken word to monitor and adjust the effects that selected words and phrases seem to exercise on other words we utter. The spoken word is irrevocable in a manner that is rarely true of the written word. Of course, we can apologize for some things that may have slipped our tongue. We may try to deny that we said what has been heard. We may correct ourselves, and say what it is that we "really meant to say." We may add meaning through a certain tone of voice or physiognomic expression. We may repeat or paraphrase our earlier points when we feel that we are being misunderstood or when we feel that our words do not seem to have their intended or hoped-for effect. And yet, what has been heard has been heard; therefore, what we say can never be completely revoked. Indeed, our spoken words someday may be brought back to us, to remind us of things we may wish forgotten. Of course, all of this is even truer when our words have been electronically recorded.

In contrast, the space of writing has a different temporal-spatial quality of immediacy that is near and distant. Writing is not just translating speech into text. In writing and reading, one inevitably adopts a relation to language that is reflective and that Gadamer (1976) and Ricoeur describe as distanciation.

> What happens to discourse when it passes from speaking to writing? . . . What the text signifies no longer coincides with what the author meant; henceforth textual meaning and psychological meaning have different destinies . . . . Thanks to writing, the "world" of the text may explode the world of the author . . . . The text must be able to "decontextualize" itself in such a way that it can be "recontextualized" in a new situation—as accomplished, precisely, by the act of reading. (Ricoeur, 1991, p. 83)

As one writes it may happen that the space opened by the text becomes charged with a signification that is, in effect, more real than real. As readers, many of us know this phenomenon.

> The freeing of the written material is the most significant effect of writing. It implies that the relation between writing and reading is no longer a particular case of the relation between speaking and hearing.

> The first important hermeneutical consequence of the autonomy of the text is this: distanciation . . . is constitutive of the phenomenon of the text as writing. (Ricoeur, 1991, p. 84)

Many readers have at one time or another been profoundly moved at the realization of being touched by a human insight. And this insight might not have affected us this deeply if we had undergone the experience in the sober light of day, rather than in the realm of the novel, story, or poem. "Reading a text oralizes it," says Walter Ong (2013, p. 175). This accounts for the strange sensation of immediacy of presence that a vocative text can induce (Steiner, 1989). But the world of the text has its own special reality, an unreality, where words may acquire depthful meaning or a certain indeterminacy of meaning.

> The world of the text is therefore not the world of everyday language. In this sense, it constitutes a new sort of distanciation that could be called a distanciation of the real from itself . . . new possibilities of being-in-the-world are opened up within everyday reality . . . what could be called the imaginative variation that literature carries out on the real. (Ricoeur, 1991, p. 84)

There is something paradoxical about the unreality of a powerful text: it can be experienced by the writer or reader as real, as unreally real, as nearer than the nearness that things may have in ordinary reality. And yet, this effect of nearness is gained through the hyper-reality of textual distanciation. This super-reality turns the insights we gain in the space of the text essentially virtual, unencumbered by the presence of all the other memories, impressions, and factualities that permeate the affairs of our everyday life. The phenomenologist as writer is an author who starts from the midst of life and yet is transported to that writerly space where meanings resonate and reverberate with reflective being.

In an oral culture, in a society dominated by orality, phenomenology would be quite impossible. Why? Not only because phenomenology is a certain mode of reflection done traditionally by scholars who write, but also because a certain form of consciousness is required, a consciousness that is created by the act of literacy: reading and writing. Walter Ong (1971, 1977, 1981) has argued that the cultural and historical fact of literacy has led to a transformed consciousness that has created a certain distance and tension between understanding and experience, reflection and action. So, when we speak of action-sensitive understanding, then we are orienting ourselves to this tension. One place where this tension is experienced in an acute form is in the act of phenomenological research as writing. In other words, it is a certain kind of writing that we are concerned with here. It is the minded act of writing that orients itself reflectively to a notion that is a feature of lived experience.

Research Writing

In all research, including in traditional (experimental or more positivistic) research, there comes a moment when the researcher needs to communicate in writing what he or she has been up to. One speaks here of the research report, which suggests that a clear separation exists between the activity of research and the reporting activity in which the research is made public. Also, in the work of various qualitative researchers, writing is conceived largely as a reporting process. In such a framework, there is no place for thinking about research itself as a poetic textual (writing) practice. For phenomenological work, writing is closely fused into the research activity and reflection itself.

Writing fixes thought on paper or the screen. It externalizes what in some sense is internal; it distances us from our immediate lived involvements with the things of our world. As we stare at what we have written, our objectified thinking now stares back at us. Thus, the distanciation of writing creates the reflective cognitive stance that generally characterizes the theoretic attitude in the social sciences. The object of radically qualitative research is essentially a linguistic project: to make some aspect of our lived world, of our lived experience, reflectively understandable and intelligible. Researchers recognize this linguistic nature of research in the imperative reminder: Write! Phenomenological research requires a commitment to write. But writing for a phenomenological researcher is not just a supplementary activity. The imperative Write, as Barthes puts it, is intended to recall research to its epistemological condition: whatever it seeks, it must not forget its nature as language, and it is this which ultimately makes an encounter with writing inevitable (Barthes, 1986, p. 316).

Research does not merely involve writing: research is the work of writing. Writing is its very essence (p. 316). For scholars such as Heidegger, Sartre, Lingis, Derrida, and Serres, the activities of researching and reflecting on the one hand, and reading and writing on the other hand, are indeed quite indistinguishable. When one visits the Husserl Archives at the University of Louvain, this close connection between research and writing becomes evident in the symbolic value of Husserl's desk, which occupies a prominent place in the archival room. It is at this desk where phenomenology received its fundamental impetus.

More so than Husserl, Sartre was a phenomenologist who stood and acted in the middle of the hustle and bustle of social and political life. But as writing became very difficult for the aging Sartre, thinking became difficult as well. I still think, the seventy-year-old Sartre said once in an interview, but because writing has become impossible for me the real activity of thought has in some way been repressed (1977, p. 5). Sartre was speaking about the difficulty that the loss of sight created for him as reader and author. It is obvious that, for Sartre, writing was not just a mere moment in the intellectual life of the thinker. Writing was somehow at the center of this life of thinking. The only point to my life was writing, he said. "I would write out what I had been thinking about beforehand, but the essential moment was that of writing itself" (p. 5). With this line, Sartre has given us his most succinct definition of his methodology. Writing is the method. And to ask what method is in phenomenological inquiry is to ask for the nature of writing. Writing is a producing activity. The writer produces text, but he or she produces more than text. The writer produces himself or herself. The writer is the product of his or her own product. Writing is a kind of self-making or forming. To write is to measure the depth of things, as well to come to a sense of one's own depth.

Inner Speech and Inner Writing

Anyone who has been engaged in writing a paper that involves descriptive or interpretive insight may be aware of the phenomenon of inner speech. Inner speech is what goes on when we seem to be thinking aloud in our head, so to speak. We may even catch ourselves with the awareness that we have caught an important idea that we want to hold onto. However, since we are doing something else (waiting for a bus, going for a walk, sitting in a train, or driving a car), we keep musing along the percolating of thought of the inner speech. Practically, we are not in a position to write what we are thinking, and so we promise ourselves to write it as soon as we are in possession of a writing tool. We may even speak the words aloud for ourselves in order to commit them to memory. Hopefully, we will not forget the phrases that seemed so relevant—the words that in some sense we were already writing, though still virtually.

And now what happens when we are sitting down and writing the stuff that earlier we were writing virtually? We hope we can recall some words that seem to be key in remembering the thoughts we had. If we are lucky, we can pick up the train of thought of inner speech and work with it in a concrete, writerly fashion with pen on paper or fingers on the keyboard. So, how is this process of writing different from the experience of inner speech that preceded it? Perhaps it is not very different. Inner speech already seems to be a kind of writing, except that the inner speech during our walking or waiting was more fluid, less determined, less precise, perhaps, than when we started writing. Now, while typing these words, what I am doing is rewriting the writing of inner speech. At the same time, it may appear that in the experience of writing, we do not catch satisfactorily what we seemed to be thinking earlier. Perhaps it is because as we write concretely on paper or on the computer keyboard, we are constantly reading. We are indeed our own first reader, but this reading leads to further prompts, and we are writing again.

Phenomenology Is Already Writing

To reiterate, a major theme of the phenomenology of practice, as described in this book, is that phenomenological reflection cannot be separated from phenomenological writing, or, better, phenomenological reflection is writing. And it seems like a strange oversight that so few phenomenologists have addressed the phenomenon of phenomenological writing. Phenomenological inquiry cannot really be separated from the practice of writing.

One scholar, who is generally identified as being concerned with writing in virtually all his work is Jacques Derrida. In his *Speech and Phenomena* (1973), Derrida poses questions fundamental to the work of Husserl that have important consequences for phenomenology and the problem of writing. Derrida's study of Husserl's foundational text *Logical Investigations* is not easy reading for nonphilosophers, but it nevertheless had a major impact on the Husserlian project of phenomenology. In his preface to the English translation of *Speech and Phenomena*, Garver suggests that the best way to understand Derrida's critique of phenomenology (i.e., Husserlian phenomenology) is in terms of the radical turn in philosophy from a logic- to a rhetoric-based approach to language and meaning. Garver uses the old medieval triad of grammar, logic, and rhetoric to explain this shift in the tradition of philosophy and the wider human sciences. Although it might be an exaggeration to say that Derrida reversed the role of logic and rhetoric, it is nevertheless obvious that he loosened the boundaries between philosophy, literature, ethics, and critical approaches in the arts.

Within this frame, Derrida's deconstructionist reading of Husserl's phenomenology is very much in keeping with what had been happening in the works of other scholars such as Heidegger (1982), the later Wittgenstein (1982), and Ricoeur (1976). In their writings, there is a shift away from understanding meaning in terms of the relation between name and reference, perceived objects and mental objects, and a move toward the changing contexts of meaning in which human beings find themselves, and to the complexity and instability of textual meaning, the language games and narrative practices that give expression and interpretation to human experience. Garver's (1972) commentary seems particularly pointed when we consider the present scene of phenomenology. Furthermore, these considerations are critical for thinking about the work done in the phenomenological human sciences, where inquiries are placed in the service of professional practices such as health science, pedagogy, education, clinical psychology, and so forth. We now see in the work of scholars such as Serres, Lingis, Nancy, and many others a decisive turn toward rhetorical practices that are still disconcerting in the eyes of some philosophers. Why? Because they imply different ways of thinking about meaning and language, literature and philosophy, narrative and scientific discourses, ontics and ethics, and therefore about the very project of inquiry and writing itself.

A provocative example can be gleaned from the text *A Taste for the Secret* that contains conversations between Derrida and the Italian philosopher Ferraris (Derrida and Ferraris, 2001). These are largely discussions about the role and significance of writing. Ferraris complains that so much philosophy seems to have taken a narrative turn, and he poses the question to Derrida: "How does writing enter philosophy?" (2001, p. 7). Ferraris questions the generally accepted version of this entrance, which holds that after the end of metaphysics, philosophers are no longer dealing with truth but are serving something like "a sort of social welfare service based on conversation" (p. 7). Ferraris is troubled by the new tolerance for letting philosophers do whatever they wish, with the exception of their proper work, which is, in his words, "the search for truth" (p. 8). This tolerance is actually repressive, he says, as it leads to the historical circumstance in which philosophy has become just another form of "literature."

Not unexpectedly, Derrida provocatively contradicts Ferraris: "Writing did not 'enter' philosophy, it was already there." And he continues, "This is what we have to think about—about how it went unrecognized, and the attempts to repudiate it" (p. 8). However, in passing, Derrida agrees with Ferraris that truth is not outmoded. Truth is not a value one can renounce. Derrida points out that writing is essential to all philosophic reflection and that it is worthwhile to think about the relation between phenomenology or philosophy in general and writing in general.

It is in the act of reading and writing that insights emerge. The writing of work involves textual material that possesses hermeneutic and interpretive significance.

It is precisely in the process of writing that the data of the research are gained as well as interpreted and that the fundamental nature of the research questions is perceived. In a phenomenological sense, the research produces knowledge in the form of texts that not only describe and analyze phenomena of the lifeworld, but also evoke immediate understandings that otherwise lie beyond their reach.

Presence and Absence

To understand the role of writing in phenomenological inquiry, we go back again to Derrida's *Speech and Phenomena* (1973), in which he examines the problem of signs in Husserl's phenomenology. Derrida questions some of the key assumptions that make possible approaches to phenomenological inquiry that are supported by Husserlian notions of the relation between worldly objects and intentional objects. He also questions the meaning of the prereflective nature of primal impressional consciousness, with its retentional and protentional aspects, and whether there is anything like simple and pure experience that can serve as the source or foundation for the meaning of signs or acts of consciousness that can provide access to the intentional object.

It is, of course, naïve to say that the qualitative researcher aims to describe "what appears in consciousness," "lived experience," "the intentional object," or "the things themselves." All of these notions begin to disintegrate when we ask what is really meant in them. As discussed in earlier chapters, Husserl's famous motto "back to the things themselves" (1981, p. 196) is usually interpreted as an opposition to constructions and premature conceptualizations and systematizations, and a return to the immediate data as given to us in consciousness. However, the problem is, of course, that the data are not unambiguously immediately given at all, and certainly not in a form that would permit the unequivocal descriptions of the so-called intentional objects. In fact, what is so compelling about Husserl's (1991) accounts of the irreducible sphere of primal impressional consciousness is that it somehow constitutes an awareness of self as a function of internal time consciousness, as well as an access to the elusive nature of the moment of the now that is always somehow at the very center of all phenomenological reflection.

How can primal impressional consciousness be the source of meaning of that which is given in experience if primal impressional consciousness is never experienced as such? Levinas (2001) had already suggested that what presents itself in consciousness is always haunted by the alterity of what withdraws itself as absence and so always presupposes an "othering." Therefore, in *Speech and Phenomena*, Derrida (1973) insists that the presence of what is given in consciousness is always preceded by, and thus profoundly compromised by, the absence of the retentional trace that gives us the experience of the now and of our awareness of self as existing now.

The upshot of all this is that writing is much less "writing down" the results of a phenomenological analysis of the data given in consciousness or experience. Why? Because the data are not unequivocally "given" as such at all. What seems given or what seems to present itself in the primal or prereflective immediacy of every moment of the now is always haunted by the not now in which we are forever caught and by the absence or void that always echoes in everything that we seem to locate in the so-called things to which we turn: the act of consciousness, or the primordiality of lived experience.

Moreover, the so-called essences or eidetic structures of intentional objects are ultimately those of language. As Merleau-Ponty says in his much-quoted "Preface" to the *Phenomenology of Perception*, "It is the office of language to cause essences to exist in a state of separation which is in fact merely apparent, since through language they still rest upon the ante-predicative life of consciousness" (1962, p. xvii). The experience of phenomenological reflection is largely (though not exclusively) an experience of language, and so phenomenological reflection on prereflective life would be much better described in terms of an experience of writing, as explicated in the provocative works of Maurice Blanchot. But Blanchot is more interested in the experience of writing itself than in the product of this experience. Writing creates a unique and separate universe, the space of the text that puts the reality of everyday life out of play. In the experience of writing, words lose their taken-for-granted significations.

We all know how writing makes something or someone disappear and then reappear in words. In *The Gaze of Orpheus* (1981) Blanchot tells how Love had driven Orpheus into the dark, the darkness of the text. His consuming desire was to see Love's essence and to feel its form, but such glance is not permitted to mortals. What lies on the other side belongs to the great silence, to a "night" that is not human. So, the gaze of Orpheus expresses a desire that can never be completely fulfilled: to see the true being of something. Yet, it is this veil of the dark that every writer tries to penetrate. This is the very nature of writing: "The act of writing begins with Orpheus' gaze" (Blanchot, 1981, p. 104), and one writes only if one has entered that space under the influence of the gaze, or perhaps it is the gaze that opens the space of writing. "When Orpheus descends toward Eurydice, art is the power by which night opens" (p. 99). Thus, Blanchot says that we can read the whole myth as an event of writing. Orpheus, the poet, tries to capture the love that has ensnared him to Eurydice with words.

The writer uses words to uncover a truth that seems almost within reach. Indeed, at first it seems that Orpheus' words (his poetic songs) bring his love into presence. His words and songs have made her flesh and visible, so to speak. As Blanchot tells it, Orpheus dimly discerns the image of his love in the dark of the Underworld, but this is not enough. He desires to see more clearly. He must bring her back from the dark of night to the light of day. Orpheus is not satisfied with the image evoked by his words. He wants the immediacy of a presence—a presence that is not mediated by words or other means. This description is uncannily close to the ambition of any phenomenologist motivated by the desire to bring to nearness that which constantly eludes our grasp—a human truth. The ambition of the phenomenological author is to grasp the naked now and rescue it from the just now.

Seeing the World Nude

It is not surprising, therefore, that Blanchot's provocative portrayals of phenomenological writing (1981, 1986) have resonated in the works of contemporary

French philosophers Jacques Derrida (1978) and Hélène Cixous (1997). What the writer tries to see is the nakedness of the now. In the words of Cixous, "What is most true is poetic. What is most true is naked life. I apply myself to 'seeing' the world nude" (1997, p. 3). However, to see the nakedness of the now directly requires that one move into that space at the edge of existence, in the twilight between the Underworld and the world of daylight. The now is the moment that is constantly past, no longer now when we try to apprehend it, and that is why Orpheus must turn around in this space where human understanding evaporates into nothingness (no-thingness), where knowing is dying. It is here, on the other side of everyday reality, that "things" exist without real existence, before they have gotten names attached to them, before they can hide themselves behind words, as if they were more real than real.

It is inevitable that Orpheus defies the law forbidding him to "turn around," because he has already violated it the moment he takes his first step toward the shadows. This observation makes us sense that Orpheus has actually been turned toward Eurydice all along: he saw her when she was invisible and he touched her intact, in her absence as a shadow, in that veiled presence that did not conceal her absence, that was the presence of her infinite absence. If he had not looked at her, he would not have drawn her to him, and no doubt she is not there, but he himself is absent in this glance, he is no less dead than she was, not dead with the tranquil death of the world, the kind of death which is repose, silence, and ending, but with that other death, which is endless death, proof of the absence of ending.

Blanchot is suggesting that Orpheus turns around twice: the first turn is eventuated in the act of writing itself—the inspired desire that makes him descend into the darkness of the night to reach that "point" of origin of his writing of Eurydice. It is where the shadow of Eurydice pulls him. And in this writing he arrives "at the instant towards which one can only move through space opened up by the movement of writing" (1981, p. 104). Language opens and transcends itself into image—the image wherein meaning speaks and resonates. This opening space eventuates a second turn, the forbidden gaze at Eurydice who is present in her absence but who must be made visible and tangible by the work. However, this ambition is doomed. Eurydice, the origin of Love, becomes the appearance of disappearance. The work crumbles, and Eurydice is twice lost.

Thus, Orpheus turns around and gazes at Eurydice. What does he see? In this writingly wondering gaze, one may hope to gain a glance of truth in its naked appearance, peer past the veneer of human constructs. Is this possible? If so, how is this possible? Does such a realm exist? There are many philosophical reasons to answer "yes" and "no." But, perhaps the writer can find the answer to this question in the experience of writing itself, in the virtuality of the text, where one can run up against the human wall of language or where one might be permitted a momentary gaze through its crevices.

Writing creates a space that belongs to the unrepresentable. It is in this writerly space where there reigns the ultimate incomprehensibility of things, the unfathomable infiniteness of their being, the uncanny rumble of existence itself, but in this fleeting gaze, we also sense the fragility of our own existence, of our own death, that belongs to us more essentially than anything, says Derrida (1995a).

To see Eurydice in her invisibility, and to make her visible in her infinite immortality, Orpheus has entered the dark, and so it happens that in this fleeting glance Orpheus sees and does not see, touches and does not touch, hears and does not hear his beloved, whereas she still belongs to the uncanniness of the night.

The problem of writing is that one must bring into presence a phenomenon that cannot be represented in plain words—it would escape all representation. So, we may distinguish between the presentative (immediate) and the representative (mediated) modes. The presentative mode is immediate or direct—the representative mode is mediate or indirect. The writer who aims to bring the object of his or her gaze into presence is always involved in a tensional relation between presentation (immediate "seeing" and understanding) and representation (understanding mediated by words). This writing is a first reading "from now on understood as the vision of a presence immediately visible, that is to say intelligible," says Blanchot (1993, p. 422). Language substitutes itself for the phenomenon that it tries to describe. In this sense, language re-presents what is already absent, and, yet, absence is a sign of presence, a nonabsent absence. The contradiction is that to bring something into presence, one would have to write without recourse to language and concepts and without the help of discourses of representation—but compelled by the gaze of Orpheus, one has to write.

Orpheus is the writer, and Eurydice is the secret meaning (the feminine?) that the writer's work seeks and desires. Thus, the gaze of Orpheus and the image he sees of Eurydice belong to the essential act of writing. The writer is the solitary figure who leaves the everyday reality of ordinary daylight and whose writerly gaze creates the space of the text and then enters, dwells in this space of the text, to bring back what cannot be brought back: the object of desire. The writer's problem is that the Orphean gaze unwittingly destroys what it tries to rescue. In this sense, every word kills and becomes the death of the object it tries to represent. The word becomes the substitution of the object.

Even the subtlest poem destroys what it names. For this reason, Blanchot (1981) says that the perfect book would have no words. The perfect book would be "blank," as it tries to preserve what it can only destroy if it tried to represent it in language (see Nordholt, 1997; Blanchot, 1981, pp. 145–160). Perhaps this is why writing can be so difficult. The author becomes tacitly aware that language annihilates or "kills" whatever it touches. The result is the terrible realization that one has nothing to say. There is nothing to say, or, rather, it is impossible to truly "say" something. The writer desires to capture meaning in words, but the words constantly substitute themselves, destroying the things that they are meant to evoke. There are no "things"—only evocations, nothings.

At the level of raw existence, there are no "things," only the darkness of the night from which human insight and meaning arises. In the space of the text, we witness this birth of meaning and death of meaning—or meaning becomes indistinguishable from the dark. This dark may be experienced as the frightful allure of Existence itself that fascinates the writer but that cannot be written: the "there is" or the *il-y-a*. Levinas (1985) described the *il-y-a* as something that resembles what one hears when holding an empty seashell against one's ear, as if the emptiness is full, as if the silence is a murmuring, as if one hears the silent whispering of the *Real*.

471

We could say that the night is the very experience of the *there is* . . .

When the forms of things are dissolved in the night, the darkness of the night, which is neither an object nor the quality of an object, invades like a presence. In the night, where we are riveted to it, we are not dealing with anything. But this nothing is not that of pure nothingness. There is no longer *this* or *that*; there is not "something." But this universal absence is in its turn a presence, an absolutely unavoidable presence [. . .] *There is*, in general, without it mattering what there is, without our being able to fix a substantive to this term. There is an impersonal form, like it rains, or it is warm. Its anonymity is essential . . .

It makes things appear to us in a night, like the monotonous presence that bears down on us in insomnia . . .

The rustling of the *there is* . . . is horror. We have noted the way it insinuates itself in the night, as an undetermined menace of space itself disengaged from its function as receptable for objects, as a means of access to beings. (Levinas, 1985, pp. 52–55)

This Orpheic image of the difficulty of writing might seem overly trite for the philosopher, who already knows this intellectually, or it might seem totally absurd for the non-philosopher, who regards this image as unacceptably intellectual. But is this not what a writer experiences? Furthermore, as phenomenologists, should we not draw from it practical conclusions? Whether one ponders the meaning of the most consequential or the most trivial of human concerns, the act of phenomenological writing, if done with utmost seriousness, confronts the writer with the dark, with the enigma of phenomenality.

This is what it means to dwell in the space of the text, where the desire for meaningfulness leads. "The act of writing begins with Orpheus' gaze," says Blanchot (1981, p. 104), but to write, one must already be possessed by the desire to descend into the darkness of the night: "one can only write if one arrives at the instant towards which one can only move through space opened up by the movement of writing" (p. 104). Like Orpheus, the writer must enter the dark, the space of the text, in the hope of seeing what cannot really be seen, hearing what cannot really be heard, touching what cannot really be touched. This is like what Robert Frost once called "falling forward into the dark." Darkness is the method (see van Manen, 2001).

Although method (in the usual sense of following directions, procedures, or orientations) can, indeed, give guidance, one cannot rely on it. Therefore, Derrida argues, it is important to distinguish between bad writing (*hypomnesis*, low or inferior thinking) and good writing (*anamnesis*, upward or mindful thinking): "Good writing is thus always hauté [haunted] by bad writing" (Derrida and Ferraris, 2001, p. 8). The distinction between good writing and bad hinges on a reliance on method, not on method as such but on method conceived as prescriptions, strategies, procedures, and techniques. Derrida points out that in Plato as well as Heidegger, we can already find the distinction between bad writing and good writing, hypomnesis and anamnesis—between mere philosophic technique, on the one side, and poetic thinking as a kind of writing, on the other.

For Heidegger genuine phenomenological method consists of creating one's path, not in following a path: "When a method is genuine and provides access to the objects, it is precisely then that the progress made by following it . . . will cause the very method that was used to become necessarily obsolete" (1982, p. 328). After all, when we try to reflect on the originary dimensions of meaning of some phenomenon, we would abandon the single-mindedness of reflection for reflection relying on some preconceived method. Moreover, says Heidegger, it is difficult to commit oneself to certain phenomenological research methods, as even within the tradition of philosophy, "there is no such thing as one phenomenology, and if there could be such a thing it would never become anything like a philosophical technique" (p. 328).

Thus, qualitative method as writing is often difficult, as it requires sensitive interpretive skills and creative talents from the researcher. Phenomenological method, in particular, is challenging, because it can be argued that its method of inquiry constantly has to be invented anew and cannot be reduced to a general set of strategies or research techniques. Methodologically speaking, every notion has to be examined in terms of its assumptions, even the idea of method itself.

One might dismiss this cautionary tale about method by proposing that the literature of the great philosophers is contradictory: Heidegger (1982) warns us against a reliance on method, yet he and others describe phenomenology in terms of method. Phenomenology "is accessible only through a phenomenological method . . . each person trying to appropriate phenomenology for themselves," says Merleau-Ponty (1962, p. viii). How do we reconcile these claims? It appears that Heidegger is warning against reducing phenomenology to a set of philosophical strategies and techniques, and Merleau-Ponty refers to method not as techniques but as something like an attitude: "*Phenomenology can be practiced and identified as a manner and a style of thinking*" (1962, p. viii).

Indeed, it is apt to think of the basic method of phenomenology as the taking up of a certain attitude and practicing a certain attentive awareness to the things of the world as we live them rather than as we conceptualize or theorize them. "Doing phenomenology" as a reflective method is the practice of bracketing, or the "reduction," of what prevents us from making primitive contact with the concreteness of lived reality (Merleau-Ponty, 1962).

Although, according to Derrida (Derrida and Ferraris, 2001), all reflection of a general philosophic nature can be seen as a form of writing. Derrida is not speaking of the act of writing in only a metaphorical manner. What is critical about the Ferraris–Derrida discussion of the entrance and place of writing in phenomenological thinking is not only that writing has a place in phenomenology, but that phenomenological reflection is, first of all, an experience of writing.

Writing does not need to be understood here as writing to or for someone. Derrida admits, "My own experience of writing leads me to think that one does not always write with a desire to be understood—there is a paradoxical desire not to be understood" (Derrida and Ferraris, 2001, p. 30). One does not write primarily for being understood; one writes for having understood being.

Writing Desire

Now, some might feel that phenomenological research and writing, writing that truly addresses the meaning of something, is an entitled endeavor that can be claimed only by a talented author and scholar. Phenomenology does not just aim for the clarification of meaning, it aims for meaning to become experienced as meaningful. Meaningfulness happens when meaning speaks to our existence in such a way that it makes "contact" and touches us. If the goal of writing is to touch something meaningful in order to be touched by it, however, then this is no privileged pursuit.

I am only a student of phenomenological writing myself. I have become reconciled with the difficulties of writing—but no, that is not quite right. Writing is not something with which we make peace. Rather, one learns to obey its demand with the hope of an uncertain promise: to satisfy the desire really to "write" something, to see what we try to write in its nakedness. Of course, we know that the promise of writing is impossible. There is no naked truth, no understanding of naked reality, but not unlike Orpheus, we face the impossible promise: to really write something, to see what cannot be seen.

Of course, in the beginning a reluctant student writer may need encouragement. Pedagogical encouragement sometimes has to make false promises: promises of a clear view. Indeed, there is a strange contradiction at work in helping students write. The student writer is someone who studies and practices writing in the agogical hope of making something clear. Every now and then, he or she may find an updraft and suddenly soar, reaching the perspective of the gaze. Phenomenologically, this could be described as really "seeing" something. One experiences a sensation of something perceived and understood. Often, further encouragement is no longer needed. In fact, external encouragement might now be brushed off, dismissed. Something strange animates the writing from now on: we can call this desire. I have seen this over and over in my students.

No encouragement is needed, because real desire has been ignited. To write is to be driven by desire. So, perhaps, in a moment like this, one has become a real writer, propelled to cross the space of the text in search of another updraft—the perspective of the gaze. But it is then, and only then, that the true nature of writing can reveal itself: This is not a perspective at all. There is nothing to see. What happens is that one realizes that there was no soaring height to reach from which things could be grasped in Heideggerian brightness. One aimed for the light of insight, but one ends up facing the darkness of the night. The intimation of the gaze yielded only something inimitable, ineffable. Perhaps, in a sensation of being surrounded by transcendence, one was caught confusedly in a downward movement, plunging into the Orphean depths of desire. So, the original motivation to write was based on a false promise. It was, however, a promise that needed to be believed in, for the sake of being brought to the edge, where one may take off, on (perhaps) an impossible but fine flight to finally write.

Bibliographic References

Abé, K. (1964). *The Woman in the Dunes.* (E. D. Saunders, transl.) New York: Alfred A. Knopf.

Achterhuis, H. (ed.) (2001). *American Philosophy of Technology: The Empirical Turn.* Bloomington: Indiana University Press.

Adams, C. (2006). "PowerPoint, Habits of Mind, and Classroom Culture." *Journal of Curriculum Studies* 38(4): 389–411.

Adams, C. (2008a). "The Poetics of PowerPoint." *Explorations in Media Ecology* 7(4): 43–58.

Adams, C. (2008b). "PowerPoint and the Pedagogy of Digital Media Technology." Unpublished dissertation. University of Alberta, Edmonton, AB.

Adams, C. (2008c). "PowerPoint's Pedagogy." *Phenomenology and Practice* 2(1): 63–79.

Adams, C. (2010). "Teachers Building Dwelling Thinking with Slideware." *The Indo-Pacific Journal of Phenomenology* 10(2): 1–12.

Adams, C. (2012). "Technology as Teacher: Digital Media and the Re-Schooling of Everyday Life." *Existential Analysis* 23(2): 262–273.

Adams, C. and T. L. Thompson. (2011). "Interviewing Objects: Including Educational Technologies as Qualitative Research Participants." *International Journal of Qualitative Studies in Education* 24(6): 733–750.

Adams, C. and M. van Manen. (2006). "Embodiment, Virtual Space, Temporality and Interpersonal Relations in Online Writing." *College Quarterly* 9(4). www.senecac.on.ca/quarterly/2006-vol09-num04-fall/adams_van_manen.html (accessed January 29, 2014).

Afloroaei, S. (2010). "Descartes and the 'Metaphysical Dualism': Excesses in Interpreting a Classic." *META: Research in Hermeneutics, Phenomenology, and Practical Philosophy II (I)*: 105–138.

Agamben, G. (1993). *The Coming Community.* Minneapolis, MN: University of Minnesota Press.

Agamben, G. (1995). *Idea of Prose.* Albany, NY: SUNY Press.

Agamben, G. (2002). "What Is a Paradigm?" Lecture at European Graduate School. Available: www.egs.edu/faculty/giorgio-agamben/articles/what-is-a-paradigm/

Agamben, G. (2005). *Potentialities: Collected Essays in Philosophy.* Stanford, CA: Stanford University Press.

Allmark, P. (1995). Can There Be an Ethics of Care? *Journal of Medical Ethics* 21: 19–24.

Alpers, S. (1983). *The Art of Describing: Dutch Art in the Seventeenth Century.* Chicago: University of Chicago Press.

Arendt, H. (1951). *The Origin of Totalitarianism.* New York: Schocken.

Arendt, H. (1958a). *Between Past and Future: Six Exercises in Political Thought.* New York: Viking.

Arendt, H. (1958b). *The Human Condition.* Chicago: University of Chicago Press.

Arendt, H. (1978). *Life of the Mind.* 2 vols. New York: Harcourt Brace Jovanovich.

Aristotle (1941). *The Basic Works.* (R. McKeon, ed.) New York: Random House.

Austin, J. L. (1962). *How to Do Things with Words.* Cambridge, MA: Harvard University Press.

Bachelard, G. (1964a). *The Poetics of Space.* Boston: Beacon Press.

Bachelard, G. (1964b). *The Psychoanalysis of Fire.* Boston: Beacon Press.

Bachelard, G. (1969). *The Poetics of Reverie.* Boston: Beacon Press.

Bachelard, G. (1983). *Water and Dreams.* Dallas: Pegasus.

Bachelard, G. (1988). *Air and Dreams.* Dallas: Pegasus.

Bachelard. G. (2013). *Intuition of the Instant.* Evanston, IL: Northwestern University Press.

Baker-Ward, L., B. N. Gordon, P. A. Ornstein, D. M. Larus, and P. A. Clubb (1993). "Young Children's Longterm Retention of a Pediatric Examination." *Child Development* 64(5): 1519–1533.

Barrett, L. F. (2018). *How Emotions Are Made: The Secret Life of the Brain.* New York: HarperCollins.

Barthes, R. (1975). *The Pleasure of the Text.* New York: Hill and Wang.

Barthes, R. (1981). *Camera Lucida: Reflections on Photography.* New York: Hill and Wang.

Barthes, R. (1986). *The Rustle of Language.* New York: Hill and Wang.

Beekman, A. J. (1975). *Dienstbaar Inzicht: Opvoedingswetenschap als Sociale Planwetenschap.* Groningen, the Netherlands: H. D. Tjeenk Willink.

Beekman, A. J. (1983). "De Utrechtse School Is Dood! Leve de Utrechtse School!" *Pedagogische Verhandelingen* 6(1): 61–70.

Beekman, A. J. (2001). *"Het Wilde Denken." Wetenschapstheoretische Verhandelingen.* Zwolle, the Netherlands: Noordhoff.

Beekman, A. J., L. Barritt, H. Bleeker, and K. Mulderij (1984). *Researching Educational Practice.* Grand Forks, ND: University of North Dakota.

Beekman, T. (1983). "Human Science as a Dialogue with Children." *Phenomenology + Pedagogy,* 1: 36–44.

Beets, N. (1975). *Verstandhouding en Onderscheid: Een Onderzoek naar de Verhouding van Medisch en Pedagogisch Denken.* Amsterdam: Boom Meppel.

Benner, P. (1984). *From Novice to Expert: Excellence and Power in Clinical Nursing Practice.* London: Prentice Hall.

Benso, S. (2000). *The Face of Things: A Different Side of Ethics.* Albany, NY: SUNY Press.

Bergson, H. (1899). *Le Rire: Essay sur la Signification du Comique.* Paris: Revue de Paris.

Bergson H. (1955). *An Introduction to Metaphysics.* New York: Macmillan.

Bergson H. (1991). *Matter and Memory.* New York: Zone Books.

Bergson, H. (2001). *Time and Free Will: An Essay on the Immediate Data of Consciousness.* New York: Dover Publications.

Bergson, H. (2005). *Laughter: An Essay on the Meaning of the Comic.* New York: Dover Publications.

Bernasconi, R. (1990). "The Ethics of Suspicion." *Research in Phenomenology* 20: 3–18.

Bernasconi, R. (1995). "Sartre's Gaze Returned: The Transformation of the Phenomenology of Racism." *Graduate Faculty Philosophy Journal* 18(2): 201–221.

Bernasconi, R. (2020). "Frantz Fanon's Engagement with Phenomenology: Unlocking the Temporal Architecture of Black Skin, White Masks." *Research in Phenomenology* 50: 386–406.

Bernasconi, R. (2020). "Almost Always More than Philosophy Proper." *Research in Phenomenology* 30: 1–11.

Binswanger, L. (1963). *Being in the World.* New York: Basic Books.

Blanchot, M. (1981). *The Gaze of Orpheus.* New York: Station Hill Press.

Blanchot, M. (1986). *The Writing of Disaster.* Lincoln, NE: University of Nebraska Press.

Blanchot, M. (1988). *The Unavowable Community.* New York: Station Hill Press.

Blanchot, M. (1989). *The Space of Literature.* Lincoln, NE: University of Nebraska Press.

Blanchot, M. (1993). *The Infinite Conversation.* Minneapolis, MN: University of Minnesota Press.

Bollnow, O. F. (1960). "Lived-space." *Universitas* 15(4): 31–39.

Bollnow, O. F. (1974). "The Objectivity of the Humanities and the Essence of Truth." *Philosophy Today* 18(1): 3–18.

Bollnow, O. F. (1979). "What Does It Mean to Understand a Writer Better than He Understood Himself?" *Philosophy Today* 22(1/4): 10–22.

Bollnow, O. F. (1982). "On Silence—Findings of Philosophico-Pedagogical Anthropology." *Universitas* 24(1): 41–47.

Bollnow, O. F. (1988). "The Pedagogical Atmosphere." *Phenomenology + Pedagogy* 7(2): 5–78.

Bourdieu, P. (1985). "The Genesis of the Concepts of Habitus and Field." *Sociocriticism* 2(2): 11–24.

Bowden, P. (1997). *Caring: Gender-Sensitive Ethics.* London: Routledge.

Brentano, F. (1995). *Psychology from an Empirical Standpoint.* New York: Routledge.

Burms, A. and H. de Dijn (1990). *De Rationaliteit en haar Grenzen: Kritiek en Deconstructie.* Assen/Maastricht: Van Gorcum.

Buytendijk, F. J. J. (1961). *Academische Redevoeringen.* Utrecht: Dekker & Van de Vegt.

Buytendijk, F. J. J. (1962). *De Psychologie van de Roman: Studies over Dostojevski.* Utrecht: Aula Boeken.

Buytendijk, F. J. J. (1970a). "Naar een Existentiële Verklaring van de Doorleefde dwang." *Tijdschrift voor Filosofie* 32(4): 567–608.

Buytendijk, F. J. J. (1970b). "Some Aspects of Touch." *Journal of Phenomenological Psychology* 1(1): 99–124.

Buytendijk, F. J. J. (1973). *Pain: Its Modes and Functions.* Westport, CT: Greenwood Press.

Buytendijk, F. J. J. (1974). *Prolegomena to an Anthropological Physiology.* Pittsburgh, PA: Duquesne University Press.

Buytendijk, F. J. J. (1988). "The First Smile of the Child." *Phenomenology + Pedagogy* 6(1): 15–24.

Cairns, H. (1971). *Introduction. Plato, the Collected Dialogues.* (E. Hamilton and H. Cairns, eds.). Princeton, NJ: Princeton University Press.

Camus, A. (1980). "The Guest." In A. Camus, *Exile and the Kingdom.* Franklin Center, PA: Franklin Library, pp. 65–84.

Canetti, E. (1979). *The Tongue Set Free: Remembrance of a European Childhood.* New York: The Seabury Press.

Caputo, J. D. (1988). "Beyond Aestheticism: Derrida's Responsible Anarchy." *Research in Phenomenology 18*: 59–73.

Carr, D. (1969). "Translator's Introduction." In E. Husserl (1970). *The Crisis of European Sciences and Transcendental Phenomenology.* Evanston, IL: Northwestern University Press, pp. xv–xliii.

Casey, E. S. (1981). "Literary Description and Phenomenological Method." *Yale French Studies, No. 61, Towards a Theory of Description.* New Haven, CT: Yale University Press, pp. 176–201.

Casey, E. S. (1997). *The Fate of Place: A Philosophical History.* Berkeley, CA: University of California Press.

Casey, E. S. (2000). *Imagining: A Phenomenological Study.* Bloomington, IN: Indiana University Press.

Casey, E. S. (2007). *The World at a Glance.* Bloomington, IN: Indiana University Press.

Chrétien, J.-L. (2002). *The Unforgettable and the Unhoped For.* Oxford: Oxford University Press.

Chrétien, J.-L. (2003). *Hand to Hand: Listening to the Work of Art.* Oxford: Oxford.

Chrétien, J.-L. (2004a). *The Ark of Speech.* London: Routledge.

Chrétien, J.-L. (2004b). *The Call and the Response.* Oxford: Oxford University Press.

Cixous, H. (1976). *The Laugh of the Medusa.* London: Routledge.

Cixous, H. (1977). *La Venue à l'Écriture.* Paris: Union Générale d'Éditions.

Cixous, H. (1994). *Hélène Cixous Reader.* London: Routledge.

Cixous, H. (1997). *Rootprints: Memory and Life Writing.* London: Routledge.

Cixous, H. (1998). *Stigmata.* London: Routledge.

Cohen, G. and D. M. Burke (eds.). (1993). *Memory for Proper Names.* Hillsdale, NJ: Lawrence Erlbaum Associates.

Cohen, M. H. (1999). "The Technology-Dependent Child and the Socially Marginalized Family: A Provisional Framework." *Qualitative Health Research, 9*(5): 654–668.

Cox, G. (2009). *Sartre and Fiction.* New York: Continuum.

Damasio, A. (2010). *Self Comes to Mind: Constructing the Conscious Brain.* New York: Vintage Books.

Davis, P. J. and R. Hirsh. (2005). *Descartes' Dream: The World According to Mathematics.* Mineola, NY: Dover Publications.

De Beauvoir, S. (1967). *The Ethics of Ambiguity.* New York: Citadel Press.

De Beauvoir, S. (1985). *Adieux: A Farewell to Sartre.* New York: Pantheon Books.

De Beauvoir, S. (2011). *The Second Sex.* New York: Vintage Books.

De Boer, T. (1980). "Inleiding." In T. de Boer (ed.), *Edmund Husserl: Filosofie als Strenge Wetenschap.* Amsterdam: Boom Meppel.

De Cusa, N. (1960). *The Vision of God.* New York: Frederick Ungar.

DeGowin, E. L. and R. L. DeGowin. (1976). *Bedside Diagnostic Examination.* New York: Macmillan.

Derrida, J. (1973). *Speech and Phenomena and Other Essays on Husserl's Theory of Signs.* Evanston, IL: Northwestern University Press.

Derrida, J. (1976). *Of Grammatology.* Baltimore, MD: Johns Hopkins University Press.

Derrida, J. (1978). *Writing and Difference.* Chicago: University of Chicago Press.

Derrida, J. (1995a). *The Gift of Death.* Chicago: University of Chicago Press.

Derrida, J. (1995b). *On the Name.* Stanford, CA: Stanford University Press.

Derrida, J. (2005). *The Politics of Friendship.* London: Verso Press.

Derrida, J. and M. Ferraris. (2001). *A Taste for the Secret.* Cambridge, UK: Polity Press.

Descartes, R. (1989). *The Passions of the Soul.* (S. Voss, transl.) Cambridge, MA: Hackett Publishing Company.

Descartes, R. (2003). *Discourse on Method and Related Writings.* (D. M. Clarke, transl.) London: Penguin Books.

Descartes, R. (2008). *Meditations on First Philosophy with Selections from the Objections and Replies.* (M. Moriarty, transl.) Oxford: Oxford University Press.

Descartes, R. (2012). *The Principles of Philosophy.* (J. Veitch, transl.) Whitefish, MT: Kessinger Publishing.

Dilthey, W. (1976). *Dilthey: Selected Writings*. (H. P. Rickman, ed.) Cambridge, UK: Cambridge University Press.

Dilthey, W. (1985). *Poetry and Experience. Selected Works, Vol. 5*. Princeton, NJ: Princeton University Press.

Dilthey, W. (1987). *Introduction to the Human Sciences*. Toronto: Scholarly Book Services.

Dreyfus, H. L. (1972). *What Computers Can't Do: The Limits of Artificial Intelligence*. New York: HarperCollins.

Dreyfus, H. L. (1979). *What Computers Still Can't Do: A Critique of Artificial Reason*. Cambridge, MA: The MIT Press.

Dreyfus, H. L. (1991). Toward a Phenomenology of Ethical Expertise. *Human Studies 14*: 229–250.

Dreyfus, H. L. (2008). *On the Internet (Thinking in Action)*. London: Routledge.

Dreyfus, H. L. (2012). "A History of First Step Fallacies." *Minds and Machines 22*: 87–99.

Dreyfus, S. E. and H. L. Dreyfus. (1980). *A Five-Stage Model of the Mental Activities Involved in Directed Skill Acquisition*. Operations Research Center, University of California, Berkeley, CA.

Eagleman, D. (2011). *Incognito: The Secret Lives of the Brain*. New York: Viking.

Eliot, G. (1861). *Silas Marner*. Harmondsworth: Penguin Books.

Fadiman, C. (ed.). (1985). *The Little, Brown Book of Anecdotes*. Boston, MA: Little, Brown.

Fanon, F. (1961, 2004). *The Wretched of the Earth*. (R. Philcox, transl.; J.-P. Sartre, Preface.) New York: Grove Press.

Fanon, F. (1967). *Black Skin, White Masks*. (Charles Lam Markmann, transl.). New York: Grove Press.

Fanon, F. (2008). *Black Skin, White Masks*. (Richard Philcox, transl.) New York: Grove Press.

Feenberg, A. (1999). *Questioning Technology*. London: Routledge.

Figal, G. (1998). *For a Philosophy of Freedom and Strive: Politics, Aesthetics, Metaphysics*. Albany, NY: SUNY Press.

Figal, G. (2004). "Life as Understanding." *Research in Phenomenology 34*: 20–30.

Figal, G. (2010). *Objectivity: The Hermeneutical and Philosophy*. Albany, NY: SUNY Press.

Figal, G. and D. Espinet. (2012). "Hermeneutics." In S. Luft and S. Overgaard (eds.), *The Routledge Companion to Phenomenology*. New York: Routledge.

Fink, E. (1970). "The Phenomenological Philosophy of Edmund Husserl and Contemporary Criticism." In R. O. Elveton (ed.), *The Phenomenology of Husserl: Selected Critical Readings*. Seattle, WA: Noesis Press, pp. 70–139.

Fink, E. (2016). *Play as Symbol of the World and Other Writings*. Bloomington, IN: Indiana University Press.

Flusser, V. (2011a). *Does Writing Have a Future?* Minneapolis, MN: University of Minneapolis Press.

Flusser, V. (2011b). *Into the World of Technical Images*. Minneapolis, MN: University of Minneapolis Press.

Flusser, V. (2012). "The Gesture of Writing." *New Writing: The International Journal for the Practice and Theory of Creative Writing 9(1)*: 24–41.

Flyvbjerg, B. (1991). "Sustaining Non-Rationalized Practices: Body-Mind, Power and Situational Ethics. An Interview with Hubert and Stuart Dreyfus." *Praxis International 11(1)*: 93–113.

Foucault, M. (1988). "Technologies of the Self." In L. H. Martin, H. Gutman, P. Hutton, and H. Patrick (eds.), *Technologies of the Self*. Amherst, MA: University of Massachusetts Press, pp. 16–59.

Frege, G. (1892). *On Sense and Reference*. Glasgow: Good Press.

Furst, B. (1963). *What an Executive Should Know about Remembering Names and Faces*. Chicago: Dartnell Press.

Gadamer, H.-G. (1975). *Truth and Method*. New York: Seabury.

Gadamer, H.-G. (1976). *Philosophical Hermeneutics*. Berkeley, CA: University of California Press.

Gadamer, H.-G. (1986). *The Relevance of the Beautiful and Other Essays*. Cambridge, UK: Cambridge University Press.

Gadamer, H.-G. (1996). *The Enigma of Health: The Art of Healing in a Scientific Age*. Oxford: Polity Press.

Gadamer, H.-G. (1998). *Praise of Theory*. New Haven, CT: Yale University Press.

Garver, N. (1972). "Preface." In J. Derrida. (1973). *Speech and Phenomena and Other Essays on Husserl's Theory of Signs*. Evanston, IL: Northwestern University Press, pp. ix–xxix.

Geertz, C. (1973). *The Interpretation of Cultures*. New York: Basic Books.

478

Gendlin, E. T. (1988). "Befindlichkeit: Heidegger and the Philosophy of Psychology." In K. Heller (ed.). *Heidegger and Psychology. A Special Issue from the Review of Existential Psychology and Psychiatry* 43–71.

Ghaemi, N. (2001). "Rediscovering Existential Psychotherapy: The Contribution of Ludwig Binswanger." *American Journal of Psychotherapy* 55(1): 51–64.

Gilligan, C. (1993). *In a Different Voice: Psychological Theory and Women's Development.* Cambridge, MA: Harvard University Press.

Giorgi, A. (1970). *Psychology as a Human Science: A Phenomenologically Based Approach.* New York: Harper & Row.

Giorgi, A. (2009). *The Descriptive Phenomenological Method in Psychology: A Modified Husserlian Approach.* Pittsburgh, PA: Duquesne University Press.

Giorgi, A. (2011). "IPA and Science: A Response to Jonathan Smith." *Journal of Phenomenological Psychology* 42: 195–216.

Gosetti-Ferencei, J. A. (2003). *After the Palace Burns: Poems.* Paris: Zoo Press.

Gosetti-Ferencei, J. A. (2004). *Heidegger, Hölderlin, and the Subject of Poetic Language.* New York: Fordham University Press.

Gosetti-Ferencei, J. A. (2007). *The Ecstatic Quotidian: Phenomenological Sightings in Modern Art and Literature.* Philadelphia, PA: Pennsylvania State University Press.

Gosetti-Ferencei, J. A. (2011). *Exotic Spaces in German Modernism.* Oxford: Oxford University Press.

Gusdorf, G. (1965). *Speaking (La Parole).* Evanston, IL: Northwestern University Press.

Harmann, G. (2011). *The Quadruple Object.* Alresford, Hants, UK: Zero Books.

Harmann, G. (2013). *Bells and Whistles: More Speculative Realism.* Alresford, Hants, UK: Zero Books.

Hegel, G. W. F. (1977). *The Phenomenology of Mind.* New York: Humanities Press.

Hegel, G. W. F. (1979). *System of Ethical Life and First Philosophy of Spirit (Part III of the System of Speculative Philosophy).* (H. S. Harris and T. M. Knox, eds. and transl.) Albany, NY: SUNY Press.

Heidegger, M. (1962). *Being and Time.* (J. MacQuarrie and E. Robinson, transl.) New York: Harper & Row.

Heidegger, M. (1971a). *Poetry, Language, Thought.* New York: Harper & Row.

Heidegger, M. (1971b). *On the Way to Language.* New York: Harper & Row.

Heidegger, M. (1977). *The Question Concerning Technology and Other Essays.* New York: Harper & Row.

Heidegger, M. (1982). *The Basic Problems of Phenomenology.* Bloomington, IN: Indiana University Press.

Heidegger, M. (1985). *History of the Concept of Time.* Bloomington, IN: Indiana University Press.

Heidegger, M. (1993). *Basic Concepts.* Bloomington, IN: Indiana University Press.

Heidegger, M. (1994). *Basic Questions of Philosophy: Selected "Problems" of "Logic."* Bloomington, IN: Indiana University Press.

Heidegger, M. (1995). *The Fundamental Concepts of Metaphysics.* Bloomington: Indiana University Press.

Heidegger, M. (1998). *Parmenides.* Bloomington, IN: Indiana University Press.

Heidegger, M. (1999). *Contributions to Philosophy (from Enowning).* (P. Emad and K. Maly, transl.) Bloomington, IN: Indiana University Press.

Heidegger, M. (2000). *Elucidations of Hölderlin's Poetry.* (K. Hoeller, transl.) Amherst, NY: Humanities Books.

Heidegger, M. (2001). *Phenomenology of Intuition and Expression.* New York: Continuum.

Heidegger, M. (2010). *Being and Time.* (J. Stambaugh, transl.) New York: Harper & Row.

Heidegger, M. (2011). *Introduction to Philosophy—Thinking and Poetizing.* Bloomington, IN: Indiana University Press.

Heidegger, M. (2012a). *Bremen and Freiburg Lectures: Insights into That Which Is and Basic Principles of Thinking.* (A. J. Mitchell, transl.) Bloomington, IN: Indiana University Press.

Heidegger, M. (2012b). *Contributions to Philosophy (of the Event).* (R. Rojcewicz and D. Vallega-Neu, transl.) Bloomington, IN: Indiana University Press.

Heidegger, M. (2013a). *Basic Problems of Phenomenology—Winter Semester 1919/1920.* New York: Bloomsbury.

Heidegger, M. (2013b). *The Event.* Bloomington, IN: Indiana University Press.

Heidegger, M. (2014). *Gesamtausgabe (HGA)* [Complete Edition] 96, pp. 216–217.

Heim, M. (1987). *Electric Language: A Philosophical Study of Word Processing.* New Haven, CT: Yale University Press.

Henry, M. (1973). *The Essence of Manifestation*. The Hague: Martinus Nijhoff.

Henry, M. (1975). *Philosophy and Phenomenology of the Body*. The Hague: Martinus Nijhoff.

Henry, M. (1999). "Material Phenomenology and Language (or, Pathos and Language)." *Continental Philosophy Review* 32: 343–365.

Henry, M. (2003). *I Am the Truth: Toward a Philosophy of Christianity*. Stanford, CA: Stanford University Press.

Henry, M. (2008). *Material Phenomenology*. New York: Fordham University Press.

Henry, M. (2009). *Seeing the Invisible: On Kandinsky*. New York: Continuum.

Herakleitos and Diogenes. (1979). *Herakleitos & Diogenes*. (Translated from the Greek by Guy Davenport.) San Francisco, CA: Grey Fox Press.

Hermsen, J. (2014). *Kairos: Een Nieuwe Bevlogenheid*. Utrecht: De Arbeiderspers.

Hermsen, J. (2017). *Kairos Castle: The Right Time*. Amsterdam: Terra Lannoo Publishers.

Høiseth, M., M. M. Keitsch, and M. H. Hopperstad. (2014). "Interactions between Caregivers and Young Children: Exploring Pedagogical Tact in Nebulizer Treatment." *Qualitative Health Research* 24(12): 1622–1634.

Holme, B. (1979). *Bulfinch's Mythology*. New York: The Viking Press.

Hussain, S. (2011). "Toes That Look Like Toes: Cambodian Children's Perspectives on Prosthetic Legs." *Qualitative Health Research* 21(10): 1427–1440.

Husserl, E. (1931). *Ideas: General Introduction to Phenomenology*, Vol. 1. (W. R. R. Gibson, transl.) London: George Allen & Unwin.

Husserl, E. (1950). *Cartesian Meditations: An Introduction to Phenomenology*. (D. Cairns, transl.) The Hague: Martinus Nijhoff.

Husserl, E. (1964a). *The Idea of Phenomenology*. The Hague: Martinus Nijhoff.

Husserl, E. (1964b). *The Phenomenology of Internal Time-Consciousness*. Bloomington, IN: Indiana University Press.

Husserl, E. (1964c). *The Paris Lectures*. (P. Koestenbaum, transl.) The Hague: Martinus Nijhoff.

Husserl, E. (1970). *The Crisis of the European Sciences and Transcendental Phenomenology: An Introduction to Phenomenology*. (D. Carr, transl.) Evanston, IL: Northwestern University Press.

Husserl, E. (1973). *Experience and Judgment*. Evanston, IL: Northwestern University Press.

Husserl, E. (1980). *Filosofie als Strenge Wetenschap*. Amsterdam: Boom.

Husserl, E. (1981). "Philosophy as Rigorous Science." In P. McCormick and F. Elliston (eds.), *Husserl Shorter Works*. Notre Dame, IN: University of Notre Dame Press, pp. 166–197.

Husserl, E. (1982). *Logical Investigations, Vol. 1*. London: Humanities Press International.

Husserl, E. (1983). "Ideas Pertaining to a Pure Phenomenology and to a Phenomenological Philosophy." *First Book: General Introduction to a Pure Phenomenology*. (F. Kersten, transl.) Dordrecht, the Netherlands: Kluwer.

Husserl, E. (1991). *On the Phenomenology of the Consciousness of Internal Time (1893–1917)*. Dordrecht, the Netherlands: Kluwer.

Husserl, E. (1999). *Cartesian Meditations*. Dordrecht, the Netherlands: Kluwer.

Husserl, E. (2012). *Ideas: General Introduction to Pure Phenomenology*. London: Routledge.

Husserl, E. (2014). *Ideas I. Ideas for a Pure Phenomenology and Phenomenological Philosophy. First Book: General Introduction to a Pure Phenomenology*. Indianapolis, IN: Hackett Publishing Company.

Ihde, D. (1979). *Technics and Praxis*. Boston, MA: D. Reidel.

Ihde, D. (1983). *Existential Technics*. Albany, NY: SUNY Press.

Ihde, D. (1986). *Experimental Phenomenology*. Albany, NY: SUNY Press.

Ihde, D. (1990). *Technology and the Lifeworld: From Garden to Earth*. Bloomington, IN: Indiana University Press.

Ihde, D. (1993). *Postphenomenology: Essays in the Postmodern Context*. Evanston, IL: Northwestern University Press.

Ihde, D. (2009). *Postphenomenolog and Technoscience: The Peking Lectures*. Albany, NY: SUNY Press.

Ihde, D. (2010). Interview with Don Ihde, by Laureano Ralón. Figure/Ground, September 4. http://figureground.org/fg/interview-with-don-ihde/

James, I. (2006). *The Fragmentary Demand: An Introduction to the Philosophy of Jean-Luc Nancy*. Stanford, CA: Stanford University Press.

Janicaud, D. (2000). "Toward a Minimalist Phenomenology." *Research in Phenomenology* 30(1): 89–106.

Janicaud, D. (2005a). *On the Human Condition*. New York: Routledge.

Janicaud, D. (2005b). *Phenomenology "Wide Open" after the French Debate*. New York: Fordham University Press.

Janicaud, D., J.-F. Courtine, J.-L. Chrétien, and M. Henry. (2000). *Phenomenology and the "Theological Turn": The French Debate*. New York: Fordham University Press.

Jaspers, K. (1955). *Reason and Existenz*. New York: The Noonday Press.

Jaspers, K. (1997). *General Psychopathology, Vol. 1*. Baltimore, MD: Johns Hopkins University Press.

Jay, M. (2005). *Songs of Experience: Modern American and European Variations on a Universal Theme*. Berkeley, CA: University of California Press.

Kandinsky, W. (1977). *Concerning the Spiritual in Art*. New York: Dover Publications.

Kant, I. (1999). *Critique of Pure Reason*. (P. Guyer and A. W. Wood, transl.) Cambridge, UK: Cambridge University Press.

Kearney, R. (2004). *Debates in Continental Philosophy: Conversations with Contemporary Thinkers*. New York: Fordham University Press.

Kierkegaard, S. (1983). *Fear and Trembling/Repetition*. Princeton, NJ: Princeton University Press.

Kierkegaard, S. (2004). *The Sickness unto Death*. (A. Hannay, transl.) London: Penguin Books.

Klein, E. (1979). *A Comprehensive Etymological Dictionary of the English Language*. New York: Elsevier Scientific Publishing Company.

Kockelmans, J. J. (ed.). (1987). *Phenomenological Psychology: The Dutch School*. Dordrecht: Kluwer.

Korczak, J. (2007). *Loving Every Child: Wisdom for Parents*. New York: Workman Publishing.

Korczak, J. (2018). *How to Love a Child and Other Selected Works*. Chicago: Valentine Mitchell.

Kot, P. (n.d.). "An Overview of Physical Examination Techniques." Course handout, Nursing 104, Faculty of Nursing, University of Alberta.

Kounios, J. and M. Beeman. (2015). *The Eureka Factor: Aha Moments, Creative Insight, and the Brain*. New York: Random House.

Kouwer, B. J. (1953). "Gelaat en Karakter." In J. H. van den Berg and J. Linschoten (eds.), *Persoon en Wereld*. Utrecht: Erven J. Bijleveld, pp. 59–73.

Kripke, S. (1980). *Naming and Necessity*. Oxford: Basil Blackwell.

Kristeva, J. (1980). *Desire in Language: A Semiotic Approach to Literature and Art*. New York: Columbia University Press.

Kruger, D. (1985). *The Changing Reality of Modern Man: Essays in Honour of Jan Hendrik van den Berg*. Pittsburgh, PA: Duquesne University Press.

Lampert, J. H. (1976). *Cosmological Letters on the Arrangement of the World-edifice*. (S. L. Jaki, transl.) New York: Science History Publications.

Langeveld, M. J. (1964). "In Memoriam." Prof. Dr. J. Linschoten. *Nederlands Tijdschrift voor de Psychologie 19*: 101–103.

Langeveld, M. J. (1979). *Beknopte Theoretische Pedagogiek*. Groningen: Wolters-Noordhoff.

Langeveld, M. J. (1983a). "The Secret Place in the Life of the Child." *Phenomenology + Pedagogy 1(2)*: 181–189.

Langeveld, M. J. (1983b). "The Stillness of the Secret Place." *Phenomenology + Pedagogy 1(1)*: 11–17.

Latour, B. (1992). "Where Are the Missing Masses? The Sociology of a Few Mundane Artifacts." In W. E. Bijker and J. Law (eds.), *Shaping Technology/Building Society: Studies in Sociotechnical Change*. Cambridge, MA: MIT Press.

Latour, B. (2007). *Reassembling the Social: An Introduction to Actor-Network-Theory* (Clarendon Lectures in Management Studies). Oxford: Oxford University Press.

Le Guin, U. K. (1987). *Buffalo Gals and Other Animal Presences*. Markham, ON: Penguin.

Levering, B. and M. van Manen. (2002). "Phenomenology and Philosophical Anthropology in the Netherlands." In A.-T. Tymieniecka (ed.), *Phenomenology World-Wide*. Dordrecht: Kluwer, pp. 274–286.

Levinas, E. (1979). *Totality and Infinity: An Essay on Exteriority*. The Hague: Martinus Nijhoff.

Levinas, E. (1981). *Otherwise than Being or Beyond Essence*. The Hague: Martinus Nijhoff.

Levinas, E. (1985). *Ethics and Infinity: Conversations with Philippe Nemo*. Pittsburgh, PA: Duquesne University Press.

Levinas, E. (1995). *Conversations with French Philosophers*. (F. Rötzer, ed.) Atlantic Highlands, NJ: Humanities Press.

Levinas, E. (1996a). *The Levinas Reader*. (S. Hand, ed.) Oxford: Blackwell.

Levinas, E. (1996b). *Proper Names*. Stanford, CA: Stanford University Press.

Levinas, E. (1998). *On Thinking of the Other: Entre Nous*. New York: Columbia University Press.

Levinas, E. (2001). *Existence and Existents*. Pittsburgh, PA: Duquesne University Press.

Levinas, E. (2003). *Humanism of the Other*. Urbana, IL: University of Illinois Press.

Levinas, E. (2008). *Basic Philosophical Writings*. (A. T. Peperzak, S. Critchley, R. Bernasconi, eds.) Bloomington, IN: Indiana University Press.

Lingis, A. (1983). *Excesses: Eros and Culture*. Albany, NY: SUNY Press.

Lingis, A. (1986a). *Libido: The French Existential Theories*. Bloomington, IN: Indiana University Press.

Lingis, A. (1986b). *Phenomenological Explanations*. The Hague: Martinus Nijhoff.

Lingis, A. (1986c). "The Sensuality and the Sensitivity." In R. A. Cohen (ed.), *Face to Face with Levinas*. Albany, NY: SUNY Press, pp. 219–230.

Lingis, A. (1994). *The Community of Those Who Have Nothing in Common*. Bloomington, IN: Indiana University Press.

Lingis, A. (1996). *Sensation: Intelligibility in Sensibility*. New York: Humanity Books.

Lingis, A. (1997). "Travelling with Lingis: An Interview with Alphonso Lingis." (D. J. Huppatz, A. Rubens, S. Tutton, interviewers.) *Melbourne Journal of Politics 24*: 26–42.

Lingis, A. (1998). *The Imperative*. Bloomington, IN: Indiana University Press.

Lingis, A. (2000). *Dangerous Emotions*. London: University of California Press.

Lingis, A. (2001). *Abuses*. Berkeley, CA: University of California Press.

Lingis, A. (2011). *Violence and Splendor*. Evanston, IL: Northwestern University Press.

Lingis, A. (2018). *Irrevocable: Philosophy of Mortality*. Chicago: University of Chicago Press.

Linschoten, J. (1953a). "Aspecten van de Sexuele Incarnatie." In J. H. van den Berg and J. Linschoten (eds.), *Persoon en Wereld*. Utrecht: Erven J. Bijleveld, pp. 74–126.

Linschoten, J. (1953b). "Nawoord." In J. H. van den Berg and J. Linschoten (eds.), *Persoon en Wereld*. Utrecht: Erven J. Bijleveld, pp. 244–253.

Linschoten, J. (1954). *On the Way toward a Phenomenological Psychology: the Psychology of William James*. Pittsburgh, PA: Duquesne University Press.

Linschoten, J. (1964). *Idolen van de Psycholoog*. Utrecht: Erven J. Bijleveld.

Linschoten, J. (1979). *The Inevitability of Phenomenology*. In A. Giorgi, R. Knowles, and D. L. Smith (eds.), *Duquesne Studies in Phenomenological Psychology, Vol. 3*. Pittsburgh, PA: Duquesne University Press. pp. 49–59.

Linschoten, J. (1987). "On Falling Asleep." In J. J. Kockelmans (ed.). *Phenomenological Psychology: The Dutch School*. Dordrecht: Kluwer, pp. 79–117.

Linschoten, J. (2021). "On Humor." In M. A. van Manen and M. van Manen (eds.), *Classic Writings for a Phenomenology of Practice*. London: Routledge, pp. 146–179.

Løgstrup, K. E. (1997). *The Ethical Demand*. Notre Dame, IN: University of Notre Dame Press.

Low, D. (2000). *Merleau-Ponty's Last Vision: A Proposal for the Completion of the Visible and the Invisible*. Evanston, IL: Northwestern University Press.

Madjar, I. (1998). *Giving Comfort and Inflicting Pain*. Edmonton, AB: Qual Institute Press.

Madjar, I. and J. Walton (eds.). (1999). *Nursing and the Experience of Illness: Phenomenology in Practice*. London: Routledge.

Marcel, G. (1949). *Being and Having*. London: The Dacre Press.

Marcel, G. (1950). *Mystery of Being. Vols. 1 and 2*. South Bend, IN: Gateway Editions.

Marcel, G. (1978). *Homo Viator*. Gloucester, MA: Smith.

Marion, J.-L. (2002a). *Being Given: Toward a Phenomenology of Givenness*. Stanford, CA: Stanford University Press.

Marion, J.-L. (2002b). *In Excess: Studies of Saturated Phenomena*. Bronx, NY: Fordham University Press.

Marion, J.-L. (2002c). *Prolegomena to Charity*. Bronx, NY: Fordham University Press.

Marion, J.-L. (2004). *The Crossing of the Visible*. Stanford, CA: Stanford University Press.

Marion, J.-L. (2007). *The Erotic Phenomenon: Six Meditations*. Chicago: University of Chicago Press.

Marion, J.-L. (2008). *The Visible and the Revealed*. Bronx, NY: Fordham University Press.

Marramao, G. (2007). *Kairos: Towards an Ontology of 'Due Time'*. Aurora, CO: The Davies Group.

Martin, W. (2008). *Descartes and the Phenomenological Tradition*. http://privatewww.essex.ac.uk/~wmartin/DandPhT.pdf (accessed January 29, 2014).

Massie, P. (2007). "The Secret and the Neuter: On Heidegger and Blanchot." *Research in Phenomenology 37*: 32–55.

McGowin, D. F. (1993). *Living in the Labyrinth: A Personal Journey through the Maze of Alzheimer's*. New York: Dell Publishing.

McLuhan, M. (1964). *Understanding Media: The Extensions of Man*. Cambridge, MA: The MIT Press.

McWeeny K. H., A. W. Young, D. C. Hay, and A. W. Ellis (1987). "Putting Names to Faces." *British Journal of Psychology* 78: 143–146.

Meillassoux, Q. (2009). *After Finitude: An Essay on the Necessity of Contingency*. London: Continuum.

Merleau-Ponty, M. (1962). *Phenomenology of Perception*. (C. Smith, transl.) London: Routledge & Kegan Paul.

Merleau-Ponty, M. (1964a). *The Primacy of Perception; and Other Essays on Phenomenological Psychology, the Philosophy of Art, History and Politics*. Evanston, IL: Northwestern University Press.

Merleau-Ponty, M. (1964b). *Signs*. Evanston, IL: Northwestern University Press.

Merleau-Ponty, M. (1964c). *Sense and Non-Sense*. Evanston, IL: Northwestern University Press.

Merleau-Ponty, M. (1968). *The Visible and the Invisible*. Evanston, IL: Northwestern University Press.

Merleau-Ponty, M. (1973). *The Prose of the World*. Evanston, IL: Northwestern University Press.

Merleau-Ponty, M. (2003). *Nature: Course Notes from the Collège de France*. (R. Vallier, transl.) Evanston, IL: Northwestern University Press.

Merleau-Ponty, M. (2010a). *Child Psychology and Pedagogy: The Sorbonne Lectures 1949–1952*. Evanston, IL: Northwestern University Press.

Merleau-Ponty, M. (2010b). *Institution and Passivity: Course Notes from the Collège de France (1954–1955)*. Evanston, IL: Northwestern University Press.

Merleau-Ponty, M. (2012). *Phenomenology of Perception*. (D. A. Landes, transl.) London: Routledge & Kegan Paul.

Mesquita, B. (2022). *Between Us: How Cultures Create Emotions*. New York: W. W. Norton.

Mill, J. S. (1843). *A System of Logic*. London: Longmans.

Minkowski, E. (2019). *Lived Time*. Evanston, IL: Northwestern University Press.

Minty, J. (1982). "From the Diary of Judith Minty. September 19, 1972." In L. Lifshin (ed.), *Ariadne's Threat: A Collection of Contemporary Women's Journals*. New York: Harper & Row, pp. 215–219.

Montaigne, M. de (2003). *The Complete Works of Michel de Montaigne*. (S. Hampshire, intro., D. M. Frame, transl.) London: Everyman's Library.

Mood, J. J. L. (1975). *Rilke on Love and Other Difficulties*. New York: Norton.

Moran, D. (2000). *Introduction to Phenomenology*. London: Routledge.

Moran, D. and T. Mooney. (2002). *The Phenomenology Reader*. London: Routledge.

Morse, J. M., J. Bottorff, W. Neander, and S. Solberg. (1991). "Comparative Analysis of Conceptualizations and Theories of Caring." *IMAGE: Journal of Nursing Scholarship* 23(2): 119–126.

Morse, J. M., S. Solberg, W. Neander, J. Bottorff, and J. L. Johnson. (1990). "Concepts of Caring and Caring as a Concept." *Advances in Nursing Science* 13(1): 1–14.

Morton, T. (2013). *Hyperobjects: Philosophy and Ecology after the End of the World*. London: Routledge.

Moustakas, C. (1974). *Portraits of Loneliness and Love*. Englewood Cliffs, NJ: Prentice Hall.

Moustakas, C. (1990). *Heuristic Research: Design, Methodology, and Applications*. Thousand Oaks, CA: SAGE Publications.

Moustakas, C. (1994). *Phenomenological Research Methods*. Thousand Oaks, CA: SAGE Publications.

Moustakas, C. (1996). *Loneliness: How to Deal Constructively with Feelings of Loneliness*. Northvale, NJ: Jason Aronson Publishers.

Mulhall, S. (1993). *On Being in the World*. London: Routledge.

Myers, K. A. (2011). "Metanoia and the Transformation of Opportunity." *Rhetoric Society Quarterly* 41(1): 1–18.

Nancy, J.-L. (1991). *The Inoperative Community*. Minneapolis, MN: University of Minnesota Press.

Nancy, J.-L. (1993). *The Birth to Presence*. Stanford, CA: Stanford University Press.

Nancy, J.-L. (1994). *The Experience of Freedom*. Stanford, CA: Stanford University Press.

Nancy, J.-L. (1997a). *The Muses*. Stanford, CA: Stanford University Press.

Nancy, J.-L. (1997b). *The Sense of the World*. Minneapolis, MN: University of Minnesota Press.

Nancy, J.-L. (2000). *Being Singular Plural*. Stanford, CA: Stanford University Press.

Nancy, J.-L. (2005). *The Ground of the Image*. New York: Fordham University Press.

Nancy, J.-L. (2007a). *L'Evidence du Film*. Paris: Klincksieck.

Nancy, J.-L. (2007b). *The Fall of Sleep*. New York: Fordham University Press.

Nancy, J.-L. (2007c). *Listening*. New York: Fordham University Press.

Nancy, J.-L. (2008). *Corpus*. New York: Fordham University Press.

Nietzsche, F. (1954). "On Truth and Lie in an Extra-Moral Sense." In W. Kaufmann (ed.), *Nietzsche*. New York: Viking Press.

Nietzsche, F. (1968). *The Will to Power*. (W. Kaufmann, transl.) New York: Viking Press.

Nietzsche, F. (1981). *On the Advantage and Disadvantage of History for Life*. Cambridge: Hackett Publishing Company.

Nietzsche, F. (1986). *Human, All Too Human: A Book for Free Spirits*. Cambridge, UK: Cambridge University Press.

Nietzsche, F. (2010). *On Truth and Untruth*. New York: HarperCollins.

Noddings, N. (1984). *Caring: A Feminine Approach to Ethics and Moral Education*. Berkeley, CA: University of California Press.

Noddings, N. (1992). *The Challenge to Care in Schools*. New York: Teachers College Press.

Nordholt, A. S. (1997). "Het Schuwe Denken." In A. S. Nordholt, L. ten Kate, F. van de Verre (eds.), *Het Wakende Woord: Literatuur, Ethiek en Politiek bij Maurice Blanchot*. Nijmegen: SUN, pp. 11–43.

Olson, C. T. (1993). *The Life of Illness*. Albany, NY: SUNY Press.

O'Neill, J. (1989). *The Communicative Body: Studies in Communicative Philosophy, Politics, and Sociology*. Evanston, IL: Northwestern University Press.

Ong, W. J. (1967). *The Presence of the Word*. Minneapolis, MN: University of Minnesota Press.

Ong, W. J. (1971). *Rhetoric, Romance and Technology: Studies in the Interaction of Expression and Culture*. Ithaca, NY: Cornell University Press.

Ong, W. J. (1977). *Interfaces of the World: Studies in the Evolution of Consciousness and Culture*. Ithaca, NY: Cornell University Press.

Ong, W. J. (2013). *Orality and Literacy*. London: Routledge.

Ovid. (2000). *The Metamorphoses*. (A. S. Kline, transl.) New York: Borders Classics Books.

Pallasmaa, J. (2005). *The Eyes of the Skin: Architecture and the Senses*. Chichester, West Sussex, UK: John Wiley & Sons.

Pallasmaa, J. (2009). *The Thinking Hand*. Chichester, West Sussex, UK: John Wiley & Sons.

Patočka, J. (1989). *Jan Patočka: Philosophy and Selected Writings*. (E. Kohák, ed.) Chicago: University of Chicago Press.

Patočka, J. (1998). *Body, Community, Language, World*. (E. Kohák, transl.) Chicago: Open Court.

Payne, M. and J. Schad. (2003). *Life.after.theory*. London: Continuum.

Perniola, M. (2004a). *Art and Its Shadow*. New York: Continuum.

Perniola, M. (2004b). *The Sex Appeal of the Inorganic: Philosophies of Desire in the Modern World*. New York: Bloomsbury.

Pettman, D. (2006). *Love and Other Technologies: Retrofitting Eros for the Information Age*. New York: Fordham University Press.

Pinkard, T. P. (2001). *Hegel: A Biography*. Cambridge, UK: Cambridge University Press.

Plato (1927). *Plato XII: Charmides, Alcibiades I & II, Hipparchus, Lovers, Theages, Minos, Epinomis*. (W. R. M. Lamb, transl.) Harvard, MA: Harvard University Press.

Plessner, H. (1970). *Laughing and Crying: A Study of the Limits of Human Behavior*. Evanston, IL: Northwestern University Press.

Polt, R. (2006). *The Emergency of Being: On Heidegger's Contributions to Philosophy*. Ithaca, NY: Cornell University Press.

Poole, D. A. and L. White. (1991). "Effects of Question Repetition on the Eyewitness Testimony of Children and Adults." *Developmental Psychology*, 27(6), 975–986.

Potapov, E. V., B. Stiller, and R. Hetzer. (2007). "Ventricular Assist Devices in Children: Current Achievements and Future Perspectives." *Pediatric Transplantation* 11(3), 241–255.

Price, D. W. and G. S. Goodman. (1990). "Visiting the Wizard: Children's Memory for a Recurring Event." *Child Development* 61(3): 664–680.

Rehm, R. S. and J. F. Bradley. (2005). "Normalization in Families Raising a Child Who is Medically Fragile/Technology Dependent and Developmentally Delayed." *Qualitative Health Research* 15(6): 807–820.

Reinach, A. (1968). "Concerning Phenomenology." *The Philosophical Forum* 1(2): 234–256.

Reinach, A. (1983). "The Apriori Foundations of the Civil Law." *Aletheia. An International Journal of Philosophy*. Volume III, *Philosophy of Law*: 1–142.

Ricoeur, P. (1966). *Freedom and Nature: The Voluntary and the Involuntary*. Evanston, IL: Northwestern University Press.

Ricoeur, P. (1969). *The Symbolism of Evil*. Boston: Beacon Press.

Ricoeur, P. (1976). *Interpretation Theory: Discourse and the Surplus of Meaning*. Fort Worth, TX: Texas Christian University Press.

Ricoeur, P. (1983). *Hermeneutics and the Human Sciences*. New York: Cambridge University Press.

Ricoeur, P. (1991). *From Text to Action: Essays in Hermeneutics*, Vol. 2. London: Continuum.

Ricoeur, P. (1992). *Oneself as Another*. Chicago: University of Chicago Press.

Rilke, R. M. (1964). *The Notebooks of Malte Laurids Brigge*. (M. D. Herter Norton, transl.) New York: W. W. Norton and Company.

Rilke, R. M. (1977). *Possibility of Being: A Selection of Poems*. New York: New Directions.

Rilke, R. M. (1987). *Rilke and Benvenuta: An Intimate Correspondence*. New York: Fromm International.

Rilke, R. M. (1990). *The Notebooks of Malte Laurids Brigge: A Novel*. New York: Vintage International.

Rockmore, T. (2011). *Kant and Phenomenology*. Chicago: University of Chicago Press.

Romano, C. (1999). *L'Événement et le Temps*. Paris: PUF.

Romano, C. (2009). *Event and World*. Bronx, NY: Fordham University Press.

Rorty, R. (1979). *Philosophy and the Mirror of Nature*. Princeton, NJ: Princeton University Press.

Rosen, H. (1986). "The Importance of Story." *Language Arts 63*(3): 226–237.

Rosen, S. (2002). *The Elusiveness of the Ordinary*. New Haven, CT: Yale University Press.

Ross, K. (1997). "French Quotidian." In L. Gumbert (ed.), *The Art of the Everyday: The Quotidian in Postwar French Culture*. New York: New York University Press.

Rötzer, F. (1995). *Conversations with French Philosophers*. New York: Humanity Books.

Rümke, H. C. (1953). "Over Afkeer van de Eigen Neus." In J. H. van den Berg and J. Linschoten (eds.), *Persoon en Wereld*. Utrecht: Bijleveld, pp. 46–58.

Rümke, H. C. (1988). *Fenomenologie en Psychiatrie*. Kampen: Kok Agora.

Sartre, J. P. (1948/1976). *Black Orpheus*. New York: French & European Publications.

Sartre, J. P. (1956). *Being and Nothingness*. New York: Philosophical Library.

Sartre, J. P. (1963). *In Search of a Method*. New York: Vintage Books.

Sartre, J. P. (1974). *Selected Prose: The Writings of Jean-Paul Sartre*. Evanston, IL: Northwestern University Press.

Sartre, J. P. (1977). *Life/Situations: Essays Written and Spoken*. New York: Pantheon Books.

Sartre, J. P. (1978). *Sartre by Himself*. New York: Urizen Books.

Sartre, J. P. (1991). *The Transcendence of the Ego: An Existentialist Theory of Consciousness*. New York: Hill and Wang.

Sartre, J. P. (1993). *Essays in Existentialism*. New York: Citadel Press.

Sartre, J. P. (2007). *Nausea*. New York: New Directions Books.

Sawicki, M. (1998). "Personal Connections: The Phenomenology of Edith Stein." Lecture delivered at St. John's University in New York. www.library.nd.edu/colldev/subject_home_pages/catholic/personal_connections.shtml (accessed January 29, 2014).

Scheler, M. (1970). *The Nature of Sympathy*. Hamden, CT: Archon Books.

Scheler, M. (1972). *Ressentiment*. New York: Schocken Books.

Scheler, M. (1973). *Formalism in Ethics and Non-Formal Ethics of Values*. Evanston, IL: Northwestern University Press.

Schleiermacher, F. D. E. (1977). *Hermeneutics: The Handwritten Manuscripts*. Missoula, MT: Scholars Press.

Schleiermacher, F. D. E. (1978). "The Hermeneutics: Outline of the 1819 Lectures." *New Literary History 10*(1): 9.

Schutz, A. (1970). *On Phenomenology and Social Relations*. Chicago: University of Chicago Press.

Schutz, A. (1972). *The Phenomenology of the Social World*. London: Heinemann Educational Books.

Schutz, A. (1970; 1973; 1974). *Collected Papers*. 3 vols. The Hague: Martinus Nijhoff.

Schutz, A. (1973). *The Structures of the Life-World*. Evanston, IL: Northwestern University Press.

Serres, M. (1997). *The Troubadour of Knowledge*. Minnesota, MN: University of Minnesota Press.

Serres, M. (2007). *The Parasite*. Minnesota, MN: University of Minnesota Press.

Serres, M. (2008). *The Five Senses: A Philosophy of Mingled Bodies*. New York: Continuum.

Shapiro, K. (1968). *Selected Poems*. New York: Random House.

Simms, E. M. (2008). *The Child in the World: Embodiment, Time, and Language in Early Childhood.* Detroit: Wayne University Press.

Sipiora, P. and J. S. Baumlin (eds.) (2012). *Rhetoric and Kairos: Essays in History, Theory, and Praxis.* Albany, NY: SUNY Press.

Sloterdijk, P. (1983). *Kritik der Zynischen Vernunft.* Vols. 1 and 2. Frankfurt am Main: Suhrkamp Verlag.

Spiegelberg, H. H. (1959/1982). *The Phenomenological Movement: A Historical Introduction.* The Hague: Martinus Nijhoff.

Spiegelberg, H. (1972). *Phenomenology in Psychology and Psychiatry.* Evanston, IL: Northwestern University Press.

Spiegelberg, H. (1975). *Doing Phenomenology: Essays on and in Phenomenology.* The Hague: Martinus Nijhoff.

Spock, B. and M. B. Rothenberg. (1992). *Dr. Spock's Baby and Child Care.* New York: Dutton.

Spradley, J. P. and D. W. McCurdy. (1972). *The Cultural Experience: Ethnography in Complex Society.* Long Grove, IL: Waveland Press.

St. Augustine. (1960). *The Confessions.* New York: Doubleday.

Steeves, H. P. (2006). *The Things Themselves: Phenomenology and the Return to the Everyday.* Albany, NY: SUNY Press.

Stein, E. (1989). *On the Problem of Empathy.* Washington, DC: ICS Publications.

Stein, E. (1994). "Der Aufbau der Menschlichen Person." In L. Gelber and M. Linssen (eds.), *Edith Steins Werke*, Vol. 17. Freiburg im Breisgau: Herder.

Stein, E. (2000). *Philosophy of Psychology and the Humanities.* Washington, DC: ICS Publications.

Stein, E. (2009). *Potency and Act.* Washington, DC: ICS Publications.

Steiner, G. (1989). *Real Presences.* Chicago: University of Chicago Press.

Sternberg, R. J. and J. E. Davidson. (1994). *The Nature of Insight.* Cambridge, MA: The MIT Press.

Stevenson, A. and M. Waite. (2017). *The Concise Oxford English Dictionary.* Oxford: Oxford University Press.

Steward, M. S. and D. S. Steward. (1996). "Interviewing Young Children about Body Touch and Handling." *Monographs of the Society for Research in Child Development* 61(4, Serial No. 248).

Stewart, J. L. (2003). "'Getting Used to It': Children Finding the Ordinary and Routine in the Uncertain Context of Cancer." *Qualitative Health Research* 13(3): 394–407.

Stiegler, B. (1998). *Technics and Time, 1: The Fault of Epimetheus.* Stanford, CA: Stanford University Press.

Stiegler, B. (2009a). *Acting Out.* Stanford, CA: Stanford University Press.

Stiegler, B. (2009b). *Technics and Time, 2: Disorientation.* Stanford, CA: Stanford University Press.

Stiegler, B. (2010). *Taking Care of Youth and the Generations.* (S. Barker, transl.) Stanford, CA: Stanford University Press.

Strasser, S. (1974). *Phenomenology and the Human Sciences.* Pittsburgh, PA: Duquesne University Press.

Strasser, S. (1985). *Understanding and Explanation.* Pittsburgh, PA: Duquesne University Press.

Straus, E. W. (1966). *Phenomenological Psychology.* New York: Basic Books.

Straus, E. W. (1982). *Man, Time, and World.* Pittsburgh, PA: Duquesne University Press.

Taminiaux, J. (1991). *Heidegger and the Project of Fundamental Ontology.* Albany, NY: SUNY Press.

Terwee S. J. S. (1990). "The Case of Johannes Linschoten's Apostasy: Phenomenological Versus Empirical-Analytical Psychology." In S. J. S. Terwee (ed.), *Hermeneutics in Psychology and Psychoanalysis: Recent Research in Psychology.* Berlin: Springer.

Thomas, D. (1954). "Reminiscences of Childhood." In *Quite Early One Morning.* London: Aldine House, pp. 1–14.

Thomson, I. (2000). "From the Question Concerning Technology to the Quest for a Democratic Technology: Heidegger, Marcuse, Feenberg." *Inquiry: An Interdisciplinary Journal of Philosophy* 44(3): 243–268.

Thomson, I. (2005). *Heidegger on Ontotheology: Technology and the Politics of Education.* Cambridge, UK: Cambridge University Press.

Tolstoy, L. (1981). *The Death of Ivan Ilyich.* New York: Bantam Dell.

Tønnessen, H. (1966/67). "Happiness is for the Pigs: Philosophy versus Psychotherapy." *Journal of Existentialism VII*(26): 181–214.

Toombs, S. K. (ed.). (2001). *Handbook of Phenomenology and Medicine.* Dordrecht: Kluwer.

Tronto, J. (2005). "An Ethic of Care." In A. E. Cudd and R. O. Andreasen (eds), *Feminist Theory: A Philosophical Anthology*. Oxford, MA: Blackwell Publishing, pp. 251–263.

Tronto, J. (2013). *Caring Democracy: Markets, Equality, and Justice*. New York: New York University Press.

Van den Berg, J. H. (1961). *The Changing Nature of Man*. New York: Dell Publishing.

Van den Berg, J. H. (1966). *The Psychology of the Sickbed*. Pittsburgh, PA: Duquesne University Press.

Van den Berg, J. H. (1970). *Things—Four Metabletic Reflections*. Pittsburgh, PA: Duquesne University Press.

Van den Berg, J. H. (1972). *A Different Existence*. Pittsburgh, PA: Duquesne University Press.

Van den Berg, J. H. (1974). *Divided Existence and Complex Society*. Pittsburgh, PA: Duquesne University Press.

Van den Berg, J. H. (1987). "The Human Body and the Significance of Human Movement." In J. J. Kockelmans (ed.), *Phenomenological Psychology: The Dutch School*. Dordrecht: Martinus Nijhoff Publishers, pp. 55–77.

Van den Berg, J. H. (2021). "The Conversation." In M. van Manen and M. van Manen (eds.), *Classic Writings for a Phenomenology of Practice*. London: Routledge, pp. 31–46.

Van den Berg, J. H. and J. Linschoten (eds.). (1953). *Persoon en Wereld*. Utrecht: Bijleveld.

Van Hezewijk, R. and H. J. Stam. (2008). "Idols of the Psychologist Johannes Linschoten and the Demise of the Phenomenological Psychology in the Netherlands." *History of Psychology* 11: 185–207.

Van Lennep, D. J. (1987a). "The Hotel Room." In J. J. Kockelmans (ed.), *Phenomenological Psychology: The Dutch School*. Dordrecht: Kluwer, pp. 209–215.

Van Lennep, D. J. (1987b). "The Psychology of Driving a Car." In J. J. Kockelmans (ed.), *Phenomenological Psychology: The Dutch School*. Dordrecht: Kluwer, pp. 217–227.

Van Manen, M. (1977). "Linking Ways of Knowing to Ways of Being Practical." *Curriculum Inquiry* 6(3): 205–228.

Van Manen, M. (1979). "The Phenomenology of Pedagogic Observation," *The Canadian Journal for Studies in Education*, 4(1): 5–16.

Van Manen, M. (1982). "Phenomenological Pedagogy," *Curriculum Inquiry*, 12(3): 283–299.

Van Manen, M. (1985). "The Phenomenology of the Novel, or How Do Novels Teach?" *Phenomenology + Pedagogy* 3(3): 177–187.

Van Manen, M. (1986). *The Tone of Teaching*. Portsmouth, NH: Heinemann.

Van Manen, M. (1989a). "By the Light of Anecdote." *Phenomenology + Pedagogy* 7: 232–253.

Van Manen, M. (1989b). "Pedagogical Text as Method: Phenomenological Research as Writing," *Saybrook Review* 7(2): 23–45.

Van Manen, M. (1990/1997). *Researching Lived Experience: Human Science for an Action Sensitive Pedagogy*. 1st and 2nd eds. London: Routledge.

Van Manen, M. (1991). *The Tact of Teaching: The Meaning of Pedagogical Thoughtfulness*. London: Routledge.

Van Manen, M. (1997). "From Meaning to Method." *Qualitative Health Research: An International, Interdisciplinary Journal* 7(3): 345–369.

Van Manen, M. (1999a). "The Language of Pedagogy and the Primacy of Student Experience." In J. Loughran (ed.), *Researching Teaching: Methodologies and Practices for Understanding Pedagogy*. London: Falmer Press, pp. 13–27.

Van Manen, M. (1999b). "The Pathic Nature of Inquiry and Nursing." In I. Madjar and J. Walton (eds.), *Nursing and the Experience of Illness: Phenomenology in Practice*. London: Routledge, pp. 17–35.

Van Manen, M. (ed.). (2001). *Writing in the Dark: Phenomenological Studies in Interpretive Inquiry*. London: Routledge.

Van Manen, M. (2002a). "Care-as-Worry, or 'Don't Worry Be Happy.'" *Qualitative Health Research: An International, Interdisciplinary Journal* 12(2): 264–280.

Van Manen, M. (2002b). "Writing in the Dark." In M. van Manen (ed.), *Writing in the Dark: Phenomenological Studies in Interpretive Inquiry*. London, ON: Althouse Press.

Van Manen, M. (ed.). (2002c). *Writing in the Dark: Phenomenological Studies in Interpretive Inquiry*. London: Routledge.

Van Manen, M. (2007). "Phenomenology of Practice." *Phenomenology and Practice* 1(1): 11–30.

Van Manen, M. (2012). "The Call of Pedagogy as the Call of Contact." *Phenomenology and Practice* 6(2): 8–34.

Van Manen, M. (2013). "The Ecstatic-Poetic Phenomenology of Jennifer Anna Gosetti-Ferencei." *Phenomenology and Practice* 7(1): 139–143.

Van Manen, M. (2014a). Phenomenology of Practice: *Meaning-Giving Methods in Phenomenological Research and Writing*. London: Routledge.

Van Manen, M. (2014b). *Weten Wat te Doen Wanneer Je Niet Weet Wat te Doen*. Driebergen, Netherlands: NIVOZ.

Van Manen, M. (2015). *Pedagogical Tact: Knowing What to Do When You Don't Know What to Do*. London: Routledge.

Van Manen, M. (2019). "Takt, Kairos und pädagogisches Handeln." In A. Gastager and Jean Luc Patry (eds.), *Pädagogischer Takt: Analysen zu Theorie und Praxis*. Graz: Leykam Buchverlag Pädagogische Momente.

Van Manen, M. and C. Adams. (2009). "The Phenomenology of Space in Writing Online." *Educational Philosophy and Theory, 41*(1): 10–21.

Van Manen, M. and B. Levering. (1996). *Childhood's Secrets: Intimacy, Privacy, and the Self Reconsidered*. New York: Teachers College Press. http://archive.org/details/childhoodssecret00vanm (accessed January 29, 2014).

Van Manen, M. A. (2011). "Looking into the Neonatal Isolette." *Medical Humanities* 38(1): 38.

Van Manen, M. A. (2012a). "The Medium, the Message, and the Massage of the Neonatal Monitor Screen." In Y. van den Eede, J. Bauwens, J. Beyl, M. van den Bossche, and K. Verstrynge (eds.), *Proceedings of 'McLuhan's Philosophy of Media'—Centennial Conference/Contact Forum, October 26–28*. Brussels: Royal Flemish Academy of Belgium for Science and the Arts.

Van Manen, M. A. (2012b). "Technics of Touch in the Neonatal Intensive Care." *Medical Humanities*. 38(2): 91–96.

Van Manen, M. A. (2012c). "Ethical Responsivity and Pediatric Parental Pedagogy." *Phenomenology and Practice* 6(1): 5–17.

Van Manen, M. A. (2012d). "Carrying: Parental Experience of Hospital Transfer of their Baby." *Qualitative Health Research* 22(2): 199–211.

Van Manen, M. A. (2013). "Phenomena of Neonatology." Unpublished dissertation. University of Alberta, Edmonton, AB.

Van Manen, M. A. (2014). "On Ethical (In)Decisions Experienced by Parents of Infants in NICU." *Qualitative Health Research* 24(1): 279–287.

Van Manen, M. A. (2019). *Phenomenology of the Newborn: Life from Womb to World*. London Routledge.

Van Manen, M. A. (2021). *The Birth of Ethics: Phenomenological Reflections on Life's Beginnings*. London Routledge.

Van Manen, M. A. and M. van Manen. (2021). *Classic Writings for a Phenomenology of Practice*. London: Routledge, pp. 31–46.

Van Manen, M. A. and M. van Manen. (2021). "Doing Phenomenological Research and Writing." *Qualitative Health Research* 31(6): 1069–1082.

Van Manen, M. A. and M. van Manen. (2021). *Classic Writings for a Phenomenology of Practice*. London: Routledge.

Verbeek, P.-P. (2005). *What Things Do: Philosophical Reflections on Technology, Agency, and Design*. Philadelphia, PA: Penn State University Press.

Verbeek, P.-P. (2011). *Moralizing Technology: Understanding and Designing the Morality of Things*. Chicago: University of Chicago Press.

Verhoeven, C. (1967). *Inleiding tot de Verwondering*. Baarn: Ambo.

Verhoeven, C. (1972). *The Philosophy of Wonder*. (M. Foran, transl.) New York: Macmillan.

Verhoeven, C. (1987). *De Letter als Beeld*. Baarn: Ambo.

Verhoeven, C. (1992). *Alleen Maar Kijken*. Baarn: Ambo.

Verhoeven, C. (1995). *Het Geheugen Herdacht*. Baarn: Ambo.

Visker, R. (1998). "Dis-Possessed: How to Remain Silent 'after' Levinas." In S. Harasym (ed.), *Levinas and Lacan: The Missed Encounter*. Albany, NY: SUNY Press, pp. 182–210.

Wahl, J. (2017). *Transcendence and the Concrete*. New York: Fordham University Press.

Waldenfels, B. (2007). *The Question of the Other: The Tang Chun-I Lecture for 2004*. Albany, NY: SUNY Press.

Waldenfels, B. (2011). *Phenomenology of the Alien: Basic Concepts*. Evanston, IL: Northwestern University Press.

Wall, T. C. (1999). *Radical passivity: Levinas, Blanchot, and Agamben*. Albany, NY: SUNY Press.

Welton, D. (ed.). (1999). *The Body: Classic and Contemporary Readings*. Oxford: Basil Blackwell.

Wittgenstein, L. (1922/1961). *Tractacus Logico-Philosophicus*. New York: Humanities Press.

Wittgenstein, L. (1968). *Philosophical Investigations*. (G. E. M. Anscombe, transl.) Oxford: Basil Blackwell.

Wittgenstein, L. (1982). *Last Writings on the Philosophy of Psychology*, Vol. 1. Oxford: Basil Blackwell.

Wolf, M. (2007). *Proust and the Squid: The Story and Science of the Reading Brain*. New York: Harper.

Wood, D. (2002). *Thinking after Heidegger*. Malden, MA: Basil Blackwell.

Zaner, R. M. (1971). *The Problem of Embodiment: Some Contributions to a Phenomenology of the Body*. The Hague: Martinus Nijhoff.

Name Index

Abé, Kobo, 28
Achterhuis, Hans, 287, 414
Adams, Cathy, xix, 353, 415
Afloroaei, Stefan, 196
Agamben, Giorgio, 7, 202, 306, 319, 45
Alpers, Svetlana, 334
Aquinas, Thomas, 229
Arendt, Hannah, 37, 199, 211, 218, 232, 233–236, 257
Aristotle, 21, 151, 207, 209, 234, 304–306, 365
Austin, Wendy, xix, 352

Bachelard, Gaston, 79, 113, 182, 183, 268–270, 319, 384, 411
Baldursson, Stefan, 353
Barthes, Roland, 9, 14, 39, 150, 169, 170, 298, 449, 450, 465
Bataille, Georges, 249, 264, 294, 298
Baudelaire, Charles, 384, 385, 393, 446
Beckett, Samuel, xv
Beekman, Anthony, 351
Beets, Nicolaas, 37, 43, 74, 332, 336, 347–349, 414, 450
Benjamin, Walter, 234, 304, 305
Benner, Patricia, 290
Bergson, Henri, 34, 36, 79, 137, 204–208, 232, 243, 249, 271, 327, 332, 384
Bergum, Vangie, xix, 352
Binswanger, Ludwig, 34, 323, 327, 328, 332, 409
Blanchot, Maurice, xx–xxi, 7, 9, 36, 101, 105, 113, 157, 165, 202, 238, 263–268, 279, 291, 298, 309, 319, 396, 462, 469–472
Bollnow, Otto F., 73, 336, 344–347, 384, 411, 450
Bourdieu, Pierre, 322
Brentano, Franz, 21, 22, 197, 211, 214, 218, 262, 453
Buber, Martin, 64
Burms, Arnold and Herman de Dijn, 115, 391
Buytendijk, Frederik, 37, 43, 51, 71, 164, 186, 238, 317, 332, 333, 336–339, 350, 384, 414, 425, 445, 450, 453, 456

Cameron, Brenda, xix, 353
Camus, Albert, xv, 249, 332, 333, 388, 389
Cairns, Huntington, 152

Casey, Edward, 43, 50, 155, 156, 166, 411
Chrétien, Jean-Louis, 7, 34, 113, 114, 302–304, 361, 377, 378, 454, 455
Cixous, Hélène, xvii, 81, 114, 238, 264, 280, 283–287, 292, 396, 470
Clark, Graeme, 352
Cohen, Gillian and Deborah M. Burke, 54
Connolly, Maureen, 352
Cox, Gary, 244

Damasio, Antonio, 18, 253
Davis, Philip and Reuben Hersh, 194
De Beauvoir, Simone, xv, xvii, 22, 34, 206, 243, 249–251, 332, 333
De Boer, Theo, 129
DeGowin, Elmer and Richard DeGowin, 65
Dermot, Moran, 22, 128
Derrida, Jacques, xvii, 7, 9, 22, 33, 34, 55, 63, 91, 92, 118, 126, 147, 148, 156, 161, 202, 220, 232, 242, 264, 279–283, 287, 294, 298, 301–306, 311, 361, 366, 374, 396, 402, 457, 461, 465–473
Descartes, René, 138, 193, 194–197, 244, 298, 307
Dilthey, Wilhelm, 22, 29, 31, 32, 208–210, 257, 314, 332, 345
Dostoevsky, Fyodor, 156, 241, 317, 337
Dreyfus, Hubert, 289, 290, 414

Eagleman, David, 18, 253
Eliot, George, 91
Evans, Rodney, 352

Fanon, Frantz, xvii, 272–276
Feenberg, Andrew, 224
Ferraris, Maurizio, 366, 457, 467, 472, 473
Figal, Günter, 7, 34, 162, 164, 314–316, 382, 456
Fink, Eugen, 12, 49, 50, 215, 216, 232, 332, 357, 367
Flusser, Vilém, 140
Flyvbjerg, Bent, 290
Foran, Andrew, xix, 352
Foucault, Michel, 89, 140, 239, 264, 289, 290, 304
Frege, Gottlob, 54
Friesen, Norm, 353

Subject Index